Introduction to Cataloging and Classification

Recent Titles in the
Library and Information Science Text Series

Arlene G. Taylor

Introduction to Cataloging and Classification

TENTH EDITION

with the assistance of
David P. Miller

Library and Information Science Text Series

LIBRARIES
UNLIMITED

A Member of the Greenwood Publishing Group

Westport, Connecticut • London

Library of Congress Cataloging-in-Publication Data

Taylor, Arlene G., 1941-
   Introduction to cataloging and classification. — 10th ed. / by Arlene G. Taylor ;
with the assistance of David P. Miller.
      p. cm. — (Library and information science text series)
   Rev. ed. of: Wynar's introduction to cataloging and classification. Rev. 9th ed. 2004.
   Includes bibliographical references and index.
   ISBN 1-59158-230-X (alk. paper) — ISBN 1-59158-235-0 (pbk : alk. paper)
   1. Cataloging. 2. Anglo-American cataloguing rules. 3. Classification—Books.
I. Miller, David P. (David Peter), 1955- II. Taylor, Arlene G., 1941- Wynar's
introduction to cataloging and classification. III. Title. IV. Series.
Z693.W94 2006
025.3—dc22   2006011701

British Library Cataloguing in Publication Data is available.

Library of Congress Catalog Card Number: 2006011701
ISBN: 1-59158-230-X
     1-59158-235-0 (pbk.)

First published in 2006

Libraries Unlimited, 88 Post Road West, Westport, CT 06881
A Member of the Greenwood Publishing Group, Inc.
www.lu.com

Printed in the United States of America

∞

The paper used in this book complies with the
Permanent Paper Standard issued by the National
Information Standards Organization (Z39.48-1984).

10 9 8 7 6 5 4 3 2

Contents

Part II
ELECTRONIC FORMATTING

Part III
DESCRIPTION AND ACCESS

Part IV
AUTHORITY CONTROL

Part V
SUBJECT ACCESS

Part VI
ADMINISTRATIVE ISSUES

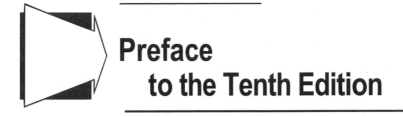

Preface
to the Tenth Edition

Since the publication of the ninth edition of this text in 2000 there have been changes in almost all areas of the organization of information, both in general, and, in cataloging and classification in particular. The world of information has changed radically with the continuing development of the World Wide Web. Cataloging tools are now almost all available on the Web. New ways of organizing information are being developed constantly. The Semantic Web is being explored; "tagging," where users of the Internet provide their own "tags" (what catalogers and indexers have called subject headings and descriptors) for information resources on the Web, is being experimented with; metadata schemes for special applications have proliferated, along with metadata registries, application profiles, gateways, and ontologies and taxonomies. These and other changes have made the task of revision formidable; nevertheless, the revision is now as up-to-date as possible given the constraints of human understanding and the passage of time between writing and publication.

The revised ninth edition, published in 2004, updated only the chapters having to do with the *Anglo-American Cataloguing Rules, Second Edition* (*AACR2*), which means that the rest of the chapters contain information from 2000. But even the *AACR2* chapters from the revised ninth edition have needed much revision for this edition, not only because of ongoing revision of *AACR2*, but also because of new thinking in the cataloging world about the approaches that should be taken in writing the next edition of cataloging rules. Therefore, all chapters in this edition have undergone thorough revision and updating. The bibliography and glossary are also substantially reworked. Only the appendix, which covers arrangement dilemmas and filing rules, remains unchanged.

There are a number of changes in this edition in addition to updating. Because authority control is so completely intertwined with the entire cataloging process, the chapter on authority control has been moved from the end of all the descriptive and subject chapters into the middle portion, immediately following the *AACR2* chapters. Authority control is now covered in Chapter 8 in Part IV. In addition, Part V, Subject Analysis, has been rearranged to better suit the needs of teachers of cataloging, most of whom teach verbal subject access in the form of controlled vocabularies before teaching the specifics of classification schemes. The chapters on verbal subject access, *Library of Congress Subject Headings*, *Sears List of Subject Headings*, and other types of verbal access now precede the chapters on classification of library materials, Decimal Classification, *Library of Congress Classification*, creation of complete call numbers, and other classification systems.

Part I, Introduction, includes chapters on the cataloging process, and the history of cataloging codes. The first chapter has been revised to incorporate new models such as *FRBR* (*Functional Requirements for Bibliographic Records*) and IFLA's new international cataloging principles and to lessen previous emphasis on paper-based products. Additional *AACR2* revisions and changes in plans for future rules, as well as a new section on international developments, have been added to the history chapter.

Part II introduces electronic formatting with a chapter introducing the MARC bibliographic format. Introductory material acknowledges newer encoding standards that may become more used in future cataloging. The MARC introduction has been updated to include recent enhancements to *MARC 21*.

In Part III we have continued the conceptual shift in description of resources that we put in place in the ninth edition in the discussion of the rules for description in chapter 4. It is divided according to the eight areas of the International Standard Bibliographic Description (ISBD), rather than according to type of material being cataloged. There continues to be such a proliferation in ways in which information can be presented that it seems appropriate to concentrate on presentation in a catalog record of the identifying data that will clearly describe information packages and aid in the provision of access to information packages, rather than to concentrate upon the physical manifestations of the information packages. The work of creating this conceptual approach in the ninth edition was ably accomplished by my colleague, David P. Miller, Levin Library, Curry College. Mr. Miller also updated the chapters covering analytic materials, choice of access points, and form of headings for names and titles. For the revised ninth edition Mr. Miller completed major updating of these four chapters to incorporate the changes that came with the 2002 revision of *AACR2*, and again for this tenth edition, he has accomplished much of the updating of these four chapters.

In Part IV, considerations of authority control have been updated to reflect current concerns with international access, where thought must be given to various cultural and verbal traditions that differ from each other. None can be considered to be superior, and ways must be found to integrate these different approaches into one means of access to all the world's information. Sections have been added discussing *FRBR* and functions of the catalog with respect to authority control.

The subject analysis chapters that constitute Part V have been thoroughly revised in addition to being rearranged to cover verbal subject approaches before classificatory ones. Results of new research have been added. Discussion of natural language processing and ontologies has been updated, and discussion of taxonomies is included. In the area of verbal subject access, the chapters on *Library of Congress Subject Headings* (*LCSH*) and *Sears List of Subject Headings* have been completely revised to reflect the changes in terminology, attitudes, and approaches manifested in the most recent editions of those lists. Chapter 11 on *LCSH* also has been updated to include the online access that is now widely available for both the list (available through *Classification Web*) and the tools needed to apply terminology from the list (available through *Cataloger's Desktop*). A section on FAST (Faceted Application of Subject Terminology) was also added. Updating for the 18th edition of *Sears* was accomplished in Chapter 12. Chapter 13 for "other" types of verbal access includes discussions of the newest editions of the thesauri described there along with new descriptions of the online versions of these thesauri that are now available.

Chapter 15 for Decimal Classification has been updated to the 22nd full edition and the 14th abridged edition of the *Dewey Decimal Classification*, and a new section on *WebDewey* has been added. Additional historical information and rationale for its creation has been added to the section on Universal Decimal Classification, along with updating to reflect the changes that have occurred in that scheme since 2000. Most of the *Library of Congress Classification* (*LCC*) schedules have been revised since the ninth edition, and Chapter 16 reflects the new revisions. Particularly noteworthy for *LCC* in the last five years is the wide availability of *Classification Web*, and information about this resource is now included.

Although the process of adding cutter numbers to classification notations to create call numbers has changed little, Chapter 17 dealing with this topic has been revised to try to present clearer explanations of certain concepts, such as cuttering of biographies, that have been noted by students as being confusing. Chapter 18 for "other" classifications has new material about taxonomies.

The administrative issues in Part VI, which consists of Chapter 19, "Processing Centers, Networking, and Cooperative Programs," and Chapter 20, "Catalog Management," have been completely updated. The changes in these areas have been dramatic, and the new chapters reflect much new work by the Library of Congress and by bibliographic networks, along with completely new ways of accomplishing the control of catalogs. In particular in Chapter 19, major updating gives information about OCLC's Connexion service, and describes major changes in the services offered by RLG and by A-G Canada. Chapter 20's revisions reflect the nearly complete move to managing catalogs and cataloging processing in online modes of operation.

The glossary includes many new terms, reflecting the major changes in the world of information since 2000. Some obsolete terms have been deleted, and many other definitions in the glossary have been updated. The selected bibliography also has listed many new resources.

Most examples of MARC records used in this edition are shown in the format that is displayed in OCLC's Connexion service. I am grateful to OCLC for permission to use their format in this book.

There are a number of people whose assistance I wish to acknowledge. Again, I acknowledge the work of David P. Miller in updating the chapters related to *AACR2*. He also revised Chapter 19, "Processing Centers, Networking, and Cooperative Programs" (previously written by Dr. Barbara B. Tillett) for this edition. Chapter 20, "Catalog Management" (with the exception of the section on "Outsourcing"), was revised and updated by Dr. Susan Hayes, Bobst Library, New York University. The section on Outsourcing was originally written by Katherine Ryner, Library & Technology Resources, St. Mary's College of Maryland, for the ninth edition, although a small amount of updating for the tenth edition was completed by myself. For all the assistance from Mr. Miller, Dr. Hayes, and Ms. Ryner, I am deeply grateful.

A person who has patiently assisted with answering my many questions is Lynn El-Hoshy, Cataloging Policy and Support Office, Library of Congress. I appreciate her assistance immensely. And I am very indebted to Dr. Daniel N. Joudrey, formerly my student, but now my colleague in a teaching position for the Graduate School of Library and Information Science, Simmons College. He has made numerous suggestions for updating various portions of this book, and he completed an initial survey of the glossary to identify terms that were obsolete, in need of attention, or were missing. I am very grateful for his support.

I wish to thank the many teachers of cataloging who use this work as a text. They continue to be supportive, to make helpful suggestions, and to encourage me to persevere in my attempts to make the book as "user-friendly" as possible. Many students, also, have made suggestions for improvements. One student, in particular, Christine Fullerton, completed a first pass at updating the bibliography for this edition.

I am most grateful to my husband, A. Wayne Benson, for his ability to understand and accept that revising books can totally consume my time and energy. His patience, encouragement, and "wordsmithing" are acknowledged and deeply appreciated.

I continue to appreciate the opportunity afforded me by Dr. Bohdan S. Wynar to work on and to eventually take over this text. Finally, I wish to thank Dr. Sue Easun, Emma Bailey, and other members of the editorial and production staffs of Libraries Unlimited for their major contributions to this work.

—Arlene G. Taylor

Part I
INTRODUCTION

Cataloging in Context

INTRODUCTION

The purposes of this chapter are to set the context in which cataloging takes place and to introduce the basic concepts of cataloging. The discussion begins with an introduction to the whole realm of bibliographic control and where catalogs fit into that realm. Catalogs are discussed, with attention given to their functions, their forms, arrangements of their entries, and their component parts. An overview of the entire process of cataloging is then given—descriptive cataloging, subject analysis, and authority control—followed by a look at cooperative and copy cataloging that makes original cataloging of all materials for every collection unnecessary. Finally, there is an introduction to the formats of bibliographic records in catalogs.

BIBLIOGRAPHIC CONTROL

Definitions

Cataloging is a subset of the larger field that is sometimes called bibliographic control, or organization of information, and it is helpful to view it in that context. Bibliographic control has been defined by Elaine Svenonius as "the skill or art . . . of organizing knowledge (information) for retrieval."[1] Richard P. Smiraglia defines it as "encompassing the creation, storage, manipulation, and retrieval of bibliographic data."[2] Arlene G. Taylor, in *The Organization of Information*, points out that "retrieval of information is dependent upon its having been organized." She goes on to say that "organization of information also allows us to keep a usable record of human endeavors for posterity."[3]

Anyone who has attempted to maintain a file of references to articles, books, and other types of materials containing information on a particular subject, or perhaps by a particular artist or author, has practiced bibliographic control over a very small part of the universe of information/knowledge. For such a project to succeed it is necessary to decide what elements of data to record about each article, book, or other container of information/knowledge, referred to hereinafter as *information package* or *resource*.[4] It may be decided to record author(s), title, keywords, abstract, and location of the information package. These become the data to be stored, manipulated, and retrieved. As the file grows, storing, manipulating, and retrieving become more and more complex. Then, art and skill become necessary for successful creation, maintenance, and use of the file.

In the universe of all knowledge (including knowledge that cannot necessarily be expressed verbally—e.g., music, art) there is a certain amount of that knowledge that has been recorded in some way—e.g., written down, printed, digitized, recorded, painted. This subset is often referred to as the bibliographic universe. Only the bibliographic universe can be controlled. Such control is performed by means of bibliographic tools in which each discrete item of knowledge is represented by a bibliographic record (also sometimes called an *entry* or *surrogate record* or *metadata*). Bibliographic tools (which are also *retrieval tools*) include bibliographies, indexes, catalogs, finding aids, registers, bibliographic databases, and search engines. We have been told by futurists that someday when all recorded information/knowledge is digitized and available online, it will be possible to gain access to needed information directly online without the intermediate step of using bibliographic tools. More and more, though, experts have realized that there must be some kind of control and some way to have preliminary information (e.g., title, author, date, subject keywords, etc.) before one tries to sort through thousands of information packages. The creation of a number of metadata standards is a result. Taylor defines *metadata* as "an encoded description of an information package (e.g., an *AACR2* [*Anglo-American Cataloguing Rules, Second Edition*] record encoded with MARC [MAchine-Readable Cataloging], a Dublin Core record, a GILS [Government Information Locator Service] record, etc.)."[5]

Component Parts of Bibliographic Control

Librarians and library users have traditionally been taught that bibliographies, indexes, catalogs, etc., are quite different tools. In fact they are all parts of the same realm of bibliographic control, but they have developed separately and in somewhat different formats for various reasons. Economic factors have been pervasive in the development of catalogs in libraries. Because libraries are generally not-for-profit agencies, there have seldom been enough resources to allow library catalogs to provide access deeper than what might be called "macrolevel indexing"—i.e., access to a whole book, entire serial, etc. Other agencies have stepped in to create indexes with what might be called "microlevel indexing"—i.e., access to articles in serials, poetry in collections, chapters in books, etc. These are sold for profit, while access to library catalogs generally has not been sold. (There are also indexes that analyze the contents of a single item—e.g., "back-of-the-book" indexes—but these are usually published at the same time as the item rather than being prepared separately for the purposes of bibliographic control.)

Although this is rapidly changing, economic constraints have dictated generally that library catalogs in the past could index only materials owned and housed in that particular library, and in this sense each one has been a microcosm of the entire bibliographic universe. On the other hand, periodical indexes have covered items owned and not owned by a library; that is, an index may cover a broader portion of the bibliographic universe. Bibliographies typically cover much smaller parts of the universe than either catalogs or indexes. That is, each bibliography usually has one subject or theme—e.g., works of an author, works on a particular subject, items published during a particular time or in a particular place. (Subsets of this category include discographies and art catalogs.) Because of their limited scope, bibliographies can easily include entries at both macro- and microlevels.

In the recent past technology has enabled bibliographic databases to be developed without the earlier economic constraints that limited the level of indexing. Many online bibliographic databases are enhanced indexes. That is, they provide microlevel indexing of bibliographic entities and provide more bibliographic data for each item indexed—e.g., more keywords, abstracts, tables of contents, etc. There are also a number of bibliographic databases that provide primarily macrolevel indexing and function as extended catalogs.

Finding aids have been developed in archives as lengthy surrogate records for whole collections housed by an archive. In archives a catalog record is often made for each finding aid. Registers have been developed in museums and provide the means for maintaining control over the artifacts housed in a museum. The Internet has retrieval tools called search engines. Most of these do not create surrogate records ahead of time, but create them "on-the-fly," using quotations from Web sites that use the word(s) sought, as requests are made by users.

An important feature of catalogs is that they typically have some kind of authority control, while the other tools typically have little or no such control over names and titles, although indexes, especially, often have some control over subject terms used. Authority control is, in part, a result of the process of maintaining consistency in the forms of the headings used in a bibliographic tool. A heading is a character string provided at the beginning of an entry in a bibliographic tool and provides one means for finding that entry. In some printed tools and in most computer systems the heading is provided at the top of a column, page, or screen on which several entries for the heading may appear. In a tool with authority control a heading is given in the "official" form representing a name, title, or subject. Authority control is defined and discussed in more detail later in this chapter.

One difficulty with the fragmentation of bibliographic control into different bibliographic tools is that users are expected to know about the existence of all of them and to be able to use them effectively. This is a somewhat unreasonable expectation since the tools overlap in their coverage of the bibliographic universe but provide their coverage in different ways. Approaches to searching the tools differ, as do the vocabularies used for searching. Once desired entries are found, conventions for displaying bibliographic data differ. In tools where there is no authority control, one cannot know whether all possible forms of a name, title, or term have been found. In an ideal bibliographic control environment a user could start with any tool and be led to other tools as needed without having to know ahead of time which tool would be appropriate.

Functions of Bibliographic Tools

Bibliographic tools have three basic functions. The first is the identifying function. All tools aim at allowing a user, who has a citation or has a particular bibliographic item in mind, to match that known item with an entry in the tool—limited, of course, by the scope of the tool. The scope of a library catalog, for example, is often the items owned by the institution; therefore, the user should be able to match or identify or find an entry for a known item that the library owns, or for an item that is elsewhere but to which the local institution can provide access.

The second function is the collocating or gathering function. Collocation is a means for bringing together in one place in a bibliographic tool all entries for like and closely related materials; for example, items about dinosaurs are grouped together. In many cases a particular work is shown in its relationship to a larger group of works—e.g., the bibliographic record for a play based upon *Huckleberry Finn* should be found with records for editions of *Huckleberry Finn*, which are in turn found with records for other works of Mark Twain. One of the best ways of accomplishing collocation is through the process of authority control. If entries for *Huckleberry Finn* are sometimes found in the H's (under *Huckleberry Finn*) and sometimes in the A's (under *Adventures of Huckleberry Finn*) with no connecting references, collocation has not been accomplished.

The third function of bibliographic tools is the evaluating function. This function allows a user to choose from among many records or entries the one that best seems to represent the knowledge/information or specific physical item desired. For example, a user looking for a particular edition of *Huckleberry Finn* should be able to select it from among several, if it is one of those listed in the tool; or, given a choice between a spoken recording on tape or CD, a user could choose the one appropriate for the equipment available. It can be seen that the three functions are somewhat interdependent.

Uses of Bibliographic Control

In *Functional Requirements of Bibliographic Records (FRBR)*[6] the functions of bibliographic control are essential for the ultimate purpose of allowing users to fulfill user tasks. These tasks as listed in *FRBR* are:

- to *find* entities that correspond to the user's stated search criteria . . .
- to *identify* an entity . . .
- to *select* an entity that is appropriate to the user's needs . . .
- to acquire or *obtain* access to the entity described . . .[7]

Catalogers, indexers, abstractors, bibliographers, and information scientists establish bibliographic control over portions of the bibliographic universe. Reference librarians, readers' advisers, and information specialists create a bridge between the user and the many bibliographic tools available. The institutional library is a major focus of these activities, but not the only one. Archives, museums, the Internet, individual freelance efforts, and commercial enterprises also play a role.[8]

The bibliographic tool *created* in the institutional library is the catalog, although extensive *use* is made of all the bibliographic tools in that setting. *Groups* of libraries work together to create some of the online databases—those that are essentially extended catalogs for the holdings of more than one library. The remainder of this book concentrates on the processes involved in creating, maintaining, and providing access to catalogs and catalog-like databases.

CATALOGS

Definition and Functions

A catalog is an organized set of bibliographic records that represent the holdings of a particular collection and/or resources accessible in a particular location. A collection may consist of any of several types of materials—e.g., books, periodicals, maps, coins, sound recordings, paintings, musical scores, to name a few. Traditionally the collection represented by a catalog has been located in one place or at least in different parts of the same institution. Increasingly, however, catalogs represent the holdings of more than one library, as libraries form consortiums and otherwise link their catalogs for the purposes of interlibrary sharing. (Such catalogs are sometimes called union catalogs.) In addition catalogs include many Internet resources that are not owned, but to which the library can provide access.

Why prepare catalogs? Catalogs are necessary whenever a collection grows too large to be remembered item for item. A small private library or a classroom library has little need for a formal catalog; the user can recall each book, sound recording, map, or other such item by author, title, subject, the item's shape, its color, or its position on a particular shelf. When such a collection becomes a little larger, an informal arrangement, such as grouping the items by subject categories, provides access to them. When a collection becomes too large for such a simple approach, a formal record is necessary. There are two major reasons to make such a formal record in larger collections: for retrieval and for inventory purposes. In addition to being unable to remember what is in a large collection for access purposes, it also becomes impossible for the owner to remember what has been acquired, lost, replaced, etc. A catalog can serve as a record of what is owned.

The functions of bibliographic control mentioned earlier—identifying, collocating, evaluating—are functions of every bibliographic tool, including catalogs. These functions for catalogs were stated by Charles A. Cutter in his *Rules for a Dictionary Catalog* in 1904. He first stated what he thought the objectives [which he called "objects"] of a catalog should be and then gave his view of the "means" by which the "objects" would be accomplished. His statement serves as the basis for today's understanding of the functions of a catalog, although in modern practice the statement is somewhat incomplete:

Objects
1. To enable a person to find a book of which either
   (A) the author
   (B) the title   } is known.
   (C) the subject

2. To show what the library has
   (D) by a given author
   (E) on a given subject
   (F) in a given kind of literature.

3. To assist in the choice of a book
   (G) as to the edition (bibliographically).
   (H) as to its character (literary or topical).

Means
1. Author-entry with the necessary references (for A and D).
2. Title-entry or title-reference (for B).
3. Subject-entry, cross-references, and classed subject-table (for C and E).
4. Form-entry and language-entry (for F).
5. Giving edition and imprint, with notes when necessary (for G).
6. Notes (for H).[9]

To conform to modern practice, the first objective needs to be rephrased as follows: To enable a person to find any intellectual creation whether issued in a print, nonprint, or electronic format.   Cutter's first object is inadequate even for printed materials inasmuch as "book" does not unambiguously encompass "periodical," "serial," or "pamphlet."

Cutter's object "E" also does not go far enough for our current understanding. Rephrased, it should read "on given and related subjects." It is clearly a prime function of a catalog to guide patrons in using the system of subject headings that any particular library may have adopted. Cutter's apparent assumption that the user always has a clearly formulated "given" subject in mind is contrary to all observation of catalog users.

Cutter's objectives remained the primary statement of catalog principles until 1961, when the International Federation of Library Associations (IFLA) at the Paris Conference approved a statement about the purpose of an author/title catalog. It stated that the catalog should be an efficient instrument for ascertaining:

1) whether the library contains a particular book specified by:
    a) its author and title, *or*
    b) if no author is named in the book, its title alone, *or*
    c) if author and title are inappropriate or insufficient for identification, a suitable substitute for the title,

and 2) a) which works by a particular author *and*
    b) which editions of a particular work are in the library.[10]

These principles, often called the "Paris Principles," were purposely restricted to an author/title catalog, and so no mention is made of subject access; but they, as well as Cutter's rules, bring out the three functions already mentioned of identifying (1.a–1.c), collocating (2.a–2.b), and evaluating (2.b).   In both Cutter's statement and the Paris Principles, the evaluating function is limited to choice of edition and to Cutter's "choice of a book . . . as to its character." With time and the advent of multiple ways of presenting the same work, both intellectually and physically, it has become more important to make certain that the catalog can assist users in making choices. This continues a long history of evolution of functions of the catalog.

New international principles are in the process of completion at this writing. In the "final" draft of these principles the functions of the catalog are to enable a user:

3.1. to **find** bibliographic resources in a collection (real or virtual) as the result of a search using attributes or relationships of the resources. . .

3.2. to **identify** a bibliographic resource or agent. . .

3.3. to **select** a bibliographic resource that is appropriate to the user's needs. . .

3.4.   to **acquire** or **obtain** access to an item described. . .

3.5. to **navigate** a catalogue (that is, through the logical arrangement of bibliographic information and presentation of clear ways to move about. . .)[11]

An additional function of a catalog brought out in the new principles is that of locating, a function not always served by other bibliographic tools. One can tell from a library catalog whether the library contains a certain information package and, if so, where it is physically located. This is true even of expanded interlibrary union catalogs in the sense that the catalog identifies which libraries house particular items, although one may need more detail to know where in a particular library to find an item. With many catalogs, the circulation system is linked, making it possible for the user to learn whether or not an item is circulating. Virtual locations of Internet information packages are provided in catalogs through their uniform resource locators (URLs).

Forms of Catalogs

A library catalog may exist in one of several physical formats: book catalog, card catalog, microform catalog, or online computer catalog, with the online catalog being the most common. The printed book catalog is the oldest type known in the United States; it was used by many American libraries as the most common form of catalog until the late 1800s. The report of the Bureau of Education in 1876 gives a list of 1,010 printed book catalogs, 382 of them published from 1870 to 1876. Because book catalogs were rather expensive to produce and quickly became outdated, they were gradually replaced by card catalogs. In a survey of 58 typical American libraries undertaken in 1893, 43 libraries had complete card catalogs and 13 had printed book catalogs with card supplements.[12] Thus, for many years book catalogs were out of favor in American libraries.

It was only with advances in less expensive printing and with the advent of automation for quicker cumulation that book catalogs again became popular with certain types of libraries. An example of a book catalog produced by more modern production techniques was the Library of Congress's (LC) *Catalog of Books Represented by Library of Congress Printed Cards*, known after 1956 as the *National Union Catalog*. It was published only in microform from 1983 through 2002, when publication ceased. As its earlier title indicates, it was, for many years, produced by photographic reduction of pre-existing catalog cards; hence, it was a by-product of a card catalog. A similar technique has been used by a number of commercial publishers (e.g., G. K. Hall), which have reproduced card catalogs of certain libraries in a book catalog format.

Beginning in the 1950s, a new type of book catalog appeared, based on the use of computers. These computer-produced catalogs, using machine-readable cataloging records, varied widely in format, typography, extent of bibliographic detail, and pattern of updating. LC began publishing its book catalog series via computer in the 1970s.

At the beginning of the 1990s the card catalog was still the library catalog most often found in the United States. It is still found in libraries that have not been able to afford the software and equipment necessary for an online catalog, and it is also found in libraries that have not been able to complete the retrospective conversion of records from card format to machine-readable format. Each entry was prepared on a standard 7.5 cm x 12.5 cm card (roughly 3" x 5"), although the size was not always standard. In the first card catalogs a variety of sizes was used from library to library, including 1½" x 5", 1½" x 10", and 4" x 6". Entries on cards were at first hand-written before the typewriter came into standard use. Typeset cards were available from LC beginning in 1901. Later, cards were often prepared by photoreproduction of a printed or typed original. Cards are now most often computer-produced from machine-readable catalog records.

Microform catalogs became much more popular with the development of computer output microform (COM). COM catalogs could be produced in either microfilm or microfiche. It was feasible with this form of catalog to provide a completely integrated new catalog every three months or so, rather than providing supplements to be used with a main catalog. However, microform catalogs were not popular with users.

The online computer catalog, often referred to as an online public access catalog (or OPAC), has rapidly become the catalog of choice. Bibliographic records stored in the computer memory are displayed on a video screen in response to a request from a user. Entries may comprise the full bibliographic record or only parts of it, depending on the system and/or the desires of the user. Until the 1990s such systems were costly, and only very large libraries were able to afford them.

Now systems have been developed for use on every size computer from mainframes to personal computers and have become quite affordable. There are so many choices of systems with operations and retrievals configured so differently that many librarians are finding it difficult to choose among them. Our current era resembles the time before the standardization of the card catalog, when sizes of cards and order of elements of bibliographic data differed from library to library. As we learn what works best, OPACs will eventually become standardized as did card catalogs.

An effective catalog in any format should possess certain qualities that will allow it to be easily consulted and maintained. If it is too difficult, too cumbersome, or too expensive, it is virtually useless. The following criteria may be considered for judging a catalog:

- **A catalog should be flexible and up-to-date.** A library's collection is constantly changing. Since the catalog is a record of what is available in that library, entries should be added or removed as items are added to or discarded from the collection. The card catalog and the OPAC are totally flexible. Records can be easily added to or removed from the files whenever necessary. However, backlogs of records to be entered can develop, especially with card catalogs.

    Book, COM, and CD-ROM catalogs are inflexible in that once they have been printed, additions or deletions cannot be made except in supplements or new editions of the catalog. On the other hand, because they are computer-produced, they can provide flexibility in making changes in existing entries for new editions of the catalog. For example, a single command can change many entries, while with a card catalog, each card must be changed individually. OPACs can be considered the most flexible and current of all catalog formats. Additions, deletions, and changes can be made at any time, and the results are usually instantly available to the user, or at least are available by the next day.

- **A catalog should be constructed so that all entries can be quickly and easily found.** This is a matter of labeling, filing, and, in the case of online catalogs, simple and clear screen instructions. So far as the card catalog is concerned, the contents of each tray must be identified to the extent that a patron who wants to locate, for example, the works of Charles Dickens can find the Dickens entries easily. The patron must know exactly what part of the alphabet each tray contains. Within the trays themselves, arrangement of entries must be such that items are not overlooked because the filing is not alphabetical, and guide cards should be sufficiently plentiful to identify coverage. Book catalogs are usually labeled on the spine, like encyclopedias. Often they have guides at the top of each page, indicating what entries are covered there.

    Microfilm catalogs typically are stored in readers that are equipped with alphabetic index strips designed to get the user to the desired part of the alphabet. Microfiche catalogs have eye-readable labels at the top of each sheet of fiche that indicate the part of the alphabet covered. Typically, each sheet of fiche has a microimage index in one corner that tells in which cross section of the fiche particular parts of the alphabet are found. Such systems are time-consuming to use, and reading the magnified fiche is often difficult. Many patrons will do almost anything to avoid using a microfiche catalog.

    Filing arrangement in computer-produced catalogs is not the same as in traditionally filed card catalogs because of the difficulty of programming computers to arrange according to traditional library filing rules. As a result, traditional rules have been re-evaluated, and now filing rules more closely resemble computer filing rules.

Entries are located in online catalogs in a variety of ways. In some the computer must be told whether an author, title, or subject search is desired. A few systems still require the user to construct "search keys" made up of combinations of letters and/or words. For example, a title search key may consist of the first three letters of the first word that is not an article plus the first letter of each of the next three words. In most systems one can enter as much of the title, author, or subject as seems useful, starting at the left of the entry as it would appear in a card catalog. Most systems also allow users to input only the words they remember in any order (called *keyword* searching), and the system searches for all records containing all the words input. The most recently created systems allow sophisticated combinations of searching certain words from an author field, other words from a title field, words from a subject field, etc., all at the same time.

Responses to searches in online catalogs also vary by system. In some of the first systems, display of multiple responses (e.g., a listing of works by Charles Dickens) was in the order of "last in, first out"—the last record cataloged or worked on in some way was the first one displayed—and there was no alphabetical collocation. Ironically, the first Web-based catalogs returned to this order of display. Most systems now alphabetize displays, but are not consistent in the way that the arrangement is accomplished. And quite a few systems now allow a user to choose display order (e.g., chronological, reverse chronological, alphabetical by author, etc.)

- **A catalog should be economically prepared and maintained.** The catalog that can be prepared most inexpensively and with greatest attention to currency has obvious advantages.

In summary, the following observations can be made about the major types of catalog:

The online catalog, with the exception of that using CD-ROM technology, is the most flexible and current. Online catalogs, including the CD-ROM versions, are compact and entries can be found quickly. Searching methods and retrieval displays, however, are not standardized, and collocation is not as reliable as in other types of catalogs. It is the most expensive type of catalog; however, expense is offset by such things as the ability to offer the catalog for searching from distant sites and the great potential for new and innovative ways of searching.

Cards for the card catalog are easy to prepare and relatively inexpensive. The chief virtue of the card catalog is its flexibility. Although it is not compact and trays cannot ordinarily be removed for long intensive study, it should be remembered that many people can use it at the same time, as long as they do not need the same drawer.

The book catalog is expensive to prepare unless numerous copies of the catalog are required; library systems that need multiple copies will find the book catalog less costly than the card catalog. Entries can be found quickly in the book catalog, and it is compact, easy to store, and easy to handle; however, it lacks flexibility.

The microform catalog is much less expensive than the book catalog, and there is evidence that its maintenance is less expensive than for the card catalog, although the initial investment in catalog conversion to machine-readable form is high. It is compact and easy to store. It can be flexible if the library can afford to run new cumulations often. However, many patrons find the microfiche versions particularly unpleasant to use.

Arrangement of Entries in a Catalog

A printed catalog (unlike an online catalog) requires multiple copies of each bibliographic record so that the record can be found under any of several access points. Traditionally there is an access point for each author and any other person or corporate body associated with intellectual creation of the work and deemed important enough that someone might search for them. There are also access points for titles, variant titles, and subject headings assigned to the record. A copy of the bibliographic record appears under each access point. In some book and microform catalogs a full copy of the record appears only at the "main" access point (a concept discussed in more detail later in this chapter and in chapter 6), and abbreviated versions appear at all other access points. In all printed catalogs each access point with its associated version of the bibliographic record is called an entry.

Online catalogs do not have "entries" in the same sense. One master copy of each bibliographic record is stored by the system. Indexes are made that link each name, title, subject heading, or other entity decided upon as an access point to any associated bibliographic record. In response to a search request, selected data elements from each relevant bibliographic record are copied to the user's screen in the display format chosen for that system.

A printed catalog (unlike an online catalog) must be arranged according to some definite plan. Depending on the subject and scope of the collection, many arrangements are possible. But no matter which one is used, it should cover the contents of the collection and guide the person who consults it to these contents.

Online catalogs must arrange the results of a search on the user's screen. In some instances the user is allowed to choose to have the display presented by main author, by date, by classification number, or by title, to name a few. The choice having been made, however, the user does not have control over any further subarrangement.

Public access catalogs are traditionally arranged according to one of two systems: classified or alphabetical. The differences between them lie in the arrangement of the entries, or in the display of responses to queries.[13]

Classified Catalogs

The classified catalog has the longest history. Many American libraries used this form before they changed to the more popular alphabetical form. It is based upon the system of classification used in a particular library. The shelflist, a record of the holdings of a library arranged by classification notation, is a classified catalog of a kind. But in a true classified catalog, a bibliographic record may be entered under as many classification notations as apply to its contents, not under just one notation as in a shelflist. In addition, the shelflist lacks an alphabetical subject index, which a true classified catalog has. In fact, classified catalogs constitute only the subject part of a divided catalog (*see* discussion below). They must be accompanied by a name/title catalog. Figure 1.1 (*see* page 14) shows a complete set of cards for a classified card catalog.

The major advantage of a classified catalog is that because it uses symbols, letters, and/or numbers, it can keep up with changing terminology and thus be up-to-date. It is also useful for in-depth study of a subject. Closely related classes are brought together in sequence—often hierarchically. This is good for scanning or for moving from general to specific. In addition this arrangement permits easy compilation of subject bibliographies. Perhaps its greatest disadvantage is that it is constructed on a particular classification scheme (even though this was an advantage as noted above). Since many patrons are not familiar with classification notations, they might need special assistance when consulting the classified catalog. Numerous Internet sites are organized by classification schemes. At these sites, the notations are not used without verbal equivalents, and in most cases, the notations are not used at all; so the user is not required to understand the meanings of notations. This approach is quite popular for browsing purposes. Perhaps Web-based catalogs will eventually offer such an option for display.

Some fields—particularly the sciences—can make good use of such a catalog, since the classified catalog is flexible and can be easily updated—e.g., only the index entries would have to be changed when terminology for a concept changes, rather than having to revise all records using the concept. Classified catalogs are also of value in locations where the patrons may speak one or two or more languages. In such a case, an alphabetical subject index may be made in each language. In Quebec, for example, where both English and French are spoken, there would be one major classified catalog with French and English indexes. There are only a few classified catalogs in use in the United States today. They are more widely used in Europe, Canada, and a few other countries. There are some predictions that international cooperation will encourage the use of classification for subject exchange, since classification symbols transcend language.

Alphabetical Catalogs

Alphabetical catalogs came into being because of their ease of arrangement and use. The alphabet is commonly understood. A user is likely to find information under direct terms—those consulted first by choice. Verbal headings are more easily understood than classification symbols. On the other hand, some terminology is quickly dated, and many terms have multiple meanings. In very large catalogs alphabetic arrangement becomes quite complex. There are two traditional arrangements of alphabetical catalogs: dictionary and divided.

Dictionary Catalogs

In the dictionary arrangement of card catalog entries, widely used in American libraries until the 1990s, all the entries—name, title, and subject—were combined, word by word, into one alphabetical file. This arrangement was said to be simple; undoubtedly it was, in the sense that only one file needed to be consulted. As libraries grew, however, the dictionary arrangement became cumbersome and complex, because all entries were interfiled. The problem became partly one of filing (are books by Charles Dickens, for example, filed before those about him?) and partly one of dispersion. The subject of "industrial relations" has many aspects. How can all these aspects be located if they are entered under headings from "A" for "arbitration" to "W" for "wages"? Two primary justifications have been offered in favor of the dictionary arrangement: most patrons seek material on one aspect of a subject rather than upon the broad subject itself, and patrons are provided with ample *see* and *see also* references, which direct them to other aspects of their subjects. Ironically, as card catalogs and cataloging backlogs grew, many libraries stopped making references for subjects in the early 1980s, saying that they would be converting to online catalogs "soon," and, therefore, inconvenience to users would not last long. However, online catalogs began to provide subject references with regularity only in the mid to late 1990s. Figure 1.2 (*see* page 15) shows a complete set of cards for a dictionary catalog.

Fig. 1.1. Card set for a classified catalog.

Series card for
name/title section
of catalog ⟶

016.282
M121c
Research studies in library science ;
no. 20

Title card for
name/title section
of catalog ⟶

016.282
M121c
Critical guide to Catholic
reference books.
McCabe, James Patrick.
Critical guide to Catholic reference books /
James Patrick McCabe ; with an introduction by

016.282
M121c

McCabe, James Patrick.
Critical guide to Catholic reference books /
James Patrick McCabe ; with an introduction by
Russell E. Bidlack. -- 3rd ed. -- Englewood,
Colo. : Libraries Unlimited, 1989.
xiv, 323 p. ; 25 cm. -- (Research studies in
library science ; no. 20)

Includes index.

Author card for
name/title
section of ⟶
catalog

282.016   016.282
                                          M121c

McCabe, James Patrick.
Critical guide to Catholic reference books /
James Patrick McCabe ; with an introduction by

270.016   016.282
                                          M121c   .n

McCabe, James Patrick.
Critical guide to Catholic reference books /
James Patrick McCabe ; with an introduction by

Cards for
classified
section of ⟶
catalog

230.016   016.282
                                       M121c   s in

McCabe, James Patrick.
Critical guide to Catholic reference books /

016.282   016.282
                                          M121c

McCabe, James Patrick.
Critical guide to Catholic reference books /
James Patrick McCabe ; with an introduction by
Russell E. Bidlack. -- 3rd ed. -- Englewood,
Colo. : Libraries Unlimited, 1989.
xiv, 323 p. ; 25 cm. -- (Research studies in
library science ; no. 20)

Includes index.
ISBN 0-87287-621-7 : $45.00

I. Title.   282.016   230.016
270.016

Fig. 1.2. Card set for an alphabetical catalog.

Series added
entry card

Title added
entry card

Subject added
entry cards

Shelflist
card

Main entry
card

Research studies in library science ;
        no. 20
Z   McCabe, James Patrick.
674   Critical guide to Catholic reference books /
.R4   James Patrick McCabe ; with an introduction by
no.20   Russell E. Bidlack. -- 3rd ed. -- Englewood,

Critical guide to Catholic reference books.
Z   McCabe, James Patrick.
674   Critical guide to Catholic reference books /
.R4   James Patrick McCabe ; with an introduction by
no.20   Russell E. Bidlack. -- 3rd ed. -- Englewood,

REFERENCE BOOKS--CATHOLIC CHURCH
Z   McCabe, James Patrick.
674   Critical guide to Catholic reference books /
.R4   James Patrick McCabe ; with an introduction by
no.20   Russell E. Bidlack. -- 3rd ed. -- Englewood,
        Colo. : Libraries Unlimited, 1989.

CATHOLIC CHURCH--BIBLIOGRAPHY
Z   McCabe, James Patrick.
674   Critical guide to Catholic reference books /
.R4   James Patrick McCabe ; with an introduction by
no.20   Russell E. Bidlack. -- 3rd ed. -- Englewood,

Z   McCabe, James Patrick.
674   Critical guide to Catholic reference books /
.R4   James Patrick McCabe ; with an introduction by
no.20   Russell E. Bidlack. -- 3rd ed. -- Englewood,
        Colo. : Libraries Unlimited, 1989.
            xiv, 323 p. ; 25 cm. -- (Research studies in
Ref   library science ; no. 20)
cop.1
            Includes index.

Z   McCabe, James Patrick.
674   Critical guide to Catholic reference books /
.R4   James Patrick McCabe ; with an introduction by
no.20   Russell E. Bidlack. -- 3rd ed. -- Englewood,
        Colo. : Libraries Unlimited, 1989.
            xiv, 323 p. ; 25 cm. -- (Research studies in
        library science ; no. 20)

            Includes index.
        ISBN 0-87287-621-7 : $45.00

            1. Catholic Church--Bibliography.
        2. Reference Books.   --Catholic Church.
        I. Title.   II. Series.

Divided Catalogs

In the 1930s the realization that dictionary catalogs were becoming more and more complex led to a modification of the dictionary arrangement. The result was the divided catalog, which, in its most common form, is in reality two catalogs: one for entries other than subject; the other for subject entries only. The divided catalog permits a simpler filing scheme than does the dictionary catalog, making it easier to consult; although the problem of scattered subjects still exists. There is a further complication implicit in this arrangement. The patron must determine whether an author or title entry or a subject entry is wanted before knowing which part of the catalog must be checked. When this divided approach is used, books about Dickens and books by Dickens are not filed together in the catalog. Catalog users need some guidance and education in this matter. OPACs have perpetuated this problem.

There were some libraries that used other types of divided catalogs, such as the three-way divided catalog consisting of separate sections for author, title, and subject entries. Although this system may have simplified the filing of cards, it can be even more confusing for a patron than the two-way divided catalog. In this arrangement, entries for books by Dickens are filed under Dickens' name in the author catalog, the titles of his individual novels are filed in the title catalog, and books about Dickens are filed in the subject catalog.

Another type of two-way divided catalog is a name/title catalog and a topical subject catalog. In such a divided catalog, names and titles that are used even as subject headings are filed in the name/title section. This type of divided catalog allows all the material by and about an author or a title to be filed together. To continue our previous example, books by and books about Dickens would be filed together in the same catalog. This system is potentially less confusing to the patron than any other form of divided catalog.

Arrangements of Online Catalogs

Because entries do not have to be arranged in a linear fashion, online catalogs do not fit easily in the earlier mentioned categories. The internal arrangements of records in the computer vary greatly from system to system and make little difference to a user. What does matter to the user is the way in which entries are displayed in response to a search request. Most online catalogs are in effect divided catalogs because a user must choose to search through one of the indexes: author, title, subject, and sometimes classification or other category. In this kind of system, a name as subject is almost always searched through the subject index, separating any records about a person from those representing works by that person. A number of systems allow searching of two indexes at once using the words *and*, *or*, and *not* or their equivalents (a form of what is called Boolean searching). These systems do, of course, allow a sophisticated user to find works by and about a person in a single search, but experience has shown that few library patrons are this capable of manipulating the system. Web-based catalogs offer forms to fill in that automatically create the Boolean search, *if* the user understands that a person's name must be typed in *both* the author field *and* the subject field. Virtually all systems also allow for keyword searching of almost any words in any record. In such a system, a keyword search for a name brings together for display all records for works by and about the person, but the display is most often arranged by date and is not collocated in any logical fashion.

In online catalogs that provide for searching by classification notation, there is a semblance of a classified catalog except that in United States cataloging practice each work is limited to one place in a classification scheme. In this respect it is more like a shelflist (*see* discussion below). In time there may be ways to gain access to bibliographic records through the hierarchy of the classification scheme used to classify the works they represent.

Components of Catalog Systems

Basically there are three components making up a whole catalog: a public access catalog, a shelflist, and an authority file or files. In printed catalogs these are separate physical components. In online catalogs the OPAC and shelflist are really different ways to search the same file; the authority file is actually a separate file. The preceding sections on form and arrangements of catalogs have, for the most part, covered public access catalogs. These are the catalogs readily available for the use of library patrons.

A shelflist is a record of the holdings of a library; entries are arranged in the order of the items on the shelf—hence the name "shelflist." With the cataloging of computer files, programs, and Internet resources, for which there is often not a physical item to be placed on a shelf, the name is less descriptive. Records of a library's holdings for such entities may be placed in order by classification notation, acquisition number, or some other device. This pattern will increase as libraries provide access to more materials of this sort in the future. The shelflist record usually contains a record of ownership of numbers of copies and/or volumes held, as well as information about locations of copies, especially when a library is made up of several collections.

Shelflists in print form have traditionally been kept in an area not accessible to the public. There have been notable exceptions to this, however, especially in situations where the areas in which materials are shelved (called stacks) are not open to the public. In these situations, browsing the shelflist can substitute for browsing in the stacks. Another change in availability of shelflists has occurred with online catalogs. When classification is an access point in the catalog, the results of classification notation searches are displayed in shelflist (i.e., classification) order, essentially making the shelflist available to everyone. In addition most online catalogs provide copy and location information at all access points.

Authority files contain records of the forms of names, uniform titles, series, and subject headings that have been chosen as the authorized forms to use as headings in a particular catalog. The authority records also contain lists of references made in the public catalog from unauthorized forms to those used for headings so that users do not have to know authorized forms to use the catalog. Traditionally, these files also have been kept in areas inaccessible to the public. Again, online catalogs have changed this. In some systems, authority files serve as indexes to the catalog.

Online catalogs usually contain these three components, but not always as distinctly separate as they are in printed catalogs. Authority files still are nonexistent in some online catalogs, and in some they are unlinked files; but increasingly they are linked to the bibliographic files so that they may serve as the index(es) to the headings used in the system, and in some cases they serve to alert catalogers automatically to inconsistencies in headings. In addition a number of other components have been added to online catalogs. For example, acquisitions and in-process records are available to the public in many systems, and circulation information—e.g., whether an item is charged out and, if so, when it is due back—is available in virtually every system.

CATALOGING

The means by which catalogs are prepared is through the process called cataloging. This process usually begins with descriptive cataloging and continues with subject analysis, and throughout both phases is intertwined the process of authority control.

Encoding

Encoding permeates the entire cataloging process. The results of each of the descriptive, subject, and authority processes are entered into a machine-readable form that is compatible with the online system in which the catalog record will be used.

Descriptive Cataloging

Descriptive cataloging is that phase of the cataloging process that is concerned with the identification and description of an information package, the recording of this information in the form of a cataloging record, the selection of name and title access points (but not topical subject access points at this stage), the formation of headings for the name and title access points, and the encoding of the data elements so that they will be machine-readable. Descriptive cataloging describes the make-up of an information package and identifies the responsibility for intellectual contents, without reference to its classification by subject or to the assignment of subject headings, both of which are the province of subject cataloging.

Description

Identification and description are interrelated processes in descriptive cataloging. Identification consists of the choice of conventional elements, guided by a set of rules. When the cataloger has properly identified the conventional elements, they are described in a catalog record in such a fashion that the description is unique and can be applied to no other entity in the collection. In other words, each information package should be distinguished from everything with which it could be confused. Elements considered essential for this purpose in describing physical information packages are title, statement of responsibility, edition information, and publication, distribution, or production information. Physical description—extent and size of item—and series data are often essential to this purpose as well. Components essential for describing virtual information packages (e.g., Internet documents) are title, statement of responsibility, edition information (if present), date information, and location information (e.g., URL). In addition the cataloger gives elements of description that may be helpful to a user in evaluating potential use of the information package, such as whether it is illustrated, what equipment is needed to use it, or that its mode of access is the World Wide Web.

Access

After describing an information package the cataloger selects name and title access points. Names of persons and corporate bodies associated with a work are chosen according to the cataloging rules used. Title access points also are chosen —in addition to the obvious main title (called title proper) there may be alternative titles, variant titles, series titles, and titles of other works related in some way with the work being cataloged.

In traditional practice one of the access points is chosen as the main one. This is called the main entry, but it should not be confused with the use of the word *entry* as defined earlier, meaning an access point with its associated version of a bibliographic record that appears as a unit in a catalog. A better term might be *primary access point*. The remaining access points are called added entries. Identification of the main entry is usually essential for identification of the work (or intellectual content) that is embodied in an information package being cataloged. A combination of main entry and title—uniform title if the work has appeared with variant titles—is the most common way of referring to a work in the realm of cataloging. Of course many works appear only once in one form and are not referred to again, so there is some controversy in the cataloging world about the necessity for choosing a main entry in all cases.[14] New rules being written are considering creation of work citations (i.e., choosing "the access point that is used as the initial element in citing a work") rather than continuing the main entry rules.[15]

The access points chosen are formatted as headings, constructed in a form that will make them readily accessible in the catalog and will enhance collocation. This is done using cataloging rules and through reference to the authority file, thus continuing the process of authority control.

Subject Analysis

Subject analysis involves determining what subject concept or concepts are covered by the intellectual content of a work. Once this has been determined, as many subject headings as are appropriate are chosen from a standard list. Again, an authority file must be consulted if the subject headings are to be properly collocated into the catalog with other works covering the same or related subject concepts.

The final step in the subject analysis process usually is to choose a classification notation from whatever classification scheme is used by the library. Traditionally in the United States the classification serves both as a means for bringing an item in close proximity with other items on the same or related subjects and, in the case of tangible information packages, as the first element of the call number, a device used to identify and locate a particular item on the shelves. The cataloger therefore must choose only the one best place in the classification scheme for the item.

Authority Control

Authority control is the result of the process of maintaining consistency in the verbal form (heading) used to represent an access point and the further process of showing the relationships among names, works, and subjects. It is accomplished through use of rules (in the case of names and titles), use of a controlled vocabulary, and reference to an authority file to create an authorized character string called a heading. An authority file is a grouping of records of the forms of names, titles, or subjects chosen for use in a catalog. Each authority record in an authority file may contain, in addition to the form chosen for use as the heading, a list of variant forms or terms that may be used as references. A very carefully prepared authority record also contains a list of sources consulted in the process of deciding upon the heading and the variant forms to use as references. It is possible to practice authority control by letting the catalog itself serve as the authority file—i.e., by assuming that the form of heading used in the catalog is correct. In large files this has proved to be difficult, and it is very difficult to keep track of references made in any size file without an authority file.

It is authority control that makes cataloging more than a process of creating a series of bibliographic records to represent discrete works without apparent relationship to any other. The process of cataloging can be defined as "creation of a catalog using bibliographic records" because authority control allows the cataloger to create headings for names, titles, and subjects that show the relationships among the works cataloged. It means that the heading for the same name in different records is always the same so that bibliographic records for all works by and about the same person or emanating from the same corporate body can be displayed together. A work heading (called a uniform title, but often consisting of the name of the author, or other main entry, followed by standardized title, as mentioned earlier) can be consistently presented so that bibliographic records for all editions, translations, sound or video recordings, adaptations, abridgements, or any other kind of manifestation of a work can be displayed together. The heading used to represent the same subject concept in different works can be used always in one form (called controlled vocabulary) so that, to the extent that works are identified as being about the same subject concept, all such works can be displayed together. Authority control of controlled vocabulary also makes it possible to refer users from terms not used to those used and from terms used to other related terms.

As we move more and more into the international arena, virtual authority control connecting national authority files with each other is becoming essential. Creators of catalogs in various countries using various languages need to be able to designate their own "authorized" forms of names, while at the same time recognizing variant names for the same person or other entity in other languages. Catalogs should not be required to use the English language "authorized" forms, but should be able to link users to entities they seek, regardless of the language used in their searches.

Cooperative and Copy Cataloging

The process of cataloging described above is often referred to as original cataloging. Fortunately it is not necessary for every information package in every library to be cataloged originally in that library. Because libraries acquire copies of many of the same items, or decide to catalog the same Internet resources, their catalogers can share cataloging by adapting for their own catalogs a copy of the original cataloging created by another library, a process commonly called *copy cataloging*.[16]

LC began to sell its standard printed catalog cards to libraries in 1901. H. W. Wilson entered the field in the 1930s with simplified catalog cards for sale. A number of other companies created and sold catalog cards from the 1950s into the 1970s. In addition LC book catalogs were available in large libraries, and methods were devised for photocopying entries from them for adaptation and use in local catalogs.

With the development of the MARC format in the late 1960s, cooperative cataloging took a new turn. At first the companies selling cards simply loaded LC's MARC tapes into their computers and printed cards from them. But the beginning of bibliographic networks based on MARC not only changed the availability of cards but also introduced the truly cooperative availability of cataloging data. The first network was OCLC—at first the Ohio College Library Center, but now the Online Computer Library Center. Libraries can become member libraries (usually through regional networks) and then contribute original cataloging to the system. Any member library can use records found in the system contributed by LC, several other national libraries, or any other member library.

At first the OCLC cataloging system was used only for the production of cards, and cards continue to be a product (although now only a very small part) of the system. Adaptations are easier online than changing photocopies or pre-printed cards. Now, however, most libraries download MARC records directly into their local online systems. Other major networks in use in the United States and Canada include the RLG (Research Libraries Group) Union Catalog and A-G Canada Ltd. Smaller regional and local networks exist in large numbers.

The amount of original cataloging remaining after use of cooperative cataloging depends upon the type and size of library. The more specialized the library, the more original cataloging it has, so specialized collections can require a high percentage of original cataloging, even though they may be quite small. In public, academic, and research libraries the percentage runs from around 5 percent to 35 percent depending upon size—in general, the larger the collection, the higher the percentage.[17]

In the mid-1990s there was a movement toward outsourcing both original and copy cataloging in some libraries. Outsourcing involves contracting with vendors outside the library to do some of the cataloging (or occasionally all the cataloging) for the library. The move has both advantages and disadvantages, and much has been written on this subject.[18]

FORMATS OF BIBLIOGRAPHIC RECORDS IN CATALOGS

The records created in the cataloging process must be displayed in some format. Uniformity of display is very desirable so that patrons can know how to read a record and where to expect to see certain elements of data. In printed catalogs the display of data elements has been quite standard. Most libraries and card production sources followed the LC pattern, because LC printed cards were so extensively used and because the order of elements devised by LC made a logical presentation of data. That order was codified by the various versions of the *Anglo-American Cataloguing Rules* (discussed in greater detail in the following chapters).

Today, the vast majority of catalog records are created using one of the MARC formats. The first MARC format was developed at LC around 1965. The version used in the United States was, for many years, referred to as USMARC to distinguish it from the versions used in other countries (e.g., RUSMARC, DenMARC, etc.). The latest version, published in 1999, is called *MARC 21*. It is a "harmonization" of CAN/MARC and USMARC, and the name is meant to show that it is ready for the 21st century.

The structure of *MARC 21* and its various formats is discussed in more detail in chapter 3. A general discussion of MARC and several other encoding standards can be found in Taylor's *The Organization of Information*.[19]

Display of MARC-formatted records is far from uniform. There have been numerous calls for standards for OPAC displays so that users may once again move from catalog to catalog (now most often while sitting at the same terminal screen), and see displays that make sense because they are predictable. IFLA has a set of guidelines for display in OPACs.[20] Figure 1.3 shows the record from figures 1.1–1.2 as displayed by OCLC's cataloging subsystem.

Fig. 1.3. Identification of information included in a MARC record. (Source: OCLC Connexion, WorldCat—record number 1912014)

Books	Rec Stat c	Entered 19890119	Replaced 20020809294902.0			
Type a	ELvl	Srce	Audn	Ctrl	Lang eng
BLvl m	Form	Conf 0	Biog	MRec	Ctry cou
	Cont b	GPub	LitF 0	Indx 1	
Desc a	Ills	Fest 0	DtSt s	Dates 1989,	

```
LC  010       89002835        ←————————— 18

    040       DLC ‡c DLC ‡d OCLCQ
                                      12
ISBN 020  16  0872876217 : ‡c $45.00

LC  050  00 {Z674 ‡b .R4 no. 20}‡a Z7837 ‡a BX1751.2
                                       17
DEW 082  00 020 s ‡a 016.282 ‡2 19

    100  1_ McCabe, James Patrick.←—1      2                        3

    245  00 Critical guide to Catholic reference books / ‡c James Patrick McCabe ; with
     14     an introduction by Russell E. Bidlack.
                                                          8
    250     3rd ed. ←——4      6          7

    260     {Englewood, Colo. : ‡b Libraries Unlimited, ‡c 1989.} ←———5

    300     {xiv, 323 p. ; ‡c 25 cm.} ←——9      10

    440  _0 Research studies in library science ; ‡v no. 20
                                      11                            13
    500     Includes indexes.←——————
  15                                19
    610  20 {Catholic Church ‡x Reference books ‡v Bibliography.}
```

Key for Fig. 1.3:

1. Heading: author's name
2. Title proper
3. Statement of responsibility
4. Edition statement
5. Publication, distribution, etc., area
6. Place of publication
7. Publisher
8. Date of publication
9. Physical description area
10. Series statement
11. Notes
12. Standard number (ISBN)
13. Subject headings
14. MARC indicator that tells computer that title will be added entry
15. MARC tag that indicates that series will be added entry
16. Library of Congress call number
17. Dewey classification number
18. Library of Congress control number
19. MARC subfield code

CONCLUSION

This chapter has presented an overview of the entire cataloging process. Greater detail about the content of description is discussed in chapters 4–5. Choice and form of headings are covered in chapters 6–7. Part IV covers authority control. Subject analysis is given thorough treatment in part V, with chapter 9 discussing the process of determining "aboutness," chapters 10–13 devoted to subject headings, and chapters 14–18 devoted to classification. The final part deals in more detail with networking, computer cataloging, and management issues.

NOTES

1. Elaine Svenonius, "Directions for Research in Indexing, Classification, and Cataloging," *Library Resources & Technical Services* 25 (January/March 1981): 88.

2. Richard P. Smiraglia, "Bibliographic Control Theory and Nonbook Materials," in *Policy and Practice in Bibliographic Control of Nonbook Media*, ed. by Sheila S. Intner and Richard P. Smiraglia (Chicago: American Library Association, 1987), p. 15.

3. Arlene G. Taylor, *The Organization of Information*, 2nd ed. (Westport, Conn.: Libraries Unlimited, 2004), p. 2.

4. Ibid., p. 368. (Taylor defines information package as "an instance of recorded information [e.g., book, article, video, Internet document or set of 'pages,' sound recording, electronic journal, etc.]".)

5. Ibid., p. 371.

6. *Functional Requirements for Bibliographic Records, Final Report*, IFLA Study Group on the Functional Requirements for Bibliographic Records (München: K.G. Saur, 1998); also available: http://www.ifla.org/VII/s13/frbr/frbr.htm or http://www.ifla.org/VII/s13/frbr/ frbr.pdf (accessed 2/14/2006).

7. Ibid., p. 82.

8. These ideas are discussed in greater detail by Ronald Hagler in *The Bibliographic Record and Information Technology*, 3rd ed. (Chicago: American Library Association, 1997), pp. 17–18; and by Taylor in *The Organization of Information*, pp. 9–19.

9. Charles A. Cutter, *Rules for a Dictionary Catalog*, 4th ed. (Washington, D.C.: GPO, 1904), p. 12.

10. International Conference on Cataloguing Principles. Paris, 9th–18th October, 1961, *Report* (London: International Federation of Library Associations, 1963), p. 26.

11. *Statement of International Cataloguing Principles*, Draft approved by the IFLA Meeting of Experts on an International Cataloguing Code, "Final" Draft Based on Responses through December 2004 showing further recommended changes from Buenos Aires, August 2004 (September 20, 2005 Draft), available: http://www.loc.gov/loc/ifla/imeicc/source/ Statement-draftsep05-clean.pdf (accessed 2/14/2006).

12. A good discussion of the historical development of cataloging practices is presented in an article written by Charles Martel, "Cataloging: 1876–1926," reprinted in *The Catalog and Cataloging*, ed. by A. R. Rowland (Hamden, Conn.: Shoe String Press, 1969), pp. 40–50.

13. *See also* discussion in: Taylor, *The Organization of Information*, pp. 38–40.

14. *See* further discussion of main entry in: Taylor, *The Organization of Information*, pp. 206–214.

15. *RDA – Resource Description and Access: A Prospectus*, Joint Steering Committee for Revision of AACR, 27 July 2005, available: http://www.collectionscanada.ca/jsc/ rdaprospectus.html or http://www.collectionscanada.ca/jsc/docs/5rda-prospectusrev.pdf (accessed 2/14/2006).

16. For an in-depth discussion of the decisions and adaptations necessary in the process of copy cataloging *see* Arlene G. Taylor, with the assistance of Rosanna M. O'Neil, *Cataloging with Copy: A Decision-Maker's Handbook*, 2nd ed. (Englewood, Colo.: Libraries Unlimited, 1988).

17. This information is based in conventional wisdom; although some libraries did conduct surveys in the 1970s and 1980s and reported their results at meetings of the American Library Association.

18. For example, *see* Claire-Lise Benaud and Sever Bordeianu, *Outsourcing Library Operations in Academic Libraries: An Overview of Issues and Outcomes* (Englewood, Colo.: Libraries Unlimited, 1998), and Marylou Colver and Karen Wilson, eds., *Outsourcing Technical Services Operations* (Chicago: American Library Association, 1997). *See also* discussion on pp. 500–501 of this text.

19. Taylor, *The Organization of Information*, pp. 69–97.

20. Martha Yee, *Guidelines for OPAC Displays*, prepared for the 65th IFLA Council and General Conference, Bangkok, Thailand, 20th–28th August, 1999, available: http://www. ifla.org/IV/ifla65/papers/098-131e.htm (accessed 2/14/2006).

SUGGESTED READING

Carpenter, Michael, and Elaine Svenonius. *Foundations of Cataloging: A Sourcebook*. Littleton, Colo.: Libraries Unlimited, 1985.

Dunkin, Paul S. *Cataloging U.S.A.* Chicago: American Library Association, 1969.

Fritz, Deborah A., and Richard J. Fritz. *MARC21 for Everyone*. Chicago: American Library Association, 2003.

Hagler, Ronald. *The Bibliographic Record and Information Technology*. 3rd ed. Chicago: American Library Association, 1997.

Harvey, Ross, and Philip Hider. *Organising Knowledge in a Global Society: Principles and Practice in Libraries and Information Centres*. Wagga Wagga, NSW, Australia: Centre for Information Studies, 2004. Chapter 1: Definitions and Introductory Concepts.

Svenonius, Elaine. *The Intellectual Foundation of Information Organization*. Cambridge, Mass.: The MIT Press, 2000. Chapter 2: Bibliographic Objectives.

Taylor, Arlene G., with the assistance of Rosanna M. O'Neil. *Cataloging with Copy: A Decision-Maker's Handbook*, 2nd ed. Englewood, Colo.: Libraries Unlimited, 1988.

Taylor, Arlene G. "The Information Universe: Will We Have Chaos or Control?" *American Libraries* 25, no. 7 (July/August 1994): 629–632.

Taylor, Arlene G. *The Organization of Information*. 2nd ed. Westport, Conn.: Libraries Unlimited, 2004.

2 Development of Cataloging Codes

INTRODUCTION

In current United States cataloging practice there is no comprehensive code of rules that tells a cataloger how to create bibliographic records that provide descriptive cataloging and subject access or how to create a catalog with those records. There is a widely accepted set of rules that covers description and name and title access and addresses authority work to some extent, but provision of subject access, authority control, and creation of catalogs depend upon following conventions—to a great extent, those established by the Library of Congress (LC). The rules for description and name and title access, the *Anglo-American Cataloguing Rules, Second Edition, 2002 Revision (AACR2R2002)*,[1] is the result of a progression of ideas about how to approach the cataloging process to prepare catalogs that provide the best possible access to library collections. *AACR2R2002* represents in print form the current agreements that have been reached to standardize descriptive cataloging practice and thereby facilitate cooperation among libraries. It expands on the agreements presented in earlier codes and forms the basis for further agreements that will be added to future codes.

The first cataloging rules were prepared by individuals. Anthony Panizzi, Keeper of the Printed Books at the British Museum, constructed a set of rules for that institution that was published in 1841.[2] This set of rules, often referred to as Panizzi's "91 Rules," was the first major modern statement of principles underlying cataloging rules; as such it has exerted an influence on every Western world code that has been created since its publication. Panizzi believed that anyone looking for a particular work should be able to find it through the catalog, and he wrote rules with that goal in mind—e.g., he insisted on entering pseudonymous works under pseudonym rather than under the author's real name. One characteristic of Panizzi's code was his occasional use of form headings as main entry—e.g., universities and learned societies were entered under the general heading "Academies," and missals, prayer-books, and liturgies were entered under "Liturgies." The concept of subject access as we know it had not yet been separated from that of main entry, and there were no provisions for subject headings as such. Clearly, though, he thought there were some kinds of publications that ought to be gathered together.

Charles A. Cutter, Librarian at the Boston Athenaeum, also created an important set of rules. His *Rules for a Dictionary Catalog*,[3] in its fourth edition at his death in 1903, gave voice to the concept that catalogs not only should point the way to an individual publication but also should assemble and organize literary units. These rules were also the first complete set of rules for a dictionary catalog. Cutter's rules were truly comprehensive, incorporating rules for subject access and filing as well as for description and name and title access. From the beginning of the twentieth century, codes have been drawn up by committees, but the influence of these early farsighted individuals has been apparent.

As mentioned earlier, the rules we have are for description and name and title access. After Cutter's rules for subject headings, two major American lists of subject headings were developed by LC and by Minnie Earl Sears—each containing introductions explaining conventions for use.[4] David Haykin enumerated principles for creating subject lists in 1951,[5] and LC issued its *Manual* for applying its headings in 1984 (5th ed., 1996),[6] but there is no comprehensive code for subject access. Some librarians began calling for such a code in the late 1980s. History related to subject headings is discussed in more detail in chapters 10–12.

Rules for descriptive cataloging have progressed through a number of different manifestations in the twentieth century: LC's *Rules on Printed Cards* (1899 through the 1930s),[7] American Library Association (ALA) and the (British) Library Association's *Catalog Rules* (1908),[8] *A.L.A. Cataloging Rules* (1941),[9] *A.L.A. Cataloging Rules for Author and Title Entries* (1949),[10] LC's *Rules for Descriptive Cataloging* (1949),[11] *Anglo-American Cataloging Rules* (1967) (*AACR*),[12] *Anglo-American Cataloguing Rules*, second edition (1978) (*AACR2*),[13] *Anglo-American Cataloguing Rules, Second Edition, 1988 Revision (AACR2R)*,[14] *Anglo-American Cataloguing Rules, Second Edition, 1998 Revision (AACR2R98)*,[15] and the present *AACR2R2002*.

The Anglo-American *Rules* of 1908 were the result of a seven-year study by a committee of ALA and the (British) Library Association. In 1901 LC had begun its printed card service, with the result that libraries became interested in ways to use LC cards along with their own cards. One of the important responsibilities of the committee was to formulate rules to encourage incorporation of LC printed cards into catalogs of other libraries. The committee attempted to reconcile the cataloging practices of LC with those of other research and scholarly libraries. The use of LC cards increased dramatically between 1908 and 1941; standardization of library catalogs progressed. However, the 1908 *Rules* were not expanded during this 33-year period, drastically curtailing attempts of cataloging practice to stay in touch with cataloging done at LC. In 1930 a subcommittee was appointed by ALA to begin work on a revision of cataloging rules, and the problems were outlined. Dissatisfaction with the 1908 code was expressed on the grounds of "omissions"; the basic rules were not in question. Expansion was required to meet the needs of large scholarly libraries or specialized collections:

> The preliminary edition, published in 1941, expanded the rules of 1908 to make more provision for special classes of material: serial publications, government documents, publications of religious bodies, anonymous classics, music and maps; to amplify existing rules to cover specific cases of frequent occurrence.[16]

The revised edition of 1949 states that in the 1949 edition:

> the chief changes from the preliminary edition are a rearrangement of the material to emphasize the basic rules and subordinate their amplifications, and to make the sequence of rules logical as far as possible;

reduction of the number of alternate rules; omission of rules for description; rewording to avoid repetition or to make the meaning clearer; and revision, where possible, of rules inconsistent with the general principles.[17]

The 1941 and 1949 rules were sharply criticized for being too elaborate and often arbitrary; emphasis had shifted from clearly defined principles to a collection of rules developed to fit specific cases rather than the conditions that the cases illustrated. Seymour Lubetzky, then a specialist in cataloging policy at LC, commented that any logical approach to cataloging problems was blocked by the maze of arbitrary and repetitious rules and exceptions to rules.[18]

Because of the omission of rules for description from the 1949 ALA *Rules*, LC published its *Rules for Descriptive Cataloging in the Library of Congress*,[19] also in 1949. This set of rules was much more simplified than had been the rules in Part II of the 1941 ALA preliminary edition. Therefore, these were not criticized, as were the rules for entry and heading, and were incorporated virtually intact into the next edition of rules published by ALA in 1967.

Because the 1949 rules for entry and heading were not satisfactory, ALA invited Lubetzky in 1951 to prepare a critical study of cataloging rules. Early drafts of Lubetzky's principles came out against complete enumeration of "cases" in rules and pointed toward a less complex code based upon well-defined principles.[20] At the International Conference on Cataloging Principles held in Paris in 1961, a draft statement of cataloging principles based upon Lubetzky's *Code of Cataloging Rules* was used as the basis for consideration. The final version of the "Statement of Principles" (often called the "Paris Principles")[21] was adopted and the participants from 53 countries agreed to work in their various countries for revised rules that would be in agreement with the accepted principles.

ANGLO-AMERICAN CATALOGING RULES **1967** *(AACR)*

The Catalog Code Revision Committee that prepared the *Anglo-American Cataloging Rules (AACR)* realized that revision must be a complete reexamination of the principles and objectives of cataloging, not merely a revision of specific rules. First, the objectives of the catalog were agreed upon; it was further decided that the Paris Principles should be the basis for rules of entry and heading. This was an important step toward international bibliographic standardization. International standardization was not accepted overnight, however. The British and Americans were attempting to produce a joint code, but American conservatives were worried about the probable costs of full implementation of the Paris Principles. When the code was finally published it was published in two texts—one British and one North American.[22]

AACR was oriented toward large research libraries, although in a few instances of obvious conflict, alternate rules were provided for use by non-research libraries. Unlike the 1949 ALA code, which was only for entry and heading, *AACR* incorporated rules for entry and heading, description, and cataloging of nonbook material. An important shift occurred in the philosophy underlying the rules for entry: "The entry for a work is normally based on the statements that appear on the title page or any part of the work that is used as its substitute."[23] This meant that information appearing only in the preface, introduction, or text was not to be considered unless title page information was vague or incomplete. Another basic shift in point of view was to that of cataloging by types of authorship rather than by types of works, and by classes of names rather than by classes of people.

Unlike earlier codes, *AACR* emphasized that choice of access points was a completely separate activity from construction of the heading used for any access point chosen. General principles became the basis for the rules for choice of main entry:

1. Entry should be under author or principal author when one can be determined

2. Entry should be under title in the case of works whose authorship is diffuse, indeterminate, or unknown

Application of rules based on these principles continued the practice of choosing a main entry, with other names and/or titles becoming added entries.   However, the choice was no longer a result of first determining the type of work involved and then finding the specific rule for that type.

The construction of the headings for names that were to be main or added entries centered on two problems: choice of a particular name, including both choice among different names (e.g., Jacqueline Onassis or Jacqueline Kennedy) and choice among different forms of the same name (e.g., Morris West or Morris L. West), and the form in which that name is presented in the heading (e.g., Seuss, Dr., or Dr. Seuss; Von Braun, Wernher, or Braun, Wernher von). Rules for form of name became based on a general principle of using the form of name used by a person or corporate body rather than the full name or official name as the 1949 ALA *Rules* directed. This meant that a person could be entered under an assumed name, nickname, changed name, etc. A person who used both his or her real name and an assumed name, however, was still entered under the real name, and a person who used a full form of a forename or used a forename initial, even though rarely, was entered under the fullest form ever used. Another change was to use a firmly established English form of name rather than the vernacular form for many well-known names (e.g., Horace, not Horatius Flaccus, Quintus).

Another important area of change was in the form of entry for corporate bodies. The general rule followed the principle of using the form of name the body itself uses. Entry was usually under that form of name except when the rules provided for entry under a higher body or under the name of the government. However, the North American text gave exceptions exempting specified bodies of an institutional nature from the principle of entry under name; these were to be entered under place as in the old rules. These exceptions were contrary to the Paris Principles and to the British text of *AACR*, but they had been requested by the Association of Research Libraries, whose member libraries feared being overburdened with the necessity for changing thousands of entries already in catalogs.

The fear of the research libraries was also eased by LC's January 1967 announcement of the policy of superimposition:

> This means that the rules for choice of entry will be applied only to works that are new to the Library and that the rules for headings will be applied only to persons and corporate bodies that are being established for the first time. New editions, etc., of works previously cataloged will

be entered in the same way as the earlier editions (except for revised editions in which change of authorship is indicated). New works by previously established authors will appear under the same headings.[24]

This policy continued throughout the duration of the application of *AACR*. As a result, thousands of headings were made between 1967 and 1981 in a form created under the 1949 ALA *Rules* or earlier rules and were placed on bibliographic records that were otherwise *AACR* records. The abandonment of the policy of superimposition with the implementation of *AACR2* was a major step toward ultimate user convenience in finding entries and improved international cooperation; but for many large libraries, thousands of entries in pre-*AACR* form already in catalogs had to be dealt with after January 1981.

In 1974 the rule in *AACR* for entry of corporate bodies under place was dropped. Because of superimposition, only new corporate bodies were established and entered under their own names. Besides this change, some 40 other rules were changed, and three chapters were totally revised in the years following publication of *AACR*. Perhaps the most significant change was the application of international standards of description, based on International Standard Bibliographic Description (ISBD), to descriptive cataloging of monographs, audiovisual media, and special instructional materials. ISBD facilitates the international exchange of bibliographic information by standardizing the elements to be used in the bibliographic description, assigning an order to these elements in the entry, and specifying a system of symbols to be used in punctuating these elements. (These symbols are discussed and illustrated in Appendix B of the 8th ed. of *Introduction to Cataloging and Classification.*[25]) In addition:

> ISBD requires that a publication be totally identified by the description. It is independent of the provisions for headings, main or added, and of the provisions for the use of uniform titles; these were internationally standardized by the Paris Principles.[26]

ANGLO-AMERICAN CATALOGUING RULES, SECOND EDITION (AACR2), AND ITS 1988, 1998, and 2002 REVISIONS

The numerous changes to rules in *AACR* and the progress toward an international standard for description not only of monographs, but also of serials and all media, were two of the reasons for the meeting in 1974 of representatives of the national library associations and national libraries of Canada, the United Kingdom, and the United States to plan for the preparation of *AACR2*. Two other reasons were a proliferation of other rules for nonbook materials that reflected dissatisfaction with *AACR* treatment of these materials and LC's announcement of intention to abandon the policy of superimposition.[27] The objectives established at that meeting were:

1. to reconcile in a single text the North American and British texts of 1967

2. to incorporate in the single text all amendments and changes already agreed and implemented under the previous mechanisms

3. to consider for inclusion in AACR all proposals for amendment currently under discussion. . . .

4. to provide for international interest in AACR by facilitating its use in countries other than the United States, Canada, and the United Kingdom[28]

The representatives at the 1974 meeting also agreed to establish a Joint Steering Committee for Revision of *AACR* (JSC) made up of one voting and one non-voting representative of each author organization.   The JSC was to appoint an editor from each side of the Atlantic and was generally to oversee the process of revision through to publication. The JSC has continued since 1974. *AACR2* has a process of continuous revision. Participating countries have committees that work continually on recommendations for revisions. Approved recommendations are passed to the JSC, which then acts to accept or reject the proposals. Before such recommendations can be accepted, they often have to be revised, and differences of opinion must be reconciled among the countries involved. The countries currently represented on the JSC are Australia, Canada, Great Britain, and the United States.

The result of the revision process was what the preface to *AACR2* calls a continuation of the first edition: "for, in spite of the changes in presentation and content which it introduces, these are still the *Anglo-American Cataloguing Rules*, having the same principles and underlying objectives as the first edition, and being firmly based on the achievement of those who created the work, first published in 1967."[29] However, *AACR2*, published in late 1978 but not implemented by the major national libraries until January 1981, had some significant differences that are worth noting here.

In the process of reconciling the North American and British texts, it was decided to use British spelling of words if the British spelling appears as an alternative in *Webster's Third New International Dictionary of the English Language, Unabridged*. In cases where terminology differs, British usages were chosen in some cases (e.g., *full stop* instead of *period*), while American usages appear in other cases (e.g., *parentheses* instead of the British *brackets*).

One significant change is in the presentation of rules for description: one general chapter presents broad provisions that can be applied in many different situations. This chapter is followed by specific chapters for different types of materials and for different conditions and patterns of publication. The rules for description are deliberately less specific in legislating ways to handle certain phenomena. The cataloger is thereby encouraged to exercise judgment in interpreting the rules in light of the needs of the user being served. One possibility for such interpretation lies in *AACR2*'s provision of three "levels" of description with increasing amounts of detail at each level. The cataloger may choose the level that provides the amount of detail relevant to the particular library's users and, at the same time, meets the standards called for in a set of international cataloging rules.

In the rules for choice of access points, it is significant that less emphasis has been placed on "main" entry, although the concept is still present. Many people have expressed the opinion that when multiple access points are readily available, and when the bibliographic description is complete by itself, there is no need to designate one of the access points as the "main" one. The original main entry concept, which remained basically unchanged from Panizzi's rules through *AACR*, was based on the idea that the purpose of the catalog is to identify works and that once the work is identified, sufficient bibliographic detail is added to facilitate finding the item that contains the work. This was based on the assumption that there is a one-to-one correspondence between work and item. This assumption worked fairly well until the latter part of the twentieth century, when the tremendous growth of literatures and formats of all kinds rendered the assumption obsolete. Now, as noted in chapter 1, use of a main entry combined with title or uniform title is the only way we have to identify the same work in several containers. It is also the most common way to identify in a note a work that is related to the work being described by the bibliographic record. As long as this is true the concept of main entry cannot be abandoned, although it is being renamed "primary access point."

A significant difference in choice of main entry in *AACR2* is that a corporate body is not considered to be an "author." Instead, there are specified categories of works that are allowed to be entered under corporate body. This concept greatly reduces the number of corporate main entries made, although those corporate bodies that would have had main entry under earlier rules are given added entry under *AACR2*, resulting in the same number of corporate access points as before.

Rules for form of headings for personal names in *AACR2* emphasize using the form of name most often used by a person (e.g., Benjamin Disraeli instead of Earl of Beaconsfield; Bernard Shaw instead of George Bernard Shaw). If a person, other than one using a pseudonym, uses more than one name, the predominant one is chosen. Rules for pseudonyms have evolved more than other rules for choice of personal name since *AACR*, in which only one form—the real name, if used—was chosen to represent a person who used more than one pseudonym or a real name and one or more pseudonyms. In the 1978 *AACR2* a predominant name was chosen; only if there was no predominant name could multiple headings be made for that author. This placed the mathematical works of Charles L. Dodgson under Lewis Carroll. *AACR2R* introduced the concept of "separate bibliographic identities," which allows separate headings in such cases as the Dodgson/Carroll example. It also called for multiple headings for all contemporary authors who use more than one pseudonym or a real name and one or more pseudonyms. This practice continues in *AACR2R2002*.

For corporate names, too, there is more emphasis on using the name as it is used by the body, removing provisions for inverting, amplifying, etc., that appeared in *AACR* (e.g., W. K. Kellogg Arabian Horse Center instead of Kellogg (W. K.) Arabian Horse Center). Geographic names are treated more internationally (e.g., states of Australia are treated like states of the United States). In the 1978 *AACR2*, counties of England, Scotland, and Wales were also treated like states of the United States, but this has been revised so that places in the British Isles now are qualified by the constituent parts of the British Isles rather than by counties.

At the time of publication of *AACR2* there were some general hopes for advantageous results from use of the new code. First, *AACR2* laid the groundwork for much more international and national cooperative cataloging, which was expected to improve greatly library service of a bibliographic nature and to result in considerable cost savings. Second, by providing the framework for standard description of all library materials, it made possible an integrated, multimedia catalog. Third, it was expected to reduce user search time by providing headings that conform more often to the forms found in works and citations. Fourth, personal name headings were expected to be more stable than formerly, thus reducing catalog maintenance costs.[30] The first two of these expected advantages have been widely accepted as having come to pass. As to the third, Elizabeth Tate demonstrated that headings do indeed conform more often to the forms found in citations.[31] In order to know if the last one has been realized, studies would have to be completed, and this has been complicated by the adoption of online catalogs, making comparisons of maintenance costs due to rule changes virtually impossible to obtain.

When *AACR2* was published in 1978, a period of time was set before implementation in order to allow libraries to prepare for the change. The date for implementation was postponed twice, but implementation finally occurred January 2, 1981, after much angst and a flurry of local *AACR2* studies to determine impact.[32] The problem was exacerbated by the fact that most libraries still had card catalogs, and changes had to be accomplished by erasing and retyping or by marking through headings and writing new forms above them. By the mid-1990s most libraries had online catalogs, in which changed headings can be changed by "global search and replace" methods, and new rule changes can be accommodated with more ease.

AACR2R and *AACR2R98* incorporated official revisions that had been approved in the 10-year periods before each publication. For the most part, the revisions had been gradually implemented in the intervening years and the new publications were accepted easily. *AACR2R2002* contained more major changes, however. Substantial changes were made to the chapters for Cartographic Materials, Electronic Resources, and Serials (renamed "Continuing Resources") . The concept of continuing resources allowed the integration of "integrating resources" (e.g., loose-leaf updates) for the first time and went a long way toward handling the problems that Web resources, which can be updated at any time, had presented for the followers of *AACR2* principles.[33]

Rule interpretations made by LC in the process of applying *AACR2* are published regularly in *Cataloging Service Bulletin*.[34] There are also official publications of rule changes that have been published annually since 2002. The work has been translated into several languages, and its influence continues to grow.

INTERNATIONAL DEVELOPMENTS

Work is now underway by the JSC to produce a new cataloging code, currently being called *RDA – Resource Description and Access*, which will have international implications.[35] A number of international developments have led to this point, and we will mention here four of the most important ones. First was the 1997 International Conference on the Principles and Future Development of AACR.[36] Held in Toronto, it included invited experts from around the world to work on developing a plan for the future of *AACR*. Recommendations from that meeting are at various stages. Some have been implemented (e.g., the concerns about continuing resources and integrating resources); some are guiding current thinking (e.g., the concern that better ways of presenting "content vs. carrier" be found); some are waiting to be considered in the future.

A second major international occurrence is the development of *Functional Requirements for Bibliographic Records (FRBR)* by a study group of the International Federation of Library Associations (IFLA).[37] It is a conceptual model for understanding how a work gets expressed and how those expressions become manifested through individual items. More importantly this model gives us a way to show relationships among works, authors, subjects, and other entities that make up a catalog, thus enabling users to be able to find, identify, select, and obtain the information they need. *FRBR* is to be an underlying structure in *RDA*.

A third international event of importance was the IFLA Meeting of Experts on an International Cataloguing Code in Frankfurt in 2003. The *Statement of International Cataloguing Principles* that came out of that meeting is expected to replace and broaden the Paris Principles—to cover all types of materials and address many more aspects of bibliographic and authority records than just choice and form of entry in textual works.[38] The draft is in the process of being reviewed worldwide and is expected to be finalized in 2007.

Finally, a development that is one impetus for including a new section on authority control in *RDA* is the concept of a virtual international authority file, where users would see headings in forms and scripts that they recognize, but where makers of catalogs would be able to link authority records for the same entity and be able to take advantage of international knowledge and expertise of other catalog creators.[39] In one model being considered there would be no single database with all the records, but rather records for the same entity being held in various national agency databases would be linked. This model is currently being tested.

More information about *RDA* is included in chapter 4. The reader should watch for rapid changes as this new cataloging code develops.

NOTES

1. *Anglo-American Cataloguing Rules, Second Edition, 2002 Revision*, prepared under the direction of the Joint Steering Committee for Revision of AACR (Ottawa: Canadian Library Association; Chicago: American Library Association, 2002). Also available on *Cataloger's Desktop* (Washington, D.C.: Library of Congress, Cataloging Distribution Service), available: http://desktop.loc.gov/ (accessed 2/14/2006). For subscription information: http://www.loc.gov/cds/desktop/ (accessed 2/14/2006).

2. Antonio Panizzi, "Rules for the Compilation of the Catalogue," in British Museum, *The Catalogue of Printed Books in the British Museum* (London, 1841), 1: v–ix.

3. Charles A. Cutter, *Rules for a Dictionary Catalog*, 4th ed., rewritten (Washington, D.C.: GPO, 1904).

4. Library of Congress, Catalog Division, *Subject Headings Used in the Dictionary Catalogues of the Library of Congress* (Washington, D.C.: Library Branch, GPO, 1910–1914); Minnie Earl Sears, *List of Subject Headings for Small Libraries* (New York: H. W. Wilson, 1923).

5. David Judson Haykin, *Subject Headings: A Practical Guide* (Washington, D.C.: GPO, 1951).

6. Library of Congress, Subject Cataloging Division, *Subject Cataloging Manual: Subject Headings* (Washington, D.C.: Library of Congress, 1984).

7. Library of Congress, *Rules on Printed Cards* (Washington, D.C.: Library of Congress, 1899–194?).

8. *Catalog Rules, Author and Title Entries*, compiled by Committees of the American Library Association and the (British) Library Association, American ed. (Chicago: American Library Association Pub. Board, 1908).

9. *A.L.A. Cataloging Rules, Author and Title Entries*, prepared by the Catalog Code Revision Committee of the American Library Association, with the collaboration of a Committee of the (British) Library Association, Preliminary American 2nd ed. (Chicago: American Library Association, 1941).

10. *A.L.A. Cataloging Rules for Author and Title Entries*, prepared by the Division of Cataloging and Classification of the American Library Association, 2nd ed. (Chicago: American Library Association, 1949).

11. Library of Congress, Descriptive Cataloging Division, *Rules for Descriptive Cataloging in the Library of Congress* (Washington, D.C.: Library of Congress, 1949).

12. *Anglo-American Cataloging Rules, North American Text*, prepared by the American Library Association, the Library of Congress, the (British) Library Association, and the Canadian Library Association (Chicago: American Library Association, 1967).

13. *Anglo-American Cataloguing Rules*, 2nd ed., prepared by the American Library Association, the British Library, the Canadian Library Committee on Cataloguing, the (British) Library Association, and the Library of Congress, ed. by Michael Gorman and Paul W. Winkler (Chicago: American Library Association, 1978).

14. *Anglo-American Cataloguing Rules, Second Edition, 1988 Revision*, prepared by the Joint Steering Committee for Revision of AACR, ed. by Michael Gorman and Paul W. Winkler (Ottawa: Canadian Library Association; Chicago: American Library Association, 1988).

15. *Anglo-American Cataloguing Rules, Second Edition, 1998 Revision*, prepared by the Joint Steering Committee for Revision of AACR (Ottawa: Canadian Library Association; Chicago: American Library Association, 1998).

16. *A.L.A. Cataloging Rules*, 1949, p. viii.

17. *A.L.A. Cataloging Rules*, 1949, p. ix.

18. Seymour Lubetzky, *Cataloging Rules and Principles: A Critique of the A.L.A. Rules for Entry and a Proposed Design for Their Revision* (Washington, D.C.: Processing Dept., Library of Congress, 1953).

19. L.C., *Rules for Descriptive Cataloging*, 1949.

20. Seymour Lubetzky, *Code of Cataloging Rules, Author and Title: An Unfinished Draft . . . with an Explanatory Commentary by Paul Dunkin* (Chicago: American Library Association, 1960).

21. International Conference on Cataloging Principles, Paris, 9th–18th October, 1961, *Report* (London: International Federation of Library Associations, 1963).

22. *Anglo-American Cataloging Rules, North American Text* (Chicago: American Library Association, 1967); *Anglo-American Cataloguing Rules, British Text* (London: Library Association, 1967).

23. *AACR, North American Text*, p. 9.

24. *Cataloging Service*, bulletin 79 (January 1967): 1.

25. Bohdan S. Wynar and Arlene G. Taylor, *Introduction to Cataloging and Classification*, 8th ed. (Englewood, Colo.: Libraries Unlimited, 1992), Appendix B, pp. 558–571, also available: http://www.pitt.edu/~agtaylor/articles/ICC8-appendixB.pdf (accessed 2/14/2006).

26. "International Standard Bibliographic Description," *Cataloging Service*, bulletin 105 (November 1972): 2.

27. "AACR 2: Background and Summary," *Library of Congress Information Bulletin* 37 (October 20, 1978): 640.

28. *AACR2*, pp. vi–vii.

29. *AACR2*, p. v.

30. "AACR 2: Background and Summary," p. 652.

31. Elizabeth L. Tate, "Access Points and Citations: A Comparison of Four Cataloging Codes," *Library Research* 1 (Winter 1979): 347–359.

32. Arlene Taylor Dowell, *AACR 2 Headings: A Five-Year Projection of Their Impact on Catalogs* (Littleton, Colo.: Libraries Unlimited, 1982), pp. 22–35.

33. Arlene G. Taylor, "Where Does AACR2 Fall Short for Internet Resources?," *Journal of Internet Cataloging* 2, no. 2 (1999): 43–50.

34. *Cataloging Service Bulletin*, no. 1– (Washington, D.C.: Processing Services, Library of Congress, 1978–).

35. *RDA – Resource Description and Access: A Prospectus*, Joint Steering Committee for Revision of AACR, 27 July 2005, available: http://www.collectionscanada.ca/jsc/ rdaprospectus.html or http://www.collectionscanada.ca/jsc/docs/5rda-prospectusrev.pdf (accessed 2/14/2006).

36. *The Principles and Future of AACR: Proceedings of the International Conference on the Principles and Future Development of AACR, Toronto, Ontario, Canada, October 23–25, 1997*, ed. Jean Weihs (Ottawa: Canadian Library Association; Chicago: American Library Association, 1998). A progress report and the discussion list archives are available: http://www.collectionscanada.ca/jsc/intlconf.html (accessed 2/14/2006).

37. *Functional Requirements for Bibliographic Records*, IFLA Study Group on the Functional Requirements for Bibliographic Records (München: K.G. Saur, 1998); also available: http://www.ifla.org/VII/s13/frbr/frbr.htm or http://www.ifla.org/VII/s13/frbr/frbr.pdf (accessed 2/14/2006).

38. *Statement of International Cataloguing Principles*, Draft approved by the IFLA Meeting of Experts on an International Cataloguing Code, "Final" Draft Based on Responses through December 2004 showing further recommended changes from Buenos Aires, August 2004 (September 20, 2005 Draft), available: http://www.loc.gov/loc/ifla/imeicc/source/Statement-draftsep05-clean.pdf (accessed 2/14/2006).

39. Barbara B. Tillett, "Authority Control: State of the Art and New Perspectives," *Cataloging & Classification Quarterly* 38, no. 3/4 (2004): 23–42; also published in: *Authority Control in Organizing and Accessing Information: Definition and International Experience*, edited by Arlene G. Taylor and Barbara B. Tillett (New York: Haworth Information Press, 2004), pp. 23–42.

SUGGESTED READING

Baker, Nicholson, "Discards." *New Yorker* 70, no. 7 (April 4, 1994): 64–86.

Cutter, Charles Ammi. *Rules for a Dictionary Catalog*. 4th ed., rewritten. Washington, D.C.: GPO, 1904.

Dowell, Arlene Taylor. *AACR 2 Headings: A Five-Year Projection of Their Impact on Catalogs*. Littleton, Colo.: Libraries Unlimited, 1982.

International Conference on AACR 2, Florida State University, 1979. *The Making of a Code: The Issues Underlying AACR 2*. Chicago: American Library Association, 1980.

Intner, Sheila S., and Jean Weihs. *Standard Cataloging for School and Public Libraries*. 3rd ed. Englewood, Colo.: Libraries Unlimited, 2001. Chapter 3: The Anglo-American Cataloguing Rules.

Lubetzky, Seymour. *Cataloging Rules and Principles: A Critique of the ALA Rules for Entry and a Proposed Design for Their Revision*. Washington, D.C.: Processing Dept., Library of Congress, 1953.

Osborn, Andrew. "The Crisis in Cataloging." *Library Quarterly* 11 (October 1941): 393–411.

The Principles and Future of AACR: Proceedings of the International Conference on the Principles and Future Development of AACR, Toronto, Ontario, Canada, October 23–25, 1997, ed. Jean Weihs (Ottawa: Canadian Library Association; Chicago: American Library Association, 1998). A progress report and the discussion list archives are available: http://www.collectionscanada.ca/jsc/intlconf.html (accessed 2/14/2006).

Russell, Beth M. "Hidden Wisdom and Unseen Treasure: Revisiting Cataloging in Medieval Libraries." *Cataloging & Classification Quarterly* 26, no. 3 (1998): 21–30.

Taylor, Arlene G. *The Organization of Information*. 2nd ed. Westport, Conn.: Libraries Unlimited, 2004. Chapter 3: Development of the Organization of Recorded Information in Western Civilization.

Part II
ELECTRONIC FORMATTING

3 > Encoding

INTRODUCTION

In the age of online catalogs the content of catalog records must use some kind of electronic encoding scheme in order to be machine-manipulable for searching and display. Encoding allows each part of a record to be set off from every other part. Then computer programs can be written so that each part will be displayed in a certain position according to the wishes of the programmer. Encoding also allows for access to a catalog record through the creation of search programs that provide for the searching of certain parts of a record (e.g., the author, the title, a subject, etc.).

Since the mid-1960s an encoding system called MARC (MAchine-Readable Cataloging) has been used to create electronic catalog records. An excellent history of its development may be found in Deborah Byrne's *MARC Manual.*[1] The most current version for use in the United States is *MARC 21*, a harmonized version of USMARC and CAN/MARC, published in 1999.[2]

Other encoding systems have been developed recently in response to the desire to make catalog records available on the Web. Standard Generalized Markup Language (SGML) is an international standard for document markup. It is a set of rules for designing markup languages that describe the structure of a document. The markup languages thus designed are SGML applications called Document Type Definitions (DTDs). DTDs often used for bibliographic data include Text Encoding Initiative (TEI), HyperText Markup Language (HTML), and Encoded Archival Description (EAD). Extensible Markup Language (XML), a subset of SGML that adds some features that solve earlier problems with SGML and HTML, has almost completely replaced SGML as the encoding scheme of choice for the Web. XML has "schemas" rather than DTDs, but they function similarly. A schema is written in XML and specifies the tags, attributes of tags, and rules for tags that will be used to encode records using the schema. Because most of the open source software is XML, and new generation systems from the computer industry support XML, the Library of Congress (LC) has developed a schema for translating MARC records into XML. Called MARCXML, it is very detailed in using all the *MARC 21* tags and codes. A simpler, but still highly compatible schema, has also been developed. This simpler schema, called MODS (Metadata Object Description Schema), has user friendly language tags. More information about these schemas may be found at the LC website.[3]

Currently, the MARC encoding system holds the position of being the one used for bibliographic records in the vast majority of the world's online catalogs. The remainder of this chapter contains an introduction to this system.

INTRODUCTION TO
MACHINE-READABLE CATALOGING (MARC)

Formats

There are *MARC 21* formats for five types of data. The following formats are currently defined:

- Bibliographic format—for encoding bibliographic data in records that are surrogates for information packages

- Authority format—for encoding authority data collected in authority records created to help control the content of those surrogate record fields that are subject to authority control

- Holdings format—for encoding data elements in holdings records that show the holdings and location data for information packages described in surrogate records

- Community information format—for encoding data in records that contain information about events, programs, services, and the like, so that these records can be integrated with bibliographic records

- Classification data format—for encoding data elements related to classification numbers, the captions associated with them, their hierarchies, and the subject headings with which they correlate[4]

This introduction is to the *MARC 21* bibliographic format.

Components of the Record

A record is a collection of fields. A field contains a unit of information within a record. A field may consist of one or more subfields. Tags, that is, three-digit numerical codes, identify each field. Every field ends with a field terminator (in OCLC, for example, the field terminator may appear as a backwards paragraph sign or as a left angle bracket or it may be invisible). Each subfield is preceded by a delimiter sign (often represented by a $ or | or ‡) followed by a single character code (usually alphabetical, but can also be numerical).

Each record has the same components:

1. Leader
2. Record directory
3. Control fields
   a. Fixed fields
4. Variable fields

Leader—The leader identifies the beginning of a new record and provides information for the processing of the record.   The leader is fixed in length and contains 24 characters.

Record directory—The record directory contains a series of fixed length entries that identify the tag, length, and starting position of each field in the record.

Control fields—Control fields carry alphanumeric (often encoded) data elements. Control field tags always begin with two zeros (00X). Most control fields are fixed in length, that is, each fixed-length field must consist of a set number of characters (*see* also "Fixed field" below). Common control fields are:

001 – Control number

005 – Date and time of latest transaction

006 – Fixed-length data elements—coding information about special aspects of the item being cataloged that cannot be coded in field 008 (i.e., separate character descriptions for books, computer files/electronic resources, maps, music, continuing resources, visual materials, and mixed materials)

007 – Physical description fixed field—physical characteristics of an item, usually derived from explicit information in other fields of the record, but expressed here in coded form (i.e., separate character descriptions for map, electronic resource, globe, tactile material, projected graphic, microform, nonprojected graphic, motion picture, kit, notated music, remote-sensing image, sound recording, text, videorecording, and one for "unspecified")

008 – Fixed-length data elements—positionally defined data elements that provide coded information about the record as a whole or about special bibliographic aspects of the item being cataloged

Fixed field—There is one fixed length control field that is commonly referred to as "*the* fixed field." Field 008 carries general information about the content of the bibliographic record. This field is often displayed in a single paragraph at the top or bottom of the screen and is often displayed with mnemonic tags. The field has 40 character positions. The data stored in this field are used to manipulate records for retrieval, filing, indexing, etc.

A fixed field from the record for a book as it is displayed in OCLC:

Type	a	**ELvl**		**Srce**		**Audn**		**Ctrl**		**Lang**	eng
BLvl	m	**Form**		**Conf**	0	**Biog**		**MRec**		**Ctry**	cou
		Cont	b	**GPub**		**LitF**	0	**Indx**	1		
Desc	a	**Ills**		**Fest**	0	**DtSt**	s	**Dates**	1999,		

Sometimes fill characters (displayed as ■ or _ or |) are used to indicate elements of the fixed field that were not in use when the record was created or were not provided by the inputting library. A blank space (sometimes written as a letter b with a forward slash through it) is meaningful. That is, a blank is input to represent a coded value. In "Srce:" above, the blank means that LC or other national cataloging agency is responsible for the creation of the record. (Because the item is published in Colorado, as indicated by "**Ctry**   cou," the source is most likely LC.)

Variable data fields—Variable data fields carry alphanumeric data of variable length. The variable fields carry traditional cataloging data elements. Three-digit numeric tags (010–999) identify variable fields. In order to talk about these tags in groups, a convention is followed in which all fields beginning with "1" are identified as 1XX fields; those beginning with "2," as 2XX fields; etc. Variable fields consist of number and code fields, heading fields, and descriptive fields. Among the most used variable fields are: (for the full lists see the *MARC 21* format)

NUMBERS AND CODES (01X–04X)

010 — Library of Congress Control Number (LCCN)

016 — National Bibliographic Agency Control Number

020 — International Standard Book Number (ISBN)

022 — International Standard Serial Number (ISSN)

033 — Date/time and place of an event

034 — Coded cartographic mathematical data

040 — Cataloging source

041 — Language code

043 — Geographic area code

047 — Form of musical composition code

048 — Number of musical instruments or voices code

CLASSIFICATION NOTATIONS AND/OR CALL NUMBERS (05X–09X)

050 — Library of Congress (LC) Call Number

070 — National Agricultural Library Call Number

060 — National Library of Medicine Call Number

080 — Universal Decimal Classification Number

082 — Dewey Decimal Classification Number

09X — Local call numbers

MAIN ENTRY FIELDS (1XX)

100 — Main entry—personal name

110 — Main entry—corporate name

111 — Main entry—meeting name

130 — Main entry—uniform title

TITLE AND TITLE-RELATED FIELDS (20X–24X)

240 — Uniform title

245 — Title proper, general material designation, remainder of title, statement of responsibility

246 — Varying form of title

247 — Former title

EDITION, IMPRINT, ETC., FIELDS (25X–28X)

250 — Edition statement

254 — Musical presentation statement

255 — Cartographic mathematical data

256 — Computer file characteristics

260 — Publication, distribution, etc. (Imprint: place, publisher, etc., date)

263 — Projected publication date

PHYSICAL DESCRIPTION, ETC., FIELDS (3XX)

300 — Physical description (extent of item, other details, size, accompanying material)

310 — Current publication frequency

321 — Former publication frequency

362 — Dates of publication and/or sequential designation

SERIES STATEMENT FIELDS (4XX)

[title proper of series, remaining title information, statement of responsibility relating to series, ISSN of series, numbering, etc.]

440 — Series statement / added entry—title

490 — Series statement (not an added entry)

NOTE FIELDS (5XX)

500 — General note

502 — Dissertation note

504 — Bibliography, etc., note

505 — Formatted contents note

506 — Restrictions on access note

508 — Creation/production credits note

510 — Citation/References note

511 — Participant or performer note

516 — Type of computer file or data note

520 — Summary, etc., note

521 — Target audience note

533 — Reproduction note

534 — Original version note

538 — System details note

546 — Language note

547 — Former title complexity note

561 — Ownership and custodial history

580 — Linking entry complexity note

59X — Local notes

SUBJECT ACCESS FIELDS (6XX)

600 — Subject added entry—personal name

610 — Subject added entry—corporate name

611 — Subject added entry—meeting name

630 — Subject added entry—uniform title

650 — Subject added entry—topical term

651 — Subject added entry—geographic name

653 — Index term—uncontrolled

654 — Subject added entry—faceted topical terms

655 — Index term—genre/form

69X — Local subject access fields

ADDED ENTRY FIELDS (70X–75X)

700 — Added entry—personal name

710 — Added entry—corporate name

711 — Added entry—meeting name

720 — Added entry—uncontrolled name

730 — Added entry—uniform title

740 — Added entry—uncontrolled related/analytical title

LINKING ENTRY FIELDS (76X–78X)

770 — Supplement/special issue entry

772 — Supplement parent entry

776 — Additional physical form entry

780 — Preceding entry

785 — Succeeding entry

787 — Nonspecific relationship entry

SERIES ADDED ENTRY FIELDS (80X–840)

800 — Series added entry—personal name

810 — Series added entry—corporate name

811 — Series added entry—meeting name

830 — Series added entry—uniform title

HOLDINGS, LOCATION, ALTERNATE GRAPHICS, ETC., FIELDS (841–88X)

852 — Location/call number

856 — Electronic location and access

880 — Alternate graphic representation

Subfields—All subfields are distinct elements within fields. Subfield definitions vary from field to field. Some of the most commonly encountered ones are:

050   LC call number
    $a   classification number
    $b   item number and date

082   Dewey Decimal Classification number
    $a   classification number
    $b   item number
    $2   edition number [edition of DDC used]

X00   Personal name
    (X00 means that these subfields apply in fields 100, 600, 700, and 800.)
    $a   personal name
    $q   fuller form of name [e.g., Lewis, C. S. $q (Clive Staples)]
    $b   numeration
    $c   titles (e.g., Mrs., Sir, Bishop)
    $d   dates
    $e   relator (e.g., ill. [for illustrator])

X10   Corporate name
    $a   corporate or jurisdiction name
    $b   subordinate unit
    $e   relator
    $k   form subheading

X11   Meeting name
    $a   meeting name
    $c   location of meeting
    $d   date of meeting
    $n   number of part/section/meeting

245   Title and statement of responsibility
    $a   title proper
    $b   remainder of title
    $c   statement of responsibility, etc.

260   Publication, distribution, etc.
    $a   place of publication, distribution, etc.
    $b   name of publisher, distributor, etc.
    $c   date of publication, distribution, etc.

300   Physical description
    $a   extent of item

$b   other physical details

$c   dimensions

$e   accompanying material

4XX and 8XX   Series

$a   title of series

$x   ISSN (4XX fields only)

$v   numbering of series

6XX   Subject access point

$a   main subject (name, topic, etc.)

$x   topical subject subdivision

$y   time period subdivision

$z   geographic subdivision

$v   form/genre subdivision

856   Electronic location and access

$a   Host name

$b   Access number

$d   Path

$h   Processor of request

$u   Uniform Resource Identifier

Indicators—The two digits that follow after the tags in a MARC field are called indicators. Each digit position has a certain meaning relating to its particular field and provides computer instructions for processing the data contained in the field. For example, in the OCLC-formatted 245 field shown below, the first indicator, "1," tells the system that there should be an access point for the title, and the second indicator, "4," tells the system that four nonfiling characters (i.e., T, h, e, and [space]) precede the first significant word of the title:

245   14   The dictionary of misinformation / $c Tom Burnam.

DISPLAY OF MARC RECORDS

MARC records are distributed in the MARC Communications Format.[5] Each record consists of one long character string beginning with the leader, followed by the record directory, followed by the fields one after another, with no breaks, to the end of the record (at which point there is a character to represent a record terminator). Such a record is practically unreadable if printed as transmitted, and so each system has a program that will display the record in a form that is more easily read. However, displays of the same record can look quite different from each other. Figures 3.1, 3.2 (*see* page 47), 3.3, 3.4 (*see* page 48) and 3.5 (*see* page 49) show the same MARC record as it is displayed in five different systems.

**Fig. 3.1. MARC record as displayed in OCLC Connexion.
(Source: WorldCat – record number 1912014).**

Books	Rec Stat c	Entered 19890119	Replaced 20020809294902.0			
Type a	ELvl	Srce	Audn	Ctrl	Lang eng
BLvl m	Form	Conf 0	Biog	MRec	Ctry cou
	Cont b	Gpub	LitF 0	Indx 1	
Desc a	Ills	Fest 0	DtSt s	Dates 1989,	

010		89002835
040		DLC ‡c DLC ‡d OCLCQ
020		0872876217 : ‡c $45.00
050	00	Z674 ‡b .R4 no. 20 ‡a Z7837 ‡a BX1751.2
082	00	020 s ‡a 016.282 ‡2 19
100	1_	McCabe, James Patrick.
245	10	Critical guide to Catholic reference books / ‡c James Patrick McCabe ; with an introduction by Russell E. Bidlack.
250		3rd ed.
260		Englewood, Colo. : ‡b Libraries Unlimited, ‡c 1989.
300		xiv, 323 p. ; ‡c 25 cm.
440	_0	Research studies in library science ; ‡v no. 20
500		Includes indexes.
610	20	Catholic Church ‡x Reference books ‡v Bibliography.

**Fig. 3.2. MARC record as displayed in the Library of Congress
Online Catalog. (Source: http://catalog.loc.gov/)**

LC Control Number: 89002835
000 01036pam 2200277 a 450
001 1034832
005 20000427134237.0
008 890119s1989 cou b 001 0 eng
035 __ |9 (DLC) 89002835
906 __ |a 7 |b cbc |c orignew |d 1 |e ocip |f 19 |g y-gencatlg
955 __ |a CIP ver. ne15/hr11 02-27-90
010 __ |a 89002835
020 __ |a 0872876217 : |c $45.00
040 __ |a DLC |c DLC |d DLC
050 00 |a Z674 |b .R4 no. 20 |a Z7837 |a BX1751.2
082 00 |a 020 s |a 016.282 |2 19
100 1_ |a McCabe, James Patrick.
245 10 |a Critical guide to Catholic reference books / |c James Patrick
    McCabe ; with an introduction by Russell E. Bidlack.
250 __ |a 3rd ed.
260 __ |a Englewood, Colo. : |b Libraries Unlimited, Inc., |c 1989.
300 __ |a xiv, 323 p. ; |c 25 cm.
440 _0 |a Research studies in library science ; |v no. 20
500 __ |a Includes indexes.
610 20 |a Catholic Church |x Reference books |x Bibliography.
991 __ |b c-GenColl |h Z674 |i .R4 no. 20 |t Copy 1 |w BOOKS
991 __ |b r-MRR |h Z674 |i .R4 no. 20 |t Copy 2 |m Alc |w GenBib bi
    90-005819

Fig. 3.3. MARC record as displayed in the OhioLINK Library Catalog. (Source: http://www.ohiolink.edu/)

```
LEADER  00000pam  2200000 a 4500c
001     19124014
008     901029s1989    cou       b      00110 eng
010     89002835
020     0872876217 :
035     0696-75260
050 00  Z674|b.R4 no.20
100 1   McCabe, James Patrick
245 10  Critical guide to Catholic reference books /|cJames
        Patrick McCabe ; with an introduction by Russell E.
        Bidlack
250     3rd ed
260     Englewood, Colo. :|bLibraries Unlimited, Inc.,|c1989
300     xiv, 323 p. ;|c25 cm
440   0 Research studies in library science ;|vno. 20
500     Includes indexes
610 20  Catholic Church|xBibliography
650   0 Reference books|xCatholic Church
```

Fig. 3.4. MARC record as displayed in the catalog of the University of Toronto Libraries. (Source: http://webcat.library.utoronto.ca)

```
090:  8  : BX 1751.2 .M252 1989|bSMCR

090:  8  : Z 7837 .M23 1989|bGENR|c1

100: 10  : McCabe, James Patrick.

245: 10  : Critical guide to Catholic reference books /|cJames
           Patrick McCabe ; with an introduction by Russell E.
           Bidlack.

250:     : 3rd ed. --

260:  0  : Englewood, Colo. :|bLibraries Unlimited,
           Inc.,|c1989.

300:     : xiv, 323 p. ;|c25 cm. --

490:  0  : Research studies in library science ;|vno. 20

610: 20  : Catholic Church|xBibliography.

650:  0  : Reference books|xCatholic Church.

500:     : Includes indexes.

020:     : 0872876217 :|c$45.00
```

Fig. 3.5. MARC record as displayed in the catalog of the New York University Libraries. (Source: http://www.bobcat.nyu.edu)

```
000 nam  a
001 NYUb12554980
003 NYU
005 20020619120746.0
008 890119s1989   cou    b   001 0 eng
010     $a  89002835
020     $a 0872876217 : $c $45.00
035     $a (CStRLIN)DCLC892835-B
040     $a DLC $c DLC $d DLC
050 00  $a Z674 $b .R4 no. 20 $a Z7837 $a BX1751.2
082 00  $a 020 s $a 016.282 $2 19
100 1   $a McCabe, James Patrick.
245 10  $a Critical guide to Catholic reference books / $c James Patrick McCabe ; with an
        introduction by Russell E. Bidlack.
250     $a 3rd ed.
260     $a Englewood, Colo. : $b Libraries Unlimited, Inc., $c 1989.
300     $a xiv, 323 p. ; $c 25 cm.
440 0   $a Research studies in library science ; $v no. 20
500     $a Includes indexes.
610 20  $a Catholic Church $x Reference books $x Bibliography.
959     $a Search with Geac Vubis Vlink $d Expand this search with Geac Vubis Vlink $i
        vlink.gif $9 0 $1
        http://bibdev.vub.ac.be/vubisweb/VlinkMenu.CSP?sid=Geac:Advance&genre=book&is
        bn=0872876217%20%3A&title=Critical%20guide%20to%20Catholic%20reference%20books%20
        %2F
852     $a NNU $b NYU $b Bobst $b REF1 $h Z674 $i .R4 no. 20 $7 12998499 $m Non-circulating
        $p 31142032829726 $y Available $5 31142032829726 $c
```

NOTES

1.   Deborah J. Byrne, *MARC Manual: Understanding and Using MARC Records*, 2nd ed. (Englewood, Colo.: Libraries Unlimited, 1998), pp. 1–15.

2.   *MARC 21 Format for Bibliographic Data: Including Guidelines for Content Designation* (Washington, D.C.: Cataloging Distribution Service, Library of Congress, 1999), 2 v.; *MARC 21 Concise Format for Bibliographic Data*, 2004 Concise Edition, available: http://lcweb. loc.gov/marc/bibliographic/ecbdhome.html (accessed 2/14/2006).

3.   Library of Congress >> MARC Standards >> MARC in XML, available: http://www.loc. gov/marcxml/ and http://www.loc.gov/mods/ (accessed 2/14/2006).

4.   Arlene G. Taylor, *The Organization of Information*, 2nd ed. (Westport, Conn.: Libraries Unlimited, 2004), p. 77.

5.   For an example of a record in the communications format, *see* Taylor, *The Organization of Information*, p. 73.

SUGGESTED READING

Avram, Henriette D. *MARC, Its History and Implications*. Washington, D.C.: Library of Congress, 1975.

Byrne, Deborah J. *MARC Manual: Understanding and Using MARC Records*. 2nd ed. Englewood, Colo.: Libraries Unlimited, 1998.

Ferguson, Bobby. *MARC/AACR2/Authority Control Tagging: Blitz Cataloging Workbook*. 2nd ed. Westport, Conn.: Libraries Unlimited, 2005.

Fritz, Deborah A., and Richard J. Fritz. *MARC21 for Everyone: A Practical Guide*. Chicago: American Library Association, 2003.

Furrie, Betty. *Understanding MARC Bibliographic: Machine-Readable Cataloging*. 7th ed. Washington, D.C.: Cataloging Distribution Service, Library of Congress, 2003. Also available: http://www.loc.gov/marc/umb (accessed 2/14/2006).

Part III
DESCRIPTION AND ACCESS

4 〉 Description

INTRODUCTION

Description as a cataloging process was briefly defined in chapter 1. This chapter discusses the process in more detail, and then introduces the rules for description in *Anglo-American Cataloguing Rules, 2002 Revision (AACR2R)*. Although this work is referred to as *AACR2R2002* elsewhere in this text, in the chapters specifically devoted to the *Anglo-American Cataloguing Rules* (chapters 4–8), the work that includes the additions and changes through 2005 is referred to as *AACR2R* unless specific quotations and/or pages from the 2002 print version or its update pages are being cited, in which case it is referred to as *AACR2R2002*. This is because in the Anglo-American cataloging community, the concept for *AACR2* has been that after its revision in 1988, any subsequent additions and changes have been equivalent to looseleaf publications, whatever their physical form may be. The work is still *AACR2R* even though additions and changes are regularly issued. This concept is made tangible with the 2002 print version, which was in fact issued in looseleaf format. (This text presumes that the cataloger has access to the 2002 revision with the 2003, 2004, and 2005 update pages interfiled or has access to the complete updated version on *Cataloger's Desktop*.)

Description is that part of the cataloging process concerned with identification of an information package, and with recording information about it in a bibliographic record in such a way that it will be identified exactly and cannot be confused with any other. Many elements contribute to the identification of an information package. A title is almost always the first identifying element, followed by the name(s) of a person or persons responsible for the contents of the work. Next, one looks for information identifying an edition; the name of the edition; the name of an editor, reviser, illustrator, translator, performer, producer, and/or publisher; the date of publication or copyright date; and a series of which the edition may be a part. Even the size, the type or number of illustrations, or the extent of the item (e.g., number of pages for a book or number of discs in a DVD set) may be helpful information for a patron seeking a particular edition of a work. When found, all these elements are useful in the description of the information package.

TECHNICAL READING OF AN INFORMATION PACKAGE TO BE CATALOGED

In order to identify conventional elements of an information package so that they can be described on a catalog record, it is necessary to know not only what to look for, but also how to look. Technical reading in this manner is scarcely the same as reading for information or for entertainment, when the entire item may be read, seen, or heard. Obviously, the cataloger will have no time for "reading" of this sort, and therefore must learn to read technically. Reading technically involves recognizing certain devices peculiar to the particular type of information package being cataloged. In this way, the cataloger can quickly determine its contents and how it can be described uniquely in such a way that this information can be passed on to potential users. The following discussion contains definitions useful to the cataloger in both descriptive cataloging and subject cataloging.

The first part of an information package that the cataloger examines in detail is the chief source of information. This source varies according to the type of material. In books, manuscripts, printed music, and printed serials, it is the title page. In microforms, films, and videorecordings it is the title frame(s). For sound recordings, it is the label and sometimes a container that is affixed to the item (e.g., cassette of a tape cassette). For cartographic and graphic materials, and for three-dimensional artifacts and realia, the chief source of information is the object itself, including permanently affixed labels or unifying containers. For electronic resources, including World Wide Web sites, any source of formally presented evidence within the resource may be used. In any of these cases, the chief source of information may be absent for some reason, in which case cataloging rules prescribe alternate sources. Usually, however, the chief source of information provides the most complete bibliographic information about the information package: the author or other person responsible for the intellectual contents; the fullest form of the title; the name and/or number of the edition; the name of the publisher, distributor, etc.; and the place and date of publication, distribution, etc. Figure 4.1 shows half the chief source of information for a sound recording. (The chief source for an audiocassette consists of all labels taken together. The side 2 label in this case differs only in the listing of contents.)

Fig. 4.1. Label from side 1 of an audiocassette.

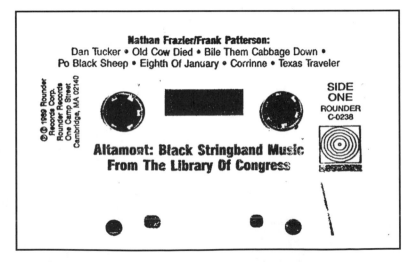

The first element that the cataloger ordinarily notices is the title. The title from the chief source of information (minus any subtitle or other title information) is called the *title proper*; as such, it is used in all library records, in trade catalogs, and in bibliographies. It may or may not adequately describe the contents of the item. The book title, *Short History of the United States*, is self-evident, but the title of the serial, *Toward Freedom*, needs an explanation. A glance through an issue will reveal that the serial discusses the development of new nations; this will be indicated as a subject heading on the catalog record.

In addition to the major part of the title, some items have secondary parts. The *alternative title* is introduced by *or* and was widely used in manifestations of works published before the twentieth century. As in Gilbert and Sullivan's *Patience, or, Bunthorne's Bride*, it amplifies the title by telling the reader that "Patience," in this case, is a woman's name rather than the name of a specific virtue. The *parallel title* is the title proper written in another language or in another script. For instance, a bilingual book on snowmobiles in the Province of Quebec has its title proper in French, *La motoneige au Québec*, and its parallel title in English, *Snowmobiling in Quebec*. *Other title information* is often used to qualify the title proper. Such qualifications are often called *subtitles*. For example, the complete title of a recorded lecture is *Behavior Control: The Psychologist as Manipulator*. "The Psychologist as Manipulator" is the subtitle. It explains the aspect of behavior control covered in the talk. There is also other title information that is not "subtitle" but does give further explanatory information. In the title, *Barbara Morgan Photography: Trisolini Gallery of Ohio University, Athens, Ohio, January 9–February 3, 1979*, the "other title" information tells where and when the show was held.

The title proper and other titles in the chief source of information, however, are not the only possible ones. Other titles exist, and the cataloger must note those that vary significantly from the title proper. When such titles are noted, the patron who knows a work only by a variant title can be directed to it. For example, Haydn's *Symphony 94 in G Major* is also known as the "Surprise Symphony"; many patrons would look for this popular form of the title instead of the title proper. Books may carry a cover title (i.e., title printed on the cover), binder's title (i.e., title lettered on the original spine of the book), or running title (i.e., title repeated at the top of each page or each alternate page of the book) that differs from the title proper. Sound recordings, videorecordings, graphic materials, or computer software may have titles on their containers that differ. World Wide Web sites may display different titles on the main body of the home page and in the title bar. Serials may have title variations on the cover or on an added title page.

The series title, however, is not a title variation, but indicates the series, if any, to which the information package belongs. A series may consist of several works all written by the same person or persons, as is the case with Will and Ariel Durant's *The Story of Civilization*, which consists of several uniform volumes. This is called an author's series. A series may also be issued by a publisher who commissions several authors to write one or more volumes on a specified subject. Such is the case with the Rinehart *Rivers of America* series of many volumes. Or perhaps an author is not commissioned but submits a work that happens to fit into a category established by the publisher. An example is Dodd, Mead's *Red Badge* series of mystery novels. Such series are called publishers' series.

The monographic series is a series that is usually issued with some regularity; each title in a monographic series ordinarily is given a number, usually in chronological order. For many patrons, the name of the series and the number of a title in it are the important identifying elements. Patrons may not remember individual authors and titles but look for these under the series name. Thus, although author and title of an individual item are major identifying elements, the series title in a monographic series assumes a significant role.

The second element to be identified by the cataloger is the statement of responsibility. This is also found in the chief source of information and is usually the author, whose name usually becomes the main entry. According to *AACR2R*, a personal author is "the person chiefly responsible for the creation of the intellectual or artistic content of a work."[1] In addition to writers of books and composers of music, this includes cartographers, artists, photographers, performers, etc. It may be necessary to locate some information about an unfamiliar author. For example, if the work is imaginative in nature, the author's nationality must be known since most classification schemes use the device of nationality to classify novels, drama, and poetry. This is discussed in the chapters 14–16 on classification in this text. It is also sometimes necessary to know an author's nationality to know how to form the heading for the name. This is discussed further in chapter 7 on form of headings for persons.

An author is not the only possibility for inclusion in a statement of responsibility. Any person or persons responsible for intellectual or artistic content or for performance, or any corporate body from which the content is issued, may need to be included in the catalog record.

The edition, if named, is usually found in the chief source of information, but may also be found in other places. In a book, a piece of printed music, or a serial it may appear in the preliminaries (i.e., title page, verso [or back] of the title page, any pages preceding the title page, and the cover), in the preface to the work, or in a colophon (i.e., a statement at the end of the work). In cartographic or graphic material, sound recordings, motion pictures and videorecordings, and three-dimensional artifacts, the edition may appear in accompanying printed material. For those items with a container, the edition may be found there.

The edition is distinguished from a printing or issue in that a new edition indicates that certain specific changes—additions, deletions, modifications—have been made from earlier versions of the item. By contrast, a new printing (or reprinting) or issue, means that more copies of the work were manufactured in order to keep up with demand. In the case of books and book-like materials, printings may have minor corrections or revisions, usually incorporated into the original type image. For other materials, a new issue may have slight variations from the original.

Editions may be named (e.g., "revised and enlarged," "abridged," "expurgated") or numbered (e.g., "5th edition"). Any of these edition statements indicates to the cataloger and the patron that some change in content or in form has been made. This information is very important to a scholar. To study the development of a poet, the literary scholar must have early and late editions of the poet's work. A physicist might want only the latest edition of a book on thermodynamics.

Because the name of the publisher or distributor, etc., might indicate the type or quality of a work, this information might be important to the patron who must choose one item from several on a specific subject. If the publisher or distributor, etc., is noted for excellence in a certain area (e.g., Skira in art; McGraw-Hill in technology), publisher/distributor information has some value to the patron. This information, including place and date, is usually found in the chief source of information, but may also be found in the same other locations as the edition statement. If the item is copyrighted, the copyright date and the holders of the copyright must be listed in or on it. This information is important when the publication date and the copyright date differ. In such a case, both dates may be given in the catalog record.

The cataloger must learn to assess quickly the details of physical description. These include the extent of the item (e.g., number of pages or volumes, number of pieces, length of playing time), dimensions (e.g., height, diameter), and physical data other than extent or dimensions (e.g., illustrations, playing speed, material, mounting, sound).

The cataloger must also be quick to identify other important and useful pieces of information about an item. Such information as variant titles of the same work (e.g., original title of a translation), other related versions of the work, language, edition history, accompanying materials, intended audience, contents of multi-volume items, and presence of bibliographies should often be noted in the catalog record. The standard number (e.g., International Standard Book Number [ISBN] or International Standard Serial Number [ISSN]) is of major importance as a means of unique international identification. It is also given in the catalog record.

If there is a preface, the cataloger should read it as an aid to determining the author's plan or objective and as an aid in identifying the edition. It also provides a key to subject matter. Similar aids are introductions, forewords, accompanying printed materials, and containers. The table of contents, with its listing of chapter titles, headings, and subheadings, is a valuable indication of the scope of a work. An index is a source for determining subject content and special emphases. A bibliography may also serve as an aid by providing important resources on the subject from the author's point of view.

During the process of the technical reading the cataloger takes note of relevant elements of information as they are found, so that they can be formed into a coherent description for the bibliographic record that will represent the information package in the catalog. Figure 4.2 shows the *AACR2R* description for the sound recording whose partial chief source of information is shown in figure 4.1 (page 54). The description was completed after a technical reading of the item. In this text, the formatting of examples is given as prescribed by *AACR2R*; online catalogs often display bibliographic information quite differently.

Fig. 4.2. Description of the item whose partial chief source of information is shown in Fig. 4.1.

Altamont [sound recording] : Black stringband music from the Library of Congress. — Cambridge, Mass. : Rounder, p1989.
1 sound cassette : analog, Dolby processed.

Credits: Nathan Frazier, vocals and banjo, Frank Patterson, fiddle (1st–7th works) ; Murph Gribble, banjo, John Lusk, fiddle, Albert York, guitar (8th–14th works).
Recorded Mar. 1942 in Nashville, Tenn. (1st–7th works), Sept. (?) 1946 (8th–13th works), and spring 1949 (14th work) in Rocky Island, Tenn.
Contents: Dan Tucker — Old cow died — Bile them cabbage down — Po black sheep — Eighth of January — Corrinne — Texas traveler — Rolling river — Old sage friend — Apple blossom — Pateroller'll catch you — Across the sea — Cincinnati — Altamont.

Bibliographic records in online systems are usually coded with the tags, indicators, and subfield codes of the MAchine-Readable Cataloging (MARC) format and are formatted with the spacing required by the system into which it will be entered. Figure 4.3 shows the description from figure 4.2 with MARC coding, formatted as it would be in the OCLC system.

Fig. 4.3. Description coded according to the MARC format and spaced and formatted as in the OCLC system. (Source: OCLC Connexion, WorldCat—record number 42552298)

Sound Recordings	**Rec Stat** c	**Entered** 19911119	**Replaced** 20001211
Type j	**ELvl** I	**Srce** d	**Audn**	**Ctrl**	**Lang** N/A
BLvl m	**Form**	**Comp** fm	**AccM**	**MRec**	**Ctry** mau
Desc a	**FMus** n	**LTxt**	**DtSt** p	**Dates** 1989,1942

007		s ‡b s ‡d l ‡e u ‡f n ‡g j ‡h l ‡i u ‡j m ‡k n ‡l n ‡m u ‡n e
040		WaO ‡c UOJ ‡d OCL
028	00	C-0238 ‡b Rounder
033	1_	194203-- ‡a 194609-- ‡a 1949----
043		n-us--- ‡a n-us-tn
047		fm ‡a cy
245	00	Altamont ‡h [sound recording] : ‡b Black stringband music from the Library of Congress.
260		Cambridge, Mass. : ‡b Rounder, ‡c p1989.
300		1 sound cassette : ‡b analog, Dolby processed.
511	0_	Nathan Frazier, vocals and banjo, Frank Patterson, fiddle (1st-7th works) ; Murph Gribble, banjo, John Lusk, fiddle, Albert York, guitar (8th-14th works).
518		Recorded Mar. 1942 in Nashville, Tenn. (1st-7th works), Sept. (?) 1946 (8th-13th works), and spring 1949 (14th work) in Rocky Island, Tenn.
505	0_	Dan Tucker -- Old cow died -- Bile them cabbage down -- Po black sheep -- Eighth of January -- Corrinne -- Texas traveler -- Rolling river -- Old sage friend -- Apple blossom -- Pateroller'll catch you -- Across the sea -- Cincinnati -- Altamont.
650	_0	African Americans ‡x Music.
650	_0	Country music ‡z Tennessee ‡y 1941-1950.
650	_0	Folk music ‡z Tennessee.
650	_0	Fiddle tunes.
700	1_	Frazier, Nathan. ‡4 prf
700	1_	Patterson, Frank, ‡c fiddler. ‡4 prf
700	1_	Gribble, Murph. ‡4 prf
700	1_	Lusk, John. ‡4 prf
700	1_	York, Albert. ‡4 prf
710	2_	Archive of Folk Song (U.S.)

DESCRIPTION OF MATERIALS USING *AACR2R*

The rest of this chapter covers in some detail the *AACR2R* rules for descriptive cataloging of materials in all formats. Not all rules are discussed, and the reader should examine the appropriate chapters of the code for more complex problems.

AACR2R does not contain instructions for MARC coding (discussed in chapter 3). The Library of Congress (LC) issues a general outline of the *MARC 21* format (the version of MARC adopted in the United States, Canada, and Great Britain) that includes definitions of all tags, indicators, and subfield codes and dictates the contents of each field and subfield, but does not indicate spacing or layout.[2] Each system that uses a MARC format creates its own spacing and layout, and it issues system documentation demonstrating how MARC records will be formatted in that system. Only *AACR2R* content, spacing, and punctuation are discussed in this chapter, although *MARC 21* field numbers and subfield codes are identified beside many of the *AACR2R* rules.

The first chapter of *AACR2R* covers description in general and is applicable to all types of materials (e.g., print, sound recordings, etc.) in all media (e.g., microform) and publication patterns (e.g., serial). Chapters 2 through 11 of *AACR2R* cover in detail various types of material and media. Chapter 12 covers continuing resources, a category which includes serials and "integrating resources" such as World Wide Web sites and looseleaf publications. These chapters often refer back to chapter 1 for rules that are generally applicable, but they also give specific guidance for situations that are peculiar to the type of material or medium under discussion. Chapters 2 through 12 of *AACR2R* cover:

2   Books, Pamphlets, and Printed Sheets
3   Cartographic Materials
4   Manuscripts (including Manuscript Collections)
5   Music
6   Sound Recordings
7   Motion Pictures and Videorecordings
8   Graphic Materials
9   Electronic Resources
10   Three-Dimensional Artifacts and Realia
11   Microforms
12   Continuing Resources

Special considerations pertaining to the cataloging of many of these materials are discussed below. It is important to keep in mind that rules from several chapters may need to be consulted in order to catalog any given information package. *AACR2R* Rule 0.24 states that the cataloger should "bring out all aspects of the item being described, including its content, its carrier, its type of publication, its bibliographic relationships, and whether it is published or unpublished. . . . As a rule of thumb, the cataloger should follow the more specific rules applying to the item being catalogued, whenever they differ from the general rules."[3]

AACR2R Chapter 13 covers a special problem in cataloging: analysis. There are purposely no chapters numbered 14 through 20 in *AACR2R*. These numbers were left vacant for later construction of rules for new types of material, in case it became necessary to develop rules for cataloging them.

FINITE VERSUS
CONTINUING RESOURCES

The most significant changes in the revisions of *AACR2R* published in 2002 have come about through the newly introduced concept of *finite* versus *continuing* resources. This is a new "division of the universe" in the code, replacing the former primary division between *monographs* and *serials*.

A monographic publication, in any medium, represents a complete bibliographic unit. The most familiar type of monographic publication is a book that is complete in one volume, or physical part. Many monographs are published in multiple physical units, of course. They may be issued in successive parts at regular or irregular intervals, even over a period of many years, but they are nevertheless not intended to continue indefinitely. Serials, by contrast, are information packages in any medium which *are* intended to be so continued. *AACR2R* defines "serial," in part, as a "resource issued in a succession of discrete parts, usually bearing numbering, that has no predetermined conclusion."[4] For decades, major aspects of cataloging practice, catalogers' job definitions, and workflow of materials were all predicated on the fundamental distinction between monographs and serials.

During the 1990s, however, the distinction between monographic and serial publications was seriously strained by new forms of electronic publication, primarily via the World Wide Web. Some electronic serials mimicked print publications in visual appearance (including pagination) and also in possessing enumeration (discrete volume and/or issue numbers) and chronology. Many others, however, dispensed with any or all of these features from the start. It became too difficult to reconcile the traditional *AACR2R* concept of "serial" with the reality of online scholarly journals that store articles in a single cumulating database, without partitioning them into separate volumes or issues. As one result, some catalogers maintained that these resources were actually monographic in nature. This led to uneasy conclusions—for example, that an online version of a print serial was an electronic monograph. It also came to seem generally absurd to treat continually changing websites of all kinds as monographs, as if they possessed the inherent monographic characteristics of stability and intended completeness. What types of information packages were these, which constantly changed while remaining arguably the same?

A breakthrough came in October 1997, when the "International Conference on the Principles and Future Development of *AACR*" was held in Toronto. The conference, which sought and received extensive comment online on a range of issues in advance, produced a number of recommendations for the further development of the code. One paper, "Issues Related to Seriality," by Jean Hirons and Crystal Graham, provided the basic thinking which, after much discussion and study by many concerned professionals, eventually led *AACR2R* out of the monograph/serial impasse.[5]

Chapter 12 of *AACR2R*, formerly titled "Serials," is now titled "Continuing Resources," as noted above. A "continuing resource" is defined as "a bibliographic resource that is issued over time with no predetermined conclusion. Continuing resources include serials and ongoing integrating resources."[6] The latter new concept addresses the dilemma of information packages that change and yet are identified as the same entity. An "integrating resource" is "a bibliographic resource that is added to or changed by means of updates that do not remain discrete and are integrated into the whole."[7] This not only expresses the nature of now-familiar Web resources, but has the added benefit of bringing a much older type of traditional resource into the fold: the updating looseleaf. Prior to this revision, looseleafs were so slightly dealt with in *AACR2R* that a compatible but separate standard was used for cataloging them: Adele Hallam's *Cataloging Rules for the Description of Looseleaf Publications*.[8] The provisions for "integrating resources" have at last removed the need for a separate standard for these materials.

It should be clear from this discussion that the concepts of monograph and serial have not disappeared from *AACR2R*, but rather have been cast in a new framework that better contains the full range of resources with which catalogers must deal. A few more points about the scope of Chapter 12 need to be noted. The chapter also covers a limited number of types of finite resources that exhibit characteristics of seriality (such as conference newsletters of limited duration, reprints of serials, and finite integrating resources). "Finite integrating resources" may seem at first to be a contradiction in terms, but simply refers to information packages which are still intended to reach a predetermined conclusion, even though changed by means of updates.

A discussion of the Library of Congress rule interpretations follows in the next section. It should be noted here, though, that LC's interpretation for *AACR2R* rule 1.0 provides very helpful guidance in determining, for doubtful cases, what kind of information package is represented by the item being cataloged (see *Cataloging Service Bulletin,* no. 103, p. 14–22).[9]

Catalogers should expect to see, within the next few years, still more in the way of significant change to AACR. The Joint Steering Committee for the Revision of AACR has begun the process of developing a significantly new edition of AACR, the provisional title of which is *Resource Description and Access* (*RDA*) rather than *AACR3*. The work plan for this revision includes, among other items,[10]

- significantly revised and expanded conceptual introductions to the rules as a whole, and to its major sections;

- a thorough revision of Part I (the equivalent of *AACR2R*'s Chapters 1–12) to provide guidelines and instructions on recording descriptive data, having chapters on identification of the resource, technical description, content description, information on terms of availability, and item-specific information;

- revision of Part II (the equivalent of *AACR2R*'s Chapters 21–26) to provide guidelines on reflecting relationships, guidelines for access points, creation of citations for related works, and special instructions for particular types of works;

- addition of a Part III giving guidelines for access point control (authority control) for names and works

- incorporation of concepts from *Functional Requirements for Bibliographic Records* (FRBR) [see discussion below], into all three parts;

- movement of ISBD punctuation rules to an appendix;

- and other changes noted in the RDA Prospectus.

Alert practitioners will wish to keep abreast of these developments. The publication of *RDA* is, as of this writing (February 2006), planned for 2008. There are no further updates planned for *AACR2R2002* beyond the small set of revisions published in 2005. To keep current, one may consult the website of the Joint Steering

Committee, which has a wealth of background documentation and links to related organizations.[11]

THE STRUCTURE OF
ANGLO-AMERICAN CATALOGUING RULES, SECOND EDITION (AACR2R) CHAPTERS 1 THROUGH 12

An important concept in using Chapters 1 through 12 of *AACR2R* is that the rule numbers are mnemonic. In International Standard Bibliographic Description (ISBD), upon which *AACR2R* is based, there are eight "areas" of description as follows:

1. Title and statement of responsibility area
2. Edition area
3. Material (or type of publication) specific details area
4. Publication, distribution, etc., area
5. Physical description area
6. Series area
7. Note area
8. Standard number and terms of availability area

Not all areas are used in describing all library materials, but in Chapters 1 to 12 of *AACR2R* all are mentioned, if only to say that the area in question is not used to describe the particular material (e.g., rule 9.3, Material (or Type of Publication) Specific Details Area: "This area is not used for electronic resources."). The rules are numbered in such a way that the number preceding the period is the chapter number and the number following the period is the rule number. Rules 1 through 8 in each chapter represent the eight "areas" named above. Thus, rule 1.2 deals with the edition area in general, while rule 5.2 covers the edition area for music, and rule 8.2 covers the edition area for graphic materials. Further, the rule numbers are subdivided by letters sometimes followed by numerals which are also mnemonic. In the general chapter, rule 1.1D is the rule for parallel titles; for books, the comparable rule is rule 2.1D, and for continuing resources it is rule 12.1D. In addition to the rules for "areas," all the chapters have general rules assigned the numeral "0." Chapters 1–3 and 5–12 also have rules 9, "Supplementary items," and 10, "Items made up of several types of materials." These rules do not all have exactly the same heading, but address the same concept (e.g., rule 10 for continuing resources is titled "Sections"). Chapters 1–3, 5, and 8 have a rule 11, "Facsimiles, Photocopies, and Other Reproductions." Chapter 2 has, in addition, rules 12 through 18 that deal specifically with early printed monographs.

Throughout *AACR2R* there are "optional" rules that allow for adding or deleting information in certain instances or that allow alternative methods of handling certain situations. Each cataloging agency must decide whether and how these options will be applied. Because so many libraries rely on LC for cataloging data, this text includes, in this chapter and the ones on *AACR2R* that follow, a discussion of LC's decision about application of each option that occurs in the rule sequences discussed in this text.

LC has issued rule interpretations that affect LC's implementation of rules in addition to the decisions about optional rules. LC rule interpretations for *AACR2R* have been published separately and are available from LC's Cataloging Distribution Service.[12] They also have been published in issues of *Cataloging Service Bulletin*. These have been cumulated by individuals outside of LC and are available at modest cost.[13] It is assumed that the version in the *Cataloging Service Bulletin* is available most widely, and so when LC's rule interpretations are referred to in this text, they are cited as *CSB* followed by the issue number and page(s) (e.g., *CSB* 45: 13–15 means *Cataloging Service Bulletin*, no. 45, pages 13 to 15). This text refers to rule interpretations published through *CSB* 109 (Summer 2005).

SPECIAL CONSIDERATIONS FOR NONBOOK MATERIALS

Chapters 3 through 10 in *AACR2R* cover materials that have been variously called "nonbook," "nonprint," "audiovisual," or "media"—the last term often including printed materials, as in "School Media Center." Often these are not handled in the same way as books or other print materials are handled. An administrative decision within each library determines whether to catalog and/or classify each of these special materials; because of their dimensions, many cannot be shelved with corresponding printed materials. The dimensions of such materials, then, become quite significant in bibliographic descriptions because this directly influences their location in a given collection, a consideration that often makes classification for shelving less significant than description.

If the librarian cannot easily remember the contents of the collection, then cataloging control is needed. If the library has only six maps, for instance, there is little need to catalog them. Sixty maps, however, or even 16, may well need to be cataloged. The disadvantage of failing to catalog descriptively any special materials is that the patron must look somewhere other than in the main catalog for the record of the material. It is strongly recommended that as many special materials as possible be cataloged descriptively and thus recorded in the catalog. Past problems in doing this were greatly eased by the publication of *AACR2*, followed by its revisions, with its integrated approach to the description of special materials. In *AACR2R* all materials are described according to the same set of principles.

Manuscripts. Collections of manuscripts can be cataloged at different levels. The collection can be described as a whole (collection-level cataloging), or individual manuscripts can be described separately (item-level cataloging). The challenge of cataloging manuscripts is that each is unique. The manuscript or the manuscript collection does not exist in another library, except perhaps in reproduction. It is not the kind of material for which catalogers can find cataloging copy already in existence. In addition, such materials often do not have any clearly defined chief source of information, and, indeed, they often do not have clearly defined titles. There may be difficulty even reading the handwriting in which a manuscript is written. It may be difficult to know whether one is dealing with an original or with a handwritten copy and, if a copy, the date it was copied and by whom. The manuscript cataloger is often dealing with events and names of persons not recorded elsewhere.

Music. One challenge in cataloging music resources is that a musical composition in printed form normally appears as a series of staves upon which notes are printed, but increasingly other systems of notation are used. The description of music written for a solo instrument, such as the piano, is relatively straightforward. The description of music written for several instrumental or vocal parts (i.e., scores) presents some special problems, especially in the title and statement of responsibility area, in the physical description area, and in the notes area.

Sound recordings. Both classification and description of sound recordings are affected by the fact that extremely disparate materials often appear on a single physical piece. This problem is addressed for description in *AACR2R*, rule 6.1G.

Motion pictures and videorecordings. Two of the complications involved in describing these materials involve the source of information and the large numbers of people responsible for them. Titles and other information, as they appear in the item itself, in accompanying materials, or on containers, often vary considerably. The large number of people involved presents problems for deciding how many "credits" will provide useful description of an item. Another problem is concerned with the ease with which videorecordings may be made, thus complicating the concepts of "copy" and "edition." These and other problems are addressed in the rules that follow, but ultimately the cataloger must use some judgment based on general principles.[14]

Graphic materials. These include, among other forms: art originals, art prints, art reproductions, charts, filmstrips, flash cards, photographs, pictures, postcards, posters, slides, study prints, technical drawings and wall charts. Many of these materials are not cataloged and/or classified in many libraries. An administrative decision within each library determines whether to catalog and/or classify these materials. Because most of them cannot be physically shelved with the corresponding monographic materials, standard classifications such as *Library of Congress Classification* (*LCC*) or *Dewey Decimal Classification* (*DDC*) often are not used. Rather, use is made of an accession or serial number to determine shelf order. On the other hand, catalog records of these materials are easily integrated in a database with records for other materials, because, in *AACR2R*, all materials are described according to the same standard—ISBD(G).

Electronic resources. The cataloging of electronic resources (formerly called "computer files") has posed some of the greatest challenges to established practice in recent times. The need for standards for cataloging these materials was recognized in 1970 when the American Library Association's (ALA's) Cataloging and Classification Section established a subcommittee to develop rules for cataloging electronic resources (then referred to as "machine-readable data files," or "MRDFs"). Since then, steady progress has been made, but the form in which bibliographic information for electronic resources can be found varies so greatly that cataloging them is somewhat more of a challenge than for most other materials. The state of the art of production of electronic resources is comparable to that of books in the early days of printing. At first there was no source of data comparable to a title page. Although program files and World Wide Web sites now usually have such a source, with non-standard and varying amounts of information, data files still usually have no such source. The rules now fully recognize the problem of "title page equivalents" by allowing the entire resource to serve as the chief source of information. As with videorecordings there is the problem of ease of duplication, complicating the ideas of "copy" and "edition."

Microcomputer software developed after the original publication of *AACR2* in 1978. As a result it was necessary to develop some supplementary interpretations for the rules in Chapter 9. These guidelines were published as a separate booklet.[15] In 1987, Chapter 9 of *AACR2* was completely revised and published as a separate publication.[16] The revision was expanded to include all types of electronic resources then existing. This revised Chapter 9 was incorporated into *AACR2R* with a number of revisions and some editing.

In similar fashion to the development of microcomputer software, widespread use of the Internet came about after the publication of *AACR2R*. In particular, the explosive growth of resources now available on the World Wide Web was chiefly enabled by the release of Mosaic browser software in 1993–1994. In consequence, remotely accessed electronic resources, intangible and easily modified without notice, have become resources of major importance in many libraries. These materials present their own set of challenges for description, classification, and management. The 2002 revision to *AACR2R* makes different provisions, where necessary, for the description of remote-access and direct-access resources, the latter being those on tangible carriers such as discs or tapes. As described above, the changing nature of most websites has been addressed by introduction of the concept of "integrating resources" in Chapter 12.

Three-dimensional artifacts and realia. Prior to the advent of *AACR2*, three-dimensional artifacts and realia were not cataloged or classified except in a few museum libraries. With a method of description consistent with that of describing other materials, however, we are seeing more cataloging of these materials—especially in media centers where emphasis is no longer on the "book" as the principal means of transmitting information.

A number of manuals have been written that supplement *AACR2R* in the area of nonbook materials. They are listed in the "Suggested Reading" section at the end of this chapter. They may be consulted for more detailed discussion of the problems of cataloging these materials, for definitions of terms unique to these types, and for in-depth examples of cataloging, although the older publications listed should be used in tandem with the latest available revisions of *AACR2R*.

SPECIAL CONSIDERATIONS FOR MICROFORMS

The cataloging of microforms requires knowledge of a number of different types of material. Books, manuscripts, maps, music, and graphic materials all can be reproduced in microform. In addition, microform can be the original means of publication of some kinds of content. According to *AACR2R*, all microforms, whether original publications or reproductions, are described in terms of the microform format with details of the original, when applicable, given in a note. As mentioned below under the discussion of rule 1.5A3, this is a controversial method for handling microforms. Those who oppose it say that the user is misled by being given a modern date in the publication, distribution, etc., area when the intellectual content of the work is much older. They are also concerned about short-entry catalogs in which the notes are not printed. Publishers that specialize in reproducing older printed material in microform say that the purpose of the reproduction is to make older materials available for scholarly study and research, not to create a new edition of it as a printed reprint of the text would do.

Earlier rules called for description of the original in the major part of the record with microform details in a note. Those opposed to this method point out that the physical form of the information package is important. A user who comes into the library wanting to borrow an item to take elsewhere to read needs to know whether it is in book form or microform. There are also potential problems for the cataloger in determining what the original was and what its physical description should be. A microform of a dissertation, for example, may be a positive copy of a negative master that is a copy of a photocopy of a printout of text originally held in a computer file. Two articles that discuss the issues involved may be read for further informa-tion.[17] Americans have tended to prefer the method of describing the original, with details about the microform in a note, but Europeans have espoused describing the original in a note. In 1980 and 1981 ALA's Committee on Cataloging: Description and Access examined this question and put forth a recommendation; its recommen-dation was that the original be described in the body of the entry, with details of the microform given in a note. The rules were not revised, but LC issued a policy deci-sion to this effect.[18] Both methods are illustrated in this text.

In December 1989 an Airlie House conference sponsored by the Council on Library Resources was held during which a solution was sought to the problem of "multiple versions." "Multiple versions" is the name given to the concept of two or more formats of the same work (e.g., a book, a negative microfilm of the book, and a positive microfilm of it; or, a published research paper, a photocopy of it, and a "pdf" file). At the conference a decision was made to pursue a possible two-tiered hierarchical solution in which the top level of the hierarchy would be a bibliographic record containing a description of the common elements of the various versions of the work, while the next level would contain the elements of description unique to each version. Although the Airlie House conference recommendations were not im-plemented, the relationship(s) between a work and its expressions remains an im-portant subject of current discussion. As with so many other questions in cataloging and classification, the "multiple versions" issue is further highlighted by the in-creasing prevalence of remote-access electronic resources, which may reproduce print materials to a greater or lesser extent, or be produced in different digital for-mats simultaneously. The simultaneous publication of moving-image works in multiple formats (particularly videotape and DVD) also points up this question.

The problem of providing intelligible, usable descriptions of "multiple ver-sions" has been reenergized by *Functional Requirements for Bibliographic Rec-ords*, a publication of IFLA (the International Federation of Library Associations and Institutions).[19] This important document (often referred to as *FRBR*) relates a hi-erarchy of bibliographic entities—*works, expressions, manifestations,* and *items*—to a set of user tasks—to *find, identify, select,* and *obtain.* It provides an analysis of those elements of bibliographic description which best suit a given user task. For ex-ample, the title of a *work* may vary in its translated *manifestations,* and the user may want to *identify* a translation in an appropriate language. Or in the context of this dis-cussion, a user may wish to *obtain* a *manifestation* of a paper in "pdf" format, rather than another format such as microfilm. A detailed discussion of *FRBR* is beyond the scope of this chapter. The reader should note, however, that the "*FRBR* model" has become an important part of the catalog code revision process. As discussed above in the section on "Finite versus Continuing Resources" (pp. 60–62), the Joint Steer-ing Committee for the Revision of AACR is planning a thorough revision of AACR by 2008. One important aspect of this revision is the incorporation of *FRBR* con-cepts and terminology throughout the code. The FRBR Working Group of IFLA's Cataloguing Section has established a website with many helpful resources, includ-ing an extensive bibliography.[20]

SPECIAL CONSIDERATIONS FOR SERIALS

As defined in *AACR2R*, a serial is a continuing resource issued in a succession of discrete parts, usually bearing numbering, that has no predetermined conclusion. Serials include both periodicals and non-periodicals. A periodical may be defined as a serial that has a distinctive title and that is issued more frequently than once a year and at regular intervals, with each issue containing articles by several contributors. Non-periodicals are all other forms of serials, such as yearbooks, annuals, memoirs, transactions and proceedings of societies, and any series cataloged together instead of separately.

There are certain types of monographs that are often treated as serials by libraries because they are not complete in one volume. These include continuations of sets, provisional serials, and pseudo-serials. Like true serials, these exhibit the characteristic of *successive issuance*, as compared with *single issuance* in the case of monographs complete when first published. A continuation of a set is a nonserial—i.e., monographic—set in process of publication. The *Oxford History of English Literature* and the *Dictionary of Literary Biography* are examples of continuations of sets. Neither publication is presently complete although many individual volumes have been issued. Such publications require a special order record—i.e., a standing order—for follow-up purposes; if such works are cataloged as sets, this creates problems for maintaining accurate records in the library's holdings record for the set. Provisional serials are those publications that are treated as serials while in the process of publication and as nonserials when complete. The justification for such treatment is often a particularly lengthy period of publication and/or a complicated numbering of individual issues. Either of the two previous examples of continuations of sets could be treated by individual libraries as provisional serials.

A pseudo-serial is a frequently reissued and revised publication that is generally treated as a monographic work at first publication but that is often treated as a serial after numerous successive editions have appeared. Serial numbering may be taken from the edition number or from the date of publication. Examples of pseudo-serials are Sir John Bernard Burke's *Genealogical and Heraldic History of the Peerage* (commonly called *Burke's Peerage*) or the *Guide to Reference Books* edited successively by Alice Bertha Kroeger, Isadore Mudge, Constance Winchell, Eugene P. Sheehy, Robert Balay, and others. Monographic treatment of a pseudo-serial requires individual descriptive cataloging for each new edition as well as additional added entries for previous editors or compilers. If a pseudo-serial is treated as a serial, the main entry is made under the title instead of the author and will require only one catalog record, as long as the title remains the same.

The principles for cataloging serials are generally the same as those for cataloging monographic publications. On the other hand, certain physical characteristics of serial publications (e.g., numerous changes in bibliographic descriptions, including changes of titles) necessitate some special rules. The aim of these special rules is to prepare an entry that will stand the longest time and will allow necessary changes to be made with a minimum of modification. If the serial is still being published or if the library has only part of the set and hopes to complete it, an open entry is prepared according to the rules that are presented in this chapter.

The descriptive cataloging of serials is generally more complex than that of monographs because of their greatly varied and possibly intricate bibliographic structure. On the other hand, classification and subject headings are likely to be somewhat more general, and therefore simpler. Indeed, in many libraries, periodicals are not classified at all but are shelved alphabetically by main entry. The detail with which serials are described may vary widely from library to library. Some consider a highly analytic description essential, while others reduce serials cataloging to the title and statement of responsibility area and a holdings note.

The serials cataloger is likely to be faced with the problem of describing a full set completely although all that may be at hand are a few volumes or current issues.

The most important sources of additional information are the *Union List of Serials*, *New Serial Titles*, *British Union Catalogue of Periodicals*, *Standard Periodical Directory*, and *Ulrich's Periodical Directory* (which now incorporates the formerly separate *Irregular Serials and Annuals: An International Directory*).[21] Other important sources are the LC catalogs and national and trade bibliographies, as well as publishers' catalogs. *Titles in Series* is useful for its lists of titles in monographic series, especially those published by university presses, and Bowker's *Books in Series in the United States 1966–1975* lists monographs distributed in popular, scholarly, and professional series.[22] In addition, the LC publication, *Monographic Series*, lists all monographs cataloged by LC that appeared as parts of series between 1974 and 1982, as well as all revised records, regardless of the date of publication.[23] Series access was incorporated in the *National Union Catalog* in 1982 and continued until it ceased publication at the end of 2002. OCLC and other databases are sources of additional information, as are published state union lists of serials.

SELECTED RULES AND EXAMPLES

The balance of this chapter is devoted to the *AACR2R* rules for description, covering *AACR2R* Chapters 1 through 12. The aim in this edition has been to integrate the parallel or analogous rules for description in each *AACR2R* chapter. Thus, for example, the rules and subrules for Area 1, Title and statement of responsibility, are discussed integrally across all chapters. To the greatest extent practicable, general principles applying to the greatest number of chapters are described first, followed by selected variations in specific *AACR2R* chapters. This organizational plan cannot always be carried out at the most detailed level, however. Despite *AACR2R*'s general parallelism across Chapters 1 through 12, analogous rule numbers in different chapters do not always discuss the same subjects. These exceptional situations are noted as they arise. Section headings for rules and subrules which have general application are designated with an X (e.g., X.5C) in place of a specific chapter number.

For each type of information package, one or more examples has been chosen to demonstrate a bibliographic record for that type. In each case, the chief source of information is illustrated. At the end of this chapter, complete bibliographic records, presented both in ISBD ("card") format and MARC format, are given. Because no one example can demonstrate every eventuality, other examples of particular instances are also given throughout the chapter.

RULE X.0. GENERAL RULES

1.0A. Sources of information

When cataloging an information package or information resource it is essential to determine whether or not it is part of a larger package. A separately published book or DVD, for example, will generally be cataloged as an independent resource. However, it may also be cataloged as a component of a larger resource, such as the *Harvard Classics* set of books or as one episode in a series of television specials. (See Chapter 5 in this text, "Description of Analytical Materials," for further discussion of "analytical" cataloging.) This rule states that the sources of information for description of an information package are dependent on this decision.

1.0A2. Basis of the description

This rule describes the basis of the description of five types of information packages: single-part resources, multipart monographs, serials, integrating resources, and assembled collections. The package as a whole is used as the basis of description for single-part resources and assembled collections. For the other three types of packages, the bases of description are as follows:

	Multipart monographs	Serials	Integrating Resources
1. Title and statement of responsibility	First or earliest available part	First or earliest available issue or part	Current iteration
2. Edition	First or earliest available part	First or earliest available issue or part	Current iteration
3. Numbering	N/A	First and/or last issues or parts for each system or sequence	N/A
4. Publication, distribution, etc.:			
a. Place and publisher, distributor, etc.	First or earliest available part	First or earliest available issue or part	Current iteration
b. Place and manufacturer	First or earliest available part	First or earliest available issue or part	Current iteration
c. Dates	First and/or last parts	First and/or last issues or parts	First and/or last iterations
5. Physical description	All parts	All issues or parts	Current iteration
6. Series	All parts	All issues or parts	Current iteration
7. Note	All parts and any other source	All issues or parts and any other source	All iterations and any other source
8. Standard number and terms of availability	All parts and any other source	All issues or parts and any other source	All iterations and any other source

Rule X.0A in Chapters 2–12 identifies the kinds of materials covered in that chapter. It also sometimes points out certain kinds of information packages *not* covered, or not covered completely, and suggests the chapter that should be consulted instead or in addition. For example, rule 4.0A directs that for the cataloging of manuscript cartographic items, one should also consult Chapter 3 of *AACR2R*.

1.0A3. Chief source of information

Once one has made a decision as to what will serve as the basis of the description (such as the resource itself, or the first part of a multipart monograph), the next step is to determine the *chief* and *prescribed* sources of information. A chief source of information is specified for each type of material or condition or pattern of publication. Information in the chief source is preferred to information found elsewhere. The rules in Chapters 2–12, describing the chief sources for those chapters, are numbered X.0B1.

This rule outlines how to determine the chief source in circumstances where there may be more than one to choose from. If an information package in one physical part presents more than one possible chief source, the first occurring potential source is used. Exceptions to this rule include sources of information that present the resource either as an independent package or as part of a larger resource, sources in multiple languages or scripts, sources with different dates of publication, incomplete title page information, and the case of a package containing manifestations of multiple works, each with its own source. The rule should be consulted for guidance in these situations.

An information package may also exist in more than one physical part. In this case, the rule specifies using the chief source on the first or earliest part. If this criterion does not apply, one should use the chief source that supplies the most information, that which serves as a unifying element for the whole package, or that belonging to the main part where the others are accompanying or otherwise dependent. Finally, this rule states that if the information package lacks a chief source, a title should be supplied based on any available source of information, with the source of the title specified in a note.

In the great majority of cases, however, the complex conditions outlined above will not apply. The following table outlines the chief sources of information for mainstream situations, where the chief source is readily identifiable.

TYPE OF MATERIAL	CHIEF SOURCE OF INFORMATION
2.0B1. Printed monographs ("Books") : i.e., all printed texts except serials (covered in *AACR2R* chapter 12) and microform reproductions of printed texts (covered in *AACR2R* chapter 11)	The title page. If there is not a title page, then the part of the item that gives the most complete information is used as a substitute. In this case, the part used as a substitute is given in a note. The information from the substitute is treated as if it were from a title page, i.e., brackets are not used. If the item has no part that can substitute, information may be taken from any available source.
	If information that would ordinarily appear on a title page is given on facing pages, both pages are treated as "the title page."
3.0B1. Atlases	Title page (same as for books).
3.0B2. Other cartographic items	a) cartographic item itself, or, if a) is inappropriate, b) container or case, or the cradle and stand of a globe.

4.0B1. Manuscript*	The manuscript itself.
	If information is scattered the order of preference is: title page if there is one and it was originally part of the manuscript, colophon, caption, heading, text itself.
	If information cannot be taken from the manuscript, use, in this order: another manuscript copy of the item, a published edition of the item, reference sources, and other sources.
5.0B1. Published music	a) If the title page consists of a "list" including the title of the work cataloged, use this list title page, cover, or caption – whichever furnishes the fullest information. Use title page or title page substitute in all other cases.
	b) If information cannot be taken from a), use, in this order: caption, cover, colophon, other preliminaries, other sources.
6.0B1. Sound recordings:	
Disc	Disc and label
Tape (open reel-to-reel)	Reel and label
Tape cassette	Cassette and label
Tape cartridge	Cartridge and label
Roll	Label
Sound recording on film	Container and label
	For all: two or more labels are treated as one chief source.
	If textual material has a collective title while the chief sources above do not, then the source of the collective title may be treated as a chief source.
	If information cannot be taken from a chief source above, use, in this order: accompanying textual material, a container, other sources. Prefer printed data to sound data.
7.0B1. Motion pictures and videorecordings	Item itself (e.g., title frames) and, if in a permanent container (e.g., a cartridge), the container and its label.
	If information cannot be taken from the chief source, use, in this order: accompanying textual material, container that is not an integral part of the piece, other sources.
8.0B1. Graphic materials	Item itself, including permanently affixed labels or containers. For an item consisting of two or more parts (e.g., slide set), use a container that provides a collective title if the items do not.
	If information cannot be taken from the chief source, use, in this order: non-integral container, accompanying textual material, other sources.
	Title screen(s). If there is no title screen, other internal sources, such as main menus, program statements and file headers may be used. The source with the most complete information is preferred.

---

* The cataloging manual *Describing Archives: A Content Standard* (*DACS*) has been accepted by LC as the standard for cataloging this type of material. One significant difference between this manual and Chapter 4 of *AACR2R* is that for Manuscript collections *DACS* allows the cataloger to supply information from a number of appropriate external sources.

9.0B1.   Electronic resources

The resource itself. Information is taken from formally presented evidence from the part of the resource that provides the most complete information. This may be the title screen(s), main menu(s), program statement(s), initial display(s) of information, home page, file header(s) including "Subject:" lines, encoded metadata and the physical carrier or its labels.

If the resource itself does not provide needed information, take it from these sources, in this order of precedence: printed or online document or other accompanying material, information printed on a container issued by the publisher or distributor.

If the information package includes two or more physical parts, and the formally presented information in the parts or their labels do not provide a collective title, take as the chief source a container or its permanently affixed label that is the unifying element.

If required information is not available from any of these sources, use the following sources, in this order of precedence: other published descriptions of the resource, other sources such as metadata records.

10.0B1.   Three-dimensional artifacts and realia

The object itself, along with any accompanying textual material and container issued with the item. Information on the item or permanently affixed to it is preferred.

11.0B1.   Microforms

Microfilm

The title frame, usually at the beginning of the item giving full title and publication details.

Aperture cards:

  set of cards   Title card

  single card   Card itself

Microfiches and microopaques

Title frame

If there is no title frame for a microfiche or a microopaque, the "header" (i.e., eye-readable data at the top of the fiche or opaque) is used unless the title there is in shortened form, while it appears in fuller form on the accompanying eye-readable materials or container. In the latter case the source of the fuller form is used as the chief source of information, and a note is made to indicate the source of the title proper. Information that is usually presented on one title frame or card may be presented on successive frames or cards. In this case, the successive frames or cards are treated as one chief source.

Information not available in the chief source is taken from other sources. The order of preference is:

    the remainder of the item
    container
    accompanying material
    other sources

12.0B. Continuing resources

12.0B1. Basis of the description

Serials: the first issue should be used for the basis of the description. If the first issue is not available, the first issue that is available is used.** LC provides a rule interpretation that gives guidance in the case of electronic serials that have been reformatted in such a way that evidence of their earlier titles and/or corporate bodies has disappeared. (*CSB* 97: 39-40)

Integrating resources: the current iteration should be used as the basis of the description, except for publication dates, which should be based on the first and/or last iterations. An "iteration" is the state of the resource as it appears at a given point in time.

12.0B2a). Printed resources

The title page (or title page substitute) is used as its chief source of information.

Sources of title page substitutes are to be used in this order: analytical title page, cover, caption, masthead, editorial pages, colophon, other pages. The source of title page substitute is given in a note. LC gives a rule interpretation that makes the following exception: if an item has two or more different titles and the title on the preferred source is known to be less stable than another title, then the source with the stable title is to be used as the title page substitute. (*CSB* 97: 41)

12.0B2b). Nonprint resources

For direct access electronic serials, the physical carrier or its labels are used as the chief source. For other resources, rule .0B of the relevant chapter is used.

** This is a change from pre-*AACR2* practice that called for using the latest issue. While there is some objection to using the first issue because of all the changes that can occur in such areas as the publication area, the former practice could not, in fact, be followed because of the extreme difficulty of examining every new issue.

1.0A4. Prescribed sources of information

Some parts of the description may be taken from "prescribed" sources rather than the chief source. Information that is either not from the chief source, where required, or from prescribed sources in other instances, must be enclosed in square brackets. The rules in Chapters 2–12, describing the chief sources covered in those chapters, are numbered X.0B2.

MATERIAL	TITLE AND STATEMENT OF RESPONSIBILITY	EDITION	[AREA 3]	PUBLICATION, DISTRIBUTION, ETC.
2.0B2 Books	Title page	Title page, other preliminaries, and colophon	[Not used]	Title page, other preliminaries, and colophon
3.0B2 Cartographic materials	Chief source of information	Chief source of information, accompanying printed material	Chief source of information, accompanying printed material	Chief source of information, accompanying printed material
4.0B2 Manuscripts	Chief source of information, published copies of the item	Chief source of information, published copies of the item	[Not used]	Chief source of information, published copies of the item (Only the date is given.)
5.0B2 Music	Chief source of information	Chief source of information, caption, cover, colophon, other preliminaries	Chief source of information	Chief source of information, caption, cover, colophon, other preliminaries, first page of music
6.0B2 Sound recordings	Chief source of information	Chief source of information, accompanying textual material, container	[Not used]	Chief source of information, accompanying textual material, container
7.0B2 Motion pictures and video-recordings	Chief source of information	Chief source of information, accompanying material	[Not used]	Chief source of information, accompanying material
8.0B2 Graphics	Chief source of information	Chief source of information, container, accompanying material	[Not used]	Chief source of information, container, accompanying material
9.0B2 Electronic resources	Chief source of information, information issued by publisher or creator, container	Chief source of information, information issued by publisher or creator, container	[Not used]	Chief source of information, information issued by publisher or creator, container
10.B2 Three-dimensional artifacts and realia	Chief source of information	Chief source of information	[Not used]	Chief source of information
11.0B2 Microforms	Chief source of information	Chief source of information, rest of the item, container	Chief source of information, rest of the item, container	Chief source of information, rest of the item, container
12.0B Continuing resources 12.0B3a) Printed resources 12.0B3b) Nonprint serials: see the chapters for the type of material, e.g., Chapter 9 for electronic serials.	Title page	Title page, other preliminaries, colophon	The whole resource	The whole resource

Each area of the description has a prescribed source or sources from which information should be taken. These prescribed sources are fairly standard from medium to medium, although there are variations. If information in an area is from a non-prescribed source, it should be enclosed in square brackets. A table of the most common prescribed sources is given below, with the variations noted.

PHYSICAL DESCRIPTION	SERIES	NOTES	STANDARD NUMBER AND TERMS OF AVAILABILITY
The whole publication	Series title page, monograph title page, cover, rest of the publication	Any source	Any source
Any source	Chief source of information, accompanying printed material	Any source	Any source
Any source	[Not used]	Any source	[Not used]
Any source	Series title page, title page, caption, cover, colophon, other preliminaries	Any source	Any source
Any source	Chief source of information, accompanying textual material, container	Any source	Any source
Any source	Chief source of information, accompanying material	Any source	Any source
Any source	Chief source of information, container, accompanying material	Any source	Any source
Any source	Chief source of information, information issued by publisher or creator, container	Any source	Any source
Any source	Chief source of information	Any source	Any source
Any source	Chief source of information, rest of the item, container	Any source	Any source
The whole resource	Series title page, analytical title page, cover, caption, masthead, editorial pages, colophon, rest of the resource	Any source	Any source

1.0C. Punctuation

An extended discussion of punctuation in *AACR2R* is given in the 8th edition of this text.[24] A substantial rule interpretation from LC provides guidance in a variety of situations (CSB 103: 22–42). Most areas in most chapters of *AACR2R* have a rule numbered .A1 (1.1A1, 1.2A1, 1.4A1, etc.) in which detailed guidance for punctuation of specific areas of the description is given.

1.0D. Levels of detail in the description

AACR2R provides three recommended levels of description. The minimum requirements for each level are specified in this rule. The rules in Chapters 1–12 of *AACR2R* provide guidance for every element of level 3. The examples in this text, for the most part, follow LC practice in cataloging at level 2. Figures 4.4 and 4.5 illustrate the first and second levels for the same item. The third level includes every possible element set out in the rules and is likely to be used only in cataloging such things as rare items.

Fig. 4.4. Rule 1.0D1. First level of description.

Scottish crofters. — Holt, Rinehart and Winston,
c1990.
    xii, 175 p.

Bibliography: p. 167-169.
Includes index.
ISBN 0-030-03754-6

Note: Cataloging to the first level of description requires use of only rules 1.1B, 1.1F, 1.2B, 1.3, 1.4D, 1.4F, 1.5B, 1.7, and 1.8B. In the use of rule 1.7, all notes are optional.

Fig. 4.5. Rule 1.0D2. Second level of description.

Scottish crofters : a historical ethnography of a Celtic village /
Susan Parman. — Fort Worth : Holt, Rinehart and Winston,
c1990.
    xii, 175 p. : ill. ; 24 cm. — (Case studies in cultural
anthropology)

Bibliography: p. 167-169.
Includes index.
ISBN 0-030-30754-6

Illustrative Examples

What follows are examples of chief and prescribed sources of information for many of the types of materials covered in *AACR2R*. These examples will be used to build descriptions throughout this chapter. Complete descriptions and MARC records for these examples are given on pages 158–173.

Chapter 2, Books

Figures 4.6–4.8 illustrate the title page and "other preliminaries" for the book that is used in this text to illustrate building a description. *Preliminaries* is defined in *AACR2R2002* as "the title page(s) of an item, the verso of the title page(s), any pages preceding the title page(s), and the cover."[25] *Colophon* is defined as "a statement at the end of an item giving information about one or more of the following: the title, author(s), publisher, printer, date of publication or printing. . . ."[26] The book used here has the title, author, and edition statement on the front cover, with the information on the spine duplicating that on the title page. It has no colophon. Colophons are not common in English-language books but are found more often in books in other languages.

Fig. 4.6. Title page of book.

A Guide to the Library of
Congress Classification

Fifth Edition

Based on the Fourth Edition of
*Immroth's Guide to the
Library of Congress Classification*

Lois Mai Chan

1999
LIBRARIES UNLIMITED, INC.
Englewood, Colorado

Fig. 4.7. Verso of title page.

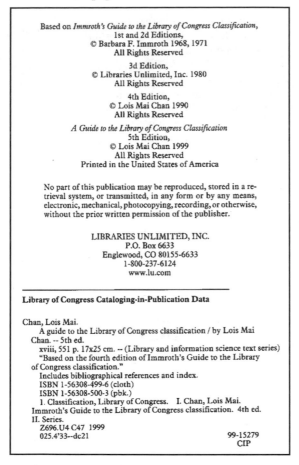

Fig. 4.8. Recto of leaf preceding title page (series title page).

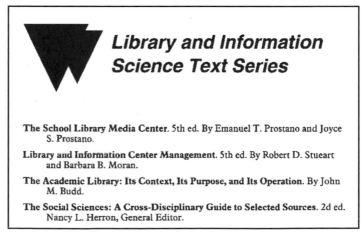

Chapter 3, Cartographic Materials

Figures 4.9–4.12 show sources of information for a map.

Fig. 4.9. Upper right corner of map.

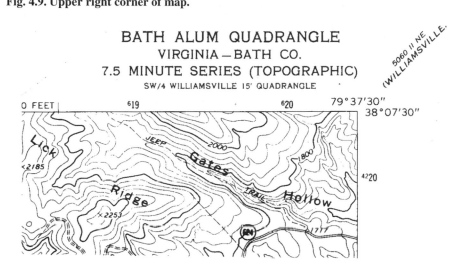

Fig. 4.10. Lower right corner of map.

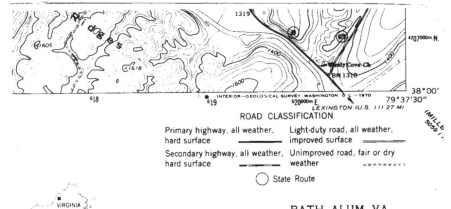

Fig. 4.11. Lower left corner of map.

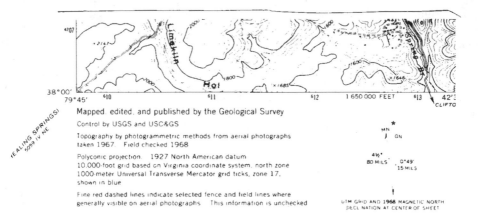

Fig. 4.12. Lower center of map.

Chapter 4, Manuscripts

Figures 4.13–4.15 show sources of information for a manuscript.

Fig. 4.13. Outside of letter shown in Fig. 4.14.

Fig. 4.14. Letter from George III to Henry Dundas. [Reproduced by permission of the Manuscript Department, William R. Perkins Library, Duke University.]

Fig. 4.15. Transcription of letter shown in Fig. 4.14.

[*Windsor, 3 Feb. 1793, 9:10 a.m.*] Mr. Secretary Dundas is to summon the Privy Council at the Queen's House for tomorrow at three o'Clock. I am glad to find the French are taking steps that must cut off the correspondence between the two Nations, and consequently puts an end to Lord Auckland's desire now before Me of intriguing with Du Mourier.

GR.

P.S. As the enclosed Warrants are all the Same and as many more will be necessary it might be a great saving of time in the Secretary's office if they were Printed and only the blanks filled up when meant to be issued I should equally as now Sign them.

Chapter 5, Music

Figure 4.16 shows the chief source of information for a piece of music.

Fig. 4.16. Chief source of information for a score.

TOMMASO ALBINONI

TRIOSONATE H-MOLL
für zwei Violinen und Basso continuo

TRIO SONATA IN B MINOR
for two Violins and Basso continuo

op. I/8

Herausgegeben von / Edited by
STEFAN ALTNER

BÄRENREITER KASSEL • BASEL • LONDON • NEW YORK
HORTUS MUSICUS 240

Chapter 6, Sound Recordings

Figures 4.17–4.18 show sources of information for a sound recording.

**Fig. 4.17. Chief source of
information from disc.**

Fig. 4.18. Information from accompanying booklet.

INSTRUMENTARIUM

Violin:
Cornelius Kleyman, Amsterdam c. 1680

Bow:
W. Baumann, Amsterdam

Recording Data: 1984-06-07, 09/11 in the Petrus Church, Stock-
    sund, Sweden
Recording Engineer & Digital Editor: Robert von Bahr
Sony PCM F1 Digital Recording Equipment, 4 Neumann U-87
    Microphones, SAM 82 Mixer, Sony Tape
Producer: Robert von Bahr
Cover Text: Stig Jacobsson
English Translation: John Skinner
German Translation: Per Skans
French Translation: Arlette Chené-Wiklander
Front Cover Picture: Conny Asberg
Back Cover Photos: Robert von Bahr
Album Design: Robert von Bahr
Type Setting: Marianne von Bahr
Lay-Out: William Jewson
Repro: KåPe Grafiska, Stockholm
Print: Offizin Paul Hartung, Hamburg, West Germany 1985

Also available as LP and MC: BIS-LP-275 & BIS-MC-275

© & ℗ : 1984/85, Grammofon AB BIS

This record can be ordered from
Grammofon AB BIS
Väringavägen 6 S-182 63 Djursholm Sweden
Phone: Stockholm (08)*(Int.: +468)* - 755 41 00
Telex: 13880 bis s
or from BIS' agents all over the world

Chapter 7, Motion Pictures and Videorecordings

Figures 4.19–4.21 show sources of information for a videotape.

Fig. 4.19. Videotape label.

Fig. 4.20. Transcription of title frames at beginning of videotape.

The Firesign Theatre presents

The Martian Space Party © 1972 TFT

Fig. 4.21. Transcription of credit frames at end of videotape.

Produced and edited by
The Firesign Theatre
and Stephen Gillmor

Camera: Stephen Winsten
Robert Guralnick
Stephen Gillmor

Sound: Peter Pilafian
Bill Driml
Phil Cross

Titles: Dr. W. Deadjellie
Bass: Cyrus Faryar
Lights: Ken Tosic

Production Assistants: Mike Rozsa
Kurt Hahn
Edina Gillmor
Alan McKay

Special thanks to dear friends:
Bill McIntyre, Rick Bralver,
Edgar Bullington and
the Grassroots and
KPFK-FM Los Angeles

Written and Performed by
The Firesign Theatre
Phil Austin   Peter Bergman
David Ossman   Philip Proctor
with Annalee and Tiny, the Firebelles

Directed by Stephen Gillmor

Chapter 8, Graphics

Figures 4.22–4.24 show sources of information for a set of stereograph reels.

Fig. 4.22. Chief source of information for set of stereograph reels.

Fig. 4.23. Unifying container for stereograph reel set.

Fig. 4.24. First page of accompanying booklet.

Chapter 9, Electronic Resources

Figures 4.25–4.26 show sources of information for computer software, a direct-access resource.

Fig. 4.25. Compact disc's chief source of information.

Fig. 4.26. Title screen print.

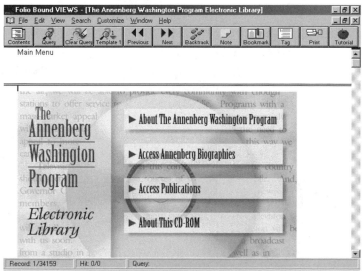

Figure 4.27 shows the chief source of information for a World Wide Web home page, a remote-access resource.

Fig. 4.27. World Wide Web home page.

Home Page: American Memory from the Library of Congress   http://memory.loc.gov/ammem/amhome.html

The Library of Congress

American Memory
Historical Collections for the National Digital Library

Over 70 Collections Now Online

Collection Finder
Select a collection or group of collections to search

Search
Search for items across all collections

Learning Page
Organized help for students, teachers, and life-long learners

Today in History
April 13, 2000

What's New!

Frequently Asked Questions

How To View | Copyright & Restrictions | Technical Information | Future Collections

Meeting of Frontiers
A multimedia English-Russian digital library

Sponsors
See who is helping to bring a virtual library to all Americans for the 21st Century

LC/Ameritech Competition

National Science Foundation Digital Libraries Initiative
Co-sponsored by the Library of Congress

Library of Congress Home | Using the Library | Thomas | Copyright Office | Exhibitions
The Library Today | Bicentennial | Help & FAQs | Search the Catalog | Search LC Site | LC Site Map

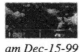

am Dec-15-99

Library of Congress
URL: www.loc.gov
Questions: American Memory Help Desk

NOTICE

Chapter 10, Three-dimensional Artifacts and Realia

Figures 4.28–4.29 show sources of information for a game.

Fig. 4.28. Top of box for dominoes game.

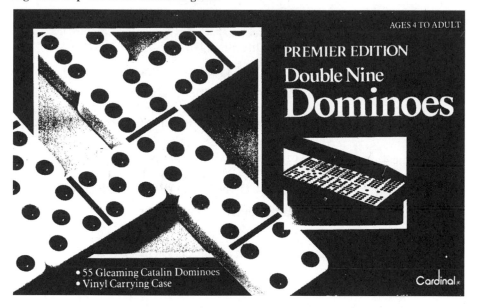

Fig. 4.29. Side of box for dominoes game.

Chapter 11, Microforms

Two items, one in microfilm format and the other in microfiche format, are used in this text to illustrate the building of description for microforms. The item illustrated in figures 4.30–4.31 is one that was assembled and filmed specifically for the purpose of bringing out an original edition in microform. The item illustrated in figures 4.32–4.34 is a microform of a previously existing work.

Fig. 4.30. Transcription of the first five frames of a microfilm.

Frame 1   WOMEN AND/IN HEALTH
                 filmed by the
                 WOMEN'S HISTORY RESEARCH CENTER
                 JULY 1974

Frame 2   WOMEN'S HISTORY RESEARCH CENTER
                 2325 Oak Street
                 Berkeley, California 94707

Frame 3   © Women's History Research Center, Inc. 1974

                 Reproduction of the material contained herein may not
                 be reproduced in any form except by express permission
                 from Women's History Research Center, Inc. and the
                 Publisher(s).

Frame 4   THIS FILM WAS MADE POSSIBLE BY A
                 REVENUE SHARING GRANT FROM THE
                 ALAMEDA COUNTY BOARD OF SUPERVISORS.

Frame 5   Filmed at a reduction ratio of 15:1

Fig. 4.31. Transcription of label on container of first reel of microfilm.

WOMEN AND HEALTH/MENTAL HEALTH
Reel No. 1   Positive
Section 1
Women's History Research Center

Fig. 4.32. Transcription of title frame of microfiche.

                                                    87-15914
BAUM, Christina Diane
      THE IMPACT OF FEMINIST THOUGHT ON AMERICAN
LIBRARIANSHIP, 1965-1985.
University of Kentucky   Ed.D. 1987

University
   Microfilms
International 300 N. Zeeb Road, Ann Arbor, MI 48106

                    Copyright 1987
                          by
                    BAUM, Christina Diane
                    All Rights Reserved

Fig. 4.33. Transcription of eye-readable data at top of fiche.

87-15914   c 1987   BAUM, Christina Diane   THE IMPACT OF FEMINIST   1 of 03
                    THOUGHT ON AMERICAN LIBRARIANSHIP, 1965-1985
Ann Arbor, Mi.; University Microfilms International 1987

Fig. 4.34. Transcription of title page of original dissertation (seventh frame of microfiche).

THE IMPACT OF FEMINIST THOUGHT ON
AMERICAN LIBRARIANSHIP 1965-1985

DISSERTATION

A dissertation submitted in partial fulfillment of the
requirements for the degree of Doctor of Education
at the University of Kentucky

By
Christina D. Baum
Lexington, Kentucky

Director: Dr. Leonard L. Baird, Professor of
Educational Policy Studies

Lexington, Kentucky

1987

Chapter 12, Continuing Resources

Figures 4.35–4.36 show the chief source for the first issue of a printed serial.
Figures 4.37–4.38 show the chief source of information for an electronic journal.

Fig. 4.35. Front cover of printed serial.

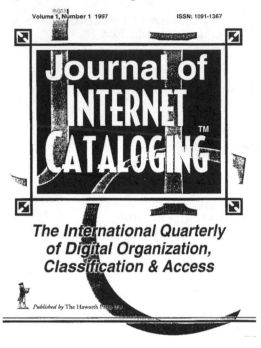

Fig. 4.36. Contents page of printed serial.

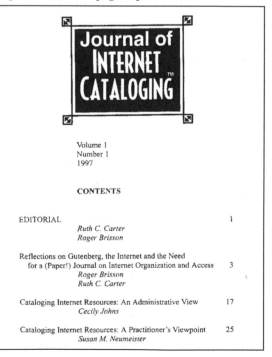

Fig. 4.37. Home Page of electronic serial.

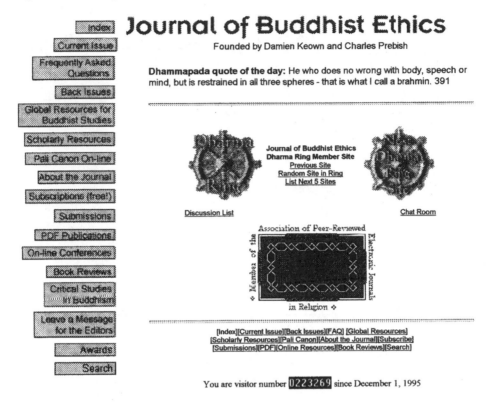

Journal of Buddhist Ethics

Founded by Damien Keown and Charles Prebish

Index
Current Issue
Frequently Asked Questions
Back Issues
Global Resources for Buddhist Studies
Scholarly Resources
Pali Canon On-line
About the Journal
Subscriptions (free!)
Submissions
PDF Publications
On-line Conferences
Book Reviews
Critical Studies in Buddhism
Leave a Message for the Editors
Awards
Search

Dhammapada quote of the day: He who does no wrong with body, speech or mind, but is restrained in all three spheres - that is what I call a brahmin. 391

Journal of Buddhist Ethics
Dharma Ring Member Site
Previous Site
Random Site in Ring
List Next 5 Sites

Discussion List   Chat Room

Association of Peer-Reviewed Electronic Journals in Religion

Member of the

[Index][Current Issue][Back Issues][FAQ] [Global Resources]
[Scholarly Resources][Pali Canon][About the Journal][Subscribe]
[Submissions][PDF][Online Resources][Book Reviews][Search]

You are visitor number 0223269 since December 1, 1995

Fig. 4.38. Contents page of electronic serial.

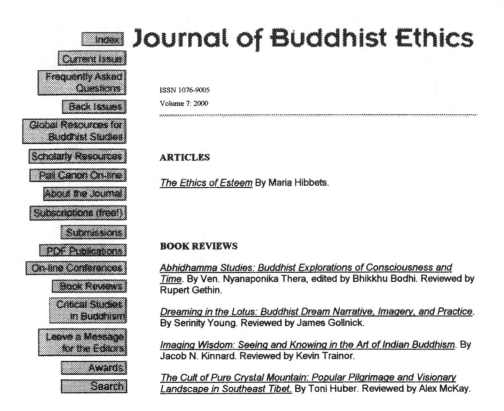

Journal of Buddhist Ethics

index

Current Issue

Frequently Asked Questions

Back Issues

Global Resources for Buddhist Studies

Scholarly Resources

Pali Canon On-line

About the Journal

Subscriptions (free!)

Submissions

PDF Publications

On-line Conferences

Book Reviews

Critical Studies in Buddhism

Leave a Message for the Editors

Awards

Search

ISSN 1076-9005

Volume 7: 2000

ARTICLES

The Ethics of Esteem By Maria Hibbets.

BOOK REVIEWS

Abhidhamma Studies: Buddhist Explorations of Consciousness and Time. By Ven. Nyanaponika Thera, edited by Bhikkhu Bodhi. Reviewed by Rupert Gethin.

Dreaming in the Lotus: Buddhist Dream Narrative, Imagery, and Practice. By Serinity Young. Reviewed by James Gollnick.

Imaging Wisdom: Seeing and Knowing in the Art of Indian Buddhism. By Jacob N. Kinnard. Reviewed by Kevin Trainor.

The Cult of Pure Crystal Mountain: Popular Pilgrimage and Visionary Landscape in Southeast Tibet. By Toni Huber. Reviewed by Alex McKay.

AREA 1.   TITLE AND STATEMENT OF RESPONSIBILITY AREA
(*MARC 21* field 245)

1.1A2.   Sources of information

Title and statement of responsibility information is to be taken from the chief source of information. There is a prescribed order for data, regardless of their order in the chief source. The prescribed order should be followed except when grammatical construction does not allow it.

X.1B.   Title proper (subfield a, *MARC 21* field 245)

1.1B1.   The exact wording, order, and spelling of the title proper should be followed in the transcription, but punctuation and capitalization may be changed. Example:

> **Chief source of information:**   Feeling Mad
> Feeling Sad
> Feeling Bad
> Feeling Glad
> **Transcription:**   Feeling mad, feeling sad, feeling bad, feeling glad.

Words or phrases which serve as introduction to the title, such as "Welcome to" or "Fox presents" are not transcribed as part of the title proper. The title which includes these words should be given in a note (see X.7B4). LC notes that this is likely to occur mainly with moving image materials, electronic resources, and popular journals. In case of doubt about whether these elements are integral to the title proper, the rule interpretation advises using the longer form as title proper and giving the shorter version in a note. (*CSB* 100: 17) Example:

> **Chief source of information:**   Welcome to the Official Web Site of
> The State of Maine
> **Transcription:**   The official Web site of the state of Maine

Three dots or square brackets in the title are replaced by a dash or by parentheses, respectively. Also, if the source of information uses a colon, slash, or equals sign, LC replaces it with other punctuation unless the space may be closed up on both sides. (*CSB* 100: 17)

1.1B2.   A statement of responsibility that is connected to the title proper with a grammatical construction (such as a case ending) is transcribed as part of the title proper. Example:

> Bill Collins' book of movies.

1.1B4.   Very long titles may be abridged if this can be done without giving up important information. The first five words may not be abridged, however. The mark of omission (i.e., ". . .") shows where omissions have been made. Example:

> Hearings before the Subcommittee on the Rules and Organization of
> the House of the Committee on Rules, House of Representatives,
> Ninety-fifth Congress, second session . . .

1.1B7.   If the chief source of information (or its substitute) lacks a title proper, one may be supplied from some other source, or may be constructed by the cataloger, if none can be found. Square brackets are used in such a case. Example:

[Map of Kerr Lake Recreation Area, North Carolina]

1.1B10.   When a chief source includes a collective title and also the titles of the separate works of the collection, the collective title is transcribed as the title proper. The separate individual titles are given in a contents note. (For transcription of titles when there is no collective title, *see* rule 1.1G.) Example:

> The great stone face & other tales [sound recording] / by
> Nathaniel Hawthorne. — Charlotte, Md. : Recorded Books, p1986.
>   2 sound cassettes (120 min.) : analog, mono.
>
>   Narrated by Nelson Runger.
>   "Unabridged."
>   In container.
>   Contents: The great stone face — The ambitious guest — The
> great carbuncle — Sketches from memory.

X.1B for AACR2R Chapters 3–10 and 12:
    Because the numbering of subrules of X.1B in Chapters 3–10 and 12 does not exactly parallel the general rules in Chapter 1, those subrules are discussed separately here.

5.1B1.   Music: If a title consists of the name(s) of one or more type(s) of composition with or without the medium of performance, key, date, and/or number, those elements are all treated as the title proper. Examples:

> Concerto in B-flat for cembalo and strings
>
> Triosonate H-moll für zwei Violinen und Basso Continuo

If, however, the medium, key, date, and/or number are present with a title other than type of composition, those elements are treated as other title information. Example:

> Short meditations : for string trio and harp

6.1B1.   *Sound recordings*: An LC rule interpretation instructs the cataloger that if the name of an author or performer is given before the titles of individual works and if it is possible that the name was meant to serve as a collective title proper, it should be treated as a title proper, unless the works are musical compositions and the name is the composer of the works, in which case the name would be given as statement of responsibility. (*CSB* 44: 25)

7.1B1.   *Motion pictures and videorecordings*: An LC rule interpretation states that credits for performer, director, etc., that precede or follow the title in the chief source are not considered part of the title proper unless they are within the title or represented by a possessive immediately preceding the title. (*CSB* 97: 32-33) Examples:

Chief source:
Twentieth Century Fox presents Star Wars
Title proper:
Star wars

Chief source:
Armstrong presents Lerner & Loewe's Brigadoon
Title proper:
Lerner & Loewe's Brigadoon

12.1B1.   Continuing resources: This rule states that obvious inaccuracies are not to be transcribed in Area 1. The title proper should be given as corrected, and the title as it appears with inaccuracies should be given in a note.

X.1B2-B3.   Rule X.1B2, and sometimes X.1B3 and following, in each chapter presents special instructions for titles proper for that type of material. In most cases rule X.1B2 gives instructions for supplying a title when the item lacks one. Examples:

[Letter] 1793 Feb. 3, Windsor [to Henry] Dundas

[Public library advertisement]

[Harris 1967 public opinion survey, no. 1702]

3.1B2.   Cartographic materials: The rules instruct one to include statement of scale if it is part of the title proper. Example:

Arabian peninsula 1:500,000 / prepared by . . .

3.1B3.   There are also directions to the cataloger on how to choose from more than one title in the chief source for cartographic materials. Choice is made on the basis of language, sequence, or layout, and if these are insufficient, then the most comprehensive title is chosen. Thus, the title proper for the map whose chief source is illustrated in figures 4.9–4.12 would be:

Bath Alum quadrangle, Virginia–Bath company

12.1B2.   Continuing resources: If the title in the chief source of information includes both an acronym or initialism and also the words represented by the initials, the full form is recorded as the title proper. Example:

Transnational data report
[Chief source and other sources read: TDR Transnational Data Report]

12.1B3.   A corporate body's name is considered to be part of the title proper only when it consistently appears as part of the title in various locations in the resource. LC applies this criterion to any word, phrase, etc., that may or may not be part of the title proper. (*CSB* 91: 20)

12.1B4-12.1B6.   These rules cover transcription of titles that are sections of, or supplements to, other resources. In general, if the title common to all sections appears with the section or supplement title, both are transcribed as title proper. An LC rule interpretation should be consulted when using rule 12.1B4. (*CSB* 97: 42–43) Examples:

Solar energy. Cumulative index

Major studies of the Congressional Research Service. Supplement

If the common title is not present with the section or supplement title, the section or supplement title is treated as title proper. Example:

Bibliography of Utah geology

Note reads:

Supplement to: Utah geology.

12.1B7. Serials: When the title proper includes a date or numbering that changes from issue to issue, the date or numbering is omitted. It is replaced by the mark of omission unless it is at the beginning. LC uses the mark of omission at the end of the title proper only if there is a grammatical reason to do so. (*CSB* 97: 43) Example:

Proceedings of the ... annual meeting

12.1B8. Serials: If there is a major change in title proper (as defined by rule 21.2C), a new description must be made for the new title. If the change is minor, the change is given in a note (see rule 12.7B4.2).

Integrating resources: If, for any iteration of the resource subsequent to that which served as the basis of its original description, there is a change in title proper, the title and statement of responsibility area should be changed to reflect the new iteration. The earlier title should be given in a note.

X.1C.   *Optional addition.* **General material designation** (subfield h, *MARC 21* field 245)

1.1C1.   *AACR2R* gives two lists of general material designations (GMDs). List 1 is for British use and list 2 is for North American and Australian use.

List 1	List 2	
braille	activity card	microscope slide
cartographic material	art original	model
electronic resource	art reproduction	motion picture
graphic	braille	music
manuscript	cartographic material	picture
microform	chart	realia
motion picture	diorama	slide
multimedia	electronic resource	sound recording
music	filmstrip	technical drawing
object	flash card	text
sound recording	game	toy
text	kit	transparency
videorecording	manuscript	videorecording
	microform	

Users of list 2 are instructed to add "(large print)" or "(tactile)" to any term in the list when cataloging material for the visually impaired. "(Braille)" may also be added to any term other than *braille* or *text*.

LC uses list 2. The examples given in this text will do likewise. The only GMDs currently supplied by LC are:

electronic resource (applicable to materials cataloged after November 2001; "computer file" was used for materials cataloged 1989–November 2001)

filmstrip (applicable to materials cataloged before 1992)

graphic (applicable to materials cataloged according to *Graphic Materials*)

microform

motion picture (applicable to materials cataloged according to Chapter 7 of *AACR2*; not applicable to materials cataloged according to *Archival Moving Image Materials*)

slide (applicable to materials cataloged before 1992)

sound recording

transparency (applicable to materials cataloged before 1992)

videorecording (applicable to materials cataloged according to Chapter 7 of *AACR2*; not applicable to materials cataloged according to *Archival Moving Image Materials*) (*CSB* 94: 11)

Some of the others would be used if LC were to begin cataloging those kinds of materials; however, the decision was made *not* to use the GMDs for manuscripts, music, and text.

A footnote to list 2 should be consulted for interpretation of particular terms. *See AACR2R2002*, p. 1–10.

1.1C2. When the GMD is used, it is added to the description in square brackets immediately after the title proper. It precedes any other title information that may be added using rule 1.1E. Examples:

Scared straight! [motion picture]

Basic concepts of humanistic psychology [sound recording]

Gargoyles [videorecording] : guardians of the gate

When an item has no collective title (see X.1G), the GMD is given immediately after the first title. This is taken to include part titles and alternative titles, but to exclude parallel titles and other title information.

1.1C3. When an item is a reproduction of a work that originally appeared in a different form (e.g., microform of a map, or sound tape of an original sound disc), the GMD for the reproduction, not the original, is given. For example, the videorecording with the following title, although originally issued as a 16mm motion picture, would be entered as:

The Americans, 1776 [videorecording]

The set of slides with the following title, which was originally issued as a filmstrip, would be entered as:

Blood pressure [slide]

1.1C4.   Some items consist of parts that fall into more than one category of the list of GMDs chosen. If one of these is predominant, that form is given as the GMD. If none is predominant, the GMD used is "kit." (*See also* rule 1.10C.) For example, the following item contains one book, one sound cassette, one poster, two puppets, and an activity guide, and would be entered as:

> Why mosquitoes buzz in people's ears [kit]

X.1D.   Parallel titles (subfield b, *MARC 21* field 245)

1.1D1.   Parallel titles are recorded in the order found in the chief source of information. Examples:

> La motoneige au Québec = Snowmobiling in Quebec
>
> Canadian journal of psychiatry = Revue canadienne de psychiatrie

> **[A space-equal sign-space precedes a parallel title.]**

X.1E.   Other title information (subfield b, *MARC 21* field 245)

1.1E1.   Other title information is transcribed using the same rules as for the title proper. Other title information includes, but is not limited to, subtitles. If there is more than one kind of other title information, each follows its own space-colon-space. Examples:

> The midnight patrol : the story of a Salvation Army lass who patrolled the dark streets of London's West End on a midnight mission of mercy

> From Poussin to Matisse : the Russian taste for French painting : a loan exhibition from the U.S.S.R.

> The scales of justice [filmstrip] : our court system

12.1E1.   Continuing resources: In cases where both an acronym or initialism and the words represented by the initials appear in the chief source of information, the acronym or initialism is given as other title information. Example:

> Transnational Data Report : TDR

Phrases that simply indicate the currency of the resource's contents are not given as other title information.

3.1E2.   Cartographic materials: If the title proper or other title information does not indicate the geographic area, this is added as other title information. Example:

> Land use and industry : [in East Germany]

4.1E2.   Manuscripts: For manuscripts, there are extensive directions (in rule 4.1B2) for creating supplied titles. If a manuscript item has a title and it lacks information required for a supplied title for that type of document, the information is added as other title information. Example:

> The duty of communicating in the Lord's Supper enforced : [sermon]

1.1E5.   When parallel titles are involved, other title information follows the title proper or the parallel title that it accompanies. Example:

> La nuit : Etüde für Klavier = Night : piano study : op. 31, Nr. 3

1.1E6.   In cases where a title proper needs explanation, an explanatory term or phrase is added in brackets as other title information in the same language as the title proper. Such additions are preceded by a colon so as to distinguish them from GMDs. Example:

> Beginnings : [poems]

X.1F.   Statements of responsibility (subfield c, *MARC 21* field 245)

1.1F1.   Statements of responsibility that appear prominently in an item are recorded as they appear. They are separated from the title or GMD information preceding them by a space-slash-space. Just as for title information, statements of responsibility that do not come from the chief source of information must be enclosed in square brackets. An LC rule interpretation suggests that only statements "that are of bibliographic significance" should be recorded, and guidelines are provided for making such a determination. (*CSB* 13: 4-6). Examples:

> And then there's always the possibility of disappearing
> altogether [motion picture] / Pegarty Long
>
> Bath Alum quadrangle, Virginia–Bath Co. / mapped, edited,
> and published by the Geological Survey
>
> Ben Oliel and Seeley / [Dorothy Wood Ewers]

6.1F1.   Sound recordings: This rule is somewhat different from that for other materials. The cataloger must make a decision as to whether the participation of the person(s) or body(bodies) involved in the recording goes beyond that of performance, execution, or interpretation of a work. If so, the statement is given as statement of responsibility. If not, the statement is given in a note. Thus, the statement on the chief source of information shown in figure 4.17 (p. 83), "Nils-Erik Sparf, The Drottningholm Baroque Ensemble," would be relegated to note position because participation seems to be "confined to performance, execution, or interpretation." Writers of spoken words, composers of music, and collectors of field material for sound recordings are included in statements of responsibility. Examples:

> Is there enough to go around? [sound recording] / Buckminster Fuller

> **(This recording consists of an interview in which Fuller is the primary speaker. In the case of a group of poems by e. e. cummings read by Spencer Tracy, for example, only e. e. cummings would be given in the statement of responsibility.)**

> Sounds of inner peace [sound recording] / composed and performed
> by Nawang Khechog

7.1F1 / 8.1F1.   Films and Graphics: These rules state that names should be given in the statement of responsibility when a person or body has had a major role in the creation of works in these media. Producers, directors, and writers (and, for graphics, artists, designers, and sponsors) are among the roles assumed to have some degree of overall responsibility. Person(s) or body(bodies) with responsibility for only segments or one aspect of a work are named in the note area.

1.1F2.   Unlike titles proper, a statement of responsibility is not essential to a description, and if one is not prominent in the item, one is not constructed.

It should be noted that serials, among other types of material, often have identical titles proper (e.g., Bulletin). When no statement of responsibility is given, non-distinctive titles become a problem when the title is the main entry and when it is necessary to make an added entry for that title on the record for another work. This problem has been solved with uniform titles. (*See* discussion in chapter 7.)

1.1F5.   Often an information package names more than three persons or corporate bodies that have all performed the same function or have had the same degree of responsibility for the work. If there are three such persons or bodies, all are given in the statement of responsibility. If there are more than three, only the first person or corporate body of each group is listed. The omission of the others is indicated by "... [et al.]" (or the equivalent of "et al." in nonroman scripts). Example:

> Studies in modality / Nicholas Rescher ; with the collaboration
> of Ruth Manor ... [et al.].

1.1F6.   Multiple statements of responsibility (i.e., for different kinds of responsibility for a work) are transcribed in the order in which they appear in the information source. They are separated from each other by a space-semicolon-space. If the layout is such that the statements are not in an obvious order, the cataloger is instructed to use "the order that makes the most sense." Example:

> Looking backwards / Colette ; translated from the French by
> David Le Vay ; with an introduction by Maurice Goudeket.

1.1F7.   Most titles of address, honor, and distinction; qualifications; dates of founding; etc., are omitted from statements of responsibility. There are four exceptions:

   1.   when the information is necessary grammatically
   2.   when only a given name or only a surname is accompanied by a title
   3.   when a title is necessary for identification
   4.   when a title of nobility or British title of honor is involved.

In the following example the title "Mrs." is necessary for identification:

> Suppression of Mutiny, 1857-1858 / Mrs. Henry
> Duberly.

1.1F8.   In instances where the relationship of the person or body in the statement of responsibility to the work is not clear, a word or phrase of explanation may be added in brackets. This does not allow, however, for the former practice of adding "by" and/or "and" in statements of authorship. Examples:

Addition with an explanatory phrase:

> About interpretation : from Plato to Dilthey : a
> hermeneutic anthology / [compiled by] Barrie A. Wilson.

Statement of responsibility without addition:

> Potters of Southern Africa / G. Clark, L. Wagner.

It should be noted that analogous rules in subsequent *AACR2R* chapters have different specific rule numbers (e.g., 2.1F2).

1.1F12.   Noun phrases sometimes appear between titles and statements of responsibility that are not clearly part of either. One has to decide whether such a noun or noun phrase seems to indicate the nature of the work or the role of the person or body responsible. If it seems to indicate the nature of the work, it is transcribed as other title information. Example:

> Walt Whitman's poetry : a study & a selection / by
> Edmond Holmes.

Otherwise it is transcribed as part of the statement of responsibility. Example:

> Innovative funding : the ABC's of supplementing LMI
> budgets / a collaborative effort initiated by the ICESA
> LMI Committee.

Preference is given the latter treatment when in doubt.

1.1F13.   The rules for transcription of title information include instructions to give statements of responsibility as part of the title when they are inseparable grammatically. When this has been done, no separate statement of responsibility is given unless there is a separate statement in the chief source of information. Examples:

No statement of responsibility:

> Horowitz in concert [sound recording] : recorded at his
> 1966 Carnegie Hall recitals.

Separate statement of responsibility:

> McGuffey's new third eclectic reader for young
> learners / by Wm. H. McGuffey.

X.1F for AACR2R Chapters 11 and 12:

11.F.   Microforms: As with other areas of the description, transcription of title and statement of responsibility may vary according to whether one is following *AACR2R* or LC policy. Examples:

Transcription of title and statement of responsibility area for the microfiche from figures 4.32–4.34 according to AACR2R:

> The impact of feminist thought on American librarianship,
> 1965-1985 [microform] / Christina Diane Baum

Transcription of title and statement of responsibility area for the same microfiche according to LC policy:

The impact of feminist thought on American librarianship, 1965-1985 [microform] / by Christina D. Baum

12.1F2.   Continuing resources: When a title includes a full or abbreviated statement of responsibility as part of the title proper no separate statement is given. Example:

ALCTS newsletter. —

*12.1F3.   For *serials*, personal editors are not recorded in statements of responsibility. If considered important, they may be given in a note. For *integrating resources*, personal editors are recorded in statements of responsibility if considered important.

X.1G.   Items without a collective title

Items that lack a collective title may or may not have a predominant part. If such a predominant part is present, the title of that part is given as the title proper for the work, and other titles are given in a note. If there is no predominant part, the rule calls for describing the item as a unit, with the option of describing each part separately and linking the separate descriptions with notes. When the item is described as a unit, the titles are transcribed in the order given in the chief source of information (or in the order in which they appear, if there is no chief source). The GMD is given following the first title, as stated in rule 1.1C2. If the parts are all by the same person(s) or body(bodies), their titles are separated by semicolons, and the statement of responsibility follows the last one. Examples:

Transcription of titles of two sides of a recording by the same person with each title taken from a separate label, and there being no linking word:

African politics [sound recording] ; More songs from Kenya / David Nzomo.

Transcription of titles of two works that are published in the same book with the title page giving the linking word and:

Fantazias ; and, In nomines / by Henry Purcell ; edited with a foreword by Anthony Ford.

If different persons or bodies were responsible for the various parts, or if it is not known whether all parts were by the same person(s) or body(bodies), each title is followed by its other title information, statement of responsibility, and a period. Example:

The suicide meet / Mary Humphrey Baldridge. Pickle / by Sheila Junor-Moore. The saga of the elk / by Jim Taylor. What it means to me to be a Canadian / compiled from Calgary school children, grades 6 and 7.

3.1G1.   Cartographic materials: This rule allows the cataloger to supply a collective title for an item that consists of a large number of physically separate parts. Example:

[Maps of the United States]

[4.1G].   Manuscripts: A collective title may also be supplied for manuscript collections, but this is authorized in rule 4.1B2 rather than here. Example:

> [Papers] / William Alexander Smith

6.1G1 / 7.1G1 / 9.1G1.   Sound recordings, Films, and Electronic resources: LC has made a decision to describe these as units in all cases. (*CSB* 94: 12) Example:

> Rhapsody in blue [sound recording] ; An American in Paris / Gershwin

11.1G.   Microforms: It is common to find several different serial titles on the same roll of microfilm. These are given separate descriptions in most libraries.

AREA 2. EDITION AREA (*MARC 21* field 250)

X.2B. Edition statement (subfield a, *MARC 21* field 250)

1.2B1.   If there is an edition statement, it is transcribed as found, with the exception that standard abbreviations found in Appendix B of *AACR2R* and numerals as found in Appendix C of *AACR2R* are used in place of the actual words from the source of information. Example:

> Export/import traffic management and forwarding / by Alfred Murr. — 3rd ed., rev. and enl.

2.2B.   Books: AACR2R does not give instructions for transcribing edition statements for multipart sets when the various parts show different edition statements. An LC rule interpretation for rule 2.2 addresses this issue. (*CSB* 41: 14)

12.2B.   Continuing resources: For *serials*, local or language edition statements, special interest, format or physical presentation statements, and reprint or reissue statements are transcribed according to the general rule. For *integrating resources*, edition statements are transcribed if considered important.

X.2C.   Statements of responsibility relating to the edition (subfield b, *MARC 21* field 250)

1.2C.   Statements of responsibility relating to the edition

1.2C1.   A statement of responsibility that applies to the edition in hand, but not to all editions of a work, is given following the edition statement, if there is one. Example:

> The Oxford school dictionary / compiled by Dorothy C. Mackenzie. — 3rd ed. / revised by Joan Pusey.

1.2C2.   When there is no edition statement, when there is doubt about whether a statement of responsibility applies to all editions, or when one is describing a first edition, all statements of responsibility are transcribed into the title and statement of responsibility area.

General notes on Area 2 in AACR2R Chapters 5, 9, 11 and 12:

5.2.   Music: An LC rule interpretation discusses the care that must be taken with music publications to distinguish between edition statements and musical presentation statements. The latter often include the word *edition*, but should not be taken as edition statements. Musical presentation statements indicate the version, arrangement, music format, etc., in which a work is presented. These go in the statement of responsibility when the music itself is meant (i.e., a version, arrangement, or transposition of the music) because an "author" is responsible for changing the original work, even if such a person is not named. When the music format is meant (e.g., edition as a set of parts), the statement is transcribed in Area 3 (see below). (*CSB* 33: 32) Only when edition statements of the book type appear are they transcribed into the edition area. Example:

> Drei Sonaten für Klavier zu vier Händen / Johann Christian
> Bach ; herausgegeben von Wilhelm Weismann. — Ed. Peters

9.2. Electronic resources: It may sometimes be difficult to interpret "edition" when cataloging electronic resources. Changes can be made to these resources very quickly and easily (e.g., data can be added, changed, or deleted). While published software has fairly standard edition statements (e.g., Version 5.6 or Release 3.0), data files do not. Published data files that are reissued on a regular basis contain a cumulation of all older data plus new data acquired since the previous issue. These are sometimes advertised as being, for example, "a complete new edition each quarter." Most libraries treat these as serials. Rule 9.2B4 instructs the cataloger not to treat as a new edition an issue including such minor changes as corrections of misspelled data, rearrangement of contents, changes in output format or display medium, and changes in physical characteristics (e.g., recording density). If deemed important, such changes may be given in a note. Examples:

> Microsoft word [electronic resource]. — Version 6.0

> Science citation index [electronic resource]. — Compact disc ed.

These rules are simplest to apply to direct-access electronic resources, where the cataloger has a physical item or set of items to inspect. There are also remote-access resources which are finite, such as reports presented on the Web and not intended to change. The recording of changing edition statements for integrating electronic resources is dealt with in rule 12.2F, which is particular to Chapter 12.

11.2. Microforms: A statement relating to an edition of a microform, rather than the edition of an original that is being reproduced, is called for in this rule. Example:

> Die Kataloge der Frankfurter und Leipziger Buchmessen 1759-1800
> [microform] / hrsg. von Bernhard Fabian. — Microfiche-Ed.

However, for reproductions of previously existing materials under current policy, LC would reverse this rule.

12.2F. Continuing resources: For *serials*, an addition, deletion, or change of edition statement on a subsequent issue or part is recorded in a note if considered important, as long as the change does not require a new description. For *integrating resources*, such a change on a subsequent iteration requires a change in the edition statement, with a note made about the earlier statement if considered important.

AREA 3.   MATERIAL (OR TYPE OF PUBLICATION) SPECIFIC DETAILS AREA

This area, at this point, is used only for cartographic materials, music, and serials. It is also used in describing microforms of cartographic materials, music, and serials. Therefore, the content of this area is discussed in the *AACR2R* chapters specifically devoted to description of these materials.

Cartographic materials:

3.3.   MATHEMATICAL DATA AREA (*MARC 21* field 255)

3.3B.   Statement of scale (subfield a, *MARC 21* field 255)

3.3B1. The first part of this area is "Statement of scale." Scale is given as a representative fraction expressed as 1:_____ and preceded by the word *scale*. This statement is given even if it is already recorded in Area 1. If the statement of scale on the item is not expressed as a representative fraction (e.g., "1 inch to 76 miles") , it is given as a representative fraction in square brackets (e.g., [1:4,815,360]). If any statement of scale is found outside the item, it also is given as a representative fraction in square brackets. If no statement is found, the scale is computed and given preceded by "ca." If it cannot be computed, the statement "scale not given" is used. An option allows giving an estimated statement of scale by comparison with another cartographic item of known scale. LC is not applying the option (*CSB* 97: 31). For electronic resources, scale is given if the resource has such a statement or if it is already recorded in Area 1; otherwise, "scale not given" is used.

3.3B2. An option allows giving additional scale information found on the item under certain circumstances. LC is applying this option. (*CSB* 8: 10) Example:

> West Indies and Central America / compiled and drawn in the Cartographic Division of the National Geographic Society, for The national geographic magazine. — Scale 1:4,815,360. 1 in. to 76 miles.

3.3B3-3.3B7. Detailed instructions for recording more than one scale value, and for handling other problems, are given in these rules, which should be consulted when one is doing in-depth map cataloging.

3.3C. Statement of projection (subfield b, *MARC 21* field 255)

If a statement of projection is found on the item or any of the accompanying materials, it is given following the scale, using abbreviations and numerals where appropriate. Example:

> Bath Alum quadrangle, Virginia–Bath Co. / mapped, edited, and published by the Geological Survey. — Scale 1:24,000 ; Polyconic proj.

3.3D. *Optional addition.* **Statement of coordinates and equinox** (subfields c-g, *MARC 21* field 255) This rule provides instructions for recording data about coordinates and equinox for terrestrial and celestial cartographic materials. Terrestrial coordinates may be expressed in degrees, minutes and seconds, or as decimal degrees.

Closed polygons may be precisely described. LC makes use of this option when the item cataloged includes the information. (*CSB* 97: 31)

3.3E. Digital graphic representation (*MARC 21* field 352)

For electronic resources, this rule provides for the provision of certain types of information, such as data type, object type, number of objects used to represent spatial information, and format name, where this information is readily obtainable.

Music:

5.3. *Optional area.* **MUSICAL PRESENTATION STATEMENT AREA** (*MARC 21* field 254)

This area calls for recording a statement found in the chief source that indicates the physical presentation of the music. As discussed above under the edition area, it is necessary to distinguish among statements that are true edition statements, those that are statements of responsibility, and those that indicate the physical presentation. LC is applying this optional area. (*CSB* 34: 25) Example:

> Aubade : trio for flute, oboe & clarinet in B^b / DeWailley ; [edited by] Jerry Kirkbride. — Score and parts

General note on Area 3 in AACR2R Chapters 3–10:

Chapters other than 3 and 5 state that area 3 is not used for the types of material described in them. The implication is that use of this area is not permitted for the types of material in question. However, although the need is rare, nonbook materials may be produced serially, and occasionally their content is cartographic (e.g., slides of maps). The scope note for Chapter 12, description of continuing resources, says that the rules in that chapter are to be used in conjunction with rules in other chapters of part I where applicable. Clearly, then, it is permissible, and certainly desirable, to use area 3 when describing other nonbook materials. For example, sound recordings that are available on a subscription basis require serial cataloging. Example:

> Musicworks [sound recording]. — No. 52 (1992)-

Microforms:

11.3.   SPECIAL DATA FOR CARTOGRAPHIC MATERIALS, MUSIC, AND SERIALS (*MARC 21* field 255, 254, OR 362)

Material specific details for cartographic materials, music, or serials are recorded as instructed in the chapters for those materials. When reproductions of previously existing works are cataloged, this area contains data relating to the original regardless of the policy being followed. Examples:

> Bulletin of the American Economic Association [microform]. — 4th ser., no. 1 (Mar. 1911)-no. 6 (Dec. 1911)

> Viewpoint [microform]. — Vol. 1 (1976)-

Continuing Resources:

12.3.   NUMBERING AREA (*MARC 21* field 362)

12.3A1.   Applicability. This rule states that Area 3 is applicable to *serials*, but not generally to *integrating resources*. LC will not apply this area to integrating resources, even where there are numbered updates (*CSB* 97: 45).

12.3B.   Numeric and/or alphabetic designation (subfield a, *MARC 21* field 362)

The numeric and/or alphabetic designation of a serial is given as it appears in the first and/or last issue or part of the serial, using standard abbreviations and numerals. The numeric and/or alphabetic designation of the original is used when a facsimile or reprint is in hand. When a serial title changes but continues its previous numbering, the numbering of the first issue with the new title is used. LC comments that numbering used alone in this area should be unique to the issue. (*CSB* 97: 44)

Rules 12.3B1–12.3B2 provide for transcription of a numeric and/or alphabetic designation.

12.3C.   Chronological designation (subfield a, *MARC 21* field 362)

Rules 12.3C1–12.3C3 treat the transcription of a chronological designation when there is no numeric or alphabetic designation. Rule 12.3C4 covers transcription of both numeric and/or alphabetic designation *and* chronological designation. It would have been clearer if this rule had been accorded a boldface rule heading. There are relatively few instances in which there is a numeric and/or alphabetic designation without also having a chronological designation; however, it is relatively common for serials of the "advances in" and "progress in" type to be dated only with an imprint date. The following title page transcription illustrates such a situation:

ADVANCES IN CHEMICAL PHYSICS

Edited by I. PRIGOGINE
University of Brussels, Brussels, Belgium

With a Preface by P. DEBYE
Cornell University, Ithaca, New York

VOLUME 1
INTERSCIENCE PUBLISHERS, INC., NEW YORK
INTERSCIENCE PUBLISHERS LTD., LONDON   1958

Such a date is recorded as part of the publication area rather than part of the numeric, alphabetic, chronological area:

Advances in chemical physics. — Vol. 1 -   — New York : Interscience Publishers, 1958-

For other examples of numeric designations see the examples under rule 12.3C4 below.

12.3C1.   A chronological designation that identifies the first and/or last issue or part of a serial is recorded as it appears, using standard abbreviations and numerals. Examples:

>Index to Title 40 of the Code of federal regulations : protection of environment. — 1978-

>HRA, HSA, CDC, OASH, & ADAMHA public advisory committees : authority, structure, functions, members. — Mar. 1978-

12.3C4.   When the first and/or last issue or part of a serial has both numbering and a chronological designation, both are given, with the numbering given first, and the chronological designation given in parentheses. Examples:

>Developmental medicine and child neurology. — Vol. 4 (1962)-

>Gas turbine electric plant construction cost and annual production expenses. Annual supplement / Office of Energy Data and Interpretation, Energy Information Administration, U.S. Dept. of Energy. —2nd (1974)-

A difficulty with this rule is that it does not refer to the potential confusion caused by a situation in which the numbering sequence is repeated every year so that there is no overall numbering, but only the dates to distinguish issues (e.g., issues published in 1998 are numbered 1 through 4, issues for 1999 are also numbered 1 through 4, etc.). If the numbering is given first, as is called for in the rules, the implication is that the numbering is continuous and a completed serial could appear to have published only a few numbers over a span of many years [e.g., No. 1 (Winter 1960)-no. 4 (Fall 1999)]. Practice indicates that the date should be followed by the number as if both were a single numeric designation. Example:

>— 1960, no. 1-1999, no. 4

In such a case a chronological designation would be recorded only when a separate one also appears on the issue.

12.3D.   No designation on first issue or part

When the first issue or part of a serial lacks numbering, but there are subsequent issues or parts available which allow inference of a pattern, numbering for the first issue or part is given, based on the inferred pattern. If such subsequent information is not available, the cataloger is instructed to record either "[No. 1] -" or its equivalent in the language of the title proper, or a chronological designation for the first issue or part. LC uses the publication or copyright date as the source for a chronological designation in cases such as yearbooks or directories (*CSB* 97: 47).

12.3F. Ceased serials

When a serial has ceased publication, the designation of the last issue or part is given following that of the first. Examples:

>Brill's content. — Vol. 1, no. 1 (Aug. 1998)-v. 4, no. 6 (fall 2001)

>ALCTS newsletter. — Vol. 1, no. 1 (1990)-v. 9, no. 4-6 (1998)

AREA 4.   PUBLICATION, DISTRIBUTION, ETC., AREA (*MARC 21* field 260)

X.4B.   General rule

All details about place(s), name(s), and date(s) of the activities involved in the publishing, distributing, issuing, releasing, and manufacture of information packages are recorded in this area. When there is more than one place, name, and/or date, they are recorded in an order appropriate to the item in hand. Names of places, persons, or bodies are given as they appear, except that prepositions that are not integral parts of the name are usually omitted, and abbreviations from Appendix B of *AACR2R* are used.

X.4C.   Place of publication, distribution, etc. (subfield a, *MARC 21* field 260)

1.4C1.   The place of publication (or production, etc.) is recorded as it appears in a prescribed source of information.

1.4C3.   The name of the country, state, province, etc., is added to the name when necessary to distinguish between places or if necessary for identification. It is added in brackets if it does not appear in the source of information. Examples:

Name of country added when city alone appeared in prescribed source of information:

Vanished fleets : sea stories from old Van Dieman's land / by Alan Villiers. — Cambridge [England]

Name of state added when name of state appeared in prescribed source of information:

Hans in luck [motion picture]. — Santa Monica, Calif.

Name of state not considered necessary to identify the city:

Troll tales of Tumble Town [filmstrip] / Don Arthur Torgersen. — Chicago

1.4C5.   When more than one place is given for a publisher, distributor, etc., the first named place is transcribed. If another place is typographically prominent, it is also transcribed. In addition, if neither the first named place nor a typographically prominent place are in the home country of the cataloging agency, the first place given that *is* in the home country is also transcribed. Places are separated from each other by a space-semicolon-space. Example:

Educational theory : an introduction / T.W. Moore. — London ; Boston

Rule 1.4D4 treats two or more places that relate to two or more publishers, etc. (see below).

1.4C6.   A probable place is given in brackets with a question mark when the place of publication, etc., is uncertain. Example:

A century in Singapore : 1877-1977 / Hongkong and Shanghai Banking Corporation. — [Singapore?]

If the place is unknown but the country, state, province, etc., is known or probable, the country, state or province, etc., is given in brackets (with a question mark if uncertain). If no country, etc., or probable country can be given, the abbreviation "s.l." (*sine loco*), or its equivalent in nonroman scripts, is given. Example:

Precious cargo / by Ralph Byrne. — [S.l. : R. Byrne]

[Note: Uppercase "S" results from its beginning an area of the description.]

1.4C8. Neither place of publication, distribution, etc., nor "s.l." is recorded for unpublished items (e.g., art originals) or for unpublished collections. *See* examples under 1.4F9-1.4F10 below.

X.4D.   Name of publisher, distributor, etc. (subfield b, *MARC 21* field 260)

7.4D Motion Pictures and Videorecordings: The function of "releasing agency" is included in this rule.

1.4D1. The name of the publisher, distributor, etc., follows the name of the place to which it relates, separated from the place by a space-colon-space.

1.4D2. The name of the publisher, distributor, etc., is given in the shortest form it can take to be understood internationally. Example:

Living with loss : a dramatic new breakthrough in grief therapy / Ronald W. Ramsay, Rene Noorbergen. — New York : W. Morrow

[Note: Publisher statement on title page reads: William Morrow and Company, Inc.]

It is important to note the term *internationally*. Because there is now more emphasis on creating bibliographic records for an international audience, the publisher, distributor, etc., area sometimes needs fuller information than was adequate in the past.

LC generally does not omit parts of a hierarchy for any corporate bodies except in the case of some commercial publishers. Also, such words as *Inc.* that appear after a serial title being recorded as a publisher are retained. (*CSB* 84: 12)

6.4D2.   Sound recordings: This rule in *AACR2R*, Chapter 6, deals with the issue of trade names, brand names, of subdivision names used by recording companies. In cases where these are used, they are recorded as the name of the publisher. Example:

Label on disc reads:
  SUNSET, a product of Liberty Records
  A division of Liberty Records, Inc., Los Angeles,
    California

Description should read:
  — Los Angeles, Calif. : Sunset

6.4D3. By contrast, if a trade name seems to be the name of a series, it is recorded as a series rather than as the name of a publisher.

1.4D3. Two particular parts of names of publishers, distributors, etc., that are to be retained are:

a) Words that indicate function other than only a publishing function. Examples:

> At the edge of megalopolis : a history of Salem, N.H., 1900-1974 / [Noyes, Turner]. — Canaan, N.H. : Published for the Town of Salem, N. H., by Phoenix Pub.

> The National labor relations act : a guidebook for health care facility administrators / Dennis D. Pointer and Norman Metzger. — New York : Spectrum Publications : distributed by Halsted Press

b) Parts of a name that distinguish between publishers, etc. For example:

> Encyclopaedia Britannica Educational Corp.
> Encyclopaedia Britannica, Inc.

> **[These are separate bodies and cannot be identified simply as Encyclopaedia Britannica.]**

5.4D3 Music: This rule has an instruction to record plate numbers and publishers' numbers in the note area.

1.4D4. There are four situations in which the transcription of a subsequently named publisher, distributor, etc. (and its place, if different from the first), is to be added after the first named body:

a) when the two bodies are linked in a single statement, e.g.,

> — London: Published for the Institute of Mediaeval Studies by Sheed & Ward.

b) when a distributor, etc., is named first, while a publisher is named later,

c) when a publisher, distributor, etc., is clearly the principal one (as shown by layout or typography) but is not named first,

d) when the first body is not in the country of the cataloging agency, while a later one is. Example:

> **Cataloging done by a U.S. cataloging agency:**

> Genetics of forest ecosystems / Klaus Stern, Laurence Roche. — London : Chapman and Hall ; New York : Springer-Verlag

An LC rule interpretation provides detailed guidance for recording multiple publishers, distributors, etc., under different circumstances. (*CSB* 100: 18–21)

(*Note*: The 2002 revisions to *AACR2R* eliminated the rule formerly numbered 1.4D4. This rule stated that when a person or corporate body appeared both in the statement of responsibility in a recognizable form, and also in the publication area, the name was given in a shortened form in the publication area. This practice is no longer allowed, due to the increasing use by automated systems of the publication area for keyword searching.)

1.4D5. An option allows addition of the name (and place if different) of a distributor when the first name is for a publisher. LC is applying this option. (*CSB* 97: 17)
Example:

> The plow that broke the Plains [videorecording] / United
> States Resettlement Administration. — Washington, D.C. :
> National Archives and Records Service : distributed by
> National Audiovisual Center

1.4D6. When the name of the publisher, etc., is not known, the abbreviation s.n.
(*sine nomine*) is given in brackets. Example:

> The story of Lanark / prepared and written by Elizabeth
> L. Jamieson. — [S.l. : s.n.]

1.4D8. Neither name of publisher, distributor, etc., nor "s.n." is recorded for unpublished items or for unpublished collections. *See* examples under 1.4F9–1.4F10
below.

X.4F.   Date of publication, distribution, etc. (subfield c, *MARC 21* field 260)

1.4F1. The date of publication of the edition in hand is the next element of this area
and follows a comma-space. An LC rule interpretation provides guidance on recording copyright dates or dates of manufacture, when a date of publication is lacking.
(*CSB* 102: 17–18)

1.4F2. The date given in the item is used even if it is known to be incorrect, in
which case the correct date is added in brackets and an explanation is given in a note
if necessary.

7.4F2. Films and videorecordings: This rule has a provision for giving in a note a
date of original production that differs from the date in Area 4. LC is applying this
option when the difference is greater than two years. (*CSB* 33: 33) Example:

> — Washington, [D.C.] : Division of Audiovisual Arts :
> distributed by National Audiovisual Center, 1989.

Note on this record:

> Made in 1985.

10.4F2. Three-dimensional artifacts and realia: This rule calls for giving only the
date for artifacts not intended primarily for communication (e.g., clothing, money,
furniture). Example:

> [White treadle sewing machine] [realia]. — 1890.

1.4F5. An option allows adding the latest copyright date to the publication, distri-
bution, etc., date if it is different. LC has applied this option since the inception of
AACR2, but does not presently do so for books and printed serials. (*CSB* 47: 15)
Example:

> Attracting birds to your backyard [videorecording] /
> with Roger Tory Peterson. — Carrboro, N.C. : Nature
> Science Network, 1990, c1986.

Note that a copyright date is always preceded by a "c," and a phonogram copyright date (the date of "pressings" of sound recordings) is preceded by a "p."

1.4F6. If the date of publication or distribution is not given in the item, the copyright date is used. Example:

> Multimedia Beethoven [electronic resource] : the ninth symphony, an illustrated interactive musical exploration / [by Robert Winter with the Voyager Company]. — [Santa Monica, Calif.] : Microsoft Corporation, c1992.

If there is no copyright date, a manufacturing date, if present, is given. In the latter case, a word such as *printing* or *pressing* is added, e.g., 1996 pressing.

LC has issued a rule interpretation for when to use copyright date, probable date of publication, and/or date of manufacture. (*CSB* 92: 11)

1.4F7. If no date of publication, etc., copyright, or manufacture can be found, the cataloger is instructed to give an approximate date. Example:

> Carrier Air Wing [videorecording]. — Seattle : Pool & Crew Communications, [1987?]

1.4F8. This rule covers dates for serials, integrating resources, and multipart information packages published over more than one year. The beginning date is given, followed by a hyphen, when the first issue, iteration, or part is available. If the resource is complete or has ceased publication, and the last issue, iteration, or part is available, the ending date is given, preceded by a hyphen. Both dates are given, separated by a hyphen, when both first and last are available. In cases where the publication date is the same for all issues, etc., only that single date is given. For incomplete multipart items, LC places the date of a second or later volume that is not the last volume within angle brackets. (*CSB* 103: 36–39) Example:

> Christ in Christian tradition / Aloys Grillmeier ; translated by John Bowden. — 2nd rev. ed. — London : Mowbrays, 1975- <1987>

In cases where the first and/or last issue, iteration, or part is not available, beginning and/or ending dates are not given in Area 4. Instead, this information is given in a note when known. Example:

> Ceased with v. 23, no. 7 (July 1998).

> **[First published issue is not available.]**

An option allows providing this information in Area 4 if it can be readily ascertained. LC does not apply this option for serials, but does apply it in individual cases for integrating resources and multipart items, when the resource itself contains an explicit statement. (*CSB* 103: 42)

1.4F9–1.4F10. No date is given for naturally occurring objects unless they have been packaged for commercial distribution. For the latter and other unpublished items the date of production is given. A date or inclusive dates are given for unpublished collections. Examples:

> [Polar bears] [art original] / Dorothy S. Taylor. —
> 1985.

> [Photographs of blue ribbon pigs, Iowa State Fair]
> [picture]. — 1927-1947.

1.4G.   Place of manufacture, name of manufacturer, date of manufacture
(subfields e, f, and g, *MARC 21* field 260)
(*Note:* This rule is titled "Place of printing, name of printer, date of printing" in AACR2R Chapters 2, 3, and 5. It is not present in Chapter 11.)

1.4G1. If the name of the publisher, distributor, etc., is not known and the place and name of the manufacturer are given, the latter are transcribed into the record after the date. (The date given in the publication date position is often the date of manufacture in this situation; if so, it is not repeated here.) Example:

> The offensive side of Lou Holtz / by Lou Holtz. — [S.l. :
> s.n.], c1978 (Little Rock, Ark. : Parkin Print. Co.)

10.4G2.   Three-dimensional artifacts and realia: If the person or body that has manufactured an object is named in the statement of responsibility (as is the case with handmade items such as hand-woven tapestries or handmade pottery), that information is not repeated in this area.

General notes on Area 4 in AACR2R Chapters 4, 9, 11, and 12:

4.4.   Manuscripts: This area in the manuscripts chapter is called the "Date Area." It omits details of place and name of publisher (this being unpublished material) and includes only date, and then only if it is not already in the title. The date of a single manuscript is given as a year, optionally followed by the month and day.

For a manuscript collection, inclusive years are given following rule 1.4F8. Example:

> [Papers] / William Alexander Smith. — 1765-1849.

9.4.   Electronic resources: All remote-access electronic resources are considered to be published. The date of creation of unpublished electronic resources is to be given in this area, and other useful dates, such as dates of data collection, should be given in a note. In cases where a resource has multiple copyright dates which apply to different aspects of production, such as graphics or programming, and there is no publication, distribution, etc., date which applies to the whole item, then only the latest copyright date should be transcribed. An option allows other dates to be given in notes; LC is applying the option on a case-by-case basis (*CSB* 94: 13).

11.4.   Microforms: The details of this area are recorded as instructed in the general chapter of *AACR2R*. Again, if one is following *AACR2R* policy, it should be remembered that the details recorded here are those of the publication of the *microform*, not those of an original being reproduced. Examples:

> Women and/in health [microform] / filmed by the Women's
> History Research Center. — Berkeley, Calif. : Women's History
> Research Center, c1974.

>   The impact of feminist thought on American librarianship,
>   1965-1985 [microform] / Christina Diane Baum. — Ann
>   Arbor, Mich. : University Microfilms International, 1987.

If one is following LC policy, the details of the original are given here for a micro-form of a previously existing work. Example:

>   The impact of feminist thought on American librarianship,
>   1965-1985 [microform] / by Christina D. Baum. — 1987.

12.4F. Continuing resources: The rules call for different treatment for serials and integrating resources with regard to changes in place of publication, distribution, etc. (12.4C2), name of publisher, distributor, etc. (12.4D2), and place and/or name of manufacturer (12.4G2). For *serials*, subsequent place and/or name information is given in notes when considered important, and when the changes do not require a new description. For *integrating resources*, the affected elements of Area 4 are changed to reflect the new iteration, and the earlier place and/or name information is given in a note if considered important. Examples:

> ***Serial***:
> *Note*:   Published: Hackensack, N.J. : MCB UP, 1999-

> ***Integrating resource***:
>   [Original iteration]
>   Washington, D.C. : OMEC International, c1988-

>   [Subsequent iteration]
>   Rockville, MD : Biotechnology Information Institute, 1990-

>   *Note*:   Published: Washington, D.C. : OMEC International,
>   1988-1990.

AREA 5.   PHYSICAL DESCRIPTION AREA (*MARC 21* field 300)

1.5A3. This preliminary rule calls for giving the physical description for the format of the information package in hand if the work is available in different formats. Optionally, notes are made to describe the other physical formats in which a work is available.
    The part of this rule that calls for describing text on microfilm as microfilm has caused much controversy in the library community. It is believed by many librarians that the importance of text on microfilm is as a version of the text. The fact that the version is in microform rather than regular print is, to these persons, less important than the description of the original in terms of number of pages of text. On the other side, there are those who say that the purpose of bibliographic description is to describe the item in hand. If it is two sheets of microfiche, it is not the same as a 350-page bound volume.
    This debate has been resolved in practice by LC's decision to catalog microreproductions of certain printed items by transcribing the physical details of the original work in the body of the description while giving the details of the microreproduction in a note. (*CSB* 77: 22–23) This practice has not been adopted as a rule revision because the other countries involved in responsibility for *AACR2R* have not had as much problem concerning the issue.
    The option of making a note describing other formats is being applied by LC. (*CSB* 84: 12) Example:

Macumba, trance, and spirit healing [videorecording] /
producer, Madeleine Richeport. — New York, NY :
Filmakers Library, 1984.
1 videocassette (43 min.) : sd., col.

Issued as U-matic ¾ in. or Beta ½ in. or VHS ½ in.
Issued also as motion picture.

X.5B.   Extent of item (including specific material designation)
(subfield a, *MARC 21* field 300)

1.5B1.   The extent of item consists of the number of physical units in Arabic numerals followed by the specific material designation. It answers the question: How many of what? The word *identical* is added before the specific material designation when appropriate (e.g., 10 identical study prints). How to record the extent of item for different types of materials is covered in detail in each *AACR2R* chapter on a type of material. Additions or qualifications to the extent are placed within parentheses.

1.5B5.   A multipart information package that is not yet complete is described with the specific material designation alone. An option allows adding the number of physical units after completion. Example:

Spy. — Oct. 1986-   . — New
York, N.Y. : Spy Pub. Partners, c1986-
v. : ill. ; 28 cm.

LC is applying the option; so if the work in the example becomes complete in, say, 30 volumes, the physical description area will read (according to *CSB* 8:9):

30 v. : ill. ; 28 cm.

2.5B. Books: This rule is called "Number of volumes and/or pagination."

Single volumes

2.5B1.   The following terms are used in recording the number of pages or leaves in a publication.

TERM USED	SITUATION
pages (abbreviated "p.")	[volume with leaves printed on both sides]
leaves	[volume with leaves printed on only one side]
columns	[volume with more than one column to a page and numbered in columns]
leaves, pages, and/or columns (in sequence)	[volume that contains sequences of leaves, pages, and/or columns]
broadside	[broadside]
sheet	[folded and other single sheets]
case	[case]
portfolio	[portfolio]

2.5B2.   Numbers of pages, leaves, or columns are recorded in accord with the numbered or lettered sequences represented. The number on the last page, leaf, or column of each sequence is recorded, followed in each case by the appropriate term or abbreviation. Examples:

92 p.	[46 leaves printed and numbered on both sides]
62 leaves	[62 leaves printed and numbered only on one side]
ix, 289 p.	[last numbered page in Roman numerals sequence and in Arabic numerals sequence]
iv leaves, 224 p.	[last numbered leaf and last numbered page]

2.5B3.   Unnumbered sequences are disregarded unless the whole item or a substantial part of a publication is unnumbered (*see* rule 2.5B7 and rule 2.5B8). An exception is made when pages in an unnumbered sequence must be referred to in a note, in which case either the estimated number is given preceded by "ca." or the exact number is given enclosed in square brackets. Example:

79, [1], 64 p.	[unnumbered page referred to in the note]
Bibliography: p. [80]	[note requiring use of the unnumbered page]

2.5B5.   When a single sequence is numbered in more than one way (e.g., when numbering changes from Roman to Arabic numerals), the first numbering scheme is ignored, and only the last number of the sequence is recorded. Example:

252 leaves	[item numbered i-vii followed by leaves 8-252, for a total of 252 leaves—not 7 leaves followed by 252 leaves as would be indicated by: vii, 252 leaves]

2.5B7.   When an entire volume is unnumbered, if it is not too large, the pages are counted and given in square brackets. The number of pages of larger items are estimated and recorded following "ca." Examples:

[12] p.	[unnumbered pages counted]
ca. 200 p.	[unnumbered pages approximated]

LC does not follow the rule except in the case of rare books. Instead, the extent statement is recorded as "1 v. (unpaged)." (*CSB* 52: 15)

The reader should consult *AACR2R*, rule 2.5B8, if dealing with complicated or irregular paging.

2.5B9.   *Leaves or pages of plates*

The number of leaves or pages of plates is recorded at the end of the numbers given for paging sequences regardless of whether the plates are placed together or are scattered through the publication. If there is only one plate, it is described as "1 leaf of plates." If plates are unnumbered, rule 2.5B7 is followed. If there are both leaves and plates, the term that is predominant is used. Examples:

vi, 224, [9] p., 26 leaves of plates	[numbered leaves of plates]
176 p., [16] p. of plates	[unnumbered pages of plates]
74 leaves, [33] leaves of plates	[unnumbered leaves of plates]

Publications in more than one volume

2.5B16.-2.5B17.   A printed monograph in more than one physical part is described with the number of whichever of the following terms is appropriate:

volumes—each bibliographic unit in its own binding

parts—bibliographic units bound several to a volume

pamphlets—collections of pamphlets bound together or assembled in a portfolio

pieces—items of varying character published, or assembled for cataloging, as a collection

case(s)—box(es) containing bound or unbound material

portfolio(s)—container(s), usually consisting of two covers joined at the back and tied at the front, top, and/or bottom, holding loose papers, illustrative materials, etc.

Examples:

5 v.	[each of five bibliographic units bound separately]
25 pts.	[each part issued separately but specified by the publisher that they should be bound several to a volume when complete]
2 cases	[unbound material held together as a bibliographic unit in two boxes]

2.5B18.   When the number of bibliographic volumes is different from the number of physical volumes, the number of bibliographic volumes is given first followed by "in" and the number of physical volumes. Example:

3 v. in 1

2.5B19.   When the volumes of a multi-volume set are paged so that the first page numbers of a succeeding volume follow the last page number of the preceding volume (ignoring any preliminary pages in the succeeding volume that may be separately paged), the total number of pages or leaves is given in parentheses after the number of volumes. Example:

2 v. (ix, 1438 p., 32 leaves of plates)

2.5B22.   Braille or other tactile systems

If an item is in braille or another tactile system, an appropriate term, such as one of the following phrases, is added to the number of pages, leaves, or volumes:

of braille

of Moon type

of jumbo braille

of computer braille

of press braille

of print and braille [eye-readable
print and braille]

of print and press braille

Examples:

3 v. of jumbo braille

484 leaves of braille

2.5B23.   Large print

Items in large print meant for use by the visually impaired should be described by adding "(large print)" to the statement of extent. Example:

58 leaves (large print)

3.5B.   *Cartographic materials:* The following specific material designations are provided:

atlas

diagram

globe

map

model

profile

remote-sensing image

section

view

Examples:

1 globe (tactile)

1 atlas (20 leaves)

4.5B.   *Manuscripts:* The manuscripts chapter directs the cataloger to record the extent of single manuscripts as one would for books. The term *bound* is added if the manuscript has been bound. Example:

128 leaves, bound

A collection that occupies one linear foot or less of shelf space is described in terms of the number of items or the number of containers or volumes. LC is applying the option to add the number of items if the collection is described in number of volumes or containers. (*CSB* 47: 35) Examples:

1 v. (208 items)

2 boxes (110 items), 2 v. (68 items)

ca. 600 items

A collection that occupies more than one linear foot of shelf space is described in terms of the number of linear feet occupied. LC is applying the option to add the number of items or containers or volumes. (*CSB* 47: 35)

5.5B1. Music: The following specific material designations are provided:

score	vocal score
condensed score	piano score
close score	chorus score
miniature score	part
piano [violin, etc.] conductor part	

Normally, specific material designations are given to different classes of materials that represent different kinds of physical objects. In the case of published music, specific material designations vary under different circumstances, one of them being whether the music is written for a solo instrument or for several instruments. The physical extent of a piece of music written for a solo instrument is described, as for any monograph, in terms of leaves, pages, or volumes. If the option of using the GMD [music], is not applied, then the term *music* is incorporated in the extent of item statement. Example:

36 p. of music.

A specific material designation using the terms *score(s)* and/or *part(s)* is to be given to a piece of music written for several instrumental or vocal parts. The type of score it is—miniature, piano, vocal, etc.—as well as its pagination and the number of copies of it issued by the publisher are to be recorded. (Definitions of different types of scores are given in the Glossary of *AACR2R*.) If the score is accompanied by parts, the number of these issued by the publisher is to be recorded.

6.5B1. Sound recordings: The following specific material designations are provided:

sound cartridge	sound tape reel
sound cassette	sound track film
sound disc	

LC adds the term "sound disc cartridge" to this list, for digitally encoded discs, such as MiniDiscs, permanently encased in a cartridge (*CSB* 109: 18). An option allows the use of terms in common usage, such as DVD-audio. A second option allows the omission of the word "sound" if general material designations are also used, as long as the resulting specific material designation is understandable. LC is not applying these options. (*CSB* 109: 18)

6.5B2.   As specified in general rule 1.5B4, playing times are given as stated, if stated explicitly on the item. If the playing time is not explicitly stated, it should be given if easily determined. As an option, an approximate time may be given if neither of these conditions apply. LC is not applying this option. (*CSB* 108: 38) In addition, the playing times of a multipart item may be given followed by the word "each" if the parts have a stated or approximate uniform playing time. Examples:

1 sound disc (73 min.)

3 sound cassettes (ca. 40 min. each)

An LC rule interpretation provides guidance for giving playing times under circumstances where there are either multiple parts, or not all durations are stated on the item. (*CSB* 108: 37–39)

7.5B1.   Films and videorecordings: The following specific material designations are provided:

film cartridge	videocartridge
film cassette	videocassette
film loop	videodisc
film reel	videoreel

An option allows the use of terms in common usage, such as DVD-video. A second option allows the omission of the words "film" or "video" if general material designations are used that clearly designate the information package as a film or videorecording.

7.5B2.   Playing times are given, as in the rule for sound recordings. Examples:

1 videocassette (88 min.)

3 film cassettes (20 min. each)

For videodiscs, the rule specifies information to be provided for discs consisting of moving images, still frames or a combination.

8.5B1.   Graphics: The following specific material designations are provided (as distributed by LC among the GMDs [in bold below] appropriate to this chapter. *CSB* 64: 12–13):

activity card	**flash card**	**slide**
activity card	flash card	slide
chart	**picture**	stereograph
chart	art print	**technical drawing**
flip chart	art reproduction	technical drawing
wall chart	photograph	**transparency**
filmstrip	picture	transparency
filmstrip	postcard	
filmslip	poster	
	radiograph	
	study print	

9.5B.   Electronic resources:

9.5B1   The following specific material designations are provided:

computer chip cartridge	computer tape cartridge
computer disk	computer tape cassette
computer optical disc	computer tape reel

The spelling "disc" is used for optical media, reflecting the standardized spelling used by the computer industry. The spelling "disk" is to be used for magnetic media only.

An option allows the use of conventional terminology, such as CD-ROM, in this area. LC is applying the option. (*CSB* 105: 38) A second option allows the use of a specific material designation to designate the content of the item, in combination with a designation for physical carrier. Use of a term taken from another subrule numbered .5B is preferred whenever possible. Example:

500 technical drawings on 1 DVD-ROM

LC is applying this second option on a case-by-case basis. (*CSB* 105: 38)

9.5B3.   Optionally, a physical description may be given for remote-access electronic resources (e.g., World Wide Web sites). Use of a term taken from another subrule numbered .5B, or a term in common use, is preferred. Examples:

15 sound files

Web site

LC is applying this option on a case-by-case basis. (*CSB* 105: 38)

10.5B.   Three-dimensional artifacts and realia:

10.5B1.   The following specific material designations are provided:

art original	game
art reproduction	microscope slide
braille cassette	mock-up
diorama	model
exhibit	toy

10.5B2.   The number and name(s) of component pieces are added to the specific material designation. The term *(various pieces)* may be added where they cannot be concisely named, or where their number is not ascertainable. In the latter case, an option allows detailing the pieces in a note. Examples:

1 game (1 board, 7 markers, 60 cards, 3 dice)

1 diorama (various pieces)

General notes on Area 5B in AACR2R Chapters 3–10:

The rules for all materials covered in these chapters, except for manuscripts, allow the cataloger to use terms other than those listed if needed. Examples:

music	**realia**
choir book	jigsaw puzzle
table book	hand puppet
sound recording	quilt
piano roll	tapestry
organ roll	statue
electronic resource	sculpture
computer optical card	bowl (cup, jar, handle holder, etc.)
	dress (coat, belt, suit, etc.)

As shown in the previous examples various pieces of information may be added in parentheses after the statement of extent of most nonbook materials if easily ascertainable from the item in hand. Numbers of pages are added after statements of extent of atlases and music. Examples:

> 1 atlas (20 leaves)
>
> 1 score (35 p.) + 4 parts

Information about systems intended for the visually impaired may be given for cartographic items, music, and graphic materials. Examples:

> 1 globe (tactile)
>
> 1 score (20 leaves, braille)
>
> 228 p. of music (large print)

Numbers of items may be given for collections of manuscripts, some kinds of graphics, and realia. Examples:

> 2 ft. (ca. 300 items)
>
> 1 transparency (3 overlays)
>
> 3 flip charts (10 sheets each)
>
> 1 game (1 board, 1 timer, 500 word cards, 1 die, 4 markers, 4 category cards, 4 pads of paper, 4 pencils)
>
> 2 dioramas (various pieces)
>
> 1 jigsaw puzzle (ca. 500 pieces)

Running/playing time may be given for sound recordings, films, and videorecordings. Examples:

> 2 sound cassettes (ca. 150 min.)
>
> 1 videocassette (15 min.)

The number of frames may be given for filmstrips, filmslips, stereographs, or videodiscs consisting of still images. Example:

4 filmstrips (ca. 40 fr. each)

In a few cases the number of intellectual units may differ from the number of physical pieces, and this may be specified. Examples:

8 maps on 2 sheets

1 aerial chart in 6 segments

Specific rules in *AACR2R* for any of the above situations should be consulted when cataloging nonbook materials.

11.5B. Microforms: The following specific material designations are provided:

aperture card

microfiche

microfilm

microopaque

LC has chosen not to follow the *AACR2R* option to drop the prefix micro when the GMD "microform" is used. The reason for LC's decision is that the resulting bibliographic description will be complete regardless of whether another library chooses to use the GMD.[27]

If the item is described in terms of "microfilm," one of the following terms is added: *cartridge, cassette,* or *reel.* Example:

13 microfilm reels

If the item is described in terms of "microfiche," the term *cassette* may be added if appropriate, and the number of frames is added in parentheses if the number can be determined easily. Example:

3 microfiches (276 fr.)

12.5B. Continuing resources:

12.5B1.   A printed resource still in progress is given the specific material designation *v.* The qualifier (*looseleaf*) is added for updating looseleafs. For nonprint resources, the specific material designation relevant to that type of material is used.

12.5B2.   When the resource is completed, the specific material designation is preceded by the number of parts in arabic numerals. An LC rule interpretation says that "parts" is to be interpreted as bibliographic units rather than physical units. (*CSB* 97: 49) Example:

The Christian's magazine [microform]. — Vol. 1
(1806)-v. 4 (1811). — Ann Arbor, Mich. : University
Microfilms, 1946-1949.
4 v. on 2 microfilm reels ; 35 mm.

X.5C.   Other physical details (subfield b, *MARC 21* field 300)
Physical details other than extent of item or dimensions are given following the extent and separated from it by a space-colon-space. These vary by type of material.

2.5C.   Books: This rule is called "Illustrative matter."

2.5C1.   If a monograph has illustrations, the abbreviation "ill." is given in the physical description. Tables are not treated as illustrations. Illustrated title pages and minor illustrations (e.g., decorations) are ignored.

2.5C2.   *Optionally,* if all of the illustrations are of one or more of the types mentioned below, the appropriate term(s) or abbreviation(s) may be given, in alphabetical order.

TERM	ABBREVIATION (IF ALLOWED)
coats of arms	
facsimiles	facsim., facsims.
forms	
genealogical tables	geneal. table(s)
maps	
music	
plans	
portraits (use for both single and group portraits)	port, ports.
samples	

If there are illustrations in addition to these types (including graphs and diagrams), they are described as "ill.," and "ill." precedes the other types in the list. Examples:

47 p. : ill., ports.	[contains illustrations, some of which are portraits]
280 p. : facsims.	[the only illustrations are facsimiles]
176 p., [24] p. of plates : ill., coats of arms, maps, plans	[illustrations include three of the specific types in rule 2.5C2, in addition to other illustrations]

LC uses only "ill." to describe an illustrated printed monograph unless there are maps present, or the publication consists wholly or predominantly of one type of illustration. (*CSB* 87: 10)

2.5C3.   If illustrations are in two or more colors, they are described as "col." or "some col." Examples:

48 p. : ill. (some col.)	[some illustrations in color]
216 p. : ill., maps (some col.), col. ports.	[some maps in color, all portraits in color]
xiv, 182 p. : col. ill.	[all illustrations in color]

2.5C4–2.5C6. Treatment of special cases (e.g., number of illustrations known, special locations of illustrations, works consisting of all or nearly all illustrations) is delineated in these rules in *AACR2R*, which should be consulted when such special cases arise.

General note on Area 5C in AACR2R Chapters 3–12:

Different kinds of "other physical details" are given for each of the materials covered in these chapters. The following outlines indicate the kinds of details specified for each type of material. These details are called for only where appropriate. Where there are several kinds of details for one type of material, they are to be given in the order specified in the list.

3.5C. Cartographic materials:

layout

production method

number of maps, etc., in an atlas

color

medium

material

mounting

Examples:

1 atlas (5 v.) : 250 col. maps

1 relief model : col., plastic

1 globe : col., plastic, mounted on wooden stand

2 maps on 1 sheet : col., mounted on linen

24 maps : photocopy, col.

4.5C. Manuscripts:

material other than paper for a single manuscript

illustrations (as noted in rule 2.5C or rule 8.5C)

Example:

42 leaves : parchment, col. ill.

5.5C. Music:

illustrations (as noted in rule 2.5C)

Example:

1 score (x, 77 p., [1] leaf of plates) : facsim.

6.5C. Sound recordings:

> type of recording
> playing speed
> groove characteristic (analog discs)
> track configuration (sound track films)
> number of tracks (tapes)
> number of sound channels
> recording and reproduction characteristics [*optional addition*]
> Examples:
>> 1 sound disc (42 min.) : digital, stereo.
>> 2 sound cassettes (ca. 150 min.) : 1½ ips, mono.
>> 1 sound disc : analog, 78 rpm, microgroove, mono.

7.5C.   Films and videorecordings:

> aspect ratio and special projection characteristics (motion pictures)
> sound characteristics
> color
> projection speed (motion pictures)
> Examples:
>> 1 videocassette (15 min.) : sd., col.
>> 1 videodisc (ca. 35 min.) : sd., b&w
>> 2 film reels (25 min.) : multiprojector, multiscreen, si., col.

8.5C.   Graphics: The other physical details required in the description depend upon the kind of graphic material being cataloged. Some require only an indication of color (e.g., col., b&w, sepia). These are:

pictures	study prints
postcards	transparencies
posters	wall charts
stereographs	

Others require some description of a characteristic in addition to color. These are:

> art prints—process in general terms (e.g., engraving, lithograph) or specific terms (e.g., copper engraving) and color
> art reproductions—method of reproduction (e.g., photogravure, collotype)
> charts and flip charts—indication of double-sided sheets (if applicable)
> filmstrips, filmslips, flash cards, and slides—indication of sound if it is integral (if sound is not integral, it is described as accompanying material)
> photographs—indication if photograph is a transparency not designed for projection or if it is a negative print. Optionally, the process used may be given. LC applies this option on a case-by-case basis. (*CSB* 47: 38)

Two kinds of items require description of a characteristic, but no indication of color. These are:

>art originals—medium (chalk, oil, pastel, etc.) and base (board, canvas, fabric, etc.) are given

>technical drawings—method of reproduction if any (blueprint, photocopy, etc.) is given

One kind of graphic item—radiograph—requires no description for other physical details.

>Examples of other physical details for graphics:

>>8 study prints : col.

>>5 filmstrips : sd., col.

>>1 art original : oil on board

9.5C.   Electronic resources:

>encoded sound
>encoded to display in two or more colors

Optional additions, if readily available and considered to be important:

>number of sides used
>recording density
>sectoring
>technical details of remote-access resources
>Examples:
>>2 computer disks : sd., col., double sided, high density
>>1 computer optical disc : sd., col.
>>15 photographs : digital, jpeg files

10.5C.   Three-dimensional artifacts and realia:

>material
>color
>Examples:
>>1 jar : clay, brown and red
>>1 jigsaw puzzle (500 pieces) : wood, col.
>>1 pair of socks : white

11.5C.   Microforms:

A negative microform is indicated here, followed by a statement of illustration using instructions in rule 2.5C. If illustrations are in color, the term *col. ill.* is used. If the microform itself is colored, terms used are *col. & ill.* Example:

>15 microfiches : negative, ill.

12.5C. Continuing resources:

Since continuing resources may be issued in many forms, other physical details are recorded according to the rule numbered ".5C" in the appropriate chapter for the type of material being treated.

The term most often used for printed **serials** is *ill.* The first issue (or issue used for cataloging) may not be totally representative of details found in later issues, but it is unlikely that one will keep returning to the record to add more details. It is better to be more general with this area of serial description. Rule 12.5C2 does, however, provide for significant changes in other physical details, for both serials and integrating resources.

X.5D. **Dimensions** (subfield c, *MARC 21* field 300)

The dimensions of an information package serve as an aid in finding it on the library shelves. Dimensions are especially valuable for libraries with separate storage areas for oversized pieces. They also serve the user who wishes to borrow an item through interlibrary loan. Dimensions are separated from either the extent or physical details by a space-semicolon-space.

2.5D. Books:

2.5D1. Size of printed monographs is given in terms of the height of volumes in centimeters. The height of the binding (or the height of the item, if unbound) is measured and recorded as the *next* whole centimeter *up* (*not* the *nearest* centimeter). Size of a volume that measures less than 10 centimeters is given in millimeters. Example:

> Critical guide to Catholic reference books / James Patrick McCabe ; with an introduction by Russell E. Bidlack. — 3rd ed. — Englewood, Colo. : Libraries Unlimited, 1989.
> xiv, 323 p. ; 25 cm.

[Note: Book actually measures 24.2 centimeters but is recorded as 25.]

2.5D2. Width of a volume is recorded only when it is less than half the height or greater than the height. Examples:

> ca. 150 p. : ill. ; 34 x 16 cm.   [width less than half the height]

> ii, 97 p. : ill., ports. ; 18 x 21 cm.   [width greater than the height]

2.5D3-2.5D5. These rules in *AACR2R* cover unusual cases and should be consulted when one is cataloging sets with items of varying sizes, or single sheets.

General notes on Area 5D in AACR2R Chapters 3–12:

For book-like materials, dimensions are given as instructed in rule 2.5D. This applies to atlases, single manuscripts, and music.

For large, flat items the height x width is given in centimeters; and if the item is stored folded, the dimensions of the folded item follow the dimensions of the extended item, preceded by a comma. This applies to maps, plans, large manuscripts, technical drawings, and wall charts. Example:

> 1 map : col. ; 67 x 97 cm., folded to 15 x 22 cm.

Round items, including globes, are described in terms of the diameter, specified as such. Sound discs and videodiscs are measured in inches, while other items are measured in centimeters. Exception: No measurements are given for stereographs, including stereograph reels, or for computer tape reels. Examples:

1 globe : col., cardboard, mounted on metal stand ; 32 cm.

1 computer optical disc ; 4¾ in.

The gauge (width) is given for motion pictures, videotapes, filmstrips, and filmslips. All are given in millimeters except for videotapes, which are given in inches. Examples:

1 film cartridge (4 min.) : si., col. ; super 8 mm.

1 film reel (12 min.) : sd., col. with b&w sequences ; 16 mm.

1 videocassette (15 min.) : sd., col. ; ¾ in.

5 filmstrips : col. ; 35 mm.

For a computer cartridge the length of the side that is to be inserted into the machine is given in inches to the next ¼ inch up. Example:

1 computer tape cartridge : sd., col. ; 3¼ in.

Most other items are measured in terms of height x width or height x depth or height x width x depth, and most are recorded in centimeters to the next whole centimeter up. This is true for relief models; manuscript collections when the containers are uniform; sound cartridges and cassettes when the dimensions are other than the standard ones (measured in fractions of inches); all graphic materials (except filmstrips, filmslips, stereographs, and slides whose dimensions are 5 x 5 cm.); computer cassettes (measured in inches to the next ¼ inch up), computer cards, and other appropriate physical carriers of electronic resources; three-dimensional artifacts and realia. Examples:

1 relief model : col., wood ; 50 x 35 x 4 cm.

2 ft. (2 boxes, ca. 300 items) ; 44 x 30 x 15 cm.

1 sound cassette (60 min.) : analog, stereo. ; 7¼ x 3½ in.

1 art original : oil on canvas ; 31 x 41 cm.

For three-dimensional artifacts and realia it may be necessary to give only one dimension. In such a case the dimension being given is specified. Examples:

1 jar : clay, brown and red ; 32 cm. high

1 paperweight : glass, col. ; 8 cm. in diam.

Three-dimensional artifacts and realia in containers should have the name of the container and its dimensions given after the dimensions of the object and preceded by a comma, or as the only dimensions. Dimensions of a container are an optional addition for cartographic materials. LC is applying the option on a case-by-case basis. (*CSB* 84: 13) Examples:

      1 relief model : col., wood ; 50 x 35 x 4 cm., in box
26 x 19 x 9 cm.

      1 jigsaw puzzle (ca. 60 pieces) : cardboard, col. ; 18 cm. in diam., in box 11 cm. in diam. x 4 cm.

No dimensions are given for sound recordings on rolls, or for sound cartridges, sound cassettes, or slides that are of standard dimensions.

The dimensions of a microfiche, a microopaque, and an aperture card mount are given as height x width in centimeters to the next whole centimeter up. Example:

12 microfiches ; 11 x 15 cm.

The width of a microfilm is given in millimeters. Example:

8 microfilm reels ; 35 mm.

Dimensions for continuing resources are recorded according to the rule numbered ".5D" in the appropriate chapter for the type of material being treated.

X.5E.   Accompanying material (subfield e, *MARC 21* field 300)

Accompanying material includes answer books, teacher's manuals, atlases, portfolios of plates, slides, sound recordings, booklets explaining audiovisual materials, and other such items. These materials often are placed in pockets inside the cover of the work being cataloged, or they may be loose inside the container. Their description may make up the fourth element of the physical description area and is separated from the dimensions by a space-plus sign-space.

1.5E1.   Four methods are suggested for handling accompanying material:

a)   It may be described in a separate entry.

b)   It may be described in a multilevel description as outlined in Chapter 13 of *AACR2R*.

c)   Details may be given in a note.

d)   Details may be given as the last element of the physical description area.

If the last method is used, an option allows addition in parentheses of further physical description of the accompanying material. LC is applying this option on a case-by-case basis, usually to items that are substantial in extent or are significant for some reason. (*CSB* 50: 23–24) Example:

> Evolution of the Arctic-North Atlantic and the Western Tethys / Peter A. Ziegler. — Tulsa, Okla. : American Association of Petroleum Geologists, c1988.
> viii, 198 p. : ill. (some col.), maps ; 29 cm. + 1 portfolio
> (30 plates : col. maps ; 28 cm.).

9.5E2.   Electronic resources: Because no physical description is given for remote-access electronic resources, the details of any accompanying material are given in a note.

12.5E.   Continuing resources: For *serials*, accompanying material is described only if it is intended to be issued regularly and used with the serial. Its frequency is given in a note. If issued only once or irregularly, such material could be described in a note, ignored, or cataloged separately if judged to be important.

AREA 6.   SERIES AREA (*MARC 21* fields 4XX)

The first definition of *series* as it appears in the *AACR2R2002* Glossary is: "A group of separate items related to one another by the fact that each item bears, in addition to its own title proper, a collective title applying to the group as a whole."[28]

LC has issued a lengthy rule interpretation regarding situations in which a series statement is to be given. It in turn refers to other rule interpretations that discuss LC practice in areas such as sources of information for the series statement, data elements in a series statement, multiple series statements and access points for series. (*CSB* 105: 22–29)

This area is not used for manuscripts (Chapter 4). When cataloging microform reproductions (Chapter 11), a series statement for an original is recorded with other details of the original. If one is following *AACR2R*, this means placing the original series in a note. If one is following LC practice, the original series is transcribed in the series area.

X.6B.   Title proper of series (subfield a, *MARC 21* fields 4XX)

1.6B1.   The title proper of a series is transcribed according to the rules for transcribing the title proper of the information package and is enclosed within parentheses. (The parentheses are not used when the series is entered into a MARC record.) Example:

> Vegetable suite : for flute and piano / Graham Powning. — London : Chester Music ; New York : W. Hansen/Chester Music, c1986.
>   1 score (6 p.) + 1 part (3 p.) ; 31 cm. — (The Chester woodwind series)

Other examples:

> *Sound recording:*   (CBS masterworks)
>
> *Game:*   (Instructo activity kit)
>
> *Microform:*   (British publishers' archives on microfilm)

Other title information is seldom recorded for series. It is recorded only if valuable for identifying the series. When other title information or parallel titles for series are recorded, they are transcribed according to the same rules used for the title and statement of responsibility area. LC's rule interpretation provides guidance for a variety of special situations, and specifies that LC practice is not to correct inaccuracies in the title proper of a series. (*CSB* 105: 29–32)

1.6B2.   This rule gives a hierarchy for choice among variant series titles that may appear in an information package. A title in the first of the prescribed sources of information for the series is preferred. If the series title does not appear in the first prescribed source, but there are different forms in other parts of the item, the order of preference for sources dictates which form should be used.

X.6E.   Statements of responsibility relating to series (subfield a, *MARC 21* fields 4XX)

1.6E1.   Statements of responsibility that appear "in conjunction with the series title" are to be recorded if "they are considered to be necessary for identification." LC's rule interpretation states that "in conjunction with" means on the same source as the series title. (*CSB* 76:16) Example:

> Post-war food and cash crop production in former
> colonial territories / compiled by B.J. Silk. — [Oxford :
> Oxford Development Records Project, 1985]
>   64 p. ; 30 cm. — (Report / Oxford Development
> Records Project ; 8)

X.6F.   ISSN of series (subfield x, *MARC 21* fields 4XX)
The ISSN is the International Standard Series Number, assigned to a serial as an internationally agreed-upon unique identifier. It is useful for identification and ordering purposes. It is recorded in the series area if it appears in the item. It follows a comma-space and precedes any numbering of the series. Example:

> Religion, intergroup relations, and social change in South
> Africa / G.E. Oosthuizen . . . [et al.] ; Human Sciences
> Research Council, Work Committee: Religion. — New
> York ; London : Greenwood, 1988.
>   xii, 237 p. ; 23 cm. — (Contributions in ethnic studies,
> ISSN 0196-7088 ; no. 24)

An LC rule interpretation states that, when using MARC format, one may not input letters "ISSN" in this subfield. (*CSB* 91: 13)

X.6G.   Numbering within series (subfield v, *MARC 21* fields 4XX)

1.6G1.   Numbering given with the series in the item is recorded as part of the series area. Abbreviations as found in Appendix B of *AACR2R* are used and Arabic numerals are substituted for non-Arabic numerals. Numbering is separated from preceding information by a space-semicolon-space. Examples:

Music: (Hortus Musicus ; 240)

Videorecording: (OCLC ; no. 6)

Electronic resource: (SRC/CPS American national election series ; no. 13)

Microform: (Columbia University oral history collection ; pt. 2, no. 24)

LC has issued a rule interpretation concerning transcription of series numbering. (*CSB* 102: 18–21)

X.6H.   Subseries (subfields n and p, *MARC 21* field 440)
AACR2R2002 defines subseries as: "A series within a series (i.e., a series that always appears in conjunction with another, usually more comprehensive, series of which it forms a section). Its title may or may not be dependent on the title of the main series."[29]
Such a subseries, if present, is transcribed after the details of the main series. Parallel titles, other title information, statements of responsibility, ISSN, and numbering are transcribed for subseries in the same way as for series. An LC rule interpretation gives guidelines for judging whether an item is part of a subseries. (*CSB* 105: 32–33) Example:

> About interpretation : from Plato to Dilthey : a
> hermeneutic anthology / [compiled by] Barrie A. Wilson.
> — New York : P. Lang, c1989.
>   xii, 208 p. ; 23 cm. — (American university studies.
> Series V, Philosophy, ISSN 0739-6392 ; v. 30)

X.6J.   More than one series statement

1.6J1.   If there is more than one series, each series is recorded in a separate series statement in its own set of parentheses (or in its own MARC field). An LC rule interpretation gives guidelines for application of this rule. (*CSB* 105: 33–34) Example:

> Conducting a successful capital campaign : a comprehensive fundraising guide for nonprofit organizations / Kent E. Dove.
> — 1st ed. — San Francisco : Jossey-Bass Publishers, 1988.
> xxii, 292 p. : ill. ; 24 cm. — (The Jossey-Bass management series) (The Jossey-Bass higher education series)

General notes on 12.6 Continuing resources:

Serials: Series numberings are not given when each issue has a separate series number. Example:

> Wage chronology : Ford Motor Company / U.S. Bureau of Labor Statistics....
> v. ; 28 cm. — (Bulletin / Bureau of Labor Statistics)

An LC rule interpretation describes three situations in which series numbers should be transcribed for a single issue or group of issues of a serial. (CSB 97: 50)

If there is a change, addition, or deletion of the series statement on a subsequent issue or part, this should be recorded in a note if considered important, unless the change, etc., can be indicated clearly in Area 6. *Continuing resources:* If such a change occurs on a subsequent iteration, Area 6 should be changed, with a note made about the earlier series statement, again, if it is considered important.

AREA 7.   NOTE AREA (*MARC 21* fields 5XX)

Many works require description beyond that presented formally in the title and statement of responsibility area through the series area. Notes qualify or amplify the formal description. Some notes contribute to identification of a work (e.g., a note giving the original title of a translated work). Some contribute to the intelligibility of the record (e.g., a note explaining the relationship of the work of a person who has been given an added entry). Other notes aid the reader who does not have in hand an exact citation (e.g., a summary or contents note). Still other notes characterize an information package (e.g., a thesis note) or give its bibliographic history (e.g., notes giving previous titles). Each *AACR2R* chapter gives rules for notes for the kind of materials covered by that chapter.

1.7A. Preliminary rule

1.7A3. Form of notes

This rule gives general guidelines for the formulation of notes.

> **Order of information.** In any one note, data that correspond to data found in descriptive areas (covered by rules numbered ".1" through ".6") are transcribed in the same order in the note. The prescribed punctuation is used with the exception that a period (full stop), space, dash, space is replaced simply by a period (full stop). Example:

Trees and shrubs of the Southeast / Blanche Evans Dean ;
illustrated by Forrest Bonner. — 3rd ed., rev. and expanded.
— Birmingham, Ala. : Birmingham Audubon Society Press, c1988.
xx, 264 p. : ill. ; 23 cm.

Rev. and expanded ed. of: Trees and shrubs in the heart of
Dixie. Rev. ed. Birmingham, Ala. : Southern University Press,
1968.

[Note contains information in the same order it would be in a description, but the period, space, dash, space area separators are omitted between areas.]

Quotations. Quotations in notes are given in quotes followed by an indication of the source, unless the chief source of information is the source of the
quotation.

Formal notes. Standard format is used for certain notes because uniformity
can assist in recognition of some types of information.

Informal notes. Informal notes should be as brief as they can be without
sacrificing clarity, understandability, or good grammar.

1.7A4.   Notes citing other editions and works

When notes are made citing other works or other manifestations of the same
work, the notes should give enough information to identify the work cited. When
giving a note for an original work from which the work in hand is reproduced, all
notes relating to the original are combined into one note. An LC rule interpretation
gives guidance and examples for applying this rule. (*CSB* 60: 14–15)

X.7B.   Notes (*MARC 21* field 500 is used unless otherwise noted.)

Notes are to be given in the order listed here, except that a note that has been
decided to be of primary importance for a particular type of material should be given
first (e.g., publishers' stock numbers for sound recordings). Upon examination, one
can determine the logic of the order. First come notes concerning the nature and language of the information package. Then come notes that relate to the areas of description from title through series in the order in which they appear in the body of the
entry. These are followed by notes that characterize and summarize the information
package.

For continuing resources, many notes (called "linking notes" by LC) refer to
another resource. *AACR2R* (rule 12.7A2) gives instructions for citing another resource in a note. It suggests using the title or name-title that is the catalog entry for
the resource. If the resource referred to is not in the catalog, or if main entry is not
used, the title proper and statement of responsibility are to be cited. An LC rule interpretation changes these instructions to include uniform title when this is appropriate. Statements of responsibility are not used in LC's linking notes. (*CSB* 99: 19–20)
Another rule interpretation clarifies the information to be provided for *serials* notes
when it is known that information in a note does not apply to all issues of a serial,
and for *integrating resources* notes when data elements such as title proper change
between iterations. (*CSB* 99: 17–19)

X.7B1.   Nature, scope, or artistic form (*MARC 21* field 500 [520 for manuscripts; 500 and 538 for computer files; 310 for serials])
When the nature, scope, or artistic form of a work is not apparent from the rest of the description, notes may be made. Examples:

Book:	Catalog of an exhibition held Aug. 16-Nov. 2, 1986, at the Fine Arts Museum of San Francisco.
Map:	Shows locations of important historical events.
Sound recording:	Organ music to demonstrate the instrument: various organists and organs.
Electronic resource:	Data base manager.
Microform:	Extensive collection of feminist serial literature published 1956 through June, 1974.

2.7B1.   Books: LC generally restricts this type of note for books to those that contain one or more literary works by one personal author *and* fall into one of several categories of languages (e.g., Turkish, Hebrew alphabet, or language indigenous to Africa and in the roman script). LC also makes notes recording the literary forms of belles lettres when their titles are misleading. Fanciful titles are not necessarily considered to be misleading. (*CSB* 54: 29–30)

4.7B1.   Manuscripts: This note prescribes terms to be used for originals and copies. The word *signed* is added if appropriate. Examples:

Printout, signed.

Mss. (photocopies)

Ms., signed (carbon copy)

Holograph (photocopy)

For collections of manuscripts, the cataloger is instructed to name the types of information packages that compose the collection and to mention any other characterizing features. Example:

[Papers] / William Alexander Smith. — 1765-1849.
51 boxes (11,573 items), 101 v. ; 44 x 30 x 9 cm.

Mss.
Capitalist and businessman operating mainly in North
Carolina from ca. 1866 to 1934. Includes correspondence,
reports, financial statements, writings, legal papers, volumes,
clippings, genealogy, pictures, bills, receipts, and promissory
notes.

5.7B1.   Music: This note is called "Form of composition and medium of performance." Musical form not apparent from the rest of the description is given briefly. Examples of forms of composition are carol, opera, concerto, and symphony. The medium of performance is given unless it has been given earlier in English or in an easily understood term in a foreign language. Example:

For harpsichord, 2 violins, viola, and violoncello.

9.7B1. Electronic resources: This note is called "Nature and scope, system requirements, and mode of access." Information on system requirements is given, when readily available, in a note beginning "System requirements:" and followed by information about the make and model of the computer(s) for which the file is designed, the amount of memory required, the name of the operating system, the software requirements, and the kind of characteristics of required or recommended peripherals. For remote-access-only resources, an additional note is made describing the mode of access. Examples:

> System requirements for Macintosh: 68030 processor or higher ; System 7 or higher ; 4 MB RAM (8 MB preferred) ; 256-color monitor ; CD-ROM drive ; mouse.

> Mode of access: World Wide Web.

12.7B1. Continuing resources: This note is called "Frequency." *AACR2R* prescribes making a note on the frequency of a *serial*, or the frequency of updates to an *integrating resource*, unless frequency is apparent from the title and statement of responsibility area or is unknown. However, an LC rule interpretation calls for a note on this information even if it is apparent from the rest of the item. (*CSB* 97: 54) Examples:

> Eight issues yearly.
>
> Bimonthly.
>
> Semiannual.
>
> Updated monthly.

X.7B2. Language of the item and/or translation or adaptation
(*MARC 21* field 546)

If the language is not evident from the description or if the fact of translation or adaptation is not apparent, notes may be made. Examples:

Book:	Translation of: Das adoptierte Kind.
Map:	Place names in Arabic and English.
Music:	German and English words.
Sound recording:	Sung in Latin.
Film:	In English; also issued in Portuguese and Spanish.
Videorecording:	Closed-captioned.
Serial:	Summaries in English, 1987-Mar./Apr. 1988; summaries in English and Spanish, May/June 1988-

An LC rule interpretation provides guidance for making language and script notes in common and less common situations. (*CSB* 99: 12–15)

X.7B3. Source of title proper
The source of the title proper is noted if it is taken from a title page substitute. In addition is it given for sound recordings and graphic materials if it is the container and also is given for sound recordings if it is accompanying textual material. The source of the title proper is *always* given for electronic resources. Examples:

Book:	Cover title.
Sound recording:	Title from publisher's catalog.
Graphic:	Title from later reproductions.
Electronic resource:	Title from home page.
Realia:	Title supplied by cataloger.

X.7B4. Variations in title (first indicator 0 or 1, *MARC 21* field 246;
2nd indicator 0, *MARC 21* field 247, *MARC 21* field 547)
Titles that differ from the title proper should be noted, if considered important.
Examples:

Book: Spine title: 1988 International Display Research Conference.

Map: Title in lower right hand corner: Bath Alum, Va.

Sound recording: Title on container: The last sixteen piano trios.
   [Label reads: The last sixteen trios.]

Electronic resource: Title on container: Pro-Cite for the Macintosh.
   [Title proper: Pro-Cite.]

Serial: Each issue has a distinctive title.

Serial: Running title: Chemical engineering catalog census.
   [Title proper is: CEC census of buyers in the chemical process industries.]

12.7B4.2. Continuing resources: This rule, "Change in title proper," is consistent with the treatment of changes in data elements in other areas. For *serials*, minor changes in title proper which occur after the first or earliest issue or part are recorded in a note. For *integrating resources*, the record is changed to reflect the title on the current iteration, and earlier titles are recorded in a note. The rule refers the cataloger to 12.1B8, which deals with changes in title proper as recorded in Area 1. Examples:

Serial: Some issues have title: Four-alarm fire signal.

Integrating resource: Former title: Arab-American news online (viewed on December 12, 1999).

LC's rule interpretations for 12.7B4.1 (*CSB* 97: 55–56) and 12.7B4.2 (CSB 105: 39–40) provide guidance on the use of *MARC 21* fields 246, 247, 500, and 547 in different situations of change in title for continuing resources.

X.7B5. Parallel titles and other title information. Example:

Realia: Subtitle on container: Tooth decay prevention kit.

Continuing resources: This note is broken out into two. 12.7B5 deals with changes in parallel titles, and 12.7B6 with changes in other title information. In both instances, the cataloger is instructed, for *serials*, to record changes after the first or earliest issue or part in a note. For *integrating resources*, the Area 1 description is changed to reflect the current iteration, with previous data recorded in a note. Example:

Serial: Parallel title, fall/winter 1967-Oct. 1980: Mental retardation.

[Title proper is in French. From 1963 to 1967 the title was in English only.]

(From this point on in Area 7 of Chapter 12, the numbering and titles of rules for notes vary considerably from the other chapters in *AACR2R* Part I.)

X.7B6.   **Statements of responsibility** (*MARC 21* fields 500, 508, and 511)

Here is a place for statements of responsibility (e.g., significant persons or bodies connected with previous editions, or persons or bodies not named in the chief source) that were not given in the title and statement of responsibility area. Examples:

Book: Prepared by the Oceanography Course Team.

[The statement of responsibility did not appear in the chief source of information but was composed by the cataloger from information that appeared elsewhere. Had it appeared in the chief source of information it would have been transcribed in the statement of responsibility area.]

Map: Grid and marginal information added by the Army Map Service.

Manuscript: Holography signed note by William Pitt appended to letter.

Music: Text based on the drama of the same name of Pushkin.

Sound recording: Violoncello: Raphael Wallfisch ; piano: Richard Markham.

7.7B6.   *Motion pictures and videorecordings*: The rule here specifies providing "cast" and "credits" notes when appropriate. The latter should include the names and functions of those who are judged to have made a major artistic or technical contribution to the production. Examples:

Cast: John Howard Davis, Alec Guinness, Robert Newton.

Credits: Editor, Lars Floden ; voices, Hans Conreid, June Forray ; music, Larry Wolff.

Continuing resources: This note is numbered 12.7B7. Examples:

Serial: Official journal of: American Academy for Cerebral Palsy and Developmental Medicine.

Serial: Issued by graduate students in the Dept. of French at the Pennsylvania State University.

Rule 12.7B7.2 addresses changes in statements of responsibility. Consistent with earlier rules distinguishing between *serials* and *integrating resources*, it states that changes in statements of responsibility for the former should be recorded in a note; for the latter, Area 1 data should be revised to reflect the current iteration, with previous data recorded in a note.

X.7B7. Edition and history (*MARC 21* fields 500, 518, and 580)

Bibliographic history notes and notes relating to the edition in hand are recorded here. Examples:

Book:	Originally published: New York : Pantheon Books, 1986.
Book:	Companion vol. to: The IMF and stabilization. 1984.
Map:	First published under title: Geographic map of the . . . Kingdom of Saudi Arabia.
Music:	Edited from ms. sources in the National Library of Turin.
Sound recording:	Recorded in San Francisco in 1999.
Sound recording:	Reissue of: Capitol SW-1804.
Videorecording:	Videorecording of play produced at Kathryn Bache Miller Theatre, Columbia University, New York, N.Y., March 10, 1998.
Electronic resource:	Full digital recording of the performance recorded in Nov. 1987 in Kirche Altstetten, Zürich, Switzerland and released on Teldec 35766.
Microform:	Filmed from the H.G. Wells collection in the Bromley Public Libraries.

2.7B7. Books: An LC rule interpretation is helpful for constructing notes about reprint editions. (*CSB* 58: 14–15)

4.7B7. Manuscripts: This note is called "Donor, source, etc., and previous owner(s)." Example:

> Gift of the estate of Mrs. Theodora Cabot, 1955.

Continuing resources: This note is split into two rules. 12.7B8 is titled "Bibliographic history and relationships with other resources." 12.7B9 is "Edition statement."

12.7B8.   Bibliographic history and relationships with other resources:

> *Continuation (including "Continued by").* When a resource continues another resource previously published, a note is made for the preceding title (*MARC 21* field 780). Example:

> Continues: Cerebral palsy bulletin.

When a resource is continued by another resource, the record for the resource before the title change should have a note added that names the succeeding title (*MARC 21* field 785). Optionally, the date of change may also be added. LC does not apply the option. (*CSB* 97: 60) Example:

> Continued by: Industrial vegetation, turf and pest management.

> *Merger.* When two or more resources are merged, the names of the previously separate resources are given on the record for the new resource (*MARC 21* fields 580 and 787). Example:

> Merger of: Mariah, and: Outside.

Each of the resources that were merged should have a note added to give the title of the new resource and the title(s) with which it has merged (*MARC 21* fields 580 and 787). Example:

Merged with: Outside, to become: Mariah/Outside.

Split. A note is made on the record for a resource that is the result of a split of a resource into two or more parts. The note should name the resource that was split (*MARC 21* fields 580 and 787). Example:

Continues in part: Transportation research.

An option allows also naming the other resource(s) resulting from the split. LC is not applying the option. (*CSB* 97: 60) The resource that was split should have a note added that gives the names of the resulting resources (*MARC 21* field 580). Example:

Split into: Transportation research. Part A, General, and: Transportation research. Part B, Methodological.

Absorption. The record for a resource that has absorbed another resource should have added to it a note giving the title of the resource that has been absorbed (*MARC 21* fields 580 and 787). An option allows giving also the date of the absorption. LC applies the option when the information is readily available. (*CSB* 97: 60) Example:

Absorbed: American Association of Stratigraphic Palynologists. Proceedings of the annual meeting.

The record for the resource that has been absorbed should have a note added that gives the title of the resource that absorbed it (*MARC 21* field 580). Example:

Absorbed by: Palynology.

Translation. Give a note for the original title of a previously published resource, when the resource cataloged is a translation. On the record for the original resource, give a note on the translation. Example:

English translation of the tables and some annexes in the publication "Nationale Rekeningen."

Simultaneous edition. A resource may be published simultaneously in two or more editions, differing in partial content and/or language. Give a note naming the other edition(s) in this case. If the name(s) of the other edition(s) are not known or are too numerous, a general note may be made. Examples:

Published in several regional editions.

Issued also in Dutch.

Supplement. (*MARC 21* fields 580 and 770). Examples:

Supplement to: Dictionary of literary biography.

Supplements, including laws, ordinances, bills, etc., accompanying some numbers.

12.7B9.2.   Change in edition information: See the discussions of rules 12.7B5-6 and 12.7B7.2, for instructions on recording changes in edition information for *serials* and *integrating resources.*

X.7B8.   Material (or type of publication) specific details

3.7B8.   Cartographic materials: This note is called "Mathematical and other material specific details." It provides for data on the magnitude of celestial charts, mathematical data not given in Area 3 for remote-sensing images, digital graphic representation data and other material specific data for electronic resources, data about multiple scales, and other types of information. Examples:

> "Contour interval 50 feet."
>
> Relief shown by hachures, shading, spot heights, etc.
>
> Scale of second map: 1:200,000

4.7B8. Manuscripts: This note is called "Place of writing." Example:

> At top of letter: Brooklyn.

5.7B8. Music: This note is called "Notation." Example:

> Shape-note notation.

9.7B8.   Electronic resources: This note is called "Type and extent of resource." Examples:

> File size varies.
>
> Weighted sample size is 2523.

Continuing resources: This rule is numbered 12.7B10 and titled "Numbering and issuing peculiarities." (*MARC 21* field 515) For *serials,* notes are given on the period covered by a volume, issue, etc., of a publication that appears annually or less frequently, and when that period is other than a calendar year. Notes are also given for complex or irregular numbering, or issuing peculiarities, when these are considered important and not already given in Area 3. Examples:

> Report year ends Mar. 31.
>
> Numbering begins each year with no. 1.
>
> Some no. irregularly issued in combined form.

A rule interpretation discusses remote-access electronic serials which reproduce some but not all volumes of an existing serial in another format. In this situation, a note is made giving the date of cataloging and the beginning of electronic coverage as of that date. If coverage changes, the note may be changed. If the first issue is subsequently digitized, the data in Area 3 must be changed. (*CSB* 97: 61)

X.7B9.   Publication, distribution, etc. (*MARC 21* field 500 or 550)
    Important publication, distribution, etc., details that cannot be given in the publication, distribution, etc., area are recorded in a note. Examples:

Book:	Printed at the Tabard Private Press, Oxshott, by Philip Kerrigan.
Map:	Based on 1972 data.
Film:	First released in France.
Graphic:	Issued in 3 parts.

2.7B9.   Books: LC interprets a date that consists of month and year or month, day, and year, and that appears in a prominent position, to be a date of release or transmittal and records it in a note in quotation marks. It is not considered to be a publication date, although the publication date may be inferred from it and given in brackets (*CSB* 44: 21–22) Example:

> "March 1990."

4.7B9. Manuscripts: This note is called "Published versions." Example:

> Published in: Some letters of George III / W.B. Hamilton. p. 416. *In* The South Atlantic quarterly. Vol. 68, no. 3 (Summer 1969).

Continuing resources: This rule is numbered 12.7B11. It provides for information on suspended or resumed publications, as well as changes in publication and distribution which do not require a new description.

X.7B10.   Physical description

Important physical details not given in the physical description area may be recorded here. Examples:

Book:	Maps on lining papers.
Map:	Maps issued in envelopes bearing copies of inset maps of cities.
Music:	Duration: 13:20.

> [given only if stated in the item; a cataloging decision made in the Music Section, Special Materials Cataloging Division, Library of Congress, indicates that for music and sound recordings, hours, minutes, and seconds are to be expressed in the note area as numerals separated by colons.[30]]

Sound recording:	Impressed on pliable surface with rectangular edge attached to hard paper cover for support.
Graphic:	For flannel board.
Puzzle:	Vertical sides in straight lines; horizontal sides form wavy lines.

11.7B10.   Microforms: Reduction ratio is given if it is outside the 16X-30X range, using one of the following terms:

Low reduction	*For less than 16X*
High reduction	*For 31X-60X*
Very high reduction	*For 61X-90X*

Ultra high reduction   *For over 90X; for ultra high reduction give also the specific ratio, e.g., Ultra high reduction, 150X*

Reduction ratio varies

Continuing resources: This rule is numbered 12.7B12. For *serials*, it provides for information about physical details which are changed or deleted on an issue or part subsequent to that which is the basis for the description. For *integrating resources*, information may be provided about physical details no longer present on the current iteration.

X.7B11. Accompanying material and supplements

Rule 1.5E1 gives four options for treating accompanying material. When giving details in a note is chosen, the details are recorded here. Examples:

Book:	Overlay grid in pocket inside back cover.
Map:	Accompanied by: Index to maps of Arabia / issued by Army Map Service. 1 sheet ; 25 x 36 cm.
Sound recording:	Program notes by Anthony Hodgson on container.
Film:	With teacher's guide and supplementary material.
Electronic resource:	Accompanied by printed Index to documents relating to the committee's hearing on the proposed tobacco settlement, November 13, 1997.
Microform:	With companion print index: American public opinion index.

Continuing resources: This rule is numbered 12.7B13.

X.7B12.   Series

Series data that cannot appropriately be given in the series area may be recorded in a note. Examples:

Originally issued in series: Research studies in library science.

Part 1 in a series.

Series statement supplied by producer.

11.7B12. Microforms: A note is made here only for a microform series of which the item has been part. The rule for a note for any series relating to the original of which the microform is a reproduction is included in Rule 11.7B22. Example:

Originally issued in series: Archives on microfilm.

Continuing resources: This rule is numbered 12.7B14. An LC rule interpretation calls for changes in series statements for *serials* to be recorded in the series area, rather than as a note. (*CSB* 97: 62)

X.7B13.   Dissertations (*MARC 21* field 502)

Dissertations or theses are described with a formal note. The English word *thesis* is followed by the degree for which the author was a candidate (e.g., Ph.D., M.A.,

Master's), the name of the institution or faculty, and the year the degree was granted. Example:

> Thesis (Ph. D.) — Texas A & M University, 1988.

Revisions, abridgments, edited editions, and publications lacking formal thesis notes are noted in *MARC 21* field 500. Example:

> Revision of thesis (Ph. D.) — Yale University, 1989.

X.7B14.   Audience (*MARC 21* field 521)

If the intended audience is stated in the publication, it may be noted here. Examples:

> For adults learning to read.
>
> Grades 3-6.
>
> For nurses' training.

4.7B14.   Manuscripts: This note is called "Access and literary rights." Example:

> Information on literary rights available in the repository.

Continuing resources: This rule is numbered 12.7B15.

X.7B15.   Reference to published descriptions (*MARC 21* field 510)

4.7B15.   Manuscripts: This rule number appears only in the general chapter and in Chapter 4. Example:

> Described in: Manuscripts for research / report of the director, 1961–1974, North Country Historical Research Center, Feinberg Library, State University College, Plattsburgh, New York. 1975. p. 31–32.

X.7B16.   Other formats (*MARC 21* field 530)

If the content of the information package has been issued in other formats, they may be noted here. Examples:

Book:	Issued also as CD-ROM.
Videorecording:	Available as cartridge or disc.
Slide:	Issued also as filmstrip.
Microform:	Library also has volumes in printed form and on microfilm.

X.7B17.   Summary (*MARC 21* field 520)

Summary notes may be given when the contents of an information package are not specified in the rest of the description. Such notes are often given for nonbook materials because of the difficulty of browsing them (as can be done with books) to determine what they contain. Examples:

Sound recording: Summary: The author presents an overview and introduction to the area of human potentialities and its implications for humankind.

Film: Summary: A sports documentary covering three snowmobile races.

Electronic resource (electronic journal): Summary: Provides image and full-text online access to back issues. Consult the online table of contents for specific holdings.

Puzzle: Summary: The picture shows a battle scene on the deck of a British war ship during the Revolutionary War. The officers are in full dress uniforms for the 1787-1795 period.

2.7B17. Books: LC practice has generally limited summary notes on printed monographs to children's books. Example:

> Summary: By falling down a rabbit hole, Alice experiences unusual adventures with a variety of nonsensical characters.

Since 1984, however, some summary notes for adult materials created by LC's overseas offices have been included in LC bibliographic records. (*CSB* 60: 15)

Continuing resources: This note is broken out into two rules. 12.7B17 is called "Indexes" (*MARC 21* field 555), and 12.7B18 is "Summary." Example:

> Indexes: Vols. 4 (1982)-8 (1986) published separately.

X.7B18.   Contents (*MARC 21* fields 504 and 505)
When parts of an information package are titled and would be useful to the user of a bibliographic record, they are brought out in notes. Examples:

Map: Each sheet includes: "Index to adjoining sheets," glossary, and "Sources of base compilation."

Music: Contents: Sonate C dur, op. 15, Nr. 15 — Sonate A dur, op. 18, Nr. 5 — Sonate F dur, op. 18, Nr. 6.

Film: Contents: The black league (20 min.) — Doing your own thing (22 min.) — Teamwork against the odds (18 min.) — A new era (15 min.)

2.7B18.   Books: The LC rule interpretation for contents notes is lengthy and should be consulted when such notes seem appropriate. (*CSB* 92: 12-14) Examples:

Contents note for collection of works of one author:

> Contents: Third girl — Poirot loses a client — Funerals are fatal.

Contents note for collection of works by different authors:

> Contents: Introduction / William Zinsser — We are not excused / Robert Stone — Writing as an act of hope / Isabel Allende — A strip of exposed film / Charles McCarry — Active in time and history / Marge Piercy — The agreed-upon facts / Gore Vidal.

Contents note for multi-volume work:

> Contents: v. 1. The gathering storm — v. 2. Their finest hour — v. 3. The Grand Alliance — v. 4. The hinge of fate — v. 5. Closing the ring — v. 6. Triumph and tragedy.

Two parts of an item that are often titled are "Bibliography" and "Index." By example, they fall under rule 2.7B18 in *AACR2R*. In LC practice formal bibliographies were traditionally given as "Bibliography:" with the page numbers on which they fall, and other bibliographical references were given as either "Includes bibliographies" or "Includes bibliographical references." The most recent policy at LC, however, is to use one form of note for bibliographical citations in any form: "Includes bibliographical references." In the case of one formal bibliography, its inclusive page numbers are given in parentheses following the note. "Discography" and "Filmography" are still given as formal notes with page numbers. (*CSB* 92: 12) Examples:

> Includes bibliographical references (p. 298–301).

> Discography: p. [109] – 111.

While the simplification is welcome, bibliography notes on past LC catalog records are now difficult to interpret. For many years "Includes bibliographical references" meant the book had citations with footnote-type numbering in the order referred to in the text, whether at the bottoms of pages or at the ends of chapters or at the end of the book. Starting in 1984 the note was used only for true footnotes at the bottoms of pages. Then in 1989 it was broadened to be the only form of note used for citations in any form. Bibliography notes in various forms continue to be shown in this text, because they are allowed by *AACR2R*. It should be noted that the rule interpretation referred to also states that electronic resources should be referred to generically as "bibliographical references."

8.7B18. Graphic materials: An LC rule interpretation for projected graphics allows the addition, after the number of frames, slides, etc., of the duration of any accompanying sound. (*CSB* 13: 17) Example:

> Contents: Return to the sea (130 fr., 25 min., 15 sec.) — To save a living sea (153 fr., 30 min., 25 sec.)

Continuing resources: This rule is numbered 12.7B19.

X.7B19. **Numbers associated with the item** (other than those covered in area 8) (*MARC 21* fields 024-032, 036, 037 and 500)
Numbers found in the item other than ISBNs or ISSNs are recorded as notes — often quoted. Examples:

Book:	"IEEE catalog number 88CH2542-9."
Map:	Publisher's no.: AMS 5060 II SW-Series V834.
Music:	Pl. no.: B.S.I. no. 31.
Graphic:	Packet no. A 792.
Realia:	"No. 1014."

6.7B19. Sound recordings: An LC rule interpretation for the transcription of a label name and number of a sound recording calls for making this note the first one. (*CSB* 109: 18) Example:

> Angel: S 37309.

Continuing resources: This rule is numbered 12.7B20.

X.7B20.   Copy being described, library's holdings, and restrictions on use
        (*MARC 21* field 506 for restrictions on access pertaining to *all* copies; local MARC field 590 for local copy information [in OCLC])
        Notes are made about the particular copy in hand, including notes about imperfections or notes giving incomplete holdings of a multipart information package. These notes are "copy specific." That is, such a note is applicable only to the copy held by the cataloger who is creating the description. This works well in an individual library. However, if the library belongs to a network and creates online original cataloging that other libraries eventually use as a basis for their cataloging, this type of note can be a source of difficulty, as is known by libraries that have had to change LC's copy-specific notes to reflect local cataloging. Such notes are tagged 590 in an OCLC MARC record and thus are readily identifiable. Examples:

Book:	"IEEE catalog number 88CH2542-9."
Map:	Publisher's no.: AMS 5060 II SW-Series V834.
Music:	Pl. no.: B.S.I. no. 31.
Graphic:	Packet no. A 792.
Realia:	"No. 1014."

This rule also calls for notes about any restrictions there may be on use of the item. Such a note may or may not be copy-specific. Examples:

Book:	Restricted use until 2010.
Electronic resource:	Available to university faculty, staff and registered students only.

Continuing resources: This rule is numbered 12.7B21.

X.7B21.   "With" notes (*MARC 21* field 501) (*See also CSB* 97: 27-28)
        For information packages lacking a collective title and described separately, a note is given beginning "With:" and then listing the other separately titled parts. Examples:

Music:	With: La plus que lente / Claude Debussy.
Sound recording:	With: Suite italienne / Igor Stravinskii — Vocalise, op. 34, no. 14 / Sergei Rachmaninoff.
Serial microform:	Filmed with: BYU studies. Vol. 11, no. 1-v. 13.

A problem in the "With" note has been commented on by music librarians. Because the rules for notes call for referring to another bibliographic item by its title proper and statement of responsibility, musical works that are entered under a uniform title may be "lost" to the user of the "With" note. Such musical works seldom have added entries for the title proper, and the filing arrangement under the main entry is usually by uniform title, not title proper. This problem, however, may be mitigated in online systems that index all MARC 245 fields in the title index.

Continuing resources: This rule, numbered 12.7B22, is called " 'Issued with' notes."

X.7B22.   Combined notes relating to the original (*MARC 21* fields 500 and 534) Two chapters besides the general chapter have this rule.

8.7B22. Graphic materials: This note is called "Note relating to the original" and calls for description of the original of a reproduced art work.

11.7B22. Microforms: This note also is called "Note relating to the original." Example:

> Reproduction of: New York : Teachers College, Columbia University, 1927. xix, 166 p. : ill. ; 24 cm.

9.7B22. Electronic resources: This rule should have been numbered B23. It is the "Item described" note, and requires giving the date on which a remote-access electronic resource was viewed (see 12.7B23 below).

X.7B23.   Two chapters besides the general chapter have a rule ".7B23."

4.7B23. Manuscripts: This note is called "Ancient, medieval, and Renaissance manuscripts" and gives instructions for more detailed notes for these manuscripts.

1.7B23.   General rules & 12.7B23 Continuing resources: This note is called "Item described." For *serials*, it is used when the description is not based on the first issue or part. Example:

> Description based on: Vol. 36, no. 1 (Winter 1989).

For *integrating resources*, the rule specifies a mandatory note which states the iteration consulted in making the distinction. The date viewed is always given here for remote-access electronic resources. In this situation the "Item described" note may be combined with the "Source of title proper" note. Example:

> Title from home page (viewed February 27, 2003).

Figures 4.39–4.43 show examples of complete cataloging for several kinds of information packages, illustrating the use of notes.

Fig. 4.39. Rule 2.7B. Transcriptions of notes for a literary work.

The poetry of Singapore / editors, Edwin Thumboo . . .
[et al.]. — [Singapore?] : ASEAN Committee on Culture
and Information, c1985.
560 p. : col. maps ; 25 cm. — (Anthology of ASEAN
literatures ; v. 1)

1 → Poems.
2 → In Chinese, English, Malay, and Tamil.
3 → Maps on lining papers.
4 → Includes index.

[1] Nature, scope, or artistic form (1.7B1)
[2] Language (1.7B2)
[3] Physical description (1.7B10)
[4] Index note (1.7B18)

Fig. 4.40. Rule 2.7B. Transcriptions of notes for a treatise.

Properties of impurity states in superlattice
semiconductors / edited by C.Y. Fong, Inder P. Batra,
and S. Ciraci. — New York : Plenum Press, c1988.
xi, 351 p. : ill. ; 26 cm. — (NATO ASI series.
Series B, Physics ; v. 183)

1 → "Proceedings of a NATO Advanced Research Workshop
on the Properties of Impurity States in Superlattice
Semiconductors, held September 7-11, 1987, at the University
of Essex, Colchester, United Kingdom"—Verso t.p.
2 → "Published in cooperation with NATO Scientific
Affairs Division."
3 → Includes bibliographies and index.

[1] Quoted note on nature of item (1.7B1)
[2] Publication information note (1.7B9)
[3] Bibliography and index note (1.7B18)

Fig. 4.41. Rule 7.7B. Transcriptions of notes for a motion picture.

Berlin [motion picture] / Polonius Film Productions ;
directors, writers, John Dooley, Tessa Dooley. — Chicago,
Ill. : International Film Bureau, 1985.
1 film reel (25 min.) : sd., col. ; 16 mm. + 1 guide.

1 → In German.
2 → Title from data sheet.
3 → Credits: Photographer, Nicholas Struthers ; narrator,
Jurgen Schweckendiek.
4 → A foreign film (England)
5 → Junior high school through adults.
6 → Issued also as videorecording.
7 → Summary: A foreign language teaching program that
introduces beginning German students to the history of Berlin
and to aspects of contemporary life in the city.

1 Language (1.7B2)
2 Source of title proper (1.7B3)
3 Statements of responsibility (1.7B6)
4 Edition and history (1.7B7)
5 Audience (1.7B14)
6 Other formats (1.7B16)
7 Summary (1.7B17)

Fig. 4.42. Rule 7.7B. Transcriptions of notes for a videorecording.

The Alphabet theatre proudly presents The Z was
zapped [videorecording] : a play in twenty-six acts / written
and directed by Chris Van Allsburg ; produced by King
Productions. — New Rochelle, N.Y. : Spoken Arts, 1988.
1 videocassette (9 min.) : sd., col. ; ½ in. +1 guide.

1 → Title on container and guide: Spoken Arts presents The
Z was zapped.
1 → Spine title on cassette and container: The Z was zapped.
2 → Credits: Music by Wayne Abravanel ; performed by the
Caslon Players.
3 → Based on the book of the same title by Chris Van
Allsburg.
4 → VHS format.
5 → Summary: As a player in a play, each letter of the alphabet
meets a fate described by a word that begins with that
letter.
6 → "SAV 9010."

1 Variations in title (1.7B4)
2 Statements of responsibility (1.7B6)
3 Edition and history (1.7B7)
4 Physical description (1.7B10)
5 Summary (1.7B17)
6 Number borne by the item (1.7B19)

Fig. 4.43. Rule 9.7B. Transcriptions of notes for an electronic resource.

Multimedia Beethoven [electronic resource] : the ninth symphony, an illustrated interactive musical exploration / [by Robert Winter with the Voyager Company]. — Version 1.10, academic ed. — [Santa Monica, Calif.] : Microsoft Corporation, c1992.
    1 CD-ROM : sd., col. ; 4 ¾ in. + 1 users' guide.

1 → System requirements: multimedia PC or equivalent (includes 386SX or higher processor, 2 MB of RAM, 30 MB hard disk, CD-ROM drive, audio board, mouse, and VGA or VGA+ display); Microsoft Windows operating system 3.1 or higher; MS-DOS CD-ROM extension (MSCDEX) version 2.2 or higher; headphones or speakers.

2 → Title from disk label.

3 → Credits: Viennese State Opera, with Wilhelm Pitz, chorus master ; Viennese Philharmonic, conducted by Hans Schmidt-Isserstedt.

4 → Summary: The program is an illustrated, interactive exploration of Beethoven's Ninth Symphony, which examines the music and historical setting in which it was created, and the concepts behind the music.

5 → Contents: Pocket guide — Beethoven's world — Art of listening — A close reading — Ninth game.

6 → "CDAC 021200."

1 Nature and scope, system requirements (9.7B1)
2 Source of title proper (1.7B3)
3 Statement of responsibility (1.7B6)
4 Summary (1.7B17)
5 Contents (1.7B18)
6 Numbers (other than Standard Numbers) (1.7B19)

AREA 8.   STANDARD NUMBER AND TERMS OF AVAILABILITY
AREA (*MARC 21* fields 020 and 022)

An LC rule interpretation should be consulted when applying this rule using standards set by LC. Included are interim guidelines for recording the new 13-digit International Standard Book Numbers. (*CSB* 109: 16–18) When cataloging microforms, it should be remembered that only a standard number assigned to the microform itself is placed here. A standard number for the original should be included in the note on details of the original. This area is not used for manuscripts.

X.8B.   **Standard number** (subfield a, *MARC 21* field 020 or 022)

X.8B1. An internationally agreed-upon standard number for the information package is given in the standard number area following the notes. The numbers usually given here are the International Standard Book Number (ISBN) or the International Standard Serial Number (ISSN). Example:

The Battle of Britain : the greatest air battle of World War II / Richard Hough and Denis Richards. — 1st American ed. — London : Hodder & Stoughton ; New York : Norton, c1989.

xvii, 413 p., [40] p. of plates : ill. (some col.), maps ; 25 cm.

Includes index.
ISBN 0-393-02766-X

X.8B2.   If there are two or more standard numbers, the one that applies to the item being described should be given. An option allows recording more than one number and adding a qualification (as prescribed in rule 1.8E). LC is applying this option. (*CSB* 8: 9) Example:

ISBN 0-8032-3093-1 (alk. paper) — ISBN 0-8032-8167-6 (pbk. : alk. paper)

When ISBNs are inserted into a MARC record, each is input into its own 020 field, each number is recorded as a block without hyphens, and the acronym *ISBN* is omitted. An ISSN is placed in a 022 field with its hyphen, but omitting the acronym *ISSN*.

X.8C. Key-title (*MARC 21* field 222)

1.8C1.   The key-title of a resource, if found on the item, is added after the ISSN, even if it is the same as the title proper. It is separated from the ISSN by a space-equal sign-space. Example:

ALCTS newsletter. — Vol. 1, no. 1 (1990)-v. 9, no. 4-6 (1998).
— Chicago, IL : Association for Library Collections &
Technical Services, American Library Association, c1990-1998.
9 v. : ill. ; 28 cm.

Eight no. a year.
Title from caption.
Continues: RTSD newsletter.
Continued by: ALCTS newsletter online.
ISSN 1047-949X = ALCTS newsletter

X.8D.   *Optional addition.* **Terms of availability** (subfield c, *MARC 21* field 020)
    It is optional to add the price or other terms of availability, separated from the ISBN or ISSN by a space-colon-space. LC does not exercise this option for current items. (*CSB* 67: 19) Example:

ISBN 0-87287-621-7 : $45.00

[*Books:* In the books chapter, the terms of availability rule is placed at 2.8C. In all other chapters which have this rule, it is placed at X.8D.]

X.8E.   **Qualification** (subfield a, *MARC 21* field 020)

1.8E1.   A brief qualification is added after the standard number when there are two or more (*see* example under X.8B2, above). If the binding type is considered important, a qualification may be added even if there is only one standard number. The terms of availability may also require a brief qualification, if, for example, there is a different price for students, institutions, etc.

RULE X.9.   SUPPLEMENTARY ITEMS (*MARC 21* field 525 [for serials]
or separate record)

All *AACR2R* chapters except that for manuscripts have this rule. Many supplementary items are described as separate entities and are given complete independent bibliographic records. The rule that identifies which supplementary works should be cataloged separately is 21.28.

In the cases where a supplementary work is described dependently, one of three methods may be chosen: 1) the supplementary item may be recorded as accompanying material (rule 1.5E1d) (*see* example under 1.10B below); 2) the item may be described in the note area (rule 1.7B11); multilevel description may be used (rule 13.6).

RULE X.10.   ITEMS MADE UP OF SEVERAL TYPES OF MATERIALS

All *AACR2R* chapters except that for manuscripts have this rule, which deals with the description of information packages with components that belong to more than one group or type of material (e.g., printed text and slides).

1.10B.   If one of the components is so predominant that the item is of no use without that component (e.g., a slide set with an accompanying script that has little value without seeing the slides), the information package should be described in terms of the predominant component with details of the other component(s) given as accompanying material or in a note. Example:

> Bushy the squirrel [filmstrip] / Cathedral Films, Inc. ;
> producers, Jim Friedrich ... [et al.] ; writer, John Calvin
> Reid. — Niles, IL : United Learning, 1987.
> 1 filmstrip (33 fr.) : col. ; 35 mm. + 1 sound cassette
> (9 min., 10 sec. : analog) + 1 study guide. — (Parables
> from nature)

> [Note: Predominant component is the filmstrip; the sound cassette and study guide
> are subsidiary components.]

1.10C.   If there is no predominant component, the information package is cataloged as described below. Note that LC does not apply 1.10C, but always designates one component as predominant. (*CSB* 103: 55)

1.10C1.   General material designation

The instructions in rule 1.1C4 are followed except when an item has no collective title. Then the appropriate GMD is given after each individual title.

1.10C2.   Physical description

The cataloger is instructed to choose the most appropriate of three methods of providing the physical description:

> a)   listing the extent of each of the individual parts. An option allows adding the
>   name of the container and its dimensions. Example:

> > Who were the Pilgrims? [kit] / National Geographic
> > Society. — Washington, D.C. : National Geographic Society,
> > c1989.
> > 30 identical booklets, 1 sound cassette, 6 activity sheets
> > (2 copies each), 8 duplicating masters, 1 teacher's guide ; in
> > box 29 x 24 x 5 cm. — (Wonders of learning)

b) giving separate physical descriptions on separate lines for each type of component. Again, naming the container and giving its dimensions is given as an option. Example:

> Element probe [kit] : an A/V game for teaching the
> chemical elements / United Learning, Inc. ; writer,
> Richard S. Treptow. — Niles, IL : United Learning, 1988.
>   100 slides : col.
>   1 sound cassette (44 min.) : analog, stereo.
>   10 duplicating masters ; 28 x 22 cm.
>   1 teacher's guide (28 p.) ; 24 cm.
>   All in container 30 x 23 x 7 cm.

c) giving a general term with the number of pieces as the extent of item for information packages with a large number of different types of materials. The same option for naming the container and giving its dimensions is allowed. Example:

> Safety begins with you [kit]. — New York : Children's
> Media Productions, c1979.
>   24 various pieces. — (School craft kits)

12.10. Continuing resources: This rule is called "Sections." It states that sections of a resource should be described as separate resources rather than using the "multi-level" structure described in chapter 5 of this text, "Description of Analytical Materials." Rules 12.1B4–12.1B6 give instructions for recording separate titles proper for sections of a serial.

RULE X.11.   FACSIMILES, PHOTOCOPIES, AND OTHER REPRODUCTIONS

The *AACR2R* chapters for printed texts, cartographic materials, music and graphics have this rule. Facsimiles, photocopies, or other reproductions of these items are described in such a way that the details of the facsimile, etc., are given in all areas except the note area. If the title of the facsimile, etc., is different from the original, the title of the facsimile, etc., is given as title proper. The same is true for edition, publication details, or series. In these cases, the details of the original are given in a single note in the notes area in the same order as they would appear in the main part of the description. Example:

> Frederic Remington / by Ernest Raboff. — 1st Harper
> trophy ed. — New York : Harper & Row, 1989.
>   [31] p. : ill. (some col.) ; 29 cm.
>
>   "A Harper trophy book."
>   Summary: A brief biography of the artist and sculptor
>   accompanies fifteen color reproductions and critical
>   interpretations of his works.
>   Reprint of: Frederic Remington / by Adeline Peter
>   and Ernest Raboff. Garden City, N.Y. : Doubleday, 1973.
>   (Art for children)

If the facsimile, etc., is in a form of material different from the original, the chapter relating to the form of the facsimile, etc., is used. For a manuscript reproduced as a book, the chapter on description of books would be used. For maps reproduced on microfilm, the chapter on description of microforms would be used.

COMPLETE DESCRIPTIONS AND MACHINE-READABLE CATALOGING (MARC RECORDS) FOR ILLUSTRATIVE EXAMPLES

Fig. 4.44. *AACR2R* **description of the printed monograph whose title page and other preliminaries are shown in figures 4.6–4.8.**

A guide to the Library of Congress classification / Lois Mai Chan. — 5th ed. — Englewood, Colo. : Libraries Unlimited, 1999.
xviii, 551 p. ; 25 cm. — (Library and information science text series)

"Based on the fourth edition of Immroth's Guide to the Library of Congress classification."
Includes bibliographical references (p. 531-537) and index.
ISBN 1-56308-499-6 (cloth) — ISBN 1-56308-500-3 (pbk.)

Fig. 4.45. MARC record for the printed monograph. (Source: OCLC Connexion, WorldCat—record number 41211262.)

Books	Rec Stat	c	Entered	19990406	Replaced	20040102		
Type a	**ELvl**		**Srce**		**Audn**	**Ctrl**	**Lang**	eng
BLvl m	**Form**		**Conf** 0		**Biog**	**MRec**	**Ctry**	cou
	Cont b		**GPub**		**LitF** 0	**Indx** 1		
Desc a	**Ills**		**Fest** 0		**DtSt** s	**Dates** 1999,		

010		99-15279
040		DLC $c DLC $d UKM $d C#P $d OCL $d SDA
015		GB99-Y0841
020		1563084996 (cloth)
020		1563085003 (pbk.)
050	00	Z696.U4 $b C47 1999
082	00	025.4/33 $2 21
100	1_	Chan, Lois Mai.
245	12	A guide to the Library of Congress classification / $c Lois Mai Chan.
250		5th ed.
260		Englewood, Colo. : $b Libraries Unlimited, $c 1999.
300		xviii, 551 p. ; $c 25 cm.
440	_0	Library and information science text series
500		"Based on the fourth edition of Immroth's Guide to the Library of Congress classification."
504		Includes bibliographical references (p. 531-537) and index.
650	_0	Classification, Library of Congress.
700	1_	Chan, Lois Mai. $t Immroth's Guide to the Library of Congress classification.

Fig. 4.46. *AACR2R* description of the map shown in figures 4.9–4.12.

Bath Alum quadrangle, Virginia–Bath Co. / mapped, edited, and published by the Geological Survey. — Scale 1:24,000 ; Polyconic proj. — Washington, D.C. : For sale by U.S. Geological Survey, 1968.
1 map section : col. ; 58 x 43 cm. — (7.5 minute series : topographic)

Title in lower right corner: Bath Alum, Va.
"Topography by photogrammetric methods from aerial photographs."
Includes quadrangle location map.
Publisher's no.: AMS 5060 II SW-Series V834.
"N3800—W7937.5/7.5."

Fig. 4.47. MARC record for the map. (Source: OCLC Connexion, WorldCat—adapted record number 39060234.)

Maps	Rec Stat	c	Entered	19980505	Replaced	19990518		
Type	e	ELvl	I	Srce	d	Relf	a	Ctrl		Lang	eng
BLvl	m	Form		GPub	f	SpFm		MRec		Ctry	dcu
CrTp	a	Indx	0	Proj	cp	DtSt	s	Dates	1968,	
Desc	a							

007		a $b j $d c
040		MFS $c MFS $d OCL
034	1_	a $b 24000
043		n-us-va
052		3883 $b B3
110	2_	Geological Survey (U.S.)
245	10	Bath Alum quadrangle, Virginia-Bath Co. / $c mapped, edited, and published by the Geological Survey.
246	1_	$i Filing title: $a Bath Alum, Va.
255		Scale 1:24,000 ; $b Polyconic proj.
260		Washington, D.C. : $b For sale by U.S. Geological Survey, $c 1968.
300		1 map section : $b col. ; $c 58 x 43 cm.
490	0_	7.5 minute series : topographic
500		Title in lower right corner: Bath Alum, Va.
500		"Topography by photogrammetric methods from aerial photographs."
500		Includes quadrangle location map.
500		Publisher's no.: AMS 5060 II SW-Series V834.
500		"N3800--W7937.5/7.5."
651	_0	Bath Alum (Va.) $v Maps, Topographic.

Fig. 4.48. *AACR2R* **description of the single manuscript shown in figures 4.13–4.15.**

[Letter] 1793 Feb. 3, Windsor [to Henry] Dundas / G.R. [George III].
1 leaf ; 38 x 46 cm., folded to 23 x 19 cm.

Holograph signed.
Purchase, 1961.
Published in: Some letters of George III / W.B. Hamilton. p. 416. *In* The South Atlantic quarterly. Vol. 68, no. 3 (Summer 1969)

Fig. 4.49. MARC record for the manuscript. (Source: OCLC Connexion, WorldCat—originally created record.)

Books	Rec Stat	n	Entered	20040214	Replaced	20040214		
Type	t	ELvl	I	Srce	d	Audn	Ctrl	Lang	eng
BLvl	m	Form		Conf	0	Biog	MRec	Ctry	xx
		Cont		GPub		LitF	0	Indx	0
Desc	a	Ills		Fest	0	DtSt	s	Dates	1793,

040		DD0 ‡c DD0
045	0_	v9v9 ‡b d17930203
090		DA506.A2 ‡b 1793
100	0_	George ‡b III, ‡c King of Great Britain, ‡d 1738-1820.
245	10	[Letter] 1793 Feb. 3, Windsor [to Henry] Dundas / ‡c G.R. [George III].
300		1 leaf ; ‡c 38 x 46 cm., folded to 23 x 19 cm.
500		Holograph, signed.
590		Purchase, 1961.
500		Published in: Some letters of George III / W.B. Hamilton. p. 416. In The South Atlantic quarterly. Vol. 68, no. 3 (Summer 1969)
651	_0	Great Britain ‡x History ‡y George III, 1760-1820.

Fig. 4.50. *AACR2R* **description of the score shown in figure 4.16.**

Triosonate H-moll für zwei Violinen und Basso Continuo = Trio sonata in B minor for two violins and basso continuo : op. I/8 / Tommaso Albinoni ; herausgegeben von Stefan Altner. — Kassel ; New York : Bärenreiter, 1987.
1 score (12 p.) + 3 parts ; 30 cm. — (Hortus Musicus ; 240)

Includes preface in German and English.
Continuo realized in score for keyboard.
Pl. no.: HM 240.

Fig. 4.51. MARC record for the score. (Source: OCLC Connexion, WorldCat—record number 17336099.)

Scores	Rec Stat c	Entered 19880112	Replaced 20011027			
Type c	ELvl I	Srce d	Audn	Ctrl	Lang N/A	
BLvl m	Form	Comp ts	AccM	MRec	Ctry gw	
Desc a	FMus a	LTxt n	DtSt s	Dates 1987,		

040		FUG $c FUG $d OCL $d RES $d OCL
019		18431132 $a 20163661 $a 21848266 $a 22990692
028	22	HM 240 $b Bärenreiter
041	0_	$g gereng
045		u9u9
048		sa02 $a ke
090		M312.4 $b .A421 op. 1, no. 8, 1987
100	1_	Albinoni, Tomaso, $d 1671-1750.
240	10	Trio sonatas, $m violins, continuo, $n op. 1. $n No. 8
245	00	Triosonate H-moll für zwei Violinen und Basso Continuo = $b Trio sonata in B minor for two violins and basso continuo : $b op. I/8 / $c Tommaso Albinoni ; herausgegeben von Stefan Altner.
260		Kassel ; $a New York : $b Bärenreiter, $c 1987.
300		1 score (12 p.) + 3 parts ; $c 30 cm.
440	_0	Hortus Musicus ; $v 240
500		Includes preface in German and English.
500		Continuo realized in score for keyboard.
650	_0	Trio sonatas (Violins (2), continuo) $v Scores and parts.
700	1_	Altner, Stefan.

Fig. 4.52. *AACR2R* description of the sound recording shown in figures 4.17–4.18.

The four seasons [sound recording] / Antonio Vivaldi. — Djursholm, Sweden : BIS, p1985.
1 sound disc (ca. 40 min.) : digital, stereo. ; 4¾ in. + 1 booklet ([10] p. ; 12 cm.)

BIS: CD-275.
Compact disc.
Nils Erik Sparf, baroque violin ; Drottningholm Baroque Ensemble. Program notes in Swedish by Stig Jacobsson with English, French, and German translations inserted in container.
Recorded June 7 and Sept. 11, 1984, in the Petrus Church, Stocksund, Sweden.

Fig. 4.53. MARC record for the sound recording. (Source: OCLC Connexion, WorldCat —adapted record number 21788480.)

Sound Recordings	**Rec Stat** n	**Entered** 19880510	**Replaced** 20020714	
Type j	**ELvl** I	**Srce** d	**Audn**	**Ctrl**	**Lang** N/A
BLvl m	**Form**	**Comp** co	**AccM** z	**MRec**	**Ctry** sw
Desc a	**FMus** n	**LTxt**	**DtSt** s	**Dates** 1985,

007		s $b d $d f $e s $f n $g g $h n $i n $j m $k l $l n $m e
040		CUY $c CUY
028	01	$b Bis $a CD-275
033	1_	19840607 $a 19840911 $b 6954
048		oa
100	1_	Vivaldi, Antonio, $d 1678-1741.
240	10	Cimento dell'armonia e dell'inventione. $n N. 1-4.
245	14	The four seasons $h [sound recording] / $c Antonio Vivaldi.
260		Djursholm, Sweden : $b BIS, $c p1985.
300		1 sound disc (ca. 40 min.) : $b digital, stereo. ; $c 4 3/4 in. + $e 1 booklet ([10] p. ; 12 cm.)
500		Compact disc.
511	0_	Nils-Erik Sparf, baroque violin ; Drottningholm Baroque Ensemble.
500		Program notes in Swedish by Stig Jacobsson with English, French, and German translations inserted in container.
518		Recorded June 7 and Sept. 11, 1984, in the Petrus Church, Stocksund, Sweden.
650	_0	Concertos (Violin with string orchestra)
650	_0	Seasons $x Songs and music.
700	1_	Sparf, Nils Erik. $4 prf
710	2_	Drottningholms barockensemble. $4 prf

Fig. 4.54. *AACR2R* description of the videorecording shown in figures 4.19–4.21.

The Martian space party [videorecording]. — Bloomington, IN : More Sugar from the Firesign Theatre [distributor], 1996, c1972.
   1 videocassette (27 min.) : sd., col. ; 1/2 in.

Cast: Phil Austin, Peter Bergman, David Ossman, and Phil Proctor.
Credits: Directed by Stephen Gillmor ; produced and edited by The Firesign Theatre and Stephen Gillmor.
Videocassette release of the 1972 film.
"Not insane! in '96" — container.
VHS format.
Summary: Filmed excerpts from a 1972 live performance by the comedy group, The Firesign Theatre, "on location at the Natural Surrealist Light Peoples' Party convention." A satirical look at political conventions and news coverage is combined with parodies of Shakespeare and low-budget television shows. The performance concludes with the liftoff of the incumbent President in a rocket to Mars, accompanied by a Japanese movie monster.

Fig. 4.55. MARC record for the videorecording. (Source: OCLC Connexion, WorldCat—originally created record.)

Visual Materials	Rec Stat	n	Entered	20040214	Replaced	20040214
Type g	ELvl	I	Srce	d	Audn	Ctrl	Lang eng
BLvl m	Form		GPub		Time 027	MRec	Ctry inu
Desc a	TMat	v	Tech	l	DtSt	r	Dates 1996,1972

007		v $b f $d c $e b $f a $g h $h o
040		DD0 $c DD0
049		DD0A
130	0_	Firesign Theatre (Performing group)
245	04	The Martian space party / $h [videorecording].
260		Bloomington, IN : $b More Sugar from the Firesign Theatre [distributor], $c 1996, c1972.
300		1 videocassette (27 min.) : $b sd., col. ; $c 1/2 in.
511		Phil Austin, Peter Bergman, David Ossman, and Phil Proctor.
508		Directed by Stephen Gillmor ; produced and edited by The Firesign Theatre and Stephen Gillmor.
500		Videocassette release of the 1972 film.
500		"Not insane! in '96" --container.
538		VHS format.
520		Filmed excerpts from a 1972 live performance by the comedy group, The Firesign Theatre, "on location at the Natural Surrealist Light Peoples' Party convention." A satirical look at political conventions and news coverage is combined with parodies of Shakespeare and low-budget television shows. The performance concludes with the liftoff of the incumbent President in a rocket to Mars, accompanied by a Japanese movie monster.
650	_0	Political conventions $v Humor.
650	_0	Presidents $z United States $x Election $y 1972 $v Humor.
655	_7	Comedy variety. $2 mim
700	1_	Gillmor, Stephen.

Fig. 4.56. *AACR2R* description of the stereograph reel shown in figures 4.22–4.24.

Smithsonian Institution, Washington, D.C. [slide]. — Portland, Or. : Sawyer's Inc., [196-?]
3 stereograph reels (7 pairs of fr. each) : col. + 1 booklet (16 p. : col. ill. ; 11 cm.). — (View-master guided picture tour)

Booklet edited by Lowell Thomas.
For use with View-master.
Summary: Shows and describes some of the major exhibits housed in three of the buildings of the Smithsonian.
Contents: Reel 1. Air and space exhibits — Reel 2. Natural history exhibits — Reel 3. History & technology exhibits.
"Packet no. A 792."

Fig. 4.57. MARC record for the stereograph reel. (Source: OCLC Connexion, WorldCat—originally created record.)

Visual Materials	Rec Stat	n	Entered	20040214	Replaced	20040214
Type g	ELvl I	Srce d	Audn g	Ctrl	Lang eng	
BLvl m	Form	GPub	Time 021	MRec	Ctry oru	
Desc a	TMat s	Tech n	DtSt q	Dates 1960,1969		

007		g $b s $d c $e u $h z
040		DD0 $c DD0
090		Q11.S8 $b S64
245	00	Smithsonian Institution, Washington, D.C. $h [slide]
260		Portland, Or. : $b Sawyer's Inc., $c [196-?]
300		3 stereograph reels (7 pairs of fr. each) : $b col. + $e 1 booklet (16 p. : col. ill. ; 11 cm.).
490	0_	View-master guided picture tour
500		Booklet edited by Lowell Thomas.
500		For use with View-master.
520		Shows and describes some of the major exhibits housed in three of the buildings of the Smithsonian.
505	0_	Reel 1. Air and space exhibits -- Reel 2. Natural history exhibits -- Reel 3. History & technology exhibits.
500		"Packet no. A 792."
610	20	Smithsonian Institution.
700	1_	Thomas, Lowell, $d 1892-1981.

Fig. 4.58. *AACR2R* description of the computer disc shown in figures 4.25–4.26.

The Annenberg Washington Program electronic library [electronic resource]. — Washington, D.C. : Annenberg Washington Program in Communications Policy Studies, Northwestern University, c1996.
1 CD-ROM : sd., col. ; 4¾ in. + 1 user guide (15 p. ; 12 cm.).

System requirements: IBM-compatible PCs, 80386 processor or better, Windows 3.1 or higher, 4 MB of RAM, 3 MB of hard disk space; Macintosh computers, 68020 processor or higher, system 6 or higher, 8 MB of RAM, 4 MB of hard disk space.
Title from title screen.
Summary: Contains more than ninety Program publications, previously published in print, addressing issues in communications, information technology, political science, medicine, and many other critical areas. Most publications include full text of the original reports.

Fig. 4.59. MARC record for the computer disc. (Source: OCLC Connexion, WorldCat—adapted record number 34777512.)

Computer Files	Rec Stat	c	Entered	19960523	Replaced	20020104
Type m	**ELvl** I	**Srce** d	**Audn**		**Ctrl**	**Lang** eng
BLvl m	**File** d	**GPub**			**MRec**	**Ctry** dcu
Desc a			**DtSt** s		**Dates** 1996,	

007		c ‡b o ‡d u ‡e g ‡f u
040		ZHM ‡c ZHM ‡d OCL ‡d OCLCQ
090		P92.U5 ‡b A5 1996
245	04	The Annenberg Washington program electronic library ‡h [electronic resource].
260		Washington D.C. : ‡b Annenberg Washington Program in Communications Policy Studies, Northwestern University, ‡c c1996.
300		1 CD-ROM : ‡b sd., col. ; ‡c 4 3/4 in. + ‡e 1 user guide (15 p. ; 12 cm.).
538		System requirements: IBM-compatible PCs, 80386 processor or better, Windows 3.1 or higher, 4 MB of RAM, 3 MB of hard disk space; Macintosh computers, 68020 processor or higher, system 6 or higher, 8 MB of RAM, 4 MB of hard disk space.
500		Title from title screen.
520		Contains more than ninety Program publications, previously published in print, addressing issues in communications, information technology, political science, medicine, and many other critical areas. Most publications include full text of the original reports.
650	_0	Communication policy ‡z United States.
650	_0	Communication ‡z United States.
710	2_	Northwestern University (Evanston, Ill.). ‡b Annenberg Washington Program in Communication Policy Studies.

Fig. 4.60. *AACR2R* description of the Web site shown in figure 4.27.

American memory [electronic resource] : historical collections for the National Digital Library / The Library of Congress. — [Washington, D.C.] : National Digital Library Program, Library of Congress.

System requirements: Web browser software; some files require audio or video players.
Mode of access: World Wide Web.
Title from home page (viewed April 13, 2000).
Title in HTML header: Home page: American Memory from the Library of Congress.
Began in 1994.

Summary: Provides information on, and access to, digitized versions of the Library's primary-source collections on American history and culture, including photographs, documents, sound recordings, and motion pictures.

Fig. 4.61. MARC record for the Web site. (Source: OCLC Connexion, WorldCat—record number 38868711.)

Computer Files	Rec Stat	c	Entered	19980330	Replaced	20040130		
Type m	ELvl I		Srce d	Audn	Ctrl		Lang	eng
BLvl m	File d		GPub f		MRec		Ctry	dcu
Desc a				DtSt m	Dates	1994,9999		

007		c ‡b r ‡d u ‡e n ‡f u
040		GPO ‡c GPO ‡d OCL ‡d GPO ‡d OKU ‡d N@F ‡d OCLCQ ‡d ZQP ‡d GPO ‡d KIDSC ‡d OCLCQ ‡d CLU ‡d LML ‡d OCLCQ
043		n-us---
082	04	027.073
090		E173
245	00	American memory ‡h [electronic resource] : ‡b historical collections for the National Digital Library / ‡c The Library of Congress.
246	30	Historical collections for the National Digital Library
246	1_	‡i Title in HTML header: ‡a Home page : ‡b American memory from the Library of Congress.
246	3_	American memory from the Library of Congress
260		Washington, D.C. : ‡b National Digital Library Program, Library of Congress.
538		System requirements: Web browser software; some files require audio or video players.
538		Mode of access: World Wide Web.
500		Title from home page (viewed April 13, 2000).
500		Began in 1994.
520	8_	Provides information on, and access to, digitized versions of the Library's primary-source collections on American history and culture, including photographs, documents, sound recordings, and motion pictures.
610	20	Library of Congress.
651	_0	United States ‡x Civilization ‡v Sources.
651	_0	United States ‡x Social life and customs ‡v Sources.
651	_0	United States ‡x History ‡v Sources.
710	2_	Library of Congress. ‡b National Digital Library Program.
856	40	‡u http://lcweb2.loc.gov/ammem/
856	40	‡u http://lcweb2.loc.gov/ammem/amhome.html
856	40	‡u http://memory.loc.gov/

Fig. 4.62. *AACR2R* description of the game shown in figures 4.28–4.29.

Double nine dominoes [game]. — Premier ed. —
L[ong] I[sland] C[ity], NY : Cardinal Industries, c1993.
    1 game (55 pieces) : plastic ; in case 12 x 20 x 5 cm. + 1
instruction sheet.

Instructions in English and Spanish.
Title on carrying case: Domino by Cardinal.
Ages 4 to adult.
"No. 511."

Fig. 4.63. MARC record for the game. (Source: OCLC Connexion, WorldCat—record number 29713225.)

Visual Materials	Rec Stat c	Entered 19940131	Replaced 19980909			
Type r	**ELvl** I	**Srce** d	**Audn** g	**Ctrl**	**Lang** eng	
BLvl m	**Form**	**GPub**	**Time** nnn	**MRec**	**Ctry** nyu	
Desc a	**TMat** g	**Tech** n	**DtSt** s	**Dates** 1993,		

040		CUM $c CUM
041		engspa
090		GV1467
092		510.7 $b DOUBLE
245	00	Double nine dominoes $h [game].
246	1_	Domino by Cardinal
250		Premier ed.
260		L[ong] I[sland] C[ity], NY : $b Cardinal Industries, $c c1993.
300		1 game (55 pieces) : $b plastic ; $c in case 12 x 20 x 5 cm. + 1 instruction sheet.
500		Instructions in English and Spanish.
500		Title on carrying case: Domino by Cardinal.
521		Ages 4 to adult.
500		"No. 511."
655	_7	Dominoes. $2 lcsh
710	2_	Cardinal Industries.

Fig. 4.64. Description of the microfilm shown in figures 4.30–4.31.

Women and/in health [microform] / filmed by the Women's History Research Center. — Berkeley, Calif. : Women's History Research Center, c1974.

14 microfilm reels : ill. ; 35 mm. + 1 guide (88 p. in various pagings ; 28 cm.)

Collection of microfilmed clippings from newspapers, professional journals, alternative newspapers, academic research papers, theses, and conference speeches. Includes leaflets, poetry, and graphic material.

Title on containers: Women and health/mental health.

"July 1974."

Low reduction (15:1).

Guide issued under title: Guide to the microfilm edition of the Women and health collection.

Contents: Section 1. Physical and mental health of women (3 reels) — Section 2. Physical and mental illnesses of women (2 reels) — Section 3. Biology, women, and the life cycle (1 reel) — Section 4. Birth control/population control (3 reels) — Section 5. Sex and sexuality (2 reels) — Section 6. Black and third world women—health (1 reel) — Section 7. Special issues of mass periodicals relating to sections I, II, III, IV, V, VI of Women and health (2 reels).

Fig. 4.65. MARC record for the microfilm. (Source: OCLC Connexion, WorldCat—adapted record number 28588259.)

Books	Rec Stat	c	Entered	19930729	Replaced	20010402			
Type	a	ELvl		Srce		Audn	Ctrl		Lang eng
BLvl	c	Form	a	Conf	0	Biog	MRec		Ctry cau
		Cont		GPub		LitF 0	Indx	0	
Desc	a	Ills		Fest	0	DtSt s	Dates	1974,	

007		h $b d $d a $e f $f a015 $g b $h b $i c $j a
040		NLM $c NLM
060	00	WA 300 $b W8715 1974
090		HQ1426 $b .W68 1974
245	00	Women and/in health $h [microform] / $c filmed by the Women's History Research Center.
246	3_	Women and, in health
246	3_	Women and health/mental health
246	3_	Women and health, mental health
260		Berkeley, Calif. : $b Women's History Research Center, $c c1974.
300		14 microfilm reels : $b ill. ; $c 35 mm. + $e 1 guide (88 p. in various pagings ; 28 cm.)
500		Collection of microfilmed clippings from newspapers, professional journals, alternative newspapers, academic research papers, theses, and conference speeches. Includes leaflets, poetry, and graphic material.
500		Title on containers: Women and health/mental health.
500		"July 1974."
500		Low reduction (15:1).
500		Guide issued under title: Guide to the microfilm edition of the Women and health collection.
505	0_	Section 1. Physical and mental health of women (3 reels) -- Section 2. Physical and mental illnesses of women (2 reels) -- Section 3. Biology, women, and the life cycle (1 reel) -- Section 4. Birth control/population control (3 reels) -- Section 5. Sex and sexuality (2 reels) -- Section 6. Black and third world women--health (1 reel) -- Section 7. Special issues of mass periodicals relating to sections I, II, III, IV, V, VI of Women and health (2 reels).
650	_0	Women $x Health and hygiene.
650	_0	Women's health services.
650	_0	Women $x Psychology.
650	_2	Health $v collected works.
650	_2	Women's Health Services $v collected works.
650	_2	Women's Health $v collected works.
710	2_	Women's History Research Center.

Fig. 4.66. Description of the microfiche shown in figures 4.32–4.34, according to *AACR2R*.

The impact of feminist thought on American librarianship, 1965-1985 [microform] / Christina Diane Baum. — Ann Arbor, Mich. : University Microfilms International, 1987.
3 microfiches (276 fr.) ; 11 x 15 cm.

Thesis (Ed.D.)—University of Kentucky, 1987.
Includes bibliographical references.
"87-15914."
Reproduction of: x, 255 leaves ; 28 cm. Typescript. Includes bibliographical references (leaves 245-254).

(If one is following LC policy, the description shown in figure 4.66 would appear as in figure 4.68.)

Fig. 4.67. MARC record for the microfiche, according to *AACR2R*. (Source: OCLC Connexion, WorldCat—originally created record.)

Books	Rec Stat	n	Entered	20040216	Replaced	20040216		
Type	t	ELvl	I	Srce	d	Audn		Ctrl		Lang	eng
BLvl	m	Form	b	Conf	0	Biog		MRec		Ctry	miu
		Cont	bm	GPub		LitF	0	Indx	0		
Desc	a	Ills		Fest	0	DtSt	s	Dates	1987,		

007		h $b e $d a $e m $f b--- $g b $h u $i c $j u
040		DD0 $c DD0
090		Z682.4.W65 $b .B38 1987
049		DD0A
100	1_	Baum, Christina D.
245	14	The impact of feminist thought on American librarianship, 1965-1985 $h [microform] / $c Christina Diane Baum.
260		Ann Arbor, Mich. : $b University Microfilms International, $c 1987.
300		3 microfiches (276 fr.) ; $c 11 x 15 cm.
502		Thesis (Ed.D.)--University of Kentucky, 1987.
504		Includes bibliographical references.
500		"87-15914."
534		$p Reproduction of: $e x, 255 leaves ; 28 cm. $n Typescript. $n Includes bibliographical references (leaves 245-254).
650	_0	Library science $z United States $x History.
650	_0	Women in library science $z United States $x History.
650	_0	Feminism $z United States $x History.

Fig. 4.68. Description of the microfiche shown in figures 4.32–4.34, according to LC policy.

The impact of feminist thought on American librarianship, 1965-1985 [microform] / by Christina D. Baum. — 1987.
x, 255 leaves ; 28 cm.

Typescript.
Thesis (Ed.D.)—University of Kentucky, 1987.
Includes bibliographical references (leaves 245-254).
Microfiche. Ann Arbor, Mich. : University Microfilms International, 1987. 3 microfiches (276 fr.) ; 11 x 15 cm. "87-15914."

Fig. 4.69. MARC record for the microfiche, according to LC policy. (Source: OCLC Connexion, WorldCat—adapted record number 22772600.)

Books	Rec Stat	c	Entered	19901204	Replaced	20031210		
Type	t	ELvl	I	Srce	d	Audn	Ctrl	Lang	eng
BLvl	m	Form	b	Conf	0	Biog	MRec	Ctry	xx
		Cont	bm	GPub		LitF	0	Indx	0
Desc	a	Ills		Fest	0	DtSt	s	Dates	1987,

007		h $b e $d a $e m $f b--- $g b $h u $i c $j u
040		SUC $c SUC $d OCL $d OCLCQ
090		Z682.4.W65 $b .B38 1987
100	1_	Baum, Christina D.
245	14	The impact of feminist thought on American librarianship, 1965-1985 $h [microform] / $c by Christina D. Baum.
260		$c 1987.
300		x, 255 leaves ; $c 28 cm.
500		Typescript.
502		Thesis (Ed.D.)--University of Kentucky, 1987.
504		Includes bibliographical references (leaves 245-254).
533		Microfiche. $b Ann Arbor, Mich. : $c University Microfilms International, $d 1987. $e 3 microfiches (276 fr.) ; 11 x 15 cm. "87-15914."
539		s $b 1987 $d xx $e n
650	_0	Library science $z United States $x History.
650	_0	Women in library science $z United States $x History.
650	_0	Feminism $z United States $x History.

Fig. 4.70. *AACR2R* description of the print serial shown in figures
4.35–4.36.

Journal of Internet cataloging. — Vol. 1, no. 1 (1997)–   . —
Binghamton, NY : Haworth Press, 1997-
    v. ; 25 cm.

Quarterly.
Title from cover.
Vol. 1 published over three years, 1997-1999.
Table of contents and abstracts from this journal can be found at
the JIC home page.
Also available via World Wide Web; OCLC FirstSearch
Electronic Collections Online; Subscription required for access
to abstracts and full text.
    ISSN 1091-1367 = Journal of Internet cataloging

Fig. 4.71. MARC record for the print serial. (Source: OCLC Connexion, WorldCat—record
number 34108984.)

Serials	Rec Stat	c	Entered	19960131	Replaced	20031115		
Type a	ELvl		Srce	d	GPub	Ctrl	Lang	eng
BLvl s	Form		Conf	0	Freq q	MRec	Ctry	nyu
S/L 0	Orig		EntW		Regl r	ISSN 1	Alph	a
Desc a	SrTp	p	Cont		DtSt c	Dates 1997,9999		

010		97-655064 $z sn96-4762
040		UOK $c UOK $d NSD $d DLC $d NYG $d AGL $d HLS $d EYM $d DLC $d IUL $d CAS $d HVL $d OCL $d AGL $d NLM $d OCLCQ
012		$i 9711 $k 1 $l 1
016	7_	9891000 $2 DNLM
016	7_	SR0089583 $2 DNLM
022	0_	1091-1367
030		JICTFP
037		$b Haworth Press, 10 Alice Street, Binghamton, N.Y. 13904-1580
042		nsdp $a lc
043		n-us---
050	00	Z695.24 $b .J68
070	0_	Z695.615 $b .J68
072	_0	X200
082	00	025.3/44 $2 21
210	0_	J. Internet cat.
222	_0	Journal of Internet cataloging
245	00	Journal of Internet cataloging.
260		Binghamton, NY : $b Haworth Press, $c 1997-
300		v. ; $c 25 cm.
310		Quarterly.
362	0_	Vol. 1, no. 1 (1997)-
500		Title from cover.

(continued)

Fig. 4.71. (Cont.)

515		Vol. 1 published over three years, 1997-1999.
530		Table of contents and abstracts from this journal can be found at the JIC home page.
530		Also available via World Wide Web; $b OCLC FirstSearch Electronic Collections Online; $c Subscription required for access to abstracts and full text.
650	_0	Cataloging of computer network resources $v Periodicals.
650	_0	Cataloging of computer network resources $z United States $v Periodicals.
776	1_	$t Journal of Internet cataloging (Online) $w (OCoLC)48388826
850		DLC $a DNAL $a InU $a MiU $a N
856	4_	$u http://firstsearch.oclc.org $z Address for accessing the journal using authorization number and password through OCLC FirstSearch Electronic Collections Online. Subscription to online journal required for access to abstracts and full text
856	4_	$u http://firstsearch.oclc.org/journal=1091-1367;screen=info;ECOIP $z Address for accessing the journal from an authorized IP address through OCLC FirstSearch Electronic Collections Online. Subscription to online journal required for access to abstracts and full text
856	41	$3 Table of contents and abstracts $u http://www.haworthpressinc.com/store/product.asp?sku=J141

Fig. 4.72. *AACR2R* **description of the electronic serial shown in figures 4.37–4.38.**

Journal of Buddhist ethics [electronic resource]. — Vol. 1 (1994)–   . — University Park, PA : [s.n.], 1994-

Text (electronic journal).
Mode of access: Electronic mail, FTP, gopher, and World Wide Web. For email subscription, send to: listserv@lists.psu.edu, the message: sub JBE-L [first name last name].
Title from title screen.
ISSN: 1076-9005 = Journal of Buddhist ethics

Fig. 4.73. MARC record for the electronic serial. (Source: OCLC Connexion, WorldCat—record number 30635286.)

Serials	Rec Stat	c	Entered	19940621	Replaced	20031101			
Type	a	ELvl		Srce	d	GPub		Ctrl		Lang	eng
BLvl	s	Form	s	Conf	0	Freq	u	MRec		Ctry	pau
S/L	0	Orig		EntW		Regl	u	ISSN	1	Alph	a
Desc	a	SrTp		Cont		DtSt	c	Dates	1994,9999		

007		c $b r $d c $e n $f u
010		sn94-2649
040		NSD $c NSD $d EYM $d OCL $d UMC $d NSD $d N@F $d OCLCQ
012		$j 0 $k 1 $l 1
022	0_	1076-9005
037		$b Journal of Buddhist ethics, c/o Charles S. Prebish, Pennsylvania State University, Religious Studies Program, University Park, PA 16802-5500 $c Free
042		nsdp $a lcd7
082	10	181 Oriental philosophy $2 12
090		BQ2
210	0_	J. Buddh. ethics
222	_0	Journal of Buddhist ethics
245	00	Journal of Buddhist ethics $h [electronic resource].
246	13	JBE
246	3_	JBE-L
260		University Park, PA : $b [s.n.], $c 1994-
362	0_	Vol. 1 (1994)-
516	8_	Text (electronic journal).
538		Mode of access: Electronic mail, FTP, gopher, and World Wide Web. For email subscription, send to: listserv@lists.psu.edu, the message: sub JBE-L [first name last name].
500		Title from title screen.
650	_0	Buddhist ethics $v Periodicals.
856	0_	lists.psu.edu $f JBE-L $h listserv $i sub $z Internet email subscription
856	1_	ftp.cac.psu.edu $d /pub/jbe $l anonymous $n Pennsylvania State University
856	1_	scorpio.gold.ac.uk $d /pub/jbe $l anonymous $n University of London (Goldsmiths College)
856	7_	ftp.cac.psu.edu $p 70 $2 gopher
856	7_	scorpio.gold.ac.uk $p 70 $2 gopher
856	4_	$u http://jbe.la.psu.edu/
856	4_	$u http://scorpio.gold.ac.uk/jbe/jbe.html

NOTES

1. *Anglo-American Cataloguing Rules, Second Edition, 2002 Revision,* prepared under the direction of the Joint Steering Committee for Revision of AACR (Chicago: American Library Association, 2002), p. 21-26.

2. *MARC 21 Format for Bibliographic Data: Including Guidelines for Content Designation* (Washington, D.C.: Cataloging Distribution Service, Library of Congress, 1999). 2v.; *MARC 21 Concise Format for Bibliographic Data,* 2004 Concise Edition, available: http://lcweb. loc.gov/marc/bibliographic/ecbdhome.html (accessed 2/14/2006).

3. *AACR2R2002,* p. I-2.

4. *AACR2R2002,* p. D-7.

5. Jean Hirons and Crystal Graham, "Issues Related to Seriality." In *The Principles and Future of AACR: Proceedings of the International Conference on the Principles and Future Development of AACR,* edited by Jean Weihs (Chicago: American Library Association, 1998), pp. 180–213.

6. *AACR2R2002,* p. D-2.

7. *AACR2R2002,* p. D-4.

8. Adele Hallam, *Cataloging Rules for the Description of Looseleaf Publications, with Special Emphasis on Legal Materials,* 2nd ed. (Washington, D.C.: Office for Descriptive Cataloging [Policy], Library of Congress, 1989).

9. *Cataloging Service Bulletin,* no. 1– (Washington, D.C.: Processing Services, Library of Congress, 1978–).

10. *RDA – Resource Description and Access: A Prospectus,* Joint Steering Committee for Revision of AACR. Available: http://www.collectionscanada.ca/jsc/rdaprospectus.html or http://www.collectionscanada.ca/jsc/docs/5rda-prospectusrev.pdf (accessed 2/25/2006).

11. *RDA – Resource Description and Access,* Joint Steering Committee for Revision of the Anglo-American Cataloguing Rules. Available: http://www.collectionscanada.ca/jsc/ rda.html (accessed 2/25/2006).

12. *Library of Congress Rule Interpretations,* 2nd ed. (Washington, D.C.: Cataloging Distribution Service, Library of Congress, 1990–), looseleaf, with updates.

13. *Library of Congress Rule Interpretations for AACR 2, 1988 Revision: Updated Through Cataloging Service Bulletin Number . . . ,* compiled with quarterly looseleaf supplements by Alan Boyd and Elaine Druesdow (Oberlin, Ohio: Oberlin College Library, 2000–).

14. A discussion of these problems in relation to *AACR2* may be found in Michael Gorman, "Cataloging and Classification of Film Study Material," in *Film Study Collections,* ed. Nancy Allen (New York: F. Ungar Publishing, 1979), pp. 113–123.

15. American Library Association, Committee on Cataloging: Description and Access, *Guidelines for Using AACR2 Chapter 9 for Cataloging Microcomputer Software* (Chicago: American Library Association, 1984).

16. *Anglo-American Cataloguing Rules, Second Edition, Chapter 9, Computer Files*, edited for the Joint Steering Committee for Revision of AACR2 by Michael Gorman, draft revision (Chicago: American Library Association, 1987).

17. Janet Swan Hill, "Descriptions of Reproductions of Previously Existing Works: Another View," *Microform Review* 11 (Winter 1982): 14–21; and Nancy R. John, "Microforms," *Journal of Library Administration* 3 (Spring 1982): 3–8.

18. *Cataloging Service Bulletin*, no. 14 (Fall 1981): 56–58; a revised version is in *Cataloging Service Bulletin*, no. 81 (Summer 1998): 20–21.

19. *Functional Requirements for Bibliographic Records, Final Report*, IFLA Study Group on the Functional Requirements for Bibliographic Records (München: K.G. Saur, 1998); also available: http://www.ifla.org/VII/s13/frbr/frbr.htm or http://www.ifla.org/VII/s13/frbr/frbr.pdf (accessed 2/14/2006).

20. IFLA Cataloguing Section, *FRBR Review Group* (*Functional Requirements for Bibliographic Records*), available: http://www.ifla.org/ VII/s13/wgfrbr/wgfrbr.htm (accessed 2/25/2006).

21. *Union List of Serials in Libraries of the United States and Canada*, 3rd ed. (New York: H. W. Wilson, 1965); coverage through 1949. *New Serial Titles: A Union List of Serials Commencing Publication After December 31, 1949* (Washington, D.C.: Library of Congress, 1953–1999); *Standard Periodical Directory* (New York: Oxbridge Communications, 1964/1965–); *Ulrich's Periodicals Directory* (New York: Bowker, 2000–); *British Union Catalogue of Periodicals* (London: Butterworths, 1955–1958); *British Union Catalogue of Periodicals. New Periodical Titles* (London: Butterworths, 1964–1980); *Serials in the British Library* (London: British Library, Bibliographic Services Division, 1981–).

22. Eleanora A. Baer, *Titles in Series: A Handbook for Librarians and Students*, 3rd ed. (Metuchen, N.J.: Scarecrow Press, 1978); *Books in Series in the United States* (New York: Bowker, 1977–1979); *Books in Series* (New York: Bowker, 1980–1989).

23. *Library of Congress Catalogs: Monographic Series* (Washington, D.C.: Library of Congress, 1974–1982); *National Union Catalog. Books* (Washington, D.C.: Library of Congress, 1983–).

24. Bohdan S. Wynar and Arlene G. Taylor, *Introduction to Cataloging and Classification*, 8th ed. (Englewood, Colo.: Libraries Unlimited, 1992), Appendix B, pp. 558–571; also available: http://www.pitt.edu/~agtaylor/articles/ICC8-appendixB.pdf (accessed 2/13/2006).

25. *AACR2R2002*, p. D-6.

26. *AACR2R2002*, p. D-2.

27. "AACR 2 Options Proposed by the Library of Congress: Chapters 2–11," *Library of Congress Information Bulletin* 38 (August 10, 1979): 316.

28. *AACR2R2002*, p. D-7.

29. *AACR2R2002*, p. D-8.

30. Richard P. Smiraglia, *Cataloging Music: A Manual for Use with AACR2*, 2nd ed. (Lake Crystal, Minn.: Soldier Creek Press, 1986), p. 29.

SUGGESTED READING

Andrew, Paige G., and Mary Lynette Larsgaard, eds. *Maps and Related Cartographic Materials Cataloging, Classification, and Bibliographic Control.* New York: Haworth Information Press, 1999.

Association for Library Collections and Technical Services, Cataloging and Classification Section, Committee on Cataloging: Description and Access, Task Force on an Appendix of Major and Minor Changes. *Differences Between, Changes Within: Guidelines on When to Create a New Record.* April 2003. Available: http://www.libraries.psu.edu/tas/jca/ccda/docs/tf-appx10.doc (accessed 2/26/2006).

Betz, Elizabeth W., comp. *Graphic Materials: Rules for Describing Original Items and Historical Collections.* Washington, D.C.: Library of Congress, 1996. Available: http://www.itsmarc.com/crs/grph0199.htm (accessed 2/26/2006).

Chan, Lois Mai. *Cataloging and Classification: An Introduction.* 2nd ed. New York: McGraw-Hill, 1994. Chapters 1–3.

Describing Archives: A Content Standard. Chicago: The Society of American Archivists, 2004.

Ferguson, Bobby. *Cataloging Nonprint Materials: Blitz Cataloging Workbook.* Englewood, Colo.: Libraries Unlimited, 1999.

————. *MARC/AACR2/Authority Control Tagging: Blitz Cataloging Workbook.* 2nd ed. Westport, Conn.: Libraries Unlimited, 2005.

Fritz, Deborah A. *Cataloging with AACR2R and MARC21, for Books, Electronic Resources, Sound Recordings, Video Recordings, and Serials.* 2nd ed. Chicago: American Library Association, 2004.

Frost, Carolyn O. *Media Access and Organization: A Cataloging and Reference Sources Guide for Nonbook Materials.* Englewood, Colo.: Libraries Unlimited, 1989.

Functional Requirements for Bibliographic Records, Final Report. IFLA Study Group on the Functional Requirements for Bibliographic Records. München: K.G. Saur, 1998. Also available: http://www.ifla.org/VII/s13/frbr/frbr.htm or http://www.ifla.org/VII/s13/frbr/frbr.pdf (accessed 2/14/2006).

Gamble, Betsy, ed. *Music Cataloging Decisions: As Issued by the Music Section, Special Materials Cataloging Division, Library of Congress in the Music Cataloging Bulletin, Through December 1991.* Canton, Mass.: Music Library Association, 1992.

Geer, Beverley, and Beatrice L. Caraway. *Notes for Serials Cataloging.* 2nd ed. Englewood, Colo.: Libraries Unlimited, 1998.

Hagler, Ronald. *The Bibliographic Record and Information Technology.* 3rd ed. Chicago: American Library Association, 1997. Chapter 2.

Hensen, Steven L. *Archives, Personal Papers, and Manuscripts: A Cataloging Manual for Archival Repositories, Historical Societies, and Manuscript Libraries.* 2nd ed. Chicago: Society of American Archivists, 1989.

Hill, Janet Swan. "Descriptions of Reproductions of Previously Existing Works: Another View." *Microform Review* 11 (Winter 1982): 14–21.

Hirons, Jean L., ed. *CONSER Cataloging Manual.* 2002 ed. Washington, D.C.: Cataloging Distribution Service, Library of Congress, 2002– . Looseleaf, with updates.

Intner, Sheila S., and Richard P. Smiraglia, eds. *Policy and Practice in Bibliographic Control of Nonbook Media.* Chicago: American Library Association, 1987, pp. 103–181.

John, Nancy R. "Microforms." *Journal of Library Administration* 3 (Spring 1982): 3–8.

Library of Congress, Program for Cooperative Cataloging, Standing Committee on Training. *Integrating Resources: A Cataloging Manual.* 2005 revision. Available: http://www. loc.gov/catdir/pcc/bibco/irman.pdf (accessed 2/14/2006).

Liheng, Carol, and Winnie S. Chan. *Serials Cataloging Handbook: An Illustrative Guide to the Use of AACR2R and LC Rule Interpretations.* 2nd ed. Chicago: American Library Association, 1998.

Mangan, Elizabeth U., ed. *Cartographic Materials: A Manual of Interpretation for AACR2, 2002 Revision.* Chicago: American Library Association, 2003.

Maxwell, Robert L. *Maxwell's Handbook for AACR2R: Explaining and Illustrating the* Anglo-American Cataloguing Rules *through the 2003 Update.* 4th ed. Chicago: American Library Association, 2004.

Olson Nancy B. *Cataloging of Audiovisual Materials and Other Special Materials: A Manual Based on AACR 2.* 4th ed. Edited by Sheila S. Intner and Edward Swanson. DeKalb, Ill.: Minnesota Scholarly Press, 1998.

Online Audiovisual Catalogers, Inc., Cataloging Policy Committee, DVD Cataloging Task Force. *Guide to Cataloging DVDs Using AACR2r Chapters 7 and 9.* 15 October 2002. Available: http://ublib.buffalo.edu/libraries/units/cts/olac/capc/dvd/dvdprimer0.html or http://ublib.buffalo.edu/libraries/units/cts/olac/capc/dvd/dvdprimer.pdf (accessed 2/14/2006).

Sandberg-Fox, Ann, and John D. Byrum. "From ISBD(CF) to ISBD(ER): Process, Policy, and Provisions." *Library Resources and Technical Services* 42 (April 1998): 89–101.

Saye, Jerry D., and Sherry L. Vellucci. *Notes in the Catalog Record Based on AACR2 and LC Rule Interpretations.* Chicago: American Library Association, 1989.

Smiraglia, Richard P. *Cataloging Music: A Manual for Use with AACR2.* 2nd ed. Lake Crystal, Minn.: Soldier Creek Press, 1986.

———. *Music Cataloging: The Bibliographic Control of Printed and Recorded Music in Libraries.* Englewood, Colo.: Libraries Unlimited, 1989. Chapters 2 and 3.

Weihs, Jean, ed. *The Principles and Future of AACR: Proceedings of the International Conference on the Principles and Future Development of AACR.* Chicago: American Library Association, 1998.

Weihs, Jean, with Shirley Lewis. *Nonbook Materials: The Organization of Integrated Collections.* 3rd ed. Ottawa: Canadian Library Association, 1989.

5 Description of Analytical Materials

INTRODUCTION

Whether or not to describe parts of a work is an ever-present problem in cataloging. When does a part of a larger work deserve description of its own? When such description is warranted, how is it accomplished in relation to the larger work? These are questions addressed by *Anglo-American Cataloguing Rules, Second Edition,* Chapter 13, "Analysis." As in the preceding chapter specific citations to the 2002 print edition with its 2003–2005 updates are referred to as *AACR2R2002*, but the work with its additions and changes is referred to as *AACR2R*.

In the Glossary of *AACR2R2002*, "analytical entry" is defined as "an entry for a part of an item for which a comprehensive entry is also made."[1] "Analytical note" is defined as "the statement in an analytical entry relating the part being analyzed to the item of which it is a part."[2] Analytical entries vary from complete bibliographic descriptions to simple added entries for parts mentioned in the description of the larger work. Obviously, preparing additional entries requires time. Usually, the decision in this matter depends on the administrative policy of an individual library and the local needs. In deciding whether analytical entries are needed, certain general situations may be taken into consideration:

- The availability of printed indexes, bibliographies, and abstracting services that will locate the material to be analyzed.

- The availability of analytics from the Library of Congress (LC) or other sources.

- The quantity and quality of material on the given subject already in the catalog.

- The quantity of material by the same creators already in the catalog. The best example in this category is provided by the library's policy regarding books in sets that usually represent various types of collections or compilations of one or more authors—e.g., *Harvard Classics* or *Harvard Shelf of Fiction*. If the library has little material by an author, the need for analytics may be greater.

- The significance of the parts to be analyzed for a given library (e.g., parts written by local noted authors, performed by local musicians, produced by locally born actors, etc.).

- The significance of the parts in a given work.

In addition, the rules in *AACR2R* give some guidance in deciding when and how analysis should be accomplished.

A basic descriptive question that must be answered before making the decision to analyze a multipart information package, and one for which there is no guidance in *AACR2R*, is: What is to be considered a multipart information package rather than two or more separate packages for cataloging purposes?

A publication issued in two or more volumes may be defined as a set. Usually, monographs in collected sets represent various types of collections or compilations by one or more authors. Many reference books are examples of monographs in collected sets. The number of physical volumes making up such a set may cause problems in cataloging and classification. If the works of a single author are collected in several volumes, the cataloger may be tempted to classify each volume separately. On the other hand, the cataloger may only have one volume of a multi-volume set to catalog and may consider classifying it as if the library had the entire set. Although both of these approaches are arguable, the fact remains that neither is really right or wrong. There are no established codes for cataloging and classifying individual titles of information packages that come in sets. The approaches presented below are provided merely for the consideration of the cataloger; they are not meant to be followed slavishly.

One usually catalogs and classifies a set of information packages together if:

- They are issued in a uniform format

- The individual items are numbered in consecutive order

- There is a general index to the entire set

Two additional criteria are:

- If patrons are likely to expect to find the information packages together as a set

- If there is a possibility that supplements and/or additional numbers will appear at a later date

However, one usually catalogs and classifies a set of information packages separately if:

- Not all the items of the set are in the library, nor are likely to be added to the library's collection

- Each item has a separate title, especially in the case of literary works

Obviously, these two sets of approaches are somewhat contradictory and demand individual application in actual practice. The following examples are designed to clarify these problems. First, it should be quite obvious that a set of books comprising an encyclopedia should be cataloged and classified together. An encyclopedia is uniform in format; the individual volumes are consecutively numbered; there is usually a general index to the entire encyclopedia; patrons do expect to find these books together as a set; and supplements and/or yearbooks often appear at a later date. Second, it similarly follows that a set of monographs that is a collection of great works (such as the *Harvard Classics* or the *Great Books of the Western World*) should be both cataloged and classified together. In these examples, however, individual items have one or more separate titles. Should individual items in such a set (both of which, for example, include the plays of William Shakespeare) be classified with other collections of Shakespeare's plays or not? Either choice will create some problems. It is unwise in either case to try to avoid a record in the catalog for each separate bibliographical unit. The catalog may be the only key the patron uses for discovering the library's holdings. Analysis is one method of solving this particular problem. The use of analytical entries under rules 13.5A and 13.6, as described below, allows these sets of monographs to be cataloged and classified together while also providing separate entries for individual bibliographical units.

The collected or complete works of one author present another problem of titles in sets. For example, Winston Churchill's *A History of the English-speaking Peoples* may be cataloged together or separately. If this work is cataloged together as a set, the individual parts or volumes are listed in a contents note, and the set receives general subject added entries and a general subject classification number (*see* figure 5.1). On the other hand, if each of the parts of this work is cataloged separately, the relationship of each part to the main work is shown by a series note. This latter approach allows for a complete publication area, including the date, for each part, and for separate specific subject added entries (*see* figure 5.2). Cataloging each part separately allows the cataloger to choose whether to classify each part separately or in the more general number. The classification problems of collected sets versus cataloging as monographs are dealt with in chapter 14 of this textbook.

Fig. 5.1. Churchill's *History of the English-speaking Peoples* cataloged as a set using a contents note for the individual bibliographical units and having a general subject heading.

Churchill, Winston, Sir, 1874-1965.
    A history of the English-speaking peoples / Winston S. Churchill.
— Toronto : McClelland and Stewart, 1988, c1956.
    4 v. : ill., maps, geneal. tables ; 22 cm.

    Includes bibliographical references and index.
    Contents: v. 1. The birth of Britain — v. 2. The new world — v. 3. The age of revolution — v. 4. The great democracies.
    ISBN: 0-8103-4573-0.

Subject heading:
    Great Britain—History.

**Fig. 5.2. One part of Churchill's work cataloged as a separate bibliograph-
ical unit using a series note to relate to the collected set and having specific
subject headings.**

Churchill, Winston, Sir, 1874-1965.
    The age of revolution / Winston S. Churchill. — Toronto :
McClelland and Stewart, 1988, c1956.
    xi, 395 p. : ill., maps ; 22 cm. — (A history of the Eng-
lish-speaking peoples / Winston S. Churchill ; v. 3)

    Includes bibliographical references and index.

Added entry made for the series:
Churchill, Winston, Sir, 1874-1965. A history of the English-speaking peoples ; v. 3.

Subject headings:
Great Britain—History—1689-1714.
Great Britain—History—18th century.

The nature of many World Wide Web sites, where an agency's home page
serves as a gateway to a number of documents or other resources maintained by the
same agency, presents another situation calling for decision making. Should one
catalog the home page alone, representing the resource at the highest level of ab-
straction? If so, should a contents note be provided (keeping in mind that websites of
this sort typically expand or alter their content)? If analytic records are provided for
individual documents, will this be in addition to, or in place of, a general record for
the site? As with the other cases examined here, the answers to these questions will
depend on the nature of the resource, the collection for which it is being cataloged,
and the needs of the library's constituency.

Figure 5.3 shows an *AACR2R* description for one of the resources found at
LC's American Memory website. The description for the entire site is shown at figure 4.60 (page 165).

**Fig. 5.3. Resource linked to the Library of Congress's American Memory
site, cataloged as a separate bibliographical unit, using an added title entry
to relate to the larger site. Specific subject headings would also be created.**

America from the Great Depression to World War II [electronic
resource] : photographs from the FSA-OWI, 1935-1945 / Prints and
Photographs Division, Library of Congress. — [Washington, D.C.] :
Library of Congress, [1998-]

    Mode of access: World Wide Web. Access: http://memory.
loc.gov/ammem/fsowhome.html
    Title from title screen (viewed on March 11, 2005).
    HTML source title: Documenting America.
    Part of the American Memory World Wide Web site, compiled
by the National Digital Library Program of the Library of Congress.
    Summary: Photographs from the Farm Security Administration-
Office of War Information Collection, created by a group of U.S.
government photographers. Subjects include rural life and the

negative impact of the Great Depression, farm mechanization, the Dust Bowl, and the later mobilization effort for World War II. The collection consists of about 164,000 black-and-white photographs. The initial online release includes approximately 45,000 of these images, with more to be added.

Added entry made for the larger site:
American memory.

SELECTED RULES AND EXAMPLES

RULE 13.1.   SCOPE
The scope of the analysis chapter in *AACR2R* is to give instructions for describing a part or parts of a larger information package. Various methods are suggested for doing this. Some of the suggestions here are also referred to in other chapters, but the point of this chapter is to gather together all the methods and to give suggestions for choosing one over another.

RULE 13.2.   ANALYTICAL ADDED ENTRIES
When the title of a part appears either in the title and statement of responsibility area or in the note area of the bibliographic record for a more comprehensive work, an added entry may be made to provide direct access to the part without having to make a separate bibliographic record for the part. Such an added entry is composed of the main entry heading and title, if title is not main entry. The title used is the uniform title if there is one, otherwise it is the title proper. *See* figure 5.4.

Fig. 5.4. Rule 13.2. Record for a comprehensive work with analytical added entry made for the second part.

Mozart, Wolfgang Amadeus, 1756-1791.
    [Symphonies, K. 543, E^b major]
    Symphony no. 39 in E flat, K. 543 [sound recording]. / Wolfgang Amadeus Mozart. Symphony no. 2 in D, op. 36 / Ludwig van Beethoven. — [Netherlands] : Philips, p1989.
    1 sound disc (64 min.) : digital, stereo. ; 4¾ in. — (Digital classics)

    Philips: 422 389-2.
    Orchestra of the 18th century (on period instruments) ; Frans Bruggen, conductor.
    Recorded June 1988, Concertgebouw, Amsterdam.
    Compact disc.
    Durations: 32:00 ; 32:00.

Analytical added entry:
Beethoven, Ludwig van, 1770-1827. Symphonies, no. 2, op. 36, D major. 1989.

RULE 13.3.   ANALYSIS OF MONOGRAPHIC SERIES AND MULTIPART MONOGRAPHS

The suggested criterion for deciding to describe a part of a monographic series or a multipart monograph independently concerns title. If the title of the part is not dependent on the title of the whole, a complete description of the part may be created, giving the title (and statement of responsibility, if applicable) of the whole set in the series area. The volume number of the part is also given in the series area. *See* figure 5.5.

Fig. 5.5. Rule 13.3. Complete independent description of a monographic title with the title of the comprehensive series given in the series area.

Austrian fiction writers after 1914 / edited by James Hardin and Donald G. Daviau. — Detroit, Mich. : Gale Research, c1989.

xi, 394 p. : ill., 29 cm. — (Dictionary of literary biography ; v. 85)

Includes bibliographical references.
ISBN: 0-8103-4563-3.

Added entry made for the comprehensive title:
Dictionary of literary biography ; v. 85.

Rule 13.3 does not go on to say what one should do if the title of an individual part is dependent on the comprehensive title or if there is no individual title. The implication is that such works would not be described separately. However, when such items appear as parts of series that are analyzed in full or that are classified separately, a separate record is necessary. An LC rule interpretation gives rules and examples for handling such situations; it should be consulted when needed. (*CSB* 109: 20–23) Its basic idea is that the comprehensive title becomes part of the title proper, no series statement is given, and an explicitly traced series added entry is made.

RULE 13.4.   NOTE AREA

If it is decided to describe the comprehensive work as a set, individual parts may be named in a contents note. This method was shown in figure 5.1 (page 181).

RULE 13.5.   "IN" ANALYTICS

Another possible way to describe a part is to provide an "In" analytic record. This is useful when one wishes to provide more information than can be given in the note area of the record for the set.

LC makes "In" analytics only in very special cases. (*CSB* 44: 36)

13.5A.   An "In" analytic shows first a description of the part. This is followed by a short description of the comprehensive work.

The description of the part contains all the elements of the eight areas of description that apply to the part. When appropriate, data for extent and specific material designation will be given to describe the physical position of the item within the whole information package.

The description of the whole information package begins with the word *In*, emphasized in a manner appropriate to the medium of the catalog. For printed catalogs, this may be accomplished through underlining or italicizing; Web-based catalogs may have other options available for display. *In* is followed by the name and/or uniform title heading (if appropriate); title proper; statement(s) of responsibility necessary for identification; edition statement; and numeric or other designation (if a serial) or publication details (if a monographic item). *See* figures 5.6 and 5.7.

Fig. 5.6. Rule 13.5A. "In" analytic where the part is contained in a monographic item.

The crisis in cataloging / Andrew D. Osborn. — p. 90-103 ; 25 cm.
In Foundations of cataloging / edited by Michael Carpenter and Elaine Svenonius. — Littleton, Colo. : Libraries Unlimited, 1985.

Fig. 5.7. Rule 13.5A. "In" analytic where the part is contained in a serial item.

Uniform titles for music : an exercise in collocation / Richard P. Smiraglia. — p. 97-114 ; 22 cm.
In Cataloging & classification quarterly. — Vol. 9, no. 3 (Spring 1989)

RULE 13.6. MULTILEVEL DESCRIPTION

An alternative to "In" analytic records is a technique called multilevel description. It is useful when one wishes to provide complete identification of both part and whole in a single record.

The first level of descriptive information shows the description of the whole manifestation of the work. The second level contains description (not repeating information given at the first level) of an individual part or groups of parts. If the second level describes a group of parts, then a third level may describe an individual part. *See* figure 5.8.

Fig. 5.8. Rule 13.6. Multilevel description showing three levels from most to least comprehensive.

The Library of America. — New York, N.Y. : Literary Classics of the U.S. : Distributed to the trade in the U.S. and Canada by Viking Press, 1982-   .   —   v. : 21 cm.

Vols. 26-27 : [Selections. 1985]. The leatherstocking tales / James Fenimore Cooper ; [edited by] Blake Nevius. — c1985.

The last of the Mohicans : a narrative of 1757. — vol. 26, p. 467-878.

LC does not use the technique of multilevel description. (*CSB* 11: 17) However, as rules are revised to include the concepts of relationships as expressed in *Functional Requirements for Bibliographic Records* (*FRBR*), better ways of displaying these multilevel relationships may be found.[3]

NOTES

1. *Anglo-American Cataloguing Rules, Second Edition, 2002 Revision*, prepared under the direction of the Joint Steering Committee for Revision of AACR (Chicago: American Library Association, 2002), p. D-1.

2. Ibid.

3. *Functional Requirements for Bibliographic Records, Final Report*, IFLA Study Group on the Functional Requirements for Bibliographic Records (München: K.G. Saur, 1998); also available: http://www.ifla.org/VII/s13/frbr/frbr.htm or http://www.ifla.org/VII/s13/frbr/frbr.pdf (accessed 2/14/2006).

SUGGESTED READING

Hagler, Ronald. *The Bibliographic Record and Information Technology*. 3rd ed. Chicago: American Library Association, 1997, pp. 332–347.

Maxwell, Robert L. *Maxwell's Handbook for AACR2R: Explaining and Illustrating the* Anglo-American Cataloguing Rules *through the 2003 Update*. 4th ed. Chicago: American Library Association, 2004.

O'Neil, Rosanna M. "Analysis and 'In' Analytics." *Serials Review* 13, no. 2 (Summer 1987): 57–63.

Choice of
Access Points

INTRODUCTION

The rules in *Anglo-American Cataloguing Rules, Second Edition*, Chapter 21, deal with the choice of access points and not the form of entry. As in chapters 4 and 5 of this text, specific citations to the 2002 print edition with its 2003–2005 updates are referred to as *AACR2R2002*, but the work with its additions and changes is referred to as *AACR2R*. Choice *of access points* means choosing all names and titles under which the description of an information package may be sought by a user. (Subject headings are also chosen as access points, but the only subjects affected by *AACR2R* are names and titles used as subjects. *See* chapters 9–18 for discussions of subject access.)

For any one item, one of the access points is chosen as a main entry, or primary access point, and the others become added entries. Originally this choice was necessary, in part, so that there could be one place in a printed catalog where all information about a work or item could be found, while other entries for the item in that catalog could be much shorter. Eventually, when *unit cards* (i.e., every card in a card set contained identical information) became standard, this need for a main entry became obsolete. And with MAchine-Readable Cataloging (MARC) records, where there is only one master record stored in a catalog, there is no need for the concept of main entry as a place to put all information. However, the main entry *heading* is also frequently used as a secondary filing element (e.g., all items under the subject heading "Psychology" are subarranged by main entry heading). In the introduction to *AACR2R2002* there is a recognition that designation of one entry as "main" may not be considered important in some libraries.[1] There is lack of agreement on this point in the cataloging community.[2]

Proponents of the main entry concept assert that one of the major outcomes of cataloging is to identify the works embodied in the information packages cataloged. This can only be done, they believe, by using one consistent means for citing any given work. This, in turn, can only be done by adhering to a set of rules for choosing the main access point and then using this access point, or main entry heading, in conjunction with other necessary elements to form a unit that identifies the work (e.g., if the main entry is the first of two authors, that name is combined with the title to form a unit that identifies the work). The unit thus formed is often referred to as the *uniform title*, although this can be misleading, since the term "uniform title" is also used to refer to a standardized title for a work that may have variant titles or that may have only a generic title. In any case, the unit formed to identify the work is used to collocate all editions, translations, criticisms, etc., of that work that may appear.

The introduction to *AACR2R2002* points out that it is necessary to distinguish the main entry from the others when one is creating a listing in which each record will be given only once, or in any other situation when one must make a single citation for a work.[3] The latter situation occurs, for example, when a related work needs to be cited on the bibliographic record for the work to which it is related, or when one work is the subject of another. *AACR2R* also points out that the concept of main entry is useful in creating uniform titles to draw those related works together. At one time it was thought that related works were probably a small proportion of all works, and therefore a great deal of time was being spent choosing main entries for many works that would never have editions, translations, etc. However, research indicates that nearly half of all information packages cataloged contain manifestations of works that are related to other works. The percentage may be as high as 75% for items held by general academic libraries, and even higher for collections of musical scores.[4]

Proponents of the idea that all access points for an information package are basically equal question the need to designate one access point as primary. They say that in most catalogs all access points are equally accessible; in online systems, the main entry is not necessarily used to subarrange records retrieved under other access points (e.g., subarrangement may be by date).

Much has been written about this controversy,[5] and its resolution may not come about without changes in the relationship between the recording of cataloging data and the means by which systems index and display such data. For example, most library systems that use *MARC 21* format, either for online access or for printed products, create the rough equivalent of uniform titles by linking the main entry headings entered in 100–111 fields with title data entered in the 240 or 245 fields. (For information packages given title main entry, a 130, 240, or 245 field is used on its own.) If catalogers no longer designate any entry as "main," the data now entered in the 100–130 fields could be moved to 700–730. This might create little difficulty where an item contains an expression of one and only one work, though for many systems some reprogramming would be necessary. For the many items which contain expressions of more than one work, and with multiple persons or bodies associated with each work, new coding would be needed to link the appropriate 7XX fields to the data entered in the 240 or 245 field. This is particularly, though not exclusively, true for music recordings. The purpose of this discussion is not to provide a detailed analysis of this technical problem, nor to suggest that this is the only aspect of the question, but rather to indicate that the "main entry debate" is not simply of theoretical interest.

In chapter 4 of this text, it was stated that the Joint Steering Committee for the Revision of AACR (JSC) is in the process of thoroughly revising the cataloging code, intended to result in an altogether new edition: *Resource Description and Access (RDA)*. As described in the prospectus produced by the JSC, part II will undergo complete revision to provide guidelines and instructions on reflecting relationships among entities that are listed in the *Functional Requirements for Bibliographic Records (FRBR)*.[6] The following chapters are proposed for *RDA*:

Chapter 7   General guidelines on reflecting relationships

Chapter 8   Access points for persons, families, and corporate bodies associated with the resource

Chapter 9   Citations for related works, etc.

Chapter 10   Special instructions for particular types of works[7]

According to this plan, Chapter 8 will "provide a set of general guidelines and instructions on choosing the primary access point (i.e., the access point used as the initial element in citing a work), as well as other access points. . . ."[8] While the exact outcome of this revision cannot be known as of this writing, it may very well give significant weight to the argument in favor of establishing standard access points for works in their various manifestations. (In addition, the coming revision may remove the so-called "Rule of Three," as discussed in rule 21.6B2 below.)

This chapter covers basic choice of *AACR2R* main entry under personal author, corporate body, and title (rule 21.1). More specific guidance is then given for choice of entry for:

- Works where there have been changes in title proper (rule 21.2) or in persons or bodies responsible for the work (rule 21.3)

- Works of single (including unknown, uncertain, or unspecified) responsibility (rules 21.4–21.5)

- Works of shared responsibility (rule 21.6)

- Collections of works by different persons or bodies (rule 21.7)

- Works of mixed responsibility and modifications of other works (rules 21.8–21.27)

- Works that are related to other works (rule 21.28)

General rules for added entries are given (rules 21.29–21.30), followed by special rules for certain legal and religious publications (rules 21.31–21.39).

The rules covered in this text deal only with basic or general instances; for more complex problems and special cases, the reader should consult *AACR2R*, Chapter 21. Examples in this text show not only the choice of main entry, but also the form of entry and the added entries. The following chapters deal with the rules for these specific forms.

GENERAL RULES:
SELECTED RULES AND EXAMPLES

RULE 21.0.   INTRODUCTORY RULES

21.0B.   Sources for determining access points
Access points for the information package being cataloged are determined from the chief source of information or its substitute (*see* rule 1.0A). Other statements appearing formally in one of the prescribed sources of information should be taken into account, but the emphasis is to be on the chief source of information, making it unnecessary for the cataloger to search in the contents or outside the item for potential access points. A rule interpretation from the Library of Congress (LC) indicates that when information in the prescribed sources is ambiguous, information may be taken from the contents or from outside the item. (*CSB* 45: 19–20)

21.0D. *Optional addition.* Designations of function

This option allows for abbreviated designations of function, such as *ed.* for *editor* and *tr.* for *translator*, to be added to a heading for a person. LC has decided not to apply this option, with two exceptions. The abbreviation *ill.* is added to the headings for illustrators that appear as added entries on bibliographic records in the Annotated Card (AC) Program (i.e., for children's books). Also, such designations are used in archival or specialist cataloging. (*CSB* 104: 23)

RULE 21.1.   GENERAL RULE

21.1A.   Works of personal authorship

Personal author is defined as "the person chiefly responsible for the creation of the intellectual or artistic content of a work."[9] This can include composers, cartographers, photographers, and performers, as well as writers and other creators. The general rule is to enter works by one or more persons under the heading for the personal author according to the specific instructions given in rules 21.4A, 21.5B, 21.6, and 21.8–21.27 and to make added entries as instructed in rules 21.29–21.30. For example, the sound recording entitled "Where the Blue of the Night Meets the Gold of the Day," which includes songs from the original sound tracks of Bing Crosby's early films, would be entered under the heading:

Crosby, Bing, 1904–1977.

There would be an added entry for the title.

21.1B.   Entry under corporate body

A corporate body is defined as "an organization or a group of persons that is identified by a particular name and that acts, or may act, as an entity."[10] Guidelines dictate that a corporate body should be considered to have a name: if the words referring to it are a specific appellation, not just a description; if the initial letters of important words are capitalized; and/or if the words are associated with a definite article. Corporate bodies include, for example, associations, institutions, business firms, governments, conferences, ad hoc events (e.g., exhibitions, festivals), and vessels (e.g., spacecraft).

LC has issued a rule interpretation that gives assistance in determining whether a conference is named. This interpretation should be consulted when needed. (*CSB* 92: 14–15)

21.1B2.   The general rule states that a corporate body may be chosen as main entry if it falls into one or more of six categories:

a.   A work that deals with the body itself, such as a report on finances or operations, or a listing of staff, or a catalog of the body's resources

b.   Certain legal, governmental, or religious types of works listed in this rule with rule numbers to consult for more guidance

c.   Works that deal with official pronouncements that represent the body's position on matters other than those covered in a) above

d.   Works of a *collective* nature that report on activities of conferences, expeditions, or events that can be defined as corporate bodies and whose names appear in the publication

e. Sound recordings, films, videorecordings, or written records of performances in which the responsibility of the group for the existence of the performance is more than a performance or execution of a previously existing script, score, etc. (e.g., improvised jazz or drama)

f. Cartographic materials for which a body does more than merely publish or distribute the materials.

A lengthy LC rule interpretation gives guidance in applying this rule, and should be consulted for more information. The rule interpretation adds a seventh category, "named individual works of art by two or more artists acting as a corporate body" (e.g., General Idea). (*CSB* 94: 13–17) *See* examples below under rule 21.4B.

21.1B3.   If a work falls outside the above categories, the main entry is chosen as if no corporate body were involved, but added entries may be made. Thus, the World Wide Web home page for the Columbus Museum of Art would be entered under the heading "Columbus Museum of Art," and an added entry would be made under the title. However, a monograph entitled "Benue through Pictures" that has been put together in the Information Division of Benue, Nigeria, does not fall under one of the five categories of rule 21.1B2; therefore, the main entry would be under the title, with an added entry under the heading: Benue (Nigeria). Information Division.

21.1C.   Entry under title

Entry under title is prescribed when there is no known personal author, or personal authorship is diffuse (*see* rule 21.6C2), *and* the work is not eligible for entry under corporate body; when the work is a collection of multiple authorship; or when the work is a text that a religious group accepts as sacred scripture.

An LC rule interpretation adds a case for title entry that is not listed in *AACR2R*. It is the situation where a work seems to give technical credit of more than one kind to several persons, and the position and typography of the statement indicates lesser importance in relation to the title. (*CSB* 18: 34–35)

RULE 21.2.   CHANGES IN TITLES PROPER

21.2A.   Multipart monographs

When the title proper of a multipart monograph changes between parts, the title of the first or earliest part is given as the title proper for the whole monograph. Any subsequent title proper is given in a note, and an added entry is made.

21.2B.   Integrating resources

For a change in title proper of an integrating resource, the description is changed to reflect the new title proper. The earlier title is given in a note, and an added entry is made.

21.2C.   Serials

This rule was significantly reconceived for the *AACR2R* revisions of 2002. As previously written, the rule prescribed conditions in which changes in the wording of titles proper were formally considered to be "title changes." These would have been regarded as significant enough to require the creation of new bibliographic records for serials. In the rule as rewritten, all changes in wording of titles proper are taken into account, but are considered to be either "major" or "minor." A major change in the title proper of a serial requires the creation of a new record.

The following changes in title proper are considered major:

a.   The addition, deletion, change of word, or change in order of any of the first five words in the title (six if the title begins with an article), unless the change is otherwise considered to be minor

b.   The addition, deletion, or change of any word after the first five (or six if the title begins with an article) which gives a different meaning to the title or indicates a change in subject matter

c.   A change in corporate body name appearing anywhere in the title, where the corporate body has changed

There are nine conditions in which changes are considered minor:

a.   A different representation of a word or words, such as a change in spelling, change in hyphenation, abbreviation vs. full spelling, etc.

b.   The addition, deletion or change of articles, prepositions, or conjunctions

c.   Differences involving a change in form of the name of the *same* corporate body

d.   An addition, deletion, or change in punctuation

e.   A different order of parallel titles appearing in the chief source, as long as the original title proper would still appear as a parallel title

f.   The addition, deletion, or change of words that link the title with numbering

g.   The alternation of two or more titles proper on different serial issues, provided that the alternation is on a regular pattern

h.   The addition, deletion, or change in order of words in a *list* (consisting of at least three terms), provided that no significant change in subject matter is indicated

i.   The addition, deletion, or rearrangement of words, such as "magazine" or "newsletter," which indicate the type of resource being described

In cases of doubt, changes are to be considered minor, and may be given in a note (cf. rule 1.7B4).

A rule interpretation from LC provides guidelines for the application of this rule to serials, including monographic series, as well as for series-like phrases. (*CSB* 105: 41–42)

RULE 21.3   CHANGES OF PERSONS OR BODIES RESPONSIBLE FOR A WORK

21.3A.   Monographs

Monographs that have been modified by a person or body different from the one responsible for the original edition are to be treated according to rules 21.9–21.23. This means that in some cases, when the nature and/or content has been changed, the main entry will be different from that of the original. Example:

Title main entry for a work whose nature has changed:

> Bambi's fragrant forest : based on the original story by Felix Salten / Walt Disney Productions

Added entries would be made for the person responsible for the original and for the corporate body responsible for modification:

> Salten, Felix, 1869-1945. Bambi.
> Walt Disney Productions.

(If a person had modified the work, main entry would be under the person. The fact that the corporate body is not main entry in this circumstance is explained above under discussion of rule 21.1B2.)

In other cases, when the modification abridges or rearranges, for example, the main entry of the original is used. Example:

Main entry for original author for an abridged work:

> Salten, Felix, 1869-1945.
>   Bambi [sound recording] / abridged by Marianne Mantell.
>   Read by Glynis Johns

Added entries would be made for the person responsible for the modification, for the reader, and for title.

> Mantell, Marianne.
> Johns, Glynis.
> Title: Bambi

21.3B.   Serials and integrating resources

AACR2R gives three conditions under which changes in persons or bodies require a new entry for a *serial*:

a. When the serial has a corporate body main entry and the name of that body changes (e.g., *Financial Report* of the Board of Trustees of the Firemen's Pension Fund, formerly the Firemen's Pension and Relief Fund)

b. When the serial has a corporate body or personal author as main entry, and the person or body is no longer responsible for the serial

c. When the serial's main entry is under a uniform title heading that must be changed, either because a corporate body used as a qualifier changes or because the body is no longer responsible for the serial

An LC rule interpretation adds three other conditions under which a new entry should be made for a serial:

d. When the serial's main entry under a uniform title heading must be changed because the title used in the heading for a translation changes

e. When there is a change in the serial's physical format (as compared with a reproduction in another format). [Note: This circumstance is included in the rule interpretation because a change of uniform title is indicated.]

f. When a change in edition statement signals a change either in subject matter or physical medium. (*CSB* 101: 30–31)

For *integrating resources*, however, these changes do not require a new entry. Instead, following the general principle involved in changes to the description of these resources, the entry is changed to reflect the latest iteration, and the earlier name or form of name is given in a note.

RULE 21.4.   WORKS FOR WHICH A SINGLE PERSON OR CORPORATE BODY IS RESPONSIBLE

21.4A.   Works of single personal authorship (*MARC 21* field 100)

An information package that contains a work or works by one personal author should have the heading for that person as its main entry. Example:

Personal author main entry:

> Bennetts, Pamela.
> > My dear lover England / Pamela Bennetts

Added entry would be made for title:

> My dear lover England

21.4B.   Works emanating from a single corporate body (*MARC 21* field 110 or 111)

An information package that contains a work or works that emanate from one corporate body should have the heading for that body as its main entry if one or more of the categories given under rule 21.1B2 applies. Examples:

Corporate body main entry for a work of single corporate responsibility (21.1B2, type a):

> Al-Anon Family Group Headquarters.
> > World directory of Al-Anon Family Groups and
> Ala-teens

Added entry would be made for title.

> World directory of Al-Anon Family Groups and Ala-teens

A work of single corporate responsibility (21.1B2, type c):

> United States. Congress. House. Select Committee to
> > Investigate Covert Arms Transactions with Iran.
> > Report of the congressional committees investigating the
> Iran-Contra Affair : with the minority views

Added entry would be made for title:

> Report of the congressional committees investigating the Iran-Contra Affair

A work of single corporate responsibility (21.1B2, type d):

> AIAA International Communication Satellite Systems Conference
> > and Exhibit (13th : 1990 : Los Angeles, Calif.)
> > A collection of technical papers : 13th AIAA International
> Communication Satellite Systems Conference and Exhibit, Los
> Angeles, CA, March 11-15, 1990

Added entry would be made for title:

A collection of technical papers

21.4D. Works by heads of state, other high government officials, popes, and other high ecclesiastical officials

21.4D1. Official communications

Two categories of official works are entered under the corporate heading for the official (*see* rules 24.20 and 24.27B):

"a) an official communication from a head of state, head of government, or head of an international body (e.g., a message to a legislature, a proclamation, an executive order other than one covered by 21.31)

b) an official communication from a pope, patriarch, bishop, etc. (e.g., an order, decree, pastoral letter, bull, encyclical, constitution, or an official message to a council, synod, etc.)."[11]

An added entry is made under the personal heading for the person. Example:

Official communication entered under corporate heading:

Maine. Governor (1975-1979 : Longley)
    Budget message address of James B. Longley, Governor of Maine, to the One hundred and seventh Legislature, State of Maine, February 6, 1975

An added entry would be made for the personal heading for the man who was governor in addition to added entries for the legislature and the title:

Longley, James B.
Maine. Legislature.
Title: Budget message address of James B. Longley

21.4D2. Other works

Other works by a government or religious official are given the personal heading for the person as main entry. One explanatory reference is made under the corporate heading rather than making an added entry under the corporate heading for each such work. Example:

Work by a government official entered under personal heading:

Jefferson, Thomas, 1743-1826.
    The portable Thomas Jefferson / edited and with an introduction by Merrill D. Peterson

Added entries would be made for the person responsible for this edition of the work and for title:

Peterson, Merrill D.
Title: The portable Thomas Jefferson

For examples of explanatory references *see* rule 26.2D in chapter 7 of this text.

RULE 21.5.   WORKS OF UNKNOWN OR UNCERTAIN AUTHORSHIP OR BY UNNAMED GROUPS

21.5A.   A work of unknown or uncertain responsibility or one that emanates from a body that lacks a name is entered under its title. Example:

Work of unknown authorship entered under title:

> The old non-conformist, touching the book of common-
> prayer and ceremonies. . . . — London : [s.n.], 1660.

21.5C.   A work is entered under a characterizing word or phrase or under a phrase naming another work by the person, if that is the only clue to authorship and it appears in the chief source of information. For example, the title page of the following work shows only a "characterizing phrase" for the name of the author. The phrase would be used as the main entry:

Work of unknown authorship entered under characterizing phrase:

> One who has tested the receipts.
> The manual of French cookery : dedicated to the housekeepers
> and cooks of England who wish to study the art : simplified for
> the benefit of the most unlearned / by one who has tested the
> receipts

Added entry would be made for title:

> The manual of French cookery

RULE 21.6.   WORKS OF SHARED RESPONSIBILITY

21.6A.   Scope

This rule is used for situations in which two or more persons or corporate bodies have made the same kind of contribution to a work. It also applies when the same kinds of contributions come from one or more persons *and* one or more corporate bodies.

Special types of collaborations are covered by rules on mixed responsibility (rules 21.8–21.27), but when those rules prescribe main entry under the heading for an adapter, for example, and when there is shared responsibility among two or more adapters, then this rule of shared responsibility is applied. This rule does not apply to multipart monographs, where there is a change of responsibility between parts, or to works that are collections of previously existing works; those are covered by rules 21.3A2 and 21.7 respectively.

21.6B.   Principal responsibility indicated

21.6B1.   A work of shared responsibility is entered under the heading for the principal person or body if one is indicated by wording or typography. Added entries are made under the headings for other persons or bodies involved, if there are not more than two. If the principal person or body is not the first named in the chief source of information, an added entry is made for the person or body whose name appears first, regardless of total number of named persons or bodies. Example:

Main entry under principal author:

Haynes, Connie
    Speed, strength, and stamina : conditioning for tennis /
by Connie Haynes, with Eve Kraft and John Conroy ; illustrated
by George Janes

Added entries would be made for subsidiary authors and for title:

Kraft, Eve F.
Conroy, John, 1908-
Title: Speed, strength, and stamina

21.6B2. When the chief source of information indicates that two or three persons or bodies have principal responsibility, main entry is made for the first named of these. Added entries are made under headings for the other principal author(s) and for a collaborator if there are two principal authors and one collaborator (i.e., there may be no more than two added entries for the same kind of contribution).

21.6C. Principal responsibility not indicated

21.6C1. If principal responsibility is not indicated and if there are not more than three names, entry is made under the one that is named first, and added entries are made for the others. Example:

Main entry under first named author when principal author is not
indicated, and there are not more than three authors:

Cheney, Gay.
    Modern dance / Gay Cheney, Janet Strader

Added entries would be made for second named author and for title:

Strader, Janet.
Title: Modern dance.

If different editions of a work have the responsible persons or bodies appearing in a different order in the chief sources of information, each edition is entered under the heading for the person or body named first in that edition.

21.6C2. If principal responsibility is not indicated and there are more than three persons or bodies, the work is entered under the title and an added entry is made for the heading for the person or body named first in the chief source of information. If editors are named prominently and there are not more than three, an added entry is made for each. If there are more than three editors named prominently, an added entry is made for the first named. Example:

Title main entry when principal author is not indicated and there are more than three
authors:

Europe reborn : the story of Renaissance civilization /
contributors, Julian Mates . . . [et al.]

Added entry would be made for the first named author:

Mates, Julian, 1927-

It should be noted that a document produced by the American Library Association's Committee on Cataloging: Description and Access, outlining changes that were being considered for the new edition of AACR, states that the recommendation to reconsider the "Rule of Three" was a trigger toward deciding to do a thorough revision of the chapter having to do with choice of access points.[12] A result may be the elimination of the restriction inherent in this rule.

RULE 21.7.   COLLECTIONS OF WORKS BY DIFFERENT PERSONS OR BODIES

21.7A.   Scope

This rule is used for situations in which contributions by different persons or corporate bodies are brought together:

1. As collections of previously existing, independent works

2. As collections of extracts from such works

3. As combinations of existing independent works and new contributions by different persons or bodies.

One should not apply this rule to works that emanate from a corporate body and fall in the scope of rule 21.1B2 or to papers or proceedings of conferences. For the latter, one should use rule 21.1B2d if the conference, etc., is named in the information package, or rule 21.5A if it is unnamed.

21.7B.   With collective title

Main entry for a work covered by this rule is title if there is a collective title. Added entries are made under the headings for prominently named editors or compilers, if there are not more than three, or for the principal one or the one named first if there are more than three. Example:

Title main entry for a collection with a collective title:

Modern music librarianship : essays in honor of Ruth Watanabe / edited by Alfred Mann.

Added entry would be made for the prominently named editor:

Mann, Alfred, 1917-

Name-title added entries are made if there are only two or three contributions or independent works included in a work covered by this rule. A name-title added entry is composed of the name of a person or corporate body followed by the title of a work for which the person or body is responsible. *See* example under 21.7C for an example of name-title added entries.

An added entry is made for each contributor when only two or three have contributed four or more works. In this case if one or two contributors have contributed only one work each, a name-title added entry is made for each.

An added entry is made for the first contributor named when more than three are named in the chief source of information.

21.7C. Without collective title

The main entry for a work that falls under this rule but does *not* have a collective title is the heading appropriate for the first work named in the chief source of information. If a chief source is lacking, the first work in the item is noted. Added entries are made as instructed in rule 21.7B. Example:

Main entry under first named author for a collection without a collective title:

Ellsworth, Ralph E., 1907-
　　　Buildings / by Ralph E. Ellsworth. Shelving / by Louis
　　Kaplan. Storage warehouses / by Jerrold Orne

Name-title added entries would be made for the second and third works plus title added entries for all three works:

Kaplan, Louis, 1909- . Shelving.
Orne, Jerrold, 1921- . Storage warehouses.
Title: Buildings.
Title: Shelving.
Title: Storage warehouses.

Note: The rule does not mention separate title added entries for the separate titles in a collection without a collective title, nor does rule 21.30J suggest such title added entries. However, an LC rule interpretation for rule 21.30J gives instructions to make separate title added entries for each of the titles listed in the title and statement of responsibility area if there are not more than three. (*CSB* 99: 33–35)

WORKS OF MIXED RESPONSIBILITY:
SELECTED RULES AND EXAMPLES

RULE 21.8.　WORKS OF MIXED RESPONSIBILITY

21.8A.　Scope

In many works the responsibility is divided. This occurs when different persons or bodies have contributed to the intellectual or artistic content performing different kinds of functions, e.g., writing, adapting, illustrating, translating, etc. Determination of main entry depends to a large extent on the relative importance of such contributions.

The rules in this section are divided into two basic categories of mixed responsibility:

1.　Modifications of previously existing works, such as revised editions, adaptations, or translations (rules 21.9–21.23)

2.　New works that consist of different kinds of contributions, such as illustrated texts or musical works with words by persons other than the composers (rules 21.24–21.27).

Works That Are Modifications of Other Works

RULE 21.9.   GENERAL RULE

Works that are modifications of other works may be entered under the heading appropriate to the new work or that appropriate to the original, depending upon the nature of the modification. If the modification has changed the nature or content of the original in a substantial way, or if the medium of expression is different, the new heading is chosen. However, if the modification is a rearrangement, abridgment, etc., where the original person or body is still seen as being responsible, the original heading is chosen. Rules 21.10–21.23 give specific guidance in applying this general rule.

Modifications of Texts (Rules 21.10–21.15)

RULE 21.10.   ADAPTATIONS OF TEXTS

Adaptations of texts are entered under the heading for the adapter or under title if the adapter is unknown. A name-title added entry is made for the original work. Examples of adaptations are paraphrases, changes of literary form (e.g., dramatization), and adaptations for children. Example:

Adapter as main entry:

> Taylor, Helen L. (Helen Louisa)
> Little Pilgrim's progress / by Helen L. Taylor

Note expanding upon statement of responsibility:

> Adaptation for children of: The Pilgrim's progress / John Bunyan.

A name-title added entry would be made for original author and title, and an added entry would also be made for the title page title:

> Bunyan, John, 1628-1688. Pilgrim's progress.
> Title: Little Pilgrim's progress.

RULE 21.11.   ILLUSTRATED TEXTS

21.11A.   General rule

When an illustrator has added illustrations to a text, the main entry is under the heading appropriate to the text. Example:

Main entry under author:

> Day, Jenifer W.
> What is a bird? / by Jenifer W. Day ; illustrated by
> Tony Chen

Added entries would be made for the artist and for the title:

> Chen, Tony.
> Title: What is a bird?

An added entry for the illustrator is made if appropriate (*see* rule 21.30K2). Works of collaboration between an artist and a writer are treated in rule 21.24.

RULE 21.12.   REVISIONS OF TEXTS

21.12A.   Original author considered responsible

The main entry for the original work is used for a revision if *either* the name of the original author appears in a statement of responsibility in the revision *or* the name of the original author appears in the revision's title proper and no other person is named in a statement of responsibility or other title information. The reviser, condenser, etc., is given an added entry. Such revisions include condensations, enlargements, revisions, and updates. Abridgments, however, are always entered under the original author, with an added entry made for the abridger, as explained above under rule 21.3A. Condensations that involve rewriting are considered to be adaptations and are entered according to rule 21.10. Example:

Revised work entered under original author:

> Gray, Henry, 1827-1861.
>   Anatomy of the human body / by Henry Gray. — 30th
> American ed. / edited by Carmine D. Clemente

Added entries would be made for the reviser and for the title:

> Clemente, Carmine D.
> **Title:** Anatomy of the human body.

21.12B.   Original author no longer considered responsible

If the wording of the chief source indicates that the original person or body is no longer responsible (i.e., it does not meet the conditions given in rule 21.12A), then entry is under the reviser, etc., or under title as appropriate. A name-title added entry is made under the original author and, if possible, the title of the latest edition to be entered under that name. Example:

Revised work entered under reviser:

> Bedingfeld, A. L.
>   Oxburgh Hall, Norfolk : a property of the National Trust / by
> A.L. Bedingfeld. — 2nd ed.

Note expanding upon statement of responsibility:

> "First edition, 1953, by Professor F. de Zulueta."

Name-title added entry would be made for original author and an added entry would also be made for title:

> Zulueta, Francis de. Oxburgh Hall, Norfolk.
> **Title:** Oxburgh Hall, Norfolk.

RULE 21.13.   TEXTS PUBLISHED WITH COMMENTARY

This rule applies to information packages comprising a text or texts by one person or body and a commentary or interpretation by another person or body. In essence, the rule calls for entry under the heading appropriate to the commentary if the chief source of information presents the manifestation as a commentary, and entry under the heading for the original work if the chief source of information presents the manifestation as an edition of the original. If the chief source is ambiguous, entry is determined by (in order of preference) emphasis in the preface, the typographic presentation of the text and commentary, or the relative extent of text and commentary. If there is still doubt, the work is treated as an edition with an added entry appropriate to the commentary. Example:

> **Text with commentary entered under first-named commentator:**
>
> Fischer, John L.
> > Annotations to the Book of Luelen / translated and edited by John L. Fischer, Saul H. Riesenberg and Marjorie G. Whiting
>
> **Note explaining the statement of responsibility:**
>
> > Annotations by J.L. Fischer, S.H. Riesenberg, and M.G. Whiting.
>
> **Added entries would be made for the 2 additional commentators and for the title, along with a name-title added entry for the original work:**
>
> Riesenberg, Saul H.
> Whiting, Marjorie G.
> Bernart, Luelen. Book of Luelen.
> Title: Annotations to the Book of Luelen.

RULE 21.14. TRANSLATIONS

A single translation is entered under the heading appropriate to the original. An added entry for the translator may be made in accordance with rule 21.30K1. Example:

> **Translation entered under original author:**
>
> Flohr, Salo, 1908-
> > Twelfth chess tournament of nations / Salo Flohr ; [translated from the Russian by W. Perelman]
>
> **Added entry would be made for title:**
>
> Twelfth chess tournament of nations.
>
> **[Note: added entries are not usually made for translators. In addition, the original title should be used in a uniform title (see chapter 7).]**

A collection of translations of works by different authors is treated as a collection (*see* rule 21.7).

RULE 21.15. TEXTS PUBLISHED WITH BIOGRAPHICAL/CRITICAL MATERIAL

Works that consist of a writer's work or works accompanied by biographical or critical material written by someone else are treated according to the way they are represented in the chief source of information. If the chief source presents the work as biography and/or criticism, the main entry is the biographer/critic. If the chief source presents the work as an edition with an editor, compiler, etc., then the original writer is used as main entry. In either case an added entry is made for the one not chosen as main entry. Examples:

Biographical work entered under biographer:

Morsc, John T. (John Torrey), 1840-1937.
Life and letters of Oliver Wendell Holmes / by John T. Morse

Added entries would be made for Holmes both as personal author of letters and as subject of the biography, and also, there would be a title added entry:

Author added entry: Holmes, Oliver Wendell, 1809-1894.
Subject added entry: Holmes, Oliver Wendell, 1809-1894.
Title: Life and letters of Oliver Wendell Holmes.

Edited biographical work entered under author:

Dover, Thomas, 1660-1742.
Thomas Dover's life and legacy / edited and introduced by Kenneth Dewhurst

Added entries would be made for the editor and for the title:

Dewhurst, Kenneth
Title: Thomas Dover's life and legacy.

Art Works (Rules 21.16–21.17)

RULE 21.16.   ADAPTATIONS OF ART WORKS

AACR2R2002 defines art works as including "paintings, engravings, photographs, drawings, sculptures, etc., and any other creative work that can be represented pictorially (e.g., ceramic designs, tapestries, fabrics)."[13]

21.16A. When an art work is adapted from one medium to another, the main entry is the adapter, or the title if the adapter is unknown. A name-title added entry is made for the original. Example:

Adaptation entered under heading for title because adapter is unknown:

[Mona Lisa] [picture] / [computer representation of the original by Leonardo da Vinci, produced via program written at IBM]

Note explaining existence of work:

Copies distributed at demonstration of IBM equipment.

Name-title added entry for original work:

Leonardo, da Vinci, 1452-1519. Mona Lisa.

Added entry for responsible corporate body:

International Business Machines Corporation.

21.16B. When an art work is reproduced, however, the main entry is the heading for the original, with an added entry for the person or body responsible for the reproduction, unless that person or body is only the manufacturer or publisher. Example:

Reproduction of art work entered under heading for the artist:

Hobbema, Meindert, 1638-1709.
    View on a high road [picture] / Hobbema ; National Gallery of Art

Added entries would be made for the body responsible for reproduction and for the title:

National Gallery of Art (U.S.).
Title: View on a high road.

RULE 21.17.   REPRODUCTIONS OF TWO OR MORE ART WORKS

21.17A.   Without text

If a work consists of reproductions of an artist's works and there is no text, the main entry is the artist.

21.17B.   With text

When text accompanies reproductions of an artist's works, entry is under the personal heading for the author of the text if that person is represented as author in the chief source of information; an added entry is made under the heading for the artist. Otherwise, or in case of doubt, entry is made under the heading for the artist with an added entry for the person mentioned in the chief source of information as having written the text. Catalogs of the holdings of a corporate body are governed by rule 21.1B2a. Art catalogs often present difficult choices. An LC rule interpretation gives guidance in this area. (*CSB* 45: 27–28) Examples:

Art reproductions with text entered under author of text:

Cassou, Jean, 1897-
    Rembrandt / par Jean Cassou

Added entry would be made for the artist:

Rembrandt Harmenszoon van Rijn, 1606-1669.

Art reproductions with text entered under artist:

Rembrandt Harmenszoon van Rijn, 1606-1669.
    More drawings of Rembrandt / introduction by Stephen Longstreet

Added entries would be made for author of text and for title:

Longstreet, Stephen, 1907-
Title: More drawings of Rembrandt.

Musical Works (Rules 21.18–21.22)

RULE 21.18.   GENERAL RULE

21.18A.   Scope

This rule applies to all kinds of arrangements of musical works where medium of performance has been changed, the original has been simplified, the new work is described as "based on" (or some equivalent), new material has been incorporated, or the harmony or style of the original has been changed.

21.18B.   Arrangements, transcriptions, etc.

A musical arrangement is a musical work or part of a musical work that has been rewritten either for a different medium of performance or to provide a simplified version. The general rule for a musical arrangement is to enter it under the heading for the original composer whenever possible. An added entry is made for the name of the arranger. Example:

Arrangement of musical work entered under original composer:

> Mozart, Wolfgang Amadeus, 1756-1791.
> > Eighth quintet, k. 614, fourth movement / W.A. Mozart ; arranged for 2 B♭ trumpets, horn, trombone & tuba by Ralph Lockwood

Added entry for arranger:

> Lockwood, Ralph.

[A uniform title would be constructed instead of a title added entry. *See* rule 25.25.]

21.18C.   Adaptations

A musical work that is an adaptation represents a more serious departure from the original work than does an arrangement. Thus, generally, the main entry is made under the heading for the adapter, with an added entry given to the author of the original work. Three types of adaptations of music are specified for entry under adapter:

"a)   a distinct alteration of another work (e.g., a free transcription)

b)   a paraphrase of various works or of the general style of another composer

c)   a work merely based on other music (e.g., variations on a theme.)"[14]

In case of doubt about whether a work is an adaptation, it is to be treated as an arrangement, transcription, etc. Example:

Adaptation of musical work entered under adapter:

> Brahms, Johannes, 1833-1897.
> > Variations and fugue on a theme by Handel, op. 24 / Johannes Brahms

Note explaining the scope of the item:

> The theme is that of the Aria con variazioni from Handel's Suite for harpsichord, 2nd collection, no. 1.

Name-title added entry for original work:

> Handel, George Frideric, 1685–1759. Suites, harpsichord, HWV 434, B♭ major. Aria con variazioni.

RULE 21.19.   MUSICAL WORKS THAT INCLUDE WORDS

21.19A.   General rule

If a musical work includes words, the main entry is for the composer with an added entry for the writer of the words, if the writer's work is represented, as in a full score or a vocal score, for example. A name-title added entry is made for an original text upon which the words have been based. Librettos are treated under another rule: 21.28. Example:

> **Musical comedy entered under composer:**
>
> Adler, Richard.
>   The pajama game : a musical comedy / music and lyrics by Richard Adler and Jerry Ross ; book by George Abbott
>
> **Note expanding statement of responsibility:**
>
> "Based on the novel '7½ cents' by Richard Bissell."
>
> **Added entries would be made for co-composer, writer, and title, and a name-title added entry would be made for the original text:**
>
> Ross, Jerry, 1926-1955.
> Abbott, George, 1889-
> **Title:** The pajama game.
> Bissell, Richard. 7½ cents.

21.19C.   Writer's works set by several composers

If the work or works of one writer are set in a collection of songs, etc., by two or more composers, entry is made according to the rule for collections, rule 21.7. Example:

> **Collection of songs with words by one writer and music by several composers; entered as a collection under title:**
>
> A Shakespeare song book / edited by H.A. Chambers.
>
> **Added entries would be made for the writer of the words, for the editor, and for the title:**
>
> Shakespeare, William, 1564-1616.
> Chambers, H. A. (Herbert Arthur), 1880-
> **Title:** A Shakespeare song book.

RULES 21.20–21.22.

These rules discuss main entry problems for musical settings for ballets, etc. (21.20), the addition of accompaniments or parts to a musical work (21.21), and liturgical music (21.22).

RULE 21.23.   SOUND RECORDINGS

It should be noted that this rule applies only to sound recordings that are modifications of other works. This includes readings of texts and performances of musical works. There is no rule specifically for sound recordings considered to constitute new works, such as recordings of improvisations and lectures. These items would be entered according to the principles of responsibility found in the basic rules. Such works as interviews made as oral history could be entered according to the principles in rule 21.25.

It should be noted also that this rule must be used in conjunction with rule 6.1G. If under rule 6.1G it is decided that a sound recording lacking a collective title should be described as a unit, then one of rules 21.23B–21.23D will be applied. If, however, it is decided to make a separate description for each separately titled work, rule 21.23A will be applied.

21.23A.   One work

Main entry for a sound recording of one work is the heading appropriate to that work. The rule specifically calls for added entries for the principal performers unless there are more than three, in which case an added entry is made for the first named principal performer. A rule interpretation from LC points out that added entries should also be made for those prescribed by the rules under which the choice of main entry for the work is made. (*CSB* 44: 37) Example:

> **Sound recording entered under author of original work:**

> Rey, Margret.
>   Curious George learns the alphabet [sound recording] / Margret & H.A. Rey

> **Note expanding statement of responsibility:**

> Read by Julie Harris.

> **Added entries would be made for the shared author, for the reader, and for the title:**

> Rey, H. A. (Hans Agusto), 1898-
> Harris, Julie.
> Title: Curious George learns the alphabet.

21.23B.   Two or more works by the same person(s) or body(bodies)

Main entry for a sound recording of works that are all the responsibility of the same person(s) or body (bodies) is the heading appropriate to those works. Added entries are made for performers and for additional responsible persons or bodies as explained above under rule 21.23A. Example:

> **Sound recording entered under composer of the several works performed:**

> Chopin, Frédéric, 1810-1849.
>   The 24 preludes [sound recording] / Chopin

> **Note expanding statement of responsibility:**

> Alexander Brailowsky, pianist.

> **Added entries would be made for the performer and for the title:**

> Brailowsky, Alexander, 1896-1976.
> Title: The 24 preludes.

21.23C.   Works by different persons or bodies. Collective title

Main entry for a sound recording of works by different persons or bodies that has a collective title is the person or body represented as principal performer. If there are two or three principal performers, main entry is the first named, with added entries for the others. A rule interpretation from LC gives guidance in deciding whom to consider "principal performers." This rule interpretation should be consulted for further detail. (*CSB* 45: 28–31) Example:

Sound recording entered under first-named principal performer:

> Klezmer Conservatory Band.
>   Yiddishe renaissance [sound recording] / Klezmer Conservatory Band

Note expanding statement of responsibility:

> H. Netsky, director.

Added entries would be made for the second named principal performer and for the title:

> Netsky, Hankus.
> Title: Yiddishe renaissance.

A sound recording with four or more principal performers or no principal performers is given main entry under title. Example:

Sound recording with more than three principal performers entered under title:

> Stay awake [sound recording]

Other title information from jacket:

> "Various interpretations of music from vintage Disney films."

Note expanding statement of responsibility:

> Performances by Betty Carter, Garth Hudson, Los Lobos, Natalie Merchant, NRBQ, Harry Nilsson, Bonnie Raitt, Sun Ra, Ringo Starr, James Taylor, Tom Waits and others.

21.23D.   Works by different persons or bodies. No collective title
This rule applies to a sound recording that contains works by different persons or bodies, that has no collective title, and that is to be cataloged as a unit. Treatment depends upon the decision about whether participation of the performer(s) goes beyond mere performance, execution, or interpretation.

Popular, rock, and jazz music are usually considered to have participation of performers beyond execution or interpretation. In these cases main entry is under principal performer, if there is one; under the first of two or three principal performers; or under the heading appropriate to the first work if there are four or more principal performers. Added entries are made for the performers not named as main entry if there are not more than three. Examples:

Sound recording entered under principal performer:

> Alan, Buddy.
>> When I turn twenty-one [sound recording] / Merle Haggard.
>> Adios, farewell, goodbye, good luck, so long / Buck Owens.

Note expanding statement of responsibility:

> Buddy Alan, vocals ; James Burton's orchestra.

Sound recording entered under main entry [title] for first work:

> Little white duck [sound recording]. Mary had a little lamb

Note expanding statement of responsibility:

> Recording sung by Betty Wells, Bill Marine and The
> Playmates with orchestra directed by Maury Laws (side A),
> The 4 Cricketones with orchestra and chorus (side B).

Classical and other "serious" music is usually considered to have participation of performers that does not go beyond execution or interpretation. For these works, main entry is under the heading appropriate to the first work with added entries for the other works if appropriate as explained under rule 21.7C.

Mixed Responsibility in New Works

RULE 21.24.   COLLABORATION BETWEEN ARTIST AND WRITER
If a work appears to be a collaborative effort between an artist and a writer, rather than an artist's illustrations of a writer's text (covered by rule 21.11A), main entry is under the one named first in the chief source of information, unless the other one is given greater prominence by typography, etc. Example:

Collaborative work entered under artist named first on title page:

> Mair, A. J. (Alice Joy).
>> More homes of the pioneers and other buildings : pen and
>> wash drawings / by A.J. Mair ; with text by J.A. Hendry

Added entries for the author of the text and for the title:

> Hendry, J. A. (John A.).
> Title: More homes of the pioneers and other buildings.

RULE 21.25.   REPORTS OF INTERVIEWS OR EXCHANGES
Whether to give main entry to the reporter or to one of the other participants in an interview or exchange depends upon how much the words are those of the reporter and how much they are those of the other participant(s). If the report gives essentially the words of the interviewee or other participant, main entry is the principal participant, first named participant, or title if there are more than three equal participants. An added entry is made for an openly named reporter. If the report, for the most part, consists of the words of the reporter, main entry is for the reporter, with

added entry(s) for the persons interviewed if they are named in the chief source of information (or for only the first if there are more than three). Examples:

Interview entered under the first named participant:

> Scott, David Randolph.
>   Interview from deep space [sound recording] / by
> David Randolph Scott, Alfred Merrill Worden, and James
> Benson Irwin

Added entries would be made for the other participants and for the title:

> Worden, Alfred Merrill.
> Irwin, James B. (James Benson).
> Title: Interview from deep space.

Interview entered under reporter:

> Schneider, Duane.
>   An interview with Anaïs Nin / Duane Schneider

Added entries would be made for the person interviewed and for the title:

> Nin, Anaïs, 1903-1977.
> Title: An interview with Anaïs Nin.

RELATED WORKS:
SELECTED RULES AND EXAMPLES

RULE 21.28.   RELATED WORKS

21.28A.   Scope

According to rule 1.9, supplementary items may be described separately or dependently (i.e., described as accompanying material; or in a note; or in a multilevel description, further described in rule 13.6). This rule (21.28) applies only to separately cataloged works that are related to another work. It includes continuations, sequels, supplements, indexes, concordances, incidental music to dramatic works, cadenzas, scenarios, screenplays, choreographies, subseries, special numbers of serials, and collections of extracts from serials. It does not apply to works that have only subject relationship to other works or to the particular types of relationships covered in rules 21.8–21.27.

In *AACR2R* proper, this rule includes librettos, but an alternative rule for librettos is given in a footnote. LC has decided to apply the alternative rule for librettos because "librettos are normally sought as an adjunct to the music."[15] Therefore, librettos are entered by LC under the heading for the musical work, with an added entry under the personal heading for the librettist. A name-title added entry is also made under the heading for the original text on which the libretto is based, if this applies. Example:

Libretto entered under heading appropriate to the musical work [composer] according to rule 21.28A, footnote 7:

> Laderman, Ezra.
> [Galileo Galilei. Libretto. English]
> Galileo Galilei : an opera-oratorio in three acts / libretto by Joe Darion ; music by Ezra Laderman

Note providing other title information:

> Original title: The trials of Galileo.

Added entries would be made for librettist, for the title page title, and for the original title:

> Darion, Joe, 1917-
> Title: Galileo Galilei.
> Title: The trials of Galileo.

21.28B. General rule

Main entry for a related work is the heading appropriate to it as if it were an independent work. An added entry is made for the name-title or title (whichever is main entry) of the related work. An added entry is not made, however, for the related work in the case of a sequel by the same author. LC has made some other exceptions to making added entries for the related works that apply to excerpts from serials, indexes, census data, and Bible texts. (*CSB* 101: 31–32) Examples:

Supplement cataloged separately and entered under author:

> Gore, Marvin.
> Elements of systems analysis for business data processing. Instructional supplement / Marvin Gore, John Stubbe

Added entries for co-author of supplement and for title:

> Stubbe, John.
> Title: Elements of systems analysis for business data processing.

[Note that a name-title added entry for the related work is not made because it would, in essence, be a duplication of the main entry and title given before the words *Instructional supplement*.]

Concordance entered under its own author:

> Williams, Mary.
> The Dickens concordance, being a compendium of names and characters and principal places mentioned in all the works of Charles Dickens . . . / by Mary Williams

Added entries for author of works to which this work is related and for title:

> Dickens, Charles, 1812-1870.
> Title: The Dickens concordance.

Collection of extracts from a serial entered as a collection under title as appropriate to the related work in hand. [Joyce is the subject of these essays.]:

James Joyce essays / by Brian Nolan . . . [et al.]

Note providing bibliographic history:

"These essays were first published in Envoy, 1951."

Added entries for first named author and for serial from which essays were extracted:

O'Brien, Flann, 1911-1966.
Envoy (Dublin).

[Note: Flann O'Brien has written under many names, including Brian Nolan. All works are brought together by LC under: O'Brien, Flann, 1911-1966.]

ADDED ENTRIES:
SELECTED RULES AND EXAMPLES

RULE 21.29.   GENERAL RULE

The preceding rules have indicated the added entries required in typical circumstances to supplement the main entry by providing additional bibliographical access to materials represented in the catalog. In general, added entries are suggested to provide access to other names of persons or titles under which a work may be known and under which catalog users might reasonably search. Persons, corporate bodies, and works related to the work at hand are considered, providing these are openly stated in the work. Added entries may also be made for names of persons and corporate bodies to reflect subsequent parts of a multipart monograph, previous iterations of an integrating resource, or subsequent issues or parts of a serial. It is a matter of local library policy to establish whether or not to make all required added entries, a decision that must be related to the extent of the collection, the needs it serves, and some economic considerations.

It is prescribed here that if the cataloger believes an added entry is needed, and if the reason for an added entry is not clear from the body of the description, a note should be provided to justify the added entry.

An option provides for explanatory references in place of certain added entries (as in rule 26.6); LC is not applying this option. (*CSB* 97: 65)

LC has given guidelines in addition to those in *AACR2R* for making added entries for audiovisual materials and for sound recordings. These should be consulted when appropriate. (*CSB* 45: 32–34)

RULE 21.30.   SPECIFIC RULES

21.30A–21.30H, 21.30K, 21.30M.   These specific rules for added entries for collaborators, writers, editors and compilers, corporate bodies, other related persons or bodies, related works, other relationships, translators, illustrators, and analytical entries have been touched on in the rules for choice of main entry. When particular guidance is needed for one of these cases, these rules in *AACR2R* should be consulted. One should also consult LC rule interpretations for rule 21.30E, Corporate bodies (*CSB* 94: 17); rule 21.30F, Other related persons or bodies (*CSB* 109:

23–24); rule 21.30G, Related works (*CSB* 109: 24–26); rule 21.30H, Other relationships (*CSB* 108: 57–58); rule 21.30K1, Translators (*CSB* 77: 44); rule 21.30K2, Illustrators (*CSB* 104: 23); and rule 21.30M, Analytical entries (*CSB* 63: 11–12). Examples:

Bibliographic entry with an added entry for editor:

> Shakespeare, William, 1564-1616.
> As you like it / [by William Shakespeare] ; edited by Peter Hollindale

Added entries made:

> Hollindale, Peter.
> **Title:** As you like it.

Bibliographic entry with an added entry for translator:

> Busch, Wilhelm, 1832-1908.
> The bees : a fairy tale / by Wilhelm Busch ; translated by Rudolph Wiemann

Notes providing information on translation:

> Translation of: Schnurrdiburr.

Added entries made:

> Wiemann, Rudolph.
> **Title:** The bees.

Two added entry rules are used with such frequency that they warrant special mention:

21.30J. Titles

Added entries are made for the title proper of every information package entered under either a personal name or corporate heading, or under a uniform title. (The 2003 update to *AACR2R* removed earlier conditions under which such added entries were not to be made).

Added entries may also be made for minor changes in the title proper of a serial, for an earlier title proper of an integrating resource, for the later title proper of a multipart item, and for any other version of the title (e.g., cover title) that differs significantly from the title proper.

An extensive rule interpretation gives guidelines for making title added entries and for tracing them. Guidance is also given for added entries for spelled-out forms of abbreviations, numerals, etc., as well as the non-spelled-out forms. (*CSB* 108: 58–81)

See examples throughout this chapter.

21.30L. Series

An added entry is made for a series on each record for each work in the series if it is judged to be a useful access point. Adding the numeric or other designation to each added entry is optional. This option is applied at LC. (*CSB* 108: 82) Example:

Bibliographic entry with an added entry for series:

> Dundes, Alan.
> Analytic essays in folklore / by Alan Dundes

Use of series area:

> — (Studies in folklore ; 2)

Added entries made:

> Title: Analytic essays in folklore.
> Series: Studies in folklore ; 2.

According to *AACR2R*, series added entries are not made if the series shares only common physical characteristics or if the series numbering appears to be only publisher's stock control numbers. For a number of years LC placed certain additional restrictions on tracing series, but in 1989 a decision was made to begin tracing every series. The cataloger should consult LC's rule interpretation for assistance with the form of series added entry tracings. (*CSB* 108: 81–87)

SPECIAL RULES:
SELECTED RULES AND EXAMPLES

Certain Legal Publications

Rules 21.31 through 21.36 cover the following legal publications:

21.31 — legislative enactments and decrees that have the force of law except for ones that are covered by later rules

21.32 — administrative regulations

21.33 — constitutions and charters

21.34 — court rules

21.35 — treaties and intergovernmental agreements

21.36 — court decisions and cases

The reader is referred to these rules for choice of entry for these publications. Examples:

Laws governing a single jurisdiction entered under name of jurisdiction:

> United States.
> [Tax reduction act of 1975]
> Tax reduction act of 1975, P.L. 94-12, as signed by the President on March 29, 1975 : law and explanation. —
> Chicago : Commerce Clearing House, [1975]

Added entries for corporate body issuing or compiling the law and for title:

Commerce Clearing House.
Title: Tax reduction act of 1975.

[For Uniform titles for laws, *see* rule 25.15]

U.S. administrative regulation entered under promulgating agency:

United States. Internal Revenue Service.
    Estate tax regulations under the Internal Revenue Code of 1954 / [United States Treasury Department, Internal Revenue Service]

Added entries for heading for uniform title for authorizing law and for title:

United States. [Internal Revenue Code of 1954]
Title: Estate tax regulations under the Internal Revenue Code of 1954.

Treaty involving two countries entered under country alphabetically first:

France.
    [Treaties, etc. United States, 1984 Jan. 3]
    Atomic energy, radioactive waste management : arrangement between the United States of America and France, signed at Washington and Paris January 3 and 10, 1984.

Added entries for the second named country and for title:

United States. Treaties, etc. France, 1984 Jan. 3.
Title: Atomic energy, radioactive waste management.

Certain Religious Publications

Rules 21.37 through 21.39 cover the following religious publications:

21.37 — sacred scriptures

21.38 — theological creeds, confessions of faith, etc.

21.39 — liturgical works

The reader is referred to these rules for choice of entry for these publications. Examples:

Sacred scripture entered under uniform title main entry:

Tipiṭaka. Suttapiṭaka. English. Selections.
Some sayings of the Buddha, according to the Pali canon /
translated by F.L. Woodward ; with an introduction by Christmas
Humphreys

Added entries for persons associated with the work and for title page title:

Woodward, F. L. (Frank Lee), 1870 or 71-1952.
Humphreys, Christmas, 1901–
Title: Some sayings of the Buddha, according to the Pali canon.

Liturgical work entered under heading for the church:

Catholic Church.
[Rite of ordination. English]
The ordination of deacons, priests, and bishops : provisional
text prepared by the International Committee on English in the
Liturgy, approved for interim use by the Bishops' Committee on
the Liturgy, National Conference of Catholic Bishops, and
confirmed by the Apostolic See.

Added entry for title:

The ordination of deacons, priests, and bishops.

NOTES

1. *Anglo-American Cataloguing Rules, Second Edition, 2002 Revision,* prepared under the
direction of the Joint Steering Committee for Revision of AACR (Chicago: American Library Association, 2002), p. 2 (paragraph 0.5).

2. For further discussion of "main entry" as a theoretical concept *see* Arlene G. Taylor, *The
Organization of Information,* 2nd ed. (Westport, Conn.: Libraries Unlimited, 2004), chapter 8.

3. *AACR2R2002,* p. 2 (paragraph 0.5).

4. Richard P. Smiraglia, Barbara B. Tillett, and Sherry L. Vellucci have done notable research in this area:

Smiraglia: "Authority Control and the Extent of Derivative Bibliographic Relationships," Ph.D. dissertation, University of Chicago, 1992; and "Derivative Bibliographic Relationships: Linkages in the Bibliographic Universe," in *Navigating the Networks: Proceedings of the ASIS Mid-Year Meeting, Portland, Oregon, May 21–25, 1994* (Medford, N.J.: Learned Information, 1994), pp. 167–183.

Tillett: "Bibliographic Relationships: Toward a Conceptual Structure of Bibliographic Information Used in Cataloging." Ph.D. dissertation, University of California, Los Angeles, 1987; "A Taxonomy of Bibliographic Relationships," *Library Resources and*

Technical Services 35 (April 1991): 150–158; "A Summary of the Treatment of Bibliographic Relationships in Cataloging Rules," *Library Resources and Technical Services* 35 (October 1991): 393–405; "The History of Linking Devices," *Library Resources and Technical Services* 36 (January 1992): 23–36; and "Bibliographic Relationships: An Empirical Study of the LC Machine-Readable Records," *Library Resources and Technical Services* 36 (April 1992): 162–188.

Vellucci: "Bibliographic Relationships Among Musical Bibliographic Entities: A Conceptual Analysis of Music Represented in the Library Catalog with a Taxonomy of the Relationships Discovered," D.L.S. dissertation, Columbia University, 1995; and "Bibliographic Relationships," in *The Principles and Future of AACR2*, ed. Jean Weihs (Chicago: American Library Association, 1998), pp. 105–146.

A team at the OCLC Office of Research, headed by Edward O'Neill, has carried out related research aimed at applying the "work" concept from IFLA's *Functional Requirements for Bibliographic Records* to records in OCLC's WorldCat database. Information about their research is available at http://www.oclc.org/research/projects/frbr/default.htm (accessed 2/26/2006).

5. For example, see Seymour Lubetzky, "The Fundamentals of Bibliographic Cataloging and *AACR 2*," in International Conference on *AACR 2*, Florida State University, 1979, *The Making of a Code* (Chicago: American Library Association, 1980), pp. 18–23; Michael Gorman, "*AACR 2*: Main Themes," in ibid., pp. 45–46; and Elizabeth L. Tate, "Examining the 'Main' in Main Entry Headings," in ibid., pp. 109–140. More recent discussions include Michael Carpenter, "Does Cataloging Theory Rest on a Mistake?" in *Origins, Content, and Future of AACR2 Revisited,* ed. Richard P. Smiraglia (Chicago: American Library Association, 1992), pp. 95–102; and Ronald Hagler, "Access Points for Works," in *The Principles and Future of AACR2*, ed. Jean Weihs (Chicago: American Library Association, 1998), pp. 214–228.

6. *Functional Requirements for Bibliographic Records, Final Report*, IFLA Study Group on the Functional Requirements for Bibliographic Records (München: K.G. Saur, 1998); also available: http://www.ifla.org/VII/s13/frbr/frbr.htm or http://www.ifla.org/VII/s13/frbr/frbr.pdf (accessed 2/14/2006).

7. *RDA – Resource Description and Access: A Prospectus*, Joint Steering Committee for Revision of AACR, 27 July 2005. Available: http://www.collectionscanada.ca/jsc/rdaprospectus.html or http://www.collectionscanada.ca/jsc/docs/5rda-prospectusrev.pdf (accessed 2/26/2006).

8. Ibid., p. 4.

9. *AACR2R2002*, p. 21-6.

10. *AACR2R2002*, p. 21-6.

11. *AACR2R2002*, p. 21-15.

12. ALA/ALCTS/CCS, Committee on Cataloging: Description and Access, *The Future of AACR*, April 2003. Available: http://www.libraries.psu.edu/tas/jca/ccda/future1.html (accessed 2/14/2006).

13. *AACR2R2002*, p. 21-31.

14. *AACR2R2002*, p. 21-34.

15. "AACR 2 Options to Be Followed by the Library of Congress, Chapters 1–2, 12, 21–26," *Library of Congress Information Bulletin*, 37 (July 21, 1978): 425.

SUGGESTED READING

Chan, Lois Mai. *Cataloging and Classification: An Introduction.* 2nd ed. New York: McGraw-Hill, 1994. Chapter 4.

Fritz, Deborah A. *Cataloging with AACR2R and MARC21 for Books, Electronic Resources, Sound Recordings, Video Recordings, and Serials.* 2nd ed. Chicago: American Library Association, 2004.

Hagler, Ronald. *The Bibliographic Record and Information Technology.* 3rd ed. Chicago: American Library Association, 1997, pp. 247–252.

Maxwell, Robert L. *Maxwell's Handbook for AACR2R: Explaining and Illustrating the* Anglo-American Cataloguing Rules *through the 2003 Update.* 4th ed. Chicago: American Library Association, 2004.

Tate, Elizabeth L. "Examining the 'Main' in Main Entry Headings." In International Conference on *AACR 2*, Florida State University, 1979, *The Making of a Code.* Chicago: American Library Association, 1980, pp. 109–140.

7 ▷ Form of Headings for Names and Titles

INTRODUCTION

The previous chapter dealt with choice of access points; this chapter presents rules for the form of heading regardless of whether the access point is to be a main entry (i.e., primary access point) or an added entry. Once it has been decided what is to be the main entry and what are to be added entries, it must be determined how those entries are to be displayed in the record. Choice of entry rules deal with who or what is to be an entry; form of entry rules deal with how an entry is to be recorded as a heading.

HEADINGS FOR PERSONS

Most headings in American library catalogs consist of a personal name entered under the surname followed by forenames (like the white pages of a telephone directory). However, as the following rules for headings for persons show, there are certain complexities that must be considered in a library catalog. Rules—i.e., principles and practices—must be followed consistently for those persons known by more than one name.

There are many possible instances when a person may be known and/or writes under more than one name. Some authors deliberately disguise their real names and write under a pseudonym or pen name—such as Charles Lutwidge Dodgson, who wrote his children's fantasies under the pseudonym of Lewis Carroll. Others consistently write under initialized forenames (e.g., H. G. Wells), while still others, such as Bernard Shaw (also known as George Bernard Shaw), consistently omit one of their forenames. If someone's original name is written in a nonroman alphabet, different romanization systems may create different spellings of the name (such as Chekhov, Chekov, or Tchekhov). A married woman traditionally may have two possible surnames—her birth surname and her husband's surname. Further, compound surnames—i.e., surnames consisting of two or more parts—create problems. Granville-Barker is an example of a compound, hyphenated English surname. Prefixes to surnames create another type of compound surname. De Gaulle and von Goethe are examples of surnames with prefixes; O'Brien and MacPherson are other examples. Individuals who are members of nobility may have two names—a titled name and a common surname (such as Lord Byron, George Gordon Byron). Certain individuals are known under their bynames or forenames rather than their surnames; these include royalty (Elizabeth II), saints (Joan of Arc), popes (Paul VI), and individuals in ancient and medieval periods prior to the development of surnames (Horace). Bynames or forenames often exist in different forms in different languages (such as Horace in English, but Horatius in Latin).

The purpose of this section is to demonstrate the general rules used to resolve all of the aforementioned multiple-name situations. For more complicated situations with personal names, the reader should carefully examine Chapter 22 in the *Anglo-American Cataloguing Rules, Second Edition* in one of its formats. (As in chapters 4–6 of this text, specific citations to the 2002 print edition with its 2003–2005 updates are referred to as *AACR2R2002*, but the work with its additions and changes is referred to as *AACR2R*.)

AACR2R Chapter 22 is divided into four sections, the first three of which suggest the order of the steps taken by the cataloger to establish the form in which the name will appear as a heading in the catalog. The first section, rules 22.1–22.3, is entitled "Choice of name." This "choice" is a separate action from "choice of access points," discussed in the preceding chapter. Once it has been decided through choice of access points that a person will be given an access point, rules 22.1 and 22.2 prescribe the choice of name when that person has used more than one name. Rules 22.1 and 22.3 prescribe the choice to be made between or among different manifestations of the same name. After making a choice of name and/or choice of manifestation of a name, the cataloger uses the next section, rules 22.4–22.11, "Entry element," to decide which element of the name will be the first and in what order the other elements will follow. The final step is to make any additions to the name that may be necessitated because of the kind of name involved (rules 22.12–22.16) or because two or more names are identical (rules 22.17–22.20). The fourth section of *AACR2R*, Chapter 22, is "Special Rules for Names in Certain Languages." These are for selected languages in which heading form does not follow the typical "western" style.

It should be noted that the rules in this section apply to the choice and form of personal names whether they are access points because of some kind of responsibility for the creation of a work or because they are the subject of a work. That is, a personal name subject heading is constructed in the same manner and according to the same rules as is a personal name main or added entry heading for an author, painter, performer, etc.

The Library of Congress (LC) adopted *Anglo-American Cataloguing Rules, Second Edition (AACR2)* for new names beginning January 2, 1981. It also abandoned the policy of *superimposition* at that time so that a number of already established name forms were changed to agree with the prescribed *AACR2* form. Superimposition was a policy established with the adoption of *Anglo-American Cataloging Rules (AACR)* in 1967. Under that policy any name that had been established prior to *AACR* continued to be used on new cataloging as already established, even if its form according to *AACR* would have been different. Even though this policy was officially abandoned with the adoption of *AACR2*, established names in certain defined categories were considered to be "*AACR2* compatible," and the established form continued to be used even on new records. After the initial impact of adopting *AACR2* was over, it became counterproductive to continue the "compatible" policy, because it took more time to decide on such headings than to change the old forms. Therefore, the "compatible" policy was abandoned on September 1,

1982.[1] All pre-*AACR2* headings coded as compatible between January 2, 1981, and September 1, 1982, remain in that form at LC, and as a result, it is useful to be aware of some of the major cases. These are summarized with examples in an issue of *Cataloging Service Bulletin*, which should be consulted by anyone who works with cataloging copy from LC.[2]

A heading created using *AACR2R*, Chapter 22, is coded 100, 600, 700, or 800 in the *MARC 21* (MAchine-Readable Cataloging) format, depending upon whether it functions as a main entry, a subject heading, or an added entry or begins a series added entry.

Choice of Name: Selected Rules and Examples

RULE 22.1.   GENERAL RULE

22.1A.   The name by which a person is commonly known is the one that should be chosen, whether that name be the person's real name, nickname, pseudonym, shortened form of name, or other form of name customarily used by a person. Thus the following choices might be made:

Pseudonym

Mathew James

not birth name: James D. Lucey

Nickname

Billy Graham

not William Franklin Graham

Name in religion

Maria Teresa dell'Eucaristia

not birth name: Maria Teresa Tosi

Short form of name

Virginia Knight Nelson

not Alyce Virginia Knight Nelson

Real name

Sally Benson

not pseudonym: Esther Evarts

22.1B.   The name by which a person is commonly known is to be determined from chief sources of information of works in that person's language. This, of course, may not be possible if the person is only a subject of works or creates only nonverbal works (e.g., unsigned paintings). In these cases the name is to be determined from reference sources in the person's language or from the person's country of residence or activity. A footnote to this rule in *AACR2R* indicates that "reference sources" include books and articles written about a person.

A rule interpretation from LC indicates that chief sources used for this rule may be from works published both during and after a person's lifetime. There are special instructions, also, about treatment of music composers, names without forenames, names containing abbreviations rather than initials, and other more unusual situations. (*CSB* 103: 60–63)

Throughout this chapter of *AACR2R* there are references to "commonly known" and "predominant" when referring to choosing one name or one form of name. *AACR2R2002* defines predominant name as, "The name or form of name of a person or corporate body that appears most frequently (1) in the person's works or works issued by the corporate body, or (2) in reference sources, in that order of preference."[3]

At the time of implementation of *AACR2* in 1981 there was indication from those involved in its creation that "most frequently" should not be taken to mean 51 percent of the instances; yet there were no guidelines otherwise. For a number of years before 1981, LC had used 75 percent in interpreting the "fullness of name" rule. That is, until a name appeared in a different form in an author's works 75 percent of the time (counting works by the person issued after the person's death as well as during the person's lifetime), the form of heading was not changed. They continued to apply this concept with *AACR2*, except the percentage was changed to 66 percent during the early years of *AACR2* and later was changed to 80 percent. They are continuing this policy with *AACR2R*. A note with the rule interpretation that gives the figure of 80 percent to be used with the rule for fullness (22.3A) cautions that this figure is to be applied only to rule 22.3A—that no formula has been assigned to the other rules. (*CSB* 91: 22–23) However, other libraries might still use this as a guideline for changes. When a name is first established, "predominant" could be 51 percent or more; but a change would not be called for until the name had appeared differently 80 percent of the time.

22.1C–22.1D.   Terms and punctuation associated with a name

Rules 22.1C–22.1D refer to inclusion of titles of nobility or honor, diacritical marks, and hyphens. At first glance it may not be clear how these relate to choice of name. However, the intention here is to give rules for choosing those elements that should be included in the heading. The order in which these elements appear is the subject of rules 22.4–22.17.

The general principle, again, is to follow the form customarily used by the person. Titles, words, or phrases that commonly appear with the name are included when the person is primarily known by either a forename or a surname only. Accents, other diacritical marks, and hyphens are included as used by the person, except that a hyphen that is used between a forename and a surname is not included.

RULE 22.2.   CHOICE AMONG DIFFERENT NAMES

Rules 22.2 and 22.3 give more specific guidelines for adhering to the principle stated in rule 22.1. Rules in 22.2 help choose among different names for the same person, and those in rule 22.3 help in the choice among different forms of the same name. Both may have to be used in a particular instance, because a name chosen from among different names may itself appear in varying degrees of fullness or with variant spellings. For example, once it has been decided that the name used should be George Novack, not William Warde, one then has to decide whether to use George Novack, George E. Novack, or George Edward Novack.

22.2A.   Predominant name ·

This rule applies only when a pseudonym is not involved. If a person is *known* by more than one name, and if there is a name that is clearly most common, it is used. If not, the following order of preference is used in making a choice:

"a)   the name that appears most frequently in the person's works

b)   the name that appears most frequently in reference sources

c)   the latest name."[4]

LC has issued a rule interpretation to be used for an author who simultaneously uses different forms of a real name. (*CSB* 96: 10) Another rule interpretation notes that if a person's name is shown with a nickname in quotation marks or parentheses, the nickname should be omitted in the heading. (*CSB* 43: 32)

22.2B.   Pseudonyms

22.2B1.   One pseudonym

When a person has used one pseudonym on all works, it is used for the heading, with a reference from the real name, if known. Example:

> Ford, Ford Madox, 1873-1939.
> It was the nightingale / Ford Madox Ford

[Note: Refer from[5] real name: Hueffer, Ford Madox.]

22.2B2.   Separate bibliographic identities

The concept in this rule was new with *AACR2R*. When works of one type always appear under one pseudonym and works of another type always appear under the person's real name or under another pseudonym, the person is considered to have established different bibliographic identities, and each separate group of works is entered under the name used for that identity. The cataloger is instructed to consult also rule 22.2B3 if the person involved is contemporary. Example:

Entry under real name:

> Clemens, Samuel Langhorne, 1835-1910.
> Republican letters / by Samuel L. Clemens

Note on bibliographic record:

> Articles published in the Chicago Republican in 1868.

Entry under pseudonym:

> Twain, Mark, 1835-1910.
> A Connecticut Yankee in King Arthur's court / Mark Twain

[Note: References are made from each name to the other and to Snodgrass, Quintus Curtius, 1835-1910—another pseudonym used by this author.]

The impetus for a rule establishing bibliographic identities came from those who were dissatisfied with the previous provision for entering all works of a person using two or more names under the name that had been used predominantly in the person's works or had become predominant in reference sources. The result was that the scholarly works written under a person's real name (e.g., Charles L. Dodgson) sometimes were entered under the name that person used on works of fiction (e.g., Lewis Carroll). In addition manuscript writings from a person's personal life (e.g., letters to family members) could be entered under a pseudonym used in published works. Establishing bibliographic identities solves these problems, and with advances in authority control in online systems, the need for pulling a person's works together in the same catalog drawer is no longer urgent.

22.2B3.   Contemporary authors

When a contemporary author uses more than one pseudonym or a real name and one or more pseudonyms, each work is given a heading based upon the name used in it. References are made to connect the names. Example:

Entry under pseudonym:

> Cross, Amanda, 1926-
>> Death in a tenured position / Amanda Cross

Entry under real name:

> Heilbrun, Carolyn G., 1926-
>> Hamlet's mother and other women / Carolyn G. Heilbrun

[Note: References are made from each name to the other. It should be noted that if this author were not a contemporary, both names would still be used because of separate bibliographic identities. She wrote mysteries under the pseudonym of Cross and literary criticism under her real name of Heilbrun. Although she died in 2003, LC has had a policy to not add a death date unless a change is required in the heading for some other reason. That policy changed early in 2006. See discussion at rule 22.17.]

When different editions of a work of a contemporary author have appeared with different names of the author, the name most often used should be the heading for all editions. If no one name is predominant, one should use the name that appears in the latest available edition. In all cases name-title references are made from the other name(s) used for editions of that work.

22.2B4.   When a person who falls under rule 22.2B is not a contemporary and does not have separate bibliographic identities under different names, one name is chosen based on the following order of preference:

1.   The name used in later editions of his or her works

2.   The name most used in critical works

3.   The name by which the person has come to be identified in reference sources

References are made from other names not chosen.

In a rule interpretation for all of rule 22.2B, LC points out that the intent of this rule is that for contemporaries who use at least one pseudonym, there will be as many headings as there are names. For non-contemporaries, the same may be true, but only if the cataloger can establish that there are separate bibliographic identities. If such identities cannot be identified, then there will be only one heading for non-contemporaries, regardless of number of names. The rule interpretation then gives guidelines for identifying "contemporary" and "separate bibliographic identities." (*CSB* 71: 53–55)

22.2C.   Change of name

When a person who has not used a pseudonym has changed his or her name or has acquired and become known by a title of nobility, the latest name should be used for the heading. Example:

Latest name used:

> Cochrane, Pauline A. (Pauline Atherton), 1929-
>   Improving LCSH for use in online catalogs : exercises
> for self-help with a selection of background readings /
> Pauline A. Cochrane

[Note: A reference is made from Atherton, Pauline, 1929- , name used in earlier writings.]

RULE 22.3.   CHOICE AMONG DIFFERENT FORMS OF THE SAME NAME

22.3A.   Fullness

When a name is found in forms that vary in fullness, the form most commonly found should be used as the heading, with references from the other forms when they would be useful. Example:

> **Predominant form:** John P. Hamilton
> **Occasional form:** J.P. Hamilton
> **Rare form:** "Bud" Hamilton
> **Heading:** Hamilton, John P.

[Note: Because Hamilton is a common surname, the second forename, Peter, may be required in parentheses to distinguish between two identical names (*see* rule 22.18). Also, references are needed from the two forms of name not chosen.]

When a form cannot be decided upon as most common, *AACR2R* prescribes use of the latest form; but if the latest form is in doubt, then one should use the fullest form. LC skips the possibility of "latest form" and goes directly to fullest form if one form cannot be determined to be most common. (*CSB* 91: 22)

LC's rule interpretation also suggests that if the name appears in two or more forms in the same work, one should choose the form in the chief source. If the name does not appear in the chief source, then a form in another prominent source should be used, if the name appears only once in a prominent source. Otherwise, the fullest form should be chosen. (*CSB* 91: 23)

LC applies the "80% rule" when a heading is already coded as "AACR" but subsequent items are received showing the name in a different form. If an established heading is coded "AACR2 compatible," LC generally will not reconsider the heading, although exceptions are made in a few instances (e.g., when an author has notified LC that another form of name is preferred). (*CSB* 91: 23) Examples:

> **Established heading:** Rouse, John Edward, 1942-
>   **Has written later as:** John E. Rouse
>   **Heading coded "AACR2 compatible."**
>   **Established heading retained.**

> **Established heading:** Sánchez E., Rodrigo
>   **Has now written over 80% as:** Rodrigo Sánchez Enríquez
>   **New heading:** Sánchez Enríquez, Rodrigo

22.3B.   Language

22.3B1.   Persons using more than one language

The heading for a person who writes in more than one language should be the form that corresponds to the language of most of the works. Example:

> **Names found on works:**   William More
> Guillermo Mora
> **Lived and worked in both U.S. and Venezuela.**
> **Most works in Spanish.**
> **Heading:** Mora, Guillermo

If there is doubt about which language is used in most of the works, the form found most in reference sources of the person's country of residence or activity should be used. LC practice when reference sources cannot be found, or the person is not listed, is to use the form of the name in the person's native language but to change to another language if 80% of the works eventually use the name in that language. (*CSB* 47: 52) The choice made according to this rule may be altered by application of rules 22.3B2, 22.3B3, or 22.3C.

22.3B2.   Names in vernacular and Greek or Latin forms

The heading for a name that appears in both Latin or Greek and the vernacular in reference sources and/or in the person's works should be given in the form found most often in reference sources. For cases of doubt, the Latin or Greek is chosen for persons active before 1400 A.D. and the vernacular for persons active after 1400. Example:

> **Name in vernacular:** Dante Alighieri (with various spellings)
> **Name in Latin:** Dantes Aligerius
> **Form most commonly found in reference sources:** Dante
>   Alighieri
> **Heading:** Dante Alighieri, 1265-1321

22.3B3.   Names written in the roman alphabet and established in an English form

The heading for a person entered under given name according to rule 22.8 or for a Roman of classical times is the English form if an English form is well established in English-language reference sources. The vernacular or Latin is used in cases of doubt. Example:

> **Name of saint in Latin:** Justinus
> **Name in English-language reference sources:** Justin
> **Heading:** Justin, Martyr, Saint

22.3B4.   Other names

The heading for all other names found in two or more languages is the form found most often in reference sources of the person's country of residence or activity. Example:

> **Name on original work:** John Boyer Noss
> **Name on translation of original work:** Jān B. Nūs
> **Place of author's residence:** U.S.
> **Heading:** Noss, John Boyer

22.3C.   Names written in a nonroman script

Names that must be romanized or transliterated present many problems. Some languages have a number of systems for romanization, and use of the different systems results in different spellings. In addition, there may be one or more English-language forms of some better known names. The rules in 22.3C give some guidance.

22.3C1.   Persons entered under given name, etc.

This rule, like 22.3B3, calls for entry under an English-language form, if one has become well established in English-language reference sources. (If more than one exists, choose the one that appears most frequently.) Example:

> **Romanizations of name:**   Movses Khorenat͡si
> Moses Xorenc'i
> **English-language form of name:** Moses of Khoren
> **Heading:** Moses, of Khoren, 5th cent.

If there is no English form, or if one romanization cannot be determined to be predominant, the name should be romanized according to the cataloging agency's adopted romanization table.

LC's policy for nonroman alphabet names entered under a given name or a surname is to search the name in *Academic American Encyclopedia*, *The Encyclopedia Americana*, and *Encyclopaedia Britannica* (15th ed.). If the name is in all three sources in a single form, that form is used. If it varies, the form in *Encyclopaedia Britannica* is used. If it is not found in all three sources, the systematic romanization is used. An exception is made for persons entered under *given* name who are not found in all three sources because of "specialized fame." In such cases major specialized encyclopedias, such as *New Catholic Encyclopedia*, are used. Another exception is for persons of very recent fame. For these, yearbooks to the encyclopedias and indexes to major newspapers are consulted. (*CSB* 40: 29–31)

22.3C2.   Persons entered under surname

Unlike the preceding rule, this one directs the cataloger to romanize a name entered under surname according to the table adopted by the cataloging agency. References are made from other romanized forms. If a name is found only in romanized form in the works involved, that form is used.

An alternative rule is given for 22.3C2: An English form, well established in English-language reference sources, may be used for the heading. This corresponds to the treatment of persons entered under given name, but is counter to the principle of entry under the name elements most commonly found in writers' works or in reference works in the language or country of residence or activity for persons other than writers. The Library of Congress is following the alternative rule. (*CSB* 40: 29–31) Their policy for application of the alternative rule is discussed above under rule 22.3C1. Example:

> **Romanized form appearing in the item:** Fyodor Dostoevsky
> **Systematic romanization according to LC's adopted tables:**
> Dostoevskiĭ, Fedor
> **Form most often found in English-language reference sources:**
> Dostoyevsky, Fyodor
> **Heading:** Dostoyevsky, Fyodor, 1821-1881

It should be noted that the alternative rule makes no provision for names for which there are no entries in English-language reference sources, unless the person uses Hebrew or Yiddish, in which case the romanized form found in the person's works is called for. Otherwise, when there are no entries in English-language sources, presumably, one should use the provision given in rule 22.3C1 for persons entered under given name: "If no English romanization is found . . . romanize the name according to the table for the language adopted by the cataloguing agency."[6] Example:

> **Romanizations found in chief sources of information,**
> **but not in reference sources:**
>   Maſsiūte, Regina
>   Maciūte, Regina [romanization according to adopted table]
> **Heading:** Maciūte, Regina

If variant spellings occur that are not the result of different romanizations, the form that represents an official orthographic change should be used, if this is applicable. Otherwise, one should choose the predominant spelling, or, in case of doubt, the spelling found in the first item cataloged. Example:

> **Variant spellings found:**   Thomas Decker
>   Thomas Dekker
>   Thomas Deckar
> **Predominant spelling:** Thomas Dekker
> **Heading:** Dekker, Thomas, ca. 1572-1632

Entry Element: Selected Rules and Examples

RULE 22.4.   GENERAL RULE

22.4A.   When a person's name consists of more than one part, a choice must be made about which part will be the entry element. In general the entry element is the one that would usually be used in authoritative alphabetic lists in the person's own country or language. "Authoritative" is defined as meaning "who's who" type publications, not telephone directory type publications. However, if it is known that the person prefers some other entry element than would be the usual usage for that language or country, the person's preference is followed.

22.4B.   Order of elements
The entry element is chosen according to rules 22.5–22.9, but the order of other elements is given here, covering the entry element as the first element in a name (22.4B1–22.4B2), the entry element not the first element of a name (22.4B3), or the entry element as the proper name in a title of nobility (22.4B4).

RULE 22.5.   ENTRY UNDER SURNAME

22.5A.   General rule
If a name contains a surname, the entry element should be the surname unless one of the following rules provides for a different entry element. (*See also* rules 22.6, 22.10, and 22.28.) Example:

Name on chief source of information: Jill S. Slattery
Surname entry element: Slattery
Heading: Slattery, Jill S., 1943-

22.5B.   Element other than the first treated as a surname

A name that functions as a surname, even though it is not really a surname, is treated as if it were. Example:

Name on chief source of information: Muhammad Sā'īd Bāyirlī
Heading: Bāyirlī, Muhammad Sa'īd

22.5C.   Compound surnames

22.5C1.   Preliminary rule

Compound surnames consist of two or more proper names. The rules under rule 22.5C treat these and also some names that appear to be compound surnames. The rules are applied in the order given. References should be made from elements of a compound surname not chosen for entry.

22.5C2.   Preferred or established form known

The entry element for a compound surname of a person with a known preference should be the person's preferred entry element. Otherwise, the entry element should be the element under which it is given in reference sources from the person's country or in the person's language. Example:

Lloyd George, David, 1863-1945
    War memoirs of David Lloyd George

[Note: Refer from: George, David Lloyd. George is his paternal surname.]

22.5C3.   Hyphenated surnames

Compound surnames that are hyphenated (even if only sometimes) should be entered under the first element. Example:

Heading under first part of hyphenated surname:
    Boswell-Taylor, Harold
    Refer from: Taylor, Harold Boswell-

22.5C4–22.5C5.

Rules 22.5C4–22.5C5 cover all other compound surnames, including those of married women whose surnames consist of a surname before marriage and a husband's surname.

22.5D.   Surnames with separately written prefixes

LC's rule interpretation should be consulted for guidance on placement of constituent parts of a name in headings and references once the appropriate entry element has been determined according to the following rules. (*CSB* 96: 11–12)

22.5D1.   Articles and prepositions

Names that contain an article or a preposition or a combination of the two as part of the surname should be entered under the element that would normally be used in alphabetical lists from the person's country or in the person's language.

In *AACR2R* this rule contains many specific examples of names in different languages. Only the most basic of the rules for Western names are cited here.

DUTCH. Dutch names are entered under the part following the prefix with one exception: a name with the prefix *ver* is entered under the prefix. Example:

Heading: Ver Mooten, Willem
Refer from: Mooten, Willem Ver

Heading: Beek, Jan M. van der
Refer from: Van der Beek, Jan M.

ENGLISH. English names are entered under the prefix. Example:

Heading: Van Buren, Ariane
Refer from: Buren, Ariane van

FRENCH and GERMAN. French and German names in which the prefix is an article or a contraction of an article and a preposition are entered under the prefix. Examples:

Heading: Le Bihan, Alain
Refer from: Bihan, Alain Le

Heading: Vom Scheidt, Jürgen, 1940-
Refer from: Scheidt, Jürgen vom

All other French and German names with prefixes are entered under the element following the prefix. Examples:

Heading: La Fontäine, Jean de, 1621-1695
Refer from: Fontaine, Jean de la

[Note: Entry is under the article following the preposition.]

Heading: Weizsäcker, Carl Christian von

ITALIAN. Modern Italian names are entered under the prefix. Example:

Heading: De Filippo, Peppino
Refer from: Filippo, Peppino de

In order to determine the correct entry element for medieval and early modern Italian names, reference sources should be consulted. Example:

Heading: Medici, Lorenzo de'

SPANISH. Spanish names that have a prefix that consists only of an article are entered under the prefix. Otherwise, a name is entered under the element following the prefix. Example:

Heading: Lorenzo, Pedro de

22.5D2–22.5E.   Other prefixes
In all languages, when the prefix is not an article or a preposition or a combination of the two, or when the prefix is hyphenated or combined with the name, the entry element should be the prefix. Example:

Heading: MacIntyre, Elisabeth

RULE 22.6.   ENTRY UNDER TITLE OF NOBILITY

If a person is commonly known by a title of nobility, the proper name in that title should be the entry element. This rule applies to persons who use titles rather than surnames in their works or, if there are no textual works to consult, to those persons who are listed by title in reference sources. (Reference sources that list all members of the nobility under title should not be used for this decision.) The proper name in the title is followed by the personal name in direct order, and the personal name is followed by the term of rank. Unused forenames are not included. A reference is made from the personal surname unless it is the same as the proper name in the title. The rule in *AACR2R* should be consulted for further details.

This rule is closely related to rules 22.4B4 and 22.12. The three result in the same form of name, but they approach this type of name from the three viewpoints of order of elements, entry element, and additions to names.

RULE 22.8.   ENTRY UNDER GIVEN NAME, ETC.

If a person is not identified by a title of nobility and the name does not include a surname, the entry element should be the part of the name that is the entry element in reference sources. Any words or phrases that are commonly associated with the name in that person's works or in reference sources should be included, preceded by a comma. Example:

Heading: Paul, of Aleppo, Archdeacon, fl. 1654-1666

Specific parts of this rule address names that include a patronymic and names of royal persons. LC rule interpretations give guidelines for more complicated given name entries and should be consulted for more guidance. (*CSB* 44: 46; *CSB* 71: 55–56)

22.10–22.11

Rules 22.10–22.11 give instructions for entry elements when all one has for a name are initials, letters, numerals, or phrases. These are to be entered in direct order if they do not contain a real name. More specialized rules cover entry of phrases that contain names, and these should be consulted when needed.

Additions to Names: Selected Rules and Examples

General

RULE 22.12.   TITLES OF NOBILITY

22.12A. If a nobleman or noblewoman is not entered under title according to rule 22.6, but the title or a part of the title usually appears with the name, the title of nobility should be added in the vernacular to the personal name. Example:

Heading: John, of Gaunt, Duke of Lancaster, 1340-1399

Note that terms of honor (Sir, Dame, Lord, Lady) formerly used in headings are now authorized only under the conditions given in rule 22.20 (see below).

RULE 22.13.   SAINTS

The word *Saint* is added after a saint's given name unless the person was a pope, emperor, empress, king, or queen. In those cases the latter epithet takes precedence over *Saint*, and one follows rules 22.16A–22.16B. Example:

Heading: Joan, of Arc, Saint, 1412-1431

RULE 22.15.   ADDITIONS TO NAMES ENTERED UNDER SURNAME

22.15A.   When a name consists only of a surname with an accompanying word or phrase in the person's works or in reference sources, the associated word or phrase should be added after the surname. A reference is made from the name in direct order if it would be useful. LC generally makes the direct order reference only when such a heading is a pseudonym or assumed name. (*CSB* 39: 13) Example:

> **Heading:** Jefferson, Mr., of Gray's Inn
> **Refer from:** Mr. Jefferson of Gray's Inn

22.15B.   Terms of address of married women
When a woman is identified only by "Mrs." with her husband's name, the term "Mrs." is added. Example:

> **Heading:** Bruce, William, Mrs.

22.15C.   Titles or terms other than those in the preceding rules are not added to names entered under surname except when necessary to distinguish between otherwise identical names for which dates are not available. Example:

> **Name on chief source of information:** Dr. Mary Lyon
> **Heading:** Lyon, Mary

RULE 22.16.   ADDITIONS TO NAMES ENTERED UNDER GIVEN NAME, ETC.

22.16A.   Royalty
This rule in *AACR2R* has four specific subsections with accompanying examples. The essence of the rule is that royal persons are entered under the names by which they are known. A royal name may include a house, dynasty, or surname (*see* rule 22.8C in *AACR2R*) or a Roman numeral. A phrase (in English, if possible) consisting of title and state governed follows the name of a person with the highest royal status in a state. Other epithets are not added, but are "referred from." Consorts, children, and grandchildren of rulers have a title added to their names (again in English, if possible) plus the name of the ruler to whom related. Examples:

> **Heading:** Nikolaĭ Mikhaĭlovich, Grand Duke of Russia, 1859-1919

> **Heading:** William, Prince, grandson of Elizabeth II, Queen of Great Britain, 1982-

22.16B.   Popes

22.16C.   Bishops, etc.

22.16D.   Other persons of religious vocation
Rules 22.16B–22.16D call for addition of the words *Pope*, *Bishop*, *Archbishop*, *Cardinal*, and other titles in English (if there is an English equivalent) to the names of persons who are high ecclesiastical officials. The name of the latest see is also added to some titles. For other persons of religious vocation who are entered under given name, titles or terms of address are added in the vernacular. Initials of a Christian religious order regularly used by the person are also added. Examples:

Heading: John Paul II, Pope, 1920-

Heading: Maria Crocifissa di Gesu, madre, 1713-1787

Additions to Distinguish Identical Names

RULE 22.17.   DATES

Birth and death dates are added as the last element of a heading in order to distinguish between two otherwise identical headings. An option to this rule allows adding the date(s) even when there is no conflict. LC is applying this option when the date is known at the time the heading is first established or later if the heading must be revised anyway. For persons living in the twentieth century or later, LC only adds precise dates. Less precise dates may be added to the headings for pre-twentieth century persons. (*CSB* 108: 87–88) Examples:

Addition of dates for a living person:

Vieweg-Marks, Karin, 1957-

Addition of dates when references differ as to year of birth; 1496 is probable:

Fox, Edward, Bishop of Hereford, 1496?-1538

Addition of dates when year of birth unknown:

Timberlake, Henry, d. 1626

Addition of dates when years of birth and death unknown, but date of activity is known. (Not used for twentieth century):

Gardiner, Richard, fl. 1599-1603

[Note: "fl." is the AACR2R abbreviation for "flourished."]

Day, month, and year of birth added to distinguish from others of same name and same year of birth:

Fischer, John, 1910 Apr. 27-

Fischer, John, 1910 Nov. 3-

Addition of probable dates:

Ford, John, 1586-ca. 1640

It should be noted that after a name for a contemporary person has been established in the authoritative form with the birth date only, LC has had a policy to not add the death date to the authorized form when the person died unless the authorized form had to be changed for some other reason. The assumption was that authorized forms are intended to identify persons and to distinguish among them, not to serve as reference sources. However, catalog users found this confusing, and early in 2006, LC changed the policy to make it optional to add death dates to headings that have open birth dates. Readers should follow the new rule interpretation for addition of death dates.

RULE 22.18.   FULLER FORMS

When two names as prescribed by the preceding rules are identical and a fuller form of one or both names is known, the fuller form is added in parentheses in order to distinguish between the two names. The rule calls for a reference from the full form when appropriate. In many catalogs such references are superfluous, especially when the initial in the name is for a second or later forename. Example:

> **Heading:** Roberts, J. O. (Jack O.)
> **Refer from:** Roberts, Jack O.

This rule allows the option of making the above additions even when not necessary to distinguish identical names except that, when following the option, one is not to add:

> "unused forenames to headings that contain forenames
>
> initials of names that are not part of the heading
>
> unused parts of surnames to headings that contain surnames."[7]

LC is following the option when the information is known with certainty. A rule interpretation gives guidelines for how much of the name to include in the parenthetical statement and where to place it. Once a heading has been established without the names in parentheses, they are not added if they become known later unless the heading must be changed for some other reason (e.g., it comes in conflict with another heading). (*CSB* 57: 20–21)

RULE 22.19.   DISTINGUISHING TERMS and
RULE 22.20.   UNDIFFERENTIATED NAMES

When dates or fuller forms are not available to distinguish between identical names, certain other additions may be made following rule 22.19. For given names, a brief term may be devised (e.g., "poet") and added in parentheses. For surname entries, a term of address, title of position, initials of academic degree, term of honor, etc., that appears with the name in works or reference sources may be added. Examples:

> **Heading:** Chapman, William H., M.A.

> **Heading:** Hill, Barbara, Dame

Otherwise, according to rule 22.20 the same heading is used for all persons with the same name.

22.21–22.28

Rules 22.21–22.28 are special rules for names in certain languages and should be consulted as needed.

HEADINGS FOR GEOGRAPHIC NAMES

This section covers Chapter 23 in *AACR2R*, which treats the form of heading for any geographic name that may be used as a main or added entry heading. This includes names for places that now are or once were jurisdictional entities. It does not include names that cannot be jurisdictions, such as continents, mountains, and rivers. Yet there is an attempt in *AACR2R* to separate rules for place names that are "only" geographic names from those that are names of jurisdictions. Therefore, one rule in Chapter 24, "Headings for Corporate Bodies" (rule 24.6), deals with what seem to be geographic names; but the rule actually deals with jurisdictions. Another rule, 24.3E, covers "conventional" names of governments and gives instructions to use the geographic name as constructed in Chapter 23. Other rules throughout Chapter 24 cover additions of geographic names to corporate names for the purpose of identification or distinction. It can be seen, then, that the cataloger cannot rely solely on Chapter 23 for the construction of names that appear to be geographic.

In Chapter 23 of *AACR2R* there are rules for choice of name (rules 23.2–23.3), additions to place names (rule 23.4), and modification of place names (rule 23.5). Problems involved in choice of name often involve choice between an English form and a form in some other language. Choice may also involve which name to use when the name of a place has changed. For additions to place names, problems may involve decisions about which larger place names are most useful for identification. (For example, should the name of the county, state, and/or country be added to the name of a town?) A problem that may require modification of a name involves the use of a term indicating type of jurisdiction. The problem is whether that term comes first, while the name is commonly known or listed under another element of the name (e.g., Kreis Lippe, a county in Germany, is commonly listed under Lippe). The purpose of this chapter is to demonstrate the rules used to resolve these problems.

A heading created using *AACR2R*, Chapter 23, is coded 110, 651, 710, or 810 in the *MARC 21* format, depending upon whether it functions as a main entry, subject heading, or added entry or begins a series. Codes 110, 710, and 810 are for corporate names, and in these cases the name of a jurisdiction alone is coded as a corporate name. However, in the subject fields there are separate numbers for corporate names (610) and geographic names (651). Jurisdictions that stand alone are coded as geographic names.

Selected Rules and Examples

RULE 23.2.   GENERAL RULES
These general rules involve choice of a name from among variant forms of a name that may be found.

23.2A.   English form
AACR2R calls for use of the English form of a place name and specifies that this form should be determined from gazetteers and other reference sources from English-speaking countries. When there is doubt as to whether the English form is generally used, the vernacular form is to be used. Examples:

Forms of name found:	Brasil
	Brazil
Heading: Brazil	

Forms of name found:	Bucharest
	Bucuresti
	Bucuresci̇̆
	Bukharest
	Bucarest
Heading: Bucharest (Romania)	

LC bases headings for United States names on the Geographic Names Information System (GNIS), the United States Board on Geographical Names' (BGN) domestic names system. The *Rand McNally Commercial Atlas and Marketing Guide* is used as backup when Web access is unavailable. Names from Australia and New Zealand are based on the GEOnet Names Server (GNS) of the Defense Mapping Agency, again with a recent gazetteer used as backup. Names from Great Britain are based on a recent edition of *The Ordnance Survey Gazetteer of Great Britain*; headings for place names in Canada are those provided by the National Library of Canada. For other names, the heading is based on the form found in the work being cataloged, in consultation with the form found on the GNS Web site. An English form in general use is always used, even when the BGN-approved form is in the vernacular. LC's rule interpretation provides the current Web address for the resources mentioned in this paragraph. (*CSB* 109:26–27)

LC has issued special decisions in a number of complicated cases, even where they contradict the prescriptions of *AACR2R*. These include China, Germany (pre- and post-unification), Great Britain, Korea, the several entities referred to as "London," the former Soviet Union, and Washington, D.C. (*CSB* 109: 30–32)

23.2B. Vernacular form

23.2B1. If there is no English form in general use, the form in the official language of the country is used. Examples:

Headings: [no English form in use]
Pistoia (Italy)
Tétaigne (France)
Tromsø (Norway)
Heading: [English form, Brunswick, not in general use]
Braunschweig (Germany)

In cases where there is more than one official language in a country, the most common form found in English-language reference sources is used. Example:

Forms of name found: Bruxelles
Brüssel
Brussels
Form most often found in English-language sources: Brussels
Heading: Brussels (Belgium)

Note: There is no rule for variations of spelling of the name in the same language. Because of the close association in the rules of geographic names and corporate names, it is assumed that needed rules, such as the one for spelling, may be taken from *AACR2R* chapter 24 and applied to geographic names. Rule 24.2C states that for a name with variant spellings, the one that represents an official change in orthography should be used if this applies or else the predominant spelling should be used. Example:

Original spelling: Tandjungpinang, Indonesia
New official spelling: Tanjungpinang, Indonesia
Variants also found: Tandjoengpinang
Tandjung Pinang
Tanjung Pinang
Heading: Tanjungpinang (Indonesia)

RULE 23.3.   CHANGES OF NAME

The essence of this rule is that if the name of a place changes, one should use on catalog records as many of the names as are required by rules in *AACR2R*, Chapter 24. The rule mentions specifically rules 24.3E, 24.4C4, and 24.7B4 but allows for other relevant rules as well. Examples:

In 1971, the Town of Whitchurch-Stouffville was created, incorporating the Village of Stouffville in Ontario.

A work requiring Stouffville as a heading prior to 1971 would use the heading:
Stouffville (Ont.)

A work requiring Stouffville as a heading in 1971 or later would use the heading:
Stouffville (Whitchurch-Stouffville, Ont.)

In 1971 East Pakistan became Bangladesh. A corporate body whose lifetime spanned the change would have the latest name of the country added, even for items relevant only to the body during the time the country was known as East Pakistan, e.g.,
Institution of Engineers (Bangladesh)
not Institution of Engineers (East Pakistan)

RULE 23.4.   ADDITIONS

23.4A.   Punctuation

Additions to place names that are used as entry elements are made in parentheses. Example:

Staunton (Va.)

When the whole place name is used as an addition, it is enclosed in parentheses with a comma preceding the larger place. Example:

Second Presbyterian Church (Staunton, Va.)

23.4B.   General rule

Any place name (other than that of a country or that of a state, etc., listed in rule 23.4C1 or rule 23.4D1) should have added to it the name of a larger place, following rules 23.4C–23.4F. Additional instructions for place names used as headings for governments are given in rule 24.6. Instructions for abbreviations for additions are given in Appendix B of *AACR2R*.

In a rule interpretation for this rule, LC addresses three situations not covered by rules 23.4C–23.4F: (*CSB* 41: 44–45)

1)   If an island or island group is a jurisdiction, the name of the larger jurisdiction should be added only when the island or island group is located near the larger jurisdiction. Examples:

Guardia Island (Spain)
Madeira Islands

2)   When a larger place that is being added has changed its name and if the smaller place existed through the name change, the current larger place name should be added, with a reference from the place with the earlier larger place name. Example:

Georgetown (Guyana)

with a reference from:

Georgetown (British Guiana)

3)   The additions prescribed in rule 24.6 should not be added as part of the qualifier being added under rule 23.4B. Example:

St. Romuald (Québec)
not St. Romuald (Québec, Province)

23.4C.   Places in Australia, Canada, Malaysia, United States, U.S.S.R., or Yugoslavia

23.4C1.   States, etc.
No addition should be made to the name of a state, province, etc., of one of the countries covered by this rule. Examples:

California
not California (U.S.)

Hrvatska Croatia
not Hrvatska Croatia (Yugoslavia)

LC makes references from the names of states of Malaysia qualified with "(Malaysia)." (*CSB* 41: 46) Example:

Kedah

with reference from:

Kedah (Malaysia)

For the constituent republics of the former Soviet Union (before 1992), and their successor states (after 1991), LC uses the following headings: (*CSB* 109: 31–32)

Armenian S.S.R.	Armenia (Republic)
Azerbaijan S.S.R.	Azerbaijan
Byerlorussian S.S.R.	Belarus
Estonia	Estonia
Georgian S.S.R.	Georgia (Republic)
Kazakh S.S.R.	Kazakhstan
Kirghiz S.S.R.	Kyrgyzstan
Latvia	Latvia
Lithuania	Lithuania
Moldavian S.S.R. [before 1990]	Moldova [after 1989]
Russian S.F.S.R.	Russia (Federation)
Tajik S.S.R.	Tajikistan
Turkmen S.S.R.	Turkmenistan
Ukraine	Ukraine
Uzbek S.S.R.	Uzbekistan

23.4C2.   Other places

Add the name of the state, province, or territory to a place located in one of the countries covered by this rule. Places located in cities are treated according to rule 23.4F2. Examples:

> Delmont (Pa.)
> Montreal (Québec)
> Melbourne (Vic.)

23.4D.   Places in the British Isles

23.4D1.   No addition should be made to the names of the parts of the British Isles: England, the Republic of Ireland, Northern Ireland, Scotland, Wales, the Isle of Man, and the Channel Islands.

23.4D2.   For a place located in one of the above-named parts of the British Isles, one of the following names is added to the heading, as appropriate: England, Ireland (for the Republic of Ireland), Northern Ireland, Scotland, Wales, Isle of Man, or Channel Islands. Examples:

> Antrim (Northern Ireland)
> Warwickshire (England)
> Ayrshire (Scotland)
> Cambridge (England)
> Mold (Wales)
> Tralee (Ireland)

23.4E.   Other places

If a place is not covered by 23.4C–23.4D, the name of the country in which it lies is added. Examples:

> Lund (Sweden)
> Siena (Italy)
> Rio de Janeiro (Brazil)

23.4F.   Further additions

If two places with the same name are not sufficiently distinguished with additions as instructed in rules 23.4C–23.4E, a word or phrase commonly used with them may be used or an appropriate smaller place may be added before the larger place. Examples:

> Mount Vernon (Westchester County, N.Y.)
> Mount Vernon (Erie County, N.Y.)

A place otherwise difficult to identify, such as a community within a city, may also have an appropriate smaller place added before the larger place. Examples:

> Bregninge (Svendborg, Denmark)
> Chinatown (San Francisco, Calif.)

RULE 23.5.   PLACE NAMES INCLUDING OR REQUIRING A TERM INDICATING A TYPE OF JURISDICTION

23.5A. When the first element of a place name indicates a type of jurisdiction but the place is usually listed under another name element in reference sources of the country, the term indicating type of jurisdiction should be omitted. Example:

Kreis Lippe in Germany is commonly listed under Lippe in German lists.
Heading: Lippe (Germany : Kreis)

[Note: In this example, *Kreis* is omitted from the first element according to this rule, but it is added in the qualifier to distinguish it from the principality that had the name *Lippe*, as called for in the *AACR2R* chapter on corporate names.]

The type of jurisdiction is included in all cases that do not fit the above criteria. Example:

> Dutchess County (N.Y.)

Note: The term *county* should be included for U.S. counties, even though many U.S. atlases list counties by name only under the caption *counties* and therefore omit the word *county* with the name. Note that *county* is spelled out. Most U.S. counties have been established by LC and other libraries in the past using *Co.* and are being changed by LC as new occasions for use of each county name arise.

23.5B. Occasionally a place name does not include a term indicating type of jurisdiction, but such a term is required for differentiating between two identical names. If this is the case, rule 24.6 should be applied. Example:

> Chimaltenango (Guatemala : Dept.)

[Note: There is also a municipality named Chimaltenango.]

Note: LC continues to abbreviate *Department* as *Dept.*, even though it is not allowed to be abbreviated in headings according to *AACR2R*, Appendix B, "Abbreviations." (*CSB* 32: 58)

HEADINGS FOR CORPORATE BODIES

This section covers the rules for construction of names of corporate bodies. *Corporate body* is defined in rule 21.1B1 of *AACR2R2002* as "an organization or a group of persons that is identified by a particular name and that acts, or may act, as an entity."[8] In general, entry of a corporate body is under the name the body itself uses except when the rules specify entry under a higher or related body or under the name of a government. Like the principle in use for personal names, the principle for corporate names is to choose the name the corporate body itself generally uses (including conventional names), even if that name is not the official one. Unlike personal names, however, when the name of a corporate body changes, a new heading is made under that name with cross references to and from various other former and related names.

Following the general rule (rule 24.1), there are rules for choice of names (rules 24.2–24.3) and for additions, omissions, and modifications (rules 24.4–24.11). These are followed by rules for subordinate and related bodies in general (rules 24.12–24.16), for government bodies and officials (rules 24.17–24.26), and for religious bodies and officials (rule 24.27). Problems involved in choice of name include choice among variant forms found in items issued by a body, such as official name or acronym or short form, choice among variant spellings (including differences in romanization), and choice among different languages. Problems requiring additions, omissions, or other modifications include the need to distinguish between two or more bodies with the same name, the need to provide adequate identification for a name that does not convey the idea of a corporate body, and the desire to omit unnecessary or excess terms such as *incorporated* or *biennial*.

In dealing with a subordinate body, the cataloger must decide whether the body can be entered directly under its own name or must be entered under its higher body, and because government and religious bodies present special problems in this area, the cataloger must know whether a subordinate body belongs in one of these two groups before applying the rules. The purpose of this section is to demonstrate only the most important problems of corporate entry. For more detail, the cataloger should consult *AACR2R*, Chapter 24.

As with personal names, there are certain previously established headings for corporate bodies that LC considered "*AACR2* compatible" from January 2, 1981, to September 1, 1982 (*see* discussion on pages 220–221 in the personal names section of this chapter). These are summarized with examples in *Cataloging Service Bulletin*. (*CSB* 108: 92–94)

A heading created using *AACR2R*, Chapter 24, is coded 110, 111, 610, 611, 710, 711, 810, or 811 in the *MARC 21* format, depending upon whether it functions as a main entry, subject heading, or added entry or begins a series. The codes ending in "11" are for conference names. The codes ending in "10" are for all other corporate names.

General Rules: Selected Rules and Examples

RULE 24.1.   GENERAL RULE

24.1A. A corporate body is to be entered directly under its own name unless later rules instruct that it be entered subordinately to a higher body or to a government. Although the rule does not say so, there are also religious bodies that must be entered subordinately. Therefore, the cataloger must first determine whether a body is a government or religious body and start with those rules if it is: rules 24.17–24.26 for government bodies; rule 24.27 for religious bodies. If a body is neither government nor religious but is subordinate to another body, rules 24.12–24.16 must be consulted. In many cases one will be referred back to this rule (rule 24.1), because the body can be entered under its own name even though it is a subordinate body.

LC has issued a rule interpretation which lists the types of "ambiguous entities," such as arboretums, chambers of commerce, motels, shipyards, and zoos, that should be treated as corporate bodies for the purpose of establishing headings. (*CSB* 108: 89–90)

The form of the name of a corporate body is determined from items issued by the body in its language, if possible, or from reference sources. The punctuation usage of the body should be followed (e.g., whether or not periods are included after initials depends upon the predominant usage by the body).

References from different forms of a corporate body name are prescribed in the *AACR2R* reference chapter, rule 26.3. Examples:

> **Heading:** Lawyer's Committee for Civil Rights Under Law

> **Heading:** W.K. Kellogg Arabian Horse Center
> **Refer from:** Kellogg Arabian Horse Center

> **Heading:** Nelliston Community Group

> **Heading:** Pro Musica Antiqua, Prague
> **Refer from:** Symposium "Pro Musica Antiqua" Prag

A rule interpretation from LC gives guidance for punctuating and spacing corporate names. (*CSB* 108: 90–92)

It should also be noted here that for a corporate name that itself includes the name of a place at the end, the punctuation used by the body is retained. This means that some names may be established ending with a place preceded by a comma and a space, and others may be established with a place enclosed in parentheses. These have nothing to do with the additions prescribed in rule 24.4 and should not be interpreted as "errors." Example:

> California State University, San Diego
> *not* California State University (San Diego)

24.1B.   Romanization

The name of a body that is written in a nonroman script is romanized using the table adopted by the cataloging agency. This means that even if a romanized form of the name appears in items issued by a body, that form may be used only if it corresponds to the table adopted by the cataloging agency. References are made from other romanizations. Example:

> **Romanization of name originally in nonroman script**
> **with reference from the English form of the name:**

> **Heading:** Akademiíâ nauk SSSR
> **Refer from:** Academy of Sciences of the U.S.S.R.

A footnote in *AACR2R* allows an alternative to this rule: a romanized form appearing in items issued by the body is used, and references are made from other romanizations. LC is not applying the alternative rule. (*CSB* 44: 53)

24.1C.   Changes of name
When a corporate body changes its name, a new heading is established for the new name. A bibliographic record for an item relating to the old name has the old name as a heading, while a bibliographic record for an item relating to the new name has the new name as a heading. References are made referring to each name from the other. Example:

Explanatory reference showing each name a corporate body has used:

> The Long Range Planning Service of the Stanford Research Institute became the Business Intelligence Program in April 1976. On May 16, 1977, the Institute changed its name to S.R.I. International.
> Works by these bodies are found under the following headings according to the name used at the time of publication:
> Stanford Research Institute. Long Range Planning Service
> Business Intelligence Program (SRI International)

RULE 24.2.   VARIANT NAMES. GENERAL RULES
Variant names here do not include those resulting from official changes of names. Such changes are covered by 24.1. LC has a rule interpretation that explains what are to be treated as variant names. (*CSB* 47: 54–55)

24.2B.   When different name forms are found in various places in items issued by a corporate body, the form found in chief sources of information should be used. Example:

> **Name on chief source of information:** Michael Bradner Associates
> **Forms of name found elsewhere in work:**
> Mike Bradner & Associates
> Mike Bradner and Associates
> **Heading:** Michael Bradner Associates
> **Refer from:**   Mike Bradner & Associates
> Mike Bradner and Associates
> Bradner Associates

24.2C.   When there are variant spellings of a name in items issued by the body, the one that represents an official change in orthography should be used, if this applies, or if not, the predominant spelling should be chosen. Example:

> **Name on some chief sources:** Allgemeines deutsches Commersbuch

> **Name on most chief sources:** Allgemeines deutsches Kommersbuch
> **Heading:** Allgemeines deutsches Kommersbuch
> **Refer from:** Allgemeines deutsches Commersbuch

24.2D.   When different name forms appear in the chief source of information, the one presented formally should be used if that is applicable, or the predominant form should be used if no form is presented formally or all are equally presented. *AACR2R* prescribes that if no form is predominant, a short form that distinguishes this body from others with a similar name should be used in preference to a longer form. However, a rule interpretation from LC indicates that if a body's initials or acronym appear formally with the full form, the full form should be chosen for the heading. (*CSB* 44: 53–54) Example:

> **Names on chief source of information:** GAAG, the Guerrilla Art
> Action Group
> **Neither form formally presented. No predominant form.**
> *AACR2R* **heading:** GAAG
> > **Refer from:** Guerrilla Art Action Group
> **LC choice of heading:** Guerrilla Art Action Group
> > **LC reference from:** GAAG

If a brief form does not differentiate a body from another with the same name, a form found in reference sources or the official form, in that order of preference, should be used. For example, the short form *NEA* for the National Education Association of the United States does not distinguish it from other bodies known as NEA: Nouvelles Editions africaines, National Endowment for the Arts, or the OECD Nuclear Energy Agency.

RULE 24.3   VARIANT NAMES. SPECIAL RULES

24.3A.   Language
This rule sets up an order of precedence to follow when the name of a body appears in different languages:

1.   The form in the official language of the body
2.   An English-language form if there is more than one official language and one is English
3.   The predominant language
4.   English, French, German, Spanish, or Russian, in that order
5.   The language that comes first in English alphabetic order

An LC rule interpretation inserts another criterion between 3 and 4: if one does not know the official language of the body, the official language of the country in which the body is located is used (if the country has a single official language). (*CSB* 45: 54) Example:

> **Names on publications:**
> > Schweizerische Hochschulrektoren-Konferenz, Kommission für
> Hochschulplanung
> > Commission de planification de la Conférence des recteurs des
> universités suisses
> **Official language:** German
> **Heading:** Schweizerische Hochschulrektoren-Konferenz
> Kommission für Hochschulplanung
> > **Refer from French form.**

An alternative to this rule allows use of a form of language appropriate to the catalog's users if the application of the rule results in a language not familiar to the users. LC is not following this alternative. (*CSB* 45: 54)

24.3B.   Language. International bodies
The English form of an international body is used if the name appears in English in its publications. Otherwise, the preceding rule, rule 24.3A, is used. Example:

>**Names on chief source of information:**
>al-Maṣrif al-'Arabī lil-Tanmiyah al-Iqtiṣādīyah fī Afrīqyā
>Arab Bank for Economic Development in Africa
>Banque Arabe de développement économique en Afrique
>**Heading:** Arab Bank for Economic Development in Africa
>**Refer from the names in Arabic and French.**

24.3C.   Conventional name

24.3C1.   General rule
A conventional name that is often used to identify a corporate body in reference sources in its own language should be used in place of an official name. Example:

>**Conventional name:** Abbey of Bury St. Edmunds
>**Official name:** Benedictine Abbey of Bury St. Edmunds
>in Suffolk

[Heading consists of conventional name, with reference from official name.]

24.3C2.   Ancient and international bodies
When an English form of name of an ancient body or of a body of international character has become very well known in English-language usage, this form should be used. A footnote comments that this rule applies to such bodies as religious bodies, fraternal and knightly orders, church councils, and diplomatic conferences. Examples:

>**Heading:** Orthodox Eastern Church
>**Refer from:** [Hēmerologion tēs Ekklēsias tēs Hellados]
>'Ημερολόγιον τῆς 'Εκκλησίας τῆς 'Ελλάδος

>**Heading:** Catholic Church. Canadian Catholic Conference
>**Refer from French forms of name.**

24.3D.   Religious orders and societies
The best known form of name for a religious order or society should be used. An English form is preferred, if one exists. Otherwise, the language of the country of origin is used. Example:

>**Heading:** White Fathers
>**Refer from:** Pères blancs

24.3E.   Governments
The conventional name of a government is preferred unless there is an official name in common use. The name of the geographic area over which the government has jurisdiction serves as the conventional name. Examples:

>Jersey City (N.J.)
>*not* City of Jersey City

Korea (North)
not Democratic People's Republic of Korea

San Marino
not Most Serene Republic of San Marino

24.3F.   Conferences, congresses, meetings, etc.
When variant forms of a conference name appear in the chief source of information, one that includes the name (or initials) of a body associated with the conference should be chosen, if possible. If, however, the meeting is *subordinate* to the body, rule 24.13A, Type 6 should be applied. Example:

Name of meeting: ALI-ABA Course of Study: Partnerships:
UPA, ULPA, Securities, Taxation, and Bankruptcy
**Name appears both with and without the initials of the
American Law Institute and the American Bar Association.**
Heading: ALI-ABA Course of Study: Partnerships: UPA, ULPA,
Securities, Taxation, and Bankruptcy (1990 : Seattle)
Refer from: Course of Study: Partnerships: UPA, ULPA,
Securities, Taxation, and Bankruptcy

Additions, Omissions, and Modifications: Selected Rules and Examples

RULE 24.4.   ADDITIONS

24.4A.   General rule
The subrules under rule 24.4 give general directions for making additions to corporate names. Special types of corporate names may need more specialized types of additions, which are covered in rules 24.6–24.11. All additions to corporate names are enclosed in parentheses.

24.4B.   Names not conveying the idea of a corporate body
When a corporate body name does not suggest that of a corporate body, a designation is added in English. A rule interpretation from LC that gives guidance in determining when such designations are needed (e.g., for ships, performing groups, etc.) should be consulted when needed. (*CSB* 95: 17-19) Examples:

ABBA (Musical group)

International Road Safety (Association)

But (Yacht)

24.4C.   Two or more bodies with the same or similar names
24.4C1.   General rule
When two or more corporate name headings are identical or so similar that they could be easily confused, a word or phrase must be added to each according to the subrules under rule 24.4C. Such additions may also be made when they would merely assist understanding. A rule interpretation explains how LC is applying this rule. In general, additions are made to every government body name that is entered

under its own name unless the government's name (or an understandable substitute for it) is already part of the name. An exception is made for government institutions (e.g., schools, libraries, hospitals). If one of these or if a nongovernment body is entered under its own name, a qualifier is added if it is needed for understanding the nature or purpose of the body. The rule interpretation goes on to elaborate upon choice of qualifiers and the forms qualifiers should take. (*CSB* 65: 20–21)

24.4C2–24.4C7.   Rules 24.4C2–24.4C4 authorize addition of place names—country, state, province, etc.—for a body that is national, provincial, etc., in character or of local place names for a body whose character is essentially local. If a place is not appropriate, rules 24.4C5–24.4C7 provide for addition of the name of an institution, the inclusive years of existence, or some other appropriate general designation in English. Example:

Addition of country to corporate name:

National Committee on the Status of Women (India)

[Note: This name could be held by similar groups in several countries. Therefore, the name of the country is added.]

It should be noted that when a place is used as a qualifier, if it is a place that is itself qualified by a larger place according to *AACR2R* chapter 23, the smaller and the larger place are both used in the qualifier of the corporate body. Thus, for a corporate body in Oklahoma City, the name of the city alone cannot be used as qualifier. It must be: (Oklahoma City, Okla.).

RULE 24.5.   OMISSIONS

24.5A–24.5C.   These rules require omission of certain elements from corporate names: initial articles are omitted unless the heading is to be filed under the article; terms indicating incorporation, etc., are omitted unless they are an integral part of the name or are needed to clarify the fact that the name is that of a corporate body. Other required omissions occur in rare instances, and the cataloger should consult *AACR2R* for them. Examples:

Entry of name omitting initial article:

Note giving title as shown on item in hand:
At head of title: The Daily Telegraph.

Heading made with initial article omitted:
Daily Telegraph (London, England)

Entry of name omitting term indicating incorporation:

Name appearing on publications:
Firestone Tire and Rubber Company, Inc.

Cataloger's judgment: *Inc.* not necessary for clarification as a corporate body

Heading: Firestone Tire and Rubber Company

Entry of name retaining term indicating incorporation:

Information in source about corporate body:
[Produced and distributed by Alternate Choice, Inc.]

Heading made for body with term of incorporation retained:
Alternate Choice, Inc.

RULE 24.6.   GOVERNMENTS. ADDITIONS

As mentioned in the geographic names section of this chapter, this rule is an attempt to give directions for entry of names of jurisdictions—distinct from the rules given for strictly geographic names. However, they are not totally separate, because this rule says that if names have not been differentiated by use of rule 23.4, then further addition according to rule 24.6 should be made.

LC has elaborated upon how it interprets this rule (*CSB* 78: 62–63), because it is not clear from the rule whether additions should be made to *both* conflicting names in all cases.

A succession of jurisdictions that have had the same name are all entered under one heading. Examples:

North Carolina		Hawaii	
not	North Carolina (Colony)	*not*	Hawaii (Kingdom)
	North Carolina (State)		Hawaii (Republic)
			Hawaii (State)

The name of a sovereign nation that is the same as the name of another place is not qualified. Example:

Italy
Italy (Tex.)

A third elaboration on this rule distinguishes between situations where the name of a place within a jurisdiction conflicts with the name of the jurisdiction and situations where the name of a jurisdiction conflicts with the name of a place in another jurisdiction. In the first situation, the name of the larger jurisdiction is qualified with the name of the type of government. Example:

Québec (Québec)   **[name of city]**
Québec (Province)   **[name of larger jurisdiction]**

In the second situation, only the name of the place in another jurisdiction is qualified. Example:

Alberta (Va.)
Alberta
not Alberta (Province)

An exception is made for the state of Washington. It is entered:

Washington (State)

24.6B.   If a jurisdiction is not a city or town and must have an addition because of conflict with another name, the type of jurisdiction is given in English, if there is an English equivalent; otherwise, it is given in the vernacular. Examples:

São Paulo (Brazil)
São Paulo (Brazil : State)
Alessandria (Italy : Province)
Esberg (Denmark : Kommune)

RULE 24.7.   CONFERENCES, CONGRESSES, MEETINGS, ETC.

24.7A.   Omissions

Words that express number, frequency, or year of meeting are omitted from the name of a conference. Example:

> **Name on chief source of information:** II Jornadas de Derecho Natural
> **Heading:** Jornadas de Derecho Natural

An LC rule interpretation states that, with some exceptions, an abbreviated form of the year will be retained as part of a conference name when that abbreviation is combined with an acronym or initialism. (*CSB* 92: 17–18)

24.7B.   Additions

The number of a conference, etc., the year, and the place in which it was held are added in parentheses to the name. If any of these elements are not known, they are omitted. Examples:

> **Heading:** International Ocular Trauma Conference
> (1st : 1988 : Zhengzhou, Henan, China)

> **Heading:** International Symposium on Viral Hepatitis
> and Liver Disease (1987 : Barbican Centre for Arts
> and Conferences)

For further guidance in selecting qualifiers for conferences, etc., the LC rule interpretation on this rule should be consulted. (*CSB* 92: 18)

Subordinate and Related Bodies

The problem of entry of corporate bodies that are subordinate to or closely related to other bodies is a difficult one. No completely unambiguous set of rules (including *AACR2R*) has yet been devised to handle it. The last sixteen rules in chapter 24 of *AACR2R* (rules 24.12–24.27) deal with this issue; yet even with this exhaustive treatment the end result may still depend upon the judgment of the individual cataloger.

There are three parts to this section: general rules, government body rules, and religious organization rules. The cataloger must first know if a body is a government or religious body. This is important because, in some cases, the results of applying the nongovernment rules to a government body may yield a heading not intended by the makers of the code. However, once into the sequence for government or religious bodies, the cataloger may be referred back to the general sequence for further instructions.

If it is determined that a body is a government body, rules 24.17–24.26 must be consulted before any others in chapter 24, because a government body is always a subordinate body—that is, it is always subordinate to a jurisdiction. Once into the rules, the cataloger may find that the result is the same as if subordination were not involved—that is, the body may be entered under its own name. (For example, the University of California, Los Angeles, a state institution, and the University of Southern California, a private institution, both end up entered under "University of. . . .") But if the body is one of the types listed in rule 24.18, it will be entered subordinately, and then rule 24.19 for direct or indirect subheading must be consulted; and if it is one of Types 6 through 11, one of rules 24.20–24.26 must also be consulted. The cataloger must also be concerned with the level of subordinate body involved. If it is subordinate to another government body that is entered under its *own name* because it is not one of the types listed in rule 24.18, then general rules 24.12–24.14 must be consulted for formulation of the heading for the subordinate body. If it is subordinate to another body that is entered under *jurisdiction*, then the cataloger continues to use government body rules 24.17–24.19 for formulation of the heading for the subordinate body.

If it is determined that a body is a religious body, rule 24.27 and its subparts are consulted first. Certain kinds of religious subordinate bodies are specified for subordinate entry in these rules. All others are to be treated according to general rules 24.12–24.14.

For all subordinate bodies other than government or religious, the cataloger uses general rules 24.12–24.16, which refer back to rules 24.1–24.3 for construction of headings for subordinate bodies that should be entered under their own names.

Subordinate and Related Bodies: Selected Rules and Examples

RULE 24.12.   GENERAL RULE

If a subordinate body is not a government body entered under jurisdiction, it is to be entered under its own name according to rules 24.1–24.3 unless it is one of the types listed under rule 24.13. A reference is made from the name formulated as a subheading of its higher body to the name as an independent heading. (Note the similarity of this rule to rule 24.17 for government bodies.) Examples:

Headings for subordinate bodies under their own names:

Information on title page of exhibition catalog: Baxter Art
   Gallery, California Institute of Technology, Pasadena
Heading: Baxter Art Gallery
   Refer from: California Institute of Technology. Baxter Art
   Gallery

Information on chief source of information: National
   Affiliation for Literacy Advance, Laubach Literacy
   International's programming arm in the U.S. and Canada
Heading: National Affiliation for Literacy Advance
   Refer from: Laubach Literacy International. National
   Affiliation for Literacy Advance

RULE 24.13.   SUBORDINATE AND RELATED BODIES ENTERED SUBORDINATELY

When a subordinate or related body's name belongs to one of Types 1–6 below, the heading for that body is constructed so that the higher body is named first, followed by the name of the subordinate or related body. If the name or abbreviation of the higher body is included in the name of the subordinate body in noun form, it is omitted from the subheading, unless it does not make sense to omit it. There may or may not be names of intervening bodies that are part of the hierarchy, depending on the application of rule 24.14. (Note the similarity of this rule to rule 24.18 for government bodies. Note also that Types 1–4 in the two rules are nearly identical, but that the other types are quite different.)

Type 1.   If a name contains a term that implies the body is part of another body, it is entered subordinately. Examples of such terms: *department, division, section, branch*, and their equivalents in other languages. Example:

> **Name on chief source of information:** Section of International Law and Practice, American Bar Association
> **Heading:** American Bar Association. Section of International Law and Practice

An LC departure from *AACR2R*, mentioned at the end of the geographic names section above, affects headings constructed by many rules, and is illustrated again here. LC continues to abbreviate *Department* as *Dept.* even though this is not authorized for use in headings by *AACR2R*, Appendix B, "Abbreviations." (*CSB* 32: 58) Example:

> **Previously established heading:** Notre Dame, Ind. University. Dept. of Economics
> **LC's heading under *AACR2R*:** University of Notre Dame. Dept. of Economics

> **[Note: Even though the heading had to be reconstructed for other reasons, the abbreviation *Dept.* was retained.]**

Type 2.   If a name contains a term that implies that the body is subordinate to another in an administrative sense, it is entered subordinately *if* the name of the higher body is required to identify the subordinate body. *AACR2R* gives two words as examples: *committee* and *commission*. LC has created lists of words in English, French, and Spanish that imply administrative subordination. (*CSB* 71: 64–65) For the second part of the rule, judgment is to be used by LC's catalogers to determine whether the name of the higher body is required for identification. Example:

> **Information on chief source of information:** NAIS Teacher Services Committee
> **Heading:** National Association of Independent Schools. Teacher Services Committee
> **Refer from:** NAIS Teacher Services Committee

Type 3.   If a name is "general in nature" or indicates only that it is a geographic, chronological, numbered, or lettered subdivision of a higher body, it is entered subordinately. For LC "general in nature" means that the name has no distinctive elements, such as proper names, nor does it have subject words. (*CSB* 25: 67–68) Example:

Name in credits of motion picture: Brigham Young University,
     Media Productions
Cataloger's judgment: *Media Productions* is general in nature
Heading: Brigham Young University. Media Productions

Type 4.   If a name does not give the impression of being that of a corporate
body, it is entered subordinately. Example:

Name on chief source of information: National Student Ministries
Cataloger's judgment: Name does not clearly give the impression
     of being that of a corporate body
Heading: Southern Baptist Convention. National Student Ministries

Type 5.   If a name of a unit of a university simply indicates that it encompasses a particular field of study, it is entered subordinately. A rule interpretation
adds *college* as well as *university* and also adds *interest* and *activity* to *field of study*
as criteria for the type of field encompassed by the unit. (*CSB* 44: 58) Example:

Name on chief source of information: School of Graduate and Professional
     Studies, Emporia State University
Heading: Emporia State University. School of Graduate and
     Professional Studies

Type 6.   If the name of a subordinate or related body includes the entire name
of the higher or related body, it is entered subordinately. LC has issued a lengthy
rule interpretation for rule 24.13, Type 6, including exceptions and exclusions and
discussing its application to named meetings. (*CSB* 44: 58–62) Example:

Name on chief source of information: Chaucer Group of the Modern
     Language Association of America
Heading: Modern Language Association of America. Chaucer
     Group

RULE 24.14.   DIRECT OR INDIRECT SUBHEADING
A body that belongs to one of the types listed in rule 24.13 and that, therefore,
is to be entered subordinately is entered as a subdivision of the element closest
above it in its hierarchy that is entered under its own name. If there are elements in
the hierarchy that fall between the subdivision and the name that is to be the entry element, they are omitted unless they are needed to distinguish this body from another
that does or might have the same entry form (e.g., several sections of the same institution might have an office called the "Personnel Office"). A reference is made from
the form that includes the name of an intervening body that has been omitted from
the heading. (Note the similarity of this rule to rule 24.19 for government bodies.)
Examples:

Name on chief source of information: University of Washington
     Libraries, Manuscripts Section
Heading: University of Washington. Libraries. Manuscripts Section

**[Note: Even though the University of Washington is a government body, its subordinate
bodies are entered according to rules 24.12–24.14 because the university is entered under its own name, not under jurisdiction.]**

Name on chief source of information: Radiological Research Laboratory, Department of Radiology, Columbia University, New York, N.Y.
Heading: Columbia University. Radiological Research Laboratory
Refer from: Columbia University. Dept. of Radiology. Radiological Research Laboratory

Omission of elements of a hierarchy is another area where the results of different catalogers' judgments may vary. The words *or is likely to be* often mean differences in judgment. LC has identified for its catalogers two categories where judgment should not vary. In the first category, names of bodies performing functions common to many higher bodies (e.g., Personnel Office; Planning Dept.), the hierarchy should be included. In the second category, names of bodies performing major functions unique to the higher body (e.g., Division of Fisheries; Division of Transport [under the Ministry of Transport, Industry, and Engineering]), intervening elements of the hierarchy should be omitted. Common sense must dictate the inclusion of hierarchy for the great middle ground. The cataloger should consider whether the name would be appropriate for another subordinate body within the same higher body structure and whether some word or phrase in a name in the hierarchy expresses an idea necessary to the identification of the subordinate body. (*CSB* 18: 76–78)

Government Bodies and Officials: Selected Rules and Examples

RULE 24.17.   GENERAL RULE
A government body that is not one of Types 1–11 under rule 24.18 below is entered under its own name according to rules 24.1–24.3 or is entered subordinately to a higher body that is entered under its own name according to rules 24.12–24.14. A reference is made from the form the name would have if it were a subheading under the name of the government. Example:

Heading: National Institutes of Health (U.S.)
Refer from: United States. National Institutes of Health
N.I.H.
United States. Public Health Service.
National Institutes of Health
United States. Federal Security Agency.
National Institutes of Health

LC treats the United Nations as a government body when applying these rules. (*CSB* 45: 58)

**RULE 24.18.   GOVERNMENT AGENCIES ENTERED
SUBORDINATELY**
When a government body's name belongs to one of Types 1–11 below, it is entered subordinately. If the name or abbreviation of the government is included in the name of the subordinate body in noun form, it is omitted from the subheading, unless it does not make sense to omit it. There may or may not be names of intervening bodies between the name of the government and the name of the subordinate body being established, depending on the application of rule 24.19.

A rule interpretation from LC should be consulted for guidance when a government agency name contains the entire name of its parent body (there is no equivalent to rule 24.13, Type 6, under rule 24.18). (CSB 44: 62–64)

Type 1.   If a name contains a word that implies the body is part of another body, it is entered subordinately. The same terms given as examples under rule 24.13, Type 1, apply here. Example:

> **Name on chief source of information:** Division of Planning, City of Jersey City
> **Heading:** Jersey City (N.J.). Division of Planning

Type 2.   If a name contains a word that implies that the body is subordinate to the government in an administrative sense, it is entered subordinately *if* the name of the government is required to identify the agency. Example:

> **Information on chief source of information:** Legislative Commission on Correctional Programs [seal]: The Great Seal of the State of North Carolina
> **Heading:** North Carolina. Legislative Commission on Correctional Programs

In LC's rule interpretation for catalogers at LC, there are two tests to be applied here. One is a judgment as to whether the name contains a word that implies "administrative subordination." The cataloger should ask whether the word is commonly used in a particular jurisdiction for names of government subdivisions. If in doubt, the word is considered not to have such an implication. The same list of terms in English, French, and Spanish given for rule 24.13, Type 2, is given under the rule interpretation for this rule and should be consulted when needed. (*CSB* 71: 65–67)

If the name passes the first test, it is then evaluated as to whether the name of the government is required for identification. "If the name of the government is stated explicitly or implied in the wording of the name, enter it independently; in all other cases, enter the name subordinately."[9] Thus, the United States Travel Service, which includes the government in its name, is entered independently: United States Travel Service. The Soil Conservation Service, however, is entered subordinately: United States. Soil Conservation Service.

If the body is entered independently according to this interpretation, the name of the government is added as a qualifier unless the name or an understandable surrogate for the name of the government (e.g., *American* for U.S.) appears in the name. (*CSB* 71: 67) *See* example under rule 24.17 above.

Type 3.   If a name is "general in nature" or indicates only that it is a geographic, chronological, numbered, or lettered subdivision of a government or a government agency, it is entered subordinately. Example:

> **Name on chief source of information:** U.S. Public Health Service. Region V
> **Cataloger's judgment:** Region V is a name that is general in nature
> **Heading:** United States. Public Health Service. Region V

LC policy for interpreting this rule states that if the body is at the national level, it is to be considered general and entered subordinately if the name contains neither distinctive words nor subject words and does not contain either the term *national* or *state* or one of their foreign language equivalents. (*CSB* 44: 63) For example, enter subordinately:

>   Research Center
>   Library
>   Technical Laboratory

but enter independently:

>   Population Research Center (U.S.)
>   Nuclear Energy Library (U.S.)
>   Technical Laboratory of Oceanographic Research (U.S.)
>   National Gallery (U.S.)

If the body is below the national level and it is not any of the other types under rule 24.18, LC enters it under the name of the government unless that name is explicitly or implicitly included in the subordinate body's name or the name contains some other word that tends to make it absolutely unique (e.g., a proper noun). (*CSB* 44: 63)

As under Type 2, a body entered independently under Type 3 will have the name of the government added as a qualifier unless it is already part of the body's name. (*CSB* 44: 63)

Type 4.   If the name does not give the impression of being that of a corporate body *and* it does not contain the name of the governing jurisdiction, it is entered subordinately. Example:

>   **Name on chief source of information:** Naval Oceanography and Meteorology
>   **Heading:** United States. Naval Oceanography and Meteorology

Type 5.   If the name represents a major executive agency (as defined by official publications of the government) it is entered subordinately. Example:

>   **Name on chief source of information:** Oyo State Executive Council
>   **Heading:** Oyo State (Nigeria). Executive Council

LC restricts application of this rule to major executive agencies of *national* governments. (*CSB* 44: 63)

Type 6.   Government legislative bodies are entered subordinately according to the provisions in rule 24.21. *See* example under rule 24.21.

Type 7.   Government courts are entered subordinately according to the provisions in rule 24.23. *See* example under rule 24.23.

Type 8.   Principal armed services are entered subordinately according to the provisions in rule 24.24. *See* example under rule 24.24.

Type 9.   Chiefs of state and other heads of government are entered subordinately according to the provisions in rule 24.20. *See* example under rule 24.20.

Type 10.   Embassies, consulates, etc., and **Type 11**, Delegations to international and intergovernmental bodies, are also entered subordinately.

RULE 24.19.   DIRECT OR INDIRECT SUBHEADING

This rule is the same as rule 24.14 except that the body is entered under the heading for the government instead of under the lowest element in the hierarchy that is entered under its own name. Other elements in the hierarchy are interposed or omitted in the same way and with the same difficulties in judgment. (*See* discussion under rule 24.14.) Examples:

Indirect subordinate entry of an office:

> **Name on chief source of information:** Office of the Executive Director, Colorado Department of Natural Resources
> **Heading:** Colorado. Dept. of Natural Resources. Office of the Executive Director

Direct subordinate entry of an office:

> **Name on chief source of information:** U.S. Department of Commerce Maritime Administration, Office of Commercial Development, Office of Port and Intermodal Development
> **Heading:** United States. Office of Port and Intermodal Development
> > **Refer from:**   United States. Maritime Administration. Office of Port and Intermodal Development
> >
> > United States. Maritime Administration. Office of Commercial Development. Office of Port and Intermodal Development

Special Rules

RULE 24.20.   GOVERNMENT OFFICIALS

24.20B.   Heads of state, etc.

The heading for a head of state who is acting in an official capacity is made up of the name of the government followed by the title of the office in English, if possible, the inclusive years the person held that office, and a brief form of name of the person in the language used for the person's personal heading. Non-gendered terminology is used, e.g., *Sovereign*, not *Queen* or *King*. Example:

> **Heading for governor as an official:** New York (State). Governor (1983-1994 : Cuomo)

An explanatory reference should be made to the incumbent as a person (*see* rule 26.3C1 in *AACR2R*).

RULE 24.21.   LEGISLATIVE BODIES

A legislature is entered under the name of the jurisdiction for which it makes laws. Chambers of legislative bodies are entered subordinately to the legislative body, and committees are entered subordinately to the legislature or to a chamber, whichever is appropriate. A subcommittee of the U.S. Congress is entered as a sub-heading of the committee to which it is subordinate. If legislatures are numbered, the number and year(s) are added. Session numbers may also be added [e.g., United States. Congress (106th, 1st session : 1999)]. Example:

Entry of a state legislative committee:

Name on chief source of information: Committee on Motor Vehicles, Illinois House of Representatives
Heading: Illinois. General Assembly. House of Representatives. Committee on Motor Vehicles

It should be noted that, although *AACR2R* shows in its examples "United States. Congress. House of Representatives," which is the official name of that body, LC continues to use the conventional name "House" in its headings for the body. (*CSB* 44: 64)

RULE 24.23.   COURTS
Civil and criminal courts are entered as subheadings of the jurisdiction. A place name for the place a court sits or the area it serves is omitted but added as a conventional addition if needed to distinguish it from others of the same name. Example:

Name on chief source of information: Court of Common Pleas of Crawford County, Pa.
Heading: Pennsylvania. Court of Common Pleas (Crawford County)

RULE 24.24.   ARMED FORCES
A principal service of the armed forces of a government is entered as a sub-heading of the government. A branch, district, or unit is entered as a subheading for the principal service, and if it is numbered, the numbering in the style used in the name follows the name. Example:

Name on chief source of information: Air Defense Command, U.S. Air Force
Heading: United States. Air Force. Air Defense Command

RULE 24.27.   RELIGIOUS BODIES AND OFFICIALS

24.27A.   Councils, etc., of a single religious body
Councils, etc., of a single religious body are entered as subheadings of that body. Appropriate additions may be made as for conferences, etc. (rule 24.7B). General councils are entered according to the general rules for subordinate bodies (rules 24.12–24.13). Example:

Name on chief source of information: Il Concilio romano del 1725
Heading: Catholic Church. Concilio romano (1725)

24.27B.   Religious officials
The heading for a religious official acting in an official capacity looks very much like the heading for a head of state (rule 24.20B). It consists of the heading for the diocese, order, patriarchate, etc., followed by the title in English (unless there is no English equivalent), the inclusive years of incumbency, and the name of the person. Example:

Name on chief source of information: His Holiness John Paul II
Heading: Catholic Church. Pope (1978-2005 : John Paul II)

[Note: An explanatory reference should refer to the personal heading for John Paul II.]

24.27C.   Subordinate bodies

Provinces, dioceses, synods, and other subordinate units having jurisdiction over geographic areas are entered as subheadings of the religious body. For the Catholic Church, the English form of name should be used. Example:

Name on chief source of information: Arzobispado del Cuzco
Heading: Catholic Church. Archdiocese of Cuzco (Peru)
Refer from: Catholic Church. Arzobispado del Cuzco

UNIFORM TITLES

When a work has appeared under more than one title, a uniform title may be used for cataloging purposes in order to bring all editions of the work together. Uniform titles may also be used to *distinguish* different works which have the same titles proper. Uniform titles of the first type have traditionally been used for sacred scriptures, creeds, liturgical works, and anonymous classics. In more recent practice, uniform titles of the second type have been found useful for distinguishing works such as serials with generic titles (such as *Report*). *Bible* is a very common example in library catalogs of the first type of uniform title; similarly, editions of the Mother Goose verses are assembled under the uniform title *Mother Goose.* In these cases the uniform titles represent main entry headings. In other instances the uniform title follows the main entry, as in the cases of music, laws, liturgical works, and translations. *AACR2R*, Chapter 25, contains many further suggestions for extending these rules to other instances.

One of the problems faced in constructing uniform titles of the first type is the choice of a title when titles of a work appear in more than one form. Titles may be in different languages, in one or more long forms and one or more short forms, or in two simultaneous versions (as when a work is published simultaneously in England and the United States under different titles). Some works may be published in parts and need identification of the part *without* identification of the whole (as in the case of one title from a trilogy) or *with* identification of the whole (as in the case of a book from Homer's *Iliad*, called only "Book 1"). Additions may be needed to distinguish uniform titles from each other or from other headings, to identify the language in which the work appears, to identify the version, or to date the particular edition. The purpose of this chapter is to demonstrate the general rules used to resolve these problems. Much more detail can be found in *AACR2R*, Chapter 25.

In addition to the first rule, which sets down the conditions for use of uniform titles, the *AACR2R* chapter comprises three groups of rules: basic rules for choice and form of the title itself (rules 25.2–25.4 and 25.12), rules for additions to uniform titles (rules 25.5–25.11), and special rules for certain materials (rules 25.13–25.35). The materials given special treatment are manuscripts and manuscript groups (rule 25.13), incunabula (rule 25.14), legal materials (rules 25.15–25.16), sacred scriptures (rules 25.17–25.18), liturgical and other religious works (rules 25.19–25.24), and music (rules 25.25–25.35).

A title heading created using *AACR2R*, Chapter 25, is coded 130, 240, 630, 730, or 830 in the *MARC 21* format, depending upon whether it functions as a main entry, a supplementary title between main entry and the title proper, a subject heading, an added entry, or a series added entry. A name-title entry may also be made with the uniform title coded as subfield *t* in a 600, 700, or 800 field.

RULE 25.1.   USE OF UNIFORM TITLES

Whether or not uniform titles are used may depend on the type and size of catalog one has. *AACR2R2002* gives six criteria to use in deciding whether to use uniform titles:

"1)   how well the work is known

2)   how many manifestations of the work are involved

3)   whether another work with the same title proper has been identified (*see* 25.5B)

4)   whether the main entry is under title (*see* 21.1C)

5)   whether the work was originally in another language

6)   the extent to which the catalogue is used for research purposes."[10]

In essence this rule states that the entire set of rules on uniform titles is optional, and a policy decision should be made in each cataloging agency as to whether some or all of the rules should be applied.

General Rules: Selected Rules and Examples

RULE 25.2.   GENERAL RULE

25.2A.   In a printed record the uniform title is given before the title proper and enclosed in square brackets. If the main entry is title, *AACR2R* calls for it also to be enclosed in brackets, but an option allows omitting the brackets if the uniform title is used as main entry. The Library of Congress is following the option, which is a continuation of LC's past practice. In addition it is LC practice not to enclose uniform titles in brackets when used in added entries. (*CSB* 64: 28–29) It is also LC practice in the case of anonymous classics that have been published in many editions, translations, and differing titles to use the uniform title for all editions, even when it does not differ from the title proper. (*CSB* 64: 28–29) Example:

Uniform title as main entry without square brackets—LC practice:

Beowulf.
    Beowulf : an edition with manuscript spacing notation
and graphotactic analyses / Robert D. Stevick

25.2B.   Uniform titles are not used for revisions or updated versions of a work in the same language as the original. Instead, these are related by giving a note about the earlier edition in the bibliographic record for the later edition. Example:

New title, not uniform title, used for new edition in the same language:

> Hawker, Pat.
>   Amateur radio techniques / Pat Hawker. — 6th ed. — London :
> Radio Society of Great Britain, 1978.
>   336 p. : ill. ; 25 cm.
>
>   First ed. published with title: Technical topics for the radio
> amateur.

25.2C.   Initial articles

Initial articles are omitted unless the uniform title is to be filed under that article. Example:

Initial article not included in uniform title:

> Dickens, Charles, 1812-1870.
>   [Pickwick papers]
>   The Pickwick papers / Charles Dickens ; edited with
> an introduction and notes by James Kinsley

[Note: In MARC records the square brackets are not recorded, and display is dependent upon the programming of the system.]

Individual Titles

RULE 25.3.   WORKS CREATED AFTER 1500

25.3A. For a work created after 1500 the title in the original language by which the work has become known is used as its uniform title. The "known" title is judged from its use in manifestations of the work or in reference sources. Example:

Uniform title in original language:

> Suder, Joseph, 1892-
>   [Dona nobis pacem]
>   Festmesse in D [sound recording] / Joseph Suder

Other titles given to this work:

> Messe Dona nobis pacem
> Grosse Messe Dona nobis pacem

25.3B.   If none of the titles in the original language can be established as being the "best known," the title proper of the original edition is used. In using such original titles, one should omit introductory phrases and statements of responsibility that can be grammatically separated. LC also omits alternative titles. (*CSB* 44: 65) Example:

Use of title proper of the original edition when there are variant titles in the original language:

> Cross, Amanda, 1926-
>   [Death in a tenured position]
>   A death in the faculty / Amanda Cross. — London :
> Virago, 1988, c1981.

Note explaining uniform title:

>   Originally published as: Death in a tenured position. New
> York : Dutton, 1981.

25.3C.   Simultaneous publication under different titles

25.3C1.   When a work is published in two or more editions simultaneously in the same language with different titles, the cataloger should use as uniform title the one for the edition published in the cataloging agency's country, if this applies. If it does not apply, the title of the edition received first should be used. Example:

> **American title used as uniform title for work whose British title is different:**
>
> Mansfield, Peter, 1928-
>   [Arab world]
>   The Arabs / Peter Mansfield. — Harmondsworth :
> Penguin, 1982.

> **Note explaining uniform title:**
>
> American ed. published under title: The Arab world.

RULE 25.4.   WORKS CREATED BEFORE 1501

25.4A.   If a work was created before 1501, the title in the original language by which the work is identified in modern reference sources is used. If none of the titles can be established in reference sources, the title found most frequently in modern editions, early editions, or manuscript copies (in that order of preference) is used. This rule, however, is superseded by rules 25.4B–25.4C and 25.14, if they apply. Example:

> **Uniform title for pre-1501 work as identified in reference sources:**
>
> Gawain and the Grene Knight.
>   Sir Gawain and the Green Knight / translated with an
> introduction by Brian Stone

25.4B–25.4C.   In general, a well-established English title, if there is one, is used for a pre-1501 Greek work or anonymous work in nonroman script. Example:

> **Anonymous pre-1501 work originally in nonroman script entered under
> established English title with the language of the translation in hand added
> (rules 25.4 and 25.5C1):**
>
> Arabian nights. English.
>   More fairy tales from the Arabian nights / edited and
> arranged by E. Dixon ; illustrated by J.D. Batten

RULE 25.5.   ADDITIONS TO UNIFORM TITLES

25.5B.   Conflict resolution

25.5B1.   If uniform titles used as main entries are identical to each other or to the form used as the heading for a person, corporate body, or reference, additions are made in parentheses to the uniform title. Example:

> **Additions in parentheses to distinguish between two otherwise identical uniform titles:**
>
> Jungle book (1942)
>   Jungle book [motion picture]
> Jungle book (1967)
>   The jungle book [motion picture]

Identical uniform titles that are entered under the same personal or corporate heading also need additions in parentheses to distinguish them. Example:

> United States.
>   [Census (1960)]
> United States.
>   [Census (1970)]

For this rule LC has made a lengthy rule interpretation that prescribes the kinds of additions that are to be made to distinguish between otherwise identical titles for *continuing resources*. (*CSB* 108: 99–114) For *serials*, such conflicts are generally handled by adding a uniform title to the bibliographic record for the serial in hand, not to the one cataloged earlier.

Place of publication is LC's generally preferred qualifying term for conflicting serial titles. Example:

> Times (Charleston, S.C.)
> Times (Kansas City, Mo.)

However, if the title consists only of an indication of type and/or periodicity of publication, or if the place is inadequate to resolve the conflict, or if the conflicting titles include initials of their issuing bodies' names, then the heading for the body that originated or issued the serial is used as the qualifying term. Examples:

Occasional paper (Canberra College of Advanced Education. Library)
Occasional paper (London Public Library and Art Museum (Ont.))

[Note: title only indicates periodicity]

European physics series (McGraw-Hill)
European physics series (Wiley)

[Note: both series are published in New York, N.Y.]

Other qualifiers may be added when the above provisions do not suffice. Other qualifiers may be place and date, corporate body and date, date, edition statement, other title information, etc. The LC rule interpretation should be consulted for elaboration on these qualifiers and on other special situations such as may occur with radio and television programs, comics, motion pictures, U.S. Census publications, choreographic works, named individual works of art, and other situations in which conflict may arise.

25.5C.   Language

25.5C1.   When the item in hand is in a different language from the original, the name of the language of the item is added to the uniform title. LC catalogers use the language name as established in the latest edition of *MARC Code List for Languages*. (*CSB* 99: 53) Example:

Modern translation with original title as uniform title, followed by language of translation:

> Leys, Simon, 1935-
>   [Habits neufs du président Mao. English]
>   The Chairman's new clothes : Mao and the cultural
> revolution / Simon Leys ; translated by Carol Appleyard
> and Patrick Goode

AACR2R rule 25.5C and LC's rule interpretation on multilingual works should be consulted when more than one language is involved. (*CSB* 99: 53–54)

25.5D.   An option allows addition of General Material Designations (GMDs) at the end of uniform titles. LC is not applying this option. (*CSB* 44: 67)

RULE 25.6.   PARTS OF A WORK
This rule is not applied to parts of the Bible and certain other sacred scriptures (*see* rules 25.17–25.18) or to parts of musical works (*see* rule 25.32).

25.6A.   One part

25.6A1.   When a separately cataloged part of a work has a title that is not dependent for its meaning upon the title of the collected work, the title of the part alone is used as the uniform title. A reference is made from the form the heading would have if the title of the part were a subheading of the title of the whole work. Example:

Separately cataloged part with its own title as uniform title:

> Hesse, Hermann, 1877-1962.
> [Tractat vom Steppenwolf. English]
> Treatise on the Steppenwolf / Hermann Hesse ; [translated from the German] ; paintings by Jaroslav Bradac

[Note: The title of the whole work is *Der Steppenwolf*.]

> **Refer from:** Hesse, Hermann, 1877-1962. Steppenwolf. Tractat vom Steppenwolf. English

25.6A2.   When a separately cataloged part of a work has a title that *is* dependent for its meaning upon the title of the whole work, the uniform title is the title of the whole work followed by the title of the part as a subheading. Arabic numerals are used to record part numbers. Example:

Separately cataloged part given as subheading of the title of the whole work:

> Milton, John, 1608-1674.
> [Paradise lost. Book 4]
> Paradise lost, book IV / John Milton ; edited by S.E. Goggin

LC specifies that words such as "Volume" included in the part title should not be abbreviated here, even if included in the list of abbreviated words in *AACR2R* Appendix B. (*CSB* 87: 31)

25.6B.   More than one part
When an item consists of consecutively numbered parts, the designation of the parts in the singular is used as a subheading of the title of the whole work and is followed by the inclusive numbering of parts. Example:

Separately cataloged consecutive parts of a work given as subheading of the title of the whole work:

> Milton, John, 1608-1674.
> [Paradise lost. Book 9-10]
> Paradise lost, books IX and X / John Milton ; edited by Cyril Aldred

When an item has two parts not consecutively numbered, the uniform title is made for the first part, and a name-title added entry is made for the second. When an item has three or more parts not consecutively numbered, the uniform title of the whole work is used, followed by "Selections."

RULE 25.7.   TWO WORKS ISSUED TOGETHER

25.7A.   When an item contains two works entered under a personal or corporate main entry, uniform titles are assigned to the two works. The uniform title of the first work is given following the main entry, and a name-title added entry using the second uniform title is made for the second work. Example:

Separate uniform titles made for two works appearing in the same item:

> Poe, Edgar Allan, 1809-1849.
> [Tell-tale heart]
> The telltale heart ; and, The cask of Amontillado [sound recording]

Added entry for second work:

> Poe, Edgar Allan, 1809-1849. Cask of Amontillado.

Collective Titles

Collective titles can be general (e.g., "Works," "Selections") or more specific (e.g., "Novels," "Poems," "Laws, etc.") . When these are used alone, the effect is to separate originals from translations, different editions from each other, etc., if the titles proper are different. They also are inadequate when being used in added entries. Therefore, LC emphasizes using the principle found in rule 25.5B in conjunction with collective titles when needed to bring together items with different titles proper or to refer to a work in an added entry. The designation to be enclosed in parentheses may be title proper, editor, translator, publisher, etc.—whichever best fits each case. Example:

> Maugham, W. Somerset (William Somerset), 1874-1965.
> [Short stories (Heinemann)]
> Complete short stories

This technique is applied only after the need arises; thus, earlier entries must be revised. (*CSB* 99: 47–49)

RULE 25.8.   COMPLETE WORKS

If an information package contains, or claims to contain, the complete works of a person, the collective title "Works" is used as uniform title. Example:

> Posada, José Guadalupe, 1852-1913.
> [Works. English & German. 1976]
> Das Werk von Jose Guadalupe Posada = The works of José Guadalupe Posada / edited and with an introduction by Hannes Jähn

A rule interpretation from LC indicates that "Works" occurs so frequently that there should always be additions made to such uniform titles to make them distinctive. The interpretation outlines the additions to be made. (*CSB* 100: 58-60)

RULE 25.9.   SELECTIONS

When an item contains three or more works in various forms, all by the same person, the collective title "Selections" is used as uniform title. Example:

> Twain, Mark, 1835-1910.
> [Selections. 1987]
> The outrageous Mark Twain : some lesser-known but extraordinary works : with "Reflections on religion" now in book form for the first time / selected and edited, with an introduction, by Charles Neider

LC calls for the same additions here that are made to the collective title "Works." (*CSB* 60: 22)

RULE 25.10.   WORKS IN A SINGLE FORM

The following collective titles are used for collections of the works of a person all in one form:

Correspondence	Poems
Essays	Prose works
Novels	Short stories
Plays	Speeches

LC applies this rule only when the title proper of the collection is not distinctive or when there is no collective title proper. (*CSB* 60: 22–23)

Special Rules for Certain Types of Work: Selected Rules and Examples

Laws, Treaties, Etc.

RULE 25.15.   LAWS, ETC.

25.15A.   Modern laws, etc.

25.15A1.   Collections

A collection of legislative enactments is given the uniform title "Laws, etc.," unless the compilation is on a particular subject. LC, when using "Laws, etc.," makes further additions, in parentheses, and revises existing records that lack the additions. The additions may consist of a brief title and, if needed, edition or date. The LC rule interpretation should be consulted. (*CSB* 36: 33–38) Example:

> India.
> [Laws, etc. (Statutes of India)]
> The statutes of India : a manual of central arts & rules : exhaustive commentary on all central acts with important central rules

When a compilation of laws is on a particular subject, a citation title, if there is one, should be used as uniform title. If there is no citation title, a uniform title should be constructed according to rule 25.3. LC adds that if a subject compilation lacks both a citation title and a collective title, the uniform title of the first law in the collection should be used. (*CSB* 36: 38)

25.15A2.   Single laws, etc.

Single laws are assigned, as uniform title, one of the following (in order of preference): an official citation title (or official short title), an unofficial short or citation title used in legal literature, the official title, or any other official designation. Example:

Official short title used as uniform title:

> Québec (Province)
> [Labour code. English & French]
> Code du travail : Titre 1, des relations du travail =
> Labour code : Title, labour relations

RULE 25.16.   TREATIES, ETC.

The uniform title for treaties is "Treaties, etc." Various additions are made depending upon the circumstances: the second party for a collection of treaties between two parties or for single treaties between two parties; the date or earliest date of signing (in the form: year, abbreviated name of the month, number of the day) for a single treaty. A single treaty between four or more parties is entered under the name by which the treaty is known (in English, if possible) followed by the year of signing in parentheses. Added entries for individual signers, if made, are formulated with the uniform title "Treaties, etc.," followed by date of signing. *See* treaty example following rule 21.36 on p. 215 in chapter 6.

Sacred Scriptures

RULE 25.17.   GENERAL RULE

The uniform title for a sacred scripture should be the title that is usually used in English-language reference sources that discuss the particular religious group that uses the scripture.

RULE 25.18.   PARTS OF SACRED SCRIPTURES AND ADDITIONS

25.18A.   Bible

When appropriate, the testaments (designated O.T. and N.T.) are added after the word "Bible." Then books are designated. If the books are numbered, the number is given as an ordinal Arabic numeral after the name. The name of a group of books may also be a subdivision of the testament (e.g., Minor Prophets, Apocrypha, Gospels). Next are added, as appropriate: 1) language; 2) version, translator, name of manuscripts or repository, or reviser; and 3) year. A single selection with a distinctive title is entered directly under that title with a reference from the appropriate "Bible" uniform title. If a work consists of more than two selections, they are entered under the most specific Bible heading appropriate to all, with the term *Selections* added after language and version but before the year. Examples:

Bible. [parts] [language] [versions] [selections] [date]

Bible.   N.T. Corinthians, 1st . . .
Bible.   N.T. English. Stern. 1989.
Bible.   N.T. Gospels . . .
Bible.   O.T. Esther. Hebrew. 1990.
Bible.   O.T. Genesis XII, 1 - XXV, 11 . . .
Bible.   O.T. Historical books . . .
Bible.   O.T. Leviticus. Hebrew. Samaritan. 1959.
Bible.   English. New Century. Selections. 1990.
Bible.   English. New Jerusalem Bible. 1990.
Bible.   English. New Life. 1990.

25.18B–25.18M.   Rules 25.18B–25.18M are special rules for the Talmud, Mishnah and Tosefta, Midrashim, Buddhist scriptures, Vedas, Aranyakas, Brahmanas, Upanishads, Jaina Agama, Avesta, and Koran. Rules are given for parts and additions as for the Bible.

Liturgical Works, Theological Creeds, Confessions of Faith, Etc.

RULE 25.19.   GENERAL RULE
When a liturgical work is entered under an English-language corporate body name, the uniform title should also be in English if there is an established English title; if not, the uniform title is given in the language of the liturgy. Example:

Uniform title for a liturgical work:

Catholic Church.
[Mass, Epiphany. German]
Messe an Epiphanias

RULES 25.20–25.23
Rules 25.20–25.23 are special rules for Catholic and Jewish liturgical works, for variant and special texts, and for parts of liturgical works.

Musical Works

RULE 25.25.   GENERAL RULE
The general rule outlines the rules in the remainder of the chapter.

Uniform titles for:	Rule(s):
one musical work	25.26–25.31
one or more parts of a musical work	25.32
two works of a composer issued together	25.33
collections of music	25.34

The last rule, rule 25.35, is for additions to a uniform title to designate a particular manifestation. The cataloger is instructed to use rules 25.1–25.7 whenever they are applicable and are not contradicted by rules 25.26–25.35.

Individual Titles

RULE 25.26.   GENERAL RULE

The initial title element of the uniform title for a musical work is created as instructed in rules 25.27–25.29. Rules 25.30–25.32 and 25.35 give instructions for additions to the initial title element, although additions are not always required.

RULES 25.27–25.31

Uniform titles are frequently used in cataloging music because the same musical composition is often issued in numerous editions with variations in the language and the wording of the title pages. Composer-title references are made from forms of the title not used as uniform title, as needed. Examples:

> Beethoven, Ludwig van, 1770-1827.
>> Battle of Vitoria
>> see
>> Beethoven, Ludwig van, 1770-1827.
>> Wellingtons Sieg

> Beethoven, Ludwig van, 1770-1827.
>> Cantata on the death of Emperor Joseph II
>> see
>> Beethoven, Ludwig van, 1770-1827.
>> Kantate auf den Tod Kaiser Josephs II

In the selection and construction of uniform titles the most reliable bibliographical sources are consulted, such as thematic indexes, bibliographies, music encyclopedias, etc. Information given in the work cataloged is not used without an attempt at verification. LC catalogs are useful in constructing a uniform title, but only after the cataloger has identified the work in thematic or other musical sources.

Rules 25.27–25.31 give the principles for construction of a uniform title for a single work. The basic rule for choice of uniform title instructs the cataloger to use the composer's original title unless a later title in the same language has become better known. If the title is distinctive, it is left unmodified unless there is a conflict. Example:

> Bach, Johann Sebastian, 1685-1750.
>> [Kunst der Fuge]

If the title is distinctive and there *is* a conflict, the title is followed by some modification as instructed under rule 25.31B1. Example:

> Bach, Johann Sebastian, 1685-1750.
>> [Wachet auf, ruft uns die Stimme (Cantata)]

> Bach, Johann Sebastian, 1685-1750.
>> [Wachet auf, ruft uns die Stimme (Chorale prelude)]

However, if the title consists solely of the name of one type of composition, the title is constructed as instructed under rule 25.29A. Additions are then made according to rule 25.30: the medium of performance (the instruments for which it was written), followed by further identifying elements to distinguish the work from other compositions by the same composer, generally the serial number, opus (or thematic index) number, and the key. Examples:

> Mozart, Wolfgang Amadeus, 1756-1791.
> [Quartets, strings, K. 387, G major]
> Quartett für 2 Violinen, Viola und Violoncello

> Dvořák, Antonín, 1841-1904.
> [Symphonies, no. 8, op. 88, G major]
> From the new world : symphony no. 8 by Dvořák

Titles of works in the larger vocal forms (operas, oratorios, etc.) generally require additional modification because of the various versions in which they are likely to be issued. Example:

> Puccini, Giacomo, 1858-1924.
> [Manon Lescaut]
> [Manon Lescaut. Vocal score]
> [Manon Lescaut. Libretto. English]

RULE 25.32.   PARTS OF A WORK
A separately published part of a musical work uses the title of the whole work, followed by the title of the part. This is counter to rule 25.6A1 for other types of works. Examples:

> Arne, Thomas Augustine, 1710-1778.
> [Artaxerxes. Soldier tir'd]

> Schumann, Robert, 1810-1856.
> [Fantasiestücke, piano, op. 12. Nr. 7. Traumes Warren]

RULE 25.33.   TWO WORKS ISSUED TOGETHER
When two works are published together, a uniform title is constructed as specified in rule 25.7.

Collective Titles

RULE 25.34
This rule gives principles for construction of a uniform title for items containing more than two works. Complete works (rule 25.34A) are treated as in rule 25.8. A collection of selections of various types of compositions originally composed for various instrumental and/or vocal media is assigned the uniform title "Selections" (rule 25.34B). However, if a collection contains works of various types all in a broad or specific medium, the designation of that medium is used (rule 25.34C1). For example:

> [Instrumental music]
> [Vocal music]
> [Brass music]
> [Piano music]
> [Violin, piano music]

If the collection contains works of one type, the name of that type is used, with the addition of medium in appropriate cases (rule 25.34C2). For example:

[Operas]
[Quartets, strings]
[Sonatas, piano]

Additions

RULE 25.35.   ADDITIONS TO UNIFORM TITLES FOR MUSIC

Further additions are made to distinguish sketches for a musical composition, arrangements of a musical work, translations of texts of vocal works, etc. Example:

Cowell, Henry, 1897-1965.
    [Concerto brevis; arr.]
    Concerto brevis : for accordion and orchestra

REFERENCES

The rules in the preceding sections of this chapter have referred to "references" needed when one name or form of heading is chosen from among more than one possible name or form of heading. This section is a summary of all those situations where references are called for explicitly or implicitly in the earlier rules. This section also gives examples of the different types of references. Chapter 26 of *AACR2R*, "References," begins with introductory notes that define different kinds of references, explain the form to use, and set up the conditions under which references should be made. Following this introduction are specific rules for and examples of references for persons, corporate bodies and geographic names, uniform titles, and added entries for series and serials. Finally, there is a rule allowing references instead of certain added entries that are common to many editions.

References are not included in the bibliographic records for the information packages being cataloged when the references are made. Instead they are recorded in an authority record. An authority record is a separate record for each name or title established as a heading to be used in the library's public catalog. It contains the established form for the heading, the forms from which references should be made to the established form, and, often, notes about the sources of information used in establishing the heading. In manual authority files the forms from which references are to be made are preceded by x's—one x precedes a *see from* reference, and two x's precede a *see also from* reference. In a machine-readable authority file headings and references are preceded by codes similar to those used in bibliographic records. There is a separate *MARC 21* format for authority records. In this format 1XX codes precede headings, 4XX codes precede *see from* references, and 5XX codes precede *see also from* references. Sample authority records and further information about authority files are given in chapter 8 of this text.

It has been noted in previous chapters that a successor to *AACR* is under development. The Joint Steering Committee for the Revision of AACR proposes in its RDA Prospectus that *Resource Description and Access* include a new Part III, titled "Access Point Control." The current *AACR2R* chapters 22 through 26 will become a core of Part III, which will provide "guidelines and instructions on formulating access points and recording data used in access point control."[11]

Selected Rules and Examples

RULE 26.1.   GENERAL RULE

26.1A.   References are to be made as instructed in the previous sections of this chapter and also according to the more general instructions in *AACR2R*, chapter 26. References should be made only to a heading for which there is an entry in the catalog. (References made to headings that are not in the catalog are called *blind references* because they direct a user to something that cannot be seen.) A record of every reference made should be kept under the heading to which the reference refers. (This record is usually kept on an authority record for the heading that is being referred to. The record, among other things, enables one to correct or delete a reference when the heading is changed or deleted.)

26.1B.   *See* references
    See references are used to direct users from a form of name or title of a work that they have looked under to the form that has been chosen as the heading for that name or title. A *see* reference says to the user, "No, you won't find what you're looking for here; but if you'll look under _____, you will find something."

26.1C.   *See also* references
    See also references are used to direct users from a name or uniform title heading to a related name or uniform title heading. A *see also* reference says to the user, "Yes, there is some information here, and you may also be interested in related information that you can find under _____."

26.1D.   Name-title references
    Name-title references are used when a title has been entered under a personal or corporate name and either *see* or *see also* references are needed from another form of the title. When such references are needed, the name is given before the title in both the form referred from and the form referred to.

26.1E.   Explanatory references
    Explanatory references are used when more guidance or explanation than can be given in simple references is necessary. These are coded 260 or 360 in the *MARC 21* authority format.
    Terminology used in references is undergoing change with the expansion of online catalogs. In an online environment the codes 4XX and 5XX can be translated into other words or phrases than *see* and *see also*, if the creator of the system believes that other terminology would be more understandable to users. Popular substitutes are "search under" or "the heading used in this catalog is" for *see*, and "search also under" or "related information may be found under" for *see also*. Because *AACR2R* uses *see* and *see also*, these terms are used in the remainder of this chapter for ease of explanation.
    There is a lengthy LC rule interpretation that explains the forms that references should take on LC authority records, explaining, for example, how references for "compatible headings" might differ from those for "pure" *AACR2* headings. (*CSB* 47: 57–60)

26.1F.   Form of references
    AACR2R suggests that the form of name from which a reference is made should have the same structure it would have if it were the heading rather than a reference to the heading. *AACR2R* also calls for making only one reference rather than

two or more when one form is used to refer to more than one catalog heading. Examples:

> Taylor, J. R.
>   see also
>   Taylor, James Robert
>   Taylor, John Roberts

> ACU
>   see
>   Arbeitskreis Computer im Unterricht (Germany)
>   Association of Commonwealth Universities
>   Association of Computer Users (U.S.)

LC makes individual references rather than combined references in these instances. (*CSB* 47: 60) Presumably this is because of the difficulty of maintaining records of such combined references in an automated system. However, in most online systems that have access to authority records a search for initials brings up a response screen that lists all the headings with authority records that have a reference from those initials. The wording of the examples of references in *AACR2R* and in this text is not intended to be prescriptive, but only to provide examples.

RULE 26.2.   NAMES OF PERSONS

26.2A.   *See* references

26.2A1.   Different names
When a person has used a name different from that chosen for the heading for that person, or when a different name is found in reference sources, a reference is made from the different name to the heading. (*See also* rule 26.2C1 and rule 26.2D1.) Examples:

> Tosi, Maria Teresa, 1918-
>   see
>   Maria Teresa dell'Eucaristia, suor, 1918-

> Beyle, Marie Henri, 1783-1842
>   see
>   Stendhal, 1783-1842

> Skłodowska-Curie, Maria, 1867-1934
>   see
>   Curie, Marie, 1867-1934

26.2A2.   Different forms of the name
If a form of name used by a person is significantly different from the form used for the heading for the person, a reference is made. For LC catalogers the policy for normal inverted headings is to make references from forms that have any variations to the left of the comma or in the first element to the right of the comma. (*CSB* 99: 31) Examples:

> Burt, Stanley G.
>   see
>   Burt, S. G. (Stanley G.)

Abe, Suehisa, 1622-1709
see
Abe, Suenao, 1622-1709

Ruth, George Herman, 1895-1948
see
Ruth, Babe, 1895-1948

Homerus
see
Homer

26.2A3.   Different entry elements
A reference should be made from any element of a name heading under which a user might reasonably look for a name. Examples:

Van Zuidam, R. A.
see
Zuidam, R. A. van

Buren, Ariane van
see
Van Buren, Ariane

Damas, Bernardo Valverde
see
Valverde Damas, Bernardo

Ram Acharya
see
Acharya, Ram

Wellesley, Arthur, Duke of Wellington, 1769-1852
see
Wellington, Arthur Wellesley, Duke of, 1769-1852

26.2C.   *See also* references
When a person is entered under two headings (e.g., two pseudonyms), *see also* references are made at each heading to direct the user also to search under the other heading. Example:

Baker, Ray Stannard, 1870-1946
see also
Grayson, David, 1870-1946

Grayson, David, 1870-1946
see also
Baker, Ray Stannard, 1870-1946

An LC rule interpretation provides for the situation in which the names of one or more members of a group are included in the group name itself. In this case, references are made in both directions: from the individual names to the name of the group, and vice versa. (*CSB* 94: 23) Example:

Crosby, Stills & Nash
see also
Crosby, David, 1941-
Stills, Stephen
Nash, Graham

Crosby, David, 1941-
see also
Crosby, Stills & Nash

[Similar references would be made for Stills and Nash.]

26.2D.   Explanatory references

26.2D1.   Explanatory references are provided when more information is needed for guidance than can be given with a *see* or *see also* reference. Examples:

Stone, Rosetta
The joint pseudonym of Michael K. Frith and Dr. Seuss.
For separate works entered under each name search also under:
Frith, Michael K.
Seuss, Dr.

Hunter, Evan, 1926-
For works of this author written under pseudonyms, see
Collins, Hunt, 1926-
McBain, Ed, 1926-
Marsten, Richard, 1926-

26.2D2.   An option allows making an explanatory reference under each separately written prefix that can be used in a number of surnames. The purpose of such a reference is to explain how names with this prefix are entered in the catalog. Example:

Van
Some names beginning with this prefix are also entered under the name following the prefix (e.g., Zuidam, R. A. van)

LC is not applying this option. Instead, individual references are traced for each heading. (*CSB* 30: 22)

RULE 26.3.   GEOGRAPHIC NAMES AND NAMES OF CORPORATE BODIES

26.3A.   *See* references

26.3A1.   Different names
When a corporate body or place has appeared in works or reference sources with a different name or names than that used for the catalog heading, a reference is made from the different name. If, however, the name represents a name *change*, use rule 26.3C1. Example:

Detroit (Mich.). Police Dept. God Squad
see
Detroit (Mich.). Police Dept. Chaplain Corps

26.3A3.   Different forms of the name

If a different form of name for a body or place is found in works or reference sources or if different romanizations result in different forms, references are made from the differing form(s). Examples:

A.B.E.D.I.A.
> see
> Arab Bank for Economic Development in Africa

Wien (Austria)
> see
> Vienna (Austria)

Pharmaceutical Society of Korea
> see
> Taehan Yakhakhoe

Kellogg Arabian Horse Center
> see
> W.K. Kellogg Arabian Horse Center

General Aniline and Film Corp. Ansco
> see
> Ansco

Society of Jesus
> see
> Jesuits

Bradner Associates
> see
> Michael Bradner Associates

26.3A5.   Numbers

If headings are arranged so that numbers expressed as words are displayed in a different place than numbers expressed as numerals, make references from the opposite form to the one used in the heading, if the number is in a position to affect the arrangement. Example:

3 Bridges Reformed Church (Three Bridges, N.J.)
> see
> Three Bridges Reformed Church (Three Bridges, N.J.)

26.3A6.   Abbreviations

If headings are arranged so that abbreviations are displayed in a different place than the equivalent words, refer from the full form to an abbreviation, if the abbreviation is in a position to affect the arrangement. Example:

Mount Auburn Associates (Somerville, Mass.)
> see
> Mt. Auburn Associates (Somerville, Mass.)

LC includes ampersands or other symbols that represent *and* here. If such a symbol occurs in the first five words, a reference from the name using *and* or its equivalent in the language of the heading is made. For other abbreviations to have a reference made, LC requires that they be in the first five words, not be listed in Appendix B.9 of *AACR2R*, *and* not represent a proper name. (*CSB* 21: 45)

26.3A7.   Different forms of heading

References are made from different forms of a corporate name that seem to be reasonable forms under which a user might search. Examples:

> Cambridge University
> > see
> > University of Cambridge

> California Institute of Technology. Baxter Art Gallery
> > see
> > Baxter Art Gallery

> Project Introspection
> > see
> > Virgin Islands of the United States. Project Introspection

> United States. Maritime Administration. Office of Commercial Development.
> > Office of Port and Intermodal Development
> > see
> > United States. Office of Port and Intermodal Development

> Treviso (Italy). Cathedral
> > see
> > Treviso Cathedral

26.3B.   *See also* references

26.3B1.   *See also* references are made between corporate headings that are related. This includes names that represent corporate name changes. LC calls the latter "earlier/later heading references," and instead of reading *see also*, the message of the reference reads "search also under the earlier heading" or "search also under the later heading." (*CSB* 109: 33–34) Examples:

> Gemeentelijke Archiefdienst Amsterdam
> > see also
> > Amsterdam (Netherlands). Gemeentearchief

> Automotive Transport Association of Ontario
> > search also under the later heading
> > Ontario Trucking Association

> Ontario Trucking Association
> > search also under the earlier heading
> > Automotive Transport Association of Ontario

26.3C.   Explanatory references

26.3C1.   General rule

Explanatory references are made when more guidance is required. Examples:

United Nations. Missions.
  Delegations, missions, etc. from member nations to the United Nations and to its subordinate units are entered under the name of the nation followed by the name of the delegation, mission, etc., e.g.
  United States. Mission to the United Nations
  Uruguay. Delegación en las Naciones Unidas

A. Harris & Co.
  Sanger Brothers was established in 1857. A. Harris & Co. was established in 1886. In 1961 they merged to form Sanger-Harris.
  Works by these bodies are found under the following headings according to the name used at the time of publication:
  Sanger Brothers
  A. Harris & Co.
  Sanger-Harris

LC no longer makes references of this type. Instead each related body is connected with the earlier or later name by a *see also* reference. References like the "United Nations. Missions" example above are handled by placing specific *see* references on each applicable authority record. (*CSB* 109: 44)

26.3C2.   Acronyms
When a system arranges initials separated by periods in a different place from initials not separated by periods, *AACR2R* allows for making an explanatory reference. Examples:

N.A.C.
    see
  National Automobile Club
  Naval Avionics Center (U.S.)
    When these initials occur in a title or other heading without spaces or periods, they are arranged as a single word.

NAC
    see
  National Automobile Club
  Naval Avionics Center (U.S.)
    When these initials occur in a title or other heading with spaces or periods, they are arranged as if each initial is a single word.

LC no longer makes explanatory references for acronyms. They are converted to simple *see* references on the authority record for each name involved. (*CSB* 109: 30)

RULE 26.4.   UNIFORM TITLES

26.4A.   A rule calling for a reference to or from a uniform title, in some cases, means that the reference may require a name heading preceding the uniform title.

26.4B.   *See* **references**

26.4B1.   Different titles or variants of the title

When different titles have been used in other editions of a work than the one(s) held by the library, or when variant titles have been used to cite a work in reference sources, references may be made from these variants. Examples:

> Laderman, Ezra. Trials of Galileo
> > see
> Laderman, Ezra. Galileo Galilei

> Córdoba (Argentina : Province). Ley no. 4051
> > see
> Córdoba (Argentina : Province). Ley orgánica del poder judicial (1942)

> Suder, Joseph, 1892-   . Festmesse, in D
> > see
> Suder, Joseph, 1892-   . Dona nobis pacem

> Revueltas, Silvestre, 1899-1940. Chit-chat music
> > see
> Revueltas, Silvestre, 1899-1940. Música para charlar

> **[Title page title: Música para charlar = Chit-chat music. Title added entries would be made for both titles. In the other cases, a title added entry would be made for the title proper of the information package being cataloged.]**

When translated titles are involved, the reference is made from the translated version of the title to the uniform title followed by the appropriate language sub-heading. Examples:

> Song of Roland
> > see
> Chanson de Roland. English

> Naft, Stephen, 1878-1956. Kyōsanshugi ni taisura nijū no shitsumon
> > see
> Naft, Stephen, 1878-1956.
> Answer please! Questions for communists. Japanese

26.4B2.   Titles of parts of a work cataloged independently

When a part of a work is cataloged so that the part is entered independently, a reference is made from the uniform title of the whole work with the part as a sub-heading to the title of the part as an independent entry. Example:

> Hesse, Hermann, 1877-1962. Steppenwolf. Tractat vom Steppenwolf
> > see
> Hesse, Hermann, 1877-1962. Tractat vom Steppenwolf

26.4B3.   Titles of parts cataloged under the title of the whole work

When a part of a work is cataloged so that the part is a subheading of the whole work, and if the title of the part is distinctive, a reference is made from the title of the part to the uniform title of the whole work with the part as a subheading. Examples:

Strauss, Richard, 1864-1949. Breit über mein Haupt dein schwarzes Haar
   see
   Strauss, Richard, 1864-1949. Licder, op. 19. Breit über mein Haupt dein schwarzes Haar

Mu`awwidhatan
   see
   Koran. Mu`awwidhatān

26.4B4. Collective titles

If a collection or selection of works of one person has been given a collective uniform title, and if the title proper is distinctive, a name-title reference is made from the title proper to the uniform title. Example:

Shepp, Archie. Further fire music
   see
   Shepp, Archie. Instrumental music. Selections

RULE 26.5.   REFERENCES TO ADDED ENTRIES FOR SERIES AND SERIALS

This rule states that, when making an added entry for either a series to which individually cataloged parts belong, or under the heading for a serial, references should be made from different forms of the series or serial heading that users might reasonably search under. A lengthy LC rule interpretation for rule 26.5A provides guidance for making such references in the case of series added entries. (*CSB* 105: 84-95)

NOTES

1. *Cataloging Service Bulletin*, no. 17 (Summer 1982): 31.

2. *Cataloging Service Bulletin*, no. 101 (Summer 2003): 55–57.

3. *Anglo-American Cataloguing Rules, Second Edition, 2002 Revision,* prepared under the direction of the Joint Steering Committee for Revision of AACR (Chicago: American Library Association, 2002), p. D-6.

4. *AACR2R2002*, p. 22-6.

5. For examples of references, *see* the section on references in this chapter: "References" (p. 270).

6. *AACR2R2002*, p. 22-11.

7. *AACR2R2002*, p. 22-36.

8. *AACR2R2002*, p. 21-6.

9. *Cataloging Service Bulletin*, no. 41 (Summer 1988): 54.

10. *AACR2R2002*, p. 25-5.

11. *RDA – Resource Description and Access: A Prospectus,* Joint Steering Committee for Revision of AACR, available: http://www.collectionscanada.ca/jsc/rdaprospectus.html or http://www.collectionscanada.ca/jsc/docs/5rda-prospectusrev.pdf (accessed 2/25/2006), p. 5.

SUGGESTED READING

Bratton, Robert, ed. "Authority Tools for Audiovisual and Music Catalogers: An Annotated List of Useful Resources." Online Audiovisual Catalogers, Inc., 2003- . Available: http://ublib.buffalo.edu/libraries/units/cts/olac/capc/authtools.html (accessed 2/14/2006).

Chan, Lois Mai. *Cataloging and Classification: An Introduction.* 2nd ed. New York: McGraw-Hill, 1994. Chapters 5–6.

Hagler, Ronald. *The Bibliographic Record and Information Technology.* 3rd ed. Chicago: American Library Association, 1997. Chapter 6.

Maxwell, Robert L. *Maxwell's Guide to Authority Work.* Chicago: American Library Association, 2002.

———. *Maxwell's Handbook for* AACR2R*: Explaining and Illustrating the* Anglo-American Cataloguing Rules *through the 2003 Update.* 4th ed. Chicago: American Library Association, 2004.

Smiraglia, Richard P. *Cataloging Music: A Manual for Use with AACR2.* 2nd ed. Lake Crystal, Minn.: Soldier Creek Press, 1986. Chapter 3: Uniform Titles.

———. *Music Cataloging: The Bibliographic Control of Printed and Recorded Music in Libraries.* Englewood, Colo.: Libraries Unlimited, 1989, pp. 54–61.

Part IV
AUTHORITY CONTROL

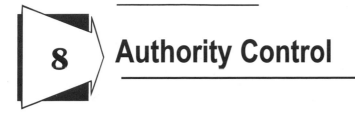

Authority Control

INTRODUCTION

Authority control, as currently practiced, is the result of the process of maintaining consistency in the verbal form used to represent an access point in a catalog and the further process of showing the relationships among headings for names, works, and subjects. The goal is to make possible the identifying and collocating functions of the catalog. (This chapter includes discussion of authority control of subject headings in addition to authority control of names and works, although discussion of subject analysis and creation of subject headings follows in the next chapters.)

As mentioned in several earlier chapters, international authority control is increasingly of concern. This is true because of the need to allow the creators of catalogs in various countries using various languages to designate their own "authorized" forms of names and subject terms. Everyone should not be required to use English language "authorized" forms, but we all should be able to use the same authority control. Therefore, several projects are experimenting with various potential methods of creating "virtual international authority files."[1]

FRBR

An international development that will allow us to move more easily toward international authority control is *Functional Requirements for Bibliographic Records (FRBR)*.[2] *FRBR* is a conceptual model of the bibliographic universe developed by the International Federation of Library Associations and Institutions (IFLA) that provides a way of describing entities and relationships between them. *FRBR* describes three groups of entities. Group 1 identifies entities that are the products of intellectual endeavors: work, expression, manifestation, item. Description of Group 1 entities has been considered the province of the descriptive chapters of *AACR2R*, which are covered in this text in chapters 4 and 5. Group 2 in *FRBR* identifies entities responsible for the products of intellectual endeavors: person, corporate body. These entities have been considered to be the province of the *AACR2R* processes of choosing access points and creating headings for them—processes that are covered in this text in chapters 6 and 7. The creators of *AACR*, who are working on a revision, promise to incorporate *FRBR* more fully into the new rules. Group 3 identifies entities that may serve as the subjects of intellectual or artistic endeavor: concept, object, event, and place, in addition to all entities in Groups 1 and 2. Entities as subjects are dealt with in this text in chapters 10–13.

It is the part of the model that provides a way of identifying relationships be-tween entities that is the province of authority control, but relationships are not fully developed in the *FRBR* model. The *FRBR* introduction acknowledges that the model does not develop those relationships between and among entities that are considered to be the province of the syndetic structure of a catalog. IFLA recognized the need for an extension of the model to incorporate authority data, and set up a new working group in 1999 to define functional requirements of authority records. A draft of the conceptual model for authority records (being referred to as *Functional Requirements for Authority Records*, or *FRAR*) was made available for comments to be submitted by the end of October 2005.[3] The reader should be alert to developments.

AUTHORITY CONTROL AND
FUNCTIONS OF THE CATALOG

FRBR maps the relationships it identifies to four "user tasks," which are quite similar to the functions of the catalog discussed in chapter 1 of this text. *FRBR*'s user tasks are:

- to *find* entities that correspond to the user's stated search criteria
- to *identify* an entity
- to *select* an entity that is appropriate to the user's needs
- to acquire or *obtain* access to the entity described[4]

The functions of a catalog given in chapter 1 are: identifying, collocating, evaluat-ing, and locating. Whatever the terminology used, authority control greatly en-hances a user's ability to have success in using a catalog.

Identifying Function

Authority control enhances the identifying, or finding, function of the catalog through the use of consistent forms of access points with references from forms not used. In a system under authority control, a user can assume that all works relating to a name or a concept will be found together or will at least be connected with refer-ences. Once one determines, for example, that records are found under Cochrane, Pauline A., and not under Atherton, Pauline, one can assume that everything by this person will be found at this heading. It is not necessary to look under Cochrane, P. A., or the alternate spelling, Cochran, or to try to think of other possible spellings or forms.

It is also possible to identify titles through use of a consistent heading for works that have different titles. A particular edition of the Bible, for example, can be found under "Bible." One does not have to remember an exact title such as *Holy Bible*, or *Good News for Modern Man*, although specific editions can also be found un-der these titles if one remembers them.

Likewise, once one determines that works about psychological help for fami-lies are found under "Family psychotherapy" and not under "Family therapy," one can assume that everything on that topic will be found there. Identification of works on a particular subject is made easier by using only one of the terms when there are two or more synonyms or by always using the words of a phrase in the same order —e.g., "Serials control systems," not "Control systems for Serials."

Collocating Function

Authority control enhances the collocating, or gathering, function of the catalog through the linking of consistent headings in a syndetic structure. *Syndetic* is an adjective meaning "connective, connecting." It is used to characterize the nature of a catalog under authority control because of the connecting that is brought about by using consistent headings and by providing references to and among those headings.

Names are collocated by bringing everything by and about a person or corporate body together under the same form of name; or in some cases where a person or body actually has used two or more different *names* (not just different forms of a name), collocation may be accomplished by connecting the names with references. Examples of the latter are:

University of North Carolina at Chapel Hill.   School of Information and Library Science
> For works issued by this body under its earlier name see:

University of North Carolina at Chapel Hill.   School of Library Science.

Dodgson, Charles Lutwidge, 1832–1898
> For works written under this author's pseudonym see:

Carroll, Lewis, 1832–1898.

Works are collocated by creating a uniform title for every work that has appeared under more than one title and by providing references from titles not chosen for the heading. In this way, for example, all manifestations of the Bible can be found together; and, as another example, Dickens's *Life and Adventures of Nicholas Nickleby* can be found with editions of the same work titled *Nicholas Nickleby*. Uniform titles also aid in showing relationships among works. Bibliographic records for the musical stage play and the film version of *Nicholas Nickleby* contain added entries for the uniform title for Dickens's original work, and can be found collocated with it. References also can help to show relationships among works. An example of such a reference is:

Tolkien, J. R. R. (John Ronald Reuel), 1892–1973.   Lord of the rings. 2. Two towers
> see

Tolkien, J. R. R. (John Ronald Reuel), 1892–1973.   Two towers.

The heading chosen for the work in this example collocates the bibliographic records for the work under the title of the part, but the reference collocates with the title of the whole larger work, letting the user know that parts of the whole work are available in addition to the whole work.

Authority control assures that subjects are collocated by providing consistent headings for discrete concepts, by assuring that there are references to those headings from terms not used, and by providing a network of references to and among broader terms, narrower terms, and related terms. For example, let us suppose that someone is using a catalog in which the subjects are from the *Library of Congress Subject Headings (LCSH)* and in which appropriate references have been provided. If this person looks up "Heart attack," a reference will show that this term is not used, but that "Myocardial infarction," is used instead. At "Myocardial infarction," in addition to finding bibliographic records representing works on the subject, the user will find a reference to the narrower term "Cardiogenic shock." In an ideal world there would also be a reference to the broader term "Coronary heart disease," although, traditionally, library catalogs have referred only to narrower and related terms because it was felt that to refer to broader terms made an impossibly complicated network. (This was true in manual systems. Most libraries even gave up providing related and narrower term references in manual catalogs.) If the broader term reference is made, however, the user can follow up with a search under "Coronary heart disease" and is referred to the related term "Type A behavior" and two other narrower terms besides the one that led to this term: "Angina pectoris" and "Coronary artery stenosis." There could also be a reference to the broader term "Heart—Diseases."

SYSTEM DESIGN

It should be emphasized that authority control of names, works, and subject terminology does not ensure that everything by and about a person or corporate body or everything on a subject will be found together. The design of the system in which the names, titles, and subject headings are displayed is a major factor. Excellent discussions of how system design can supplement and enhance authority control can be found in Yee and Layne's *Improving Online Public Access Catalogs* and in several other sources.[5] In addition, the Subject Analysis Committee of the American Library Association has published recommendations for system design for the best use and display of subject reference structures.[6] Finally, a chapter in *The Organization of Information* addresses issues of system design that can assist or deter users in their successful use of a catalog.[7]

It should also be pointed out that not all forms of name or all terms thought of by a user will match a reference if they do not match a heading. For example, a user of an authority-controlled online catalog with references who searches for "heart attacks" will be told there are no matches, because the reference is from "heart attack" in the singular. Or, a person may search for a name spelled as it sounds (e.g., "Kirshenbaum, Baruk" instead of "Kirschenbaum, Baruch"). Systems can be designed with enhanced search capabilities to supplement authority control in such situations.

And, of course, in the case of subject headings, subject analysis, as discussed in chapter 9, is also a factor. Only if an item were determined to be *about* "heart attacks" as a result of the process of subject analysis, would it be found under "Myocardial infarction." In library catalogs, even that would be true only if at least 20 percent of a work were on the subject.

LACK OF AUTHORITY CONTROL

In systems without authority control, it is up to the user to try to think of all possible ways that a name, work, or subject could be verbally represented, while at the same time eliminating all possible representations that will not satisfy the need. For example, a user wanting material on "Mercury" as a metal must eliminate that which concerns the planet or the Roman god; and a user wishing to consult works by John F. Murphy on cash management (*see* figure 8.1) must sort out these from works by other John F. Murphys who write about chemical engineering, education, geology, law, parenting, and other subjects, and who do not always use titles that are descriptive of their contents.

**Fig. 8.1. Partial authority records for five authors who use the name "John F. Murphy".
(Source: OCLC Connexion, Authorities)**

010	n 83175165
040	DLC ‡b eng ‡c DLC ‡d DLC
100 1_	Murphy, John F.
670	Murphy, A.M. Successful parenting, c1983 (a.e.) ‡b CIP t.p. (John F. Murphy, Ed. M.)

010	n 80072584
040	DLC ‡b eng ‡c DLC
100 1_	Murphy, John F., ‡d 1922-
400 1_	Murphy, Jack, ‡d 1922-
670	His Mary's immaculate heart, 1951.

010	n 83016187
040	DGPO ‡b eng ‡c DLC
100 1_	Murphy, John F. ‡q (John Francis), ‡d 1913-
670	His Sound cash management and borrowing, 1981: ‡b t.p. (John F. Murphy, retired bank exec. and member Manasota SCORE Chapter, Sarasota, Fla.)

010	no 90025472
040	DGPO ‡b eng ‡c DGPO
100 1_	Murphy, John F. ‡q (John Francis), ‡d 1922-
670	Richmond, G.M. Preliminary quaternary geologic map of the Dinwoody Lake area, Fremont County, Wyoming [MI], 1989?: ‡b t.p. (John F. Murphy; U.S. Geological Survey)

010	n 78011669
040	DLC ‡b eng ‡c DLC ‡d MoSpS-AV
100 1_	Murphy, John Francis, ‡d 1937-
400 1_	Murphy, John F. ‡q (John Francis), ‡d 1937-
670	American Society of International Law. Legal aspects ... 1978 (a.e.) ‡b t.p. (John F. Murphy)
670	International criminal law [VR] 1995: ‡b guide (Professor John F. Murphy, Villanova University School of Law; speaker)

In fact, in many of today's supposedly authority-controlled online catalogs, users must do this same sorting because works by all John F. Murphys, regardless of variant qualifiers or birth dates, are interfiled and subarranged alphabetically by the titles of their various works, or are subarranged in reverse chronological order, or are subarranged in some indeterminate fashion, and there is no reference to the John F. Murphy who is entered as "Murphy, John Francis, 1937–   ". (*See* figure 8.2.) This is a step backward from card catalogs where all works by the person whose heading is "Murphy, John F. (John Francis), 1913–   " were filed together before works by the person whose heading is "Murphy, John F. (John Francis), 1922–   ".

Fig. 8.2. Partial listing of titles in OCLC of at least nine different authors named "John F. Murphy". (Source: OCLC Connexion, WorldCat)

101.	Murphy, John F.	The Chemical safety board's reactive hazard investigation "improving r	Distributed by American Instit	2003	
102.	Murphy, John F.	A Comparison study of patient's overall perception of acute pain after		1989	
103.	Murphy, John F.	Elder law handbook /	OSBA,	2004	
...					
106.	Murphy, John F. (John Francis)	Implications of the Irish past :		1983	
107.	Murphy, John F.	LPS 2002 :	American Institute of Chemical	2002	
...					
109.	Murphy, John F. (John Francis)	Perceived effectiveness of Illinois secondary schools by superintenden		1986	
110.	Murphy, John F.	Performance of a mass-spectrometric method for the analysis of gene ex	Distributed by American Instit	2002	
111.	Murphy, John F. (John Francis), 1922-	Preliminary Quaternary geologic map of the Dinwoody Lake area, Fremont	Dept. of the Interior, U.S. Ge	1989	
112.	Murphy, John F.	Sex education and successful parenting /	Pauline Books & Media,	1996	D
...					
115.	Murphy, John F. (John Francis), 1913-	Sound cash management and borrowing /	U.S. Small Business Administra	1989	G
116.	Murphy, John F. (John Francis)	Success in spelling /	Laidlaw Brothers,	1985	
117.	Murphy, John F.	Success in spelling,	Laidlaw Brothers,	1985	
...					
126.	Murphy, John F.	Successful parenting /	St. Paul Editions,	1983	D
127.	Murphy, John F.	"Woven Hymns" of lyric and narrative :		1988	
128.	Murphy, John F., 1960-	The ecology and population biology of two litter decomposing basidiomy		1992	
...					
130.	Murphy, John F., 1922-	Petrography and geochemistry of the Cape Neddick Gabbro, Maine /		1984	
131.	Murphy, John Francis, 1937-	Cases and materials on the regulation of international business and ec	M. Bender,	1991	
...					
145.	Murphy, John Francis, 1937-	Sword of Islam :	Prometheus Books,	2002	P
...					
148.	Murphy, John Francis, 1937-	The United States and the rule of law in international affairs /	Cambridge University Press,	2004	P

It has been argued by some that users have for some time now been finding material in uncontrolled online databases that index papers and articles. This is true, but the process is not without some frustration. And the free text searching in search engines on the Internet can yield hundreds of "hits," many of which are unrelated to the desired search. A series of articles in 1985 and 1986 in *DATABASE* and *ONLINE* addressed the problem of searching for names in such databases.[8] Even though these articles are now more than twenty years old, they still apply when searching any database, including the Internet, that is not under authority control. Upon reading these articles the reader may be struck by the immense number of complications waiting to sabotage the uninitiated, and may wonder how any searcher could possibly remember all the tricks necessary for a complete name search. These articles are mini-lessons in performing authority work, except that it is up to the user, not the cataloger, to do the work over and over as searches are performed.

AUTHORITY WORK

Authority control, of course, cannot be achieved automatically. It requires authority work to be done by catalogers and indexers. First, it is necessary to discover all available evidence related to the naming of a person, body, work, topic, etc., and then to choose the form to use as the heading and the forms to use as references according to some rule. Then there must be creation of authority records. A carefully prepared authority record contains the form chosen for use as the heading, a list of variant forms or terms that may be used as references, and a list of sources consulted in the process of deciding upon the heading.

Name and Title Authority Work

The process followed for names, uniform titles, and series is somewhat different from that used for subjects. The first step in the process used for names, uniform titles, and series is verification, which means determining the existence of an author or other entity and the accepted form of heading to use. The name or title is first recorded as it appears in the work being cataloged. The next step usually is to check the library's catalog and authority files to determine if the heading already has been established for the library. If it has, the authorized form is noted and used in the cataloging in hand. If the heading is not already established, the cataloger checks the LC name authority file (LCNAF) either online at LC's website[9] or through a utility in which the library holds membership, or in a CD-ROM or microfiche version. If the name or title is in the LCNAF and is coded as being in *Anglo-American Cataloguing Rules, Second Edition* (*AACR2*) form, the record is copied for the local file. This may be accomplished by downloading the authority record from the bibliographic utility to the local system, if the library has an online catalog. Another method, if the library relies on cards, is to download the authority record from the machine-readable version used onto a personal computer. Then the record can be printed on card stock from the machine-readable record. There are several programs available for this operation.

If the name or title is not in the LCNAF or is not coded as being in *AACR2* form, then *Anglo-American Cataloguing Rules, Second Edition, 2002 Revision* (*AACR2R2002*) is consulted for the appropriate rules for form. If verification problems emerge, such as the existence of different names or different forms of the same name, further sources of information must be consulted. Such sources that might be consulted include other works by the same author or issued by the same body, publisher sites on the Internet, reliable directories or biographical dictionaries, or other reference sources. An authority record must then be made. The one or more sources used as authoritative may be cited in the authority record. Pertinent references are listed. References also should be made, as well as a revised authority record, for any conflicting heading that had to be changed in the process of creating the authority heading for the name or title in hand.

If a library is a NACO participant the cataloger submits the authority record to the international database through the NACO program. NACO is the name authorities program of the Program for Cooperative Cataloging (PCC), an international program operating out of LC, but consisting of a cooperative group of several hundred institutions. NACO participants receive special training upon joining NACO.[10] Following training, participants submit newly created or modified authority records to a liaison at LC who provides feedback for three to six months, after which the participants become independent. Independent catalogers enter the records directly into either OCLC or the RLG Union Catalog.

Many authority records are created in the *MARC 21* format (MAchine-Readable Cataloging format for the U.S., Canada, and Great Britain) by LC and by NACO libraries, and most libraries try to use these as much as possible in order to reduce their local authority work. Figure 8.3 shows a name authority record coded according to the *MARC 21* authorities format and formatted as is done in the OCLC system. In the *MARC 21* format the authorized heading is given in a field beginning with 1 (100, 110, 111, 150, 151, etc). *See from* references are given in fields beginning with 4 (400, 410, etc.). *See also from* references are given in fields beginning with 5 (500, 510, etc.). Notes are given in fields beginning with 6 (667, 670, 675, 678, 680, 681, 682, 688). Special kinds of references are given in fields 663 through 666. MARC records, of course, can be displayed in any fashion that a system programmer chooses.

Fig. 8.3. MARC name authority record. (Source: OCLC Connexion, Authorities—record number 00256371)

ARN	00256371							
	Rec stat	n	Entered	19790314	Replaced	19840322000000.0		
	Type	z	Upd status	a	Enc lvl	n	Source	
	Roman	|	Ref status	a	Mod rec		Name use	a
	Govt agn	|	Auth status	a	Subj	a	Subj use	a
	Series	n	Auth/ref	a	Geo subd	n	Ser use	b
	Ser num	n	Name	a	Subdiv tp	n	Rules	c
010		n 79022593						
040		DLC ‡b eng ‡c DLC						
100	1_	Van Buren, Ariane.						
400	1_	Buren, Ariane van						
400	1_	Van Buren, E. Ariane						
670		Nuclear or not? 1978 (a.e.) ‡b t.p. (Ariane van Buren) jkt. (E. Ariane van Buren, research assoc., International Inst. of Environment & Development)						

A few libraries continue to use card authority files. Figure 8.4 shows one format that a manual name authority card might take. In this format the rules used are indicated in the upper right corner, the heading is given on the top line at the left margin, sources are given next, and references follow. A single *x* is equivalent to a 4xx field in *MARC 21* and means that there will be a *see* reference from that form to the heading. A double *xx* is equivalent to a 5xx field in *MARC 21* and is used to mean that a *see also* reference would be made from that form, in cases where headings have been created for two or more names for the same person or body, e.g.:

Carroll, Lewis, 1832–1898.

xx   Dodgson, Charles Lutwidge, 1832–1898

Fig. 8.4. Sample name authority record in card format.

AACR2

Van Buren, Ariane.

LCAF: n   79022593

Work cat: Nuclear or not?   1978 (a.e.): t.p. (Ariane van Buren) jkt. (E. Ariane van Buren, research assoc., International Inst. of Environment & Development)

x   Buren, Ariane van
x   Van Buren, E. Ariane

Subject Authority Work

Subject authority work is almost always done by verifying a heading as being the latest terminology used in the official list used by the library. The online version of the *Library of Congress Subject Headings (LCSH)*, for example, can be searched through a bibliographic utility, through *Classification Web*, or in the latest book version (the 29th edition was published early in 2006). In most libraries with online catalogs, the subject authority file is linked with the bibliographic file so that all recommended references are presented to users who search for those terms. In a manual system it is necessary to determine which of the headings that follow the codes for *see also from* references are already represented in the catalog. The cataloger using a manual system may also choose from the list of recommended terms those from which *see* references should be made.

If a subject string is being constructed for original cataloging, and one is using *LCSH*, it is necessary also to consult the *Subject Cataloging Manual: Subject Headings*, either in print form or through *Cataloger's Desktop*, and *Free-Floating Subdivisions: An Alphabetical Index* (so far only available in print form). SACO participants may submit proposals to LC for either new subject headings not found in *LCSH*, or proposals to change headings that are found in *LCSH* but are deemed to be outdated, incomplete, or exhibit other such deficiencies.[11] SACO is the subject authorities program of the PCC. NACO institutions are automatically members of SACO, and in addition, any institution may apply to become a SACO-only member. Such membership requires an institutional commitment to an annual goal of 10–12 proposals for new or changed LCSH headings and/or new or changed LC Classification numbers. It is expected that a cataloger making a proposal is using the latest versions of *LCSH* and the manuals. It is also expected that research be performed to assure that the proposed heading is not a duplicate and that the necessary sources be cited to demonstrate that the term is used in writing and is needed. It is also possible to propose a new classification number. Persons making classification proposals should be using the latest available LC classification schedules and the *Subject Cataloging Manual: Classification.*

Figure 8.5 shows a subject authority record in the *MARC 21* format as displayed in OCLC. Terms coded 450 are "used for" terms from which *see* or *use* references should be made. Terms coded 550 can be either related terms or broader terms. The difference is made known through use of "$w g" following the broader terms. Both related and broader terms should have references made from them to *see also* the term in the 150 field. *MARC 21* authority records do not show narrower terms, working on the assumption that the narrower terms are automatically taken care of when the system is programmed to display all the references from broader terms on every record.

Fig. 8.5. Sample MARC subject authority record. (Source: OCLC Connexion, Authorities —record number 02110833)

ARN	02110833						
Rec stat c		**Entered** 19860211		**Replaced** 19980416155519.3			
Type	z	**Upd status**	a	**Enc lvl**	n	**Source**	
Roman	l	**Ref status**	a	**Mod rec**		**Name use**	b
Govt agn	l	**Auth status**	a	**Subj**	a	**Subj use**	a
Series	n	**Auth/ref**	a	**Geo subd**	i	**Ser use**	b
Ser num	n	**Name**	n	**Subdiv tp**	n	**Rules**	n

010	sh 85018276
040	DLC ‡b eng ‡c DLC ‡d DLC
053	HD69.C6
150	Business consultants
450	Efficiency engineers
450	Management advisory services
450	Management consultants
550	Consultants ‡w g
550	Interim executives
670	UMI business vocab. ‡b (Management advisory services)

Although very few libraries use card subject authority files, for the few who do, Figure 8.6 is an example of one format for a subject authority card, indicating the source of the information. In manual subject authority records, the initials NT (narrower term), UF (used for), RT (related term), and BT (broader term) are often used, although *x* and *xx* may be used as in name authority records.

Fig. 8.6. Sample subject authority record in card format. (Source: *Library of Congress Subject Headings*, 28th ed.)

Business consultants (May Subd Geog)
  [HD69.C6]
    UF Efficiency engineers
          Management advisory services
          Management consultants
    BT Consultants
    RT Interim executives
    NT Hospital consultants
          Marketing consultants
          Risk managers
                                        LCSH 28th ed.

CREATION OF AUTHORITY FILES

Following creation of authority records, the next step in authority work is the addition of the records into an authority file, either manual or machine-readable. In order for the authority file to serve its purpose it must be linked in some way to the bibliographic file. In card or paper systems the link is implicit. That is, the link is in the mind of a human who perceives the presence of an identical form on both the authority record and the catalog record and also perceives the presence in both files of the appropriate reference(s).

In many machine systems, also, the authority system linkage is implicit. In those systems the authority file, although automated, is a completely separate file from the bibliographic file, and authority control of new records is dependent upon the cataloger finding the correct form of a heading in the authority file and then entering it correctly into the bibliographic record. There are no references in these files, although the authority files may be searched under the forms from which references are authorized. In such systems changes in headings mean that unless there are strict procedures for checking headings already in a file against every new heading entered, two or more forms of a heading may appear simultaneously with different bibliographic records displayed at each heading. A recent catalog search by the author returned the following headings with numbers of bibliographic records to the left of the heading:

    1   Williams, Tennessee, 1911– 1983.
  156   Williams, Tennessee, 1911–1983.
    1   Williams, Tennessee, 1914–1983.

The first heading has a space after the hyphen before the death date. The third heading has an incorrect birth date. A sophisticated automated linked authority control system should "catch" the first and third headings as being one-of-a-kind (and perhaps either new to the system or in error) and would identify them so that a catalog manager could check their validity.

Subject headings also can cause display problems when authority control is only implicit. Changes are made to *LCSH* headings with some frequency. In September 2004, for example, "Trials—Drama" was changed to "Legal drama." In an authority file with only implicit authority control the cataloger first using the new heading must notice the change and take steps to have the records with the former heading changed to the current one. In such situations it is possible occasionally to run the bibliographic file against the authority file to check for headings that match references and to change any matches found to the new form; but it is not feasible to do this often, and in the meantime multiple forms exist unless someone notices and changes them individually.

In more sophisticated systems the linkage between authority file and bibliographic file is explicit. That is, a direct internal linkage exists between a heading stored in the authority file and the same heading stored in the bibliographic file. In such systems the headings for every new record are checked against the authority file, and new or changed headings are flagged for review. In these systems also, references are displayed from unused terms to used ones and from used terms to narrower terms and usually also to related terms. References to broader terms are often not displayed, however (as discussed earlier in this chapter).

In the most sophisticated systems there is a linkage that uses relational file techniques to link a bibliographic record with only identification numbers as headings to a system of authority records that store all the headings linked to an identification number for each. The advantage here is that each heading is stored only once, and thus matching of bibliographic and authority headings is unnecessary. In addition when a heading has to be changed, the change is made only in the authority record. What the user sees in such a system is no different from what is seen in the previously described linked systems.

CATALOG AS AUTHORITY FILE

While it is possible to do authority work without making separate authority records, this is done less and less often. In manual card catalogs, libraries formerly would let the catalog itself serve as the authority file. That is, the heading used in the catalog was assumed to have been verified, and necessary references were tracked on the back of one of the main entry cards for the heading in question. This method became difficult when notes were needed to resolve conflicting headings or when the set of cards on which the references were recorded was withdrawn from the catalog.

In online catalogs, too, the bibliographic record may be considered to contain the authoritative heading in situations where no notes or references are required. In some systems authority work is done for every heading, but authority records are made only when references or notes are required. In these latter systems the heading index is created from authority file headings and references combined with headings from bibliographic records that have no associated authority records. When storage space was an issue, the advantage of this system was the saving of disk space necessary to store MARC authority records that contained no information that was not already available in bibliographic records. This advantage was offset in systems using relational file techniques, because in the latter, much space was/is saved by storing each heading only once instead of in every associated bibliographic record. Storage space is no longer an issue in most systems, and authority records are now often made for every heading so that a search for a heading can place the searcher in the authority file, where a particular heading can be chosen before the user is given a list of bibliographic records.

MAINTENANCE OF AUTHORITY SYSTEMS

In order to maintain an authority system, it is necessary to have routine error checking between authority and bibliographic files. There must also be routine error checking among authority records for consistency. For example, if a changed heading authority record does not replace the older heading record properly, it would be possible to have a response to a search for one term refer to another term only to have a reference at that term referring back to the first (e.g., "Trials—Drama *see* Legal drama" and "Legal drama *see* Trials—Drama" in the same catalog).

Updating is necessary when a library is using LC authority data as the basis of its authority system. Names are changed to reflect new usages by some authors; subjects are constantly changed to update terminology, add references, etc.; and new headings are added. There must be procedures for replacing the changed records and adding the new ones. Changed records are particularly difficult because there is not yet a mechanism for notifying a library that has used a bibliographic record in the past that its terminology or name form has now been changed. For example, the authority record for "Cochrane, Pauline Atherton, 1929–   " was changed in 1990 to "Cochrane, Pauline A. (Pauline Atherton), 1929–   " because 80 percent of her works as represented in OCLC's database were found to use the form with the initial "A." Records that appeared in LC's MARC file at the time were changed and reissued, but many records in the bibliographic networks and in local online catalogs remained in the old form for a number of years. One problem in such a case is that the titles of works of such authors appear in two or more separate alphabetical subsets—the same problem that can result when no authority work was done in the first place. Later, at OCLC and in other systems, special projects ran the authority file against the bibliographic file to check for and correct such discrepancies. Some systems (e.g., OCLC) now routinely run new authority records from LC against the bibliographic file on a regular basis, although it is not difficult to find catalogs where this has not been done and in which old forms of names and subjects abound.

CONCLUSION

There are several potential uses for authority control that have not yet been realized. One is the idea mentioned earlier of providing access to broader subject terms. Another is the potential for controlling elements of records not now perceived as access points (e.g., names of publishers). A third potential lies in further control of works. Editions of works, for example, are now related only by either the fact of their having identical author and/or title access points or the provision of notes on bibliographic records giving earlier titles or authors. If authority control of works, which is only in its infancy, were extended to such relationships as editions and other derivative works, identifying works in fields such as music and literature would be greatly enhanced.[12]

NOTES

1.   See discussions of projects in Arlene G. Taylor and Barbara B. Tillett, eds., *Authority Control in Organizing and Accessing Information: Definition and International Experience* (New York: Haworth Information Press, 2004).

2.   International Federation of Library Associations and Institutions, IFLA Study Group on the Functional Requirements for Bibliographic Records, *Functional Requirements for Bibliographic Records, Final Report* (München: K.G. Saur, 1998). Also available: http://www.ifla.org/VII/s13/frbr/frbr.htm or http://www.ifla.org/VII/s13/frbr/frbr.pdf (accessed 2/14/2006).

3.   *Functional Requirements for Authority Records: A Conceptual Model: Draft 2005-06-15*, IFLA UBCIM Working Group on Functional Requirements and Numbering of Authority Records (FRANAR). Available: http://www.ifla.org/VII/d4/FRANAR-Conceptual-M-Draft-e.pdf (accessed 2/14/2006). For additional information see: Glenn E. Patton, "FRANAR: A Conceptual Model for Authority Data," *Cataloging & Classification Quarterly* 38, no 3/4 (2004): 91–104; also published in *Authority Control in Organizing and Accessing Information: Definition and International Experience*, edited by Arlene G. Taylor and Barbara B. Tillett (New York: Haworth Information Press, 2004), pp. 91–104.

4.   *FRBR*, p. 82.

5.   Martha M. Yee and Sara Shatford Layne, *Improving Online Public Access Catalogs* (Chicago: American Library Association, 1998). For additional discussion of how system design can supplement authority control, *see*: Marcia Bates, "Subject Access in Online Catalogs: A Design Model," *Journal of the American Society for Information Science* 37, no. 6 (November 1986): 357–376; Christine L. Borgman, "Why Are Online Catalogs *Still* Hard to Use?" *Journal of the American Society for Information Science* 47, no. 7 (July 1996): 493–503; Arlene G. Taylor, "Authority Control and System Design," in *Policy and Practice in the Bibliographic Control of Nonbook Media*, edited by Sheila S. Intner and Richard P. Smiraglia (Chicago: American Library Association, 1987), pp. 64–81.

6.   American Library Association, Association for Library Collections and Technical Services, Subject Analysis Committee, Subcommittee on Subject Reference Structures in Automated Systems, *Recommendations for providing access to, display of, navigation within and among, and modifications of existing practice regarding subject reference structures in automated systems, December 1, 2003.* Available: http://www.ala.org/ala/alctscontent/catalogingsection/catcommittees/subjectanalysis/subjectreference/RefStructuresFinal.doc (accessed 2/14/2006). For additional information see: David Miller, Tony Olson, and Sara Shatford Lane, "Promoting Research and Best Practices in Subject Reference Structures: A Decade of Work by the Subject Analysis Committee," *Library Resources & Technical Services* 49, no. 3 (July 2005): 154–166.

7.   Arlene G. Taylor, *The Organization of Information* (Westport, Conn.: Libraries Unlimited, 2004), Chapter 5.

8. Catherine E. Pasterczyk, "Russian Transliteration Variations for Searchers," *DATABASE* 8 (February 1985): 68–75; Anne B. Piternick, "What's in a Name? Use of Names and Titles in Subject Searching," *DATABASE* 8 (December 1985): 22–28; David M. Pilachowski and David Everett, "What's in a Name? Looking for People Online—Social Sciences," *DATABASE* 8 (August 1985): 47–65; David M. Pilachowski and David Everett, "What's in a Name? Looking for People Online—Current Events," *DATABASE* 9 (April 1986): 43–50; David Everett and David M. Pilachowski, "What's in a Name? Looking for People Online—Humanities," *DATABASE* 9 (October 1986): 26–34; Bonnie Snow, "Caduceus: People in Medicine: Searching Names Online," *ONLINE* 10 (September 1986): 122–127.

9. Library of Congress Authorities. Available: http://authorities.loc.gov/ (accessed 2/14/2006).

10. "NACO: Program for Cooperative Cataloging." Available: http://www.loc.gov/catdir/pcc/naco/naco.html (accessed 2/14/2006).

11. "SACO Program Description: Program for Cooperative Cataloging." Available: http://www.loc.gov/catdir/pcc/saco/saco.html (accessed 2/14/2006).

12. Richard Smiraglia, "Authority Control of Works: Cataloging's Chimera?" *Cataloging & Classification Quarterly* 38, no 3/4 (2004): 291–308; also published in *Authority Control in Organizing and Accessing Information: Definition and International Experience*, edited by Arlene G. Taylor and Barbara B. Tillett (New York: Haworth Information Press, 2004), pp. 291–308.

SUGGESTED READING

Burger, Robert H. *Authority Work: The Creation, Use, Maintenance, and Evaluation of Authority Records and Files*. Littleton, Colo.: Libraries Unlimited, 1985.

Clack, Doris Hargrett. *Authority Control: Principles, Applications, and Instructions*. Chicago: American Library Association, 1990.

Maxwell, Robert L. *Maxwell's Guide to Authority Work*. Chicago: American Library Association, 2002.

Smiraglia, Richard. *The Nature of "A Work": Implications for Knowledge Organization*. Lanham, Md.: Scarecrow Press, 2001.

Talmacs, Kerrie. "Authority Control." In *Technical Services Today and Tomorrow*. 2nd ed., edited by Michael Gorman, pp. 129–139. Englewood, Colo.: Libraries Unlimited, 1998.

Taylor, Arlene G. "Authority Control: Where It's Been and Where It's Going," and other papers from the "Authority Control: Why It Matters" conference sponsored by NELINET, 1 November 1999, Worcester, Mass. Available: http://www.nelinet.net/edserv/conf/cataloging/cts/1999/taylor.htm (accessed 2/14/2006).

Taylor, Arlene G., and Barbara B. Tillett, eds. *Authority Control in Organizing and Accessing Information: Definition and International Experience*. New York: Haworth Information Press, 2004.

Tillett, Barbara B. "Authority Control: State of the Art and New Perspectives." *Cataloging & Classification Quarterly* 38, no. 3/4 (2004): 23–42; also published in *Authority Control in Organizing and Accessing Information: Definition and International Experience*, edited by Arlene G. Taylor and Barbara B. Tillett, pp. 23–42. New York: Haworth Information Press, 2004.

Part V
SUBJECT ACCESS

9 ▷ Subject Access to Library Materials

INTRODUCTION

Subject analysis is the part of cataloging that deals with determining what the intellectual content of an item is "about," translating that "aboutness" into the conceptual framework of the classification or subject heading system being used, and then translating the conceptual framework into the specific classificatory symbols or specific terminology used in the classification or subject heading system.

First, one must have a clear idea about the level of exhaustivity that is to be applied. Exhaustivity has to do with the number of concepts that will be considered in the conceptual framework of the system. A. G. Brown identifies two basic degrees of exhaustivity: depth indexing and summarization.[1] Depth indexing aims to extract all the main concepts dealt with in an item, recognizing many subtopics and subthemes. Summarization recognizes only a dominant, overall subject of the item, recognizing only concepts embodied in the main theme. In library cataloging, traditionally, subject analysis has been carried out at the summarization level, reserving depth indexing for other enterprises such as periodical indexes.

Determining what an item is about at the summarization level can be a difficult matter. In chapter 1 Charles A. Cutter's statement of the basic functions of a catalog was quoted, including "To show what the library has . . . on a given subject." (*See* p. 7) This implies that it is obvious what being "on a given subject" means. Patrick Wilson has discussed this matter at some length and has suggested that part of the problem is that catalogers and others are taught to look for *the* subject of an item.[2] He observes that if a person is writing a book or paper, and you ask what the person is writing about, he or she can tell you. If you go further and ask what is the subject about which the person is writing, this seems to be an equivalent question; but using the definite article *the* in front of *subject* implies that there will be just one thing to mention in answer to the question. Wilson's further explication demonstrates the fallacy of this assumption.[3]

Although some items *seem* to have an easily determined subject, it may not be so. A work titled *History of Mathematics* is about the discipline of mathematics; but it is more specifically about mathematics from a historical perspective while not being about the discipline of history. This distinction has a certain subtlety that is learned through education in our present-day Western tradition. It is possible that in another place and time history would be considered to be the major subject of anything historical, regardless of the specific topic. Let us take another example: *Nature in Italian Art: A Study of Landscape Backgrounds from Giotto to Tintoretto.* This work is about landscape painting—specifically in Italian art during a set period of time. Is it *about* Italian art? Who is to say that it would not be useful to someone searching for information on Italian art? Is it about Giotto and Tintoretto and all the landscape artists in between? Of course it is, and if one were doing depth indexing, all would be indexed; but if one is looking for *the* subject, a listing of names of numerous artists will not do.

Determining what something is about depends to some extent upon one's knowledge or opinions about the world and upon understanding a work in different ways depending upon one's experiences. Many people could read a list of names that included Giotto and Tintoretto and not know that the list was a list of Italian artists, not to mention that they were landscape painters. A person could understand each individual sentence in a writing and still not know what the writing as a whole was about.

In addition determination of "aboutness" may depend on judgment. This problem has been elaborated upon by W. C. Berwick Sayers:

> If [a] book on Scotland is not mainly geographic and historical, but consists of descriptive and narrative chapters together with a melange of literary and scientific observations and reflections on the national traits and institutions, also considerable social philosophy in the last chapters, the judgment is indeed complex and the decisions may be uncertain.[4]

Because it is difficult to define what "on a given subject" means, and because determining "aboutness" depends upon the indexer's or cataloger's knowledge, opinions, experiences, and judgment, Marcia Bates has observed that "it is practically impossible to instruct indexers or catalogers [on] how to find subjects when they examine documents. Indeed, we cataloging instructors usually deal with this essential feature of the skill being taught by saying such vague and inadequate things as 'Look for the main topic of the document.' "[5]

Although there is no one correct way to determine "aboutness," one suggested method is presented in Arlene G. Taylor's *The Organization of Information*.[6] The book also includes an appendix that gives a workform listing concepts to consider.[7] Two other works that are useful for someone faced with the need to determine "aboutness" are *Documentation: Methods for Examining Documents, Determining Their Subjects and Selecting Indexing Terms*, published by the International Organization for Standardization, and *Subject Analysis: Principles and Procedures*, by D. W. Langridge.[8] These give suggested guidelines on what to look for when doing subject analysis. In a recent study, Daniel Joudrey found that a group of untrained analysts used multiple approaches to determining aboutness and also used various strategies for examining both the physical item and the intellectual content. Each participant used a different combination of techniques to gain an understanding of aboutness. However, patterns were identified that Joudrey intends to explore in further research.[9]

Prior to the 1980s there was considerable antipathy toward subject access in the United States based in part on studies that showed that academic library card catalog users used a subject approach only about 30 percent of the time. However, Karen Markey constructed a grid of card catalog use studies in several types of libraries completed between 1967 and 1981 that shows that subject approaches in card catalogs varied from 10 percent to 62 percent and the median was about 40 percent.[10] More recent studies of online catalog users have showed that subject access in online catalogs is quite popular—one study of many types of libraries with different online systems showed that subject approaches were about 59 percent of all catalog uses.[11] It must be assumed, therefore, that subject analysis has been done well enough that people find it useful, if not perfect. In fact there is evidence that subject headings add considerable value to a record. In recent research, Tina Gross and Arlene G. Taylor found that "if subject headings were to be removed or no longer included in catalog records, users performing keyword searches would miss more than one third of the hits they currently retrieve. On average 35.9% of hits would not be found."[12] That is, for one third of records retrieved by users conducting keyword searches, the keyword(s) being sought appear in the record *only* in subject headings.

Once the cataloger has decided what he or she thinks an item is about, that "aboutness" must be translated into the conceptual framework of the system. If one is using a verbal subject system, completion of a sentence beginning, "This information package is about . . ." serves well as a translation device into the conceptual framework of thinking about words that can be used to identify the intellectual content of the information package. If one is classifying, this usually means one must determine disciplines, subdisciplines, subtopics, space (i.e., place in which the subject is set), time, and form (e.g., historical treatment, dictionary). A. G. Brown gives an excellent introduction to the process of learning to place one's subject into a conceptual framework necessary for classification.[13]

Finally, the cataloger assigns subject headings either according to a set of rules, as was the case with PRECIS headings (*see* discussion of PRECIS in chapter 13), or from a controlled list of headings, which may also have rules for using the list, as is the case with *Library of Congress Subject Headings* (*LCSH*; discussed in chapter 11) or with the *Sears List of Subject Headings* (*Sears*; discussed in chapter 12). The cataloger also assigns classification symbols from the particular classification scheme being used (discussed in chapters 14–18). The subject term(s) most often appear as access points for the item in the library's catalog. The classification notation is usually used as the basis for a call number for a physical information package, that will determine the position of the item on the library's shelves.

ALPHABETIC VERSUS CLASSIFIED APPROACH TO INFORMATION

During cataloging, the cataloger must take into account the dual manifestations of the items to be added to the collection. Such items are both intellectual and physical entities. In descriptive cataloging the physical description addresses the physical entity, while name and title headings are constructed to allow for access to the intellectual work. For access to the intellectual contents, subject catalogers choose one or more subject terms to insert into the bibliographic record. However, they traditionally choose only one classification notation, which will place all copies of a given physical item together on the shelves. Classifiers strive for the optimum location in view of the content of the item, the accepted classification schedule, and the needs of the clientele. Such decisions are not always easy to make. For instance, the same historical treatise might go equally well into political or economic history, or perhaps under social history or biography. In the choice of subjects to be represented in the catalog or index for this hypothetical treatise, all the aspects can be brought out through choice of multiple subject access points. And, of course, virtual information packages (e.g., web pages) are not limited to only one place on any shelf. As discussed in chapter 1, classified catalogs allow several classification notations to be assigned, but few catalogs in the United States are classified. However, categorization of websites allows classifying each one in more than one category. If classified catalogs are to make a comeback, it probably will be because the alphabetical "index" will be combined with the classified display arrangement. Getting to a subject area using words, the user will be able to browse up and down a hierarchy (or browse surrounding related concepts in a visual subject display) and will be able to explore related concepts through hyperlinks.

Each approach in a catalog requires a different pattern of communication. The alphabetical catalog gives a "horizontal" approach through its random scattering of access points throughout the entire linguistic finding apparatus. The classified catalog offers a "vertical" (hierarchical) approach through its closely related classes and categories, under which materials can be identified by means of logical, orderly sequences from general to specific.

With online catalogs it is possible to have both approaches in the same catalog, and some experimentation with this has been done.[14] For the most part, so far, access by classification notation in online catalogs is a shelflist approach—that is, there is only one classification notation for any one item.

Users who want information on a certain subject usually approach a catalog with questions formulated in their own words. These words must be translated into the predetermined access terminology of the catalog. The connection between users and subject headings (the "alphabetical" approach) has been facilitated by the use of keyword searching. Instead of the user's terminology having to coincide with that of a controlled list, the user may enter his or her own terminology. If one record can be identified that seems to match the user's subject need, subject headings in the record can be searched specifically to find other records on the subject and to find the subject's reference structure of broader terms, narrower terms, and related terms. Likewise, classification notations in a relevant record can be searched to find other records that have been given the same classification.

It may be that keyword searching will soon be enhanced by the power of ontologies. The field of Natural Language Processing (NLP) uses lexical ontologies to provide analysis of language. An ontology may include an analysis of each term as to its usage as different parts of speech; and within each part of speech, it may give the various senses in which a term may be used. For example, a fence may be a structure built to set off a particular area, or a fence may be a receiver of stolen goods. Then within each sense, synonyms, antonyms, related terms, broader terms, narrower terms, etc., may be given. Other ontologies show more underpinnings of categorization/classification. In all cases ontologies are intended to be used to assist humans and computers to "share knowledge." The potential for ontologies in catalogs is that when a user searches the catalog for a particular keyword, the system could present the user with the various senses of that word, from which the user could choose the one wanted. A further step could be to ask the user if he or she wishes to search for all synonyms to the sense chosen.[15]

CONCLUSION

This chapter has discussed the topic of subject analysis and arrangement of library materials both by verbal/alphabetical approaches and by classification. In the chapters that follow, these two approaches are considered separately along with systems and schemes for implementing each approach. The reader should remember, however, that these are two sides of the same coin and that both are attempts to provide users with access to the intellectual contents of the items being analyzed. For more discussion of controlled vocabularies, ontologies, and classification theory and concepts, the reader is referred to Taylor's *The Organization of Information*.[16]

NOTES

1.   A. G. Brown, in collaboration with D. W. Langridge and J. Mills, *An Introduction to Subject Indexing*, 2nd ed. (London: Bingley, 1982), frames 48 and 51.

2.   Patrick Wilson, "Subjects and the Sense of Position," in *Theory of Subject Analysis: A Sourcebook*, edited by Lois Mai Chan, Phyllis A. Richmond, and Elaine Svenonius (Littleton, Colo.: Libraries Unlimited, 1985), p. 309.

3.   Wilson, "Subjects and the Sense of Position," pp. 309–320.

4.   W. C. Berwick Sayers, *Sayers' Manual of Classification for Librarians*, 3rd ed. rev. by Arthur Maltby (London: Andre Deutsch, 1955), pp. 235–236.

5.   Marcia J. Bates, "Subject Access in Online Catalogs: A Design Model," *Journal of the American Society for Information Science* 37, no. 6 (November 1986): 360.

6.   Arlene G. Taylor, *The Organization of Information*, 2nd ed. (Westport, Conn.: Libraries Unlimited, 2004), Chapter 9: Subject Analysis.

7.   Ibid., pp. 347–351.

8.   *Documentation: Methods for Examining Documents, Determining Their Subjects and Selecting Indexing Terms* (Geneva, Switzerland: International Organization for Standardization, 1985); D. W. Langridge, *Subject Analysis: Principles and Procedures* (London: Bowker-Saur, 1989).

9.   Daniel N. Joudrey, "Building Puzzles and Growing Pearls: A Qualitative Exploration of Determining Aboutness." Ph. D. dissertation, University of Pittsburgh, 2005. Available: http://edt.library.pitt.edu/ETD/available/etd-12132005-155713/ (accessed 2/14/1006).

10.   Karen Markey, *Subject Searching in Library Catalogs: Before and After the Introduction of Online Catalogs* (Dublin, Ohio: OCLC, 1984), pp. 75–77.

11.   *Using Online Catalogs: A Nationwide Survey*, edited by Joseph R. Matthews, Gary S. Lawrence, and Douglas K. Ferguson; sponsored by the Council on Library Resources (New York: Neal-Schuman, 1983), p. 144.

12.   Tina Gross and Arlene G. Taylor, "What Have We Got to Lose? The Effect of Controlled Vocabulary on Keyword Searching Results," *College & Research Libraries* 66, no. 3 (May 2005): 212–230.

13.   Brown, *Introduction to Subject Indexing*, frames 91–130.

14.   For an example of research using terminology associated with classification, see Karen Markey and Anh Demeyer, *Dewey Decimal Classification Online Project: Evaluation of a Library Schedule and Index Integrated into the Subject Searching Capabilities of an Online Catalog: Final Report to the Council on Library Resources* (Dublin, Ohio: OCLC, 1986).

15.   For more about ontologies *see*: Noy, Natalya F., and Deborah L. McGuinness. *Ontology Development 101: A Guide to Creating Your First Ontology* (Knowledge Systems Laboratory, Stanford University, 2000). Available: http://www.ksl.stanford.edu/people/dlm/papers/ontology-tutorial-noy-mcguinness-abstract.html (accessed 2/14/2006).

16.   Arlene G. Taylor, "Systems for Vocabulary Control," Chapter 10, and "Systems for Categorization," Chapter 11 in *The Organization of Information*, 2nd ed. (Westport, Conn.: Libraries Unlimited, 2004).

SUGGESTED READING

Brown, A. G., in collaboration with D. W. Langridge and J. Mills. *An Introduction to Subject Indexing*. 2nd ed. London: Bingley, 1982 [programmed text].

Chan, Lois Mai. *Cataloging and Classification: An Introduction*. 2nd ed. New York: McGraw-Hill, 1994. Chapter 7: Subject Cataloging.

Documentation: Methods for Examining Documents, Determining Their Subjects and Selecting Indexing Terms. Geneva, Switzerland: International Organization for Standardization, 1985.

Foskett, A. C. *The Subject Approach to Information*. 5th ed. London: Library Association Publishing, 1996.

Fugmann, Robert. *Subject Analysis and Indexing: Theoretical Foundation and Practical Advice*. Frankfurt am Main: Indeks Verlag, 1993.

Hagler, Ronald. *The Bibliographic Record and Information Technology*. 3rd ed. Chicago: American Library Association, 1997. Chapter 7: Subject Access.

Harvey, Ross, and Philip Hider. *Organising Knowledge in a Global Society: Principles and Practice in Libraries and Information Centres*. Wagga Wagga, NSW, Australia: Centre for Information Studies, Charles Sturt University, 2004. Chapter 6: Subject Access Concepts.

Langridge, D. W. *Subject Analysis: Principles and Procedures*. London: Bowker-Saur, 1989.

Subject Indexing: Principles and Practices in the 90's: Proceedings of the IFLA Satellite Meeting Held in Lisbon, Portugal, 17–18 August 1993. München: K.G. Saur, 1995.

Taylor, Arlene G. *The Organization of Information*. 2nd ed. Westport, Conn.: Libraries Unlimited, 2004. Chapter 9: Subject Analysis.

Wilson, Patrick. "Subjects and the Sense of Position." In *Theory of Subject Analysis: A Sourcebook*, edited by Lois Mai Chan, Phyllis A. Richmond, and Elaine Svenonius. Littleton, Colo.: Libraries Unlimited, 1985.

Verbal Subject Access

INTRODUCTION

A common means of providing access to the intellectual contents of a library is the use of a list of controlled vocabulary terms and references, giving an alphabetical approach to the concepts. The other traditional approach to subject access is classification, which provides a linear hierarchical approach. The two techniques offer alternative, and to some extent complementary, modes of access to the collection, comprising that aspect of bibliographic control and access known as subject cataloging.

BASIC CONCEPTS AND STRUCTURE OF SUBJECT HEADINGS

Subject heading has been defined as a "subject concept term or phrase found in a subject heading list and used in catalog records."[1] The use of subject headings in catalog records is to serve as access points by which works can be searched. Most such subject headings in library catalogs are precoordinated, while their counterparts in indexes, which are called "descriptors," are meant to be used in postcoordinated systems. Information analysts distinguish precoordinate indexing, by which appropriate terms are chosen and coordinated into phrases or subject-subdivision combinations at the time of indexing or cataloging, from postcoordinate indexing using single concept terms, which are then coordinated by users after the encoded records have been stored. All standard published lists of "subject headings" were developed with precoordinate indexing techniques. Lists called "thesauri" are usually used in postcoordinate systems.

Subject headings have dual objectives: 1) to identify pertinent material on a given subject or topic; 2) to enable the inquirer to find material on related subjects. Both objectives pose problems of communication; both demand a set of terms that match, as far as possible, the terms likely to be in the minds of inquirers wishing to locate material on a given topic or in a given discipline. A number of years ago E. J. Coates warned:

This would be fairly simple to achieve if there were an uncomplicated, one-to-one relationship between concepts and words: that is to say, if there were a single word corresponding to each separate concept and a single concept corresponding to each separate word. In fact, we have on the one hand concepts that can be rendered by any one of a number of words, and on the other hand, concepts for which no single word equivalent exists in the natural language.[2]

Modern subject heading practice has its roots in Charles A. Cutter's *Rules for a Dictionary Catalog*.[3] Later theorists refined and expanded Cutter's work in various ways. David Judson Haykin, former Chief of the Library of Congress (LC) Subject Cataloging Division, enumerated the principles that he believed underlay the choice of terms for a subject list.[4] They may be summarized as follows:

1. *The reader as focus.* "[T]he heading, in wording and structure, should be that which the reader will seek in the catalog, if we know or can presume what the reader will look under. . . . [In] the face of a lack of sufficient objective, experimental data, we must rely for guidance in the choice of terms upon the experience of librarians and such objective findings as are available."

2. *Unity.* "A subject catalog must bring together under one heading all the books which deal principally or exclusively with the subject, whatever the terms applied to it by the authors of the books and whatever the varying terms applied to it at different times. [It] must [use] a term which is unambiguous and does not overlap in meaning other headings in the catalog, even where that involves defining the sense in which it is used."

3. *Usage.* "The heading chosen must represent common usage or, at any rate, the usage of the class of reader for whom the material on the subject within which the heading falls is intended. . . . Whether a popular term or a scientific one is to be chosen depends on several considerations. If the library serves a miscellaneous public, it must prefer the popular to the scientific term."

4. *Specificity.* "The heading should be as specific as the topic it is intended to cover. As a corollary, the heading should not be broader than the topic; rather than use a broader heading, the cataloger should use two specific headings which will approximately cover it."

The following discussion touches on some of the most important problems encountered in construction and use of subject headings.

The Choice of Subject Headings

Linguistic usage determines correctness of form in natural language, as all grammarians and dictionary compilers well know. Language changes constantly, not only in response to new discoveries and formulations of knowledge, but also in response to dynamic forces of its own, some but not all of which have been codified by linguists. In choosing subject terms, librarians try to consider both the author's usage and the patron's needs and preferences; but authors and patrons are likely to use different terms for the same subject. Without a record of choices, the cataloger may enter the same subject under two or more different headings. Two types of decision are especially likely to miscarry: those for which more than one adequate term is available and those for which no adequate term is available.

Selecting a term from among verbal equivalents. The cataloger or compiler of a subject heading list must sometimes choose one subject term from among several synonyms or very similar terms. Cutter suggested the following sequence of preferences when selecting from synonymous headings:[5]

1. *The term most familiar to the general public.* Cutter no doubt was thinking of the local library's public. We shall see that one of the major differences between *LCSH* and *Sears* is that *LCSH*, being designed for use in a comprehensive research library, favors scientific terminology (e.g., **"Myocardial infarction"** with a reference from "Heart attack"), whereas *Sears* tends to use more popular terms (e.g., **"Heart attack"** with a reference from "Myocardial infarction").

2. *The term most used in other catalogs.* Since patrons frequently change libraries or consult more than one library catalog, it is comforting to find that terminology remains stable, even standardized, so long as it does not violate the usage of the local library's public. Broad bibliographic networks, using consolidated computer files, make reliably standardized terminology even more desirable. A different, but related, argument is that new concepts and terms are often introduced into the periodical literature before they form the topics of full-scale books. If a library's subject heading list does not yet include such a term, the cataloger might consult the *New York Times Index*, or commonly used periodical indexes and abstracting tools, to discover what usage, if any, has been established.

3. *The term that has fewest meanings.* The clear intent here is to avoid ambiguity wherever possible.

4. *The term that comes first in the alphabet.* This is the type of arbitrary, procedural decision that can be invoked when semantic considerations have been exhausted.

5. *The term that brings the subject into the neighborhood of other, related subjects.* It was previously noted that a serious drawback of alphabetic arrangement is its fragmentation of subject matter and that most alphabetic subject lists indulge in some "classing." Here is Cutter's recognition that the technique is valid, but only after all other modes for choosing among synonymous terms have been exhausted.

Supplying a term that is not contained in a single word. Some concepts must be expressed by phrases (combinations of words); although phrase headings present certain disadvantages. Coates, speaking about card catalogs indicated that most catalog users try to formulate search topics in single words, even when a phrase would be used in natural language.[6] Research in online catalogs has tended to verify this observation. Various uncertainties shadow the introduction of phrases into a controlled vocabulary. In determining the order of words, should a heading always retain the order of natural language, or should modifications and transpositions be allowed in the interests of brevity and clarity? Should a variety of syntactic forms be used, or should the syntax of phrase headings be confined to a few simple forms that occasionally make them seem awkward and artificial? Some theorists feel that, lacking cleanly enunciated rules, phrase-makers have produced a number of troublesome headings. Modern usage condones several varieties, which different subject lists usually adapt to their own uses. The specific rules printed in *Sears List of Subject Headings* (*Sears*) and in *Library of Congress Subject Headings* (*LCSH*) simplify but do not solve this problem, since they are purely arbitrary.[7] The problem of communication still exists. Many information packages are listed under subject headings that patrons would not immediately think of as the appropriate ones under which to search. For the most part they can be roughly categorized as follows. All examples are taken from the LC list:

1. *Modified nouns.* Modifiers can take different syntactic forms:
   a. Nouns preceded by adjectives or other modifiers, e.g., "**Regional planning**," "**Fur-bearing animals**," or "**Country life**"
   b. Nouns followed by adjectives or other modifiers, e.g., "**Insurance, Malpractice**," or "**Molds (Fungi)**"

2. *Conjunctive phrases.* The conjunction is nearly always *and*, e.g., "**Mills and mill-work**," "**Instrumentation and orchestration**," or "**Mind and body**"

3. *Prepositional phrases. In* and *of* are most common, but other prepositions may be used to form phrases, e.g., "**Segregation in education**," or "**Freedom of speech**"

4. *Serial phrases*, e.g., "**Plots (Drama, novel, etc.)**"

5. *Complex phrase forms*, e.g., "**Artificial satellites in telecommunication**," "**Glass painting and staining**," "**Justice, Administration of**," "**Right and left (Political science)**," or "**Fortune-telling by tea leaves**"

6. *Subdivided topical phrases*, e.g., "**Book industries and trade—Exhibitions**," "**Mines and mineral resources—United States**," or "**Military service, Voluntary—Law and legislation**"

The Number of Subject Headings

The number of subject headings entered into a catalog for a single item depends on many factors. As long as library catalogs were in card form, rapidly increasing bulk was both an economic and a use hazard. Maintenance costs (housing, filing, revising) were high, and users grew confused or wasted considerable time moving from one point to another in a roomful of several thousand trays.

The conventional wisdom has been that the larger the number of subject entries provided, the greater the cost of cataloging a title. On the other hand, limiting the number of subjects to one or two per record can be even more expensive, because the cataloger must take longer to determine what should be the *best* heading to represent the content in question. A major consideration should be that the assignment of more headings per item makes the total resources of the library more available and may bring out special aspects and bits of unusual or significant information.

In the early 1980s LC was adding about two subject entries per cataloged item. This was up from fewer than two entries per record prior to the implementation of *Anglo-American Cataloguing Rules, Second Edition (AACR2)*. The tendency over the decades prior to 1980 was to reduce the average number of subject entries. However, this trend has reversed, and more entries per record are being made. Indexes and abstracting tools in science and technology, by contrast, tend to use specific subject entries to a point of minute analysis. Twenty to forty subject terms for one brief article are not rare. Subject analysis of library titles has expanded with the increased use of automated bibliographic and authority control. Current online catalogs have made increasing the number of subject entries proportionately less expensive in time, effort, and cost of retrieval.

The computer is facilitating more, and better, studies of library use, to discern optimum types and quantities of subject headings for full subject retrieval. A 1983 Council on Library Resources (CLR) study of online catalog use of 15 online catalogs showed that in catalogs with subject access, about 59 percent of all searches were for subject information rather than for "known items."[8] This was quite different from earlier studies of card catalog use, many of which showed that over two-thirds of searches in academic libraries were known-item searches (although subject searching in public libraries was often higher).[9] The CLR researchers recommended that system designers implement keyword searching for subjects and browsing of the subject index or thesaurus, which have now been almost universally accomplished. The researchers also recognized that such systems can only find subject terms that exist in bibliographic records, and therefore they recommended increased subject information in bibliographic records along with strict authority control to restrict the number of synonymous and related terms.[10]

Location of Material on Related Subjects

Consistency is one of the most important criteria for assigning subject headings. The cataloger should choose one subject term, and one alone, to index all materials on the same topic. References should then be made to the chosen heading from all other likely terms. They help the inquirer to locate available material on the topic, plus collateral topics, at the level of specificity and from the point of view most useful for the particular need. References consist primarily of three types: references from unused terms, coordinate references, and hierarchical references.

An unused term is one under which no items are entered. Instead, a reference is made from that term to the one that is used, e.g., "Lunar expeditions *USE* **Space flight to the moon**." The instruction given may be something other than the word *USE*, e.g., "For material on this subject search under" or "see." It is also possible for an online catalog to give no reference in a situation where a *see* reference would be given in a manual catalog, but instead to automatically send the user to the used term. For example, a user searching under "lunar expeditions" might be automatically given a list of the library's material that had been assigned the heading "space flight to the moon." This practice is called "invisible referencing."

Coordinate references are most often related term references that suggest to the user that if the material already located is more or less relevant, there are other related headings that might also yield some relevant material. The instruction given is often "*See also*" or "Related material on this topic may be found under"; e.g., "**Hearing** *See also* **Deafness**" or "**Deafness.** Related material on this topic may be found under **Hearing**." The connections and relationships shown by coordinate references (often called "related terms") are horizontal rather than vertical. They usually overlap in such ways that reciprocal or multilateral entries are deemed to be necessary, e.g., "**Reforestation** *See also* **Tree planting**," "**Tree planting** *See also* **Reforestation**." Others suggest associative rather than overlapping relationships, e.g., "**Police misconduct** *See also* **Police—Complaints**," "**Police—Complaints** *See also* **Police misconduct**."

Hierarchical references move vertically, rather than horizontally, leading the user to topics at a different level of specificity. In current library practice references of this type nearly always move "down" from a general term to one or more specific topics subsumed under it, e.g., "**Cruelty**, see also the narrower term **Atrocities**," although in indexing practice, many systems provide for moving either up or down the hierarchy. (*See* discussion of this issue in chapter 9.)

While unused term references are most often synonymous terms, they are occasionally hierarchical or coordinate in their relationship to the used term. A few of them move "up" from a specific term that is not used to the broader term that contains it, e.g., "Heirs *Use* **Inheritance and succession**." This happens more often in *Sears* than in *LCSH*, because *Sears* is intended for smaller collections, and there is a need to collocate concepts at a broader level. A few other unused term references show an "illustrative" relationship, e.g., "Economic entomology *Use* **Beneficial insects**."

Besides simple references, subject heading lists sometimes include scope notes to define and delimit a subject term. These may or may not suggest further terms for the user to consult. Some catalog systems allow these notes or guides to be displayed preceding all subject entries given under those terms in their catalogs. Other systems do not allow such display and the libraries involved may keep one or more copies of the printed list near the catalog for public consultation. The following two examples come from *LCSH*:

Community and school
> Here are entered works on ways in which the community at large, as distinct from government, may aid the school program.

Migrant labor
> Here are entered works on laborers who migrate from one section to another section of the same country. Works on nationals of one country working in another country are entered under "**Alien labor**." Works on employment opportunities in foreign countries are entered under "**Employment in foreign countries**."

Some lists include key headings or pattern headings, with instructions to the cataloger on how to construct other headings of similar form that have been omitted from the list for reasons of brevity. The following example is from *Sears*:

Hijacking of airplanes
Use same form for the hijacking of other modes of transportation.

To assure maximum consistency, a careful, up-to-date record of all subject term selections and references should be kept, either by checking the terms used and the additions made in a standard printed list or by maintaining a separate subject authority file.

The Concept of Specific Entry

One of Haykin's principles on which the choice of terms for a subject list must rest was "specificity." The idea had been enunciated a half century earlier by Cutter:

> Enter a work under its subject heading, not under the heading of the class which includes that subject. . . . Put Lady Cust's book on "the cat" under "Cat," not under Zoology or Mammals, or Domestic animals. . . . Some subjects have no name. They are spoken of by a phrase or phrases not definite enough to be used as headings. It is not always easy to decide what is a *distinct* subject. . . . Possible matters of investigation . . . must attain a certain individuality as objects of inquiry and be given some sort of *name*, otherwise we must assign them class-entry.[11]

It should be noted that the concept of specific entry is not the same as the concept of coextensive entry. At least one system for subject analysis, *PRECIS* (discussed in greater detail in chapter 13), attempts to make subject headings coextensive with the concept/topics covered in the item analyzed. That is, the precoordinated subject heading will cover all, but no more than, the concepts or topics covered in the item. A very simple example can be drawn by elaborating upon the idea from Cutter above. If one had a book about cats and dogs, the concept of *specific* entry would require two headings: "Cats" and "Dogs." There is no one specific term to cover these two kinds of animal. In order to have a heading that is *coextensive* with the subject of the items the heading would have to be "Cats and dogs."

A great weakness of the concept of specific entry is that subjects must be described in terms that are constantly changing. Material very often has to be cataloged before a suitable term has been added to any standard list. Many subjects now represent a cross-fertilization among once traditional disciplines, and new concepts are being generated almost daily. In addition particular terms can fluctuate in meaning. There is also a tendency for any alphabetic subject list based on the ideal of specific entry to develop sequences of topical subdivisions or modifications that convert true random alphabetical access into an inadvertent categorizing device. All such lists show marks of a split personality in this respect.

The two most popular American lists, *LCSH* and *Sears*, are reviewed in the next two chapters. Chapter 13 presents some other indexing systems that are used as modes of subject access to organized library collections.

NOTES

1.   Arlene G. Taylor, *The Organization of Information*, 2nd ed. (Westport, Conn.: Libraries Unlimited, 2004), p. 379.

2.   E. J. Coates, *Subject Catalogues: Headings and Structure* (London: Library Association, 1960), p. 19.

3.   Charles Ammi Cutter, *Rules for a Dictionary Catalog*, 4th ed. (Washington, D.C.: GPO, 1904; republished, London: Library Association, 1972). The original version of this work was Charles A. Cutter, "Rules for a Printed Dictionary Catalogue," in *Public Libraries in the United States of America: Their History, Condition, and Management*, U.S. Bureau of Education (Washington, D.C.: GPO, 1876), Part II.

4.   David Judson Haykin, *Subject Headings: A Practical Guide* (Washington, D.C.: GPO, 1951), pp. 7–9.

5.   Cutter, *Dictionary Catalog*, p. 19.

6.   Coates, *Subject Catalogues*, p. 19.

7.   For the development of phrase heading forms in *Library of Congress Subject Headings* and in *Sears List of Subject Headings*, *see* chapters 11 and 12 of this text.

8.   *Using Online Catalogs: A Nationwide Survey*, edited by Joseph R. Matthews, Gary S. Lawrence, and Douglas K. Ferguson (New York: Neal-Schuman, 1983), pp. 144–146.

9.   Karen Markey, *Subject Searching in Library Catalogs: Before and After the Introduction of Online Catalogs* (Dublin, Ohio: OCLC Online Computer Library Center, 1984), pp. 75–87.

10.   *Using Online Catalogs*, pp. 177–179.

11.   Cutter, *Dictionary Catalog*, pp. 66–67.

SUGGESTED READING

Chan, Lois Mai, Phyllis A. Richmond, and Elaine Svenonius. *Theory of Subject Analysis: A Sourcebook.* Littleton, Colo.: Libraries Unlimited, 1985.

Coates, E. J. *Subject Catalogues: Heading and Structure.* London: Library Association, 1960.

Foskett, A. C. *The Subject Approach to Information.* 5th ed. London: Library Association Publishing, 1996. Chapter 8: Alphabetical Subject Headings: Cutter to Austin.

Mann, Thomas. *Library Research Models: A Guide to Classification, Cataloging, and Computers.* New York: Oxford University Press, 1993. Chapter 4: The Traditional Library Science Model. Part Two: The Vocabulary-Controlled Catalog.

Pettee, Julia. *Subject Headings: The History and Theory of the Alphabetical Approach to Books.* New York: H. W. Wilson, 1946.

11 Library of Congress Subject Headings (LCSH)

INTRODUCTION

The official list, *Library of Congress Subject Headings* (*LCSH*), consists of terms, with references, that have been established over the years since 1898 for use in the Library of Congress' (LC's) subject catalogs. Although developed to give subject access to the vast collections of one particular library, this list can be, and has been, adopted by libraries of all sizes, including many with non-LC classification schemes. The National Library of Canada, for example, has for many years used it as basic, supplementing it with a special set of terms for Canadian material.[1] It is used in the United States by most large public libraries, college and university libraries, and special libraries that do not have technical subject lists of their own. Since bibliographic records created by LC often carry *Dewey Decimal Classification* (*DDC*)[2] numbers as well as LC call numbers, but have only LC subject headings, some smaller libraries also use the LC subject list. Others retain the shorter, less frequently revised *Sears List of Subject Headings* (*Sears*) list as their primary source, but consult the LC list for suggestions when *Sears* cannot provide the specificity or the diversity they want.[3] (*Sears* is discussed in chapter 12.)

BACKGROUND

Library of Congress subject headings come from a long tradition of theory and practice that is generally held to begin with Charles A. Cutter's *Rules for a Dictionary Catalog*.[4] A brief review of Cutter's approach and of the major developments stemming from his work can be found in chapter 10, "Verbal Subject Access." The purpose in the present chapter is to highlight trends leading directly to the current manifestations of LC subject headings.[5]

On July 1, 1909, J. C. M. Hanson, Chief of the Catalog Division of LC, addressed the Catalog Section of the American Library Association (ALA) at its Bretton Woods Conference "The Subject Catalogs of the Library of Congress."[6] He alluded to a two-volume subject catalog published by LC in 1869, but called the subject heading developments of the intervening 40 years too radical to permit a meaningful comparison. The many changes brought about by a new classification scheme (see chapter 16 for the history of the *LC Classification* [*LCC*]) and the move into a new building required a new approach to subject indexing. LC catalogers agreed to start from the ALA *List of Subject Headings for Use in Dictionary Cata-*

logs (1895)[7], which embodied much of Cutter's theory and which originally formed an appendix to his *Rules*. The ALA *List* was designed for smaller libraries of "generally popular character," but with LC's printed card distribution plans, such an orientation was advantageous.

When the first cards carrying the new headings were published, subject terms were given only if an LC call number was available to print. Since schedules for many of the new *LCC* classification letters were still undeveloped, the list of subject headings grew slowly in the first decade. Proposed new headings were compared to those in the ALA *List* before final selection. Separate publication of the new list did not start until 1909, when the annotated and interleaved copies of the ALA *List* grew unwieldy. It was assumed from the first that cumulations of additions and changes would be issued periodically to supplement the main list, which itself appeared in parts until March 1914.

The practice of subordinating place to subject in scientific and technical headings, as well as under many economic and educational topics, was established at this time. But other subjects—historical, political, administrative, social, and descriptive—were to be subordinated to place, although Hanson admitted to "a number of subjects so nearly on the border line, that it has been difficult in all cases to preserve absolute consistency in decisions."[8] Besides the place/subject versus subject/place precedents, other syntactic forms evolved:

> There is undeniably a strong tendency in the Library of Congress catalog to bring related subjects together by means of inversion of headings, by combinations of two or more subject-words, and even by subordination of one subject to another.[9]

Hanson recognized that subordination within the dictionary arrangement of his new subject list was a concession to the alphabetico-classed or systematic organization of the 1869 catalog. He argued:

> the student and the investigator . . . are best served by having related topics brought together so far as that can be accomplished without a too serious violation of the dictionary principle.[10]

The practice of inversion of certain types of modified headings was firmly established by 1951 when David Judson Haykin wrote:

> It is unlikely that the reader will look under an adjective denoting language, ethnic group, or place for material on a subject limited by language, ethnic group, or place, although, in the case of ethnic groups particularly, the interest in the group may outweigh that in the subject. On this basis it has been assumed, although it has not been demonstrated, that a reader interested in French art . . . would be much more likely to look under *Art, French* (or *Art—France*) . . . than under the respective uninverted forms.[11]

These and other practices have been questioned and modified in recent years but were basic premises in the establishment of subject headings at LC for many years and are still reflected in the list.

FORMATS AND SUPPLEMENTARY TOOLS

LC subject headings are made available in several forms. The longest running format is the printed and bound version. For many years these lists were published in new editions every five years or so, but starting in 1988 with the eleventh edition, they have been published annually.[12] Beginning with the ninth edition, it was necessary to publish the list in two volumes, which quickly expanded, and the last several editions have been published in five volumes. The volumes have for many years been published in red bindings and are affectionately known as "The Big Red Books." The print format can be supplemented with *LC Subject Headings Weekly Lists*, available on the World Wide Web.[13] These give information about new and changed subject headings, class numbers, references, and scope notes. A fully updated version is available through *Classification Web* by subscription.[14]

MARC (MAchine-Readable Cataloging) format authority records for LC subject headings became available online through OCLC in 1987 and through RLG's database in 1988. The authority records are also available on LC's official website, through a subsite called "Library of Congress Authorities."[15]

The concept of the official headings authorized by LC is referred to in this chapter as LCSH (standing for Library of Congress subject headings). The online version available at the time of writing yields the examples found in this chapter.

When catalogers make use of LCSH there are several supplementary tools that must be used. The rules and guidelines used by LC catalogers when applying LCSH have been published as *Subject Cataloging Manual: Subject Headings (SCM: SH)*, issued in looseleaf form with periodic updates.[16] It is an essential tool for anyone who wishes to apply the subject headings correctly. It is also available and kept up-to-date through *Cataloger's Desktop*, available by subscription on the Web.[17]

Catalogers can also keep up-to-date on LCSH through the *Cataloging Service Bulletin (CSB)*.[18] *CSB* gives information about changes to *SCM: SH*, lists some new subject headings that have been established, lists headings that have been changed, and gives information about new publications that may be useful to the subject cataloger.

TYPES OF TOPICAL SUBJECT HEADINGS
(*MARC 21* bibliographic field 650, 2nd indicator 0; *MARC 21* authority field 150)

Library of Congress topical subject headings are constructed in a variety of ways, ranging from a single noun to complex descriptive phrases. As was discussed in chapter 10, Cutter enumerated six varieties according to their grammar or syntax.[19] They covered only primary headings, i.e., headings without further subdivision. The categories below are his, but the examples come from the current LCSH:

- A single word (e.g., "**Skating**")

- A noun preceded by an adjective (e.g., "**Administrative law**")

- A noun preceded by another noun used like an adjective (e.g., "**Energy industries**")

- A noun connected with another noun by a preposition (e.g., "**Radioisotopes in cardiology**")

- A noun connected with another noun by *and* (e.g., "**Libraries and society**")

- A phrase or sentence (e.g., "**Show driving of horse-drawn vehicles**")

While Cutter did tolerate modifier inversions (e.g., "**Etching, Anonymous**") "only when some other word is decidedly more significant or is often used alone with the same meaning as the whole name," he made no explicit provision for parenthetical qualifiers (e.g., "**Kairós (The Greek word)**") or other such complicated forms as "**Internal combustion engines, Spark ignition**," which, like subdivisions, are usually reminiscent of the alphabetico-classed approach. There are various alternative groupings. This discussion follows that of Lois Mai Chan in her treatise on subject headings.[20]

Single Noun Headings

Cutter's Rule No. 172 reads: "Enter books under the word which best expresses their subject, whether it occurs in the title or not."[21] He worked primarily in terms of the simple concept-name relationship on which the noun forms of all languages are based. LC over the years has experimented with slight variations of this single-word heading, for example, inclusion of an initial article (e.g., "**The West**"), sometimes inverted (e.g., "**State, The**") in the interests of clarity. Subject headings are no longer established with an English article in the initial position. "**The West**" has been changed to "**West (U.S.)**."[22]

Another variation was the distinction drawn, particularly in literature and art, between singular nouns (denoting the activity or the form, e.g., "**Essay**" and "**Painting**") and plural nouns (denoting the objects, e.g., "**Essays**" and "**Paintings**"). In general no new plural noun headings are being established, and some old plurals (e.g., "**Paintings**") have been cancelled in favor of the singular form.

Adjectival Headings

Adjectival headings start with a modifier followed by a noun or noun phrase (e.g., "**Municipal officials and employees**"). The modifier may be an adjective or it may be a noun used as an adjective. Examples of some of these are:

Common adjective (e.g., "**Dental records**")

Ethnic, national, or geographic adjective (e.g., "**African American librarians**")

Participial modifiers (e.g., "**Applied anthropology**" or "**Hearing aids**")

Common noun used as a modifier (e.g., "**Household pests**")

Proper noun used as a modifier (e.g., "**Bernstein polynomials**")

Conjunctive Phrase Headings

Headings composed of two or more nouns, with or without modifiers, connected by *and* or ending with *etc.* belong in this group. Those that are additive may comprise similar elements (e.g., **"Wit and humor"** or **"Charitable uses, trusts, and foundations"** or **"Chapters, Cathedral, collegiate, etc."**) or the elements may be contradictory (e.g., **"Right and wrong"**). Headings of this type are now established only when a work being cataloged discusses a relationship between two topics from both perspectives and in such broad terms that the relationship could not be described by use of a main heading with a subdivision.[23] Many older additive headings have been separated (e.g., **"Buddha and Buddhism"** has been replaced by **"Buddhism"** and **"Gautama Buddha"**).

Prepositional Phrase Headings

Prepositions sometimes enable the subject cataloger to express single but complex ideas for which there is no one word. Some express relationships for which an "and" phrase would be artificial (e.g., **"Photography in psychiatry"** or **"Police services for juveniles"**). Some are inverted (e.g., **"Justice, Administration of"**). Examples of other prepositions used are:

against (e.g., **"Offenses against the person"**)

as (e.g., **"Alfalfa as feed"**)

from (e.g., **"Theft from motor vehicles"**)

on (e.g., **"Mothers on television"**)

to (e.g., **"Ceramic to metal bonding"**)

with (e.g., **"Double bass with band"**)

Many of these circumlocutions are replaced when a simpler expression gains currency (e.g., **"Psychoanalysis in historiography"** was replaced by **"Psychohistory"**). "As" headings for classes of persons have been restricted to certain situations where the resulting connotation will not be seen as disparaging (e.g., **"Physicians as authors"**). Old headings in which men or women are identified as professionals (e.g., **"Men as nurses"** or **"Women as teachers"**) have been replaced by adjectival phrases (e.g., **"Male nurses"** and **"Women teachers"**).[24]

Parenthetical Qualifiers

Nouns or phrases in parentheses following primary terms have in the past resulted in a variety of linguistically inept headings. LC no longer adds them to designate special applications of a general concept, although it has no plans to change established headings such as:

Vibration (Marine engineering)
Cookery (Frozen foods)
Excavations (Archaeology)

For newly established situations, three different techniques are available:

- "In" and "of" headings:

    Information theory in biology (*not* **Information theory (Biology)**)

    Abandonment of automobiles (*not* **Abandonment (Automobiles)**)

- Phrase headings:

    Combinatorial enumeration problems (*not* **Enumeration problems (Combinatorial analysis)**)

- Subdivisions under a primary heading (preferred when practicable):

    Public health—Citizen participation (*not* **Citizen participation (Public health)**)

A few situations are recognized in which it may be necessary to use parenthetical qualifiers. If the term or phrase has more than one dictionary definition, the following types of qualifiers may be added in order to:

- Specify a discipline, especially if the heading represents a concept:

    "Analysis (Philosophy)"

- Identify the category if a heading designates a kind of "object"

    "Trunks (Luggage)"

It is also LC practice to use parenthetical qualifiers to:

- Remove ambiguity or to make an obscure word or phrase more explicit:

    "Cluttering (Speech pathology)"

- Identify the category for a named entity:

    "Arulo (Artificial language)"[25]

Parenthetical expressions are also used for some headings for buildings and other structures and for musical works.

Inverted Headings

Inversions, while awkward syntactically (e.g., **"Older people's writings, American"**), serve the alphabetico-classed function of subordinating specific descriptors under their broad generic categories (e.g., **"Education, Bilingual"** or **"Asylum, Right of"**). Here too, much inconsistency is apparent.

In the course of its efforts to modernize and systematize LCSH, LC has attempted to set policy for creation of new inverted headings. For example, topical headings modified by adjectival qualifiers referring to ethnic groups are to be established in the inverted form (e.g., **"Proverbs, Korean"**) with certain exceptions, one of which is for ethnic groups of the United States (e.g., **"Mexican American proverbs"**).[26] LC occasionally changes an existing heading, especially in cases where every instance of the concept but one is in direct order.

SEMANTICS

Not only have syntactic forms of subject headings come under close scrutiny and revision in recent years, but also LCSH terminology has been reconsidered. Word meanings, particularly their connotative aspects, mutate rapidly; social and political upheavals cause many changes, and scientific and technological developments account for many more. The problem of shifting terminology is particularly troublesome for a subject access list based on specific entry, avoidance of synonyms, and controlled references, that was originally designed for use with card or printed book catalogs.

A ringing complaint that LCSH terminology was obsolete and prejudicial came from Sanford Berman in 1971.[27] As Head of the Hennepin County, Minnesota, Library Catalog Department for many years, Berman edited the *HCL Cataloging Bulletin*, a bimonthly publication that contained lists of subject headings and references added to the HCL catalogs.[28] Many new concepts were added as headings at HCL before being added by LC. Unfortunately, with Berman's retirement, the Hennepin County Library no longer provides this service, but the awareness that Berman raised is still at work at LC.

Other writers have also criticized the stance at LC on conceptual and linguistic shifts. Doris Clack's 1975 analysis of black literature resources started from a critique of LC subject analysis. She observed:

> Inadequate subject analysis is not just a problem with black literature—though admittedly there the level of adequacy is critically low—nor has it only in recent years been brought to the attention of the library world.[29]

Clack devoted the bulk of her treatise to various lists of LC class numbers and subject terms from the black perspective. Since her book was published, LC has made many changes. The one cited below involved changing approximately 12,000 cards:

> A basic function in the maintenance of a subject heading system is that of updating headings to conform to changing terminology or altered concepts. In general, the Library of Congress is and has been conservative in making changes since it involves altering reference structures surrounding a given heading as well as accommodating the change in both the card catalogs and the machine-readable data base. However, after a long period of great reluctance in effecting major changes, the Library has recently been involved in a number of changes represented in the following list . . .
>
> **Negroes.** This heading discontinued February 1976.
> See **Afro-Americans** for later materials on the permanent residents of the United States. See **Blacks** for later materials on persons outside the United States. . . .[30]

It can be seen in this statement that a major deterrent to LC's making changes was the card catalog. Since they closed the card catalog at the beginning of 1981 and have had only machine-readable records to update, terminology changes have been made more readily; but because LC's home-grown computer system did not have global search and replace capabilities, changes still had to be made record by record. This made it difficult to consider massive changes such as changing "Afro-Americans" to the more popular "African Americans" of the 1990s. At the end of 1999, the implementation of a new integrated library system (ILS) promised to make such changes easier, and "Afro-American" was changed to "African American" in November of 2000.

Reflecting another socio-linguistic revolution was Joan K. Marshall's 1977 critique of gender bias in *LCSH*.[31] She used six principles developed by ALA's Social Responsibilities Round Table Task Force Committee on Sexist Subject Headings to replace logically and consistently the guesswork that had evolved over the years from Cutter's concern for the "convenience of the public." Basing her work on the six principles, she submitted an alphabetical, annotated "Thesaurus for Nonsexist Indexing and Cataloging." As in the case of the subject concepts for people of African descent, LC has overhauled most of its more obsolete or offensive sexist headings.

PROPER NAME HEADINGS

Any proper name can be used as a subject heading in the LC system. Names are not, however, all included in the subject list or given subject authority records. The only ones appearing in the list are those that are used as pattern headings (*see* discussion below), or as examples, or that need special subject subdivisions or instructions printed under them.

Personal and Corporate Names and Uniform Titles
(*MARC 21* bibliographic fields 600, 610, 611, 630;
MARC 21 authority fields 100, 110, 111, 130)

The correct forms of personal names, names of corporate bodies, names of jurisdictions, names of conferences and meetings, and uniform titles (i.e., names of works) are found in LC's Name Authority File (LCNAF; discussed in chapter 8). When any of these is the subject of a work, the correct form is taken from LCNAF and placed in a subject field in the bibliographic record. These names are established in accordance with LC's interpretation of *Anglo-American Cataloguing Rules, Second Edition* (*AACR2R*).

Geographic Names
(*MARC 21* bibliographic field 651;
MARC 21 authority field 151)

Geographic, jurisdictional, and physiographic names form a large part of any library's subject network. Prior to the mid-1970s, only key examples to illustrate modes of entry and types of subdivision were listed in LCSH. Libraries had to locate bibliographic records using the names to verify them. With the acceptance of *AACR2* in 1981 it was decided to create subject geographic names in a form consistent with the jurisdictional forms controlled by *AACR2*. Subject authority records are now created for all non-jurisdictional geographic and physiographic names, except for those that are created as free-floating phrase headings (*see* discussion below, p. 325), and they are listed in the printed versions of LCSH. Although the form of jurisdictional names is taken from LCNAF, subject authority records are sometimes made and printed when needed in order to add a topical and/or chronological subdivision (e.g., "**Chicago (Ill.)—History—To 1875**").

Place names reflecting political or jurisdictional changes are treated somewhat differently as subject headings than as descriptive cataloging access points. In descriptive cataloging, the name used for the place at the time of the creation of the work is used as the access point. In subject cataloging, however, when the name of a country, state, city, etc., has been changed without substantially affecting the jurisdictional area covered, it is LC's policy to make all subject entries under the new name regardless of the time period covered. Subject entries under an old name are changed to the new name. These changes are referred to as "linear jurisdictional name changes."[32] This policy is followed regardless of whether the government changed the jurisdiction name or the change was made to accommodate cataloging rules. Examples:

Old Form	Latest Form
Argentine Republic	**Argentina**
British Honduras	**Belize**
Ceylon	**Sri Lanka**
Zaire	**Congo (Democratic Republic)**
Formosa	**Taiwan**

When jurisdictions have merged or split, various headings may be appropriate depending on the time period covered by the work in hand. In general the headings should correspond to the area and time period being discussed.[33]

GENRE/FORM TERMS
(*MARC 21* bibliographic field 655; *MARC 21* authority field 155)

"Form" is a concept that has been associated with subject analysis from the inception of the idea that books could be entered in catalogs and placed on shelves according to the category they belonged to. Early categories included such things as encyclopedias, biographies, and histories, as well as chemistry and religion. Later, as subject headings evolved to mean what an item is "about" instead of a category to which the book belonged, the idea of "form" remained as part of the subject heading process. Because it was often difficult to separate the ideas of "aboutness" and form, as in the case of "history," which seems to incorporate elements of both, the concept of form has only recently finally been given its own treatment in bibliographic records.

A definition, created by a Subcommittee of ALA's Subject Analysis Committee, was approved by appropriate ALA bodies in January 1993:

Form data are those terms and phrases that designate specific kinds or genres of materials. Materials designated with these terms or phrases may be determined by an examination of:

their physical character (e.g., videocassettes, photographs, maps, broadsides)

the particular type of data that they contain (e.g., bibliographies, questionnaires, statistics)

the arrangement of information within them (e.g., diaries, outlines, indexes)

the style, technique, purpose, or intended audience (e.g., drama, romances, cartoons, commercials, popular works)

or a combination of the above (e.g., scores)

A single term may be modified by other terms, in which case the whole phrase is considered to be form data (e.g., aerial photographs, French dictionaries, conversation and phrase books, wind ensemble suites, telephone directories, vellum bound books, science fiction).[34]

LC does not yet create form/genre *headings* that are treated differently from topical headings (i.e., that are coded 655 in the MARC format instead of 650), although they do designate subdivisions of headings as form terms (see discussion below). However, a project to incorporate genre/form headings for moving images into LCSH has begun at this writing. A goal is to release in 2006 a draft list along with instructions (as a SCM: SH memo) for applying such headings in bibliographic records.

There are a number of specialized lists of form terms in the rare books, art, audiovisual, and map communities, among others. One commonly used list in public and school libraries is the *Guidelines on Subject Access to Individual Works of Fiction, Drama, Etc.*[35] Terms from this list are added in 655 fields to catalog records by many public libraries.

HEADINGS OMITTED FROM
LIBRARY OF CONGRESS SUBJECT HEADINGS (LCSH)

A troublesome corollary of the principle of specific entry is the inevitable, and seemingly endless, proliferation of subject terms for individual members of certain subject categories. Until the early 1980s LC omitted from its printed list a wide variety of such terms. These terms were included in the library's official records but were not spelled out in the printed editions of *LCSH*. They included such categories as names of sacred books, fictitious and legendary characters, works of art, chemicals, geographic regions, archaeological sites, and buildings. Authority records are now being made for the individual names in such groups, but only those established after 1976 (1981 if affected by *AACR2*) are in the file. There are still many general *See also* references to cover such situations (e.g., "**Lumber**, SA *kinds of lumber*, e.g., Cypress; Walnut"). Such general references are gradually being replaced as the narrower headings are established.

Categories of headings currently intentionally omitted from *LCSH* include headings residing in the LCNAF and free-floating phrase headings. Headings in the LCNAF are discussed above. Free-floating phrase headings are composed as needed without creation of authority records. In free-floating phrase headings the initial word changes. This type is still limited to a very few pattern phrases. The following are listed in the *Subject Cataloging Manual*:

> [name of city] Metropolitan Area ([geographical qualifier])
> > e.g., **Atlanta Metropolitan Area (Ga.)**
>
> [name of city] Region ([geographical qualifier])
> > e.g., **Dallas Region (Tex.)**
>
> [name of city] Suburban Area ([geographic qualifier])
> > e.g., **Atlanta Suburban Area (Ga.)**
>
> [name of geographic feature] Region ([geographic qualifier, if part of the name as established])
> > e.g., **Himalaya Mountains Region**
>
> [name of river] Region ([geographic qualifier, if part of name as established])
> > e.g., **Tweed River Region (Scotland and England)**[36]

LC formerly used some free-floating ". . . in . . ." phrase headings, but these have been discontinued. For example "[topic] in art" is no longer used and now must be individually established (i.e., not free-floating). The free-floating phrase "[name heading (except personal names)] in art" (e.g., **Manhattan (New York, N.Y.) in art**") has been replaced by the free-floating subdivision "—In art" used under names of corporate bodies and under countries, cities, etc. (e.g., "**Manhattan (New York, N.Y.)—In art**"). LC's formerly used phrase ". . . as a profession" (e.g., "**Medicine as a profession**") now uses the free-floating subdivision "—**Vocational guidance**" instead (e.g., "**Medicine—Vocational guidance**").

It should be pointed out that this list of categories of headings omitted from *LCSH* refers only to main headings. In the discussion under "Subdivisions" below, it can be seen that there are *many* headings with subdivisions that are not individually listed in the subject authority file.

GENERAL CHARACTERISTICS OF *LIBRARY OF CONGRESS SUBJECT HEADINGS (LCSH)*

The appearance of LCSH differs depending upon whether one is dealing with a "printed" version or with a MARC version. In the printed book version and in *Classification Web* all primary subject terms and subjects with subdivisions appear in boldface type, while reference tracings and references interfiled with the main headings are in lightface type. References interfiled with primary terms are followed by the instruction USE, which is in turn followed by the preferred term. The instruction SA (see also) is given in some entries and precedes terms, phrases, etc., that show related headings or subdivisions. The directions UF (used for), BT (broader term), RT (related term), and NT (narrower term) precede reference tracings in printed entries. In *Classification Web* the terms following BT, RT, and NT are linked so that a click on one of these terms takes the user to that term with its associated references.

In the *MARC 21* authorities format, functions of terms are identified by coding. Primary terms are given a three-digit code beginning with *1* (e.g., 150, 151). "Used for" terms are assigned codes beginning with *4* (e.g., 450, 451); "see also" references are coded 360; and broader and related terms are assigned codes beginning with *5* (e.g., 550, 551). Narrower terms are not shown in *MARC 21* authority records except in the relatively few cases where general "reference records" are made showing the unused term coded 150 and the preferred term in a field coded 260. In such a record there is a fixed field code to show that the record is a reference record and that the term in the 150 field should not be used as a heading.

Syndetic (Reference) Structure

Figures 11.1 and 11.2 (page 328) illustrate the usages of the abbreviations in the print formats and of the codes in the MARC format.

Fig. 11.1. Printed entry for subject heading "Maintenance."

Maintenance

UF	Preventive maintenance
	Upkeep
BT	Maintainability (Engineering)
RT	Repairing
	Service life (Engineering)
SA	*subdivision* Maintenance and repair *under kinds of objects, including machinery, vehicles, structures, etc., e.g.* Automobiles—Maintenance and repair; Dwellings—Maintenance and repair; Nuclear reactors—Maintenance and repair
NT	Buildings—Repair and reconstruction
	Grounds maintenance
	Military bases—Maintenance
	Plant maintenance

In figure 11.1 the two terms following UF serve as tracings to indicate that there are references that read:

Preventive maintenance
    USE Maintenance

Upkeep
    USE Maintenance

This also serves as an instruction that when the heading "Maintenance" is first entered into the catalog, these two references should be added to the catalog also. In online systems with linked authority files, this is done automatically.

The BT line not only indicates that the term following BT is a broader term in the hierarchy of the concept, but also serves as a tracing to indicate that there should be a reference in the catalog that reads:

Maintainability (Engineering)
Search also under the narrower term Maintenance

In traditional library practice it has been considered improper to provide a reference from a narrower term to its broader term, on the assumption that there would be no place to stop until one arrived at "General Knowledge," and the catalog would be overflowing with reference cards. Now that catalogs are mostly online, however, there is no reason to limit references, and there is evidence that users like to be able to browse "up" a hierarchy to the broader terms in addition to being able to browse narrower and related terms.

The terms following RT are related terms. Neither is hierarchically above the other. The instruction here is to make references both from and to these terms:

Maintenance
Search also under   Repairing
                          Service life (Engineering)

Repairing
Search also under   Maintenance

Service life (Engineering)
Search also under   Maintenance

SA means "see also" and is currently used for special instructions concerning how the concept embodied in this heading may be used as a subdivision or to refer to groups of headings that are all related to the heading concept. In the example shown above, the concept as a subdivision may be expressed as "Maintenance and repair" under kinds of objects.

The terms following NT are narrower in the concept hierarchy, and there is an implicit instruction to make a reference that reads:

Maintenance
Search also under the narrower terms
Buildings—Repair and reconstruction
                   Grounds maintenance
                   Military bases—Maintenance
                   Plant maintenance

This last reference, in some cases, could be combined with the "related terms" reference from "Maintenance" shown above unless the wording of the reference is of the type that refers specifically to related terms and/or narrower terms.

The *MARC 21* format version of the same record (see figure 11.2, page 328) shows the heading coded 150. The "used for" terms are coded 450. In some records a term coded 450 may be followed by "‡w nne" ("e" meaning "earlier"), which indicates that the now unused term was once used as the heading for the concept, but the correct heading now is the one in the 150 field. The broader term and the related terms are all coded 550. The broader term is distinguished from the two related terms by the "‡w g" following the term. The special instructions about the concept used as a subdivision are coded 360. Narrower terms are not included in *MARC 21* authority records on the assumption that if all references are made from broader terms listed in all authority records in an online system, references to the narrower terms will automatically be taken care of. This does, in fact, work, as can be seen in the sample screen display from OCLC (see figure 11.3) in which all terms that have "maintenance" in a 550 field in their records are displayed.

Fig. 11.2. *MARC 21* Subject Authority Record as formatted in OCLC. (Source: OCLC Connexion, Authorities)

ARN	02080919			
__	Rec stat c Entered 19860211 Replaced 19891011120233.6			__
__	Type z	Upd status a	Enc lvl n	Source	__
__	Roman |	Ref status b	Mod rec	Name use b	__
__	Govt agn |	Auth status a	Subj a	Subj use a	__
__	Series n	Auth/ref a	Geo subd |	Ser use b	__
__	Ser num n	Name n	Subdiv tp n	Rules n	__

010	sh 85079931
040	DLC ‡b eng ‡c DLC ‡d DLC
150	Maintenance
360	‡i subdivision ‡a Maintenance and repair ‡i under kinds of objects, including machinery, vehicles, structures, etc., e.g. ‡a Automobiles--Maintenance and repair; Dwellings--Maintenance and repair; Nuclear reactors--Maintenance and repair
450	Preventive maintenance
450	Upkeep
550	Maintainability (Engineering) ‡w g
550	Repairing
550	Service life (Engineering)

Fig. 11.3. Display of narrower terms and related terms in OCLC.

6 records found searching for Topicals (expanded) - MAINTENANCE — [550] in Authorities

Search Results

1. Buildings ‡x Repair and reconstruction [150]
2. Grounds maintenance [150]
3. Military bases ‡x Maintenance [150]
4. Plant maintenance [150]
5. Repairing [150]
6. Service life (Engineering) [150]

The instructions for references imbedded in the abbreviations and codes are not to be followed blindly, but should be applied where useful and needed. If, for example, a catalog lacks entries under the narrower terms "Grounds maintenance," "Military bases—Maintenance," and the related term "Service life (Engineering)," then the reference from "Maintenance" would omit these and read only:

Maintenance
>*Search also under*
>>Buildings—Repair and reconstruction
>>Plant maintenance
>>Repairing

If all six headings are lacking, then the reference should not be made at all. Online systems can be programmed to display only references to headings that actually appear in the catalog.

The related and broader term references to "Maintenance" present a complicated problem. If there were no entries in the catalog under "Repairing," strictly speaking it would be inaccurate to make a reference reading:

Repairing
>*Search also under* Maintenance

Some theorists argue that it is nonetheless justifiable to make such references on the assumption that the term referred from will eventually be activated. Even if it is not, they say, the reference serves to move users from a term not included in the catalog to one where there may be pertinent materials. Some libraries convert such ambiguous references into USE references:

Repairing
>USE Maintenance

If the term referred from is later activated, they change the instruction on the reference. This system is difficult to handle, and as more catalogs are automated it is necessary to write unambiguous programs that create references only as authorized in the authority file. The problem can be solved by using *Broader terms, Narrower terms*, etc., in catalogs instead of *See also*, or *Search also under* (a phrase currently used in numerous systems). There should be no semantic problem with telling a user that a related term for "Repairing" is "Maintenance," even if there are no entries under "Repairing." In fact, the traditional ban on referring users from narrower terms to broader terms should also be lifted. The problem is also being solved in some systems by giving the number of postings beside each term. Listing a referred-to term with zero postings alerts the user to the term's presence in the subject heading list, but indicates that the particular database in use does not have any records with the term.

A number of writers have criticized LCSH's syndetic structure and its lack of ability to show hierarchical relationships in a "tree" structure. E. J. Coates wrote in 1960 that LCSH merely linked an "indeterminate selection" of related terms—that at times there was more than one level of hierarchy in a list under one primary term, while at other times intermediate hierarchical terms were omitted from the chain of references.[37] George Sinkankis demonstrated in his 1972 study, in which he followed the *See also*s under the heading "Hunting," that a user was quickly led away from the subject. By following the references he was led to "Migrant labor,"

"Pimps," "Liturgy and drama," and "Panic," among other terms.[38] Toni Petersen wrote in 1983 that during a project to create the *Art and Architecture Thesaurus* (*AAT*), the designers chose to keep LCSH terms as a base and to modify and expand them. But the *See also*s and *See also from*s in LCSH had to be ignored because they could not be converted to broader, narrower, and related terms. There were too many types of reference present.[39] Mary Dykstra was critical in 1988 of the format LC began using in *LCSH11 (LCSH, 11th edition)*, the first edition to use the abbreviations BT, RT, NT, etc., instead of the previous system that used *x* and *xx* to trace *See* and *See also* references. Dykstra believed that LC was trying to make *LCSH* look like a true thesaurus, which it is not because of its use of "headings" instead of "terms."[40]

LC has recognized the problems but has not been able to eliminate all inappropriate references created in the past; staff time has not always been available for "clean-up" projects. However, beginning in the mid-1980s, subject catalogers at LC put into effect a fairly strict policy for creating new references for all *new* headings created. The general rule is to make a broader term reference from the class of which the heading is a class member (e.g., "**Cinematography**, BT Photography"), to make a reference for a whole/part relationship (e.g., "**Toes**, BT Foot"), and to make a reference for cases in which a specific heading is an instance or example of a broader category (e.g., "**Erie, Lake**, BT Lakes—United States"). Broader term references are made only from the next broader level in a hierarchy. Related terms are used to link two headings not in the same hierarchy (e.g., a concept and an object). One of the headings should be strongly implied whenever the other is considered (e.g., "**Boats and boating**, RT Ships").[41] While this reference policy moves LCSH toward answering its critics, the problem will not be solved completely until all "clean-up" projects have been completed.

Scope Notes

Scope notes are sometimes inserted into subject authority records. In printed versions they are between the heading and its references; in *MARC 21* records they are tagged 680. Such notes specify the range of application for a term or draw distinctions between related terms. In the past, a few libraries with card catalogs copied these notes on cards and filed them in the catalog just ahead of the subject entries under the same heading. But most libraries simply provided one or more copies of *LCSH* near the catalog for reference use by patrons doing subject searches. With the advent of online catalogs, it was not possible at first to display scope notes, but more online catalogs now have this capability, and there is encouragement to provide more such information to users. A typical example of a heading with a scope note is figure 11.4.

Fig. 11.4. Printed entry for a subject heading with a scope note.

Sexism   *(May Subd Geog)*
   Here are entered works on sexism as an attitude as
well as works on attitude and overt discriminatory behavior.
Works dealing solely with discriminatory behavior directed
toward both of the sexes are entered under Sex discrimination.
   UF   Sex bias
   BT   Attitude (Psychology)
          Prejudices
          Sex (Psychology)
          Social perception
   RT   Sex role
   NT   Heterosexism
          Sex discrimination

In the *MARC 21* authorities format the scope note is in a field coded 680 as can be seen in figure 11.5, the record for "Sexism" as it is formatted in the OCLC database.

Fig. 11.5. *MARC 21* **authority record showing a scope note in the 680 field. (Source: OCLC Connexion, Authorities)**

ARN	02102436			
Rec stat c	Entered 19860211	Replaced 19870326163626.7		
Type z	Upd status a	Enc lvl n	Source	
Roman		Ref status b	Mod rec	Name use b
Govt agn		Auth status a	Subj a	Subj use a
Series n	Auth/ref a	Geo subd i	Ser use b
Ser num n	Name n	Subdiv tp n	Rules n

010		sh 85120678
040		DLC ‡b eng ‡c DLC ‡d DLC
150		Sexism
450		Sex bias
550		Attitude (Psychology) ‡w g
550		Prejudices ‡w g
550		Sex (Psychology) ‡w g
550		Social perception ‡w g
550		Sex role
680		‡i Here are entered works on sexism as an attitude as well as works on attitude and overt discriminatory behavior. Works dealing solely with discriminatory behavior directed toward both of the sexes are entered under ‡a Sex discrimination.
681		‡i Note under ‡a Sex discrimination

Subdivisions

(*MARC 21* subfields ‡x, ‡y, ‡z, and ‡v)

It was mentioned earlier that the practice of establishing subdivisions for headings was firmly set in Hanson's time as a concession to alphabetico-classed organization of catalogs. The introduction to *LCSH* states:

> The application of Library of Congress subject headings requires extensive use of subject subdivisions as a means of combining a number of different concepts into a single subject heading. Complex topics may be represented by subject headings followed by subdivisions. Some subdivisions are printed in *LCSH* but a greater number of subdivisions may be assigned according to rules specified in the *Manual*. Only a fraction of all possible heading-and-subdivision combinations are listed in *LCSH*.[42]

Subdivisions fall into several broadly defined categories: topical and chronological subdivisions specific to particular headings; geographic subdivisions; form subdivisions; free-floating subdivisions; and subdivisions under pattern headings.

Topical Subdivisions Specific to Particular Headings

(*MARC 21* bibliographic and authority subfield ‡x;
MARC 21 subdivision authority record field 180)

Some headings need topical subdivisions that are specific to the concepts in the headings and that, therefore, must be authorized specifically for the headings. Such subdivisions in printed versions of *LCSH* are introduced by a long dash; if two subdivisions are used, there are two long dashes; etc. Figure 11.6, shows subdivisions for the heading "**Lumber**" As printed in the book version of LCSH.

Fig. 11.6. Printed entry for subject heading "Lumber" and its subdivisions.

Lumber
    [TS800-837]
    BT   Forests and forestry
          Wood products
    RT   Timber
    SA   *kinds of lumber, e.g.* Cypress; Walnut
    NT   Hardwoods
          Pit-wood
          Planing-mills
          Sawmills
—Advertising
    USE Advertising—Lumber
—Drying
    [TS837]
    UF   Lumber—Seasoning
           Lumber drying
           Seasoning of Lumber
           Wood—Drying
    BT   Wood—Preservation
—Law and legislation   *(May Subd Geog)*
—Mensuration
—Rate-books
    [HE2116.L8]
—Seasoning
    USE   Lumber—Drying
—Storage
—Transportation
    [HE199.5.L84 (Freight)]
    [HE595.L8 (Ships)]
    [HE2321.L8 (Railroads)]
— —**Law and legislation**   *(May Subd Geog)*

The interpretation of the subdivisions in figure 11.6 should be as shown below, which is, in fact, the way the terms are displayed in *Classification Web.*

    Lumber—Advertising
      USE **Advertising—Lumber**
    Lumber—Drying
    Lumber—Law and legislation
    Lumber—Mensuration
    Lumber—Rate-books
    Lumber—Seasoning
      USE **Lumber—Drying**
    Lumber—Storage
    Lumber—Transportation
    Lumber—Transportation—Law and legislation

In the MARC version of LCSH, each of these headings is given a separate authority record. The MARC records for the main heading and four of its subdivision records are shown as figures 11.7 to 11.11. In these records the dashes that appear in the printed list are represented by the code ‡x.

Fig. 11.7. MARC record for the main heading "Lumber". (Source: OCLC Connexion, Authorities)

ARN 02070743			
Rec stat c Entered 19860211 Replaced 19871021111358.5			
Type z	Upd status a	Enc lvl n	Source
Roman |	Ref status b	Mod rec	Name use b
Govt agn |	Auth status a	Subj a	Subj use a
Series n	Auth/ref a	Geo subd |	Ser use b
Ser num n	Name n	Subdiv tp n	Rules n

010	sh 85078804
040	DLC ‡b eng ‡c DLC ‡d DLC
053	TS800 ‡b TS837
150	Lumber
360	‡i kinds of lumber, e.g. ‡a Cypress; Walnut
550	Forests and forestry ‡w g
550	Wood products ‡w g
550	Timber

Fig. 11.8. MARC record that generates a "USE" reference from "Lumber—Advertising" (*see* second 450 field). (Source: OCLC Connexion, Authorities)

ARN 03645412			
Rec stat c Entered 19940607 Replaced 19961004125910.7			
Type z	Upd status a	Enc lvl n	Source
Roman |	Ref status a	Mod rec	Name use b
Govt agn |	Auth status a	Subj a	Subj use a
Series n	Auth/ref a	Geo subd i	Ser use b
Ser num n	Name n	Subdiv tp n	Rules n

010	sh 94004017
040	DLC ‡b eng ‡c DLC ‡d DLC
053	HF6161.L9
150	Advertising ‡x Lumber
450	Advertising ‡x Lumber trade ‡w nne
450	Lumber ‡x Advertising
670	Work cat.: NUCMC data from Forest History Soc. for Laughead, W.B. Papers, 1897-1958 ‡b (William B. Laughead, advertising manager for Red River Lumber Company, popularizer of folk hero Paul Bunyan through advertising pamphlets of the company)

Fig. 11.9. MARC record for "Lumber—Drying". (Source: OCLC Connexion, Authorities)

	ARN 02070757						
	Rec stat c	Entered 19860211	Replaced 19950918171534.2				
	Type	z	Upd status	a	Enc lvl	n	Source
	Roman	|	Ref status	b	Mod rec		Name use	b
	Govt agn	|	Auth status	a	Subj	a	Subj use	a
	Series	n	Auth/ref	a	Geo subd	i	Ser use	b
	Ser num	n	Name	n	Subdiv tp	n	Rules	n

010	sh 85078805
040	DLC ‡b eng ‡c DLC ‡d DLC
053	TS837
150	Lumber ‡x Drying
450	Lumber ‡x Seasoning
450	Lumber drying
450	Seasoning of lumber
450	Wood ‡x Drying
550	Wood ‡x Preservation ‡w g

Fig. 11.10. MARC record for "Lumber—Transportation". (Source: OCLC Connexion, Authorities)

	ARN 02070790						
	Rec stat c	Entered 19860211	Replaced 19960305120606.5				
	Type	z	Upd status	a	Enc lvl	n	Source
	Roman	|	Ref status	n	Mod rec		Name use	b
	Govt agn	|	Auth status	a	Subj	a	Subj use	a
	Series	n	Auth/ref	a	Geo subd	i	Ser use	b
	Ser num	n	Name	n	Subdiv tp	n	Rules	n

010	sh 85078810
040	DLC ‡b eng ‡c DLC ‡d DLC
053	HE199.5.L84 ‡c Freight
053	HE595.L8 ‡c Ships
053	HE2321.L8 ‡c Railroads
150	Lumber ‡x Transportation

Fig. 11.11. MARC record for "Lumber—Transportation—Law and Legislation". (Source: OCLC Connexion, Authorities)

ARN 02070794				
Rec stat n	Entered 19860211	Replaced 19860211000000.0		
Type z	Upd status a	Enc lvl n	Source	
Roman |	Ref status n	Mod rec	Name use b	
Govt agn |	Auth status a	Subj a	Subj use a	
Series n	Auth/ref a	Geo subd i	Ser use b	
Ser num n	Name n	Subdiv tp n	Rules n	

010	sh 85078811
040	DLC ‡b eng ‡c DLC
150	Lumber ‡x Transportation ‡x Law and legislation

Chronological Subdivisions Specific to Particular Headings

(*MARC 21* bibliographic and authority subfield ‡y;
MARC 21 authority record field 182)

Chronological subdivisions are sometimes assigned in LCSH. The most common assigned time periods are for historical or political time periods under particular jurisdictions. It is also possible to have time periods assigned under topical headings. The assignment of century time periods is "free-floating" and is discussed below. Chronological subdivisions appear in the printed book version list as in figure 11.12.

Fig. 11.12. Printed entry for a place with established chronological subdivisions.

Papua (Indonesia) *(Not Subd Geog)*
. . .
—Politics and government
— —To 1963
— —1963-

In *MARC 21* authority records chronological subdivisions are preceded by the code ‡y. Again, every heading/subdivision combination has its own separate authority record. MARC records for Papua (Indonesia) and its chronological subdivisions are shown in figures 11.13 to 11.16.

Fig. 11.13. MARC name authority record for "Papua (Indonesia)". (Source: OCLC Connexion, Authorities)

ARN 05786797				
Rec stat c	Entered 20020614	Replaced 20050119114051.0		
Type z	Upd status a	Enc lvl n	Source	
Roman |	Ref status a	Mod rec	Name use a	
Govt agn |	Auth status a	Subj a	Subj use a	
Series n	Auth/ref a	Geo subd n	Ser use b	
Ser num n	Name n	Subdiv tp n	Rules c	

010	no2002052215
040	DLC-OI ‡b eng ‡c DLC-OI ‡d DLC ‡d WaU ‡d DLC
043	a-io---
151	Papua (Indonesia)
451	Provinsi Papua (Indonesia)
451	Tanah Papua (Indonesia)
451	West New Guinea (Indonesia)
451	West Papua (Indonesia)
551	Irian Jaya (Indonesia) ‡w a
670	Papua menggugat, 2002: ‡b t.p. (Papua; Tanah Papua)
670	Undang-Undang Republik Indonesia nomor 21 Tahun 2001 Tentang Otonomi Khusus Bagi Provinsi Papua, 2001: ‡b p. 5 (art. 1: Provinsi Papua adalah Provinsi Irian Jaya yang diberi Otonomi Khusus dalam kerangka Negara Kesatuan Republik Indonesia)
670	GEOnet, June 3, 2003 ‡b (Papua [short form], Provinsi--ADM1, 05? 00? S 138? 00? E, variants: West New Guinea; West Irian; Tanah Papua; Nieuw-Guinea; Nieuw-Guinea; Netherlands New Guinea; Netherland New Guinea; Nederlands Nieuw-Guinea; Nederlandsch Nieuw-Guinee; Irian Jaya, Propinsi; Irian Barat, Propinsi; Irian Barat, Daerah Tinghat I; Irian Barat; Irian; Dutch New Guinea; ID09)
670	West Papua action update, no. 2 ‡b (West Papua)
670	West Papua action Web site, Jan. 19, 2005 ‡b (West Papua, the western half of New Guinea island, termed "Irian Jaya province," or, more recently, "Papua" under Indonesian control)
781 _0	‡z Indonesia ‡z Papua

Fig. 11.14. MARC subject authority record for the "Politics and government" subdivision. (Source: OCLC Connexion, Authorities)

ARN 02121129				
Rec stat c	Entered 20030421	Replaced 20030529125830.0		
Type z	Upd status a	Enc lvl n	Source	
Roman |	Ref status n	Mod rec	Name use b	
Govt agn |	Auth status a	Subj a	Subj use a	
Series n	Auth/ref a	Geo subd |	Ser use b	
Ser num n	Name n	Subdiv tp n	Rules n	

010	sh 85068061
040	DLC ‡b eng ‡c DLC ‡d DLC
151	Papua (Indonesia) ‡x Politics and government

Fig. 11.15. MARC record for the first chronological subdivision. (Source: OCLC Connexion, Authorities)

ARN 02121131			
Rec stat c	Entered 20030421	Replaced 200030529125802.0	
Type z	Upd status a	Enc lvl n	Source
Roman |	Ref status n	Mod rec	Name use b
Govt agn |	Auth status a	Subj a	Subj use a
Series n	Auth/ref a	Geo subd |	Ser use b
Ser num n	Name n	Subdiv tp n	Rules n

010	sh 85068062
040	DLC ‡b eng ‡c DLC ‡d DLC
151	Papua (Indonesia) ‡x Politics and government ‡y To 1963

Fig. 11.16. MARC record for the second chronological subdivision. (OCLC Connexion, Authorities)

ARN 02121132			
Rec stat c	Entered 20030421	Replaced 200030529125900.0	
Type z	Upd status a	Enc lvl n	Source
Roman |	Ref status n	Mod rec	Name use b
Govt agn |	Auth status a	Subj a	Subj use a
Series n	Auth/ref a	Geo subd |	Ser use b
Ser num n	Name n	Subdiv tp n	Rules n

010	sh 85068063
040	DLC ‡b eng ‡c DLC ‡d DLC
151	Papua (Indonesia) ‡x Politics and government ‡y 1963-

Geographic Subdivisions
(*MARC 21* bibliographic and authority subfield ‡z;
MARC 21 subdivision authority record field 181)

The code words "*(May Subd Geog)*" in parentheses after any entry in the printed list tell us that place names may be added without having been spelled out in the list and without separate MARC authority records having been created. In a MARC authority record the code for geographic subdivision is given in byte 06 of the 008 fixed field. The letter *i* indicates that geographic subdivision is allowed. In the OCLC system the fixed field byte is labeled "Geo subd:". The printed and MARC codes are illustrated in figures 11.17 and 11.18.

Fig. 11.17. Printed entry showing a heading that may be subdivided geographically.

Lumbering   *(May Subd Geog)*
  [TS800-837 (Manufactures)]
    Here are entered works on the manufacturing of
  logs into lumber. Works on the felling of trees through
  the transporting of logs to sawmills or to a place of sale
  are entered under Logging.
  BT   Forest products industry
  RT   Lumber trade
  NT   Communication in lumbering
        Explosives in lumbering
        Logging
        Lumbermen

Fig. 11.18. MARC record showing "i" in fixed field subfield "Geo subd:" meaning that the heading can be subdivided geographically. (Source: OCLC Connexion, Authorities)

ARN 02070847						
Rec stat c	Entered 19860211	Replaced 19970902143428.1				
Type z	Upd status a		Enc lvl n		Source	
Roman |	Ref status b		Mod rec		Name use b	
Govt agn |	Auth status a		Subj a		Subj use a	
Series n	Auth/ref a		Geo subd i		Ser use b	
Ser num n	Name n		Subdiv tp n		Rules n	

010	sh 85078820
040	DLC ‡b eng ‡c DLC ‡d DLC
053	TS800 ‡b TS837 ‡c Manufactures
150	Lumbering
550	Forest products industry ‡w g
550	Lumber trade
680	‡i Here are entered works on the manufacturing of logs into lumber. Works on the felling of trees through the transporting of logs to sawmills or to a place of sale are entered under ‡a Logging.
681	‡i Note under ‡a Logging

It will be noted that in the earlier example shown for the heading "Lumber" (*see* figure 11.7 on page 334), geographic subdivision is not called for. The code shown following "Geo subd:" in that record is a "fill character" (shown in the example as "l").

The code "i" stands for the word "indirect" which was a former term used to indicate that geographic subdivision was allowed. It still describes the manner in which LCSH goes about providing geographic subdivision. Indirect subdivision means that the elements of the geographic name are to be arranged hierarchically, with a broader place name preceding the local name, e.g., "**Lumbering—Oregon —Portland**."

Formerly, "direct" subdivision was allowed (and is still used in *Sears*, as explained in chapter 12). This meant that the place name was written as it would be written to address a letter (e.g., "**Opera—Santa Fe, N.M.**"). Late in 1976, "direct" subdivision was abandoned by LC, although there are a few exceptions, which are well defined. The advantage of indirect subdivision is the collocation of material on one topic for one country or state, while direct subdivision separated such material by the first letters of the names of cities. On the other hand, indirect subdivision can sometimes be difficult to apply (e.g., when a geographic entity falls within two countries), whereas direct subdivision allowed use of the established name without alteration.

The following are subdivided "direct" in exception to the "indirect" policy:[43]

- Names of countries (not divided through continent)

- Names of first-order subdivisions (e.g., states) of the United States, Canada, and Great Britain (while there are five countries that are qualified by first-order subdivision rather than country under *AACR2R*, only three of these are subdivided indirectly this way in LCSH)

- Inverted headings for regions (e.g., "**Italy, Northern**")

- Names of geographical entities not wholly within one country

- Two cities: Washington (D.C.), and Jerusalem. (Vatican City is treated as a country and is thus also assigned directly)

- Islands "at a distance" from "owning" land masses

- Antartica (entities on the continent are divided through "**Antartica**")

The following list shows some results of the above policy:

> **Catholic Church—France—Paris**
> **Children—Ontario—Toronto**
> **Children—Australia—New South Wales** [only two
>   levels are allowed; so a city in New South Wales
>   would follow "**Australia—**":
>   **Children—Australia—Newcastle (N.S.W.)**]
> **Education—Washington (D.C.)**
> **Geology—Aegean Islands (Greece and Turkey)**
> **Geology—Indonesia—Ambon Island**
> **Lumbering—Pyrenees**

For geographic subdivisions, as for geographic headings, local name changes are observed. For instance, works that formerly would have received the heading "**Banks and banking—Leopoldville, Belgian Congo**" are now found under "**Banks and banking—Congo (Democratic Republic)—Kinshasa**." In card catalogs it was very difficult to keep up with such subdivision changes because of the difficulty of finding all occurrences of, for example, "Belgian Congo" used as a subdivision. In online catalogs, keyword searching is making such changes easier, although some critics still object to making such changes "regardless of the form of the name used in the work cataloged."[44]

If both geographical and topical subdivisions are established in the same heading, the last provision for geographical subdivision prevails. For example, the subject heading "Children" may be subdivided geographically. The subdivision "Quotations" is not divided. Therefore, a correct heading would be:

Children—Illinois—Quotations

The subdivision "Dental care" under "Children" *is* divided. Therefore, a correct heading would be:

Children—Dental care—Illinois

Other explanations and illustrations of geographic headings and subdivision practice are issued from time to time. Their best sources are the *Cataloging Service Bulletin*, and the *Subject Cataloging Manual: Subject Headings*.

Form/Genre Subdivisions
(*MARC 21* bibliographic and authority subfield ‡v;
MARC 21 authority record field 185)

Although form/genre subdivisions have been assigned in subject heading strings from the beginning of LCSH, they have only been coded separately in the MARC format since February 1999. The need to code form subdivisions differently has occasioned the reevaluation of the use of these subdivisions and their location in subject strings. At the current time, wording of form subdivisions is such that quite often the same word form is used to indicate that the work is *about* a particular form as the word form used to indicate that the work is *an example of* a particular form. Coding is according to the function of the word in the subject string, resulting in the possibility of identical subject string constructions being coded differently. For example, "**Science ‡x Periodicals**" represents a work about science periodicals, while "**Science ‡v Periodicals**" represents a work that is a periodical that deals with scientific subjects. LC's publication, *Free-Floating Subdivisions: An Alphabetical Index*[45] includes a column for subfield codes, in which a letter "v" appears beside each subdivision that may be coded as a form subdivision.

Free-Floating Subdivisions
(*MARC 21* bibliographic and authority subfield ‡x and/or ‡v)

For many kinds of primary headings there are a number of identical, or nearly identical, subdivisions that can be applied in specifically defined situations, according to LC's rules, policies, and practices, and that, therefore, do not have separate authority records made for each heading with subdivision combination in which they appear. These are collectively designated "free-floating," but they may not be assigned indiscriminately, for they fall into different groups, each with its own rules and examples. There are five broad groups: general free-floating subdivisions; subdivisions used under classes of persons and ethnic groups; subdivisions used under names of corporate bodies, persons, and families; subdivisions used under place names; and subdivisions controlled by pattern headings. Each group is explained briefly below. All free-floating subdivisions are listed in *Free-Floating Subdivisions: An Alphabetical Index*.[46] In this list they are in alphabetical order, each with a reference to the category in which it appears in *SCM: SH* and with citations to special instructions in the manual when applicable.

• General Free-Floating Subdivisions

General free-floating subdivisions are listed in *SCM: SH*, H1095. Along with each subdivision is a scope note, followed by *See also* references to other subdivisions, when applicable. With some there are also references to other memo numbers in the manual, often because the concept represented by the subdivision has an entire instruction sheet about it. Some also include the instruction *"(May Subd Geog)."* Example:

> **—Political aspects** *(May Subd Geog)*   *(H1942)*
> Use under individual religions and topical headings for works on the political dimensions or implications of nonpolitical topics.
> See also **—Politics and government** under names of countries, cities, etc., and under ethnic groups.

An example of a heading using this subdivision is:

Environmental education—Political aspects

• Subdivisions Used under Classes of Persons and Ethnic Groups

These subdivisions are listed in *SCM: SH*, H1100 and H1103. The primary headings under which the list in H1100 may be used include all kinds of classes of persons except ethnic groups and nationalities, which is covered by H1103. Examples of classes of persons are: **Mothers**; **Youth**; **Political prisoners**; **Lungs—Cancer—Patients**; **Baseball coaches**; and **African American dentists**. Examples of ethnic groups are: **French-Canadians**; **Dinka (African people)**; **Jews**. Headings for nationalities (e.g., **Ukrainians**) are included when they designate those nationalities *outside* their native countries. Many of the subdivisions in these two lists carry the instruction *"(May Subd Geog)."* Only a few have scope notes. Examples using these subdivisions: **Women—Information services**; **Cuban Americans—Job stress**.

• Subdivisions Used under Names of Corporate Bodies, Persons, and Families

Subdivisions to be used under names of corporate bodies are given in H1105. H1110 lists subdivisions used under names of persons, and H1120 lists those for family names. The subdivisions in H1105 may be used under names of all types of corporate bodies except names of conferences, congresses, meetings, or names of jurisdictions. Some terms in H1105 have scope notes and references to other subdivisions. Example: **Princeton University. Art Museum—Catalogs**.

Subdivisions listed in H1110 may be used under persons of all categories. A separate list that once existed for literary authors was discontinued in 1998. Like the previous lists, H1110 contains some scope notes and references to other subdivisions. Unlike the other lists, this one has a number of unused terms with "see" references to the terms that should be used instead. Example: **Lincoln, Abraham, 1809-1865—Correspondence**.

The list of subdivisions to be used under family names (H1120) is relatively short with no scope notes or references. Example: **Lull family—Coin collections**.

- Subdivisions Used under Place Names

Subdivisions to be used under place names are given in two lists: H1140 lists subdivisions used under names of places, and H1145.5 lists those to be used with names of bodies of water. Like the list for subdivisions under corporate bodies, the list of subdivisions in H1140 is a list with some scope notes that limit the use of some subdivisions. Example: **Chicago (Ill.)—Ethnic relations**. The list of subdivisions used with names of bodies of water is very short. Example: **Allegheny Reservoir (Pa. and N.Y.)—Water rights.** An instruction states that appropriate subdivisions from the list to be used under names of places may also be used under names of bodies of water. Example: **Okmulgee Lake (Okla.)—Maps**.

- Subdivisions Controlled by Pattern Headings

Pattern headings are examples of a particular primary heading type that have been entered into the *LCSH* authority file to show all the possible subdivisions that might be used with other specific headings of the same type. A very few may not even apply to the heading under which they are found.

Several categories of specific subjects have distinctive sets of subdivisions applicable to all examples of their genre. These include such categories as educational institutions, religious and monastic orders, languages, musical instruments, industries, military services, animals, diseases, and chemicals. Pattern headings are represented by examples in the printed *LCSH* and in the online authority file, but one must have a table to find them. A table in alphabetical order by category is found in the introduction to the printed list (also in the "Introduction" in *Cataloger's Desktop*). A table grouped by subject field is found in *SCM: SH*, H1146. For each pattern heading there is also a separate memo in *SCM: SH* that explains what is included in the category and lists all allowable subdivisions for that category.

The following table shows some of the pattern headings available:

Subject Field	**Category**	**Pattern Heading(s)**
Religion	Religions	**Buddhism**
History and geography	Legislative bodies	**United States. Congress**
Social sciences	Individual educational institutions	**Harvard University**
The arts	Music compositions	**Operas**
Science and technology	Organs and regions of the body	**Heart; Foot**

Following the pattern, if one were cataloging a work about "kidneys," for example, it would be appropriate to find "**Heart**" in LCSH and choose appropriate subdivisions found there to be used with the heading "**Kidneys**." General free-floating subdivisions as found in H1095 (discussed above) are not usually printed under pattern headings, but they may also be used as appropriate.

Subdivision Authority Records

In February 1999 LC began distributing subdivision records for the more than 3,000 topical, form, and chronological free-floating subdivisions in LCSH. These records contain subdivision data in 18x fields. Codes in 073 fields identify location of instructions concerning the subdivisions in *SCM: SH*. Each record contains a basic usage statement, and some records have references. A typical subdivision record is shown in figure 11.19.

Fig. 11.19. MARC authority record for the subdivision "Indexes." (Source: OCLC Connexion, Authorities)

ARN 04933911			
Rec stat c Entered 19990225 Replaced 20010205144605.0			
Type z	Upd status a	Enc lvl n	Source
Roman |	Ref status a	Mod rec	Name use b
Govt agn |	Auth status a	Subj a	Subj use a
Series n	Auth/ref d	Geo subd |	Ser use b
Ser num n	Name n	Subdiv tp b	Rules n

010	sh 99001477
040	IEN ‡b eng ‡c DLC
073	H 1095 ‡a H 1100 ‡a H 1103 ‡a H 1105 ‡a H 1110 ‡z lcsh
185	‡v Indexes
485	‡v Bibliography ‡v Indexes
485	‡v Dictionaries, indexes, etc. ‡w nne
680	‡i Use as a form subdivision under subjects.
681	‡i Reference under the heading ‡a Indexes

Classification Aids
(*MARC 21* bibliographic field 053)

Many primary subject terms, and some subject subdivisions under those terms, are accompanied by *LC Classification* (*LCC*) notations. Sometimes more than one *LCC* notation is given, with a term from the schedule to show the various aspects of classification represented by the subject heading (see figure 11.20). Frequently a range of notations is supplied as shown in figure 11.17 (page 339).

**Fig. 11.20. Printed entry showing *LCC* notations in three
different areas for the subject heading "Chestnut."**

Chestnut   *(May Subd Geog)*
      [QK495.F14 (Botany)]
      [SB401.C4 (Nut trees)]
      [SD397.C5 (Forestry)]
      UF   Castanea sativa
            Castenea vesca
            Castanea vulgaris
            Chestnut tree
            Common European chestnut
            English chestnut
            European chestnut
            Italian chestnut
            Spanish chestnut
            Sweet chestnut
      BT   Castanea
      RT   Cookery (Chestnuts)

In the *MARC 21* authorities format the classification numbers are given in a field
with the tag 053 as shown in figure 11.21. When a term is used to identify the particular aspect the classification represents, that term is coded ‡c in the 053 field.

**Fig. 11.21. MARC authority record showing LCC notations in 053 fields.
(Source: OCLC Connexion, Authorities)**

	ARN 02140296			
	Rec stat c Entered 19860211 Replaced 19910620144255.2			
	Type z	Upd status a	Enc lvl n	Source
	Roman		Ref status b	Mod rec	Name use b
	Govt agn		Auth status a	Subj a	Subj use a
	Series n	Auth/ref a	Geo subd i	Ser use b
	Ser num n	Name n	Subdiv tp n	Rules n
010	sh 85023154			
040	DLC ‡b eng ‡c DLC ‡d DLC			
053	QK495.F14 ‡c Botany			
053	SB401.C4 ‡c Nut trees			
053	SD397.C5 ‡c Forestry			
150	Chestnut			
450	Castanea sativa			
450	Castanea vesca			
450	Castanea vulgaris			
450	Chestnut tree			
450	Common European chestnut			
450	English chestnut			
450	European chestnut			
450	Italian chestnut			
450	Spanish chestnut			
450	Sweet chestnut			
550	Castanea ‡w g			
550	Cookery (Chestnuts)			
681	‡i Example under ‡a Nuts			

Classification notations are usually supplied when a term is first established. Occasionally they are added at a later time. But there is no systematic checking or revision of these notations unless changes are being made in an existing record for some other reason. Thus, a classification notation could be changed or its meaning revised in the *LCC* schedules, but it might not be changed in LCSH. Therefore, these notations are only a guide and should not be assigned without verification.

Filing Arrangement

The list proper in printed versions is given in alphabetical order. Filing rules were revised in 1980 to facilitate computer manipulation, and the revised rules continue to be used for the book version of LCSH. Basic arrangement is word by word. Numbers given in digits precede alphabetic characters in the order of increasing value. Initials separated by punctuation file as separate words. Abbreviations without interior punctuation file as single whole words:

4-H clubs
A3D bomber   USE Skywarrior bomber
A4D (Jet attack plane)   USE Skyhawk (Jet attack plane)
A-36 (Fighter-bomber planes)   USE Mustang (Fighter planes)
A.J.S. motorcycle   USE AJS motorcycle
A priori
Aage family   USE Agee family
ACI test   USE Adult-child interaction test
ACTH
AK 8 motion picture camera
Alaska—History
ALGOL (Computer program language)

In the book version of LCSH punctuation of subject terms affects filing order more immediately than it does in lists such as *Sears*, which sacrifice categorical to straight alphabetical arrangement. Subject headings from LCSH that contain subordinate elements preceded by one or more dashes fall into three groups:

a)   period subdivisions (MARC subfield ‡y), arranged chronologically according to explicit dates, regardless of whether a descriptive term is used,

b)   topical and form subdivisions (MARC subfield ‡x and subfield ‡v), arranged alphabetically, and

c)   geographical subdivisions (MARC subfield ‡z), arranged alphabetically.

The secondary subdivisions under "**United States—Foreign relations**" illustrate all three groups in order:

a)   **United States—Foreign relations—To 1775**
       United States—Foreign relations—1775-1783
       United States—Foreign relations—1783-1865
       United States—Foreign relations—1789-1809
       United States—Foreign relations—1812-1815

b) **United States—Foreign relations—Executive agreements**
United States—Foreign relations—Historiography
United States—Foreign relations—Juvenile literature
United States—Foreign relations—Law and legislation
United States—Foreign relations—Speeches in Congress
United States—Foreign relations—Treaties

c) **United States—Foreign relations—Iran**
United States—Foreign relations—Latin America
United States—Foreign relations—Middle East

However, in *Classification Web* these three groups generally collapse into two: numerals first, followed by words in alphabetical order. And, in fact, period subdivisions beginning with a word are found alphabetically:

United States—Foreign relations—1775-1783
United States—Foreign relations—Executive agreements
United States—Foreign relations—Iran
United States—Foreign relations—Speeches in Congress
United States—Foreign relations—To 1775

Prior to 1974 period subdivisions were sometimes indicated only by descriptive terminology (e.g., "**United States—History—Civil War**"), and one may still find these forms in old card catalogs.

In *LCSH* book version all subject subdivisions (identified by dashes) file ahead of inverted modifiers, which are punctuated by commas. Inverted modifiers, in turn, file ahead of parenthetical qualifiers. Last of all come phrases that start with the primary term:

Children
Children—Attitudes
Children—Growth
Children—Quotations
Children—Surgery
Children, Ashanti
Children, Blind
Children, Yoruba
Children (Christian theology)
Children (International law)
Children (Roman law)
Children and animals
Children and strangers
Children as inventors
Children in literature
Children of working parents

Online versions both in *Classification Web* and in OCLC display the main heading with its subdivisions first, but following those, all other headings beginning with that main heading (i.e., phrases, inverted forms, parenthetical terms) are alphabetical without regard for punctuation:

Children
Children—Attitudes
Children—Growth
Children—Quotations
Children—Surgery
Children and animals
Children and strangers
Children as inventors
Children, Ashanti
Children, Blind
Children (Christian theology)
Children in literature
Children (International law)
Children of working parents
Children (Roman law)
Children, Yoruba

SUBJECT HEADINGS FOR CHILDREN'S LITERATURE
(2nd *MARC 21* indicator "1" in bibliographic record 650 field;
authority record fixed field 008/11 code "b")

Since 1965 LC has issued a special service for children's catalogers. Known originally as the Annotated Card Program, and now often referred to as AC cataloging, it was originated in order to provide "more appropriate and in-depth subject treatment of juvenile titles."[47] The "Introduction" to LCSH gives a description of the program, a history, an explanation of application, a review of commonly used subdivisions, and general instructions for applying and modifying standard LC subject terms. In the *MARC 21* bibliographic format they are tagged specifically as subject terms for children with a second indicator of *1* in 6XX fields. Some comparative examples are:

LCSH	Annotated Card List
Cliff-dwellers	Cliff dwellers
Enuresis	Bedwetting
Navel	Belly button
Phytogeography	Plant distribution
Zoogeography	Animal distribution

FAST

Because the complex syntax and rules for constructing LCSH headings tend to limit its application to situations where highly skilled personnel are available and also limit the effectiveness of automated authority control, recent calls have been made for simplification for easier use, clear understanding, straightforward application, and uncomplicated automated adaptation. Rebecca Dean states, "The purpose of adapting the LCSH with a simplified syntax to create FAST (Faceted Application of Subject Terminology) headings is to retain the very rich vocabulary of LCSH while making the schema easier to understand, control, apply and use."[48]

After a subcommittee of the Subject Analysis Committee of the American Library Association studied the issue of semantic interoperability, it reported in 1999 that a controlled vocabulary should be simple and easy to apply, should be intuitive enough to not require sophisticated training to use, should be logical, and should be scalable from the simplest implementation to the most sophisticated.[49] A research group at OCLC working on the issue decided to develop a new schema derived from LCSH but applied with a simpler syntax.[50] This takes advantage of the vocabulary control exercised by LC catalogers and does not require development of new terminology. FAST is defined by Edward T. O'Neill and Lois Mai Chan to have the following characteristics:

- A controlled vocabulary with all headings established in the authority file, with the exception of headings containing numeric values only;

- Based on the LCSH vocabulary;

- Designed for an online environment;

- A post-coordinated faceted vocabulary;

- Usable by people with minimal training and experience;

- Compatible with automated authority control.[51]

FAST has eight facets: topical, geographic (place), form (type, genre), chronological (time, period), personal name, corporate name, title, and meeting name. In each facet main headings can be subdivided only by subdivisions from the same facet. Topical headings may be subdivided by topical subdivisions; geographic headings may be subdivided by geographic subdivisions; etc. Each such heading-with-subdivision combination is established with its own authority record in the FAST authority file. Therefore, instead of a list of free-floating subdivisions that one would consult to find appropriate subdivisions for a particular main heading, there is an authority record found, for example, for the combination "**Education— Dictionaries—Spanish**" as well as for the combination "**Chemistry— Dictionaries—Spanish**."

In the geographic facet, geographic names are established and used in indirect order. For example, Pittsburgh, Pennsylvania is always represented as "**Pennsylvania —Pittsburgh**" in FAST instead of "**Pittsburgh (Pa.)**" as it appears when it is a main heading in LCSH. The form facet consists of terms that have been identified as those to be coded with the subfield "v" code by LC. The chronological facet goes against LC policy, and follows some earlier recommendations (rejected by LC for LCSH) that chronological headings should consist of the actual time periods of coverage reflected in the resources being described. Therefore, chronological headings in

FAST consist of a beginning date and an ending date covering the time period of the resource.

The personal name facet (including family names) and the corporate name facet use names as they are established in the LC Name Authority File. A name is included in the FAST authority file only if it has been used as a subject in at least one record in the OCLC database and only if the name is valid for subject use. The title facet and the meeting facet are still in the process of development. They are to be clarified in the next phase of the development agenda.

Evaluation of FAST is ongoing with several experimental projects using it, and with a Subject Analysis Committee subcommittee conducting research to determine its efficacy. The reader should be alert to developments.

CONCLUSION

In spite of perennial criticisms on grounds of its outdated terminology, illogical syntax, and general inefficiency for precise subject retrieval, LCSH is the most widely accepted controlled vocabulary list in use in English-language libraries today. LC, with prompting and assistance from interested bystanders, now and again assesses its virtues and disadvantages. Intensive efforts continue the work toward modernizing and systematizing this tool. Many of the features discussed in this chapter represent steps in that direction. The Subject Authority Cooperative Program (SACO) is one way that libraries have to assist LC with improving LCSH.[52] Being a member of SACO allows a library's catalogers to submit proposed new subject headings and classification numbers to LC via the Program for Cooperative Cataloging (PCC). For the foreseeable future, this venerable subject list gives every sign of retaining its vitality and preeminence for subject access to library collections.

NOTES

1. *Canadian Subject Headings*, 3rd ed. (Ottawa: National Library of Canada, 1992); and *Canadian Subject Headings: Supplement*, 3rd ed. (Ottawa: National Library of Canada, 1996).

2. Melvil Dewey, *Dewey Decimal Classification and Relative Index*, Edition 22, edited by Joan S. Mitchell, et al. (Dublin, OH: OCLC, 2003); *Abridged Dewey Decimal Classification and Relative Index*, Edition 14, edited by Joan S. Mitchell, et al. (Dublin, OH: OCLC, 2004). DDC, Dewey, Dewey Decimal Classification, and WebDewey are registered trademarks of OCLC.

3. *Sears List of Subject Headings*, 18th ed., Joseph Miller, editor; Joan Goodsell, associate editor (New York: H. W. Wilson, 2004).

4. Charles Ammi Cutter, *Rules for a Dictionary Catalog*, 4th ed., rewritten (Washington, D.C.: GPO, 1904; republished, London: The Library Association, 1972). The original version of this work was: Charles A. Cutter, "Rules for a Printed Dictionary Catalogue," in *Public Libraries in the United States of America: Their History, Condition, and Management*, United States Bureau of Education (Washington, D.C.: GPO, 1876), Part II.

5.   For fuller information on the origin and development of the LC subject list, *see* Lois Mai Chan, *Library of Congress Subject Headings: Principles and Application*, 4th ed. (Westport, Conn.: Libraries Unlimited, 2005); and Richard S. Angell, "Library of Congress Subject Headings—Review and Forecast," in *Subject Retrieval in the Seventies: New Directions*, edited by Hans (Hanan) Wellisch and Thomas D. Wilson (Westport, Conn.: Greenwood Publishing Co., 1972), pp. 143–163.

6.   J. C. M. Hanson, "The Subject Catalogs of the Library of Congress," *Bulletin of the American Library Association* 3 (September 1909): 385–397.

7.   American Library Association, *List of Subject Headings for Use in Dictionary Catalogs* (Boston: Library Bureau, 1895).

8.   Hanson, "Subject Catalogs," p. 387.

9.   Ibid., p. 389.

10.   Ibid., p. 390.

11.   David Judson Haykin, *Subject Headings: A Practical Guide* (Washington, D.C.: GPO, 1951), p. 11.

12.   *Subject Headings Used in the Dictionary Catalogues of the Library of Congress*, [1st]–3rd eds. (Washington, D.C.: Library of Congress, Catalog Division, 1910–1928); *Subject Headings Used in the Dictionary Catalogs of the Library of Congress*, 4th–7th eds. (Washington, D.C.: Library of Congress, Subject Cataloging Division, 1943–1966); *Library of Congress Subject Headings*, 8th–12th eds. (Washington, D.C.: Library of Congress, Subject Cataloging Division, 1975–1989); *Library of Congress Subject Headings*, 13th– eds. (Washington, D.C.: Library of Congress, Office for Subject Cataloging Policy, 1990–).

13.   *Library of Congress Subject Headings Weekly Lists* (Washington, D.C.: Library of Congress, Cataloging Policy and Support Office, January 1984–). 1997, no. 1–date. Available: http://www.loc.gov/catdir/cpso/cpso.html#subjects (accessed 2/14/2006).

14.   *Classification Web* (Washington, D.C.: Library of Congress, Cataloging Distribution Service) Available: http://classificationweb.net/ [requires ID and password] (accessed 2/14/2006). For subscription information: http://www.loc.gov/cds/classweb/ (accessed 2/14/2006).

15.   Library of Congress Authorities. Available: http://authorities.loc.gov/ (accessed 2/14/2006)

16.   *Subject Cataloging Manual: Subject Headings*, 5th ed. (Washington, D.C.: Cataloging Distribution Service, Library of Congress, 1996). Updates, 1997– . (Also available in *Cataloger's Desktop*.)

17.   *Cataloger's Desktop* (Washington, D.C.: Library of Congress, Cataloging Distribution Service). Available: http://desktop.loc.gov/ [requires ID and password] (accessed 2/14/2006). For subscription information: http://www.loc.gov/cds/desktop/ (accessed 2/14/2006).

18.   *Cataloging Service Bulletin*, no. 1– (Washington, D.C.: Library of Congress, Processing Services, 1978–).

19. Cutter, *Rules*, pp. 71–72.

20. Chan, *Library of Congress*, pp. 48–59.

21. Cutter, *Rules*, p. 71.

22. *Subject Cataloging Manual: Subject Headings*, H290; H690, p. 7.

23. *Subject Cataloging Manual*, H310.

24. *Subject Cataloging Manual*, H360.

25. *Subject Cataloging Manual*, H357.

26. *Subject Cataloging Manual*, H320, H350, H351.

27. Sanford Berman, *Prejudices and Antipathies: A Tract on the LC Subject Heads Concerning People* (Metuchen, N.J.: Scarecrow Press, 1971).

28. Hennepin County Library, Cataloging Section, *Cataloging Bulletin*, May 1973–Nov./Dec. 1999.

29. Doris H. Clack, *Black Literature Resources: Analysis and Organization* (New York: Marcel Dekker, 1975), p. 10.

30. *Cataloging Service*, bulletin 119 (Fall 1976): 22, 24.

31. Joan K. Marshall, *On Equal Terms: A Thesaurus for Nonsexist Indexing and Cataloging* (Santa Barbara, Calif.: American Bibliographical Center–Clio Press, 1977).

32. *Subject Cataloging Manual*, H708.

33. *Subject Cataloging Manual*, H710.

34. American Library Association, Subject Analysis Committee, 1993, "Definition of Form Data." Available: http://www.pitt.edu/~agtaylor/ala/form-def.htm (accessed 2/14/2006).

35. Subject Analysis Committee, Subcommittee on the Revision of the Guidelines on Subject Access to Individual Works of Fiction, Drama, etc., *Guidelines on Subject Access to Individual Works of Fiction, Drama, Etc.* 2nd ed. (Chicago: American Library Association, 2000).

36. *Subject Cataloging Manual*, H362.

37. E. J. Coates, *Subject Catalogues: Headings and Structure* (London: Library Association, 1960).

38. George M. Sinkankis, "A Study in the Syndetic Structure of the Library of Congress List of Subject Headings." Ph.D. dissertation, University of Pittsburgh, 1972.

39. Toni Petersen, "The AAT: A Model for the Restructuring of LCSH," *Journal of Academic Librarianship* 9 (September 1983): 207–210.

40. Mary Dykstra, "LC Subject Headings Disguised as a Thesaurus," *Library Journal* 113 (March 1, 1988): 42–46.

41. *Subject Cataloging Manual*, H370.

42. *Library of Congress Subject Headings*, "Introduction" in *Cataloger's Desktop*, 2006, issue 1, February 2006.

43. *Subject Cataloging Manual*, H830, H807, H980, H1045, H1050.

44. *Cataloging Service*, bulletin 120 (Winter 1977): 10.

45. *Free-Floating Subdivisions: An Alphabetical Index*, 1st ed.– (Washington, D.C.: Library of Congress, 1989–).

46. Ibid.

47. *LCSH*, "Introduction."

48. Rebecca J. Dean, "FAST: Development of Simplified Headings for Metadata," in *Authority Control in Organizing and Accessing Information: Definition and International Experience*, edited by Arlene G. Taylor and Barbara B. Tillett. New York: Haworth Information Press, 2004, pp. 331–332.

49. *Subject Data in the Metadata Record: Recommendations and Rationale: A Report from the [ALA/ALCTS/SAC] Subcommittee on Metadata and Subject Analysis*, July 1999. Available: http://www.ala.org/ala/alctscontent/catalogingsection/catcommittees/subjectanalysis/metadataandsubje/ subjectdata.htm (accessed 2/14/2006).

50. FAST [Research Project], OCLC Office of Research Team (Edward T. O'Neill, Lead). Available: http://www.oclc.org/research/projects/fast/default.htm (accessed 2/17/2006).

51. Edward T. O'Neill and Lois Mai Chan, "FAST (Faceted Application of Subject Terminology): A Simplified LCSH-Based Vocabulary," World Library and Information Congress: 69th IFLA General Conference and Council, 1–9 August 2003, Berlin. Available: http://www.ifla.org/IV/ifla69/papers/010e-Oneill_Mai-Chan.pdf (accessed 2/14/2006).

52. "SACO Program Description: Program for Cooperative Cataloging." Available: http://www.loc.gov/catdir/pcc/saco/saco.html (accessed 2/14/2006).

SUGGESTED READING

Berman, Sanford. *Prejudices and Antipathies: A Tract on the LC Subject Heads Concerning People*. Metuchen, NJ: Scarecrow Press, 1971.

Chan, Lois Mai. *Library of Congress Subject Headings: Principles and Application*. 4th ed. Westport, Conn.: Libraries Unlimited, 2005.

Dean, Rebecca J. "FAST: Development of Simplified Headings for Metadata." *Cataloging & Classification Quarterly* 39, no. 1/2 (2004): 331–352; also published in *Authority Control in Organizing and Accessing Information: Definition and International Experience*, edited by Arlene G. Taylor and Barbara B. Tillett. New York: Haworth Information Press, 2004, pp. 331–352.

Ferguson, Bobby. *Subject Analysis: Blitz Cataloging Workbook.* Englewood, Colo.: Libraries Unlimited, 1998. Chapter 1: Library of Congress Subject Headings.

Foskett, A. C. *The Subject Approach to Information.* 5th ed. London: Library Association Publishing, 1996. Chapter 23: Library of Congress Subject Headings.

Intner, Sheila S., and Jean Weihs. *Standard Cataloging for School and Public Libraries.* 3rd ed. Englewood, Colo.: Libraries Unlimited, 2001. Chapter 9: Library of Congress Subject Headings.

Library of Congress Subject Headings: "Introduction." Washington, D.C.: Library of Congress, Cataloging Distribution Service [current issue]; also published in *Cataloger's Desktop* (Washington, D.C.: Library of Congress, Cataloging Distribution Service). Available: http://desktop.loc.gov/ (accessed 2/14/2006).

Mann, Thomas. *Doing Research at the Library of Congress: A Guide to Subject Searching in a Closed Stacks Library.* Washington, D.C.: Library of Congress, Humanities and Social Sciences Division, 1994.

———. *Library Research Models: A Guide to Classification, Cataloging, and Computers.* New York: Oxford University Press, 1993.

Olson, Hope A., and John J. Boll. *Subject Analysis in Online Catalogs.* 2nd ed. Englewood, Colo.: Libraries Unlimited, 2001. Chapter 6: Subject Headings and Descriptors.

O'Neill, Edward T., and Lois Mai Chan. "FAST (Faceted Application of Subject Terminology): A Simplified LCSH-Based Vocabulary." World Library and Information Congress: 69th IFLA General Conference and Council, 1–9 August 2003, Berlin. Available: http://www.ifla.org/IV/ifla69/papers/010e-Oneill_Mai-Chan.pdf (accessed 2/14/2006).

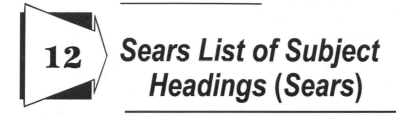

Sears List of Subject Headings (Sears)

INTRODUCTION

The *Sears List of Subject Headings* (*Sears*), now in its eighteenth edition, is widely used by small public libraries and by school libraries. It is very much smaller in scope and more general in treatment than *Library of Congress Subject Headings* (*LCSH*), which is commonly used in academic and research libraries. Its history of continuous publication is not so long-standing as that of the Library of Congress (LC) list. The preface states:

> Minnie Earl Sears prepared the first edition of this work in response to demands for a list of subject headings that was better suited to the needs of the small library than the existing American Library Association and Library of Congress lists. Published in 1923, the List of Subject Headings for Small Libraries was based on the headings used by nine small libraries that were known to be well cataloged.[1]

For many years *Sears* followed *LCSH* fairly closely, differing mainly in level of specificity (although its principles encourage specific entry and creation of headings of greater specificity when needed). In its earlier editions *Sears* used the broader headings from *LCSH*. However, in the most recent editions, *Sears* has shown more independence.

Wilson also has published a special interest companion volume for Canadian libraries and a Spanish language translation.[2] A new Spanish-language thesaurus based on *Sears* is currently being prepared,[3] and it is expected that both English and Spanish versions of *Sears* will be made available on WilsonWeb, the online reference database service of The H.W. Wilson Company, as well as in print.

TERMINOLOGY

New headings for recent editions of *Sears* were suggested by librarians representing various sizes and types of libraries, by commercial vendors of bibliographic records, and by H. W. Wilson catalogers responsible for the Standard Catalog series, *Book Review Digest*, and various periodical indexes. Examples of completely new headings in the eighteenth edition are: "Aromatherapy," "DVDs," "Journaling,"

"Optical scanners," "Racially mixed people," and "Test bias." *LCSH* was consulted, but modifications of *LCSH* were made to meet the needs of smaller collections. Included among the terms in *Sears* are some terms from LC's "Subject Headings for Children's Literature." The editors of the eighteenth edition tried to keep revisions to existing headings to a minimum, but they did change a few things, including changing the subdivision "—**Description**" to "—**Description and travel**," which is the usage of *LCSH* and other subject lists.

A comparison of *Sears* headings with comparable ones from *LCSH* can be helpful in understanding the differences between the lists. An example of *Sears*'s comparative brevity and simplicity is that *Sears* uses "**Litigation**" alone for this concept, while *LCSH* uses "**Actions and defenses**," "**Complex litigation**," and "**Government litigation**" as primary headings that represent various versions of the concept. Examples of *Sears'* use of broader concepts are: *Sears* uses "**Hallucinogens**" and "**Silk screen printing**"; *LCSH* uses only narrower terms: "**Hallucinogenic drugs**," "**Hallucinogenic plants**," "**Screen process printing**," and "**Serigraphy**." An example of *Sears'* use of less technical terms is: *Sears* uses "**Heart attacks**"; *LCSH* uses "**Myocardial infarction**." An example of *Sears'* use of common phraseology instead of subdividing one concept with another is: *Sears* uses "**Lung cancer**"; *LCSH* uses "**Lungs—Cancer**."

Modernization of Terminology

Through the years, *Sears* has undergone the same attempts to eliminate racist, sexist, and pejorative headings that have been made with LCSH. For example, the heading "**Negro actors**," was replaced by "**Black actors**" and its narrower term, "**African American actors**," while "**Air lines—Hostesses**" became "**Flight attendants**," and "**Man (Theology)**" was changed to "**Human beings (Theology)**." Other headings with prejudicial connotations disappeared or underwent purification rites. The tenth edition's "**Jewish question**" disappeared along with "**Women in aeronautics**" and most other "**Women in . . .**" and all "**Women as . . .**" headings. "**Underdeveloped areas**" was downgraded into a USE reference to "**Developing areas**" in the eleventh edition, changed to a USE reference to "**Third World**" in the twelfth edition, and then became a USE reference to "**Developing countries**" in the thirteenth edition. "**Insanity**" was converted into a USE reference to "**Mental illness —Jurisprudence**" in the fourteenth edition, which, in turn, became "**Insanity defense**" in the sixteenth edition. "**Man, Primitive**" became "**Nonliterate man**" in the fourteenth edition, followed by becoming "**Primitive societies**" in the sixteenth edition. A major feature of the seventeenth edition was the revision for the native peoples of the Western Hemisphere. Headings beginning with "**Indians . . .**" were canceled in favor of "**Native Americans**."

Modernization has also occurred with time periods. "**Renaissance**," used as an adjective, has been replaced by the subdivision "—**15th and 16th centuries**" (e.g., "**Renaissance decoration and ornament**" became "**Decoration and ornament —15th and 16th centuries**"). The adjective "Modern" has been eliminated (e.g., "**Modern architecture—1800–1899 (19th century)**" has been replaced by "**Architecture—19th century**," and the former "**Modern art**" is now either "**Modernism in art**" or "**Art—20th century**," or both).

Sears has, for many editions, deleted certain headings of decreasing interest. For example, "**Iran-Contra Affair, 1985–1990**" was deleted from the eighteenth edition. Such headings are still valid and may be used in catalogs, however. Other deleted headings are no longer valid; in this case, they are given as references to other headings, and some have the label "[Former heading]" in the UF list under the established heading. Example:

Aboriginal Australians
UF Australian aborigines *[Former heading]*

Problems of Updating Terminology

Some linguistic change would have occurred, no doubt, regardless of the social climate. However, formal subject lists have tended to be conservative in their response to new terminology. In attempting to retain the goodwill of their constituents, they are understandably sensitive to the disruptions caused to a library's cataloging routines when an unduly large number of new subject forms are mandated at one time. Still, the argument that an obsolete form reflects usage in the bulk of the literature indexed is specious. Furthermore, it becomes misleading as new materials with new terminology are added. On the other hand, librarians with card catalogs feared not only the time and effort required to change large numbers of entries, but also the stresses placed on the filing apparatus when revised cards had to be moved from one section of the catalog to another. As online catalogs have become the norm, this problem has eased.

SEARS LIST OF SUBJECT HEADINGS' USE OF SUBJECT HEADING THEORY

The general philosophy of *Sears* is contained in two phrases, both of which the cataloger should remember as he or she makes specific application of the list to the individual materials in the library's collection: the principle of specific entry and the principle of unique heading.[4]

"The principle of specific entry" means that a specific heading is preferred to a general one. For a book about cats alone, "**Cats**" is preferred to "**Domestic animals**." On the other hand, the headings "**Siamese cats**" or "**Seal-point Siamese cats**" might be too specific for some libraries, although the principle of specific entry would place a work on Siamese cats under that heading, and *Sears* has a general reference under "**Cats**" that reads: "SA names of specific breeds of cat [to be added as needed]." The cataloger must know the collection, know its emphases, and know something of the way people use it to be prepared to assign subject headings to it. Are users likely to look for very specific headings, or do they expect to find information under a more general collocating category?

"The principle of unique heading" means that one subject heading, and one alone, is chosen for all items on that subject. The choice of subject headings must be logical and consistent. References should be inserted in the catalog wherever it is anticipated that patrons are likely to approach the topic through different terminology. A few general principles or guidelines are useful for constructing unique subject headings that are logical and consistent:

- Prefer the English word or phrase unless a foreign one best expresses the idea. *Sears*, for example, carries the reference "Laissez faire. USE **Free enterprise**."

- Try to use terms that are used in other libraries as well, unless the library in question is highly specialized or otherwise unique.

- Try to use terms that will cover the field, i.e., terms that will apply to more than one item.

References

Sears breaks down references into three main categories, and the introduction discusses each in some detail: specific *See* references; specific *See also* references; and general references.[5] (References in *Sears* carry the same designations as in *LCSH*, that is, USE, UF, SA, BT, NT, and RT; however, the *Sears* introduction still identifies these as "see," "see also," and "general" references, possibly because of the number of smaller catalogs that still contain references designated in this way rather than "search also under" or other newer reference forms.)

See references are considered essential to the success of the catalog. Yet the cataloger in a local library may not find necessary every *See* reference suggested in the list. For example, *Sears* proposes "Plants, Edible USE **Edible plants**." There is also a narrower term reference under "**Plants**" to "**Edible plants**," and in a small catalog, the inverted reference could be superfluous. The most frequent and helpful varieties of *See* references direct the user from:

- Synonyms or terms so nearly synonymous that they would cover the same kind of material, e.g., "Chemical geology USE **Geochemistry**" and "Pay equity USE **Equal pay for equal work**."

- The second part of a compound heading, e.g., "Illusions USE **Hallucinations and illusions**" and "Motels USE **Hotels and motels**."

- Variant spellings or initialisms to the accepted spelling or full form, e.g., "Gipsies USE **Gypsies**" and "ESP USE **Extrasensory perception**."

- Opposites when they are included without being specifically mentioned, e.g., "Disobedience USE **Obedience**" and "Truth in advertising USE **Deceptive advertising**."

- The singular to the plural when the two forms would not file together, e.g., "Goose USE **Geese**."

See also references pose theoretical and practical problems that jeopardize their efficacy. Yet both *Sears* and *LCSH* make heavy use of them. The above warning against making references simply because they are suggested in a standard list holds as true for *See also* references as it does for *See* references.

It was stated in chapters 10 and 11 that *See also* references normally move downward from a general term to a more specific term or terms, e.g., "**Conservation of natural resources** *See also* **Energy conservation; Nature conservation**." In this example the general term refers to two more specific terms. The user who pursues the reference by looking under "**Nature conservation**" will find a still more specific downward reference to more headings: "**Nature conservation** *See also* **Endangered species; Landscape protection; Natural monuments; Plant conservation; Wildlife conservation**." Although the reference in the catalog may appear as just shown, the designation in the *Sears* list for these terms is "NT," for "narrower term(s)." The list also includes terms designated "BT," for "broader term(s)." As mentioned in chapter 11, some catalogs also make *See also* references to broader terms.

Sears also indulges in a high number of bilateral or reciprocal references, where the movement is horizontal, between related subjects of more or less equal specificity. These terms are designated "RT," for "related term(s)," in the list. The following examples have been pruned of extraneous terms, to make their reciprocity more visible:

Gods and goddesses *See also* **Mythology; Religions**

Mythology *See also* **Gods and goddesses**

Religions *See also* **Gods and goddesses**

Mollusks *See also* **Shells**

Shells *See also* **Mollusks**

In the case of "general" *See* and *See also* references, the terms being referred to are not specific headings, but instead are general groups or categories of things that may be established as headings as needed. Examples:

Faculty
    USE types of educational institutions and names of
                individual educational institutions with the
                subdivision *Faculty*, e.g. **Colleges and**
                universities—Faculty [to be added as needed]

Furniture
    SA   furniture of particular countries, e.g. **American**
            furniture; types of furniture, and names of
            specific articles of furniture, e.g. **Tables**;
            Chairs; etc. [to be added as needed]

The results of these general references may be so diverse or numerous that it is suggested that specific references be made from a broader term to all narrower terms on the next level of specificity. Example:

Furniture
    See also **Beds**
               Bookcases
               Chairs
               Desks
               Tables

Only those headings that actually appear in the catalog would be included in such a specific list.

General references to terms with subdivisions present another problem. That is, when the list gives "Illustrations USE subjects, names, and uniform titles with the subdivision *Pictorial Works*; e.g., **Animals—Pictorial works; United States—History—1861–1865, Civil War—Pictorial works**; etc. [to be added as needed]," and the library that has subject entries for both referrals adds a book consisting largely of pictures of children, should the cataloger revise the reference entry by inserting "**Children—Pictorial works**" as a third illustration? Or can he or she depend on the "etc." to cover all subsequent examples? Most libraries follow the second option, thus throwing the burden of search on the user, who probably either will not understand the instructions or, after a bit of desultory searching, will give up, unless the catalog is online and the system allows the possibility of doing a search on just the "Pictorial works" segment of headings. However well the user copes, valuable materials may be overlooked.[6]

The following list enumerates some major types of general references:

1. Common names of various members of a class, e.g., "**Dogs** SA types of dogs, e.g. **Guide dogs**; and names of specific breeds of dogs [to be added as needed]"

2. Names of individual persons, etc., e.g., "**Presidents—United States** SA names of presidents [to be added as needed]"

3. Names of particular institutions, buildings, structures, societies, etc., e.g., "**Bridges** SA types of bridges and names of individual bridges [to be added as needed]"

4. Names of particular geographic features, e.g., "**Natural monuments** SA names of individual natural monuments [to be added as needed]"

5. Names of places subdivided by subject, e.g., "Defenses USE types of defenses, e.g. **Air defenses**; and names of continents, regions, countries, and individual colonies with the subdivision *Defenses*, e.g. **United States—Defenses** [to be added as needed]"

6. Subjects followed by form subdivisions, e.g., "Case studies USE subjects with the subdivision *Case studies*, e.g. **Juvenile delinquency —Case studies** [to be added as needed]"

7. Subjects with national adjectives, e.g., "**Essays** . . . Collections of literary essays by American authors are entered under **American essays**; by English authors, under **English essays**; etc. . . ."

STRUCTURE OF SUBJECT HEADINGS

Like LCSH, *Sears* terms consist of a variety of forms, ranging from a single noun to different kinds of complex descriptive phrases:[7]

- The single noun is the most desirable form of subject heading if it is specific enough to fit the item at hand and the needs of the library. In general, if there is a significant difference between the singular and plural forms, the plural is preferred (e.g., "Mouse USE **Mice**"). However, there are situations where the singular form is used to cover abstract ideas or general usage (e.g., "**Essay**" as a literary form), while the plural designates individual examples of the form.

- The modified noun takes at least two forms: a) normal word order (e.g., "**Health maintenance organizations**"), and b) explanatory modifier added in parentheses (e.g., "**Hotlines (Telephone counseling)**"). Formerly, inverted word order was used, but now it is only used as a "used for" term from which a reference is made to the normal word order (e.g., "Technical assistance, American USE **American technical assistance**").

- The compound heading is usually two nouns joined by *and*, but the nouns are sometimes also modified (e.g., "**Coal mines and mining**"). The terms are conjoined for various reasons:

  —To link related topics. Usually both ideas are covered in a single treatise, e.g., "**Anarchism and anarchists**," "**Clocks and watches**," and "**Puppets and puppet plays**."

  —To link opposites. Again, the pairs are often discussed together, e.g., "**Corrosion and anticorrosives**," "**Good and evil**," and "**Joy and sorrow**."

  In most cases, usage dictates the order of terms, but when that fails, alphabetical order is preferred. If a library should acquire enough materials under one of two such terms to make searching difficult or tiresome, the cataloger might consider splitting the subject heading into its two components, with linking references. For example, *LCSH* has broken its former heading "**Antigens and antibodies**" into "**Antigens**" and "**Immunoglobulins**."

- The phrase heading may be prepositional (e.g., "**Cost and standard of living**"), serial (e.g., "**Stories, plots, etc.**"), or an intriguing combination of forms (e.g., "**Superhero comic books, strips, etc.**" or "**Life support systems (Medical environment)**").

TYPES OF SUBDIVISIONS

Subject subdivisions indicate a specialized aspect of a broad subject or point of view (e.g., "**Artificial satellites—Orbits**"). They are set off from the primary heading by a dash. Unlike the *LCSH* book version, *Sears* does not separate the category from references that are inverted with commas (e.g., "Artificial satellites, American USE **American artificial satellites**") or from phrases beginning with the same words (e.g., "**Artificial satellites in telecommunication**"), but interfiles all entries in straight alphabetical order, letter by letter to the end of each word, disregarding punctuation, as instructed in the American Library Association (ALA) filing rules that are discussed in the Appendix.[8]

A primary purpose of the subject subdivision is to subdivide topics that are broad in scope or that have much written about them (e.g., "**Education**"). Without subdivision, there would be many entries under such headings subarranged only by main entry or by date. Headings with large numbers of entries can be tedious for a catalog user to search. Subdivision allows grouping of the entries in meaningful ways, e.g.,

Education—Aims and objectives

Education—Curricula

Education—Experimental methods

There are several types of subdivisions, including topical subdivisions, geographic subdivisions, chronological subdivisions, and form subdivisions. Subdivisions may be compounded under a given topic. Three are used to show subtopics in the example: "**United States—History—1861–1865, Civil War—Medical care**."

Subdivisions of Broad Application

Form subdivisions are used to indicate the physical (e.g., ". . . —**Bibliography**") or philosophical (e.g., ". . . —**Research**") form of the work and may be used by the cataloger to divide practically any subject heading in the list, if local policy allows the cataloger to add such subdivisions even if they are not "established" in the list.

In addition there are many general and topical subdivisions that may be used under subjects as appropriate. These are given in the main list with instructions for their use as subdivisions with appropriate subject headings. There is also a list in the front of the volume that gives all subdivisions in the list except geographic or chronological.[9] This is a simple alphabetical list for handy reference only. The cataloger should always check the main list for instructions for the use of each subdivision.

Sears, like *LCSH*, has a group of headings that serve as patterns for the subdivisions that may be used under all headings of the same type. Some of these "Key Headings" are:[10]

Public figures:
Presidents—United States (to illustrate subdivisions that may be used under presidents, prime ministers, governors, and rulers of any country, state, etc.)

Authors:
Shakespeare, William, 1564–1616 (to illustrate subdivisions that may be used under any voluminous author)

Places:
United States; Ohio; Chicago (Ill.) (to illustrate subdivisions—except for historical periods—under geographic names)

Languages and Literatures:
English language (to illustrate subdivisions that may be used with any language)

English literature (to illustrate subdivisions that may be used with any literature)

In order to use the subdivisions under the key headings, one finds the appropriate example (e.g., "**English language—Idioms**") and then applies the subdivision to the heading for the item in hand (e.g., "**French language—Idioms**").

Subdivisions of Limited Application

Some special topic divisions cannot readily be transferred from one heading to another because they are specially tailored to bring out important aspects of individual topics, e.g., "**Deaf—Means of communication**" or "**Airplanes—Piloting**." One could not reasonably use "**Deaf—Piloting**" or "**Airplanes—Means of communication**." Such divisions are listed both in the alphabetical reference list and in the main list. A cataloger is expected to use common sense in applying them.

Chronological Subdivisions

Time divisions, which apply most frequently to history, define a specific chronology for the primary topic. Some consist merely of dates (e.g., "**Europe—History —1789–1900**"). Often the date or dates are followed by a descriptive phrase (e.g., "**Church history—30–600, Early church**"). Prior to the twelfth edition the descriptive phrase preceded the dates in such headings. The change in position facilitates filing in chronological order both manually and by machine. Occasionally the chronological designation is an inverted qualifier rather than a subdivision (e.g., "**Gettysburg (Pa.), Battle of, 1863**").

Geographic Subdivisions

Geographic divisions are of two forms: a) area—subject, e.g., "**Chicago (Ill.)—Census**," and b) subject—area, e.g., "**Geology—Bolivia**." *Sears* adds parenthetical instructions to those headings in its list that may be divided by place, e.g., "**Geology** (May subdiv. geog.)." Under some headings the instructions are more detailed, e.g., "**American hostages** (May subdiv. geog. except U.S.)."

Unlike LCSH, *Sears* does not dictate the form of geographic subdivisions. The introduction specifies that *Sears* uses, in the main list, direct place subdivision (in which the name of the place discussed in the work is used directly as the subdivision) rather than indirect place subdivision (in which the name of a larger geographic area is interposed between the subject and a smaller area discussed in the work). *Sears* uses the *AACR2* form of a place name in using direct subdivision (i.e., "**—Chicago (Ill.),**" not just "**—Chicago**"), but it does not mandate this usage for the libraries using its list. Some libraries may wish to follow LCSH practice and use indirect place subdivision. If direct place subdivision is chosen, it is wise to use *AACR2* form for the sake of consistency.

Geographic area subdivided by subject situations are less conspicuous in the list, but play an important role in most library catalogs. Instructions may take the form: "**Italy** . . . May be subdivided like United States except for *History*."

Subject headings in various fields, especially in the fields of science, technology, and economics, usually are subdivided by place. Those in history, geography, and politics usually are made subdivisions under place.[11] It is assumed that the real subject of a book about Colorado history, and the one the patron will most likely consult, is "**Colorado**," not "**History**." In *Sears*, the main subject heading "**History**" is used only for general works on history as an intellectual discipline.

HEADINGS FOR BELLES-LETTRES

Individual works of belles-lettres (e.g., novels, plays, and poetry) are not always assigned subject headings. It has often been assumed that patrons are more likely to seek access to these materials through author or title. However, there are many themes of literature that may be used as subject headings. In the list of form subdivisions supplied by *Sears* ". . . —**Fiction**" appears as a suggested option for libraries that prefer to make subject headings for fictionalized history or biography. Thus, a novel about the Six Day War in the Middle East might be given the subject heading, "**Israel-Arab War, 1967—Fiction**." In addition other genre headings, such as "**Mystery fiction**" or "**Science fiction**," can be assigned to these works. The eighteenth edition of *Sears* is the first to include in its "Principles of the Sears List" guidance to libraries that choose to assign topical and geographic headings to individual works of fiction, drama, and poetry.[12]

For literary anthologies it is common to give a genre heading with the subdivision "—**Collections**" (e.g., "**Poetry—Collections**"; "**American drama—Collections**"), but *Sears* sometimes uses the plural noun (e.g., "**Essays**") rather than using the subdivision.[13] Topical headings reflecting themes of the work as a whole are also common (e.g., "**Love poetry**"; "**Dogs—Fiction**").

PHYSICAL CHARACTERISTICS AND FORMAT OF *SEARS LIST OF SUBJECT HEADINGS*

The eighteenth edition of *Sears* opens with a preface that gives its historical setting and identifies the authoritative sources and the new features incorporated in it. It is followed by an explanatory essay that has become a *Sears* tradition, undergoing considerable expansion in scope and detail over the years. This essay is called "Principles of the Sears List of Subject Headings."[14] It treats both the theoretical and practical aspects of subject heading work. It merits careful reading, not only by those planning to use the *Sears* list, but also by anyone wishing to gain knowledge of traditional subject list usage. The discussion of "Principles" is followed by an explanation of what kinds of headings are expected to be added by the cataloger, a list of "Key" headings, a list of canceled and replacement headings, a list of revisions of special interest to Canadian users, explanations of the use of subdivisions in *Sears*, an explanation of the symbols used, and finally the list proper.

In the list proper, subject entries are printed in boldface type. USE references appear in lightface type in the same alphabet. Filing in *Sears* has already been discussed under "Types of Subdivisions." The following excerpt shows the various elements that may be included under a subject entry, although not every entry requires all of these elements:

Children's poetry   808.81

>Use for individual poems, collections, or materials about poetry written for children. Individual works and collections of poetry written by children are entered under **Children's writings**. Materials about poetry written by children are entered under **Child authors**.

UF   Poetry for children

SA   subjects and personal, corporate,
        and place names with the
        subdivision *Juvenile poetry*;
        e.g. **Christmas—Juvenile po-
        etry** [to be added as needed]

BT   **Children's literature**
        Poetry

NT   **Children's songs**
        Lullabies
        Nonsense verses
        Nursery rhymes
        Tongue twisters

DDC numbers from the fourteenth edition of the *Abridged Dewey Decimal Classification* are given with the permission of the publisher, OCLC.[15] The above example shows the associated *DDC* number in its customary place, on the same line with the subject entry. Two or three numbers may be specifically included to remind the user that he or she might profitably seek further in the *DDC* to find the best number for the particular need.

Scope notes have been used more extensively in each new edition of *Sears*. The one in the example above is typical. The reader receives first a positive instruction on appropriate use of the entry. Then comes a negative instruction (albeit stated positively) on the kinds of material that should be placed under a different entry.

The initials UF (standing for "used for") normally follow the scope note or, if there is no scope note, the entry proper. The letters UF before one or more terms mean that a USE reference is recommended from each such term to the heading under which the UF appears. Terms preceded by UF are never used as subject headings. Next come the letters SA followed by an explanation of general kinds of terms that may be related. Then we have the letters BT followed by terms that represent concepts broader than the concept represented in the heading. Next come the letters NT. They precede a list of more specific headings that the user might like to explore. Although not present in the above example, many entries end with a list of terms of related significance that follow the letters RT. Each boldface entry in the lists following BT, NT, and RT is a legitimate subject heading. Reference to these headings might very well lead to further headings that could help expand or modify the search to reveal the full range of materials available in the particular collection. But a reference is not usually made in the catalog unless the catalog actually has material under the heading referred to (*see* discussion of this issue in chapter 11).

Thus, *Sears* suggests the following references for the subject entry "**Children's poetry**," but the local cataloger is expected to consider each on its merits, in view of the terminology used by the library's clientele and the presence of other subject entries in the catalog:

Poetry for children
    USE   **Children's poetry**

Children's literature
    See also   **Children's poetry**

Poetry
    See also   **Children's poetry**

Children's poetry
    See also   **Children's songs**
                     Lullabies
                     Nonsense verses
                     Nursery rhymes
                     Tongue twisters

The cataloger should also consider whether a *see also* reference needs to be made in response to the "SA" instruction under "**Children's poetry**."

Sears includes a list of "Headings to Be Added by the Cataloger."[16] Several varieties of proper names and common names are identified for which there is no attempt to include all possibilities in the printed list. One or two obvious names of each variety can be found in the list proper, to serve as examples or because important or typical subdivisions have been given. The cataloger is also reminded that "general" *See also* references imply other specific names that the cataloger is to add as needed, using available reference sources to establish correct entry forms.

UPDATING

Sears updates its usage by successive editions. New print editions are published every few years. A machine-readable version, available on tape, is updated annually. The relatively limited scope of *Sears*, for use in small and medium-size libraries, makes comprehensive revision manageable for both editors and users. The results are more coherently integrated than the ad hoc revisions issued for *LCSH*. However, some may believe that one to three years is too long to wait for updated terminology in today's rapidly changing environment. LC's publication of the "Weekly Lists" and weekly updating of the online LCSH permit (if they do not always ensure) easy professional response on the part of one enormous library to inevitable, but generally unpredictable, shifts in publishing interests and emphases. Actually neither approach monopolizes all the advantages. What matters is that every viable subject access mode remain under constant surveillance and revision, offering a dynamic compromise between rigid custom and assimilative change.

Plans are being made to make the Sears list available on the Web using the Thesaurus module and search capabilities of WilsonWeb. Readers should watch for this development.

CONCLUSION

The assigning of subject headings is a discipline that inevitably seems complicated and bewildering to the neophyte cataloger. Unlike other cataloging disciplines, it has no logical progression other than the linguistic development of knowledge itself. Even the assigning of a classification number to a book is less forbidding, for the novice usually has some sort of previous orientation to the Dewey system and can see, if dimly, the divisions of knowledge and why they should exist. Subject headings are, however, not difficult once the cataloger learns to handle them. Both *Sears* and *LCSH* are quite explicit in their directions; both contain lists of general subdivisions with specific instructions for their use. If followed consistently, they will provide useful reference guides for the user, including the reference librarian.

A beginning cataloger should study the subject list used in the local library. It would be helpful to choose a subject in which he or she is personally interested, tracing it throughout the list and observing the interrelation of references. There are other aids, such as the reference tools in the library. They amplify subjects and clarify aspects not immediately understood, especially in an age when no one can expect to know everything. The library's shelflist and public catalog are also helpful. The former can suggest subject headings if the cataloger has a classification number in mind, since most card shelflists consist of full unit records, with tracings for the subject entries of each cataloged item. Online catalog searches by classification number allow retrieval of full MARC records, complete with subject headings. The main catalog can suggest classification numbers if the cataloger has a subject heading in mind. Neither is a completely reliable crutch. Books are very often written about new subjects and about more than one subject. The vagaries of past and present individual catalogers, however experienced, may mislead. Yet both resources are generally helpful; both serve to characterize the practices of the local library. To become a successful cataloger, one must know what is current local practice and work within that frame of reference. Major changes should not be put into effect until the reasons for what is done are fully understood and the reactions of other users and fellow librarians can be anticipated.

NOTES

1. *Sears List of Subject Headings*, 18th ed., Joseph Miller, editor; Joan Goodsell, associate editor (New York: H. W. Wilson, 2004), p. vii.

2. Lynne Isberg Lighthall, ed., *Sears List of Subject Headings: Canadian Companion*, 6th ed., with the assistance of Shana Bystrom, et al. (New York: H. W. Wilson, 2001); *Sears—Lista de Encabezamientos de Materia: Traducción y Adaptación de la 12a. Edición en Inglés*, ed. por Barbara M. Westby; trans. por Carmen Rovira (New York: H. W. Wilson, 1984) [Spanish translation now out-of-print].

3. *Encabezamientos Sears Siglo 21*, edited by Joanna F. Fountain (New York: H.W. Wilson [in preparation]).

4. For more detailed discussion of the theory of subject headings, refer to chapter 10, "Verbal Subject Access."

5. The list of reference types is adapted from *Sears*, p. xxxiv-xxxvii, but the examples are changed, to give alternative insights.

6. *Sears*, pp. xxxvi-xxxvii, also discusses this problem.

7. For a review of the structure of *LCSH* and further comment on some of the points mentioned here, *see* "Types of Topical Subject Headings" in chapter 11 and "The Choice of Subject Headings" in chapter 10.

8. *See* pp. 346–348 of this text to compare the filing used in the book version of *LCSH* with that found in *Sears*.

9. *Sears*, p. xlv-l.

10. *Sears*, p. xli.

11. *Sears*, p. xxii-xxiii.

12. *Sears*, p. xxviii-xxxi.

13. *Sears*, p. xxviii.

14. Much of the foregoing discussion is based on this essay.

15. Melvil Dewey, *Abridged Dewey Decimal Classification and Relative Index*, Edition 14, edited by Joan S. Mitchell, et al. (Dublin, OH: OCLC, 2004). DDC, Dewey, Dewey Decimal Classification, and WebDewey are registered trademarks of OCLC.

16. *Sears*, p. xl.

SUGGESTED READING

Ferguson, Bobby. *Subject Analysis: Blitz Cataloging Workbook*. Englewood, Colo.: Libraries Unlimited, 1998. Chapter 2: Sears List of Subject Headings.

Foskett, A. C. *The Subject Approach to Information*. 5th ed. London: Library Association Publishing, 1996, pp. 348–353.

Intner, Sheila S., and Jean Weihs. *Standard Cataloging for School and Public Libraries*. 3rd ed. Englewood, Colo.: Libraries Unlimited, 2001. Chapter 8: Sears List of Subject Headings.

"Principles of the Sears List of Subject Headings." In *Sears List of Subject Headings*. 18th ed., Joseph Miller, editor; Joan Goodsell, associate editor. New York: H. W. Wilson, 2004, pp. xv–xxxix.

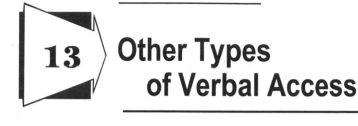

Other Types
of Verbal Access

INTRODUCTION

For well over a century libraries have provided subject retrieval from their holdings through the use of pre-coordinate lists of integrated and cross-referenced topical headings. The preceding chapters have discussed *Library of Congress Subject Headings* (*LCSH*) and *Sears List of Subject Headings* (*Sears*), which remain the most universally recognized linguistic tools for analyzing library collections. Recent developments in information science offer new modes of indexing that throw both practical and theoretical light on traditional subject lists. Some of the techniques are offered as supplements, or substitutes, for traditional subject catalogs. This chapter reviews those enterprises most pertinent to library subject retrieval and explains briefly the applications of the more successful ones.

DEVELOPMENTS IN DOCUMENT
INDEXING

The word *index* still connotes book and periodical indexes more often than it does subject catalogs for library collections. However, library indexes and catalogs are nearly as old as alphabets, being present in some form with almost every organized collection of written records as far back as the early Mesopotamian and Egyptian archives. In the final years of the nineteenth and the early years of the twentieth centuries, catalogers frequently made numerous "analytics" for significant informational works in their libraries. Books were expensive. The high cost of acquisitions and the relative scarcity of printed materials were countered with efforts to exploit collections intensively. Librarians were a captive labor force, often with "disposable time" on the job. And what more profitable "pick-up work" could there be than making analytic indexes to anthologies and treatises? If the cards followed standard cataloging practices they were filed into the official catalog. If they were less carefully constructed, they might be kept in a desk drawer or a shoe box in the reference department. John Rothman wrote about a continuing reciprocity between library classification and indexing:

Although indexing is often clearly differentiated from cataloging and classification, there is considerable overlapping in practice, and the development of new cataloging techniques or new classification systems is bound to affect indexing practices. Thus the development of the Dewey and other decimal classification systems for library catalogs was paralleled by the development of decimal, coded, and faceted topical indexing systems.[1]

Hierarchical Controlled Vocabularies

Controlled vocabularies with their systematized language that subsums narrower terms or subdivisions under broader terms are familiar to librarians in many contexts. We spoke in previous chapters of their use for library subject catalogs. The commercial arena, where indexes are created to analyze periodical articles, anthologies, report literature, patents, and the like for rapid retrieval in nearly all disciplines, has also turned to controlled vocabularies, usually called *thesauri*.

The terms *thesaurus* and *subject heading list* are often used interchangeably in the literature, but they are not really the same. Since 1974 there have been international standard guidelines for thesauri.[2] There have been no such standards for subject heading lists. However, at this writing, a revision of ANSI/NISO Z39.19 is going through the approval process.[3] Its title has been changed to reflect a change from a standard for thesauri to one for controlled vocabularies, including subject heading lists, synonym rings, taxonomies, and thesauri. Another difference is that thesauri are composed of "terms," while subject heading lists are composed of "subject headings." This difference has been described by Mary Dykstra.[4] She said that in general a term denotes a single concept, while a subject heading may consist of composites of terms, although a subject heading may also consist of a single concept. Yet another difference lies in the way terms and subjects are related to each other (i.e., the syndetic structure). The guidelines for thesauri give rules for establishing hierarchical relationships and for assigning related (or associative) terms. While LCSH also has rules that are used when establishing new headings, composite headings are more difficult to relate than terms, and there remain many headings and relationships that were established before the rules were made. Dykstra argued that by adopting the abbreviations used by thesauri to show these relationships, LCSH exacerbated the confusion that already existed.[5] A final difference is that a thesaurus is likely to cover a limited discipline or cross-disciplinary area, whereas subject heading lists tend to be designed for subject application to general or multi-disciplinary collections.

Discussed below are four thesauri from different disciplines that illustrate the range available. These four began their availability in print form. But with the rapid growth in online databases, thesauri have also moved online. For three of these (all except the *Art & Architecture Thesaurus* [*AAT*]), the online version is available only with a subscription to the database they are used to index. These three can also be purchased in book format, and at least one is available on CD.

Thesaurus of Psychological Index Terms

Thesauri usually have introductory material that explains how to use them. Introductory material from the *Thesaurus of Psychological Index Terms*[6] is available on the website of the American Psychological Association. That introduction provides a typical explanation:

> The Relationship Section is the most powerful section of the Thesaurus because it provides all the information about each term, including its definition, hierarchical relationship to other terms, and other data to help you decide whether or not to use the term in your search.

> The Thesaurus lists each term alphabetically and cross-references and displays each term with its broader, narrower, and related terms.

> PsycINFO periodically updates the indexing vocabulary with new terms. The year of the term's addition in the Thesaurus appears as a four-digit superscript.[7]

The introduction then goes on to explain posting notes (i.e., the number of times the term has been used in indexing records in the PsycINFO database), scope notes, and history notes. Term relationships are then explained and include "USE," "UF (Used For)," "B (Broader Term)," "N (Narrower Term)," and "R (Related Term)."

It can be seen that such designations of terms and term relationships influenced the usages now found in LCSH. An example of an entry from the print version of this thesaurus is:

Communication Skills[1973]
PN   3724   **SC** 10540
SN   Individual ability or competency in any type
of communication. Limited to human populations.
    UF   Communicative Competence
    B   Ability [1967]
    N   Language Proficiency [1988]
       Rhetoric
       Writing Skills [1985]
    R   ↓ Communication [1967]
       ↓ Communication Disorders [1982]
       Communication Skills Training [1982]
       Pragmatics [1985]
       Social Cognition [1994]
       ↓ Verbal Communication [1967]

(Use of a down arrow in front of any narrower or related term indicates that that term has narrower terms itself.)

The online version, shown in figure 13.1, appears somewhat differently.[8] The indication in the online version that a narrower term has narrower terms itself is "[+NT]" instead of a down arrow. The scope note and date of entry are viewable by clicking on the "i" button beside the term.

Fig. 13.1. Sample online record from the *Thesaurus of Psychological Index Terms*.

Select	Subject Heading	Hits	Explode	Focus	Scope Note
▲	[Back up in List]				
☐	Communication	6875	☐	☐	ⓘ
	Communication (Privileged)				
	Communication (Professional)				
	Communication Apprehension				
☐	Communication Disorders	1014	☐	☐	ⓘ
☑	**Communication Skills**	3731	☐	☐	ⓘ
	[Used For]				ⓘ
	Communicative Competence				
	[Broader Terms]				ⓘ
	☐ Ability	3799	☐	☐	ⓘ
	[Narrower Terms]				ⓘ
	☐ Language Proficiency	1486	☐	☐	ⓘ
	☐ Rhetoric	667	☐	☐	ⓘ
	☐ Writing Skills	2717	☐	☐	ⓘ
	[Related Terms]				ⓘ
	☐ Communication [+NT]	6875	☐	☐	ⓘ
	☐ Communication Disorders [+NT]	1014	☐	☐	ⓘ
	☐ Communication Skills Training	1534	☐	☐	ⓘ
	☐ Pragmatics	1358	☐	☐	ⓘ
	☐ Social Cognition	3412	☐	☐	ⓘ
	☐ Verbal Communication [+NT]	10965	☐	☐	ⓘ
☐	Communication Skills Training	1534	☐	☐	ⓘ

Thesaurus of ERIC Descriptors

The *Thesaurus of ERIC Descriptors* uses the abbreviations for the relationships that were adopted by LCSH: UF—*Used for*; NT—*Narrower term*; BT—*Broader term*; RT—*Related term*.[9] "Use" is the mandatory reciprocal of UF, putting a non-postable term into place. Unlike LCSH, however, SN precedes a scope note. Under postable terms other kinds of information are also given. The date is the "add date" (date of first entry). Search strategies for materials entered into the database prior to that time should in most instances use different terminology. A posting count (the number of citations available when the current edition of the print version of the *ERIC Thesaurus* was published) is given for the number of times the term has been used as a descriptor or identifier in *Current Index to Journals in Education* (*CIJE*) and *Resources in Education* (*RIE*). A Group Code (GC) number is given to assist the user in identifying other Descriptors that are conceptually related to the term. Examples of *ERIC Thesaurus* entries are:

Dress Design
　　USE   Clothing Design

Drill Presses
　　USE   Machine Tools

Drinking		*May 1974*
Postings: 2,154	GC: 210	
SN	Consumption of alcoholic beverages	
UF	Alcohol Consumption	
	Alcohol Use	
	Social Drinking	
NT	Alcohol Abuse	
BT	Behavior	
RT	Alcohol Education	
	Alcoholic Beverages	
	Drug Use	
	Health Behavior	
	Health Education	
	Recreational Activities	

Again, the online version, shown in figure 13.2, appears differently.[10] The plus sign beside a term indicates that it has narrower terms displayed in its record. Interestingly, the scope note is not available in the record for the term itself. Note that the scope notes for broader, narrower, and related terms for "Drinking" are shown in this record. The scope note for "Drinking," itself, is shown in records for which "Drinking" is a broader, narrower, or related term.

Fig. 13.2. Sample online record from the *Thesaurus of ERIC Descriptors*.

☐   Drinking [+]

05/10/1974

Use For

Alcohol Consumption

06/09/1988

Alcohol Use

06/09/1988

Social Drinking

05/10/1974

Broader Terms

☐   Behavior [+]

The aggregate of observable responses of an organism to internal and external stimuli (Note: Use a more specific term if possible)

07/01/1966

Narrower Terms

☐   Alcohol Abuse [+]

Excessive or otherwise inappropriate ingestion of alcoholic beverages, often causing risk or injury to health and impaired social functioning (Note: If possible, use the more specific term "Alcoholism")

06/09/1988

Related Terms

☐   Alcohol Education

07/01/1966

☐   Alcoholic Beverages

02/11/1974

☐   Drug Use [+]

Medicinal or nonmedicinal use of drugs

03/05/1980

☐   Health Behavior

Actions, practices, or habits that have an impact on health

06/30/2000

☐   Health Education [+]

Educational activities that promote understanding, attitudes, and practices consistent with individual, family, and community health needs (Note: For study and training in the health/health-related occupations, use "Medical Education" or "Allied Health Occupations Education")

07/01/1966

☐   Recreational Activities [+]

07/01/1966

Inspec Thesaurus

A more complex example comes from the *Inspec Thesaurus* of the Institution of Electrical Engineers.[11] (INSPEC was once an acronym for Information Services for the Physics and Engineering Communities, but has now evolved into the word "Inspec.") The print version uses the following abbreviations:

UF:	*Used for*	indicates a 'lead-in' term from which reference is made
NT:	*Narrower Term(s)*	indicates one or more specific terms, one level lower in the hierarchy
BT:	*Broader Term(s)*	indicates one or more general terms, one level higher in the hierarchy
TT:	*Top Term(s)*	indicates the most general term(s) in the hierarchy
RT:	*Related Term(s)*	indicates conceptual relationships between terms, not related hierarchically
CC:	*Classification Code(s)*	one or more INSPEC classification codes used to indicate subjects related to that represented by the Thesaurus term
DI:	*Date of Input*	indicates the date the term was first used in the Thesaurus
PT:	*Prior Term(s)*	indicates terms used for the concept before establishment of the current preferred term.

Examples of *Inspec Thesaurus* listings are:

```
dynamic braking
    USE    braking

dynamic nuclear polarisation
    UF     dynamic nuclear polarization
           solid effect
    NT     CIDNP
           Overhauser effect
    BT     magnetic double resonance
    TT     resonance
    RT     nuclear polarisation
    CC     A0758   A3335D   A7670E
    DI     January 1977
    PT     magnetic double resonance
```

The *Inspec Thesaurus* is also available online within a database called "Engineering Village 2."[12] The record for "dynamic nuclear polarisation" is shown in figure 13.3. Online, the abbreviations are not used, and categories are in a different order with broader terms, related terms, and narrower terms in a horizontal line rather than underneath each other.

Fig. 13.3. Sample online record from the *Inspec Thesaurus*.

Search: **dynamic nuclear polarisation** >> dynamic nuclear polarisation

dynamic nuclear polarisation (Select) ⓘ

Used for: *dynamic nuclear polarization*
              solid effect

Prior Terms:
              magnetic double resonance   (Select)

Top Terms:
              resonance   (Select)

Broader Terms	Select	Related Terms	Select	Narrower Terms	Select
magnetic double resonance	⌐	nuclear polarisation	⌐	CIDNP	⌐
				Overhauser effect	⌐

Art & Architecture Thesaurus (AAT)

A thesaurus that is truly arranged in hierarchical order is the *AAT*. It is arranged in seven facets or categories: Associated Concepts, Physical Attributes, Styles and Periods, Agents, Activities, Materials, and Objects. Each facet is subdivided into subfacets, called "hierarchies." In the hierarchies the descriptors are displayed to show their broader term/narrower term relationships. For example, in the "furnishings hierarchy" one finds:[13]

      Objects Facet
      . . . Furnishings and Equipment
      . . . . . . Furnishings
      . . . . .furnishings
      . . . . <furnishings by form or function>
      . . . . furniture
      . . . . <furniture by location or context>
      . . . . outdoor furniture

At any concept in the hierarchy, one can look at the term record to see synonyms and spelling variants, related concepts, and a scope note. The record for "outdoor furniture" is shown in figure 13.4.

The *AAT* has strict rules for the establishment of hierarchical relationships and for related terms, which it calls "associative relationships." It has attempted to resolve much of the subjectivity that has plagued other thesauri.

Fig. 13.4. Sample record from the *Art & Architecture Thesaurus® Online*.

ID: 300165810

Record Type: concept

🔁 **outdoor furniture** (<furniture by location or context>, furniture, ... Furnishings and Equipment)

Note: Term generally applied to a great variety of furniture specially designed for use outdoors.

Terms:

outdoor furniture (preferred, C,U,D,American English-P)
furniture, garden (C,U,UF,American English)
furniture, outdoor (C,U,UF,American English)
furniture, patio (C,U,UF,American English)
furniture, porch (C,U,UF,American English)
garden furniture (C,U,UF,American English)
patio furniture (C,U,UF,American English)
porch furniture (C,U,UF,American English)

Facet/Hierarchy Code: V.TC

Hierarchical Position:

🔁　　　　　　　　Objects Facet
🔁　　　　　　　　.... Furnishings and Equipment
🔁　　　　　　　　........ Furnishings
🔁　　　　　　　　........... furnishings
🔁　　　　　　　　.............. <furnishings by form or function>
🔁　　　　　　　　.................. furniture
🔁　　　　　　　　...................... <furniture by location or context>
🔁　　　　　　　　........................... outdoor furniture

Related concepts:

related to .... **Adirondack chairs**
.... (armchairs, <chairs by form>, ... Furnishings and Equipment) [300171702]
related to .... **deck chairs**
.... (<chairs by location or context>, chairs, ... Furnishings and Equipment) [300037837]
related to .... **gliders (furniture)**
.... (<multiple-seating furniture>, seating furniture, ... Furnishings and Equipment) [300164278]
related to .... **picnic benches**
.... (<benches by location or context>, benches, ... Furnishings and Equipment) [300038524]
related to .... **picnic tables**
.... (<tables by function>, tables (support furniture), ... Furnishings and Equipment) [300039755]
related to .... **Westport chairs**
.... (<chairs by form>, chairs, ... Furnishings and Equipment) [300133811]

Sources and Contributors:

furniture, garden............ [VP]

(continued)

Fig. 13.4. (*Cont.*)

```
                        ...................... Getty Vocabulary Program
furniture, outdoor........... [VP]
                        ...................... Getty Vocabulary Program
furniture, patio........... [VP]
                        ........................ Getty Vocabulary Program
furniture, porch........... [VP]
                        ........................ Getty Vocabulary Program
garden furniture........... [VP]
                        ........................ Avery Index (1963-)
                        ........................ Gloag, Short Dictionary of Furniture (1965)
                        ........................ Stephenson, Rustic Furniture (1979) 90
outdoor furniture........... [VP Preferred]
                        ........................ Candidate term AVERY - 10/87
                        ........................ CDMARC Subjects: LCSH (1988-)
                        ........................ Fehrman, Popular Interior Design (1987) 44
patio furniture........... [VP]
                        ........................ Avery Index (1963-)
porch furniture........... [VP]
                        ........................ Avery Index (1963-)

Subject: ..... [VP]
          ........... RILA, Subject headings, unpub. (1975-1990) garden ornaments and furniture

Note: .......... [VP]
```

The PREserved Context Indexing System (PRECIS)

From 1970 through 1990 a system was used for subject access to *The British National Bibliography* (*BNB*) that was neither a subject heading list nor a thesaurus. It was called *PRECIS* (*PREserved Context Indexing System*). Derek Austin, one of the originators of the system and long-time director of the service, described it as follows:

> The system is firmly based upon the concept of an open-ended vocabulary, which means that terms can be admitted into the index at any time, as soon as they have been encountered in literature. Once a term has been admitted, its relationships with other terms are handled in two different ways, distinguished as the syntactical and the semantic sides of the system.[14]

PRECIS was a theoretically elegant system that relied on creation of controlled vocabulary following rules and principles rather than starting from an existing vocabulary. *PRECIS* indexers began by creating a phrase that described what the item was about. From this phrase, index strings were established in which each term had a meaningful relationship with the preceding and following terms. For example, in the string "Training. Personnel. Cotton industries. India." each word relates to the next.

But if a simple permutation places Cotton industries first, followed by the rest of the string (i.e., "Cotton industries. India. Training. Personnel."), the concepts of personnel and cotton industry are separated. In *PRECIS*, a two-line printout was used so that each term in a permuted index could always remain in context, e.g.,

> Cotton industries. India.
> Personnel. Training.

In this example, the concepts of cotton industries and personnel are still "next to" each other, and meaning is preserved.

The second main feature of *PRECIS* was the open-ended vocabulary which allowed new terminology to be adopted as soon as it was used. Each term was semantically defined and syntactically related by *see* and *see also* references to synonyms and other associated words. The term was assigned a Reference Indicator Number (RIN) that identified the semantic/syntactic package. When an index string was created, a subject package consisting of the string itself, associated classification numbers, and pertinent RINs was created and assigned a Subject Indicator Number (SIN). In this way, whenever the SIN was assigned to an information package the terms controlled by the RINs would be displayed in the bibliographic record. The terms could be updated without having to update every occurrence of the term in every record in the system.

The widespread availability of online keyword searching and the time-consuming nature of syntactic analysis and coding of *PRECIS* concept strings led the BNB to discontinue use of *PRECIS* at the end of 1990.[15] When a subject string is retrieved via keyword in an online system, it need not be displayed with the keyword in the lead position. It can always be displayed with the keyword in its context as it was placed in the original string, and therefore a major benefit of PRECIS has been made into a moot point by technological advances.

Coordinate Indexing

The post–World War II information explosion dramatized the values of good indexing. Older methods that had gone into eclipse were revived and improved. New theories sprang up to support other techniques. A major departure from the relatively simple hierarchical use of subordinate divisions and inverted modifiers in traditional subject heading lists was the idea of postcoordinate searching, in which the searcher could play a more active role. A coordinate index consists of a list of subject terms in a standard format. Each term is independent of all others, except for cross references, and is designed to retrieve all documents for which it is specifically relevant. A user can stop at the single-term level of search if he or she is satisfied with the results. True postcoordinate searching moves on to a second level. Taking two or more terms that together delimit a still more specific search topic, and requesting the records indexed with both or all of them, the searcher retrieves only those items that have been indexed under all the chosen terms.

Suppose the searcher is looking for material on the use of solar energy for drying grain. The index might offer the terms "Solar energy," "Heat engines," and "Grain." Perhaps five document citations emerge because they are all entered under all three terms. In a traditional printed subject catalog this type of postcoordinate searching is awkward and difficult. The underlying assumption is that the list itself is precoordinate. That is, the assimilation and matching of concepts has already been done by the cataloger and is implicit in the terminology of the list. For example, *LCSH* offers the subject headings "**Solar energy in agriculture**" and

"**Grain—Drying**" as subject identifiers for the above items. In a printed catalog there would be no way of matching the two concepts to specify the available items except by comparing subject entries under each heading or examining full bibliographic records to find those on which both headings were traced.

In postcoordinate indexing, the coordination of terms is the responsibility of the searcher, rather than of the subject cataloger. The terms are usually single nouns, and the specific documents may be identified with accession numbers rather than hierarchical classification or call numbers. In 1953 Mortimer Taube introduced what he called the Uniterm index, to emphasize its postcoordinate use of single terms as opposed to composite headings.[16] It was primarily a manual system, using cards with headings displayed at the top and 10 columns in which document accession numbers could be entered according to the number's final digit. For example, documents 56A, 306, 96, 1176, and 1006 might all be listed in column 6 of each of the three cards bearing the Uniterms "Solar energy," "Heat engines," and "Grain." The technique, known as terminal digit posting, has been most successful in its computerized applications, where some of the tediousness and error-proneness of manual listing is forestalled.

To overcome the disadvantages of a visual search, other modes of postcoordinate indexing were soon developed. Mechanical scanning devices were based on the fact that cards could be precisely gridded for punched holes to replace the columns of written or printed numbers. Two or more of these punched cards (e.g., the three carrying the headings "Solar energy," "Heat engines," and "Grain") could be laid together and held up to the light, or otherwise probed, to extract the reference numbers that they indexed in common. Several brands of these cards were marketed, variously called optical coincidence cards, peek-a-boo cards, or feature cards.

A newer form of coordinate indexing is that created by keyword access in online catalogs and other databases. This has been described by Bates (italics original):

> [I]n fact, *online search capabilities themselves constitute a form of indexing*. Subject access to online catalogs is thus a combination of original indexing and what we might call "search capabilities indexing." . . .
>
> Typical online search capabilities are keyword searching, Boolean searching, truncation, and multi-index searching (that is, combining query terms from more than one index, e.g., "FIND TITLE Grapes AND FIND AUTHOR Steinbeck").
>
> . . . When an online catalog simply possesses the capability of being searched by title keyword, in effect a whole new index is added to the catalog, with every title word an index term, even though the whole index is not seen printed out.[17]

Typically, online catalogs with keyword access allow the user to input several search terms to be searched at once with an implicit Boolean "and" in operation. That is, a keyword search may be "solar energy grain," which the system interprets to mean "Find bibliographic records that have the words 'solar' AND 'energy' AND 'grain'." While this method can yield false drops (e.g., "Electrical energy characterization of grain boundaries in gallium arsenide and their relationship to solar cell performance"), it can also yield a number of useful retrievals in much less time than that needed for manual indexing. It cannot be a complete substitute for manual indexing, however, because keyword vocabulary is not controlled (i.e., no connections are made between synonyms, variant word forms, related terms, etc.), not all titles contain subject-content words, and authors writing on the same concepts use different words to express those concepts.

The commands used to retrieve information from computer databases nearly all make use of the Boolean logic operators *and*, *or*, and *not*. With these machine-manipulated instructions, search commands that are highly sophisticated and very powerful examples of postcoordinate searching can be executed. For example, someone using the ERIC database might want to examine material on the consumption of alcohol in clubs, at social gatherings, and the like, but not have to wade through all those discussing related problems of health. Using the *ERIC Thesaurus*, he or she could construct the search command "(Drinking *or* Alcoholic Beverages) *and* ((Behavior *or* Recreational Activities) *not* (Health *or* Health Education))." Since the commands within parentheses are executed first, all documents indexed under the following rubrics would be retrieved:

Drinking *and* Behavior *but not* Health
Drinking *and* Behavior *but not* Health Education
Drinking *and* Recreational Activities *but not* Health
Drinking *and* Recreational Activities *but not* Health Education
Alcoholic Beverages *and* Behavior *but not* Health
Alcoholic Beverages *and* Behavior *but not* Health Education
Alcoholic Beverages *and* Recreational Activities *but not* Health
Alcoholic Beverages *and* Recreational Activities *but not* Health Education

AUTOMATIC INDEXING METHODS

Indexers, like other human beings, are fallible, often are inconsistent, are subject to extraneous influences on their work, operate at a slow pace, and are therefore the most expensive component of an indexing operation. The idea of replacing human indexers by feeding part or all of a text into a machine that would assign index terms automatically, impartially, and with unfailing consistency and accuracy arose, therefore, quite early in the computer age. Success has, however, largely eluded the best efforts of many investigators and inventors.

KWIC and KWOC Indexing

The earliest automatic indexing method relying on the power of computers to perform repetitive tasks at high speed was invented by Hans Peter Luhn, an IBM engineer, who in 1958 produced what became known as KWIC (Key Word In Context) indexing. Luhn reported his system in 1960.[18] On the assumption that titles of scientific and technical articles generally include words indicating the most significant concepts dealt with, he wrote a program that printed strings of title words, each word appearing once in alphabetical order in the center of a page, with all other words to the left or right of the center word printed in the order in which they appeared in the title; when the right-hand margin was reached, the rest of the title (if any) was "wrapped around" to the left-hand margin and continued inward. A user had only to scan the left-justified middle column for a desired keyword and could, when the word was found, read the rest of the title "in context." The method worked indeed fully automatically (i.e., without any human intervention other than the keyboarding) and resulted in a quickly and inexpensively produced display of potentially sought terms. Most KWIC programs also employ so-called stop lists to eliminate common words such as articles, prepositions, and conjunctions from the middle column where they presumably would not be sought. A specimen of a typical KWIC index is shown in figure 13.5. This earlier and rather crude form of automatic indexing has, ironically, remained the only one that has proven itself to be practical and is still being used.

Fig. 13.5. Sample from a KWIC index.

```
ORMATION AT THE NUCLEAR  SAFETY INFORMATION CENTER.    & INF    AINPBX-0005-0346A
UNCEMENT MEDIA ON CFSTI  SALES.=               & OF VARIOUS ANNO  AINPBX-0005-0327
        IMPACT OF A LARGE  SCALE COMPUTERIZED SDI SYSTEM ON A    AINPBX-0005-0223
WITH NASA/SCAN, A LARGE  SCALE SELECTIVE ANNOUNCEMENT SERVI      AINPBX-0005-0217
     OF INFORMATION-SMALL  SCALE. DISSEMINATION - CHOOSE IT      AINPBX-0005-0239
     OF INFORMATION-SMALL  SCALE. EXPERIMENTAL TRIAL OF SELEC    AINPBX-0005-0243
     OF INFORMATION-LARGE  SCALE. IMPACT OF A LARGE SCALE        AINPBX-0005-0223
  OF INFORMATION.  LARGE  SCALE. KWOC INDEX AS AN AUTOMATIC      AINPBX-0005-0211
     OF INFORMATION-SMALL  SCALE. MANAGEMENT OF SMALL, SPECIA    AINPBX-0005-0233
     OF INFORMATION-LARGE  SCALE. OPᶜ .TING EXPERIENCE WITH      AINPBX-0005-0217
ON OF INFORMATION-LARGE  SCALE. POL? MAN/S SDI.&DISSEMINATI     AINPBX-0005-0227
    EXPERIENCE WITH NASA/  SCAN, A LARGE SCALE SELECTIVE         AINPBX-0005-0217
TO THE DISSEMINATION OF  SCIENTIFIC AND EDUCATIONAL INFORMA     AINPBX-0005-0350A
         FOR FEDERAL  SCIENTIFIC AND TECHNICAL INFORMATI        AINPBX-0005-0311
   FORUM FOR SPECIALIZED  SCIENTIFIC COMMUNICATION.=            AINPBX-0005-0031
ATION.  LARGE SCALE. &  SCIENTIFIC DISSEMINATION OF INFORM      AINPBX-0005-0211
ATION-LARGE SCALE. &   SCIENTIFIC DISSEMINATION OF INFORM       AINPBX-0005-0217
ATION-LARGE SCALE. &   SCIENTIFIC DISSEMINATION OF INFORM       AINPBX-0005-0223
ATION-LARGE SCALE. &   SCIENTIFIC DISSEMINATION OF INFORM       AINPBX-0005-0227
```

An adaptation of the KWIC method, known as KWOC (Key Word Out Of Context), simply prints the sought words in the left-hand margin instead of in the middle of the page, the rest of the title (or the entire title, including the keyword itself) being printed to the right or beneath the keyword (*see* figure 13.6).

KWIC and KWOC indexing have, however, some severe limitations. For example, only words that appear in titles can be sought, while the article itself may deal with many other concepts not mentioned in the title. Since there is absolutely no vocabulary control (other than the elimination of stop-list words), synonymous terms are not available to users as potential access points for searching (i.e., there are no *see* references, say, from AGRICULTURE to FARMING or from SODIUM CHLORIDE to SALT). Also, many titles are not representative of the subject dealt with or are on purpose written to catch the attention of prospective readers without indicating the subject at all, e.g., "On the care and construction of white elephants" (on cataloging) or "The money-eating machines" (on computer management).

Fig. 13.6. Sample from a KWOC index.

CHEMICUS	Index Chemicus 4377.400 Q
CHEMISTRY	Abstracts of Bulgarian Scientific Literature: Chemistry 0554.515 X
	Berichte: Physiologie Physiologische Chemie und Pharmakologie (Chemistry) 1936.870
	Bibliographic Series: Institute of Paper Chemistry 1967.700
	Bibliography on the High Temperature Chemistry and Physics of Materials 2002.870
	Current Abstracts of Chemistry and Index Chemicus 3494.030 Q
	Current Titles in Electro Chemistry 3504.860 X
	Key to Turkish Science Chemistry 5091.830
	Papers and Patents from Olin Research (Chemistry) 6394.700
	Selected Bibliography of Pure Chemistry 8233.005
	Selected Bibliography of Applied Chemistry 8233.006
	USSR and East Europe Scientific Abstracts: Chemistry 9135.1014 X
CHEMISTS	Bibliographies of Chemists 1993.120
CHEMOTHERAPY	Cancer Chemotherapy Abstracts 3046.465
CHEST	Journal of Specialist Medicine: Heart and Chest including Tuberculosis 5066.130
CHEST DISEASES	Excerpta Medica: Chest Diseases Thoracic Surgery and Tuberculosis 3835.824 X
CHILD DEVELOPMENT	Child Development Abstracts and Bibliography 3172.942
CHILD EDUCATION	Exceptional Child Education Abstracts 3835.200
CHILDREN'S	'Courrier' of the International Children's Centre 3482.600
CHINA	Index to People's Republic of China Press etc. 4385.100

In addition, lengthy KWIC indexes are tiresome to scan, especially when they are printed in small type and in all capitals, as is often the case. Thus, contrary to the pun intended by the acronym KWIC, such indexes are neither quick for the user nor really indexes to concepts dealt with in texts but rather are listings of words that authors happened to put into titles. On the other hand, after the introduction of KWIC indexes, titles of scientific and technical articles became more indicative of their contents because authors and editors became aware of the fact that inexpressive titles would be overlooked in KWIC and similar indexing techniques.[19] In the social sciences and humanities, however, the custom of authors to give catchy and uninformative titles to their papers is continuing unabated.

Extraction of Words

KWIC indexing was only the first of the so-called derivative indexing methods, all of which are based on the principle of extracting words from machine-readable text—a title, an abstract, or even the full text of a document. Automatic extraction of words is generally coupled with *truncation* in searching, that is, the possibility of searching for a word stem without regard to its prefixes or suffixes, in order to retrieve a maximum of potentially useful occurrences of that word. Thus, a physicist looking for the presence of the concept "pressure" may search for *PRESS* (the asterisks indicating that prefixes and suffixes are also to be searched), which may give:

COMPRESS
COMPRESSION
IMPRESSION
SUPPRESSION
PRESS
PRESSER
PRESSES
PRESSURE
PRESSURIZE
PRESSURIZATION
PRESSWORK

While truncation (or "stemming") does increase recall, it lowers precision because it may result in unwanted and irrelevant items being retrieved (the latter known as "false drops"). At least two phenomena dictate this. First, homonyms cannot be detected by mere extraction methods—that is, in the example just cited, IMPRESSION, SUPPRESSION, and PRESSWORK do not pertain to "pressure" in the physical sense, while PRESS may pertain both to mechanical equipment and to newspapers, the latter being of no interest to a physicist. Second, the elimination of "common" words by a stop list may also result in false drops whenever relationships are of importance, e.g., a Boolean search for TEACHERS *and* STUDENTS *and* EVALUATION will retrieve both teachers' evaluation of students and students' evaluation of teachers, because the elimination of the crucial words "of " and "by" makes it impossible to know who does what to whom.

For a time it was tried to correct the lack of indicators of relationships in derivative indexing by so-called *links* and *roles*, the former making explicit which words were linked to each other in a relationship, while the latter indicated functions (e.g., acting "as" or "for" something). These devices led indeed to higher precision, but they had to be assigned at the input stage by human beings. As that greatly diminished any gains made by automatic extraction of terms, the method was soon abandoned.

Term Frequency Methods

On the assumption that terms (other than common words) to be indexed are those occurring either very frequently in a text (and therefore indicating concepts dealt with) or very seldom (indicating a topic mentioned expressly only once or twice in the title or first paragraph but then being referred to by "it" or "this" and the like), methods were designed to perform automatic indexing on the basis of frequency of occurrence and co-occurrence of terms, using probabilistic models. Some investigators tried to couple such methods of determining how often a term is used (term frequency methods) with term weighting, i.e., assigning different degrees of importance to terms on the basis of what terms are used in a search request or on the basis of where and how terms appear (e.g., in the title, in an abstract, or in the first or last paragraph of a text, and whether they are italicized or capitalized), all of which can to some extent be determined automatically. While these methods are of interest to statisticians and mathematicians, and some have produced acceptable results under tightly controlled laboratory conditions when applied to very limited subject fields, they have as yet not found any practical large-scale application.

Linguistic Methods

A quite different approach to automatic indexing is by syntactic and semantic analysis. Syntactic analysis is concerned with the automatic recognition of significant word order in a phrase or sentence and with inflections, prefixes, and suffixes that indicate grammatical relationships, while the semantic analysis approach seeks to analyze noun phrases automatically with the aid of stored dictionaries and other linguistic aids. The two methods are often used in conjunction. Research in the field of Natural Language Processing (NLP) has proliferated in recent years, and progress has been made; although the dream of information retrieval systems that can respond to a user's need through use only of natural language queries in full text databases analyzed only by computer has not been realized.

Searching of full text of websites by search engines such as Google makes use of linguistic methods when returning responses such as "Did you really mean . . .?" when a misspelled word has been used in a search. Such search engines do not yet have ontologies (see below) that pull together synonyms, suggest hierarchical relationships, or distinguish among several meanings for the same word.

Ontologies

Linguistic ontologies are used in NLP to assist in the analysis of natural language text. Ontologies in the field of Artificial Intelligence are formal representations of what, to a human, is common sense. Linguistic ontologies must formalize the reality of using language for communication, and include the realities of grammar, semantics, and syntax. Ontologies are similar to subject heading lists and thesauri in that they organize words into sets of synonyms, and then use relationships like broader, narrower, and related terms to organize the synonym sets. They are unlike subject lists and thesauri in their analysis of categories such as nouns, verbs, adjectives, and adverbs. They also do not necessarily designate preferred terms in the synonym sets.

Not all ontologies are linguistic ontologies. Some have strong underpinnings of categorization or classification. Others emphasize vocabulary and definitions. Most are designed to represent one particular area of knowledge. The OWL Web Ontology Language defines ontology as that which "defines the terms used to describe and represent an area of knowledge." The OWL document further states that "Ontologies include computer-usable definitions of basic concepts in the domain and the relationships among them."[20] The vision for the Semantic Web requires that computers and humans share knowledge. Ontologies provide the definitions of basic concepts which allow that sharing of meaning and thus are the building blocks of the Semantic Web. For more information on NLP, ontologies, and the Semantic Web readers are referred to Taylor's *The Organization of Information*.[21]

Computer-Aided Indexing

As indicated above, except for KWIC and KWOC indexing, none of the other automatic indexing methods has been applied on a large scale. For the time being, the large access services and databases still use human indexers and abstractors, even though their work is far from perfect or consistent, because none of the methods of automatic indexing invented so far has shown itself to be able to compete in terms of indexing quality or economic viability. Focus in research is no longer on automatic indexing methods, but computers, as discussed above, are increasingly aiding information retrieval in various other ways. In addition, computers are now widely used by indexers in computer-aided indexing, relying on stored dictionaries of synonyms and homonyms, lists of authors' names for automatic verification, lists of trade names and names of chemical compounds, plants and animals, etc. They are also used to take the drudgery out of indexing by automatically arranging entries in alphabetical order or subordinating subheadings and cross references in exact sequence under a heading, and by performing many other functions that previously had to be done manually and therefore were quite expensive and often subject to errors.

SWITCHING LANGUAGES

We have made a cursory examination of a number of subject access systems available for use in modern library cataloging. Most are self-contained, providing their own categories and terminology, with syntactical rules designed to express complex or multi-faceted concepts. Each exhibits both strengths and weaknesses. Not one has yet proved sufficient to meet all needs nor is demonstrably better than all others in every situation.

The information explosion, together with rapid developments in automation, has made intercommunication among subject disciplines, libraries, and nations both a possibility and a growing necessity. Several possible solutions to this problem have been proposed. One has been a movement toward "switching languages." With a multilateral translation program, materials already indexed would be more readily available, while libraries and information centers could avoid future duplication by joining systems of shared cataloging without discarding or revamping their own catalogs and indexes.

A number of attempts, such as umbrella (i.e., broad) classifications, have been tried and failed. A somewhat different approach was that of the BRS/TERM database, which was created to enhance online searching.[22] The vocabularies of six thesauri were organized into concept records that included hierarchical information and free-text searching suggestions. This kind of approach has an inherent linguistic interest that has led researchers to reexamine the structure and properties of indexing languages.

Another such project is the Unified Medical Language System® (UMLS®).[23] Started in 1986 by the National Library of Medicine (NLM), the UMLS aims to aid the development of systems to help health professionals and researchers in the retrieval of biomedical information from a variety of sources. Relevant information is scattered across many databases that use very different controlled vocabularies and/or classifications. The UMLS is comprised of three "knowledge sources": the Metathesaurus®, a lexicon, and a semantic network. The Metathesaurus brings together in a uniform format more than 100 different vocabularies and links different terminology used for the same concepts. It does not attempt to make judgments about the "best" terminology to use—the usages in the source vocabularies are preserved; but it does establish new relationships among terms from different vocabularies.

Projects in specialized subject areas like the one covered by the UMLS hold great promise. With these, the ideal of long-sought "switching languages" may finally be realized.

CONCLUSION

A number of approaches for providing access to information packages by their subject matter have been discussed in this chapter. Subject headings have traditionally been used in library catalogs, but indexes that provide access to journal articles, patents, and documents being published on the Internet have been making use of thesauri specific to specialized subject areas, and more recently have used ontologies and various automatic indexing techniques. Given the explosion of information and its availability, research into and development of new ways to provide subject access quickly must continue.

NOTES

1. John Rothman, "Index, Indexer, Indexing," in *Encyclopedia of Library and Information Science*, Vol. 11 (New York: Marcel Dekker, 1974), p. 289.

2. International Organization for Standardization, *Documentation: Guidelines for the Establishment and Development of Monolingual Thesauri*, 2nd ed. ISO 2788 (Geneva: ISO, 1986, first edition published in 1974); British Standards Institution, *British Standard Guide to Establishment and Development of Monolingual Thesauri*, BS 5723 [Rev. ed.] (London: BSI, 1987); American National Standards Institute, *American National Standard Guidelines for Thesaurus Structure, Construction, and Use*, ANSI Z39.19–1980 (New York: ANSI, 1980).

3. National Information Standards Organization, *Guidelines for the Construction, Format, and Management of Monolingual Controlled Vocabularies*, ANSI/NISO Z39.19-200x (draft standard) (Bethesda, Md.: NISO Press, 2005).

4. Mary Dykstra, "LC Subject Headings Disguised as a Thesaurus," *Library Journal* 113 (March 1, 1988): 42–46.

5. Dykstra, "LC Subject Headings Disguised," p. 43.

6. *Thesaurus of Psychological Index Terms*, 10th ed. (Washington, D.C.: American Psychological Association, 2005).

7. *Introductory Material from the Thesaurus of Psychological Index Terms* (Washington, DC: American Psychological Association, 2005). Available: http://www.apa.org/psycinfo/training/thesintro.html (accessed 2/19/2006).

8. Entry from online *Thesaurus of Psychological Index Terms*. Available: http://gateway.ut.ovid.com/gw1/ovidweb.cgi [requires subscription] (accessed 2/19/2006).

9. *Thesaurus of ERIC Descriptors*, 14th ed. (Phoenix, Ariz.: Oryx Press, 2001).

10. Entry from online *ERIC Thesaurus*. Available: http://oh1.csa.com/ids70/thesaurus.php [requires subscription] (accessed 2/19/2006).

11. *Inspec Thesaurus*, 2004 [ed.] (London: Institution of Electrical Engineers, 2004). Also available as part of the *Inspec Search Aids CD-ROM*. (See: http://www.iee.org/publish/support/inspec/document/thes/ for publication and purchase information; accessed 2/19/2006.)

12. *Inspec Thesaurus* in "Engineering Village 2." Available: http://www.engineeringvillage2.org/ [requires subscription] (accessed 2/19/2006).

13. *Art & Architecture Thesaurus® Online*. Available: http://www.getty.edu/research/conducting_research/vocabularies/aat (accessed 2/19/2006).

14. Derek Austin, "Progress in Documentation: The Development of PRECIS: A Theoretical and Technical History," *Journal of Documentation* 30 (March 1974): 47. In addition to this excellent article, the serious student is referred to: Derek Austin, *PRECIS: A Manual of Concept Analysis and Subject Indexing*, 2nd ed. (London: British Library, 1984); *The PRECIS Index System: Principles, Applications, and Prospects*, Proceedings of the Interna-

tional PRECIS Workshop, ed. by Hans H. Wellisch (New York: H. W. Wilson, 1977); and M. Mahapatra and S. C. Biswas, "PRECIS: Its Theory and Application—An Extended State-of-the-Art Review from the Beginning up to 1982," *Libri* 33 (December 1983): 316–330.

15.   National Bibliographic Service, *Newsletter* no. 1 (June/July 1990): 3–4.

16.   Mortimer Taube and Associates, *Studies in Coordinate Indexing* (Washington, D.C.: Documentation, Inc., 1953).

17.   Marcia J. Bates, "Rethinking Subject Cataloging in the Online Environment," *Library Resources & Technical Services* 33, no. 4 (October 1989): 401.

18.   Hans Peter Luhn, "Keyword in Context Index for Technical Literature (KWIC Index)," *American Documentation* 11 (1960): 288–295.

19.   J. J. Tocatlian, "Are Titles of Chemical Papers Becoming More Informative?" *Journal of the American Society for Information Science* 21 (1970): 345–350.

20.   *Web Ontology Language (OWL) Use Cases and Requirements*, W3C Recommendation, 10 February 2004. Available: http://www.w3.org/TR/webont-req/ (accessed 2/19/2006)

21.   Arlene G. Taylor, *The Organization of Information*, 2nd ed. (Westport, Conn.: Libraries Unlimited, 2004), pp. 282–288.

22.   Sara D. Knapp, "Creating BRS/TERM, a Vocabulary Database for Searchers," *Database* 7, no. 4 (December 1984): 70–75.

23.   National Library of Medicine, "Unified Medical Language System (UMLS)." Available: http://www.nlm.nih.gov/research/umls/ (accessed 2/19/2006).

SUGGESTED READING

Anderson, James D., and José Pérez-Carballo. *Information Retrieval Design: Principles and Options for Information Description, Organization, Display, and Access in Information Retrieval Databases, Digital Libraries, Catalogs, and Indexes.* St. Petersburg, Fla.: Ometeca Institute, 2005. Chapter 8: "Analysis and Indexing Methods."

Bates, Marcia J. "Rethinking Subject Cataloging in the Online Environment." *Library Resources & Technical Services* 33, no. 4 (October 1989): 400–419.

Foskett, A. C. *The Subject Approach to Information.* 5th ed. London: Library Association Publishing, 1996. Part IV (Chapters 25–27): Post-coordinate Indexing Languages.

Harvey, Ross, and Philip Hider. *Organising Knowledge in a Global Society: Principles and Practice in Libraries and Information Centres.* Wagga Wagga, NSW: Centre for Information Studies, 2004. Chapter 8: "Alphabetical Subject Access Mechanisms," and Chapter 9: "Subject Access to Web Content."

Lancaster, F. W. *Indexing and Abstracting in Theory and Practice.* 3rd ed. Champaign, Ill.: University of Illinois, Graduate School of Library and Information Science, 2003.

Mann, Thomas. *Library Research Models: A Guide to Classification, Cataloging, and Computers*. New York: Oxford University Press, 1993. Chapter 5: The Traditional Library Science Model. Part Three: Published Bibliographies and Indexes.

McKiernan, Gerry. *Beyond Bookmarks: Schemes for Organizing the Web*. Available: http://www.public.iastate.edu/~CYBERSTACKS/ CTW.htm (accessed 2/14/2006).

Classification
of Library Materials

INTRODUCTION

Collections in libraries of any appreciable size are arranged according to some system, and the arrangement is generally referred to as classification. Whereas subject headings give a random alphabetic approach to the concepts inherent in documents, classification provides a logical, or at least a methodical, approach to the arrangement of those documents. Classification traditionally provides formal, orderly access to the shelves. In online environments it is beginning to be used to bring order out of chaos and to provide hierarchical means for browsing for relevant resources.

No matter what scheme is chosen, the purpose of classification is to bring related items together in a helpful sequence from the general to the specific. Ease of access is especially important if the collection is heterogeneous. It is convenient and desirable—particularly in the open-shelf collections to which many libraries in the United States are committed—to have, for example, all histories of the United States together, or all items on symbolic logic, or all symphony scores, so that the patron, who may or may not have one title in mind, can find related works in one location.

The ultimate aim of any classification system is to lead an information seeker to the information packages required. Traditionally in the United States this has been accomplished either through direct search of the shelves (open stacks) or through the help of a library attendant whose duty is to retrieve the materials on demand (closed stacks). Each system has its virtues. Open stacks encourage browsing, and thus stimulate intellectual awareness and foster serendipity. They work best with a logical, fairly comprehensible system of classification that encourages the patron's self-reliance in seeking items on a particular subject or its specific aspects. Closed stacks lessen the chances that materials will be mishandled, misplaced, or stolen, but they force a searcher to limit his or her own searching to the catalog and to wait for a library employee to bring items specifically requested. Closed stacks are valuable in a storage library situation where items may not be shelved in subject groups at all, but ranged in more or less fixed location by size, with consecutive numbers assigned as addresses. ["Fixed location" means that each item has one specific, fixed position on a particular shelf in the library as was the case in many libraries prior to the mid-nineteenth century. "Relative location" is a fluid, constantly changing arrangement of items according to their relationship to one another and resulting from the addition of new materials or the removal of old, weeded, or lost materials. In this system items may be moved from shelf to shelf without altering or disturbing their classified sequence.] Now, in addition to the traditional approaches, some libraries offer classified access to Internet resources through the catalog. And many websites, themselves, offer a classified arrangement to the hyperlinks accumulated at the site.

LIBRARY CLASSIFICATION

Organized documentary collections have existed since early civilizations learned to convert their spoken languages to written forms. Even before the codex book appeared, early record depositories received some form of utilitarian arrangement. Groupings were made by title, by broad subject, by chronology, by author, by order of acquisition, by size, etc. One of the earliest catalogs was the one known as *Pinakes*, compiled for the great Alexandrian library by the poet Callimachus in the third century B.C. Although this catalog did not survive, it is known that it arranged the entries in at least 10 (and possibly more) main classes, subdivided alphabetically by author. In the Middle East and in the Byzantine Empire it served as a model for other catalogs and bibliographies until the early Middle Ages. The monastery libraries of that time in Western Europe were mostly small and had almost no need for classification, but the university libraries of the late Middle Ages arranged books corresponding to the Trivium (Grammar, Rhetoric, Logic) and Quadrivium (Arithmetic, Music, Geometry, Astronomy), the traditional seven subject fields taught. Within the classes, books had fixed locations on the shelves.

Beginning in the sixteenth century, librarians devised many different classification schemes for the arrangement of books, but fixed locations predominated in most European and early American libraries until the mid-nineteenth century. The most substantive developments in the arrangement of library collections were concurrent with the rapid growth of libraries and their use during the nineteenth century. At that time librarians felt a definite need for better methods of arrangement, so that the content of their holdings would be available, and more apparent, to the user.

The history of modern library classification corresponds to the various attempts to adapt and modify existing philosophical systems of knowledge to the arrangement of materials and to users' needs. One of the best known early American classifiers was Thomas Jefferson, third president of the United States. He adapted certain elements of Francis Bacon's outline of knowledge, not only to his own library, but also to his plans for the organization of the University of Virginia and the reorganization of the College of William and Mary.

Bacon's system classified materials as functions of the three basic faculties: history (natural, civil, literary, ecclesiastical) as the function of memory; philosophy (including theology) as that of reason; and poetry, fables, and the like as that of imagination.[1] Its influence was widespread. Jean Le Rond d'Alembert used the Baconian system for the arrangement of the famous *Encyclopédie ou dictionnaire raisonné des sciences des arts et des métiers* of the French Enlightenment (1751–1765). Jefferson's classification was based on that modification as was the *Catalogue* of Benjamin Franklin's Library Company of Philadelphia (1789). Three years before Jefferson's *Catalogue of the Library of the United States* was installed at the Library of Congress (LC), a variant of the Philadelphia scheme was used to produce the 1812 *Catalogue of the Library of Congress*.[2]

Among other early followers of the Baconian system were Thaddeus Mason Harris, librarian at Harvard (1791–1793); Edward William Johnson, librarian of the College of South Carolina and later of the St. Louis Mercantile Library; and, finally, Johnson's successor, William Torrey Harris, a Hegelian who inverted the Baconian system, creating an independent American classification. At the same time, various adaptations of the Brunet utilitarian classification scheme existed in several American libraries as a direct result of its use to arrange parts of the British Museum and the Bibliothèque Nationale.

In 1876 Melvil Dewey devised his famous classification, now known as *Dewey Decimal Classification (DDC)*, based in large part on W. T. Harris's system, with a decimal notation.[3] Soon *DDC* was spreading its influence throughout the world. At about the same time, Charles A. Cutter began his work at the Boston Athenaeum. Cutter sought to achieve, not a classification of knowledge, but a practical, useful method for arranging library materials. Nevertheless, his *Expansive Classification* shows the definite influence of Spencer and Comte, especially in the development of its subordinate classes.

Toward the end of the 19th century, when LC had grown from several thousand books to nearly one million, it was apparent that the library would need a new classification system. After much deliberation, J. C. M. Hanson and Charles Martel decided to design an independent system governed by the actual content of the collection (literary warrant). This form of classification differed from a purely philosophical approach in that it was based on the books as entities. For this reason *Library of Congress Classification (LCC)* is more enumerative than many other schemes. An *enumerative* classification attempts to assign designations for (to enumerate) all the single and composite subject concepts required in the system. *Hierarchical* classification is based on the assumption that the process of subdivision and collocation must exhibit as much as possible the "natural" organization of the subject, proceeding from classes to divisions to subdivisions and following, at least in part, the rules of division as set down by "logic." *Faceted* classifications confine their explicit lists of designations to single, unsubdivided concepts, giving the local classifier generalized rules with which to construct headings for composite subjects (*see* the section of this chapter below, "Faceted Classification").

In summary, established philosophical systems of knowledge, with various modifications, underlie most traditional library classifications. The frequent distinction between classification of knowledge and classification of materials seems to have confused the thinking of many librarians. The two processes have important interactions. Even cursory examination of any library classification, including those purporting to organize "the items themselves," reveals an intellectual concept of the item as an expression of certain ideas in one of many available media. Philosophical classification organizes knowledge itself—registering, evaluating, and classifying thoughts, ideas, and concepts for the universal purpose of adequately representing the field of human learning. Library classification arranges the records that express and preserve knowledge, making adjustments as needed because of the physical format of such records.

For more discussion of classification theory and concepts, readers are referred to Taylor's *The Organization of Information*.[4]

TRADITIONAL CLASSIFICATION SCHEMES

Most traditional classification systems are basically both hierarchical and enumerative. By contrast, the more recent schemes tend to be faceted. In this introductory text the discussion includes generally all three types. It is well to remember that materials on shelves or in files are arranged in a single order. Most items can be requested by author, title, subject, or form, but they can be organized by only one of these at a time. Linear arrangement imposes certain limitations on the classifier. Over the years efforts to meet such limitations have resulted in techniques or features that are characteristic of nearly every library classification.

One such feature is a general works class, which accommodates items that are too broad in scope for inclusion in any single class. Such works usually overlap several traditional disciplines or "classes," e.g., encyclopedias, dictionaries, general periodicals, etc. In addition, genre classes organize materials according to their form of presentation rather than their subject content. Literary works, e.g., poetry, drama, fiction, etc., are the most obvious, but books of etchings, photographs, musical scores, etc., also fall into this group. Form divisions group items in a class according to their form or mode of treatment. For example, notations for outlines, dictionaries, or periodicals are used to pull together those presentations; and notations for philosophical treatments, such as research in a subject, histories, and biographies show the "inner form" of items.

A notation is a shorthand code for the class, division, and subdivisions chosen for an item. It may be composed of letters, numerals, arbitrary signs, or a mixture of these. Notation can be of two types, pure or mixed. Pure notation uses only one kind of symbol. *DDC*, for example, uses numbers only (e.g., 152.46, meaning psychology of the emotion of fear). Mixed notation uses two or more kinds of symbols. *LCC*, for example, uses letters and numbers (e.g., BF575.F2, meaning psychology of the emotion of fear).

A final feature of traditional classification schemes is the index. The index provides an alphabetical approach to the classified part of the scheme.

FACETED CLASSIFICATION

A faceted classification differs from a traditional one in that it does not assign fixed slots to subjects in sequence, but uses clearly defined, mutually exclusive, and collectively exhaustive aspects, properties, or characteristics of a class or specific subject. Such aspects, properties, or characteristics are called *facets* of a class or subject, a term introduced into classification theory and given this new meaning by the Indian librarian and classificationist, S. R. Ranganathan, and first used in his *Colon Classification* in the early 1930s.[5] Although the term was then new to classification, the idea was not (as Ranganathan freely admitted). It had its roots in Dewey's device of place (location) using a standard number (e.g., the United States always being 73) appended to any subject number by means of digits 09, a device now known as a *facet indicator*. Dewey recognized three things:

- That certain characteristics such as "belonging to a place," "being in the form of a periodical," and some others are general and should be applicable to all subjects

- That such a number must be clearly distinguished from the class notation for the main subject to avoid confusion

- That two or more facets could be combined to express a complex subject —his "number building" device (e.g., the subject "frost damage to oranges" can be expressed by adding to the class notation 634.31 for oranges the facet indicator 9 and the last two digits taken from the subject "plant injuries: frost injury" 632.11, to result in 634.31911)

Most other classification schemes designed after Dewey also provided generally applicable facets for places and time periods, and often also for forms. Even *LCC*, which is a more enumerative scheme, included such facets, although they were specially developed for each class as a part of the enumerative structure and are not uniformly applicable in all classes. The *Universal Decimal Classification* (*UDC*) expanded Dewey's "standard subdivisions" to about a dozen generally applicable "auxiliaries" (*see* the section on *UDC* in chapter 15). Finally, the *Colon Classification* introduced the fully faceted approach by means of class notations constructed entirely from individual facets in a prescribed sequence from the most specific to the most general.

Originally, Ranganathan postulated five basic facets: personality (i.e., the focal or most specific subject), material, energy (i.e., any activity, operation, or process), space, and time, known as the "PMEST formula." These basic facets were used to analyze a class or subject and to construct a composite class notation for it. For example, the subject "the design of metal ploughshares in the 19th century U.S." shows all five facets: from the most general to the most specific, 19th century is the time facet; U.S. is the space (or place) facet; design (an activity) is the energy facet; metal is the material facet; and ploughshares, the focal subject, is personality. It was soon found that these five basic facets were too broad and that most classes or disciplines needed tailor-made facets; e.g., the field of education can be broken down into facets for students, educators, teaching methods, subjects taught, level of instruction, etc.; agriculture has the facets crops, operations (sowing, harvesting, etc.), implements and tools, etc.

Each facet must have a distinctive notation and a facet indicator to show the sequence of facets unambiguously. For example, a classification notation from Ranganathan's *Colon Classification* is: J , 381 ; 4 : 5 . 42 ' N70.[6] It is for a book on the eradication of virus in rice plants in Japan, 1971. Each punctuation mark shows what facet is coming next:

, (comma)	personality
:(semicolon)	matter
: (colon)	energy
. (period)	space
' (apostrophe)	time

In the notation given, the first category is for a main subject, not part of the PMEST formula. Main subjects correspond roughly to academic areas. The breakdown of the notation is:

J	agriculture	(main subject)
381	rice plant	(personality)
4	virus disease	(matter)
5	eradication	(energy)
42	Japan	(space)
N70	1970s	(time)

A faceted structure relieves a classification from a rigid hierarchical arrangement and from having to create thousands of fixed "pigeonholes" for subjects that happened to be known or were foreseen when a system was designed. Such systems often left no room for future developments and made no provision for the expression of complex relationships. Enumeration is, however, not entirely absent from faceted schemes: the *Colon Classification* has some 50 main classes, largely corresponding to traditional disciplines.

All traditional schemes are essentially based on the strictly hierarchical genus-species relationship for most of their subdivisions. Faceted schemes recognize this relationship where warranted, but also display others, such as whole-part, operations and processes, agents and tools, substances, physical forms, organizational aspects, and many more as needed, for each specific field or subject. The design of faceted classification schemes is treated in detail by B. C. Vickery.[7]

A faceted class notation, such as those in the examples above, is not necessarily meant to serve as a shelving device or "call number" (although all or part of it may be so used) but rather for the arrangement of items in bibliographies and access service databases, where the faceted notation provides a helpful sequence, and the individual facets can be accessed and retrieved either alone or in any desired combination. This feature is especially important for online retrieval, which has been successfully applied to faceted classification, as a complement to verbal retrieval methods by subject headings or keywords.

The faceted approach is, indeed, not limited to the construction and assignment of class notations. It is clearly discernible also in verbal subject indication, e.g., a subject heading such as "**Newspapers—United States—Bibliography**" shows "United States" as the place facet and "bibliography" as the form facet. The "List of subdivisions ..." in the *Sears List of Subject Headings* (*Sears*) is actually a list of generally applicable facets (although it is not arranged systematically as it would be in a faceted classification).

Since the 1960s all major classification schemes (with the exception of *LCC*) either have been partially restructured on a faceted basis or display a fully faceted structure. The influence of faceted classification theory has been most conspicuous in *DDC*, which now offers facets not only for its traditional "standard subdivisions" and areas, but also for individual literatures and languages, for ethnic and national groups, and in completely revised schedules for such areas as music and biology that rely heavily on faceting in their internal structures. Special faceted classifications have been designed for broad fields such as education or business management, as well as for more specialized ones such as occupational safety, the diamond industry, library and information science, and many others (*see* the section titled "Special Classification Schemes" in chapter 18).

CRITERIA FOR A SUCCESSFUL CLASSIFICATION SCHEME

Classification schemes, as indicated earlier, vary widely. Besides providing for the subject organization of the collection, a successful classification scheme may also contain devices for indicating method of treatment or form of materials treated, time periods, places, peoples, various types of persons, and other special categories.

Any or all of these devices may be justifiably and successfully used for a special situation such as a rare book collection or a collection concerned with a particular subject area or period. Following is a list of a few criteria that may be generally applied to judge a successful classification system:

- **It must be inclusive as well as comprehensive.** That is, it must encompass the whole area of knowledge in the field of knowledge that it claims to represent. It must therefore include all subjects that are, have been, or may be recognized, allowing for possible future additions to the particular body of knowledge being covered. It must make provision, not only for the records themselves, but also for every actual and potential use of the records.

- **It must be systematic.** Not only must the division of subjects be exhaustive, but it must also bring together related topics in logical, comprehensible fashion, allowing its users to locate easily whatever they want that is available. It must be so arranged that each aspect of a subject can be considered a separate, yet related, part of the scheme, and it must be so arranged that new topics and aspects can be added in a systematic manner.

- **It must be flexible and expansible.** It must be constructed so that any new subject in its knowledge area may be inserted without dislocating the general sequence of classification. It must allow for recognized knowledge in all its ramifications, and it must be capable of admitting new topics or new aspects of well-established topics. The flexibility of the notation is of first importance if the classification scheme is to be expansive and hospitable in the highest degree. It should also be current. *DDC*, for example, is kept up-to-date with the publication of "New and changed entries" on the Dewey website.[8] These notices and revisions are especially important in subject areas in which a great deal of new work is being done.

- **It must employ terminology that is clear and descriptive, with consistent meaning for both the user and the classifier.** The arrangement of terms in the schedule and the index should help reveal the significance of the arrangement. The terms themselves should be unambiguous and reasonably current, correctly identifying the concepts and characteristics present in the materials being classified.

BROAD AND CLOSE CLASSIFICATION

Close classification means classing each work as specifically as possible, using all available subdivisions in the classification scheme. Broad classification collocates works under the main divisions and main subdivisions of the scheme, without using its breakdowns into narrower concepts. When a library has relatively few items in a given subject area, broad classification might actually be more useful than isolating each item under its own specific classification notation. A library using the *DDC* with a large collection of Bibles, for example, may need to classify the King James Version in 220.5203, whereas a smaller collection might cut back to the broad number 220. Generally speaking, *DDC* provides small libraries with more opportunities than does *LCC* to cut back to broader notations, because its enumeration stresses hierarchies of subject matter, while *LCC* has relatively few notations that signify broad categories.

GENERAL PRINCIPLES OF CLASSIFYING

Most of this chapter has been directed to the broad principles, methods, and problems of constructing classification systems. Some attention should now be given to choosing the optimum location for each item.

When classifying an item with respect to a particular collection, it is often tempting to arrange items with local needs in mind, but classification schemes vary in their hospitality to local manipulation. It is assumed that such possibilities and difficulties were considered when the choice was made of one scheme over all others for use in a particular setting.

Once the particular system of arrangement is chosen, certain general precepts enable the classifier to apply it meaningfully to the information packages being organized. The following summary is designed to aid that process. These principles apply primarily to both the *DDC* and the *LCC* schemes.

- **In general classify the item first according to subject, then by the form in which the subject is represented.** There are exceptions, of course. For example in *DDC*, in literature, classification is first by country/language, then by form, then by time period, then by author; in *LCC*, classification is first by country/language, then by time period, then by author, then by form. Subject does not figure into the classification in either case.

- **Classify an item where it will be most useful.** The classifier has to consider the nature of the collection and the needs of the user. For example, should a sports biography be classified with sports or with biography? The answer to this question might be quite different in a school library than in a library that specializes in sports materials.

- **Place the item in the most specific subject division that will contain it, rather than with the general topic.** This principle, of course, may be affected by a decision to use broad rather than close classification. Most libraries, for example, classify general French histories together and then subdivide the rest of the items dealing with the history of France by the specific time periods or local places they cover. To assign the same notation to all would result in a discouragingly large assortment of volumes under one notation. On the other hand, small libraries might prefer to classify all of their few volumes dealing with this subject in the general classification.

- **When an item deals with two or three subjects, place it with the predominant subject or with the one treated first. When an item deals with more than three subjects, place it in the general class that combines all of them.** This principle requires little explanation. The subject that is treated most fully should take predominance over secondary subjects. If two subjects are coordinate (e.g., electricity and magnetism treated equally in the same volume) the information package should be classified with whichever topic comes first.

  There are some refinements to this general principle. For example, if the work covers two subjects, one of which is represented as acting upon or influencing the other, such a work should be classified under the subject influenced or acted upon. Thus, a work discussing French influence on English literature should be classified with English literature. On similar grounds a work such as *Religious Aspects of Philosophy* should be classed under philosophy, not religion, since a treatment of some particular aspect of a subject should be classed with the subject, not with the aspect.

Another, perhaps more involved difficulty arises with the monographic series or collected set. (*See* chapter 5.) Winston Churchill's *History of the English-Speaking Peoples* can be classified as an author's collection of four related volumes under a broad "history" number. Or the classifier can place volume 1 with other works on very early Britain, volume 2 with those on discovery and growth of the New World, and so on. LC, at one time, often classified series and collected sets together, but has in recent years moved to classify series volumes separately in most cases. When series are classified together, LC catalogers often provide, for optional use by other libraries, an alternative, volume-specific classification notation.

CONCLUSION

Critics have noted limitations in existing classification systems used by most libraries today.[9] A few are summarized here only as a basis for further study. There is a long-standing argument over the logical arrangement of various systems. Although a scheme may be logical within itself, it can also have inconsistencies. For example, in *DDC*, language (400s) is separated from literature (800s), and history (900s) from social sciences (300s). In *LCC* language is classified with literature (classes P-PZ), and history (classes D-F) is relatively closer to the social sciences (class H). Arguments can be advanced for both approaches. Language is closely related to literature, but it is also essential to all disciplines. History throws much light on the social sciences, but every discipline and every literature has its own history that influences, and is influenced by, general social history. There is some evidence that the current trend toward faceting has lessened concern over achieving the one incontestably correct logical arrangement.

As mentioned above, *DDC* and *LCC*, the two most popular library classifications, are both linear and therefore uni-dimensional. Concepts found in works are multi-dimensional, but because classification is most often used to arrange items on shelves, only one number is assigned to each title whether it covers one subject or many. Classified catalogs address this problem to a certain extent because they allow the classifier to assign as many numbers to the catalog record as are appropriate. But classified catalogs have not gained acceptance in the United States. Instead, the many subject relationships among items and works are shown through a verbal, alphabetical approach—i.e., subject headings with references (*see* chapters 10–13).

Other limitations include problems of reorganization and relocation arising from the need to keep any classification scheme up-to-date. *DDC* and *LCC* both are regularly revised with new numbers being added for new concepts and with some concepts being moved to more logical locations in the scheme (e.g., computer science in *DDC* was moved from 001.6 to 004–006, and in *LCC* a new class, ZA, was created for "Information Resources," to give this rapidly growing area room to expand). Occasionally, a section of a scheme is completely reorganized so that the old numbers are reused with new meanings (e.g., 560–590 for life sciences was completely reorganized for the twenty-first edition of *DDC*). While such reorganizations and relocations are very logical from a theoretical point of view, they may wreak havoc for orderly browsing in libraries. Most libraries cannot afford to reclassify older items, so they either push all items belonging to a reorganized section together on the shelves and start a new section for the new items, or they simply give up and say that the number is only a location address in any case. A more in-depth discussion of this problem may be found in *Subject Analysis in Online Catalogs*, by Hope A. Olson and John J. Boll,[10] and in Taylor's *The Organization of Information*.[11]

Another problem arising from the process of keeping a classification scheme up-to-date is that the notation tends to become more complex and awkward as the schedules are expanded to include new subjects and to define old topics more specifically. In *LCC*, for example, digits are added after decimal points to place a new concept with older equivalent concepts. For example, in Z665–Z674.2, Library and information science, Z666 is for "Bibliography," and Z667 is for "Information retrieval systems." When "Information organization," an equivalent concept to "Information retrieval," was added, it was placed at Z666.5.

Related to the problem of keeping up with revisions in classification schemes is the fact that in most libraries, most of the classification numbers are taken from cataloging provided by an outside agency (e.g., a centralized processing facility or LC). These numbers are only as current as the time period in which they were assigned. A more in-depth discussion of this problem may be found in Taylor's *Cataloging with Copy*.[12]

In an international context classification is taken much more seriously than it has been in the United States. In a setting where many languages are involved it has been found that numerical and other symbols can transcend the language barriers imposed upon verbal subject approaches. As computer technology becomes more sophisticated many of the limitations mentioned above have the potential to be overcome, and classification may become an international means for subject communication.[13]

In chapters 15–18 some of the better-known modern classifications devised by librarians and used in various contexts are discussed. Their resemblances and differences are briefly examined, to show their actual and possible uses, strengths, and limitations.

NOTES

1. Cf. Bacon's *Advancement of Learning* (1605) and his Latin translation of it: *De augmentis* (1621).

2. Leo E. LaMontagne, "Historical Background of Classification," in *The Subject Analysis of Library Materials* (New York: Columbia University School of Library Service, 1953), p. 20.

3. Melvil Dewey, *A Classification and Subject Index for Cataloguing and Arranging the Books and Pamphlets of a Library*, Amherst, Mass., 1876. Latest edition is *Dewey Decimal Classification and Relative Index*, Edition 22, edited by Joan S. Mitchell, et al. (Dublin, OH: OCLC, 2003). DDC, Dewey, Dewey Decimal Classification, and WebDewey are registered trademarks of OCLC.

4. Arlene G. Taylor, *The Organization of Information*, 2nd ed. (Westport, Conn.: Libraries Unlimited, 2004), pp. 297–324.

5. S. R. Ranganathan, *Colon Classification* (Madras: Madras Library Association; London: Goldston, 1933).

6. S. R. Ranganathan, *Colon Classification: Basic Classification*. 6th ed., completely revised (Bombay; New York: Asia Publishing House, 1960).

7. B. C. Vickery, *Faceted Classification: A Guide to the Construction and Use of Special Schemes*, 1st ed. reprinted with additional material (London: Aslib, 1968).

8. OCLC, "Dewey Services: Updates: New and changed entries" (available: http://www.oclc.org/dewey/updates/new/default.htm [accessed 2/19/2006]).

9. A helpful list of articles and books on classification theory can be found in the brief bibliography: Phyllis A. Richmond, "Reading List in Classification Theory," *Library Resources & Technical Services* 16 (Summer 1972): 364–382.

10. Hope A. Olson and John J. Boll, *Subject Analysis in Online Catalogs*, 2nd ed. (Englewood, Colo.: Libraries Unlimited, 2001), pp. 192–193.

11. Taylor, *The Organization of Information*, pp. 308–313.

12. Arlene G. Taylor, with the assistance of Rosanna M. O'Neil, *Cataloging with Copy*, 2nd ed. (Englewood, Colo.: Libraries Unlimited, 1988), pp. 170–246.

13. Russell Sweeney, "The Atlantic Divide: Classification Outside the United States," in *Classification of Library Materials*, edited by Betty G. Bengtson and Janet Swan Hill (New York: Neal-Schuman, 1990), pp. 40–51.

SUGGESTED READING

Chan, Lois Mai. *Cataloging and Classification: An Introduction*. 2nd ed. New York: McGraw-Hill, 1994. Chapter 11: General Principles of Classification.

Dunkin, Paul S. *Cataloging U.S.A.* Chicago: American Library Association, 1969. Chapter 6.

Foskett, A. C. *The Subject Approach to Information*. 5th ed. London: Library Association Publishing, 1996. Chapter 10: General Classification Schemes and Chapter 21: The Colon Classification.

Harvey, Ross, and Philip Hider. *Organising Knowledge in a Global Society: Principles and Practice in Libraries and Information Centres*. Wagga Wagga, NSW, Australia: Centre for Information Studies, Charles Sturt University, 2004. Chapter 7: Classification.

Herdman, M. M. *Classification: An Introductory Manual*. 3rd ed., revised by Jeanne Osborn. Chicago: American Library Association, 1978.

Hunter, Eric J. *Classification Made Simple*. 2nd ed. Aldershot, Eng.; Burlington, Vt.: Ashgate, 2002.

Langridge, D.W. *Classification: Its Kinds, Elements, Systems and Applications*. London: Bowker-Saur, 1992.

Mann, Thomas. *Library Research Models: A Guide to Classification, Cataloging, and Computers*. New York: Oxford University Press, 1993. Chapter 3: The Traditional Library Science Model. Part One: The Classification Scheme.

Marcella, Rita, and Arthur Maltby. *The Future of Classification*. Aldershot, Eng.; Brookfield, Vt.: Gower, 2000.

Olson, Hope A., and John J. Boll. *Subject Analysis in Online Catalogs*. 2nd ed. Englewood, Colo.: Libraries Unlimited, 2001. Chapter 7: Bibliographic Classification.

Taylor, Arlene G. *The Organization of Information*. 2nd ed. Westport, Conn.: Libraries Unlimited, 2004. Chapter 11: Systems for Categorizing.

15 Decimal Classification

INTRODUCTION

Of modern library classification schemes, the *Dewey Decimal Classification* (*DDC*)[1] is both the oldest and the most widely used in the United States. It also has a substantial following abroad. Such widespread use is a tribute to Melvil[le Louis Kossuth] Dewey, whose original plan was adaptable enough to incorporate new subjects as they emerged and flexible enough to withstand the changes imposed by the passage of time. Dewey was born on December 10, 1851, and graduated in 1874 from Amherst College, where he became assistant college librarian. He actually began developing the first draft of his system for arranging books while working as a student assistant in the college library in 1873. He soon became a leader in American librarianship, helping to found both the American Library Association (ALA) and the first American library school at Columbia University. Being a man of many interests, he was also an advocate of spelling reform. He shortened his forename to "Melvil," dropped his two middle names, and even attempted to change the spelling of his surname to "Dui." Throughout his career he promoted librarianship by his teaching, writing, and speaking. In recognizing and acting upon the need to systematize library collections for effective use, he knew of various previous attempts, but found them inadequate.[2]

Dewey never claimed to have originated decimals for classification notation, but earlier systems used them merely as shelf location devices with no significant relation to the subject matter. What Dewey did claim as original, and with some justification, was his "relativ [relative] index," compiled as a key to the "diverse material" included in his tables. His most significant contribution was perhaps the use of decimals for hierarchical divisions. Combined with the digits 0 to 9, decimals provide a pure notation that can be subdivided indefinitely.

The first edition of Dewey's scheme, prepared for the Amherst College Library, was issued anonymously in 1876 under the title *A Classification and Subject Index for Cataloguing and Arranging the Books and Pamphlets of a Library*. It included schedules to 1,000 divisions numbered 000–999, together with a relative index and prefatory matter—a total of 44 pages. The second, "revised and greatly enlarged" edition was published under Dewey's name in 1885. Since that time 20 more full editions and 14 abridgments have appeared. The fourteenth edition, published in 1942, remained the standard edition for many years because an experimental index to the fifteenth edition, published in 1951, was unsuccessful. In 1958 the sixteenth edition appeared with many changes and additions, including a complete revision of sections 546–547, "Inorganic and Organic Chemistry." Since that time most successive editions have carried, besides other, less sweeping changes, totally

403

new developments of one or more targeted portions of the system. The present twenty-second edition (*DDC22*) was published in 2003; the associated fourteenth abridged edition was published in 2004.

DDC notations are assigned the tag 082 in *MARC 21* (the current MAchine-Readable Cataloging format used by Canada, Great Britain, and the United States; see chapter 3) when they have been created for a particular item by the Library of Congress (LC) or other national cataloging agency. In OCLC and other bibliographic networks a *DDC* notation created by a local library participating in the network is placed in MARC field 092. *DDC* complete call numbers are also placed in field 092, regardless of who assigned the *DDC* notation to the item involved.

Closely related to *DDC* is the *Universal Decimal Classification* (*UDC*), which was based originally on *DDC*. It is discussed briefly at the end of this chapter.

BASIC CONCEPTS

The system arranges all knowledge as represented by library materials into ten broad subject classes numbered from 000 to 900. Using Arabic numerals for symbols, it is flexible to the degree that numbers can be expanded in linear fashion to cover special aspects of general subjects. Theoretically, expansions may continue indefinitely. The more specific the work being classified, the longer the number combination tends to grow. LC records have been known to carry suggested Dewey numbers containing 21 digits, i.e., 18 places past the decimal. Such long numbers, however accurate, are unwieldy; it is hard to crowd them onto book spines and audio-visual containers, and dangers of miscopying and mis-shelving are multiplied. For these and related reasons many larger libraries have turned from *DDC* to some other system, such as *Library of Congress Classification* (*LCC*), which has a more economical notation.

Nevertheless, the *DDC* system has many advantages. Its content is compact, consisting in *DDC22* of a volume for introductory matter, the manual, auxiliary tables, and lists of relocations, discontinuations and reused numbers; two volumes for schedule summaries and schedule development; and a fourth volume for the index. It incorporates many mnemonic devices that can be transferred from one class to another (e.g., "–03" at the end of a classification number of any length often indicates a dictionary of the subject at hand). The classifier, once familiar with the system, can apply it to incoming materials quite rapidly. It provides a limited number of optional alternative locations and allows for great detail of specification. Patrons are likely to be familiar with it, because it is the system most frequently used in school and public libraries. Furthermore, it arranges subjects from the general to the specific in a logical order, which often can be traced by analogy through more than one class. It is philosophical in conception, being based on a systematic outline of knowledge that allows for subjects not yet known. Even so, the overall arrangement is not preemptively theoretical or logical. Dewey's intent was to provide a practical system for classifying books. This primary application to the books generally found in American libraries remains one of its notable limitations, although efforts have been made in later editions to rectify that bias.

A basic premise of the Dewey approach is that there is no one class for any given subject. The primary arrangement is by discipline. Any specific topic may appear in any number of disciplines. Various aspects of such a topic are usually brought together in the relative index. For example, a work on "families" may be classified in one of several places depending on its emphasis, as can be seen in the table below. Besides the aspects shown there, other material on families may be found in still different *DDC* numbers. Use of the relative index would lead the classifier to some of them.

Some *DDC* Class Numbers Pertaining to the Family

173	Ethics of family relationships
241.63	Christian family ethics
296.4	Jewish religious family rites, celebrations, services
306.8	Marriage and family
362.82	Families with specific problems
363.96	Family planning
392.36	Dwelling places [including those for families]
616.89156	Family psychotherapy
796	Sports for families
929.2	Family histories

The basic concepts of the system are covered in two places in *DDC22*: the introduction and the manual. The introduction gives detailed explanations of the schedules and tables and detailed instructions in classifying and building numbers with *DDC*. The manual is devoted to a discussion of the tables and schedules by number, pointing out areas of difficulty and explaining what should or should not be included in certain numbers.

In addition to the manual in *DDC22*, two outside sources provide guidance: *Dewey Decimal Classification: Principles and Application*, by Lois Mai Chan and Joan S. Mitchell[3]; and *Dewey Decimal Classification, 22nd Edition: A Study Manual and Number Building Guide*, by Mona L. Scott.[4]

SCHEDULE FORMAT

Summaries

At the beginning of volume 2, *DDC22* provides three summaries, showing successively the 10 main classes, the 100 divisions, and the 1,000 sections of the basic scheme. Each class consists of a group of related disciplines.

Summary of the 10 Main *DDC* Classes

000	Computer science, information & general works
100	Philosophy & psychology
200	Religion
300	Social sciences
400	Language
500	Science
600	Technology
700	Arts & recreation
800	Literature
900	History & geography

Each main class is separated into 10 divisions, although a few of these, as well as some further subdivisions, may seem to be rather artificially located within the class. The hundred divisions are shown in the "Second Summary," from which the following numbers are taken:

Summary of the Divisions of a Typical *DDC* Class

600	Technology
610	Medicine & health
620	Engineering
630	Agriculture
640	Home & family management
650	Management & public relations
660	Chemical engineering
670	Manufacturing
680	Manufacture for specific uses
690	Building & construction

Each division is subdivided into 10 sections. Again some of these may seem artificially located. The one thousand sections are shown in the "Third Summary," from which the following numbers are taken:

Summary of the Sections of a Typical *DDC* Division

610	Medicine & health
611	Human anatomy, cytology & histology
612	Human physiology
613	Personal health & safety
614	Incidence & prevention of disease
615	Pharmacology & therapeutics
616	Diseases
617	Surgery & related medical specialties
618	Gynecology, obstetrics, pediatrics & geriatrics
619	[Unassigned]

Volume 2 presents in detail the subjects placed in 000 through 599. Fully detailed schedules for subjects placed in 600 through 999 are in volume 3. In the full schedules, each of the 1,000 numbers that has subdivisions extending over more than two pages gives a summary of the "tens" place past the decimal point, e.g.,

612   Human physiology

SUMMARY

612.001–.009	Standard subdivisions
.01–.04	[Biophysics, biochemistry, control processes, tissue and organ culture, physiology of specific activities]
.1	Blood and circulation
.2	Respiration
.3	Digestion
.4	Hematopoietic, lymphatic, glandular, urinary systems
.6	Reproduction, development, maturation
.7	Musculoskeletal system, integument
.8	Nervous functions Sensory functions
.9	Regional physiology

At a few places within the schedules, multilevel summaries are provided. An example of this can be found at "610 Medicine & health."

Entries in Schedules

In the full schedules the 1,000 sections are listed separately, followed in detail by any subdivisions they may have. There are often asymmetrics attesting to the fact that the phenomena of the world cannot always be subdivided and re-subdivided into groups of 10:

Extended Decimal Subdivision of a *DDC* Topic

612	Human physiology
612.1	Blood and circulation
612.11	Blood
612.12	Blood chemistry
612.13	Blood vessels and vascular circulation
612.14	Blood pressure
612.17	Heart
612.18	Vasomoters

Successive lengthening of the base number by one (occasionally two or three) digit(s) achieves step-wise division. This pyramidal structure means that, in subject relationships, what is true of the whole is true of the parts. For instance, the medical sciences are a branch of technology; physiology is a medical science, etc.

A Typical *DDC* Hierarchical Sequence

600	Technology
610	Medicine & health
612	Human physiology
612.1	Blood and circulation
612.11	Blood
612.112	Leukocytes (White corpuscles)
612.112 7	Counts and counting

As the notation expands beyond the decimal point, *DDC* editors introduce a space after every third number. The spaces are inserted merely to facilitate reading the closely listed digits. On library materials and bibliographic records they should be omitted, so that the number will occupy no more space than is absolutely necessary. The final number in the example above would be written "612.1127" in a bibliographic record. The schedules rarely display numbers with more than four decimal places, although the relative index sometimes expands numbers to eight or even nine decimals. In the index we find "Radiation injuries — animals — veterinary medicine 636.089 698 97." Yet the schedules proper expand "636 — Animal husbandry" only as far as "636.089 — Veterinary sciences Veterinary medicine." Instructions at 636.089 in the schedules allow the building of the longer number found in the index. The concept of building numbers is explained later in this chapter.

Certain places in the schedules where fully symmetrical expansion cannot be maintained are given *centered entries*, which represent concepts for which there is no specific number in the notational hierarchy and which, therefore, cover an abbreviated span of numbers. These appear with centered lines immediately above them and with the symbol ">" at their left margins. Centered entries are always followed by a note that tells where to class comprehensive works that cover the subject represented by the centered entry, e.g.:

A Typical *DDC* Centered Entry

>   439.6–439.8   Specific North Germanic languages

Class comprehensive works in 439.5

Other useful formatting devices are the section numbers and running titles at the top of each page of volumes 2 and 3 (the schedules), the use of boldface and light-face type in various sizes, lefthand marginal indentions to indicate hierarchical structure, and the use of square brackets for numbers from which a topic has recently been shifted (or "relocated").

Notes

Perhaps the most helpful sources of information for the *DDC* classifier are the notes. There are several major kinds of notes in the twenty-second edition: notes that tell what is found at a classification, notes that tell what is found at other classifications, "including" notes (i.e., notes that identify topics in "standing room"), notes that explain changes in schedules and tables, notes that instruct the classifier in number building, notes that prescribe citation and preference order, and notes that explain options.

Notes found in the first two groups have what is called "hierarchical force." This means that they are applicable to all the subdivisions under the number that has the note, as well as to the number with the note.

Notes that Tell What is Found at a Classification

These notes include scope notes, definition notes, number-built notes, former heading notes, variant name notes, and class-here notes. An example of a scope or definition note is found at "553 Economic geology." The first note there reads, "Quantitative occurrence and distribution of geologic materials of economic utility." The second note at this classification is an example of a class-here note: "Class here interdisciplinary works on nonmetallic geologic materials." Such notes are used to list major topics that are included at a class and also to indicate where interdisciplinary and comprehensive works are to be classified. Number-built notes explain the source of built numbers that are included in the schedules, e.g. "559.9 Earth sciences of extraterrestrial worlds. Number built according to instructions under 554-559." Former heading and variant name notes begin with those words and seem self-explanatory.

Notes that Tell What is Found at Other Classifications

These notes begin with the words *class, for*, or *see also*. For example, at "070.9 Historical and persons treatment of journalism and newspapers" is found the note, "Class historical treatment of specific topics of journalism in 070.41-070.49." At "338.5 General production economics" is the note, "For organization of production, see 338.6."

Including Notes (Notes that Identify Topics in "Standing Room")

These notes provide a location for topics that do not yet have enough works about them to justify a separate number. It is assumed that there may be more works in the future, in which case the topics could be assigned their own number. Therefore, the rules for applying *DDC* do not allow number building of any kind (including additions of standard subdivisions) for topics in "standing room." The assumption is that the number in which the topic stands may be subdivided in a later edition to create a number for the topic, and so, if no number building has been done, all items on that topic can be classified in the new number for the topic simply by adding new digits to the general number. Standing-room notes begin with the word *including*. For example, in the library and information sciences section under "Descriptive cataloging," one finds "025.322 Choice of entry and form of heading." The first note says, "Including corporate headings, personal name headings, uniform titles." There is already a subdivision "025.3222 Authority files," and it would be possible in the future that individual subdivisions for corporate headings, personal name headings, and uniform titles could be made.

Notes that Explain Changes in Schedules and Tables

These notes tell a user of the schedules that there have been changes at a particular number since the last edition of *DDC*. There may have been revisions of contents covered, a discontinuation of coverage either for a whole number or for a part of its contents, or a relocation of all or part of the contents.

Notes that Instruct the Classifier in Number Building

Number-building instructions provide ways to gain greater depth of analysis at a particular classification. Number building is discussed in detail below.

Notes that Prescribe Citation and Preference Order

These notes help a classifier decide which of more than one aspect or characteristic to use for classification. Citation order allows the use of two or more characteristics (i.e., facets) in a specified order. Preference order establishes the order in which one chooses a facet when only one can be chosen. For example:

006   Special computer methods

> . . .
> Unless other instructions are given, class subjects with aspects in two or more subdivisions of 006 in the one coming last, e.g., natural language processing in expert systems 006.35 (*not* 006.33)

Notes that Explain Options

Such notes are usually given in parentheses and may be of benefit in providing alternative methods for handling certain situations. International users find that options for religions, languages, and literatures allow them to give preferred treatment for local needs. One option often followed is:

016   Bibliographies and catalogs of works on specific subjects or in specific disciplines

> . . .
> (Option: Class with the specific discipline or subject, plus notation 016 from Table 1, e.g., bibliographies of medicine 610.16)

COMPLETELY REVISED SCHEDULES

In *DDC21* there were three significant areas that underwent complete remodeling: 350–354 — Public administration, 370 — Education, and 560–590 — Life sciences. For two of these areas, public administration and life sciences, facets and facet indicators became a basic part of the design. Faceting in this form was introduced in the music schedule that was completely revised for the twentieth edition. It allows building of numbers through use of the indicators 0 and 1. Faceting makes possible the identification of meaningful components in a number both in the classification process and in the retrieval process.

In addition to those complete revisions, *DDC21* began a two-edition plan to reduce Christian bias in 200 — Religion. *DDC22* completed the relocations and expansions that were planned for 200 — Religion.

DDC22 has no "completely revised schedules" but nonetheless has some major changes. Dealt with in the twenty-second edition are updated developments and terminology for social groups and institutions in 305–306; improvements to the 340 schedule that relates to law of nations, human rights, and intergovernmental organizations; substantial updating of 510 — Mathematics and 610 — Medicine and health; movement of numbers for facilities for travelers from 647.94 into the 910–919 area with other travel-related concepts; and updating of numerous geographic areas in Table 2. Perhaps the most striking change in *DDC22* is the removal of Table 7 (Groups of Persons), which was largely a duplication of the broad outline of the schedules themselves. Classifiers are now instructed to use notations available in the schedules and in —08 from Table 1 in place of the former Table 7.

NUMBER BUILDING

A premise in working with *DDC* is that all possible numbers are not specifically printed in the schedules, but more precise numbers than those printed can be built or synthesized using tables or other parts of the schedules.

Adding from Auxiliary Tables

Auxiliary tables 1 through 6, found in volume 1 of *DDC22*, give the classifier one way to expand existing numbers in the schedules. Each number in these tables is preceded by a dash to show that it cannot stand alone as a classification number. The dash should be omitted when the number is attached to a classification notation.

Table 1. Standard Subdivisions

As was noted under the "General Principles of Classifying" section of chapter 14, all shelf classifications provide a dual approach. Some items are grouped on the basis of their subject content, while others are placed according to their form or genre. The standard subdivisions supplied in auxiliary Table 1 derive from what was called in earlier editions a table of "form divisions." The present-day "standard subdivisions" include examples other than form. Some actually do treat form (e.g., dictionaries, encyclopedias, periodicals, etc.). Others represent "modes of treatment," covering theoretical or historical aspects of the subject, such as philosophy and theory, history, etc. The following illustrates some of the categories to be found in Table 1.

–01   **Philosophy and theory.** An exposition of any subject treated from the theoretical point of view.
        Examples: 701 Philosophy of the Arts
                 720.1 Philosophy and Theory of Architecture
                 721.01 Philosophy and Theory of Architectural Structure

–03   **Dictionaries, encyclopedias, concordances.**
        Examples: 720.3 Dictionary of Architecture
                 727.803 Encyclopedia of Library Buildings

–05   **Serial publications.** Used for publications in which the subject is treated in articles, papers, etc.
        Examples: 720.5 Architectural Record
                 727.805 Journal of Library Architecture

–08   **History and description with respect to kinds of persons.**
        Examples: 720.8 Architectural Adaptations for
                        People with Specific Needs
                 727.808 Library Building Adaptations for
                        People with Specific Needs

–09   **Historical, geographic, persons treatment.**

Examples: 720.9   Fletcher's History of Architecture

727.809 History of Carnegie Library Buildings

Most of the standard subdivisions are further subdivided in Table 1. For example, under "–01 Philosophy and theory" the following subtopics are listed:

–011   Systems

–012   Classification

–014   Language and communication

–015   Scientific principles

–019   Psychological principles

The –09 standard subdivision can be geographically divided, through the addition of area digits from Table 2, e.g., "720.973 History of Architecture in the United States." This is explained in detail below in the section titled "Table 2. Geographic Areas, Historical Periods, Persons."

Unless specific instructions indicate otherwise, standard subdivisions may be used with any number if such application is meaningful. One specific instruction not to add standard subdivisions is found only in the introduction in volume 1 and is often overlooked. When a work does not "approximate the whole of the subject of the number," the standard subdivision usually should not be added. This was mentioned above in the discussion of notes that identify topics in "standing room." If, for example, a resource is about research on corporate name headings, it should be given the number "025.322" for "Choice of entry and form of heading." Because the resource is not about research on forms of all kinds of headings, and because there is no specific number for corporate headings, the standard subdivision "–072" for research should not be attached to the number.

Although in the table each number is preceded by a single zero, e.g., "–03 Dictionaries, etc.," it is sometimes necessary in the schedules to apply a double or triple zero to introduce the subdivision. This happens when single zero subdivisions are already appropriated in the schedules for special purposes. The instructions that cover such situations are explicit and should be followed carefully. A few examples will illustrate certain basic principles:

a)   **Standard subdivisions printed in the schedules**
       In some parts of the schedules a concept that is ordinarily expressed as a standard subdivision is printed with its own number. For example, "805 Serial publications" is printed in the schedule following "800 Literature . . ." Therefore, this is the number used for a serial about literature, not 800.5 or 800.05. Likewise, "501 Philosophy and theory" is printed after "500 Natural sciences and mathematics." None of the standard subdivision breakdown for –01 found in Table 1 is printed after "501," but one can use this breakdown at this number if appropriate. For example, a work on the concept of theoretical classification in the natural sciences would be classified "501.2."

b) **Standard subdivisions not printed and no instructions given**

   The most common situation is that in which standard subdivisions are not printed and no instructions arc given. In such cases a single-0 introduces the standard subdivision. For example, the schedules give the number "371.4" for student guidance and counseling. A work on the philosophy and theory of student guidance and counseling would be given the classification number "371.401."

c) **0-divisions used for a specific purpose; standard subdivision to be introduced by a double-0**

   An example of the double-0 appears at "271 Religious congregations and orders in church history." Single-0 subdivisions are used for specific kinds of religious congregations, e.g., "271.01 Contemplative religious orders," "271.03 Teaching orders," "271.04 Preaching orders," etc. Here the instruction is to use 271.001–271.009 for standard subdivisions. Therefore, an encyclopedia of religious congregations and orders in general is classified in 271.003.

d) **00-divisions used for special purposes; standard subdivisions to be introduced by a triple-0**

   An example of the triple-0 appears at "230 Christianity   Christian theology." Single-0 numbers 230.1–230.9 are reserved for "Doctrines of specific denominations and sects. Double-0 numbers 230.01–230.09 are reserved for "Standard subdivisions of Christian theology." Therefore 230.001–230.009 (triple-0) are used for "Standard subdivisions of Christianity." An encyclopedia of Christianity would be classified as 230.003.

Table 2. Geographic Areas, Historical Periods, Persons

When a given heading can be subdivided geographically and the library has many books dealing with that subject, it is recommended that the classifier use Table 2 (the area table), which allows one to expand the number systematically by region or site. It is by far the bulkiest of the six auxiliary tables accompanying the DDC schedules. Its general arrangement is as follows:

–01–05	Historical periods
–1	Areas, regions, places in general; oceans and seas
–2	Persons (Regardless of area, region, place)
–3	The ancient world
–4	Europe Western Europe
–5	Asia Orient Far East
–6	Africa
–7	North America
–8	South America
–9	Other parts of world and extraterrestrial worlds Pacific Ocean islands

Area –1 is used for the treatment of any subject geographically but not limited by continent, country, or locality. It allows diverse elements that have natural ties to regions or groups (e.g., frigid zones, temperate zones, land forms, or types of vegetation) to be brought together under certain subjects. Area –2 permits subdivision by biography, diaries, reminiscences, correspondence, etc., of persons associated with any subject for which the schedule instructions say to add the "areas" notation directly instead of adding "standard subdivision" notation –092 from Table 1. Area –3 offers specific subdivisions for ancient countries and areas up to the fall of the Roman Empire. Area notations –4 through –9 are for specific continents and modern countries. For example, area number "–4 Europe" has the following summary subtopics:

–41	British Isles
–42	England and Wales
–43	Central Europe Germany
–44	France and Monaco
–45	Italian Peninsula and adjacent islands Italy
–46	Iberian Peninsula and adjacent islands Spain
–47	Eastern Europe Russia
–48	Scandinavia
–49	Other parts of Europe

The area notations –41 and –42 were extensively revised in the nineteenth edition to reflect a thorough reorganization of British local administration. The area concepts of "British Isles," "United Kingdom," and "Great Britain" were at the same time relocated from area –42 to area –41. Area notation –47 was extensively revised in the twenty-first edition in order to make a more logical organization for the countries of the former Soviet Union. The area notations for several areas were revised and expanded for the twenty-second edition, e.g., –682–687 Republic of South Africa, and –74 Quebec.

Area notations may be added directly to schedule numbers where so instructed. For example, a general treatise on higher education in Dundee, Scotland, is classified in 378 in the Dewey Decimal Classification. The schedule at 378.4–.9 instructs "Add to base number 378 notation 4–9 from Table 2." In Table 2 one finds "–412 7" as the number for "Dundee City" (under –412 Northeastern Scotland). This number is therefore applied to 378, giving 378.4127, as the following analysis shows:

378	Higher education
378.4	Europe
378.41	British Isles
378.412	Northeastern Scotland
378.4127	City of Dundee

Where specific instructions (as in 378.4–.9) are not given for geographical treatment in the schedules, the classifier can apply the Table 1 standard subdivision "–09 Historical, geographic persons treatment" to any number that lends itself to that approach, unless localized instructions mandate a double- or triple-0 in place of the single-0. For example, the specific DDC number for savings banks is 332.21. To classify a work on savings banks in London, the schedule gives no specific direction to use Table 2, nor does it give any direction for specific subdivisions. So the standard subdivision –09 may be used directly. In Table 1 a note under "–093–099 Treatment by specific continents, countries, localities; extra-terrestrial worlds" says to "Add to base number –09 notation 3–9 from Table 2." So works on savings banks in London are classified in 332.2109421. The number may be analyzed to show:

332.21	Savings banks
332.2109	Standard subdivision for historical and geographical treatment
332.21094	In Europe
332.210942	In England and Wales
332.2109421	In Greater London

Although these examples result in long numbers, they are quite simple to construct.

Table 3. Individual Literatures and the Arts

Table 3, "Subdivisions for the Arts, for Individual Literatures, for Specific Literary Forms," is actually three tables: Table 3A, "Subdivisions for Works by or about Individual Authors," Table 3B, "Subdivisions for Works by or about More than One Author," and Table 3C, "Notation to be Added Where Instructed in Table 3B, 700.4, 791.4, 808–809." The titles of these tables are descriptive of their uses. They are never used alone, but are used following specific instructions. Numbers "–1–8 Specific forms" in Tables 3A and 3B develop and expand the summary form numbers that appear in the full schedules under 810, 820, 830, 840, 850, and 860. These mnemonic form divisions for kinds of literature are:

–1	Poetry	(e.g., 831	German poetry)
–2	Drama	(e.g., 839.12	Yiddish drama)
–3	Fiction	(e.g., 839.313	Dutch fiction)
–4	Essays	(e.g., 869.4	Portuguese essays)
–5	Speeches	(e.g., 891.865	Czech speeches)
–6	Letters	(e.g., 895.16	Chinese letters)
–7	Humor and satire	(e.g., 896.3927	Swahili humor & satire)

[–7 does not appear in Table 3-A and is not used for individual authors.]

–8	Miscellaneous writings (e.g., 899.2118 Tagalog (Filipino) miscellaneous writings)

Flow charts for building literature numbers can be found at the Table 3 instructions in the Manual in volume 1 of *DDC22*. These are of great assistance in following the massive amount of instructions found in the literature schedules and with Table 3.

Table 4. Individual Languages

Table 4, "Subdivisions of Individual Languages and Language Families," is used with base numbers for individual languages, as explained under 420–490. In a fashion similar to that of Table 3 it provides mnemonic form divisions for languages, e.g.:

–1	Writing systems, phonology, phonetics of the standard form of the language (e.g., 431 Writing systems and phonology of standard German)
–2	Etymology of the standard form of the language (e.g., 439.12 Etymology of the standard form of Yiddish)
–3	Dictionaries of the standard form of the language. (e.g., 439.313 Dictionaries of the standard form of Dutch)

etc.

Table 5. Ethnic and National Groups

Table 5, "Ethnic and National Groups," is used according to specific instructions at certain places in the schedules or in other tables, or through the interposition of "–089 [History and description with respect to] Ethnic and national groups" from Table 1. These applications are exactly parallel to the use of Table 2, which is used either on direct instructions in the schedule or on interposition of "–09 Historical, geographic, persons treatment" from Table 1. The Table 5 summary includes:

–05	Persons of mixed ancestry with ethnic origins from more than one continent
–09	Europeans and people of European descent
–1	North Americans
–2	British, English, Anglo-Saxons
–3	Germanic peoples
–4	Modern Latin peoples
etc.	

Table 6. Languages

Table 6, "Languages," is a basic mnemonic table used to indicate the particular language of a work or the language that is the subject matter of a work. It is used as instructed in the schedules or other tables. The summary includes:

–1	Indo-European languages
–2	English and Old English (Anglo-Saxon)
–3	Germanic languages
–4	Romance languages
etc.	

To illustrate, in order to classify a Bible in French, one would start with the entry given in both index and schedules, "220.5 Modern versions and translations [of the Bible]." For "220.53–59 Versions in other languages [than English]" the schedule direction says, "Add to base number 220.5 notation 3–9 from Table 6." The notation for French in Table 6 is –41. The resulting whole number for a modern French Bible may be analyzed as follows:

220	The Bible
220.5	Modern versions and translations
220.54	In the Romance languages
220.541	In modern French

Adding from Other Parts of the Schedules

There are a number of places in the schedules where the classifier is instructed to find a number elsewhere in the schedules and to add it whole to the number at hand, as demonstrated by the following example:

750   Painting and paintings

    . . .

758   Other subjects [other than those listed for 751 through 757]

    . . .

758.9   Other [other than the ones listed for 758.1 through 758.7]
    Add to base number 758.9 notation 001–999, e.g., paintings of scientific
    subjects 758.95, of historical events 758.99 . . .

If one wanted to classify paintings of library buildings, the number for the architecture of library buildings, 727.8, would be attached to 758.9, resulting in 758.97278.

In many other places the classifier is instructed to take a part of another number and add to a base number given in the instruction. The following example illustrates this kind of instruction:

398.369   Animals [as subjects of folklore]
    Add to base number 398.369 the numbers following
    59 in 592-599, e.g., rabbits 398.369932

At 599.65 we find:

599	Mammalia (Mammals)
.6	Ungulates
.65	Cervidae (Deer)

So, for a work on deer as the subject of folklore, the notation would be 398.369965.

More complicated instructions may give more than one directive for building a number. For example:

616.994   Cancers
616.99411–.99415   Cancers of cardiovascular organs
                       Add to base number 616.9941 the numbers
                       following 611.1 in 611.11–611.15, e.g.,
                       cancer of heart 616.99412; then add further
                       as instructed under 618.1–618.8, e.g., therapy
                       for cancer of heart 616.9941206

At 611.1 is found:

.1   Cardiovascular organs
.11   Pericardium
.12   Heart
.13   Arteries
.14   Veins
.15   Capillaries

At 618.1–618.8 is a table of digits to be added where instructed. Within this table one finds:

01–03   Microbiology, special topics, rehabilitation,
04   Special classes of diseases
05   Preventive measures and surgery
052   Preventive measures
059   Surgery
06   Therapy
07   Pathology

So a work on surgery for cancer of the heart would be given the classification number 616.99412059, that is, 616.9941 (base number) followed by 2 (for heart) followed by 059 (for surgery). "Add tables" of this type are found in many places in the schedules and must be used only as instructed.

When a single work treats multiple aspects of a subject, such as age, gender, and physical characteristics, the classifier must be careful to observe citation and preference order. As mentioned earlier, citation order allows a number to be built that takes into account two or more of the aspects. Instructions are given in such cases as to the order in which the aspects may be represented in the number. If a citation order is not given, then one must choose among the aspects according to instructions for preference. Sometimes one is instructed to prefer the aspect that comes first (or last) in the schedule, while at other times there may be a table of preference given. The important point to remember is to follow instructions. More detail about number building can be found in the *Introduction* to *DDC22* and in Chan and Mitchell's *Dewey Decimal Classification: Principles and Application*.[5]

THE RELATIVE INDEX

The "relative" index is so called because it is claimed to show relationships of each specific topic to one or more disciplines and to other topics. It contains terms found in the schedules and tables, and synonyms for those terms; names of countries, states, provinces, major cities, and important geographic features; and some names of persons. It does not have phrases that contain concepts represented by standard subdivisions (e.g., "Medical education"). Many *see also* references are given (e.g., "Organizations . . . *see also* Religious organizations"). Geographic name entries usually refer the user to the appropriate area table [e.g., "Macerata (Italy : Province) T2–456 73"]. A few referrals occur to the standard subdivisions and to other auxiliary tables (e.g., "Repairs ...T1–028 8").

The *DDC* relative index enumerates alphabetically all the main headings in the classification schedules, plus certain other specific entries not actually listed in the schedules. One such instance was discussed on pages 407–408.

In other places index terminology varies from that found in the schedules for the same class number, although the general meanings coincide. For example, the schedule entry "612.792 1 Glands and glandular secretions... Including perspiration" is a generalized representation of the index entry "Sebaceous glands–human physiology 612.792 1."

The classifier should, of course, consult the index, especially in cases in which the location of the desired topic, or the precise nature of its relation to other topics, is in doubt. Yet the relative index should never become a substitute for the schedules. It is coordinated with them, but is limited for reasons of space and cannot show hierarchical progressions or topical groupings. It will guide the classifier to some, but not necessarily all, aspects of a given subject. The next important step in the classification process is to consult the schedules for verification, perspective, and possible further instructions. Only by using the two types of display together can the full potential of the scheme be realized.

BROAD AND CLOSE CLASSIFICATION

Because it offers a wide variety of techniques and nearly limitless expansions in number building, *DDC* is hospitable to all the titles that a large library might add in any subject. It also offers various ways to meet the limited needs of smaller libraries. The classifier must remember that, in general, when there are relatively few works in a given subject area, *DDC* encourages broad classification. Digits in class notations after decimal points may be cut off at any appropriate place. Formerly, LC provided two segmentation marks to show where the abridged version of the number would end and/or to show the beginning of a standard subdivision. Effective September 1, 2005, only one segmentation mark is given in a number to indicate the end of an abridged number. The segments are indicated by slash marks. An example of the former practice is 940.53/18/092, which stands for "World War II—Holocaust —Biographies." A small library with a limited collection of materials on World War II might prefer to keep them all together under 940.53. If the library has several dozen items on the war, it might keep the ones on the Holocaust together by using 940.5318. If it maintains a separate resource collection for use by researchers, it could add the standard subdivision "–092" to distinguish the biographies. This number now would be given only one segmentation mark, where the abridged number would end: 940.53/18092. When a library decides to retain entire numbers to achieve close classification at particular points in the collection, it omits the slash marks, which were used in the LC record merely to suggest break-points.[6]

In catalog records created by other members of a network, the *DDC* classification numbers do not have slash marks. If a shorter number is desired, one must consult the schedules to find an appropriate break-point. For example, in the World War II Holocaust number above, breaking the number at 940.531 places the item with other works on social, political, and economic history of the war—not a very logical option. Breaking it at 940.5318 places it with items on the Holocaust, not subdivided by standard subdivision—quite logical. The classifier needs to check the schedules and not just cut the number at an arbitrary number of digits past the decimal point, which could result in an illogical placement.

UPDATING

New editions of *DDC* have been published every few years. Between editions, updating is accomplished via publication of new and changed entries on the Dewey website at the first of each month.[7] It contains corrections of errors, clarifications, updating, and expansions. Also available on the Dewey home page are other kinds of updating tools such as "Tips," "LCSH/DDC mappings," and "WebDewey quarterly enhancements."[8] A policy for "continuous revision" has been adopted by OCLC, which means that revisions are released between editions, and new editions appear as cumulations.

ABRIDGED EDITIONS

The first *Abridged Decimal Classification and Relativ Index for Libraries, Clippings, Notes, etc.*, appeared in 1894, the year in which the fifth edition of the full schedules was published. Abridged edition 14 is based on *DDC22* and was published in 2004. Like its predecessors, it is designed primarily for general collections of 20,000 titles or fewer, such as are found in small public and school libraries. It contains many fewer entries than the full edition; and tables, schedules, index, and manual all appear in one volume. The numbers used are compatible with *DDC22* so that growing libraries can expand from the abridged to the full edition as their collections increase.

WEBDEWEY

WebDewey offers online searching and browsing access to the *Dewey Decimal Classification*. In addition, it maps *DDC* to *Library of Congress Subject Headings* (*LCSH*) and links from the mapped LCSH to the corresponding LCSH authority records. In the case of Abridged WebDewey, mapping is to the *Sears Subject Headings*. Selected Medical Subject Headings are also mapped to DDC numbers. WebDewey offers a work area where a cataloger may build a number during the process of reading the number-building instructions. Local notes can also be added that will be displayed in context so that local classification practices are appropriately available. WebDewey and Abridged WebDewey are available as add-on services to OCLC Connexion, OCLC's cataloging service.

It is considered difficult by some to learn DDC by starting with WebDewey instead of the print text, because one cannot get a sense of the "big picture" on just one screen versus being able to look at two or more pages of text at once. However, for the experienced user, WebDewey can offer advanced means of display that are found to be quite desirable. For example, searching can be done using one or multiple indexes and by using Boolean operators, proximity searches, right and left truncation, and character masking. There are browsable Key Word in Context (KWIC) indexes of the Relative Index and LCSH and browsable sequential indexes of DDC numbers. Classification and table numbers are shown in hierarchical displays that show the position in relation to broader and narrower classes. Extensive use of hyperlinks gives fast access to related records and to entries in the Manual that are cited in notes for particular numbers. Top-down navigation through DDC is possible starting with a display of the ten main classes.

A tutorial assists in introducing new users to the best approaches for using WebDewey.[9] In addition instructions are available for obtaining access to both WebDewey and Abridged WebDewey.[10]

DIFFICULTIES:
LONG NUMBERS AND TOPIC RELOCATIONS

Among the difficulties built into the *DDC* system are its long numbers, which increase rather than diminish as the system grows, nullifying some of the mnemonic character of the basic system. For example, the number 636.08969897, which was cited on page 407 as coming from the relative index entry for radiation injury in veterinary medicine, is so long that any mnemonic associations between it and the number 616.9897 (from which it was built) are obscured. Librarians who wish to retain these long numbers because of extensive holdings in one or more fields should write them on items to be shelved in several lines. The above number could be written in short segments as follows:

636

.089

698

97

Related to the long number difficulties are the topical relocations that occur from one edition to another. Such surgery is forced upon the system by its limited notational base and the swift growth and change in the world of knowledge and of publication. An article by Pat Thomas written soon after publication of *DDC20* gives pointers on adjusting to *DDC*'s expansions, reductions, relocations, and revised schedules.[11] While the big rush, particularly in academic libraries, to change from *DDC* to *LCC* seems to have run its course, no library can afford to ignore all efforts to keep shelf arrangement contemporary with the shifts in knowledge as reflected first in the literature and then in the updates to *DDC*.

Decisions about updating *DDC* are made by an editor-in-chief and assistant editors in consultation with the *DDC* Editorial Policy Committee (EPC). The *DDC* EPC, a ten-member international board, represents interests of librarians in various kinds of libraries and advises the *DDC* editors and OCLC concerning the ongoing development of *DDC*.

UNIVERSAL DECIMAL CLASSIFICATION (UDC)

UDC was begun in 1895 by two Belgian lawyers, Paul Otlet and Henri LaFontaine, for the classification of a huge catalog of the world's literature in all fields of knowledge. Otlet wrote in 1897 that "this repertory will consist of an inventory of all that has been written at all times in all languages, and on all subjects. A kind of artificial brain . . . dealing with everything."[12] Otlet and LaFontaine dreamed of universal peace coming through the help of hyper-documentation. Although they did not see either world peace or completion of an inventory of knowledge, their dream of a repertory of the world's knowledge may be coming to pass on the World Wide Web.

UDC was based on the DDC (then in its fifth edition) but was, with Dewey's permission, expanded by the addition of many more detailed subdivisions and the use of typographical signs to indicate complex subjects and what we know today as facets. DDC's decimal notation was retained (except for final zeros), but for long numbers a decimal is placed after every third digit, e.g. 546.791.027*238 (the number for elements, with *238 being the atomic number for uranium). The 10 main classes as well as some subdivisions are still the same in UDC as they are in DDC, but class 4 (i.e., DDC 400) has been amalgamated with class 8 and is currently vacant. Many major and almost all minor subdivisions are now quite different from those in DDC. The main difference lies, however, in the synthetic structure of UDC. A work dealing with two or more subjects can be classed by two or more UDC class notations, linked by a colon sign (the most commonly used of the typographical symbols), as in the following example:

362.1 : 658.3 : 681.31 Hospital : Personnel management : Computers

for a work on the use of computers in the management of hospital personnel. Such a class notation is, however, not a "call number" but is intended for a classified catalog in which each of the three class notations may serve as an access point, while the other two are shown in rotation, e.g.,

658.3 : 681.31 : 362.1

681.31 : 362.1 : 658.3

If UDC is to be used for shelf classification, one of the three class notations may be chosen as a call number for a work on this complex subject.

UDC's faceted structure has its roots in DDC's device for indication of place, namely, the intercalation of —09 followed by the class notation for a country or region, e.g., —0973 for the United States. UDC uses many of the same place notations as DDC but encloses them in parentheses. For example, "plant cultivation in the U.S." is 631.50973 in DDC but 631.5(73) in UDC (note that the main class notation is the same in both). In addition to the place facet UDC also has specific symbols and notations for the language of a work, its physical form, nationalities and peoples, time periods, materials, persons, specific points of view, and recurring subdivisions in certain classes, all of which can be appended to basic notations either alone or in combination, as in the following example:

631.5	Plant cultivation—written in Russian
631.5(038)	—Glossary
631.5"17"	—18th century
631.5(= 97)(85)	—By American Indians in Peru

Due to this highly faceted structure and largely expressive notation the *UDC* has been used successfully in computerized information retrieval.[13]

UDC schedules were first published from 1904 to 1907 in French, followed later by full editions in English. *UDC* has since been published in whole or in part in 23 languages. It is widely used in many countries where English is the main or a co-official language (e.g., the British Isles, Canada, Australia, New Zealand, India) and in countries using other languages (e.g., Germany, Japan, Russia, Spanish-speaking countries).[14]

Until 1992 *UDC* was managed by the International Federation of Documentation (FID) in The Hague (Netherlands). When it became apparent in the 1980s that a more broadly based organization was needed to administer *UDC*, FID and the publishers of the Dutch, English, French, Japanese, and Spanish editions combined to found a new body, the UDC Consortium (UDCC). An early action of the UDCC was to create an international database that would be a master file. The database, called the Master Reference File (MRF), now containing more than 66,000 entries, is held at the Royal Library in The Hague and is updated once a year. An editor-in-chief and an editorial board of international membership oversee the continuous revision and expansion.[15]

Since 1992, UDCC has maintained the scheme by reviewing its content and initiating revisions and extensions. The results are published in *Extensions and Corrections to the UDC*.[16] A two-volume, easy-to-use edition of *UDC* was published in a "complete" edition by the British Standards Institution in 2005.[17] It is derived from the MRF. Supplements are issued each year, each one cumulating all previous ones so that one has only to look in two places for the latest notations. An abridged edition, containing about 4,100 entries, was published in 2003.[18] "UDC Online" is an electronic version of the complete edition of UDC and is available by subscription. Its features are similar to features of WebDewey.[19]

In the United States *UDC* is used mainly in some scientific and technical libraries and by one abstracting database.[20] More detailed descriptions of the *UDC*, its development, and its application may be found in a number of publications.[21]

NOTES

1. Melvil Dewey, *Dewey Decimal Classification and Relative Index*, Edition 22, edited by Joan S. Mitchell, et al. (Dublin, OH: OCLC, 2003); *Abridged Dewey Decimal Classification and Relative Index*, Edition 14, edited by Joan S. Mitchell, et al. (Dublin, OH: OCLC, 2004). DDC, Dewey, Dewey Decimal Classification, and WebDewey are registered trademarks of OCLC.

2. A very short summary of Melvil Dewey's life written by Wayne A. Wiegand is available: http://www.oclc.org/dewey/resources/biography (accessed 2/20/2006). A longer biography is also available: Wiegand, Wayne A. *Irrepressible Reformer: A Biography of Melvil Dewey*. Chicago: American Library Association, 1996.

3. Lois Mai Chan and Joan S. Mitchell, *Dewey Decimal Classification: Principles and Application*, 3rd ed. (Dublin, Ohio: OCLC, 2003).

4. Mona L. Scott, *Dewey Decimal Classification, 22nd Edition: A Study Manual and Number Building Guide* (Westport, Conn.: Libraries Unlimited, 2005).

5. Chan and Mitchell, *Dewey Decimal Classification.*

6. "Segmentation Marks in Dewey Numbers," available: http://www.oclc.org/dewey/news/newsletter/ddcnews_ifla2005.pdf (accessed 2/20/2006).

7. "Dewey Services: Updates: New and changed entries," available: http://www.oclc.org/dewey/updates/new/default.htm (accessed 2/19/2006).

8. "Dewey Services: Updates," available: http://www.oclc.org/dewey/updates/default.htm (accessed 2/14/2006)

9. "Using OCLC WebDewey: An OCLC Tuturial," available: http://www.oclc.org/dewey/resources/tutorial/ (accessed 2/20/2006).

10. "Dewey Services: Latest versions: WebDewey," available: http://www.oclc.org/dewey/versions/webdewey/default.htm (accessed 2/14/2006); "Dewey Services: Latest Versions: Abridged WebDewey," available: http://www.oclc.org/dewey/versions/abridgedwebdewey/default.htm (accessed 2/14/2006).

11. Pat Thomas, "Implementing *DDC20*," *DC&* 5, no. 1 (March 1990): 7–8.

12. Quotation of Paul Otlet's writing from W. Boyd Rayward's *The Universe of Information* (Moscow: FID, 1975) as cited in "UDC Announcements," available: http://www.udcc.org/announcement.htm (accessed 2/20/2006).

13. "About Universal Decimal Classification and the UDC Consortium," available: http://www.udcc.org/about.htm (accessed 2/14/2006).

14. Ibid.

15. Ibid.

16. *Extensions and Corrections to the UDC* (The Hague: FID, 1951–). Annual.

17. British Standards Institution, *Universal Decimal Classification, Complete Edition* (London: BSI, 2005).

18. British Standards Institution, *Universal Decimal Classification*, 2nd ed., abridged (London: BSI, 2003).

19. "UDC Online," available: http://www.udcc.org/udconline.htm (accessed 2/14/2006).

20. *Meteorological and Geoastrophysical Abstracts* (Boston: American Meteorological Society, 1950–).

21.   I. C. McIlwaine, *The Universal Decimal Classification: A Guide to Its Use* (The Hague: UDC Consortium, 2000); W. Boyd Rayward, "The UDC and FID: A Historical Perspective," *Library Quarterly* 37 (July 1967): 259–278; A. C. Foskett, "The Universal Decimal Classification," in *The Subject Approach to Information*, 5th ed. (London: Library Association Publishing, 1996), pp. 281–294.

SUGGESTED READING

Chan, Lois Mai, and Joan S. Mitchell. *Dewey Decimal Classification: Principles and Application.* 3rd ed. Dublin, Ohio: OCLC, 2003.

Ferguson, Bobby. *Subject Analysis: Blitz Cataloging Workbook.* Englewood, Colo.: Libraries Unlimited, 1998. Chapter 3: Dewey Decimal Classification.

Foskett, A. C. *The Subject Approach to Information.* 5th ed. London: Library Association Publishing, 1996. Chapter 17: The Dewey Decimal Classification and Chapter18: The Universal Decimal Classification.

Intner, Sheila S., and Jean Weihs. *Standard Cataloging for School and Public Libraries.* 3rd ed. Englewood, Colo.: Libraries Unlimited, 2001. Chapter 11: The Dewey Decimal Classification.

McIlwaine, I. C. *The Universal Decimal Classification: A Guide to Its Use.* The Hague: UDC Consortium, 2000.

Miksa, Francis L. *The DDC, the Universe of Knowledge, and the Post-Modern Library.* Albany, N.Y.: OCLC Forest Press, 1998.

Olson, Hope A., and John J. Boll. *Subject Analysis in Online Catalogs.* 2nd ed. Englewood, Colo.: Libraries Unlimited, 2001. Chapter 8: Online Catalogs and the Dewey Decimal and Library of Congress Classifications.

Scott, Mona L. *Dewey Decimal Classification, 22nd Edition: A Study Manual and Number Building Guide.* Westport, Conn.: Libraries Unlimited, 2005.

16 ⟩ Library of Congress Classification (LCC)

INTRODUCTION

The Library of Congress (LC) was founded in 1800. Its earliest classification system was by size (folios, quartos, octavos, etc.), subdivided by accession numbers. By 1812 the collection had grown to about 3,000 volumes, and a better method of classification was needed. The solution was to arrange the works under 18 broad subject categories similar to the Bacon-d'Alembert system used in the 1789 *Catalogue* of Benjamin Franklin's Library Company of Philadelphia. Soon after, in 1814, British soldiers burned the Capitol, where the collection was housed. To re-establish it, Thomas Jefferson offered to sell Congress his library of around 7,000 volumes. Jefferson had cataloged and classified the works himself, using 44 main classes and divisions based on a different interpretation of the Bacon-d'Alembert system. After some debate, Congress agreed to purchase the Jefferson books. Although many were destroyed in a later fire, the classification that came with them was used until the end of the nineteenth century. By that time it had undergone so much ad hoc modification, largely based on shelving and other physical limitations, that it was barely recognizable and completely inadequate.

Many significant changes occurred at LC near the turn of the century. In 1899 Dr. Herbert Putnam, the new Librarian, with many new staff appointments and a brand new building, decided to reorganize and reclassify his rapidly growing collection. Since it was to be moved into more adequate shelving areas, the time was right to develop a better, more detailed classification system. There were already in existence the first five editions of the *Dewey Decimal Classification* (*DDC*) and the first six expansions of Charles A. Cutter's *Expansive Classification*. LC classifiers studied both, as well as the German *Halle Schema* devised by Otto Hartwig. They did not adopt any in full, but the experience they gained was invaluable, and their debt, especially to Cutter, is implicit in the basic structure of their system. While the outline and notation of their main classes are very similar to those of the *Expansive Classification*, there are no main classes I, O, W, X, or Y, as there are in the Cutter system.[1] All five letters do appear, however, as second or third symbols in the notation for various LC subclasses. The other major similarity to the *Expansive Classification* is in the structure of class "Z—Bibliography and Library Science," which was the first class devised and was adopted from Cutter with only minor variations.

After Putnam and his Chief Cataloger, Charles Martel, determined the broad outlines of the new classification, different subject specialists were asked to develop each individual schedule, or portion of the system. Within a broad general framework set up to ensure coordination, each topic or form of presentation identified as a class or subclass was further organized to display the library's holdings and to serve anticipated research needs. Schedules comprising single classes or parts of classes were separately published as they were completed. Most of them first appeared between 1899 and 1940. Many have since gone through several editions. In one sense, the scheme represents a series of special classifications. Yet special libraries, with narrowly defined collecting and service goals, often find the *Library of Congress Classification* (*LCC*), which serves broader, more interdisciplinary uses, unsatisfactory for their purposes.

To keep the system functionally up-to-date, individual schedule volumes are frequently reviewed in committee. Revisions, reallocations, and additions keep it flexible and hospitable to new subjects or points of view. For example, in the 1960s interest in Eastern religions and the increase in materials from Asia occasioned a re-allocation in 1972 of the topic "Buddhism" from the span BL1400–1495 into a whole new subclass, BQ. Revisions were likewise made in subclass PL, particularly in the sections for Chinese, Japanese, and Korean literatures. Number spans now reflect political changes in Albania, Bangladesh, Korea, Namibia, Somalia, and the like. A triple-letter subclass "DJK—Eastern Europe" was developed in 1976. Intensified foreign acquisitions programs under PL480, the National Program for Acquisitions and Cataloging (NPAC), the revised copyright law, and other developments, stimulated increased expansion and revision of the system. New revisions continue to be printed. Among recent revisions are revisions of the Social Sciences (H class), Education (L class), and many of the language and literature classes.

Hundreds of different number-letter combinations compatible with the notation have not yet been employed or have been retired in favor of new locations. The scheme will continue to accommodate for a long time the many new subjects and aspects of subjects not yet anticipated. It is particularly useful for large university and research collections because of its hospitality and inherent flexibility. It has been used effectively in smaller academic and public libraries, although its adaptability for broad classification is limited. Even special libraries frequently base their own more technical constructs on it, extending its schedules or parts of schedules to cover their unique materials. Some foreign libraries also use the system, although, in spite of LC's large foreign holdings, it is primarily designed from an American perspective.

In the *MARC 21* (MAchine-Readable Cataloging format for the U.S. and Canada) Bibliographic Format call numbers based on *LCC* that are assigned by LC or the British Library are placed in field 050. Those assigned by Library and Archives Canada or other contributing Canadian libraries, the National Library of Medicine, or the National Agricultural Library are entered in field 055, 060, or 070, respectively. In the OCLC system, members are asked to enter locally assigned call numbers based on *LCC* in field 090.

CLASSIFICATION TOOLS AND AIDS

The working schedules are contained in over 40 separate volumes. Besides the basic schedules, there are some separately published tables to be used with specific schedules and a short general *Outline*, now in its seventh edition, which gives the secondary and tertiary subclass spans for most classes. Several volumes are devoted to subclass coverage of broad areas, such as related language and literature groups. They comprise:

A	General Works (1998)
B-BJ	Philosophy, Psychology (2000)
BL-BQ	Religion (General). Hinduism. Judaism. Islam. Buddhism (2001)
BR-BX	Christianity, Bible (2000)
C	Auxiliary Sciences of History (1996)
D-DR	History (General) and History of Europe (2001)
DS-DX	History of Asia, Africa, Australia, New Zealand, etc. (1998)
E-F	History: America (2000)
G	Geography. Maps. Anthropology. Recreation (2005)
G Tables	Geographic Cutter Numbers Tables G1548-G9804 [available in PDF format]
H	Social sciences (2005)
J	Political Science (1997)
K	Law (General) (2005)
K Tables	Form Division Tables for Law (2005) (apply to all K subclasses except KD, KE, and KF)
KB	Religious Law (2004)
KD	Law of the United Kingdom and Ireland (1998)
KDZ, KG-KH	Law of the Americas, Latin America, and the West Indies (2000)
KE	Law of Canada (1999)
KF	Law of the United States (2005)
KJ-KKZ	Law of Europe (2000)
KJV-KJW	Law of France (1999)
KK-KKC	Law of Germany (2000)

KL-KWX	Law of Asia and Eurasia, Africa, Pacific Area and Antarctica (2001)
KZ	Law of Nations (1998)
L	Education (2005)
M	Music and Books on Music (1998)
N	Fine Arts (1996; new ed. expected 2006)
P-PZ Tables	Language and Literature Tables (2004)
P-PA	Philology and Linguistics (General). Greek Language and Literature. Latin Language and Literature (2005)
PB-PH	Modern European Languages (2005)
PJ-PK	Oriental Philology and Literature, Indo-Iranian Philology and Literature (2005)
PL-PM	Languages of Eastern Asia, Africa, Oceania. Hyperborean, Indian, and Artificial Languages (2001; new ed. expected 2006)
PN	Literature (General) (2004)
PQ	French, Italian, Spanish, and Portuguese Literatures (2004)
PR, PS, PZ	English and American Literatures. Juvenile Belles Lettres (2005)
PT	German, Dutch, and Scandinavian Literatures (2005)
Q	Science (2004)
R	Medicine (1999)
S	Agriculture (1996)
T	Technology (1999)
U-V	Military Science. Naval Science (1996)
Z	Bibliography. Library Science. Information Resources (2001; new ed. expected 2006)
A-Z	Outline (7th ed., 2003)

The schedules are also all available via *Classification Web.*[2] *Classification Web* offers a number of advantages over the print version. In addition to access to the classification scheme and the *Library of Congress Subject Headings* (as discussed in chapter 11), one has correlations between LCC numbers and LCSH. There are advanced search and navigation tools, and many hypertext links exist within and among the files. A notes file allows addition of local institutional or personal comments.

Updating

All files in *Classification Web* are updated weekly. Updating of the print version is accomplished by several publications, most of which are available directly from LC.[3]

- **Revised editions of individual schedules.** As seen in the list of volumes above, the various schedules have had revisions made at different times. Each one gets a full revision as the need arises. All schedules and the *Outline* are sold individually by LC's Cataloging Distribution Service (CDS), or if all are purchased at once, a package price provides a savings.

- *Library of Congress Classification—Additions and Changes.* Additions and changes are available on the Web. LC's Cataloging Policy and Support Office posts revisions in "Weekly Lists."[4] At the same site one can find the Web version of the LC Classification Outline and various memos such as one identifying obsolete and optional numbers in *LCC*.

- *SUPERLCCS™ . . . : Library of Congress Classification Schedules Combined with Additions and Changes.* These cumulations of the schedules combined with LC's once quarterly, but now weekly, *Additions and Changes* have been published since 1988, by Gale Research Company, now known as Thomson Gale, a business of the Thomson Corporation. SUPERLCCS is available both in print and on microfiche.[5]

- *Cataloging Service Bulletin.* This channel for recent decisions and experiments in technical processing at LC has been offered since 1945.[6] It has a regular quarterly publication schedule, carrying valuable data on *LCC* and shelflisting practice, as well as other aspects of subject and descriptive cataloging. Subscriptions may be placed with CDS, or it may be downloaded in PDF format for free.

Indexing

There has been no official comprehensive index to the print version of *LCC*. Rather, each volume has its own index, and an index in one volume only rarely refers to a concept in another volume. This lack has been satisfied online in *Classification Web*, where one can search in various ways for words associated with all classification notations.

If one is using the print version of *LCC*, one needs to think of various disciplines that might have notations for a topic and search in the index of the schedule for each of those disciplines. For example, the index to class "T—Technology" provides the following entries under "Baths, Public":

Baths, Public
Building construction: TH4761
Plumbing: TH6518.B3

The class "N—Fine Arts" index entry reads:

Bath houses:
Architecture: NA7010

and the class "R—Medicine" entry reads:

Public baths:
Public health: RA605-607

A possible way to find notations from more than one discipline is to search *LCSH*.[7] While it was never designed to function as an index, many entries and subdivisions refer in brackets to one or more class numbers, often including terminology used in the schedules. In it, under the heading "Public Baths" one finds the following:

Public baths *(May Subd Geog)*
[RA605-RA606 (Public health)]

The narrower terms "Bathhouses" and "Baths, Roman" have no classification notations associated with them. The broader term "Baths" has only notations for school hygiene, personal hygiene, and therapeutics. The broader term "Public buildings" has "[NA4170-4510 (Architecture)]," but this does not include the NA7010 notation for "Bath houses." LC makes no effort to maintain class notations in *LCSH*, and it can be seen that under the heading, "Public baths" one would miss the entries from the N and T schedules.

Sometimes though, *LCC* notations relating to a given concept can be grouped more quickly through *LCSH* than through the many schedule indexes, as shown in the following example:

Schedule B-BJ—Philosophy; Psychology:
Hypnotism (Parapsychology): BF1111-1156
Schedule BL, BM, BP, BQ—Religion: Religions, Hinduism, Judaism, Islam, Buddhism:
Hypnotism: BL65.H9
Schedule H—Social Sciences:
Hypnotism and crime: HV6110
Schedule Q—Science:
Hypnotic conditions
Physiology: QP425-427
Schedule R—Medicine:
Hypnotics: RM325
Hypnotism and hypnosis
Anesthesiology: RD85.H9
Dentistry: RK512.H95
Forensic medicine: RA1171
Psychiatry: RC490-499

LCSH:
 Hypnotics   *(May Subd Geog)*
  [RM325]

  . . .

 Hypnotism
  [BF1111-BF1156 (Parapsychology)]
  [HV6110 (Hypnotism and crime)]
  [RC490-RC499 (Psychiatry)]

  . . .

 Hypnotism in dentistry   *(May Subd Geog)*
  [RK512.H95]

  . . .

 Hypnotism in surgery   *(May Subd Geog)*
  [RD85.H9]

It can be seen that one would miss the entries at BL, QP, and RA when using *LCSH*, but more entries are grouped there than are not.

The best indexing is in *Classification Web*. There one finds the following by searching for "public baths," "baths, public," and "bath houses" in the LCC index:

Public baths: Ablutions: Islamic law
  KBP184.47.P82   Public baths

Public baths: Public health
  [RA605-607]   Public baths, comfort stations, etc.

Baths, Public: Ablutions: Islamic law
  KBP184.47.P82   Public baths

Baths, Public: Building construction
  TH4761   Baths

Baths, Public: Employees
  HD8039.P86-.P862   Public bath employees

Baths, Public: Plumbing
  TH6518.B3   Baths, Public

Bath houses: Architecture
  NA7010   Baths and washhouses

Bath houses: Tang and post-Tang China
  KNN345.B37   Bath houses

Bath houses (Ancient China)
  KNN195.B37   Bath houses

And the following entries are found in the LCC index in *Classification Web* when searching "hypnotic":

Hypnotic age regression
  RC499.H96   Hypnotic age regression

Hypnotic conditions: Physiology
  [QP425-427]   Sleep. Hypnotic conditions, etc.

Hypnotics
  RM325   Hypnotics. Sedatives

Hypnotism: Bibliography: Medicine
  Z6675.H9   Hypnotism

Hypnotism: Criminal law
  K5028   Criminal law and hypnotism

Hypnotism: Psychiatry
  [RC490-499]   Hypnotism and hypnosis. Suggestion therapy

Hypnotism and crime
  HV6110   Hypnotism and crime

Hypnotism and criminal law
  KK8014   Criminal law and hypnotism

Hypnotism and hypnosis: Anesthesiology
  RD85.H9   Hypnosis

Hypnotism and hypnosis: Anesthesiology: Dentistry
  RK512.H95   Hypnotism

Hypnotism and hypnosis: Forensic medicine
  RA1171   Other special

Hypnotism and religion
  BL65.H9   Hypnotism

Hypnotism in literature: General: Literary history
  PN1059.H8   Hypnotism

Hypnotism in motion pictures
  PN1995.9.H95   Hypnotism

Hypnotism (Parapsychology)
  [BF1111-1156]   Hypnotism. Animal magnetism. Odylic force.
                               Biomagnetism. Mesmerism. Subliminal projection

In 1978 the United States Historical Documents Institute, Inc., and University Microfilms International jointly sponsored the filming of 6.8 million cards of the LC shelflist, arranged by call number, covering 1968–1979.[8] This tool can be used as a kind of index, but is used most effectively for fine-tuning class number and shelflist assignments through comparison of proposed numbers for new materials with those already grouped in a given area.

Just as the Gale cumulations and the LC shelflist reproductions are commercial aids based on official, publicly accessible LC data, so a number of indexing ventures have reflected similar trade manipulation of publications or automated processing available from LC. Their problem has been in keeping up-to-date. A publication that can serve as a kind of index is Scott's *Conversion Tables: LC–Dewey, Dewey–LC, and LC Subject Headings–LC and Dewey*.[9]

BASIC FEATURES

Because *LCC* was developed as a utilitarian scheme for books at LC, it is an enumerative, rather than a deductive, system. Among the basic features borrowed from Cutter are its order of main classes, its use of capital letters for main and subclass notation, its use of Arabic numerals for further subdivision, and its modification of the Cutter author-mark idea to achieve alphabetic subarrangements of various kinds.

All the LC schedules have similar, but not identical, sequencing arrangements and appearance. Within each sequence of class numbers the order proceeds, as a rule, from general aspects of the topic or discipline to its particular divisions and subtopics. Chronological sequences may trace historical events, publication dates, or other useful time frames. Geographical arrangements are frequently alphabetical, but just as frequently are given in a "preferred order," starting with the Western Hemisphere and the United States. Class "G — Geography, etc." is distinct from the history classes, although located next to them. This distribution is similar to the *DDC* location of "910 — Geography and Travel" within class "900 — History." Neither scheme quite succeeds in solving the problem of ambiguous relationships between popular works of description and travel and other, perhaps more scholarly, books on national or regional social life and customs. The user must search both the history and the geography shelves, and even the social sciences, to find all available materials on these topics.

There are some significant differences between *LCC* and *DDC* in organizing some materials. For example, *LCC* provides broad subclasses in class P for the various national literatures, subdividing next by chronology and then by individual author. Seldom, except for anthologies, does it group literary works by form. *DDC* also starts in its 800 class with a basic separation into national literatures, but it subdivides next by form, e.g., poetry, drama, fiction, etc. Only subordinately does it provide for time divisions or individual authors.

The LC preference for grouping national literatures by time period and author extends to class "B — Philosophy" but not to music or the graphic arts. In subclass "M — Music and Scores" works are classed first by form (e.g., opera, oratorio, symphony, chamber music), then by composer. There is no attempt to keep time periods, national schools, or genres of expression (e.g., classical, romantic, modern) distinct. Subclass "ML — Literature, History and Criticism of Music" does use national, chronological, and similar groupings. In class "N — Fine Arts" materials are grouped first by form (e.g., sculpture, drawing, painting), then by nationality or chronology, and finally by artist.

The major LC use of literary grouping by form formerly was its subclass "PZ — Fiction in English; Juvenile Belles Lettres." Here a concession was made to a "reader interest" orientation that proved to be controversial and a stumbling block to the full use of *LCC* by other research libraries with large holdings in literature. Therefore, beginning July 1, 1980, LC discontinued use of PZ1, PZ3, and PZ4. American fiction is now classed in PS, English fiction in PR, and translations of fiction into English with the original national literature. Otherwise, LC's handling of literature has met with general approval. A recurring pattern of organization within each literature may give the shelf or shelflist browser a useful guide:

1. History and criticism, subdivided
   a. Chronologically
   b. Then by form
2. Collections or anthologies, subdivided by form
3. Individual authors, subdivided
   a. Chronologically
   b. Then alphabetically by author
      1) Collective works
      2) Individual works
      3) Biography and criticism

LCC breaks the "information and general works" grouping in the 000 class of *DDC* into two classes at opposite ends of the alphabet. The "A — General Works" schedule employs for its subclasses rare instances of mnemonic notation. General encyclopedias are located in subclass AE, general indexes in AI, general museum publications in AM, and so forth. By contrast, the Z class, containing bibliographies and works on the book industries and on libraries, has, until very recently, had no two-letter subclasses at all. While its subject bibliographies are arranged alphabetically by topic in the Z5001–Z8000 span, there is nothing mnemonic about their notation. A need for a new classification area for "Information Resources" precipitated the creation of subclass ZA in 1996. The only other notable instances of mnemonic class letter associations in *LCC* are for class "G — Geography, etc.," class "M — Music," subclass "ML — Music Literature," and class "T — Technology."

SCHEDULE FORMAT

Most of the *LCC* schedules exhibit certain common features of external and internal format. Many of these format features are missing from certain schedules, a reminder that the scheme was intentionally decentralized in its development. Subject specialists were encouraged to adopt standard modes of organization, but were never forced to maintain a rigid formal pattern.

External Format

The gross physical format, or external appearance, of the printed schedules has already been described. Both old and new editions, regardless of typography or binding, tend to follow a familiar pattern of organization:

1. **A preface or prefatory note** nearly always follows the title page. These introductory remarks in recent editions have become briefer and less helpful for classification purposes than they formerly were.

2. **Brief synopses** next appear in many of the schedules, to show the primary subdivisions contained in those volumes. In most cases these broad subclasses are readily identifiable by their brief double-letter notation, but class "K—Law" is issued in double-letter subclass volumes with synopses that frequently show mnemonic triple-letter divisions. We can learn at a glance that the law of Ontario is found in subclass KEO, while that of Quebec is in KEQ. A similar mnemonic arrangement applies to the American states in subclass KF, but their notation is more complicated since several states share certain initial letters. A typical synopsis is shown in figure 16.1.

    Fig. 16.1. An example of the LCC feature known as a "Synopsis."

    SYNOPSIS

H	SOCIAL SCIENCES (GENERAL)
HA	STATISTICS
HB	ECONOMIC THEORY. DEMOGRAPHY
HC	ECONOMIC HISTORY AND CONDITIONS
HD	INDUSTRIES. LAND USE. LABOR
HE	TRANSPORTATION AND COMMUNICATIONS
HF	COMMERCE
HG	FINANCE
HJ	PUBLIC FINANCE
HM	SOCIOLOGY (GENERAL)
HN	SOCIAL HISTORY AND CONDITIONS. SOCIAL PROBLEMS. SOCIAL REFORM
HQ	THE FAMILY. MARRIAGE. WOMEN
HS	SOCIETIES: SECRET, BENEVOLENT, ETC.
HT	COMMUNITIES. CLASSES. RACES
HV	SOCIAL PATHOLOGY. SOCIAL AND PUBLIC WELFARE. CRIMINOLOGY
HX	SOCIALISM. COMMUNISM. ANARCHISM

3. **An outline**, consisting not only of alphabetic subclasses, but also of significant alphanumeric subspans, is present in nearly every schedule. In schedules without synopses the outlines tend to be briefer and to show broader subdivisions; in schedules with synopses, they are longer and more detailed. Occasionally, as in the schedule for class "J—Political Science," the "synopsis" is really an outline. These two kinds of preliminary overview offer the user supplementary techniques for arriving quickly at any given portion of the schedules. The outline for the first two subclasses of class H appears in the schedule as shown in figure 16.2.

Fig. 16.2. An example of the LCC feature known as an "Outline."

OUTLINE

H		Social Sciences (General)
HA		. Statistics
	29-32	Theory and method of social science statistics
	36-37	Statistical services. Statistical bureaus
	38-39	Registration of vital events. Vital records
	154-4737	Statistical data
	154-155	Universal statistics
	175-4737	By region or country
HB		Economic theory. Demography
	71-74	Economics as a science. Relation to other subjects
	75-130	History of economics. History of economic theory
		Including special economic schools
	131-147	Methodology
	201-206	Value. Utility
	221-236	Price.
	238-251	Competition. Production. Wealth
	501	Capital. Capitalism
	522-715	Income. Factor shares
	801-843	Consumption. Demand
	846-846.8	Welfare theory
	848-3697	Demography. Population. Vital events
	3711-3840	Business cycles. Economic fluctuations

4. **The schedule proper** enumerates specific class number assignments and sequences in their most explicit form. Page formatting devices, although slightly different in each of the schedule formats (i.e., published schedules available from CDS, schedules available on *Classification Web*, and schedules available from Thomson Gale), demonstrate hierarchical subordinations and progressions. *LCC* printed schedules show left-margin indentions, with nested running titles on nearly every page or screen display to demonstrate hierarchy. These devices are not so carefully worked out, nor so consistently displayed, as they are in *DDC*. In *Classification Web* a complete hierarchy is displayed in the top frame of the divided screen for any notation on which a user clicks, although this display contains only the words of the hierarchy, not the notations; and it is not in the traditional indented form.

Many broad headings which offer a useful survey of subtopics are interpolated just ahead of the specific numbers that they embrace. They often carry no single class number of their own. For example:

> Theory and practice of education
>> Including philosophy
>> Collected writings
>>> Including essays, monographs, papers
>>> Several authors

LB5	Serial collections
LB7	Minor collections

>>>> Including selections, extracts, etc.
>> Individual authors see LB51-885

There is no notation to be assigned for just "Theory and practice of education" or even for "collected writings" on that subject. For this and related reasons *LCC* does not work well for classifying small general collections or parts of collections. Nor are these spans very often accompanied by internal summary tables such as *DDC* uses.

Most schedules do carry internal subdivision tables at key junctures, to provide schematic patterns for further localized development of class numbers or sequences. While *LCC* is basically enumerative (that is, its topical number assignments are usually not made until there is at least one work to go into the category), these generalized subdivision tables open up patterned arrangements that are usually not fully realized on the shelves.

Scope notes and footnotes occasionally refer to auxiliary tables, etc., or they sometimes give useful instructions for number building. An excerpt from the "T — Technology" schedule (*see* figure 16.3, page 439) shows most of these features.

5. **Auxiliary tables** designed for use with more than one specific classification notation or span are located externally to the schedules proper. In printed volumes they appear after the full schedule, immediately preceding the index. (Tables for classes G, K, and P-PZ are published in completely separate volumes.) In *Classification Web* there is a separate button to click in order to view tables, which are numbered with the letter of the discipline followed by the table number (e.g., N1, N2, etc., for Fine Arts tables).

   Sometimes a table number is given in parentheses beside an entry in the schedule, to alert the user that the entry should be further subdivided. Sometimes a footnote cites the table with its page number and occasionally indicates how the interpolation should be made. Sometimes the instructions for interpolation are right in the schedule. Such is the case in figure 16.3 from the TD subclass, shown on page 439.

   The excerpt in figure 16.4, page 440, from the "N—Fine Arts" external Table N1 and Table N2 shows how spans of 100 and 200 numbers can be distributed among the same list of terms. Table N1 distributes America and the United States among numbers 1 to 10, while Table N2 distributes the same geographic area among numbers 1 to 25. The notation span "N5801–5896.3—Classical art—Special regions or countries—Other [i.e., non-Greek or Ancient Italian] regions or countries" is to be distributed according to Table N1, adding the appropriate table number to N5800. On the other hand, "NB1501–1685—[Sculptured monuments in] Special regions or countries" uses Table N2 as a guide for adding country numbers to NB1500.

**Fig. 16.3. Sample excerpt from the *LCC* "T" schedule showing
many typical schedule features.**

TD	**Environmental technology. Sanitary engineering**
	Including the promotion and conservation of the public health, comfort, and convenience by the control of the environment
	Cf. GE170-190, Environmental policy
	Cf. GF51, Human beings and the environment
	Cf. RA565-600, Environmental health
	Cf. TH6014-6085, Environmental engineering in buildings
	Periodicals and societies. By language of publication
1	English
2	French
3	German
4	Other languages (not A-Z)
5	Congresses
6.A1-Z	Exhibitions. Museums
6.A1	General works
6.A2-Z	By region or country, A-Z
	Subarrange each country:
	.x General works
	.x2A-Z Special. By city, A-Z
7	Collected works (nonserial)
9	Dictionaries and encyclopedias
12	Directories
	History
15	General works
16	Ancient
17	Medieval
18	Modern to 1800
19	Nineteenth century
20	Twentieth century
21-127	Country and city subdivisions (Table T1 modified)
	Including municipal reports of public sanitary works
	Add country number in table to TD0
	Under each two number country, unless otherwise specified:
	1.A1 General works
	1.A6-Z States, provinces, etc., A-Z
	2.A-Z Local (Cities, etc.), A-Z
	Biography
139	Collective
140.A-Z	Individual, A-Z
	General works
144	Early to 1850
145	1850-
146	Elementary textbooks
148	Popular works
151	Pocketbooks, tables, etc.
153	General special
155	Addresses, essays, lectures
156	Environmental and sanitary engineering as a profession

Fig. 16.4. Distribution of the same terms among different spans of numbers.

TABLES TO Class N

TABLE N1: TABLES OF REGIONS OR COUNTRIES (100 NUMBERS)

	America
01	General
	Latin America
01.5	General
	By region or country see <u>N1 14-41</u>
	North America
02	General
	United States
03	General
03.5	Colonial period; 18th (and early 19th) century
03.7	19th century
04	20th century
04.5	Northeastern States
04.7	Atlantic States
05	New England
05.5	Middle Atlantic States
06	South
07	Central
08	West
08.5	Northwestern States
08.6	Southwestern States
09	Pacific States
10.A-W	States, A-W

Each state may be subarranged:
.x   General works
.x2A-.x2Z   Local (other than cities), A-Z

. . .

TABLE N2: TABLES OF REGIONS OR COUNTRIES (200 NUMBERS)

	America
01	General
	Latin America
02	General
	By region or country see N2 31-82
	North America
03	General
	United States
05	General works
06	Colonial period; 18th (and early 19th) century
07	19th century
08	20th century
08.5	Northeastern States
08.7	Atlantic States
10	New England
10.5	Middle Atlantic States
11	South
14	Central
17	West
18	Northwestern States
18.6	Southwestern States
19	Pacific States
25.A-W	States, A-W

Each state may be subarranged:
.x   General works
.x2A-.x2Z   Local (other than cities), A-Z

. . .

Auxiliary Table N1 from the N schedule is "simple" because it carries only one sequence of numbers that can be interpolated directly into the corresponding number spans in the schedule. In the past many tables were "compound." That is, they supplied more than one number sequence for the same list of subtopics. Someone using older copies of schedules will still find these compound tables. All tables in new schedules and in the version available on *Classification Web* are now "simple" tables. Number spans from the schedule and the table are matched according to the quantity of materials that the LC classifiers anticipate at any given location.

Geographical and chronological subdivisions are often relegated to auxiliary tables. The two concepts may be combined as shown in figure 16.4 on page 440. Other principles of division may also be found in tabular form. Tables in class "J—Political Science" contain such categories as "Periodicals," "Public administration," "Political participation," and the like. The heavily used PR, PS, PZ schedule has a separately published extensive set of tables designed for use with literary author numbers, running the gamut from long spans for prolific, often translated and discussed authors to brief expansions of cutter designations for recent or little-published authors.

6. **A detailed index** accompanies each printed schedule. These indexes vary in coverage and depth, but most of them list specific topics from their schedule. References from synonyms or related terms, alphabetized and indented subordinate topical lists, and suggestions for placing related materials in other schedules are occasionally included.

Internal Format

While Herbert Putnam and Charles Martel left the local arrangement of topical and form divisions very much to the discretion of their subject specialists, they nevertheless identified certain basic orientation features for use throughout the system. These organizational concepts were generally known as "Martel's Seven Points" of internal format. They could be incorporated into the schedules at any level of hierarchical subdivision appropriate within the given context. They encompassed:

1. **General form divisions.** The approach here was similar to Dewey's Form Division Table, which has evolved in recent *DDC* editions into the Table of Standard Subdivisions. It assumes that library materials can often be effectively grouped according to their mode of presentation. Examples are periodicals; society publications; collections; dictionaries or encyclopedias; conference, exhibition, or museum publications; annuals or yearbooks; directories; and documents. Because of their general application they belong near the beginning of any disciplinary or topical sec-

tion, but *LCC* imposes no rigid order upon their location. Their importance in subclass "L—Education (General)" is observed in the following schedule outline:

	L	**EDUCATION (GENERAL)**
	7-97	Periodicals. Societies
	101	Yearbooks
	107	Congresses
	111-791	Official documents, reports, etc.
	797-899	Educational exhibitions and museums
	999-991	Directories of educational institutions

By contrast, subclasses "LD-LG—Individual [Educational] Institutions" show no obvious use of the form division concept. Only in their auxiliary tables do a few of the forms emerge as useful ordering concepts.

2. **Theory. Philosophy.**

3. **History. Biography.**

4. **Treatises. General works.** Works falling under points 2–4 of Martel's Seven Points are often intermixed with those arranged according to physical form and with other locally useful groupings, as shown in the excerpt from QE—Geology in figure 16.5.

Fig. 16.5. Excerpt showing intermixture of different kinds of form subgroupings for the Geology subclass.

QE	**GEOLOGY**	
1	Periodicals, societies, congresses, serial publications	
3	Collected works (nonserial)	
4	Voyages and expeditions	
5	Dictionaries and encyclopedias	
6	Philosophy	
7	Nomenclature, terminology, notation, abbreviations	
	History	
11	General works	
13	By region or country, A-Z	
	Biography	
21	Collective	
22	Individual, A-Z	
	e.g. .D25 Dana, James Dwight	
	.L8 Lyell, Charles	
	.S77 Steno, Nicolaus	
23	Directories	
25	Early works through 1800	
	General works, treatises, and advanced textbooks	
26	1801-1969	
26.2	1970-2000	
26.3	2001-	
	Elementary textbooks	
28	General	
28.2	Physical geology	
28.3	Historical geology	

5. **Law. Regulation. State relations.** Until the publication in 1969 of the first "K—Law" subclass, this ordering principle was handy for grouping legal materials with their related topics, especially in the social sciences. The development of class K inverts the relationship. Whenever possible such works are now classified first as legal materials and only subordinately as being discipline-oriented. For example, resources dealing with government regulations for control of drugs as economic commodities were originally classified in HD9665.7–9. Those dealing with regulations for the manufacture, sale, and use of drugs were classified in RA402. Subclass "KF—Law of the United States" now places drug laws in KF3885–3895. Now, most works dealing with U.S. drug legislation and regulation are placed there.

6. **Study and teaching. Research. Textbooks.** Unlike *DDC*, *LCC* sometimes allows a unique place for textbooks, as well as for more theoretical works on how to study, teach, or research a topic. An example of this was shown in figure 16.5, QE28–28.3 for elementary textbooks. In other disciplines, *LCC* explicitly groups all textbooks with general works and treatises, as shown under QH581 in figure 16.6.

Fig. 16.6. Excerpt showing textbooks grouped with general works and treatises.

QH	CYTOLOGY
573	Periodicals, societies, congresses, serial publications
574	Collected works (nonserial)
575	Dictionaries and encyclopedias
	History
577	General works
578	By region or country, A-Z
	General works, treatises, and textbooks
581	Through 1969
581.2	1970-
581.5	Addresses, essays, lectures
582	Pictorial works and atlases
582.4	Popular works
582.5	Juvenile works
	Study and teaching. Research
583	General works
583.2	Laboratory manuals

7. **Subjects and subdivisions of subjects.** Most modern classification systems are disciplinary rather than topical. That is, they normally proceed from broad general divisions of knowledge to narrower subdivisions, with more or less comprehensive coverage provided for each special topic in relation to the hierarchy. Any linear arrangement of books or other materials on shelves must resort to a series of cyclic progressions if it displays subject-related groupings based on logical considerations or practical associations. Just as Martel's fourth point reminds classifiers that "general works" should be shelved together, usually near the beginning of each new topical group, so this seventh point provides for further

subject breakdown based on "literary warrant" or the amount of material requiring classification in such a group. One intermediate type that *LCC* frequently places just after "general works" is a potpourri called "general special" or "special aspects." These works treat the topic from particular points of view. Sometimes, as in TD153 (*see* figure 16.3 on page 439), such works have a single class number. At other places they must be spread out over several pages of the schedules.

NOTATION

The typical *LCC* notation contains a mixed notation of one to three letters, followed by one to four integers, and possibly a short decimal. Decimal numbers were not used much until it became necessary to expand certain sections where no further integers were available. Decimals do not usually indicate subordination, but allow a new topic or aspect to be inserted into an established context. In the excerpt from the "QH573–583.2—Cytology" schedule (*see* figure 16.6, page 443) the decimals belie the left-margin indentions of their associated topics. Clearly, "QH581.5—Addresses, essays, lectures" is hierarchically equivalent to "QH575—Dictionaries and encyclopedias," and is not subordinate to "QH581—General works . . . Through 1969."

Another method of expanding *LCC* notations is by means of mnemonic letter-number combinations, which look like Cutter's "Author numbers" but are derived from a different matrix (*see* chapter 17, "Creation of Complete Call Numbers"). These "cutter numbers" may represent topical concepts or geographic, personal, or corporate names. They are subordinated to schedule notations where an instruction to subdivide "A-Z" appears. Since they are part of the classification notation, some of the actual LC assignments, or at least some examples, are included within the schedule (*see* "QE22—Individual [biography of geologists], A-Z" in figure 16.5 on page 442). Geographic cutter numbers generally are not included, however (*see* "QH578—[History of cytology] By region or country, A-Z" in figure 16.6.

Alphabetic geographic sequences normally appear at subordinate places in the schedules, where they subdivide a single integer or decimal number. For broader disciplines or subjects, where the geographic arrangement covers an extensive number span, the organization follows a preferred pattern as was noted in the section on external format (*see* page 438). Class N, Tables N1 and N2 (*see* figure 16.4 on page 440), show how such sequences begin with "home base" (i.e., the Western Hemisphere and the United States), and then follow a pattern that covers the earth pretty much according to our American perceptions of the nearness and importance of our neighbors.

LC interpretation of "cutter numbers" is always decimal. In a typical letter(s)-number(s)/letter-number(s) combination, the primary letter(s)-number(s) group should be arranged first alphabetically, then by integer(s) until a digit is introduced following a decimal point. All schedules make the basic ordering by integer quite evident, as when PR509 follows PR51, but precedes PR5018. The secondary letter-number(s) combination, by contrast, should be filed decimally. LC carefully inserts a decimal point in front of it, even if, as at "QH541.15.M3—Mathematical Models in Ecology," a decimal is already part of the primary notation. Some libraries using LCC drop the cutter decimal from their notation, on the premise that users will remember to follow the convention. The practice may possibly cause confusion in cutter number runs where it is not clearly understood that a classification notation like PR4972.M33 should follow PR4972.M3 but precede PR4972.M5.

Occasionally a classification notation, or series of notations, appears in the schedules in parentheses. These were formerly termed "shelflist numbers," but today more often are called "alternative class numbers." Some of them represent locations once actively used, but now retired by LC. Other classification notations appear to have been reserved in parentheses for possible future use and have since been activated. "PA2025—Collections [dealing with Latin philology and language]" was so reserved in the original 1928 edition of the P-PA schedule, but now the parentheses have been removed. Alternative classification notations are nearly always accompanied by notes telling the user to "see" another notation. Subclass SD (Forestry), for example, has an entry "(SD559) [Forestry—Exploitation and utilization—Valuation, mensuration, etc. —] Assessment and taxation, see HJ4167 etc." Libraries using *LCC* are welcome to adopt these alternative notations if their own classification needs are better realized by so doing.

Following are a few examples of classification using *LCC*.

Example 1

DC203.4	Ashton, John, b. 1834.
	English caricature and satire on Napoleon I . . .

D	History (General)
DC	History of France
139–249	Revolutionary and Napoleonic period, 1789–1815
203–212.5	Biography of Napoleon
203.4	Caricature and satire

Example 2

QL696	Turner, Angela K.
.P247	Swallows & martins . . .

Q	Science
QL	Zoology
605–739.3	Chordates. Vertebrates
671–699	Birds
696	Systematic divisions. By order and family, A-Z
.P2	Passeriformes
.P247	Hirundinidae (Swallows)

Example 3

RA407.3	American Hospital Association
	Comparative statistics on health facilities and population : metropolitan and nonmetropolitan areas . . .

R	Medicine (General)
RA	Public aspects of medicine
1–418.5	Medicine and the state
407–409.5	Health status indicators. Medical statistics and surveys
407.3–407.5	By region or country

| 407.3–407.4 | United States. |
| 407.3 | General works |

Example 4

HB1237	Marriage statistics for Sweden . . .
H	Social sciences
HB	Economic theory. Demography
848–3697	Demography. Population. Vital events
1111–1317	Marriages. Nuptiality
1121–1317	By region or country. Table H2
	[Add country number in table to HB1120]
	[Table H2: 117-118 Sweden]
1201–1252.8	Europe
1229–1238	Scandinavia
1237	Sweden [General works]

CONCLUSION

Most libraries using *LCC* will continue to use officially assigned call numbers for any of their own materials that LC has already classified. However, it is a rare library that holds only information packages also available in the LC collection. Classifiers should be able to create reasonably consistent notations with which to fit their unique holdings into the system. They may stumble over special practices at local points, but the general principles of arrangement are nearly always decipherable, especially now that one can search LC's and other libraries' online catalogs by LC call number and compare the results with the *LCC* schedules. Highly specific shelflisting (i.e., the rationale underlying many cutter numbers, as explained in chapter 17) is, on the other hand, not always so easy to explain. *LCC* is loosely coordinated and essentially pragmatic. It aims first to classify closely, then to identify uniquely, particular works, or issues of works, using the most economical notation available within its broad parameters of theory and practice.

NOTES

1. A table comparing the main classes of the Cutter and the LC schemes is given on page 458.

2. *Classification Web*, http://classificationweb.net [requires ID and password] (accessed 2/14/2006]); subscription information available: http://www.loc.gov/cds/classweb (accessed 2/14/2006).

3. Library of Congress, Cataloging Distribution Service, "LC Classification Schedules and Manuals from CDS" (available: http://www.loc.gov/cds/classif.html [accessed 2/21/2006]).

4. "Library of Congress Classification," The Library of Congress Cataloging Policy & Support Office (available: http://www.loc.gov/catdir/cpso/cpso.html#class [accessed 2/21/2006]).

5. For information regarding Thomson Gale and its publication of the cumulated editions of the *Library of Congress Classification,* see: Thomson Gale (available: http://www.gale.com/ [accessed 2/21/2006]).

6. Library of Congress, *Cataloging Service*, bulletin 1 (June 1945)–125 (Spring 1978); *Cataloging Service Bulletin*, no. 1 (Summer 1978)– . PDF version (free): http://www.loc.gov/ cds/freepdf.html (accessed 2/21/2006).

7. *Library of Congress Subject Headings*, 13th– eds. (Washington, D.C.: Library of Congress, Office for Subject Cataloging Policy, 1990–). Also available in *Classification Web.* For a detailed discussion of *LCSH, see* chapter 11 of this text.

8. *Library of Congress Shelflist* (Ann Arbor, MI: UMI/Proquest, 1968–1979). Reprint information available: http://www.umi.com/products_umi/descriptions/Library-of-Congress-Shelflist-330.shtml (accessed 2/21/2006).

9. Mona L. Scott, *Conversion Tables: LC–Dewey, Dewey–LC, and LC Subject* Headings– *LC and Dewey*, 3rd ed. (Westport, Conn.: Libraries Unlimited, 2005).

SUGGESTED READING

Chan, Lois M. *A Guide to the Library of Congress Classification*. 5th ed. Englewood, Colo.: Libraries Unlimited, 1999.

Dittmann, Helena and Jane Hardy. *Learn Library of Congress Classification*. Lanham, Md.: Scarecrow Press, 2000.

Ferguson, Bobby. *Subject Analysis: Blitz Cataloging Workbook*. Englewood, Colo.: Libraries Unlimited, 1998. Chapter 4: Library of Congress Classification.

Foskett, A. C. *The Subject Approach to Information*. 5th ed. London: Library Association Publishing, 1996. Chapter 22: The Library of Congress Classification.

Intner, Sheila S., and Jean Weihs. *Standard Cataloging for School and Public Libraries*. 3rd ed. Englewood, Colo.: Libraries Unlimited, 2001. Chapter 12: Library of Congress Classification.

Olson, Hope A., and John J. Boll. *Subject Analysis in Online Catalogs*. 2nd ed. Englewood, Colo.: Libraries Unlimited, 2001, pp. 240–264.

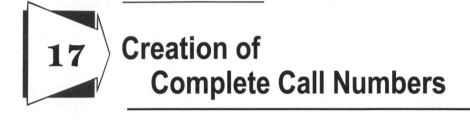

17 Creation of Complete Call Numbers

INTRODUCTION

Library call numbers serve a double function. The classification notation portion groups related materials together. The second portion of the complete call number uniquely identifies different works in the same class. Traditionally, this second part of the call number is based on the main entry, or primary access point, which has been chosen for the work through descriptive cataloging. Various terms such as *author number*, *book number*, and *cutter number* have been applied, but *author number* does not allow for those works with title main entries, while *book number* implies that it cannot be applied to nonbook materials. *Cutter number* is also misleading because the Library of Congress (LC) method of deriving it differs from the original tables devised by Charles A. Cutter.

However, the name *cutter number* has come into general use in practice regardless of the classification scheme used. Its general usage is a tribute to Cutter, who conceived the idea of using alphanumeric symbols to keep items in alphabetical order within a particular classification notation. In this text *cutter number* is used for any notation serving this function.

CUTTER NUMBERS DEVISED BY CHARLES A. CUTTER

Providing a classification notation with a supplementary cutter number enables the cataloger to design a fully unique call number for each title in a collection. The cutter numbers most often used with *Dewey Decimal Classification* (*DDC*) classification notations are taken from a set of tables devised by Cutter. These tables equate surnames and other words with alphanumeric sequences. Cutter initially produced a table in a single alphabet of all consonants except *S*, followed by an alphabet of vowels and the letter *S*.[1] This "two-figure" table (most of its combinations consist of a capital letter plus two digits) was later expanded by Kate E. Sanborn to provide more differentiation among names for use with larger collections.[2] Since she did not adhere to Cutter's schema, Cutter then developed his own expansion to permit growing libraries to assign more specific book numbers without disrupting the sequences they had already established from his two-figure table.[3] There are thus three different "Cutter" tables. The Cutter-Sanborn version is perhaps the most widely used today, being preferred by many larger libraries because of its simpler design and notation. OCLC has developed Four-Figure Cutter Tables (one is an extension of Cutter and the other an extension of Cutter-Sanborn). A "Dewey Cutter Program" can be downloaded to automatically provide cutter numbers upon input of text.[4]

While cutter numbers are most commonly used to arrange material by main entries (usually authors' surnames, but occasionally forenames, corporate names, or titles), they are also used in some instances to alphabetize material by subject, as in the case of biography. To illustrate the use of each table, let us suppose that we wish to assign a cutter number for the English poet, John Donne. The three tables carry the following sequences:

Cutter Two-figure Table

Doll	69	Foh
Dom	71	Folg
Doo	72	Foll

Cutter Three-figure Table

Donk	718	Folk
Donnet	719	Folke
Doo	72	Foll

Cutter-Sanborn Table

Donk	684	Fonti
Donn	685	Fontr
Donner	686	Foo

According to the Cutter two-figure table, the number for Donne is D71. Using the Cutter three-figure table it is D718 (an expansion of the D71 assignment). But using the Cutter-Sanborn table it is D685. The above examples also demonstrate the three-column display used in the original form of the tables. In 1969 Paul K. Swanson of the Forbes Library, Northampton, Massachusetts, and Esther M. Swift, editor of the H. R. Huntting Company, revised this arrangement into single continuous alphabets of two columns, with letters on the left corresponding to numbers on the right. The Swanson-Swift arrangement appears to be easier to use.

The work letter (or workmark) is the first letter of the title of the work, exclusive of articles. It follows the cutter number on the second line of the call number. For example, the complete Dewey Decimal call number for Henry James's novel *Wings of the Dove* is 813.4 J27w. Work letters do not inevitably ensure that a book will be placed in alphabetical sequence within the author grouping; this depends upon the sequence of acquisition of the books. One additional letter from the title may be added if necessary. For example, a copy of James's *Washington Square* might be assigned the call number 813.4 J27wa. If the third acquisition is a volume entitled *The Works of Henry James*, it would most probably be given the call number 813.4 J27, with no workmark, as most libraries prefer to place collected works of an author ahead of the individual works.

With an author such as Erle Stanley Gardner, who began the title of all of his Perry Mason mysteries with *The Case of the . . .* , such a scheme is not feasible. Depending on the library's policy, the cataloger can choose one of several alternatives. For example, the cataloger can ignore completely the common phrase *the case of the* and proceed directly to the distinctive part of the title, or use two work letters: *c* for *case,* plus an additional letter for the first distinctive word of the title (e.g., *The Case of the Mischievous Doll* might be assigned the work letters *cm*).

Biographies and criticism of a specific author pose a particular problem of library policy. The preferred way to classify biographies of literary authors in Dewey is with their work, in order to keep everything by and about a literary figure in one place. In such cases, a common method of distinguishing works "by" from works "about" an author is to insert an arbitrary letter—usually one toward the end of the alphabet (e.g., a capital "X") —after the cutter number and to follow it with the initial of the author of the biography. This device puts all books about an author directly following all books by that author. For example, if the letter "X" is chosen as the biography letter, a biography of Henry James by Leon Edel could be cuttered J27Xe, and it would follow, in shelflist order, J27w. If James had written a novel beginning with the letter *z* only the work letter *z* would be used for the novel; and the convention is to file the lower case work marks before capitals. Some libraries using this system use "Y" for criticisms and "Z" for concordances. In the Dewey schedule, 928 is an optional biography number for literary figures (920 for Biography; 8 for Literature). Using this option, biographies of authors might be classified in 928, with subdivision for nationality. The cutter number in this case would be the number for the biographee with a workmark for the author of the biography. A capital letter would not be necessary.

Biographies of persons who are not authors or are not literary authors are classified in Dewey in a number corresponding to the subject area where the person was most prominent. The standard subdivision –092 is used with such a number. The cutter number for such a work usually stands for the person the work is about with a workmark for the author of the biography.

The problem of a variety of editions occurs most frequently in literature, but classic works in all other fields are also reprinted by the same or another publisher, especially since paperbacks and audio books have revived many worthwhile books that have been long out of print. One cataloging practice is to assign the date of publication as part of the call number to all editions of a single work issued by the same publisher and to assign a number following the work letter to all editions of the same work published by different publishers. For example, the first acquired copy of *Wings of the Dove* might be assigned the call number 813.4 J27w. If the library acquired a second copy of the novel, issued by a different publisher, the number might be 813.4 J27w2. If we assume that the second publisher was Modern Library and that the library received another edition of the novel, also published by Modern Library, in 1985, the call number might then be 813.4 J27w2 1985. A completely different edition published by a third publisher could be assigned 813.4 J27w3. Many variations of these practices exist. Keeping track of such numbering, however, is daunting, and most libraries have decided just to add the date of publication to a new edition's call number in all cases (e.g., 813.4 J27w 1983).

CUTTER NUMBERS DEVISED BY THE LIBRARY OF CONGRESS (LC)

LC call numbers also consist, in general, of two principal elements: classification notation and cutter number, to which are added, as required, symbols designating a particular work. While it is possible to use Cutter-Sanborn numbers with LC classification, most libraries prefer to use LC cutter numbers constructed from a table composed by LC for this purpose.

Policies and procedures used at LC in completing call numbers have been published in the form of a shelflisting manual.[5] This manual should be consulted for more detailed information than is discussed below.

LC cutter numbers are composed of the initial letter of the main entry heading, followed by Arabic numerals representing succeeding letters on the following basis:

LC Cutter Table

(1)	After initial *vowels* for the second letter:	b	d	l-m	n	p	r	s-t	u-y
	use number:	2	3	4	5	6	7	8	9

(2)	After initial letter *S* for the second letter:	a	ch	e	h-i	m-p	t	u	w-z
	use number:	2	3	4	5	6	7	8	9

(3)	After initial letters *Qu* for the second [i.e. next] letter:	a	e	i	o	r	t	y	
	use number:	3	4	5	6	7	8	9	

For initial letters *Qa-Qt*, use: **2-29**

(4)	After other initial *consonants* for the second letter:	a	e	i	o	r	u	y	
	use number:	3	4	5	6	7	8	9	

(5)	For *expansion* for the letter:	a-d	e-h	i-l	m-o	p-s	t-v	w-z	
	use number:	3	4	5	6	7	8	9	

The following examples show cutters that would be used if entries already shelflisted conform to the table [above]. In most cases, cutters must be adjusted to file an entry correctly and to allow room for later entries.

Vowels		S		Q		Consonants	
IBM	.I26	Sadron	.S23	*Qadduri	.Q23	Campbell	.C36
Idaho	.I33	*Scanlon	.S29	*Qiao	.Q27	Ceccaldi	.C43
*Ilardo	.I4	Schreiber	.S37	Quade	.Q33	*Chertok	.C48
*Import	.I48	*Shillingburg	.S53	Queiroz	.Q45	*Clark	.C58
Inman	.I56	*Singer	.S57	Quinn	.Q56	Cobblestone	.C63
Ipswich	.I67	Stinson	.S75	Quorum	.Q67	Cryer	.C79
*Ito	.I87	Suranyi	.S87	Qutub	.Q88	Cuellar	.C84
*Ivy	.I94	*Symposium	.S96	*Qvortrup	.Q97	Cymbal	.C96

*These cutters reflect the adjustments made to allow for a range of letters on the table, e.g., **l-m**, or for letters not explicitly stated, e.g., **h** after an initial consonant.[6]

Some points need further comment. Note first of all that the numeral *1* appears nowhere in the table. LC avoids its use, so that it will not become necessary to use zeros to preserve alphabetic order. If, for instance, the name *Abbott* were given the cutter *.A1*, a subsequent cutter at the same location for *Aamondt* would have to be, say, *.A09*, while *Aagard* would go to *.A085* or something like it. While most type-fonts distinguish between the digit zero and the capital letter *O*, it is still sometimes difficult for the human eye to distinguish them. In actual practice, LC shelflisters would likely give *Abbott* a cutter such as *.A2* so that later assignments for names such as *Aagard* and *Aamodt* could have *.A12* and *.A15*, or similar decimals to ensure space for unlimited further alphabetical expansion if needed.

All this brings out another trait of LC shelflisting. There is nothing sacrosanct about the above table. It has been officially changed as shelflisting problems were encountered and new needs were perceived. The present LC shelflist contains a jumble of old and new assignments. Recently devised numbers may reflect accommodation to outmoded practices, to avoid extensive re-shelflisting, rather than following current practice as outlined in the table. Cutter numbers assigned for the same person may also vary significantly from one classification notation to another. The examples below illustrate such a variation:

TL561	Splaver, Sarah, 1921–
.S65	Some day I'll be an aerospace engineer . . .
. . . .	
Z682	Splaver, Sarah, 1921–
.S735	Some day I'll be a librarian . . .

Since cutter numbers are used by LC to extend some classification notations, as well as for shelflisting alphabetically by main entry, many works have two cutter segments in their call numbers. One example is Niles M. Hansen's *French Regional Planning*, for which the LC call number, HT395.F7H35, can be analyzed as follows:

H	Social sciences
HT	Communities. Classes. Races
395	Regional planning: countries or regions other than the United States, A-Z
.F7	France
H35	The cutter number for Hansen

While double cutters are commonplace, triple cutters are exceedingly rare. They have been used in class G for certain kinds of subject maps, but with a special disclaimer added. An example is the *New York City Community Health Atlas 1988* prepared by Melvin I. Krasner, et al. Its call number, G1254.N4 E55 K7 1988, is analyzed as follows:

G	Geography. Anthropology. Recreation
1-9980	Geography (General). Atlases. Maps
1000.3-3122	Atlases
1254	New York State sub-area atlas
.N4	New York City
E55	Public Health [from Table G1a—Subject subdivisions: "These numbers are not Cutter numbers and have no alphabetical significance."]
K7	Cutter number for Krasner
1988	Date of atlas publication

In other instances where double cutters are prescribed in the schedules to stand for two separate subdivisions of the subject, the second cutter is made to accommodate both the subject for which it stands and the alphabetical arrangement for which it stands. For example:

HD3568   Cooperatives : pivot for economic development
.A6L343   [a book about cooperatives in Lagos, Nigeria]
1996

In the classification schedules under HD3441–3570.9, the notation run assigned to industrial cooperation by country, the notation for the country (in this case, HD3568 for Nigeria) is first cuttered by *.A6* for general cooperative societies and then is subdivided further "by state, province, etc." Therefore, *L343* stands both for Lagos State and for the alphabetical arrangement of the title main entry among other works on the subject.

Reserved cutter numbers. The LC schedules and tables frequently set aside the first few *.A* or the last several *.Z* possibilities in a cutter sequence for special purposes. Observe the example at "TD21–127—Country and City Subdivisions [of Environmental technology and Sanitary engineering]" in figure 16.3 on page 439. Assume that class T, Table 1, and the internal table in the schedule have been applied to derive the classification number TD28.A1 for a general work on sanitary engineering in Mexico. Let us suppose that the first book classified here was written by a Ricardo Gomez. Using the LC cutter number table, we could complete the call number as TD28.A1G6 or TD28.A1G65. A second work on the same topic by a Rachael Goode might then receive the call number TD28.A1G66, while still a third treatise by a Ralph Goddard could be given something like TD28.A1G58.

Assume now that we have a book on sanitary engineering in the Mexican state of Aguascalientes. It cannot receive the usual cutter *.A3* or *.A33* because the internal table at TD21–126 has "reserved" .A1 through .A5 for general works and other possible future needs. One knows this because the direction for cuttering for "States, provinces, etc." is to use ".A6–Z," meaning that the first cutter that can be used for a state beginning with the letter "A" is "A6." Therefore we must accommodate the reservation by assigning the classification number TD28.A68, followed by an appropriate cutter number for main entry. Now suppose that still another book covers sanitary engineering in the city of Aguascalientes. Our classification number will probably be TD29.A38, plus a second cutter for the main entry.

.Z cutter reservations are most common in class P, where researchers like to have biography and criticism of an author shelved immediately following that author's works. In this class, separate integers frequently designate all authors of a given period whose surnames start with the same initial (e.g., PR6045 is for all English literary authors who wrote between 1900 and 1960 and whose surnames begin with "W"). The first cutter number is then based on the second letter of the surname. That is, the letter beginning the cutter is the second letter of the author's name, followed by a number representing the third letter (e.g., the cutter for Rebecca West is E8). A second cutter, based usually on an auxiliary table of reserved numbers, identifies collected works, selections, titles of separate works, adaptations, translations, or biography and criticism. *The Selected Letters of Rebecca West* carries the LC call number PR6045.E8Z48 1999, exemplifying application of auxiliary Table 40 in the *P-PZ Language and Literature Tables* of the LC classification schedules, where *Z48* is for collections of a person's letters arranged by date of publication.

Additions to LC call numbers. Workmarks, in the traditional sense of lower-case letters added to book numbers to alphabetize titles or writers of biographies, are not used by LC. Lowercase letters do serve a few special purposes in LC call numbers. They are sometimes used following dates, as discussed below. In addition, in subclass "PZ Fiction in English. Juvenile Literature" a unique combination of upper- and lowercase letters (instead of second cutter numbers) alphabetizes the titles of a given author, while dates designate reissues or new editions. For example, the original 1938 Vanguard Press edition of Dr. Seuss's *The 500 Hats of Bartholomew Cubbins* was given the call number PZ8.G326 Fi, while the 1990 Random House edition has the call number PZ8.G326 Fi 1990. (*Fi* was used in the time when this title was to be filed as if spelled out: "Five Hundred Hats. . . .") Formerly, numerals were used with juvenile literature call numbers to designate new editions, so the 1966 Collins edition of this work was given the call number PZ8.G326 Fi2.

The adding of dates to LC call numbers has increased with multiple publications in more than one country, in different imprints, in paperback as well as hardcover, in later editions, and in reprints. LC began in 1982 to add dates to all monographic call numbers.[7] One use of lowercase letters is to identify bibliographically distinct issues of the same title published in the same year. For example, Andrew M. Greeley's *Love Song* was published by G. K. Hall in a large print version the same year it was published by Warner Books. The second one to be cataloged was assigned the call number PS3557.R358 L68 1989b, the use of the letter "b" being the only difference between the two call numbers. Another use of lowercase letters following dates is to distinguish among works on the same subject and published in the same year that have the same corporate body as main entry.[8]

A few other exceptional notations show up in some schedules. For example, dates are used not only as final elements, to distinguish issues of the same title, but also they occasionally become secondary elements of classification numbers, taking precedence over cutter numbers. Classification numbers "BX830–831—General and Ecumenical Councils [within Roman Catholicism]" use this device to arrange church councils by date of opening. An example is John W. O'Malley's *Tradition and Transition: Historical Perspectives on Vatican II*, which carries the LC call number BX830 1962 .O45 1989. Also, in schedule "BL-BX—Religion" some Bible texts are so specifically classified that LC shelflisters merely add dates (no cutter numbers) to keep them in order. For example, the *NRSV-NIV Parallel New Testament in Greek and English*, with interlinear translation by Alfred Marshall, has been assigned the LC call number BS1965.5 1990.

CONCLUSION

Call numbers are of particular concern in libraries with open stacks where browsing allows patrons to find materials on similar subjects in proximity, to find works of one author on a subject together, and to find editions of a work together. Where there are closed stacks, an accession number can serve as well as a call number for retrieval, although a greater burden is then placed on the verbal subject headings to guide users to information packages in particular subject areas.

While use of cutter numbers is the most common method of creating complete call numbers, other means may sometimes be found more useful. In a science and technology collection, for example, where recency of material may be of utmost importance, subarrangement under each classification notation may be by year of imprint. In very small general collections, on the other hand, one or more letters of the first word of the main entry may be added after the classification notation, with no additional numbers given. This method, however, will usually not result in unique call numbers, which may be needed for shelving management.

NOTES

1. Charles A. Cutter, *Two-Figure Author Table*, Swanson-Swift revision, 1969. Distributed by Libraries Unlimited, Inc., Littleton, Colo. (formerly distributed by H. R. Huntting Co.).

2. Charles A. Cutter, *Cutter-Sanborn Three-Figure Author Table*, Swanson-Swift revision, 1969. Distributed by Libraries Unlimited, Inc., Littleton, Colo. (formerly distributed by H. R. Huntting Co.).

3. Charles A. Cutter, *Three-Figure Author Table*, Swanson-Swift revision, 1969. Distributed by Libraries Unlimited, Inc., Littleton, Colo. (formerly distributed by H. R. Huntting Co.).

4. "Dewey Cutter Program," OCLC (available: http://www.oclc.org/dewey/support/program/default.htm [accessed 2/14/2006])

5. *Subject Cataloging Manual: Shelflisting*, 2nd ed. (Washington, D.C.: Cataloging Distribution Service, Library of Congress, 1995). Also available in *Cataloger's Desktop*.

6. Ibid., G60, pp. 14–15

7. *Cataloging Service Bulletin*, no. 19 (Winter 1982): 25–26.

8. *Subject Cataloging Manual: Shelflisting*, G220.

SUGGESTED READING

Comaromi, John P. *Book Numbers: A Historical Study and Practical Guide to Their Use.* Littleton, Colo.: Libraries Unlimited, 1981.

Lehnus, Donald J. *Book Numbers: History, Principles, and Application.* Chicago: American Library Association, 1980.

Taylor, Arlene G. *The Organization of Information.* 2nd ed. Westport, Conn.: Libraries Unlimited, 2004. Chapter 12: Arrangement and Display.

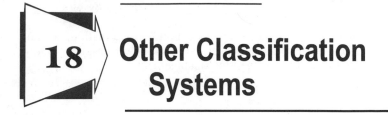

18 ▷ Other Classification Systems

INTRODUCTION

This chapter provides a brief overview of some of the more significant modern classifications besides *Dewey Decimal Classification* (*DDC*) and *Library of Congress Classification* (*LCC*). Those discussed are Cutter's *Expansive Classification*, Brown's *Subject Classification*, Bliss's *Bibliographic Classification*, and some special classifications, including some taxonomies. *Universal Decimal Classification* (*UDC*) was discussed at the end of chapter 15, "Decimal Classification," and Ranganathan's *Colon Classification* was used as an example in the discussion of faceted classification in chapter 14. While the classifications discussed here by no means exhaust modern classification research and practice, they do illustrate many of the problems and solutions, or failures, of both the seminal and the well-entrenched systems discussed in the contemporary literature.[1]

CUTTER'S *EXPANSIVE CLASSIFICATION*

The *Expansive Classification*, like the *DDC*, was the brainchild of an eminent library pioneer. Charles A. Cutter (1837–1903) was 15 years older than Melvil Dewey (1851–1931), but took 15 years longer to publish his scheme. Both men devised their systems as practical efforts to organize collections that they knew and served. Just as *DDC* came out of Dewey's student employment in the Amherst College Library, so Cutter's cataloging efforts in the Harvard College Library, and for much longer at the Boston Athenaeum, gave rise to his *Expansive Classification*.

While the lives and achievements of the two men show many parallels, there are also significant differences. In classification, Dewey chose his pure decimal notation early on, making it such a key feature of his approach that it more or less governed all subsequent growth patterns. He saw that a simple basic design, easy-to-master mnemonic devices, and a certain sturdy inflexibility could provide a general system that would be applicable to the many libraries that were being established. With characteristic energy, he started a schedule of periodic revision to keep his system responsive to the rapidly changing cultural and publishing milieu. And he marketed his invention with zest and conviction. Cutter was of a more delicate physique and temperament, less exuberant, more institution-oriented. But he, too, was imbued with the gregarious optimism of his era and worked diligently to establish librarianship as a helping profession, with "scientific" organization as one of its basic assumptions.

Cutter's scheme stressed a sequence of "classifications," or expansions, from a very simple set of categories for a small library to an intricate network of interrelated, highly specific subdivisions for the library of over a million volumes.[2] He did not live to finish his ultimate seventh expansion or to embark on a successive-edition program, but he did have the satisfaction of seeing the Library of Congress (LC) prefer many features of his scheme to that of his friendly rival. His willingness to take suggestions, and to compromise, worked to his credit and to the continuing influence of his system in spite of its limited adoption.

Cutter found the 10 broad classes of *DDC* too narrow a base for large collections. He therefore turned to the alphabet, with its easily ordered sequence of up to 26 primary groupings. For collections that "could be put into a single room" his first "classification" used only seven letters, with an eighth double-letter subclass, as follows:

A   Works of reference and general works that include several of the following sections, and so could not go to any one

B   Philosophy and Religion

E   Biography

F   History and Geography and Travels

H   Social sciences

L   Natural sciences and Arts

Y   Language and Literature

YF   Fiction

Cutter's second classification, or expansion, introduced a mixed alphanumeric notation that could be used if a small library should grow to require closer, more specific classes. It also subdivided the "F—History" and the new "G—Geography" classes by adding two Arabic numerals to the letter to signify identical geographic areas for each class. For example, F30 means History of Europe, while G30 means Geography of Europe. The second expansion holds 14 main classes, some redefinition of the original seven, and further differentiation of two classes along geographic lines.

The third expansion completes all but "P—Vertebrates" of the base 26 divisions and separates Religion from Philosophy, moving it to a second double-letter subclass. Part of the debt that *LCC* owes to Cutter can easily be traced through the outline comparison shown on page 458.

The fourth expansion subdivides 12 main classes for the first time, increasing the double-letter subclasses to 50. It also carries an extensive supplementary table expanding the double-digit geographic numbers from the F and G classes into a "place" or "local" list.

The fifth expansion introduces the twenty-sixth single-letter class "P—Vertebrates" and subdivides all remaining undivided classes, using many triple- and a few quadruple-letter sections. The sixth "classification" introduces no new techniques—only new expansions of existing classes and subclasses.

The seventh classification was published in 18 parts, edited and to some extent developed by William Parker Cutter after the originator's death.[3] All expansions were prepared on the theory that as a library outgrew its simpler modes of organization, partial dislocation and reclassification of the existing collection was preferable to complete reorganization. Although some books would have to be reclassed and relocated, not all would be, and certainly not all at once.

Cutter's *Expansive Classification* (3rd Expansion)		Library of Congress Classification (LCC)	
A	General works	A	General works
B	Philosophy	B	Philosophy. Religion
BR	Non-Judaeo-Christian religions		
C	Judaism and Christianity	C	History. Auxiliary sciences
D	Ecclesiastical history	D	History (except America)
E	Biography	E-F	History of the Americas
F	History		
G	Geography	G	Geography. Anthropology
H	Social sciences	H	Social sciences
I	Sociology		
J	Political science	J	Political science
K	Law	K	Law
L	Natural sciences	L	Education
M	Natural history	M	Music
N	Botany	N	Fine arts
O	Zoology		
		P	Language and literature
Q	Medicine	Q	Science
R	Technology	R	Medicine
S	Engineering	S	Agriculture
T	Manufactures and Handicrafts	T	Technology
U	Defensive and preservative arts	U	Military science
V	Athletic and recreative arts	V	Naval science
W	Fine arts		
X	Languages		
Y	Literature		
YF	Fiction		
Z	Book arts	Z	Bibliography and Library science

While it was never widely adopted, some 67 American, Canadian, and British libraries have been identified as past or present Cutter System users.[4] Perhaps even more important is the influence it exerted on later, more popular classifications, such as that developed at LC.

BROWN'S *SUBJECT CLASSIFICATION*

Next in chronological development is a British scheme. James Duff Brown (1864–1914) was a Scottish counterpart of Dewey and Cutter, if somewhat younger. Coming to the profession from an early apprenticeship to publishers and booksellers, he became deeply involved in the public library movement in Great Britain. It is debatable whether his advocacy of open stacks was directly influenced by his travels in the United States in 1893. His breadth of knowledge was legendary, even though he did not have a university education, and his interest in music resulted in several music reference tools that he either compiled or sponsored.

Brown recognized the lack of good organization of materials in most British libraries. To make open stack access feasible he and John Henry Quinn published in 1894 a "Classification of Books for Libraries in Which Readers Are Allowed Access to Shelves." Brown's own "Adjustable Classification" followed in 1898. As the name implies, it allowed for insertion of new divisions or topics as needed, but it was not worked out or indexed in much detail. Growing out of it, in 1906, was the first edition of the *Subject Classification*. In 1914, shortly after Brown's death, came a second edition, and in 1939 James Douglas Stewart issued a revised and enlarged third edition.[5]

The basic scaffold of Brown's *Subject Classification* consists of 11 main classes, expressing four broad divisional concepts in orderly sequence. Primary notation is alphabetical, with some classes assigned more than one capital letter, to cover all subtopics without making the notation unduly long:

A	Generalia	} Matter and force
B C D	Physical Science	
E F	Biological Science	
G H	Ethnological and Medical Science	} Life
I	Economic Biology and Domestic Arts	
J K	Philosophy and Religion	
L	Social and Political Science	} Mind
M	Language and Literature	
N	Literary forms	
O - W	History, Geography	} Record
X	Biography	

Each initial letter is followed by three Arabic numerals. Sequence, rather than length of number, reveals hierarchy, e.g.,

D600	METALLURGY
601	Smelting
602	Blast Furnaces
603	Open Hearth Furnaces
604	Ores

These schedule numbers may be expanded like decimals (without the decimal point) when new topics require insertion. The scheme allows several methods of building numbers: geographic numbers from the O-W classes may be attached to topical numbers when needed. There is a "Categorical Table" of "forms, etc. for the subdivision of subjects." Numbers from this table are attached after a period, which is not to be regarded as a decimal point. A plus sign is used to connect two facets from the same class. The underscore is used to "stack" parts of a number. Its purpose is to keep an extended notation compact.

While Brown's *Subject Classification*, like Cutter's *Expansive Classification*, never gained the widespread adoption received by its American rivals, timing and the lack of a consistent, continuing update program may be the explanation, rather than the comparative merits of the four schemes. Brown's system stimulated research and development in British classification theory, much as Cutter's did in the United States. Both are now milestones of classification history, rather than popular modern schemes for arranging library materials.

BLISS'S
BIBLIOGRAPHIC CLASSIFICATION

Henry Evelyn Bliss (1870–1955) was Librarian of the College of the City of New York, where he spent some 30 years developing and testing his ideas on library classification. After several periodical articles and books, he finished publication of his magnum opus only two years before his death.[6]

A "bibliographic" classification is, in Bliss's terminology, one designed to organize documentary materials (i.e., library collections, chiefly in print format). The sequence of main classes nonetheless preserves the discipline (rather than topical) orientation that Bliss interpreted as the basic structure of knowledge. Paul Dunkin called it "a sort of reader interest classification for scholars."[7]

According to Bliss, it is important in classifying a book to decide in what main classes it falls. The literature on concrete topics like "bees" is not kept in one place (as Brown would try to do) but is distributed, as in *DDC*, according to the "aspect" from which it is viewed. For example, a book on bees from a scientific aspect goes to class "G—Zoology," whereas a book on beekeeping is classed in "U—Useful Arts."

The Bliss system soon grew more popular in Great Britain than in the United States.[8] A British Committee for the Bliss Classification, which changed its name in 1967 to the Bliss Classification Association (BCA), draws its membership largely from libraries using the scheme. It publishes an annual *Bliss Classification Bulletin* and has an annual meeting in November each year. The Association arranges lectures and visits to libraries using the scheme. The BCA official website[9] links to several *Bibliographic Classification* (*BC*) sites, some of which are particular colleges of Cambridge University and of Oxford University.

The second edition (*BC2*) is so radically revised that it is more accurately described as a new system, although it uses the broad outline developed by Bliss. It derives techniques of facet analysis, as well as of explicit citation and filing orders, from Ranganathan's monumental contributions to classification theory. The outline of *BC2* is as follows:

	Introduction & Auxiliary schedules. 1977
2/9	Generalia, Phenomena, Knowledge, Information science & technology
A/AL	Philosophy & Logic. 1991
AM/AX	Mathematics, Probability, Statistics. 1993
AY	General science. 1999
B	Physics. 1999
C	Chemistry, Chemical Engineering. To be published 2006
D	Space & Earth sciences
	Astronomy
	Geology
	Geography
E/GQ	Biological sciences
E	Biology
	Biochemistry
	Genetics
	Virology
F	Botany
G	Zoology
GR	Agriculture
GU	Veterinary Science
GY	Applied Ecology, Human environment
H	Physical Anthropology, Human biology, Health sciences. 1980
I	Psychology & Psychiatry. 1978
J	Education. Rev. ed. 1990
K	Society (includes Social sciences, sociology & social anthropology). 1984
L/O	History, (includes Archaeology, biography and travel)
P	Religion, Occult, Morals and ethics. 1977
Q	Social welfare & Criminology. Rev. ed. 1994
R	Politics & Public administration. 1996
S	Law. 1996
T	Economics & Management of economic enterprises. 1987
U/V	Technology, Engineering. To be published 2007
W	Recreation, Arts, Music. To be published 2006
X/Y	Language, Literature

The dates following the titles indicate the volumes that have appeared to date or are scheduled for publication. Detailed draft schedules have been completed for all remaining classes, and are available from the BCA.[10]

Second edition notation consists of capital letters and numerals, omitting zero because of its similarity to the letter O. The numbers are as brief as possible, consistent with full expression of the various aspects of a topic. Each main class and each subclass is fully faceted. A comprehensive and consistent citation order is observed throughout; although it is suggested that if that order is not appropriate in a particular local situation, another order may be adopted. The notation is fully faceted and does not attempt the task of always reflecting hierarchy. The notation uses only letters and numbers divided into blocks of three. The first letter indicates the discipline of the information package, as shown in the outline above. The next letter categorizes the subject into the broad areas of the discipline. It can be subdivided again for more specificity. An example of a notation for the nursing of children with cancer is HXO QEM Y:

HXO	Pediatrics
HQE	Cancer
HMY	Nursing

The initial letter for the class is dropped when combining subclasses.

The future of the *Bibliographic Classification* is dependent in large part on the timing and public acceptance of the new edition. That Bliss's theory and practice has many advantages is a fact recognized by anyone who knows it well enough to compare it with more widely accepted schemes. That it badly needed updating and further development is also clear. The gargantuan job of complete overhaul by a few aficionados on a shoestring budget, if finished, should permit future sequential revision of different class schedules as needed (somewhat resembling the present revision program at LC). Establishment of the Bliss scheme as a major contender for library adoption will require not only efficient, dedicated work, but also a great deal of luck.

SPECIAL CLASSIFICATION SCHEMES

Classification schemes comprising the entire universe of knowledge must of necessity be general and cannot deal with specialties or fine detail. They are also largely inflexible, presenting the particular viewpoint of their designers (which in the case of *DDC* and *LCC* represents the late nineteenth century), and they often disperse subjects that, for the purposes of specialists, ought to be dealt with in close proximity (e.g., *DDC* has chemistry in 540 but chemical technology in 660, which is very unhelpful for a chemistry library). Even *UDC*, although providing for very fine detail, suffers from many of the faults inherited from *DDC* (e.g., the chemistry dispersal) and often has long notations.

Librarians of collections devoted mainly or exclusively to one specific field of knowledge, a discipline, or one of its subfields have therefore often found it necessary to design special classification schemes, sometimes called *taxonomies*. The word "classification," for most people, triggers the idea of a notation assigned to an information package in order to put it in order among other information packages. The word "taxonomy," for most people, triggers the idea of a strict scientific arrangement of class/genre/species. The word comes from the Greek *taxis* (arrangement, order) and *nomos* (law). The term is still newly being used in place of "classification" and the current definition is still in flux. It can be used to mean classification schemes, thesauri, or simply lists of categories. The Montague Institute has defined it as "a system for naming and organizing things into groups that share similar characteristics."[11] Thomas Wason has defined it as "a controlled vocabulary of terms and or phrases . . . an orderly classification of information according to presumed natural relationships. . . . The most typical form . . . is a hierarchy."[12]

The British Classification Research Group (CRG) was particularly active in designing special faceted classifications during the 1960s and 1970s, whereas in the

United States special classifications were more often the work of individuals and organizations. Such special classifications have usually been bibliographic classifications, designed to provide ways of ordering physical information packages in a specific subject area. Taxonomies have developed more recently, especially with the increased use of the Web and other computer systems for providing access to full text electronic documents in specialized subject areas. Taxonomies are often categorized lists of terms and include classification schemes, subject heading lists, Internet directories and gateways. They are often proprietary to the organizations that created them and, in such cases, they may not be freely used by others.

Special bibliographic classification schemes are mainly of two types: "general-special" schemes, which classify a special field or subject exhaustively while providing only very general class marks to peripheral or extraneous subjects, and "special" schemes, dealing only with a particular specialty in sometimes very fine detail but leaving the classing of other subjects to one of the general schemes. Hybrids of the two types are those schemes that expand an existing class of a general scheme or make use of an unused notation under which a special subject field is developed in detail.

Two examples of the latter type are widely used in U.S. libraries. *The National Library of Medicine Classification*[13] uses class W (which is vacant in *LCC*) and the medical parts of *LCC*'s class Q for the entire biomedical field. Subdivision of W is by all letters of the alphabet, including even I and O (which are avoided by *LCC* because of possible confusion with the digits 1 and 0), followed by up to three digits used enumeratively and an occasional fourth digit used decimally, followed by more detailed subdivision using cuttering, e.g.,

WD 200   Metabolic diseases

WD 205.5.A5   Amino acid metabolism

Since NLM's W class notations appear on many bibliographic records produced for distribution by NLM and also on some records produced by LC, most medical libraries use the W special classification.

Moys Classification and Thesaurus for Legal Materials,[14] which expands class K of *LCC*, found wide acceptance in law libraries after its publication in 1968, but completion of most of class K by LC in recent years has reduced the need for the separate scheme. Another expansion of *LCC* is for a highly specialized subject. *An Alternative Classification for Catholic Books*[15] takes a section of the LC classification that was not in use by LC when the schedule was developed in 1937 and develops it as Christian literature with three major subclasses: BQT, theology; BQV, canon law; and BQX, church history, all further subdivided by enumerative digits and cuttering. The introduction gives detailed instructions on how to integrate these schedules into either *LCC* or *DDC* when these are used to classify other subjects in a library. (BQ is now used in *LCC* for Buddhism.)

The following examples are representatives of the special type of classification that combines a faceted structure and high flexibility with brief notations. The *London Education Classification*[16] fulfills a double role as a classification and a thesaurus and uses a letter notation, with uppercase letters serving as facet indicators, e.g.,

Mab   Curriculum
Mabb   Curriculum development
Mabf   Curriculum classification

The *Physics and Astronomy Classification Scheme*[17] of the American Institute of Physics (AIP) uses a mixed notation of two numeric groups followed by a letter, e.g.,

84   Electromagnetic technology
84.30   Electronic circuits
84.30 L   Amplifiers

Except for two sections, the AIP scheme closely resembles the *International Classification for Physics*,[18] and parts of it have been adopted by the Institution of Electrical Engineers in London for its *Classification for the INSPEC Database*.[19] Thus, a physics library could choose among three major special schemes, all of which have the backing of professional societies.

The *London Classification of Business Studies*[20] has five major classes: management responsibility in the enterprise (A-G), environmental studies (J-R), analytical techniques (S-X), library and information science (Y), and auxiliary schedules (1-7). The notation consists of up to four uppercase letters, e.g.,

K   Industries
KCL   Alcoholic drinks industry
KCLB   Wine industry

and notations can be combined by a forward slash, e.g.,

EE/KCLB Financial management in the wine industry

The scheme is used in about 40 British libraries and more than 20 libraries elsewhere. The London Business School is responsible for updating and development of the scheme.

An example of a special scheme relying on another classification for extraneous subjects is the *Classification of Library & Information Science*,[21] designed by the Classification Research Group. This scheme, too, makes use of a letter notation with capitals as facet indicators, resulting in notations such as TogsNjrFv, which expresses the topic "Online systems:centralized:Public libraries," or ZmRnM(57), "Databases:Information Services:By subject:Biology," with 57 taken from *UDC* for a subject not germane to the central topic of library and information science.

Special classifications are sometimes developed for extremely narrow subjects, such as the *Classification for London Literature*,[22] concerned with works only on that city, with decimal subdivisions for every place and event in its long history, e.g.,

10   Religion
12   St. Paul's Cathedral
12.4   Dome and roof

A 1982 bibliography of classification schemes and subject heading lists for hundreds of different subjects gives 2,250 items in several languages.[23] It may be assumed that hundreds more have been created in the intervening years.

As already mentioned taxonomies are often not available for use by anyone other than the organization that developed them. A few (mainly government-developed) are available on the Web, however. One is the NCBI (National Center for Biotechnology Information) Taxonomy.[24] Another example is the GRIN (Germplasm Resources Information Network) Taxonomy.[25] As is true of virtually all taxonomies on the Web, these two appear in hierarchical structures in which a term can be viewed in a "tree" structure. Records for individual terms may have a "taxonomy ID" (e.g., "11103" is the ID number for "Hepatitis C Virus"), but there is no classification notation to be used for the arrangement of information resources. The latter are indexed with the term and may be retrieved in response to a term search.

The ambiguity in use of the term "taxonomy" is illustrated by a website called "Taxonomy Warehouse," which says it "aims to provide a comprehensive directory of taxonomies, thesauri, classification schemes, and other authority files from around the world."[26] When browsing the lists in various categories provided, however, very few of them use the word "taxonomy" in their titles. Rather they are called thesauri, terminology or subject lists, or other such names.

A special classification scheme or taxonomy may initially have the advantage of being more detailed and more up-to-date than any of the general schemes, but it is unfortunately often the case that such schemes, once designed, are not further developed and therefore become obsolete and lacking in detail much quicker than general schemes. When adopting a special scheme, one must take care to choose a scheme that has a reasonably good chance of being further developed and updated—that is, one that is backed by an organization rather than being the one-time effort of a librarian in a special collection. Such homemade classification schemes are generally motivated by the fact that sooner or later almost any librarian will find that the scheme he or she uses, whether general or specific, is insufficiently detailed or does not contain a classification notation for a new subject. It is then easy to succumb to the temptation to create a new subdivision or an entirely new scheme for the missing topics or for sections of a scheme that seem to be misplaced. The proper design of a special classification is, however, a task best left to someone thoroughly familiar with the theory and principles of classification design, and the novice should refrain from attempting this enterprise until some considerable experience has been gained. Many a hastily conceived and improperly designed special classification scheme has had to be abandoned sooner or later, to be replaced with an existing and proven scheme at great cost and inconvenience to a library or other organization and its users.

CONCLUSION

The classification systems briefly reviewed here differ from each other, and from the better known *DDC* and *LCC* systems, in many ways. In basic theory of the organization of knowledge, some emphasize the specific subject approach, clustering these unitary topics in related sequences, whereas most start from a broad disciplinary orientation, subdividing hierarchically, so that the various aspects or unitary topics become scattered to different parts of the system. In providing a schedule framework to arrange items on shelves, some systems (the more traditional) are primarily enumerative, whereas most newer ones are synthetic or faceted. Some maintain a comparatively pure notation, whereas others use combinations of letters and

Arabic numerals, while upper- and lowercase letters, Roman numerals, Greek letters, and a variety of arbitrary relational signs and symbols appear in still others. Systems designed for the Web may be alphabetical but most are designed to display terminology in a hierarchical order.

Timeliness is a constant problem. Some systems maintain a serials program to announce additions and changes or issue new editions at intervals of 5 to 25 years. Many have outlived their originators, but some suffer more than others from age and lack of funds or organized promotion. Each has unique attractive features; each has practical and theoretical problems. Some are more useful for shelf arrangement of books and related formats. Others are better suited to in-depth indexing of periodical articles, technical reports, documents, and the like. Centripetal forces such as networking seem at the moment to favor general acceptance of one or two well-known, widely used schemes, overlooking functional disadvantages to achieve standardization and administrative coherence. Yet classification research, like that in all other areas of bibliographic organization, is very brisk and busy in the modern world of information science. Time may show that all the schemes we study and use today, regardless of their present achievements or popularity, are chiefly important for the historic part they play as heralds of still better solutions to the problems of subject access.

NOTES

1. Four examples of specific applications using the systems discussed in this chapter, as well as *DDC* and *LCC*, are given in Bohdan S. Wynar, *Introduction to Cataloging and Classification*, 5th ed., prepared with the assistance of John Phillip Immroth (Littleton, Colo.: Libraries Unlimited, 1976), pp. 314–328.

2. Charles A. Cutter, *Expansive Classification, Part I: The First Six Classifications* (Boston: Cutter, 1891–1893).

3. Charles A. Cutter, *Expansive Classification, Part II: Seventh Classification*, largely edited by William Parker Cutter (Boston and Northampton, Mass.: Cutter, 1896–1911), 2v., with supplementary pages.

4. Robert L. Mowery, "The Cutter Classification: Still at Work," *Library Resources & Technical Services* 20 (Spring 1976): 154.

5. James Duff Brown, *Subject Classification: With Tables, Indexes, etc., for the Subdivision of Subjects*, 3rd ed., rev. and enl. by James Douglas Stewart (London: Grafton, 1939).

6. Bliss's major works are the following: *The Organization of Knowledge and the System of the Sciences* (New York: Holt, 1929); *The Organization of Knowledge in Libraries*, 2nd ed., rev. and partly rewritten (New York: H. W. Wilson, 1939); *A Bibliographic Classification: Extended by Systematic Auxiliary Schedules for Composite Specification and Notation* (New York: H. W. Wilson, 1940–1953), 4v.

7. Paul S. Dunkin, *Cataloging U.S.A.* (Chicago: American Library Association, 1969), p. 126.

8.   *See,* for instance: School Library Association (England), *The Abridged Bliss Classification: The Bibliographical Classification of Henry Evelyn Bliss Revised for School Libraries,* with corrections and minor amendments (London: The Association, 1970).

9.   Bliss Classification Association, "Bliss Classification Association," available: http://www.sid.cam.ac.uk/bca/bcahome.htm (accessed 2/14/2006).

10.   Bliss Classification Association, "The Bliss Bibliographic Classification: Outline of Bliss Classification (2nd ed.)," available: http://www.sid.cam.ac.uk/bca/bcoutline.htm (accessed 2/14/2006) and http://www.sid.cam.ac.uk/bca/bcsched.htm (accessed 2/22/2006).

11.   "Ten Taxonomy Myths," *Montague Institute Review* (November 2002; updated 12 October 2005), available: http://www.montague.com/review/myths.html (accessed 2/22/2006).

12.   Thomas D. Wason, "Dr. Tom's Taxonomy Guide: Description, Use and Selections," IMS Global Learning Consortium, Inc., Version 1.01, 15 February 2006, available: http://www.mindspring.com/~wason/TDW/drtomtaxonomiesguide.html (accessed 2/22/2006).

13.   *National Library of Medicine Classification: A Scheme for the Shelf Arrangement of Books in the Field of Medicine and Its Related Sciences,* 5th ed., rev. (Bethesda, Md.: NLM, 1999); *NLM Classification 2005,* available: http://wwwcf.nlm.nih.gov/class/ (accessed 2/22/2006).

14.   Elizabeth M. Moys, *Moys Classification and Thesaurus for Legal Materials,* 4th ed. (Munich; London: Bowker-Saur, 2001).

15.   Jeannette Murphy Lynn, *An Alternative Classification for Catholic Books,* 2nd ed., rev. by G. C. Peterson; supplement (1965) by Thomas G. Pater (Washington, D.C.: Catholic University of America Press, 1965).

16.   D. J. Foskett and J. Foskett, *The London Education Classification: A Thesaurus/Classification of British Education Terms,* 2nd ed. (London: University of London Institute of Education Library, 1974).

17.   American Institute of Physics, *Physics and Astronomy Classification Scheme, 1999* (Woodbury, N.Y.: AIP).

18.   International Council of Scientific Unions, Abstracting Board, *International Classification for Physics* (Paris: ICSU/AB, 1975).

19.   Institution of Electrical Engineers, *Classification: A Classification Scheme for the INSPEC Database* (London: IEE, 1991–).

20.   K. D. C. Vernon and V. Lang, *The London Classification of Business Studies,* 2nd ed., rev. by K. G. B. Bakewell and D. A. Cotton (London: Aslib, 1979).

21.   Classification Research Group, *A Classification of Library & Information Science,* 2nd ed. (London: CRG, 1975).

22.   Guildhall Library, *Classification for London Literature,* 3rd ed. (London: The Library, 1966).

23.   *Classification Systems and Thesauri, 1950–1982* (Frankfurt, West Germany: Indeks Verlag, 1982). International Classification and Indexing Bibliography 1.

24. *The NCBI Taxonomy Homepage.* Available: http://www.ncbi.nlm.nih.gov/Taxonomy/taxonomyhome.html/ (accessed 2/22/2006).

25. *GRIN Taxonomy for Plants.* Available: http://www.ars-grin.gov/cgi-bin/npgs/html/index.pl (accessed 2/22/2006).

26. *Taxonomy Warehouse.* Available: http://taxonomywarehouse.com/ (accessed 2/22/2006).

SUGGESTED READING

Chan, Lois Mai. *Cataloging and Classification: An Introduction.* 2nd ed. New York: McGraw-Hill, 1994. Chapter 14: National Library of Medicine Classification and Other Modern Classification Systems.

Foskett, A. C. *The Subject Approach to Information.* 5th ed. London: Library Association Publishing, 1996. Chapter 10: General Classification Schemes. Chapter 19: The Bibliographic Classification. Chapter 20: The Broad System of Ordering.

Koch, Traugott, and Michael Day. *The Role of Classification Schemes in Internet Resource Description and Discovery.* Available: http://www.ukoln.ac.uk/metadata/desire/classification/ (accessed 2/14/2006).

McKiernan, Gerry. *Beyond Bookmarks: Schemes for Organizing the Web.* Available: http://www.public.iastate.edu/~CYBERSTACKS/CTW.htm (accessed 2/14/2006).

Miksa, Francis. *The Subject in the Dictionary Catalog from Cutter to the Present.* Chicago: American Library Association, 1983. Chapter 6: Cutter's Subject Rules.

Rowley, Jennifer, and John Farrow. *Organizing Knowledge: An Introduction to Managing Access to Information.* 3rd ed. Aldershot, Eng.; Burlington, VT: Ashgate, 2000. "Other General Classifications," pp. 229–243.

Wason, Thomas D. "Dr. Tom's Taxonomy Guide: Description, Use and Selections." IMS Global Learning Consortium, Inc., Version 1.01, 15 February 2006. Available: http://www.mindspring.com/~wason/TDW/drtomtaxonomiesguide.html (accessed 2/22/2006).

Part VI
ADMINISTRATIVE ISSUES

19 〉 Processing Centers, Networking, and Cooperative Programs

INTRODUCTION

With the continued growth in volume of published materials, and the increased use of computers and telecommunications to transmit bibliographic information and documents from producer to consumer, the resultant need is for more efficient library service. The impact of computerization has significantly changed the traditional patterns of cataloging and processing of library materials. Most libraries and library systems have either centralized their technical services or entered into cooperative arrangements with other libraries through various levels of networking. Some libraries purchase their processing from commercial vendors. Thus we have centralized processing, cooperative processing, and commercial processing, most of which are automated.

For nearly all American libraries, the Library of Congress (LC) has been the primary source of bibliographic data for decades. With the advent of automation, LC's bibliographic products have been repackaged or reformatted by vendors, networks, and individual libraries. The result has been the development of large databases with LC records as the core. These databases are used directly by some libraries for their cataloging operations, are accessed by other libraries through a bibliographic network, and are also used by commercial vendors who provide processing for still other libraries.

Major cataloging operations usually have two production lines: copy cataloging and original cataloging. The copy cataloging operation is usually the larger unit, staffed by well-trained technicians called "copy catalogers," who edit existing bibliographic records primarily found in machine-readable form, but also in printed form. The original cataloging operation is usually staffed by a handful of professionally trained "original catalogers" who prepare bibliographic records when no cataloging "copy" has been found for the work in hand.

Cataloging operations are now an integral part of automated processing. The development of networking using telecommunications and computers has enhanced cooperation for processing services and systems. Automation has virtually eliminated the individual library doing its own ordering, cataloging, and physical preparation of materials in isolation.

471

BIBLIOGRAPHIC SERVICES
OF THE LIBRARY OF CONGRESS

LC's bibliographic records offer complete coverage for materials, both foreign and domestic, cataloged by the Library. LC is, of course, the copyright depository for domestic works. Two federal legislative acts significantly increased LC's coverage of foreign materials starting in the early 1960s. One authorized certain foreign countries to pay some of their debts to the United States by sending printed materials. The other authorized LC to acquire, catalog, and distribute bibliographic records for all materials of research value published in foreign countries. The thrust of the legislation benefited not only LC, but also all American research libraries.

Cataloging Distribution Service (CDS)

In 1975 the Card Division of LC changed its name to the Cataloging Distribution Service (CDS).[1] The change reflected a trend from print to machine-readable format in its distribution of bibliographic records. The distribution of print formats includes the sale of *LC Rule Interpretations*, LC's *Subject Cataloging Manuals*, the *Library of Congress Classification* schedules, *Library of Congress Subject Headings,* etc. (CDS discontinued the production and sale of printed cards in 1997.) These cataloging tools, and many others, are also available in *Cataloger's Desktop* on the Web or through *Classification Web*. LC's authority records for names and subjects and also LC's bibliographic records are available through the MARC Distribution Services of the CDS.

Cataloging in Publication (CIP)

Most current American books carry a partial bibliographic description, namely author, title, series statement, notes, subject and added entries, LC call number, *Dewey Decimal Classification* (*DDC*) number, International Standard Book Number (ISBN), and LC control number (LCCN), on the verso of the title page. The program responsible for providing this bibliographic information is known as Cataloging in Publication (CIP). This program was initiated in 1971. Publishers cooperate by sending paper or electronic data sheets and front matter for books nearing publication to LC for preliminary cataloging prior to publication of their books. The "E-CIP," or Electronic Cataloging in Publication program, allows for the submission of entire galleys to LC. This results in more consistently accurate subject analysis and classification, which may be difficult when only a few pages, or sketchy data elements, are provided. CIP records are available on MAchine-Readable Cataloging (MARC) tapes, being later supplanted when the full record becomes available. CIP records are useful as a ready source of LCCNs. They can also be used to assist in the establishment of name headings. Some libraries use the CIP records for preliminary cataloging and later enhance the record when full LC records appear. Other libraries may use the brief CIP record instead of full cataloging, satisfied with the minimal-level record it provides. The illustration below shows the format and appearance of CIP data:

Library of Congress Cataloging-in-Publication Data

Anglo-American cataloguing rules / prepared under the direction of the Joint
Steering Committee for Revision of AACR, a committee of the American
Library Association ... [et al.]. — 2nd ed., 2002 revision.
    p. cm.
    Includes bibliographical references and index.
    ISBN 0-8389-3529-X (loose-leaf with binder) — ISBN 0-8389-3530-3
(loose-leaf without binder) — ISBN 0-8389-3531-1 (binder only)
    1. Descriptive cataloging—Rules. I. Joint Steering Committee for
Revision of AACR. II. American Library Association.

Z694.15.A56 A53 2002
025.3′2—dc21   2002073596

MARC Distribution Services /
MAchine-Readable Cataloging (MARC)

The importance of LC for setting catalog practice became even more evident
with the introduction of the MARC Distribution Services.[2] After initial study began
in 1964, extensive experimentation proceeded in the MARC I and MARC II, the
Retrospective Conversion (RECON), the Cooperative MAchine-Readable Cataloging (COMARC), and the British UK/MARC pilot projects; MARC format integration in 1995; and the harmonization of USMARC and CAN/MARC to *MARC 21* in
1999.

At first, records were available only for English-language monographs, but
formats now exist for archival materials, audiovisual materials, digital resources,
films, manuscripts, maps, music, and serials as well as for books. In addition, the Library of Congress does cataloging in over 400 languages. MARC records for materials in several non–Roman-alphabet languages (Arabic, Hebrew, Chinese,
Japanese, Korean, Persian, and Yiddish) are entered with those character sets. Other
non–Roman-alphabet languages currently are transliterated as the MARC records
are created, but work is proceeding toward UCS/Unicode implementation in library
systems, after which all non–Roman-alphabet languages may be entered without
transliteration.

The Conversion of Serials (CONSER) automated database was sponsored by
the Council on Library Resources (CLR), using the online facilities of OCLC, and
distributed through the MARC Distribution Services—Serials. Starting in mid-1976
with nearly 30,000 LC/MARC serial records, and accepting input from 14 North
American libraries, it amassed over 200,000 records in its initial two years. Only
one-third of them were authenticated by LC and the National Library of Canada (the
Designated Centers of Responsibility), but the number of verifications increased
each year. Original plans were for LC to take over full support at the close of the
two-year pilot program, but when it ran into difficulties in expanding its automation
capacity, OCLC agreed to retain the master database, assuming managerial responsibility as well. LC continues to coordinate the project and maintain the CONSER
records, working with the Program for Cooperative Cataloging (PCC).

Another project to add machine-readable bibliographic records for materials
previously cataloged on cards was the REMARC project, a retrospective conversion
project. The REMARC database was created by Carrollton Press, beginning in
1980. The goal was to convert to MARC format nearly five million titles cataloged

by LC between 1897 and 1968 (the year that most English-language LC cataloging of monographs became available in MARC format). Carrollton also converted some items cataloged by LC since 1968 that were not input into the MARC database by LC (e.g., foreign-language items that were phased into the MARC program throughout the 1970s). These records are available through AutoGraphics, the current owner of REMARC. Users of LC's online catalog will see these records identified as "PREMARC," but they are not included in LC's MARC Distribution Services.

Other projects to add to the LC MARC database began as experiments in cooperative cataloging. In the early 1980s the University of Chicago and Harvard University joined with LC to create cataloging records in MARC format. Library staff at both Harvard and Chicago directly input bibliographic records into the LC database, which were then distributed along with LC records to MARC subscribers. This project expanded to become the National Cooperative Cataloging Project (NCCP), and in 1995 became the PCC.

The growth and nearly universal acceptance of the MARC formats, and even more, the publication of *Anglo-American Cataloguing Rules, Second Edition (AACR2)*, highlighted the need for machine-readable authority records. A MARC format for name authority records was developed in the late 1970s, and LC began inputting name authority records in 1978. Later the MARC format for authorities was expanded to accommodate subjects, series, and uniform titles. All new names, series, uniform titles, and subjects currently entered into the LC database in the MARC authorities format, and many records have been retrospectively converted.

It is possible to obtain a subscription to one or more of the MARC Distribution Services. One can receive only books, visual materials, music, computer files, maps, or CONSER serials, or all of these. Also available are Name Authorities and Subject Authorities. These services are described on LC's Cataloging Distribution Service website.[3] All of the major bibliographic networks subscribe to the MARC Distribution Services. Manuals on the *MARC 21* formats are available.

In addition to the *MARC 21* records created by LC and the National Library of Canada, other countries have accepted the MARC format with slight variations for creating machine-readable cataloging records. Some other countries use variations of the UNIMARC format established through the International Federation of Library Associations and Institutions (IFLA), or have their own national format, such as MAB in Germany. Mapping across these formats enables sharing of records internationally.

CENTRALIZED PROCESSING

In library systems serving an entire region, county, municipality, university, public school district, commercial enterprise, or government agency, a central processing office normally handles the acquisition and preparation of materials for all public service branches. Subunits may do a final checking of records, but if any significant revision of the work is needed, it usually goes back to the central office. This type of organization received strong emphasis with the rapid growth of library systems after World War II.

The term *centralized processing* may be broadly defined as any consolidated effort to bring under one control the technical operations necessary to prepare library materials for access and use at different service points. In the ensuing discussion several comments are made that apply equally well—perhaps with some slight modification—to cooperative efforts and even to commercial sources of cataloging.

The reader can carry over such observations into those discussions where they have a bearing.

Processing centers take a variety of forms, but can generally be grouped into broad categories according to one or more notable characteristics. Grouping by type of services rendered gives:

- Centers responsible for acquisition and complete technical processing, down to the physical marking and/or jacketing
- Centers that order, catalog, and classify
- Centers that only catalog and classify

There are, of course, advantages to setting up a processing center for a group of libraries or branches. They include:

- Increased efficiency in handling more material at less cost
- Higher quality cataloging
- Centralization and simplification of business routines
- Better deployment of staff through specialization
- Use of more sophisticated technology
- Opportunities to create union catalogs

There are problems as well. Local variations in practice have to be identified and coordinated, or, if necessary, eliminated. Economic justification must be carefully determined, both before and after decision-making, to ensure that it is real, not imaginary. Many descriptive reports of individual centers lack critical self-appraisal and follow-up studies, especially in their cost analyses. Efficiency of operation is often the function of size. The "optimum" volume of processing in a given center should be determined. Combining several different types of libraries (e.g., school and public) within one system may lead to problems that even a highly structured organization cannot solve. We often learn as much from our failures as from our more successful attempts at consolidation.

COOPERATIVE SYSTEMS

The chief trait differentiating cooperative from centralized processing is that the cooperative approach involves several independent libraries or systems. Each member usually continues to perform some of its own technical service work, depending on exchange of data to achieve broader coverage or leaving a sizeable portion of its processing to be performed as a group project. Again, better use of resources, personnel, and equipment, as well as higher discounts on bulk purchases, are anticipated. The need for more standardization in ordering, cataloging, and processing may become either an advantage or a disruptive factor.

There are a number of cooperative arrangements in which several libraries with small budgets and small staffs pool resources to share one membership in a bibliographic network. Some such libraries may use access to the membership only a few hours a month; others may use it as much as one day a week.

UNION CATALOGS

Union catalogs are not, strictly speaking, a type of processing arrangement, but they are essential to a successful processing center and can be a *sine qua non* of a cooperative system. For example, the Bibliographical Center for Research (BCR) in Denver started in 1936 with a WPA grant to develop a union catalog based on a depository set of Library of Congress cards marked to show the holdings of member libraries in the Rocky Mountain area. The catalog was designed chiefly to serve BCR as a clearinghouse for regional interlibrary loans. In 1975, after a period of waning membership and reduced revenues, new objectives were announced, including the brokerage of OCLC services, with aid to members in other, related fields of communication, systems study, and network stimulation. The union catalog and interlibrary loan (ILL) services continued, but were deemphasized in favor of newer forms of cooperation. As at BCR, most union catalog projects in printed card form are now valued primarily for having fostered early efforts at library cooperation in many kinds of consortia and networks.

Some of those consortia and networks have produced online union catalogs at various levels:

- International online union catalogs of the major bibliographic networks

- Multi-institutional regional or state networks, such as the union catalog for libraries in Illinois or Wisconsin

- Single institution union catalogs, ranging from the statewide online union catalog of the University of California to the union catalog for the branches of an individual public library

There are also specialized union catalogs for types of materials, such as the Union Catalog of Newspapers on OCLC and numerous union lists of serials, including those available through the bibliographic networks.

PROGRAM FOR COOPERATIVE CATALOGING (PCC)

Initiated in February 1995, the PCC grew out of cooperative activities of the previous 20 years. LC began NACO (then called the Name Authority Cooperative project) in the late 1970s and expanded the cooperative projects for contributing full bibliographic records in NCCP (the National Coordinated Cataloging Program—no longer in existence). In November 1992 various participants from cooperative library programs met and formed the Cooperative Cataloging Council (CCC) that conducted studies to determine a strategic direction for future cooperative projects. The result was the PCC that incorporated the CONSER program in October 1997. PCC now has four components:

NACO (name authority program)
SACO (subject authority program)
BIBCO (bibliographic record program)
CONSER (cooperative online serials program)

According to its website, PCC is "an international cooperative effort aimed at expanding access to library collections by providing useful, timely, and cost-effective cataloging which meets mutually accepted standards of libraries around the world."[4] Participants contribute records through RLIN or OCLC and LC distributes those records through the MARC Distribution Services.

One of the major initiatives of PCC has been the promotion of a standard for what PCC calls the "core" record, a bibliographic record containing all essential bibliographic data elements. The purpose is to produce bibliographic records that can be created in a timely way and can be used by others with little or no editing, thus reducing the overall cost of cataloging.

ONLINE BIBLIOGRAPHIC
NETWORKS

Various definitions of networking spell out theoretical criteria or conditions. In practice, however, the term covers any systematic interchange of materials, bibliographic data, services, information, or occasionally, the transfer of such resources from a central office to a number of libraries. *Network* has been used to describe multi-library organizations designed to facilitate interlibrary loan, reference, duplicate exchange, processing, and the like. Our concern in this section is with the last named activity.

There are at present two major online bibliographic networks in the United States: OCLC Online Computer Library Center (OCLC),[5] which absorbed the former Western Library Network (WLN), and the Research Libraries Group (RLG).[6] A third network, A-G Canada Ltd., also serves some libraries in the United States, although the majority of its members are in Canada.[7] The Network Development Office of LC coined the term *bibliographic utility* for these online processing systems in 1978.[8] However, the providers of these services objected to the term, considering themselves to be networks of members. The term *utility* was an attempt to distinguish providers of computerized cataloging records from bibliographic service centers or regional networks, e.g., the Southeastern Library Network (SOLINET), which serve as regional brokers, providing intermediate communication, training, and service for participating libraries. With the provision of much more than catalog records in recent years, the lines have blurred, in any case.

Bibliographic networks seek to make catalog data widely and conveniently available, to foster processing speed and efficiency, to reduce the staff and cost of technical operations, and to facilitate resource sharing. Emphasis varies with the types of library a network is designed to serve. RLIN, for example, caters to the needs of major research libraries, while OCLC appeals to a wider spectrum. As most bibliographic networks evolved, their goals broadened to include support for different library functions.

Although the objectives of the two major bibliographic networks are similar, their services, costs, and operating procedures differ considerably. Each offers unique features that involve advantages and disadvantages for different members. The library that has potential access to more than one network must consider carefully such factors as cost, size of database, adaptation to its needs, types of service contracts, training and support arrangements, and the membership among neighboring libraries.

OCLC Online Computer Library Center (OCLC)

This oldest and largest of the bibliographic networks was incorporated in 1967 as the Ohio College Library Center, establishing an online, shared cataloging system with an online union catalog to the 54 academic libraries of Ohio. Online operations began in 1971 and expanded rapidly. In 1978 it changed its name to the acronym OCLC, Inc., downplaying the former regional connotation. At the same time, the governing structure was altered to allow libraries outside Ohio equal participation in its governance. In 1981 the official name was changed to OCLC Online Computer Library Center, Inc., in response to the fact that many people thought "OCLC" should stand for something. By 2006 there were more than 54,400 participating libraries throughout the world, cataloging most of their incoming materials through use of the existing online records, and inputting their original catalog records for cooperative use by other members.

A Members Council, elected from participants grouped in the regional service networks, chooses from among its members six of the 15 who serve on the Board of Trustees. The Members Council also advises the Board, which is the corporation's governing body. There are also Advisory Committees on Collections and Technical Services, Resource Sharing, Reference Services, and Research. Additionally, there are a number of User Groups, which are generally independent organizations with OCLC staff liaisons. User Groups have been established for types of libraries (e.g., law libraries), types of OCLC products such as Connexion and Promptcat, types of materials (e.g., music), and geographical regions.

OCLC serves individual libraries for the most part through 16 broker networks such as AMIGOS, FEDLINK, NELINET, OHIONET, SOLINET, and BCR. The western states, Europe, the Middle East and Africa, Latin America and the Caribbean, Asia Pacific, and Canada each have a regional service center maintained by OCLC itself, and there are a few scattered independent members. The brokers negotiate group contracts on behalf of their affiliates, perform profiling and staff training according to each one's specific needs, handle billing and other business procedures, and offer general assistance in effective use of OCLC services. Most regional networks are financed through membership fees plus surcharges on OCLC's charges.

The primary OCLC service has always been the online cataloging subsystem creating a database called WorldCat (formerly known as the OCLC Online Union Catalog). Because of its widespread use, it is described briefly here, but this overview is not intended to be a full introduction to its operation.[9] A library using the subsystem has access to a database that numbers more than 60 million bibliographic records, for which there are more than 990 million locations listed (according to the 2005 annual report). LC MARC tapes and additional cataloging by affiliates are constantly expanding the database at the rate of about one record every 10 seconds. An authorized library staff member at any workstation connected to the system may access any record, then edit the data to agree with the item being processed, and add holdings statements, locations, or other in-house data. Most libraries download bibliographic and authority records directly into their local automated systems, while others receive their records on magnetic tapes. For those libraries with card catalogs, cards are produced offline at OCLC headquarters in Dublin, Ohio, and shipped daily.

Connexion is the name for OCLC's primary cataloging service, providing access to WorldCat for original and copy cataloging. Connexion software is available for use with either a Web browser or Windows-based client interface. Smaller libraries who do not need to create original catalog records may also use CatExpress, a simpler service based on the Connexion Web interface. WorldCat may be searched in a variety of ways. Keyword searching is available in over thirty indexes, from the traditional, such as Title, Author and Subject, to the more specific, such as LC Children's Subject Headings and National Agricultural Library Classification Number. Numeric searches (e.g., LCCN; ISBN; ISSN; CODEN), title browse searches, and searches via special "search keys" are available. Multiple limits are available, including language, cataloging source, material format, and others.

In addition to WorldCat, LC's name (NAF) and subject (SAF) authority files are available, for both searching and browsing, singly or in combination. Authority records are displayed in separate windows, allowing the user to toggle between them and bibliographic records. (Multiple windows for each type of record may be open simultaneously.) Using this feature in the editing process, one may "cut and paste" blocks of text into bibliographic records from either authority records or other bibliographic records. There is also a capability, available to NACO participants, to have a basic name authority record generated automatically from a heading in a bibliographic record.

OCLC's Connexion service software supports the cataloging of materials in multiple non-Roman scripts, including Chinese, Japanese, Korean, Arabic, Hebrew, Cyrillic, Greek, Thai, and Tamil scripts. OCLC's former "CJK system" was retired at the end of June, 2005.

Records are held in WorldCat and in the authority databases in the MARC formats, although responses to searches may first be displayed in truncated or brief formats. New cataloging is usually entered into a MARC workform, although it is also possible to use a Dublin Core workform, especially when cataloging Web resources. There are standard protocols for original cataloging entered into OCLC. For one, member libraries are obliged to follow the latest version of *AACR2*. They are also requested, when inputting original cataloging, to check all name, uniform title, and series headings in the LC MARC authority file. Headings found in the authority file that are coded as being *AACR2* are to be input in that form into original cataloging. Records are coded to show compliance (or not) with these standards. The system is highly flexible, allowing members to adapt local records to meet local practices and conventions.

Quality control exists in published standards to which participating libraries are expected to adhere. Participants are encouraged to report any errors they find in the database. OCLC staff members check and correct the master records from these reports. Certain authorized libraries have been able to correct errors directly since 1984. "Full cataloging members" are able to enrich records, if appropriate, by adding or updating MARC data elements ranging from many types of notes to classification numbers, subject headings, URLs, and a variety of standard numbers.

Consultation of training manuals and, above all, hands-on use are needed to gain skill in tagging, searching, and using the system software. Most people who have been properly trained find the techniques simple to master. It must be remembered that OCLC's cataloging services are constantly developing and changing. A great quantity of documentation and training materials is available, but only recent tools should be used. Suggested sources for further information include OCLC's "Connexion support" site[10] and texts produced by participating networks. Also valuable are OCLC's *Technical Bulletins*, which provide updates for using the system.[11]

OCLC also offers many other cataloging services including custom cataloging, automated copy cataloging, and retrospective conversion. OCLC's Office of Research works in a number of areas relevant to cataloging, including interoperability of controlled vocabularies, automated classification, and the application of IFLA's *Functional Requirements for Bibliographic Records (FRBR)*, among other projects.[12]

Research Libraries Group (RLG)

RLG, Inc., was originally formed in 1974 by Columbia, Harvard, and Yale universities and the New York Public Library. Stanford University joined RLG as well, at an early point in its history. Membership exceeded 160 in 2005. In addition, several hundred other institutions purchase RLG's services.

The corporate objective is to foster interinstitutional support of scholarly communication and instruction in a rapidly changing climate of increasing costs and shrinking resources. Voting officers are elected annually by the member institutions to a 19-member Board of Directors. Together with the President—RLG's executive officer who serves on the Board as a voting member—they establish policies, programs, budgets, and fee structures, and they appoint committees. The primary programs of RLG are bibliographic control and access, resource sharing, collection management and cooperative development, preservation of research materials, and RLG's subject programs.

The bibliographic component is called the RLG Union Catalog (formerly RLIN, or Research Libraries Information Network). Unlike OCLC's WorldCat, the RLG Union Catalog preserves bibliographic records in clusters with a separate bibliographic record for every title cataloged by each library. Each library has online access to its own records showing whatever local changes may have been made. Local holdings, etc., are available to each local library, and selected data are available from records of other institutions. This facilitates interlibrary loan. RLIN21 is the name of RLG's Windows-based cataloging software program, used to create and edit bibliographic and authority records; an RLIN21 Web interface is used to search for, display and export records.

RLG also provides Eureka, an easy to use search service that allows simple searches by author, title, subject, and keyword, as well as advanced searches which may combine elements from an array of alphabetical and numeric indexes, limited by date and/or language. Search terms can be used singly or in any sequence. They include LC control numbers, all or part of call numbers, ISSN/ISBN numbers, LC subject headings, form and genre headings, and many others. The Boolean logic operators *AND*, *OR*, and *NOT* help tailor search strategies. All searches are interactive and can be negotiated or changed as searching progresses. Searching is also available on authority records.

In 1999 RLG introduced automatic generation of authority records from headings in bibliographic records. Also, if a library has reason to believe an item will be cataloged by a national agency, brief bibliographic information can be keyed in once. It then is automatically searched against all new records entering the system.

The RLG Union Catalog had over 48 million titles as of February 2006, including all of the LC MARC bibliographic and authority records. RLIN21 supports the

"JACKPHY" languages (Japanese, Arabic, Chinese, Korean, Persian, Hebrew, Yiddish) as well as Cyrillic. RLG also provides access to the *English Short Title Catalogue* (*ESTC*), a research tool for scholars of British literature and culture, the Hand Press Book database, and *SCIPIO: Art and Rare Book Sales Catalogs*. The RLG Union Catalog reflects the collections of major research, academic, and national libraries, law libraries, archives and museums, art and music libraries, theological libraries, medical libraries, area studies collections, public and corporate libraries, historical societies, and book clubs.

RLG also offers "Marcadia." This service matches records that have been transmitted via FTP against the RLG Union Catalog to return records that follow a desired profile, including the insertion of standard local data. RLG offers tools and training. RLG publishes several newsletters, on the Web and in print, which provide news about product updates and general information about the system, databases, and services. Among RLG's many research projects is RedLightGreen, an interface to the RLG Union Catalog designed for students and the general public and making use of *FRBR* principles.[13]

A-G Canada Ltd.

Canadian efforts toward computer-based network cataloging were sparked largely by the University of Toronto Library Automation Systems (UTLAS), which became a separate corporation in 1983 and changed its name in 1988 to Utlas International. In 1963 the Ontario New Universities Library Project started work on computer-produced book catalogs representing the initial library collections for five new campuses in the province. The project was to facilitate selection, acquisition, and cataloging, while remaining flexible in its record format, access, and products. Implementation in 1965 led to the University's participation in the LC MARC project. By 1970 it was producing cards from MARC tapes for sale to clients, including in 1971 the College Bibliocentre, a processing center for 19 colleges of applied technology. It started supplying computer-based systems and services to libraries in 1973.

The UTLAS system was purchased in the early 1990s and became ISM Information Systems Management Manitoba Corporation. In June 1997 A-G Canada, a wholly-owned subsidiary of the library automation company AutoGraphics, was formed and purchased ISM. It offers cataloging products and services primarily to Canadian libraries, but with a number of customers in the United States.

A-G Canada offers AGent, a suite of integrated products which include library automation, cataloging, resource sharing, statistics, authentication, and portal modules. The cataloging module provides access to a union catalog of bibliographic and authority records drawn from multiple sources, including the Library of Congress and national libraries in the United Kingdom, Australia, and other countries. Customers may also contribute records to the union catalog. AGent also enables access to thousands of Z39.50-compliant databases. Broadcast searching, which sends the same query to multiple sources simultaneously, is possible in this system. One particularly noteworthy feature is AGent's support of interactive online translation of LC subject headings into French, using the *Répertoire de vedettes matières* (*RVM*) subject system, or Spanish, also using authoritative lists.

Cooperation

The obvious duplication of resources and effort among the networks has been of concern for some time. It has been felt that there should be some means for exchanging data across networks. However, there are political, technical, and economic factors that must be taken into account. In 1980 a study of this subject was completed by Battelle Institute under a grant from the Council on Library Resources. The study recommended either batch processing of search requests to be exchanged among the networks or allowing a user of one network direct online access to the others. The recommendations were not implemented, but the report drew attention to the need for cooperation.

As a result there were policy changes, and cooperative projects were initiated. In 1982, for example, OCLC began allowing partial membership and tapeload membership status. At reduced cost over full membership, this allows members of other networks (particularly RLG) to have access to the OCLC database. Partial members (now called Participants) may use noncataloging subsystems or search the database without entering their cataloging. For tapeload (now called batchload) members, the location identifier is added to the OCLC master record for records on the library's archive tapes, which are run against the OCLC database. Most of RLG's full members have become batchload members of OCLC. Similarly, RLG has loaded some OCLC records in this fashion. OCLC and RLG exchange CJK records to keep their databases synchronized for Chinese, Japanese, and Korean records. A number of RLG members that were formerly OCLC members desired access to the records they had created on OCLC. By loading their archive tapes into RLG, they were allowed that access.

FUTURE PROSPECTS

Trends in computer technology and progress in developing bibliographic standards are encouraging. For many years, libraries have used minicomputers to operate local online catalogs and other processing functions, such as acquisitions and serials control, at reasonable cost in integrated library systems. Most of these systems, whether purchased from a commercial vendor or developed in-house, have access to the bibliographic networks and to Internet resources as well as Z39.50 protocol access to the online catalogs of other libraries worldwide. Advances in telecommunication make possible distributed networks, consisting of a series of separate individual library catalogs interconnected by telecommunications links or Web access. Such a configuration is especially attractive in areas where many libraries engage in extensive resource sharing and coordinated collection development.

Even with local online catalogs, libraries still find the large network databases valuable as sources for extended record searching. It appears that cataloging will continue in much the same way as today, transferring the edited machine-readable record into the local online database. Closing of card catalogs, in many libraries, was a major step in the evolution of materials processing toward quality improvement and control in standardized entry, descriptive detail, filing, physical preparation, and economical production of records.

Networking and cooperative efforts expanded during the late 1990s to projects for bibliographic control of electronic resources and digital objects. OCLC's InterCat database was an early effort toward provision of bibliographic records for Internet resources. It was succeeded by the CORC project, which provided a cooperative means to provide Extensible Markup Language (XML) records with metadata and links to full MARC records for electronic resources. The successful results of these experiments have been incorporated as standard elements in OCLC's Connexion service. RLG, as well, has undertaken many initiatives in the areas of access to, and preservation of, digital materials, with an emphasis on the needs of repositories of scholarly material.

The professional cataloger's contribution to an exclusively online situation is sometimes questioned. It is possible that those libraries that acquire only standard trade books and accept existing cataloging without modification will no longer need professional processing staff. On the other hand, there will likely be greater coordination of the national cataloging effort. LC cannot maintain timely coverage of the world's entire publication output. Other libraries at home and abroad have taken responsibility for cataloging in specific languages or subject categories. Consistently high standards will be kept in a few cataloging centers throughout the world. The number of professional catalogers may well be reduced, but the highly skilled cataloger with special language or subject competency will be in greater demand than ever. In addition local materials, such as those of a genealogical or archival nature, are becoming highly sought on the Web and will continue to need original cataloging. Moreover, public service librarians are finding that in-depth knowledge of catalog codes and conventions, machine search strategies, and MARC or other machine-readable formats immeasurably increases their effectiveness in reference work, information exchange, bibliographic problem solving, and implementation of online public-access catalogs.

NOTES

1. *Cataloging Service*, bulletin 113 (Spring 1975): 7–8.

2. Henriette D. Avram, *MARC, Its History and Implications* (Washington, D.C.: Library of Congress, 1975).

3. Library of Congress, Cataloging Distribution Service. "Bibliographic Products & Services" (available: http://www.loc.gov/cds/ [accessed 2/14/2006]).

4. "Program for Cooperative Cataloging" (available: http://www.loc.gov/catdir/pcc/2001pcc.html [accessed 2/14/2006]).

5. "OCLC Online Computer Library Center" (available: http://www.oclc.org/ [accessed 2/14/2006]).

6. "Research Libraries Group" (available: http://www.rlg.org/ [accessed 2/14/2006]).

7. "A-G Canada, Ltd." (available: http://www.ag-canada.com/ [accessed 2/14/2006]).

8. Library of Congress, Network Development Office, "A Glossary for Library Networking," *Network Planning Paper*, no. 2 (Washington, D.C.: Library of Congress, 1978): 7.

9. For general descriptions and comparisons of the major networks *see* William Saffady, "The Bibliographic Utilities in 1993: A Survey of Cataloging Support and Other Services," Chicago: American Library Association, 1993, in *Library Technology Reports* 29, no. 1 (January/February 1993).

10.   OCLC. "Connexion Support" (available: http://www.oclc.org/connexion/support/default.htm [accessed 2/28/2006]).

11. OCLC. "Technical Bulletins" (available: http://www.oclc.org/support/documentation/technicalbulletins/ [accessed 2/14/2006]).

12   OCLC. "About Research." (available http://www.oclc.org/research/about/default.htm [accessed 2/28/2006]).

13.   RLG. "RLG – RedLightGreen" (available: http://www.rlg.org/en/page.php?Page_ID = 435 [accessed 2/28/2006]).

SUGGESTED READING

Harvey, Ross, and Philip Hider. *Organising Knowledge in a Global Society: Principles and Practice in Libraries and Information Centres*. Wagga Wagga, NSW, Australia: Centre for Information Studies, 2004. Chapter 11: Arrangements for Bibliographic Data Exchange; and Chapter 12: Bibliographic Utilities.

Intner, Sheila S., and Jean Weihs. *Standard Cataloging for School and Public Libraries*. 3rd ed. Englewood, Colo.: Libraries Unlimited, 2001. Chapter 14: Computerized Cataloging.

Oddy, Pat. "Bibliographic Standards and the Globalization of Bibliographic Control." In *Technical Services Today and Tomorrow*. 2nd ed., edited by Michael Gorman, pp. 67–78. Englewood, Colo.: Libraries Unlimited, 1998.

Reynolds, Dennis. *Library Automation: Issues and Applications*. New York: R. R. Bowker, 1985. Chapters 2–4, 10–12. [Read for historical perspective.]

Rohrbach, Peter T. *Find: Automation at the Library of Congress: The First Twenty-five Years and Beyond*. Washington, D.C.: Library of Congress, 1985.

Saffady, William. "Commercial Sources of Cataloging Data: Bibliographic Utilities and Other Vendors." Chicago: American Library Association, 1998. In *Library Technology Reports* 34, no. 3 (May/June 1998): 281–432.

20 ⟩ Catalog Management

INTRODUCTION

Efficiency of bibliographic retrieval, and the quality of bibliographic description, are affected not only by the care and standards used to catalog each item, but also by several other important factors:

- The recording of local decisions and practices

- The currency of department files and records

- The organization and routines facilitating each phase of the process

- The continuing maintenance and editing of the catalog

- The oversight of any commercial processing for which the library has contracts

- The involvement with the integrated library system (ILS) with which most libraries function

Each of these factors should be carefully evaluated and efficiently administered. Here we will consider briefly the major responsibilities involved in catalog management, summarizing those features for which patterns of implementation may vary from library to library. Organizational structure, including the specification of staff duties, is not within the scope of this text.[1]

CATALOGING RECORDS AND FILES

A catalog department maintains files essential for accuracy, efficiency, standardization, and record keeping. Historically, such files were nearly always formatted on cards or slips. For many years now, however, computer technology has offered new formats, as well as new forms of access to information and library services, that have become standard in all but the smallest libraries.

---

*This chapter has been edited, rewritten, and new material added by Susan Hayes. The section on outsourcing was written by Katherine Ryner.

Catalog Formats

The historical development and present uses of various catalog formats were reviewed briefly in chapter 1, "Cataloging in Context." Although the dictionary catalog on 3" by 5" cards still exists in some libraries, active vendor merchandising of proprietary computer databases now brings alternative catalogs increasingly within the reach of smaller public and school libraries or systems. In some cases the existing card catalog remains in use, while another format is adopted to supplement and continue it.

At the initial conversion stage, machine-readable records may be stored in a large network database, in commercial automated service facilities, on archival tapes, or in the in-house computers of individual libraries. Machine-readable records can be used to generate a book, computer output microform (COM), or compact disk-read only memory (CD-ROM) catalog. CD-ROM catalogs have the same drawbacks as book and COM catalogs, in that they are static—a snapshot of the library's database at a certain point in time. However, the searching capabilities in CD-ROM catalogs are usually enhanced over the author, title, and subject listings in book and COM catalogs, often allowing searching by keyword using Boolean operators in addition to more traditional modes of access.

The number of online computer catalogs (online public access catalogs [OPACs]) in libraries has grown so rapidly that they are now the predominant form. Even in libraries that do not yet have them, most administrators have chosen to wait until they can put their bibliographic records directly online, rather than adopting interim solutions in the forms of book or COM catalogs. The online catalog retains the continuous expansion features of the card catalog, along with the compactness, speed, and ease of access characteristic of book and COM catalogs. Cost is still prohibitive for some smaller libraries but will continue to go down, rather than up, as computer services are expanded and refined. One nearly universal refinement is the OPAC that has evolved from a catalog of the holdings of a particular collection into a "portal" that provides Web access to a wide variety of online resources such as library catalogs, reference databases, and full-text e-journals and e-books.

All of the files discussed in the remainder of this section can and do exist in card, COM, CD-ROM, or online formats. (The only one likely to appear in book format is the catalog department manual, which is now often also found online.)

The Shelflist

The shelflist is a complete record of all titles in a collection, arranged by call number as the library materials are found on the shelves. Its primary purpose is to provide an official inventory record of the collection. Its classified arrangement shows what titles have been placed in a specific class notation. It serves, then, as an important classification aid, as catalogers consult it to verify their library's past use of each notation. The shelflist also displays, within certain limitations, related materials more general and more specific on either side of the notation referred to. In addition, it furnishes the matrix on which unique cutter numbers and workmarks are assigned in order to differentiate titles collocated in the same classification.

If the library has an online system searchable by call number, this can serve as the shelflist. This is more likely to occur in situations where there is an integrated system that is used for acquisition functions as well as for cataloging. In such a system a record is initiated with the order of an item. Dates, costs, etc., are part of the record and can be maintained for as long as the item is part of the system or even after the item is withdrawn or reported missing. Some libraries, however, maintain a card form shelflist as a backup to the online system. Other libraries, following the current trend away from paper-based records, have jettisoned their traditional shelflists altogether. This decision has been notably deplored by Nicholson Baker,[2] and opinion remains divided about the value and cost-effectiveness of maintaining a shelflist in card format in addition to an online catalog. Today many libraries, in deciding that accurate online records are their first priority, have made the decision not to maintain their shelflists; others, citing space considerations, have discarded theirs.

If a library has a shelflist in card format, and if the decision has been made to maintain it, decisions need to be made about what information is to be kept there. A full description of the card shelflist and a sample shelflist card may be found in the eighth edition of this text.[3]

Authority Files

The purpose of an authority file, or files, is to standardize and control a library's use of name, title, and subject headings and their respective references. (*See also* chapter 8.) Until recently (as discussed in chapter 8) it was thought necessary to have one "authorized" form for every name, title, and subject known by variant forms. Today, in the global information world, it is recognized that multiple language forms can be "authorized" forms for access purposes, and that authority records can contain all variant forms for an entity, without designating one as the "correct" one. Since a virtual international authority file has yet to be implemented, current practice still dictates the use of an established "heading," or, the exact string of characters of the authorized form for each name, title, or subject that is to be an access point in a library's catalog.

Due to staffing and budget constraints some libraries do not maintain an authority file, and in many smaller libraries its upkeep has often been more honored in the breach than in the observance. Such libraries obviously depend on their prime cataloging sources (e.g., the Library of Congress [LC]) to suggest references and to keep the use of heading forms in standard order. The inconsistencies that inadvertently creep in, through rule changes, error, and the like, are remedied if and when found. In a limited operation there may be some economic justification for this *ad hoc* approach. In larger libraries, where inconsistent and erroneous entries cause misfiling, result in loss of entries in online catalogs, and otherwise obscure valuable entries in extensive files, the interest in authority files continues to escalate as more libraries join the name authorities program (NACO) of the Program for Cooperative Cataloging (PCC) (*see* chapter 8).

Some libraries use the public catalog as their authority list, but some information that should be available to the acquisitions or catalog librarian does not lend itself to inclusion in a public file. Such information may include the series treatment or the locations of catalogs where the heading and its references were used. Moreover, the introduction of changes in cataloging rules leads to total review of how to integrate old and new forms of headings into the library's catalog.

As noted in chapter 8, there is a difference between the existence of an authority file and the processes of creating and using an authority file. According to Arlene G. Taylor, *authority work* is

The process of determining and maintaining the form of a name, title, or subject concept to be used in creating access points. In the name and title areas, the process includes identifying all variant names or titles and relating the variants to the name or title forms chosen to be access points. In some cases it may also include relating names and/or titles to each other. In the verbal subject area, the process includes identifying and maintaining relationships among terms – relationships such as synonyms, broader terms, narrower terms, and related terms.[4]

The record that results from authority work is given in a printed or machine-readable unit, called an *authority record*, which is entered into the *authority file*. The file is then used for the process of *authority control*—i.e., for maintaining the consistency of headings in a bibliographic file and for showing relationships among names, works, and subjects. In rising numbers of online systems, the process of authority control is becoming increasingly automated, but the process of authority work remains highly tied to human endeavor.

One of the major trends in authority control today is the outsourcing of the process to commercial vendors. Currently, there are approximately six agencies that provide authority control services to American libraries. Of these, the principal vendors for large libraries are Backstage Library Works, Library Technologies, Inc. (LTI), MARCIVE, and The Library Corporation (TLC). Services include retrospective clean-up, ongoing authority maintenance, and periodic updates, and are accomplished using batch processing methods and File Transfer Protocol (FTP) technology.[5] FTP technology has facilitated the uploading and downloading of records between libraries and vendors so effectively that libraries can now choose a monthly, weekly, or daily processing schedule. At least one vendor, TLC, offers "Real-Time Authority Control" (RTAC) service based on client-server technology. "RTAC allows the cataloger to send a bibliographic record during the cataloging process, have it authorized and returned to the cataloger along with all appropriate authority records almost instantly."[6] Online Computer Library Center (OCLC) and Research Libraries Group (RLG) provide their members with LC's authority file online but do not maintain constant control over headings in their databases. In the systems that provide automated authority control, incoming headings on bibliographic records are automatically checked against the computer authority file. For systems where the bibliographic and authority records are linked, a heading on a new bibliographic record that matches one in the authority file automatically links the bibliographic record to the authority record. When a heading does not match, it is either referred to the cataloger for checking, or the system creates a mini-authority record for it.[7] For systems where the bibliographic and authority records are unlinked, a match of an incoming heading with a reference will generate an invalid heading report, and a non-match will generate a new heading report.

Some libraries that maintain authority files still do so in card form; however, most libraries with online catalogs have moved to online authority files. Many authority files, whether online or manual are divided into separate files for names, subjects, and titles. Name authority files bring together in an alphabetic list all name headings—personal, corporate, conference, or geographic—that are used in a given catalog as main, added, analytic, or subject entries. Authority records for series, uniform titles, and topical subjects may be added, creating a general authority file, or they may be handled in separate files.

In-Process Files

Certain areas of acquisitions and cataloging overlap. Each library's requirements must be studied to avoid duplication of record keeping, verification, and other such activities. This is a continuous administrative responsibility. Some file, whether maintained by the catalog manager or by the order librarian, must show "items in process." Its records continuously trace the status of each item from the time it is received in the library until it goes to the shelf, with its permanent catalog record available to the public. Libraries with card files that use multiple order forms can reserve one copy of the form for the in-process record. Some use the original requisition slip, once the book has been invoiced. Others with online systems may be able to use the order record as the in-process record and later enhance that record for the catalog record. Since the correct main entry may not be established until the item is cataloged, some libraries arrange their paper in-process files by title rather than by author. Other libraries capture full-level bibliographic records from the bibliographic networks and display these in their online catalogs attached to item records displaying "In Processing" statuses. Library patrons interested in obtaining such an "In Processing" item, may request, either directly online or through their library's circulation department, that it be rush cataloged. A library's interlibrary loan (ILL) department may also request the rush cataloging of an "In Processing" item to fill an ILL request from another institution.

Catalog Department Manuals

The purpose of a department manual is to codify all pertinent decisions and procedures. The manual should be readily available to every member of the library staff, and it should contribute to the in-service training of every new cataloging employee. Even public service staff should be able and willing to consult it on problems of local catalog interpretation and use. Until recently, most departmental manuals were in looseleaf format, so the various tagged and indexed sections could be withdrawn and replaced by updated material as needed. Today, many libraries mark up their manuals in HTML and mount them on their websites.

Foster recommends that a departmental manual give complete coverage of responsibilities and practices and that it be easy to use, to read, and to revise. He gives the following points to remember during its preparation:

1. Arrange material in logical order so that related information is found together.

2. Use precise and concrete words, not abstract words. And illustrate whenever possible.

3. Be alert to details. Write the manual so that there is no question about procedures and so that the newcomer can easily understand and follow each routine.

4. But do not over-detail. Too much detail provides no room for individual variation and will not allow for minor changes without complete rewriting.

5. Anticipate future revisions and additions.

6.   Before adding a new procedure into the manual, test it out to discover and correct unforeseen problems.

7.   Take advantage of auxiliary sources, particularly publications from LC and, if the library is part of a network, publications distributed by network headquarters.[8]

On the first and last points, both related information and LC publications can be hyperlinked in manuals that appear on websites. On the last point, the department manual may contain guidelines for input standards for automated systems or refer to those input standards of the bibliographic network to which the library belongs.

Some catalog department manuals also contain expectations for cataloging staff job performance with specific guidelines for performance standards. Such guidelines are very useful for a clear understanding of expectations when it is time for performance evaluations.

CATALOGING ROUTINES

Copy Cataloging

We know that much cataloging performed in the United States today is derived from LC copy in machine-readable form.[9] Another large amount of cataloging is derived from copy created by other members of a bibliographic network. Since LC uses International Standard Bibliographic Description (ISBD) and *Anglo-American Cataloguing Rules, Second Edition (AACR2R)*, most present-day descriptive cataloging embodies the precepts of these two compatible and internationally recognized paradigms, as well as a particular usage of the ISBD, ISBD(ER) for electronic resources. Local catalogers may use a description, as found on LC or other copy, as it stands or may alter it to reflect differences in a copy of an item received locally, to correct occasional errors made on outside copy, to adjust headings to fit the local authority file, or to add name or title added entries.

In the area of subject analysis, LC provides in many of its records a suggested *Dewey Decimal Classification (DDC)* number,[10] as well as its own full LC call number, and sometimes provides possible alternative *Library of Congress Classification (LCC)* and *DDC* classification notations for such materials as bibliographies, biographies, and the separate parts of a monographic series. It also shows the subject headings it has chosen for the work. Local copy catalogers may use LC decisions as they stand, or may modify them to reflect variations in edition, impression, or format; to complete the *DDC* classification numbers; to adjust official LC call numbers to their local shelflists; to substitute *Sears List of Subject Headings (Sears)* or other subject list terms for the LC subject headings; and to omit, add, or change other tracings. Searching for full-level bibliographic records that match the item in hand is a large part of the routine copy cataloging workflow: records are obtained in real time through pre-searching by a library's acquisitions department, through further searching by copy catalogers, or by batch processing using a programmed searching service such as Research Library Group's (RLG) Marcadia (see chapter 19). If no record is available from LC or some other reliable bibliographic agency, original cataloging is usually necessary.

It is more convenient to edit copy to local standards with online cataloging than it was when using printed cards from LC or other sources. Still, a high degree of local variation from standard LC practice tends to slow workflow, due largely to the need to consult local authority files and shelflist records.

To profit most from online cataloging, it is a good idea to review all local variations from standard practice at the time a library joins a bibliographic network and periodically thereafter. This is not to suggest that all variations are misguided. Many local prerogatives are necessary because of inconsistent precedents over the years on the part of LC itself. Others may be justified by special local conditions. Librarians should review all such variations in the light of their costs and their effects on processing efficiency. Any decision will affect online cataloging in areas such as computer workstation staffing, policies on the use of other libraries' records, and the organization of authority (integration) procedures.

Original Cataloging

There are two phases in original cataloging: descriptive cataloging and subject cataloging. While most catalogers do both, there are separate mental processes to be followed in conducting the two phases.

Descriptive Cataloging

Most libraries follow LC, conforming to ISBD and *AACR2R* requirements, or some modification thereof. Bibliographic description requires transcription from the chief sources of information according to prescribed guidelines in *AACR2R* and *Library of Congress Rule Interpretations* as modified in local practice. Although professionals may be needed to catalog some of the more complicated resources using *AACR2R* or one of the encoding standards for metadata (e.g., the Dublin Core), much of descriptive cataloging is straightforward and is a task assigned to paraprofessional staff in many libraries.

Original descriptive cataloging is described briefly as follows. *AACR2R* outlines three levels of description, with increasing detail included at each of the two higher levels. It also offers options throughout, which frequently have to do with adding further details to the record. Main and added (non-subject) entries are determined in accordance with *AACR2R*, or perhaps with some adjustments for established practice. Any changes from LC practice, or *AACR2R* options exercised, should be described in the catalog department manual. All new headings should be recorded in the local authority list, along with references as indicated. Authority control takes place as discussed earlier.

Historically, cataloging has been based on the physical item, or information package, and on the iteration of a given work contained within that information package. This has resulted in the creation of multiple records with identical or related content.[11] However, with the adoption of the *Functional Requirements for Bibliographic Records (FRBR)*,[12] and the publication of *RDA*[13] (see discussion in chapter 4), catalogers will be better able to map relationships between bibliographic entities, and to create more granular surrogates for information packages.

Subject Cataloging

In original subject cataloging the cataloger must examine the information package in order to determine what it is about. With the "aboutness" concept in mind, the subject heading list and subject authority file used by the library must be consulted for consistent selection and recording of accepted headings and references. Obsolete terminology may be caught and changed at once, although it is usually better to postpone major overhauls until a designated time, in order to expedite new cataloging in progress.

For original cataloging, classifying an information package requires judgment. The task requires the selection of an appropriate classification number that fits the existing collection in subject emphasis and then requires adjusting the resulting call number to fit uniquely into the existing collection. Research on the automatic classification of electronic resources is being conducted by OCLC,[14] but it is not yet possible to rely on automatic classification. Most information packages still need to be classified by humans when no classification is provided on cataloging copy, and for original cataloging, as well. For libraries that use *LCC*, the classification process has been facilitated by the introduction of *Classification Web* by LC's Cataloging Distribution Service.[15] *Classification Web* is an online compilation of the *LCC* schedules that features correlations between *LC Subject Headings* and LC classification numbers, and between *DDC* numbers and *LCC* numbers.

After examining the information package to be cataloged in the light of the classification schedules used by the library, the cataloger usually consults the shelflist to see if the classification notation chosen, or its possible alternative, has been previously used for similar or different materials. When the appropriate classification notation is selected, the distinguishing cutter number, with any necessary additions, such as workmark, edition date, or location symbol, is added. The full call number may be recorded in the shelflist, on the information package proper (with volume and copy number if needed), and on a workform. If the shelflist is in card form, a temporary slip may be inserted in the shelflist pending arrival of permanent cards. Libraries using COM or book catalogs, and even OPACs, sometimes maintain card shelflists for recent additions.

Use of Workforms

Workforms are useful to make procedures routine and to ensure full coverage of essential points. In print format they may be sheets, cards, or slips pre-printed to exhibit the standard categories of information that catalogers must consider. If the cataloging is based primarily on a large union file of machine-readable records and is done at a computer workstation, the operator usually can call up prepared workforms. These are completed in substantive detail directly at the keyboard. Where the MARC (MAchine-Readable Cataloging) format is used, the online workform is customized to describe a "typical" information package, using preselected fields and tags which are then changed or expanded as needed. On the other hand, although becoming the rare preference, the cataloger may prefer to start in longhand on a printed form (*see* figure 20.1, page 494), handing the completed sheet to a computer workstation operator for inputting. Figure 20.2 (*see* page 495) shows the OCLC books workform as it looks when called up online.

Following the completion of workforms, the item is generally ready for final preparation. In some libraries the workform is manually translated by a typist onto pockets and labels before the item can have its final processing. Other libraries rely on a feature of their online catalogs which allows the call number from the holdings record to be mapped into a labeling program, enabling the labeler to complete the information package's final processing. Still other libraries have this step performed by commercial suppliers, by a network central office, or by in-house automated printers.

Catalog Maintenance

Like any ongoing function a catalog is subject to obsolescence, inadvertent clerical and professional errors, inconsistency, and a variety of related ills. It therefore requires continual editing and maintaining, although libraries, being continually shorthanded, often neglect or postpone the responsibility, to the detriment of effective service. As collections grow, the efforts needed to keep a catalog in satisfactory condition tend to increase exponentially. Call number changes, location changes, treatment changes, and blind references (i.e., references to or from headings once used but incompletely or inaccurately withdrawn) are among the major maintenance problems encountered in every kind of catalog. Other problems are specific to a particular catalog type. Online catalogs frequently contain data entry errors, invalid uniform resource locators (URLs), incomplete or defective records due to faulty migration from a previous online system, and problems stemming from the reindexing of the database following implementation of a new release of catalog software. Book, COM, CD-ROM, and online catalogs are particularly vulnerable to typographical errors. Such errors cause major retrieval problems.

Fig. 20.1. An OCLC participant's paper work form.

Type: a	ELvl: I	Srce: d	Audn:	Ctrl:	Lang:
BLvl: m	Form:	Conf:	Biog:	MRec:	Ctry:
	Cont:	GPub:	LitF:	Indx:	
Desc: a	Ills:	Fest:	DtSt:	Dates:	

010		041
040		043
020		090
1 ___ ___	Main entry	
24 ___ ___	Uniform title	
245 ___	Title	
250	Edition	
260	Publication info.	
300	Phys. desc.	
4 ___ ___	Series	
5 ___	Note	
5 ___	Note	
5 ___	Note	
6 ___ ___	Subject	
6 ___ ___	Subject	
6 ___ ___	Subject	
7 ___ ___	Added entry	
7 ___ ___	Added entry	
8 ___ ___	Series traced differently	
9 ___ ___	Local option	

Fig. 20.2. OCLC workform for monographs.

Edit | Editing Bibliographic Record | ■ | Action | Action | ■ | View | MARC Template

Bibliographic Workform: Books

OCLC NEW						
Books ▼	**Rec Stat** n	**Entered** 20050827	**Replaced** 20050827225819.73			
Type a	**ELvl** |	**Srce** d	**Audn**	**Ctrl**	**Lang** |||
BLvl m	**Form**	**Conf** 0	**Biog**	**MRec**	**Ctry** |||
	Cont	**GPub**	**LitF** 0	**Indx** 0	
Desc |	**Ills**	**Fest** 0	**DtSt** |	**Dates** |||| ,	

040		DD0 $b $c DD0	Functions ▼
020			Functions ▼
041	|	$h $b	Functions ▼
050	||	$b	Functions ▼
090		$b	Functions ▼
049		DD0A	Functions ▼
1||	|		Functions ▼
245	||	$h $b $c	Functions ▼
246	||		Functions ▼
250			Functions ▼
260		$b $c	Functions ▼
300		$b $c	Functions ▼
4||	||	$v	Functions ▼
5||			Functions ▼
6||	||		Functions ▼
6||	||		Functions ▼
7||	|		Functions ▼
7||	|		Functions ▼
8||	||		Functions ▼
856	4|		Functions ▼
			Functions ▼
			Functions ▼
			Functions ▼

Create 006: ▼

Action Status Delete Holdings _ Export _ Label _ Produce _ Update Holdings _
Validate _

MARC Help:

Edit | Editing Bibliographic Record | ■ | Action | Action | ■ | View | MARC Template

Maintenance of every catalog is necessary to guard against obsolescence of terminology and to remedy the inconsistencies resulting from different rules for headings, especially in online catalogs lacking a global update capability. References must be maintained, and old name and title entries must sometimes be changed when there are conflicts with new entries to the catalog. In addition there must be concern for maintenance of the equipment necessary for use. Equipment maintenance, however, usually is not performed by catalog department staff.

Card catalogs are an even higher maintenance catalog type. Because they are subject to physical wear and tear, repair of damaged drawers or replacement of worn and soiled cards is important. Tray labels, guide cards, and instructions for use inside and outside the file should be altered whenever improvements are possible. Expansion inevitably requires occasional shifting of cards. Catalog editing is needed to eliminate unnecessary entries, to suggest improvements, and to plan for future development. Old entries may not have been removed during cancellation of a title. Inconsistent headings, misleading or blind references, filing errors, missing cards, wrong call numbers, etc., all cause perplexity and ill will.

Arrangement and Filing

Before the advent of online catalogs, some people thought that filing would become a nonissue in online catalogs. However, we have now learned that when more than ten or so entries are retrieved in response to a search, they need to appear on the screen in some logical order. Catalog users are not happy with responses in which the entries appear in the order in which the items happened to be acquired by the library. In online catalogs it is often difficult to guess how many screens "in" one has to go or how far down one has to scroll, to find a desired bibliographic record in a retrieval set of 30 or more. Filing order is somewhat less of a problem, though, in online, book, and microform catalogs than it is in card catalogs. It is easier to scan one or more columns of entries and to discern their order than it is to determine the order of cards.

Neophyte catalogers are surprised to discover many alternative filing codes. They learn that choice of catalog arrangement (dictionary or divided) not only affects arrangement issues, but also affects cataloging decisions to some extent. Filing problems resulting from entry conflicts between the old *ALA Cataloging Rules* and the *Anglo-American Cataloging Rules* (*AACR*) were a major impetus to the closing of such large card catalogs as those of the New York Public Library and LC. Some libraries have attempted to interfile old and new forms of the same entry in card catalogs. In online catalogs all forms are arranged exactly as they appear. In either case, ample use of references is necessary.

Research libraries with card catalogs in the past often maintained one or another of various kinds of "categorical filing," particularly in those parts of their catalogs where relatively large numbers of highly formalized entries were concentrated. Categorical filing was based on the assumption that the user knows enough about a subject to prefer a partially classified arrangement over straight adherence to the alphabet. For instance, LC used to arrange its entries for individual books and groups of books of the Bible in canonical order, rather than alphabetically, as part of an intricate categorical arrangement.[16] Less scholarly libraries generally preferred a simpler and therefore more readily grasped alpha-arrangement. The large academic and research collections gradually succumbed to popular demand, and to the requirements of computer filing.

There is currently very little control over the arrangement of catalog displays. When one purchases an integrated library system (ILS) with its OPAC, one accepts the arrangement that has been programmed into that system. An understanding of certain filing dilemmas can be useful in making decisions about catalog maintenance of heading forms and references. An introduction to some filing/display dilemmas may be found in Taylor's *The Organization of Information*.[17] In addition the Appendix to this text includes a discussion of filing dilemmas, an introduction to the *ALA Filing Rules*,[18] and a discussion of shelflist filing. Some libraries continue to maintain card shelflists as supplements to their OPACs, making understanding of notational arrangement an important part of catalog maintenance.

Reproducing Catalog Cards

Catalog cards can be produced by typing each one individually. More often they are purchased in sets. One source of such sets is the bibliographic network of which the library may be a member. In addition to the card sets mailed from the bibliographic network, card sets may be produced from the network's online records by downloading to a printer or by downloading to the library's own computer or personal computer. Cards are then printed using special card production software. It is also possible to photocopy a set from one master unit card by adapting information from Cataloging in Publication (CIP) or the *National Union Catalog (NUC)*, or typing one copy of one's original cataloging.[19] There are also several computer programs on the market that will produce a catalog card set when main entry information is typed into the screen form.

Reclassification and Recataloging

There is inevitably a certain amount of recataloging to be performed in any library. Recataloging may be either a mass production affair or an individualized, single item performance. During the 1960s and early 1970s many medium-sized and larger libraries, especially academic ones, mounted full reclassification projects from *DDC* to *LCC*. Large-scale reclassification was sometimes undertaken on special collections or a selected part of a collection. In the course of most such efforts, brief, inaccurate, or obsolete cataloging could be caught and redone. Many collections were at the same time weeded and surveyed for needed new materials.

More commonly, however, recataloging is performed on individual items for which the former records prove unsatisfactory. Classification notations within a given classification scheme (e.g., *DDC* or *LCC*) may need changing because the schedules have been revised or because of new interpretations and needs within the collection. Recataloging on a greater or lesser scale may also be the consequence of adopting a new or revised descriptive cataloging code. For instance, *Anglo-American Cataloguing Rules, Second Edition (AACR2)* called for many more corporate names to be entered directly under the body's own name. Previously, the rules called for entering most such names subordinately under a higher body (e.g., "Library of Congress" was entered as "United States. Library of Congress"). Catalogers whose libraries were not yet ready to close their card files and start new ones based strictly on the changed rules had to decide what to do about superseded usages, particularly changed headings for already used entries that were likely to be used again.

Today some library catalogs still contain headings constructed under old rules. As more online systems provide linked authority control, the problem can be fixed in OPACs. However, some libraries with card catalogs attempt to solve this dilemma with full sets of *See also* references linking old and new forms of headings in unified or split files without actually recataloging the older works. Other libraries recatalog under the new forms, particularly if there are only a limited number of entries under the obsolete forms. Old and new forms are often identified and corrected during preprocessing for an online catalog's database or in subsequent cleanup of the database. As mentioned previously, ongoing maintenance of changed forms of headings in online catalogs can be simplified through a global update capability.

Closing Card Catalogs

In 1965 studies were made at the New York Public Library that confirmed that a staggering number of the cards (29 percent) in the public catalog of the Research Libraries Division were illegible, damaged, dirty, badly worn, or otherwise unfit to remain. The problem was aggravated by the fact that some entries had been there for over 100 years. It was a dramatic instance of a malaise that was reaching epidemic proportions in many long-established research libraries. Besides the deterioration problem, upkeep and maintenance were expensive and unsatisfactory. Space, lighting, and furniture posed real logistics problems in files of over 10 million cards. Labor costs for filing were also rising.

Libraries began to look to technology to solve the card problem. Book or COM catalogs could be made from machine-readable records. As the 1970s progressed, it began to be apparent that the machine-readable records could be accessed directly online. LC made plans to "freeze" its existing card files on January 1, 1980, in conjunction with the appearance of *AACR2*. At that time they planned to abandon their practice of "superimposition," by which they had retained most established headings regardless of rule changes, following *AACR* dictates only for those headings being established for the first time. Superimposition had been an attempt to avoid the Herculean task of updating all forms rendered obsolete by the new rules. Even with liberal use of references, it confounded catalogers and catalog users alike, with its legacy of inconsistent access forms in a single file.

Because most other libraries, even large ones, were not yet ready to go online, LC was convinced by other large libraries to postpone this action for a year. Starting in 1981, with all obsolete headings officially frozen in a searchable but defunct catalog, headings for new materials were established according to *AACR2* regardless of whether a given entry was identified differently in the old catalog. In situations where libraries closed old catalogs, complete bibliographic access to all the records in *both* catalogs under many personal, corporate, and geographic headings required that the search be conducted under heading forms that differed from one catalog to the other. The kind and number of references to be used in one or both catalogs occasioned much discussion.

Not all librarians in 1981 were convinced that a step as radical as closing one catalog and starting afresh on another was the best solution to problems of catalog lag. For the most part, only large research collections tried it. Most libraries maintained one catalog, using combinations of interfiling, split files, references, and revising old headings.

The advent of online catalogs during the following decades precipitated more card catalog closings than did *AACR2*. Most online catalogs did not have a distinct "opening" date. Several years' worth of entries appeared in both the closed card catalog and the online catalog. Eventually most libraries converted virtually everything in the card catalogs to machine-readable form through a process called "retrospective conversion," and many libraries have thrown out their card catalogs.

Retrospective conversion for an online catalog may involve one or more of the following:

- retrospective conversion to transform every record in the card shelflist into machine-readable form

- preprocessing of archival data files and retrospective conversion data files by a commercial service on contract

- systematic database cleanup projects using global update capabilities of the online system

- ongoing database maintenance

During retrospective conversion and preprocessing operations, outdated headings may be changed to current forms. Retrospective conversion can be done through a bibliographic network by searching for the records in the database and, when a match is found, adding that record to the library's archive data file. Retrospective conversion can also be done by a commercial service on contract (*see* the "Outsourcing" section in this chapter).[20]

COMMERCIAL PROCESSING

In the mid-1800s, Charles C. Jewett, librarian of the Smithsonian Institution, proposed "A Plan for Stereotyping Catalogues by Separate Titles. . . ."[21] The Smithsonian was at that time a copyright depository. As it produced bibliographic records, they could, he suggested, be preserved on stereotype plates for a variety of applications, including the printing of cards for sale to other libraries on demand. While Jewett's proposal did not itself endure, it presaged the marketing of printed cards undertaken by LC in 1901. Neither venture was "commercial" in the strict sense, although they were later imitated by a host of business concerns. Barbara Westby defined *commercial cataloging* as "centralized cataloging performed and sold by a non-library agency operating for profit."[22] In some cases it has been a by-product of other commercial interests, e.g., the Standard Catalog compilations of H. W. Wilson, the vending emphasis of a book jobber such as Baker & Taylor, or the promotional activities of a corporation like the Society for Visual Education.

The Wilson Printed Catalog Card Service supplied many school and public libraries with simple but adequate card copy at nominal cost for widely read books from 1938 to 1975. During that period more than 100 other distributors and publishers followed the Wilson example of supplying a packet of cards with each book sold. In 1976 the first edition of *Cataloging with Copy* listed 15 commercial processing services and 5 additional commercial sources of card sets.[23] Technological advances have caused considerable changes in the scene since then. Some of the services are no longer in business. Most of the others have radically changed their character. They have supplemented their print services with microform, CD-ROM, and/or online data retrieval systems. In recent years commercial processors have added catalogers to their staffs and provide cataloging services on a contract basis (*see* the discussion in the "Outsourcing" section of this chapter below).

Outsourcing

One of the more controversial library issues of the past decade has been outsourcing. Outsourcing can be defined as the purchase from an outside vendor of specific services or functions that would otherwise be provided by in-house staff. Libraries have been contracting out services for years, but a more recent trend has been the outsourcing of entire library departments, or even entire libraries. Services that have been outsourced in libraries recently include collection development, cataloging, and processing. Although changes occur rapidly, some publications have attempted to identify such services and to analyze their impact on libraries.[24]

Libraries have been purchasing catalog cards and catalog records from LC, OCLC, and RLG for decades. Catalog departments often seek outside help for projects such as the cataloging of backlogs, special collections, and foreign language materials. The difference these days is that libraries are downsizing cataloging staff and are paying for-profit vendors for regular cataloging services.

Why would a library want an outside vendor to fulfill its cataloging needs? When a vendor can provide better quality catalog records at a faster pace and at a cheaper rate than in-house staff can provide, the library benefits. Cost savings can be realized because of reduced overhead costs such as equipment, supplies, and bibliographic network connect time. Physical space can be saved, and staff can be moved into what some might consider to be more critical areas. Some libraries have outsourced cataloging in response to problems with personnel and productivity.

Some proponents of the outsourcing of cataloging services claim that cataloging is not a core function of libraries, and that those personnel resources formerly spent in cataloging should be geared towards such core functions as reference service. That organizing information is a core library service, and that the catalog is the key to the library, is not something that all library administrators agree upon.

Many librarians, though, feel that outsourcing is anathema to the obligations of professional librarianship. Outsourcing cataloging can mean that lower-skilled, lower-paid personnel replace highly-trained (and presumably higher-paid) catalogers. Catalog records that are inaccurate and incomplete can be produced. This results in long-term problems with the catalog database; patron access to collections can be hindered rather than helped by outsourcing.

More arguments against outsourcing include the library's dependency on the vendor. If a library commits to a vendor to perform a function such as cataloging, problems can arise if the vendor changes its core service, no longer supports certain technology, or goes out of business. When cataloging staff members are replaced by outside vendors, local knowledge of collections and user needs is lost, as is loyalty to the institution. Human costs are high: jobs can be lost. If cataloging staff remain employed by the institution, they can lose promotional opportunities and benefits. If displaced staff members are moved to other departments, those other departments are affected. Morale throughout the library can be damaged, and resentment can be fostered. One research study found that it was more cost effective to keep cataloging in-house.[25]

Whether the outsourcing of library services is a wave of the future or just a temporary trend in management theory remains to be seen. The success of outsourced cataloging depends on how the vendor contract is negotiated and on how library administration manages the change. Poorly planned and/or managed outsourcing projects can be very detrimental to staff, to the catalog, and to the bottom line. When outsourcing cataloging, there must be a way to measure in-house performance and costs in order to compare them to outsourced performance and costs. Experienced catalogers must become contract managers, oversee quality control of the vendor's product, and constantly monitor costs and the value of the contract.

INTEGRATED LIBRARY SYSTEMS (ILS)

Most catalog managers are currently dealing with integrated library systems. When library automation began in the 1970s, most systems were based on a hierarchical model, involving a host mainframe computer and one or more "dumb" terminals. Eventually, minicomputers replaced mainframes, but the basic model, featuring text-based, command or menu-driven OPACs with terminal emulation software, did not change. As microcomputer technology advanced into the 1990s, tasks became distributed between the host, or server, and the requestor, or client, with standard communication methods such as Transmission Control Protocol/Internet Protocol (TCP/IP) and Z39.50 facilitating the sharing of information between client and server. According to Jamshid Beheshti, the client/server model is "based on modular programming in which a large piece of software is divided into smaller, manageable modules. Each module can then be implemented in an appropriate hardware/software environment."[26]

Today, most library networks use the client/server model, in which the online public-access catalog, or OPAC, is supported by a range of other automated services, which function to heighten its effectiveness as a retrieval tool. As the most visible part of an ILS, the OPAC displays not only location information, but also circulation/reserve status and acquisitions information in the form of "on order/in processing" records. Most OPACs provide serials check-in and bindery information, enabling users to initiate interlibrary loan and/or document delivery requests. Almost all include circulation functions. Other typical functions of an ILS include: commercial database access, flexible printing options, electronic reserves, vernacular display of languages, generation of statistics and reports, security and user authentication, and the ability to handle special enhancements, such as interfaces with acquisitions and serials jobbers or a table-of-contents service.[27]

Increasingly, the pervasiveness of the Internet in contemporary life has forced librarians and vendors to provide resources and products that can satisfy user demand for a more scaleable online environment, and for such Web-delivered services as integrated and enriched content (including graphics and images), shopping cart functionality, 24/7 access, and the metasearching of multiple information silos at once. In their quest to improve interoperability, some librarians "wonder whether the information portal of the future should be based on a single ILS, or instead be a collection of products from different ILS vendors."[28] A current trend is towards providing state-of-the-art user support outside of the ILS—electronic ILL, reserve and resource management systems, as well as "portals, metasearch tools, reference linking software, radio frequency identification tags (RFIDs) and digital asset management systems," now dominate the world of library automation.[29]

A library's online system may be integrated by using single sets of hardware or software, or it may be "functionally integrated" by linking automated modules supplied by a range of vendors. Today, in an effort to provide lower costs and increased flexibility, open source software, e.g., Linux, is being adopted by most U.S. ILS vendors.[30] Shared library standards, such as *MARC 21* (as expressed in XML), Dublin Core, Meta Object Description Schema (MODS), and NISO Circulation Interchange Protocol (NCIP), and analogous standards in the computing and networking industries, e.g., the Open Archives Initiative Protocol for Metadata Harvesting (OAI-PMH) and the Simple Object Access Protocol (SOAP), make integrated library automation possible.[31]

Within the cataloging module, catalogers may create or edit bibliographic records and update holdings information. They may retrieve bibliographic records downloaded or transmitted via FTP from a cataloging resource file, not accessible to the public, for use in copy cataloging. They can copy a record in their own database, and use it as the basis for a new bibliographic record. They can also access, with greater or lesser degrees of interaction, functions located in other modules within the integrated system, such as circulation, acquisitions, and reserve. Most online cataloging modules accommodate the creation of templates, usually called workforms, that allow catalogers to call up blank MARC records that have been customized to describe a "typical" information package of a given format. In the authority file, catalogers may create authority records, or edit records that have been generated from headings in bibliographic records.

Online Public Access Catalogs (OPACs)

Although experimentation with them began in the 1960s, OPACs did not become really functional until the 1980s. OPACs were developed locally in libraries and also commercially. Some expanded out of circulation systems that developed in the 1970s. Others were designed solely to serve as OPACs. Still others grew up as one component of integrated online systems that incorporated acquisitions and serials control functions as well as circulation and catalog functions.

Most OPACs are configured or customized according to a purchasing library's needs: all differ in the way in which data are displayed, the amount of data displayed, and the manner in which a user must interact with them. Some allow users to limit a search by language, publication date, location, or format. There are varying amounts of authority control from none at all to a complete authority record for every heading fully linked to the bibliographic records. OPACs also provide for very different kinds of access ranging from those that essentially duplicate the access points available in a card catalog to those that offer sophisticated levels of searching.

Today, most OPACs are "Webbed" OPACs or WebCats, which replace telnet sessions and their accompanying logon/logoff protocol with Web access. Through hypertext links, users can access other catalogs remotely, while Z39.50 and NCIP technology offer the capacity to search different databases located in different servers.[32] Catalogers as well as users benefit from the increased functionality of OPACs with Web interfaces. Using Windows-based workstations, catalogers can locate bibliographic records from the catalogs of other institutions, extract summary or other notes, and cut-and-paste them into records in their own online catalog.[33]

Some OPACs already feature full texts with their associated metadata and the integration of visual content as well as sound and video clips. Future developments are already on the horizon and promise multilingual systems that permit advanced query processing, probabilistic ranked searching, and relevance feedback. Christine Borgman's prediction that there would be a shift "from bibliographic data exchange between local integrated systems and between local systems and shared cataloging utilities to interoperability between digital libraries"[34] has proved accurate. Driven by rising user expectations and facilitated by the rapid pace of computer technology, the trend away from access to information repositories and towards an open, extensible metadata infrastructure will continue.

IFLA Guidelines for OPAC Displays

In 1997 at the meeting of the International Federation of Library Associations and Institutions (IFLA) in Copenhagen, members from the sections on Bibliography, Cataloguing, Classification and Indexing from the Division of Bibliographic Control, and from the section on Information Technology formed a Task Force "to bring together in the form of guidelines or recommendations a corpus of good practice to assist libraries to design or re-design their OPACs."[35] The focus of the guidelines is on the display of catalog records, rather than on circulation, serials check-in, fund accounting, acquisitions or bindery information, and they are intended to apply to all types of catalogs. The intent of the guidelines is "to recommend a standard set of display defaults, defined as features that should be provided for users who have not selected other options, including users who want to begin searching right away without much instruction."[36] The guidelines are divided into principles and recommendations, the recommendations being an expansion of the principles into actual practice, with the principles providing "a context and rationale for the recommendations."[37]

One of the major frustrations for catalog managers in the era of online catalogs has been the loss of control over the display of the cataloging records that they produce. In the card catalog, it was possible to use guide cards, "filing titles," and other such mechanisms in order to place cards where they would be the most useful. The programming of OPACs has often been done by persons with little understanding of the cataloging process. Arrangement and display of headings has too often made catalogs look as if little thought had gone into creation of headings (e.g., when headings are displayed in all capital letters with no punctuation as, for example, "LA FONTAINE JEAN DE 16211695" or "CHICAGO ILL ETHNIC RELATIONS"). The IFLA guidelines are designed to help librarians in customizing OPAC software, and to inform and educate vendors and producers of this software.

Workstations

The origins of the technical services workstation (TSW) go back to the introduction of the personal computer (PC) in the early 1980s. TSWs were first utilized in cataloging departments to facilitate inventory control and timely processing of library materials. The TSW's design and development varied from institution to institution, depending on the networking environment, system capabilities, and customization by staff.[38] However, according to Roger Brisson and Janet McCue, some features of the TSW became standard, and formed the conceptual model for the TSW used in many cataloging departments:

The platform can be an IBM-compatible PC, [or] a Macintosh, . . . although it should be noted that the majority of libraries use IBM-compatible computers. Regardless of the platform, the microcomputer must have enough computing power to run multiple applications (ideally it should be multitasking). It must also possess local storage capabilities of sufficient size, and it must support graphic-based operations with high resolution monitors that are large enough to display multiple windows.

Workstations are networked—to a LAN, to a TCP/IP ethernet link, and to the Internet. Networking supports access to resources and allows for the sharing of these resources among a work group. . . .

Workstations provide access to a variety of resources through a uniform user interface. . . .

Workstations support enhanced editing and inputting capabilities. For example, workstations possess a cut-and-paste feature so that information can be quickly moved from application to application. . . .

Workstations provide electronic access to cataloging and acquisitions support tools. These tools include locally developed documentation, standards or manuals specific to cataloging or acquisitions (an example being the Cataloger's Desktop of the Library of Congress [LC]), or reference resources such as dictionaries, encyclopedias, or language translators. . . .[39]

Today, as more and more library online systems have switched from a mainframe to a client-server environment, most library TSW's are client-based modular platforms that use vendor or local system-supplied software packages that feature update and Z39.50 search/retrieval capabilities.[40]

CATALOGING SUPPORT

As cataloging becomes increasingly automated, a range of electronic and Internet-based products, services, and resources has evolved to support the cataloging process. One of the most widespread is the previously mentioned *Cataloger's Desktop*, a product of LC, which features the following publications: *AACR2R*; *Library of Congress Rule Interpretations*; Subject Cataloging Manuals for Classification, Shelflisting, and Subject Headings; *MARC 21* Formats for Bibliographic, Authority, Holdings, and Classification Data, and Community Information; the latest editions of all five *MARC 21* Code Lists; and numerous other useful cataloging tools. Another is the Web Cataloging Assistant, a cataloging tool that extracts data from Web pages, and then creates MARC records that are first loaded into LC's cataloging client and then distributed by the Cataloging Distribution Service.[41]

OCLC, like LC, offers cataloging support services via its Connexion service. Connexion provides access to WorldCat, the OCLC union catalog, as well as to a wide variety of integrated cataloging tools, including NACO support for authorities functionality, local files, macros, and batch and real time processing.

In addition to its Marcadia searching program mentioned previously, RLG enables NACO catalogers using RLG's Union Catalog library processing system to select a heading in a bibliographic record and generate an authority record in the RLG Name Authority File. In addition, having converted its Union Catalog, Eureka Databases, and Archival Resources from a mainframe system to an open server environment, RLG now offers a full range of cataloging services via its Web-based search interface, RLIN21.

CONCLUSION

The catalog manager has responsibility for a major operating tool of the library. As can be seen in this chapter, the person(s) responsible for this area must be knowledgeable in several areas: cataloging, supervising, policies and procedures, managing contracts, and interfacing with ILS vendors. The constant growth of the database and the evolution of functionality of systems requires continuous reevaluation in order to keep the operation moving smoothly and the database operating effectively.

NOTES

1. Other reliable texts are available for this purpose. *See*, for example, G. Edward Evans and Sandra M. Heft, *Introduction to Technical Services for Library Technicians*, 6th ed. (Englewood, Colo.: Libraries Unlimited, 1994); and Donald L. Foster, *Managing the Catalog Department*, 3rd ed. (Metuchen, N.J.: Scarecrow, 1987).

2. Nicholson Baker, "Discards," *The New Yorker* 70, no. 7 (April 4, 1994): 64–86.

3. Bohdan S. Wynar, *Introduction to Cataloging and Classification*, 8th ed. by Arlene G. Taylor (Englewood, Colo.: Libraries Unlimited, 1992), pp. 518–519. For additional examples of shelflist cards and explanations, *see* Marty Bloomberg and G. Edward Evans, *Introduction to Technical Services for Library Technicians*, 5th ed. (Littleton, Colo.: Libraries Unlimited, 1985).

4. Arlene G. Taylor, *The Organization of Information*, 2nd ed. (Westport, Conn.: Libraries Unlimited, 2004), p. 356.

5. Sherry L. Vellucci, "Commercial Services for Providing Authority Control: Outsourcing the Process," *Cataloging & Classification Quarterly* 39, no. 1-2: 443–456; also published in *Authority Control in Organizing and Accessing Information: Definition and International Experience*, edited by Arlene G. Taylor and Barbara B. Tillett. New York: Haworth Information Press, 2004, pp. 443–456.

6. Vellucci, "Commercial Services," p. 447.

7. For more detailed information on automated authority control *see* Arlene G. Taylor, "Authority Control: Where It's Been and Where It's Going," and other papers from the conference "Authority Control: Why It Matters," sponsored by NELINET, November 1, 1999, Worcester, Mass., available: http://www.nelinet.net/edserv/conf/cataloging/cts/1999/taylor.htm (accessed 2/14/2006).

8. Foster, *Managing the Catalog Department*, pp. 225–226.

9. For discussion of adapting copy in the cataloging process, *see* Arlene G. Taylor, with the assistance of Rosanna M. O'Neil, *Cataloging with Copy: A Decision-Maker's Handbook*, 2nd ed. (Englewood, Colo.: Libraries Unlimited, 1988).

10. Melvil Dewey, *Dewey Decimal Classification and Relative Index*, Edition 22, edited by Joan S. Mitchell, et al. (Dublin, OH: OCLC, 2003); *Abridged Dewey Decimal Classification and Relative Index*, Edition 14, edited by Joan S. Mitchell, et al. (Dublin, OH: OCLC, 2004). DDC, Dewey, Dewey Decimal Classification, and WebDewey are registered trademarks of OCLC.

11. Roy Tennant, "A Bibliographic Metadata Infrastructure for the Twenty-first Century," *Library Hi-Tech* 22 (2004): 175.

12. *Functional Requirements for Bibliographic Records*, IFLA Study Group on the Functional Requirements for Bibliographic Records (München: K.G. Saur, 1998); also available: http://www.ifla.org/VII/s13/frbr/frbr.htm or http://www.ifla.org/VII/s13/frbr/frbr.pdf (accessed 2/14/2006)

13. *RDA – Resource Description and Access: A Prospectus*, Joint Steering Committee for Revision of AACR, available: http://www.collectionscanada.ca/jsc/rdaprospectus.html or http://www.collectionscanada.ca/jsc/docs/5rda-prospectusrev.pdf (accessed 2/25/2006).

14. OCLC Office of Research, "Automatic Classification Research at OCLC," available: http://www.oclc.org/research/projects/auto_class/default.htm (accessed 2/14/2006).

15. *Classification Web* (Washington, D.C.: Library of Congress, Cataloging Distribution Service), available: http://classificationweb.net [requires ID and password] (accessed 2/14/2006). For subscription information: http://www.loc.gov/cds/classweb (accessed 2/14/2006).

16. *A Catalog of Books Represented by Library of Congress Printed Cards Issued to July 31, 1942* (Ann Arbor, Mich.: Edwards Brothers, 1943); vol. 14, 3–13, gives full explanation of the arrangement.

17. Taylor, *The Organization of Information*. Chapter 12: Arrangement and Display.

18. *ALA Filing Rules* (Chicago: American Library Association, 1980).

19. Taylor, *Cataloging with Copy*, pp. 5–7.

20. For in-depth discussions of retrospective conversion, *see* Ruth C. Carter and Scott Bruntjen, *Data Conversion* (White Plains, N.Y.: Knowledge Industry Publications, 1983); and Dennis Reynolds, *Library Automation: Issues and Applications* (New York: R. R. Bowker, 1985), pp. 280–324.

21. Charles Coffin Jewett, *On the Construction of Catalogues of Libraries, and Their Publication by Means of Separate, Stereotyped Titles*, 2nd ed. (Washington, D.C.: Smithsonian Institution, 1853).

22. Barbara M. Westby, "Commercial Services," *Library Trends* 16 (July 1967): 46.

23. Arlene Taylor Dowell, *Cataloging with Copy: A Decision-Maker's Handbook* (Littleton, Colo.: Libraries Unlimited, 1976), pp. 248–257.

24. Clare B. Dunkle, "Outsourcing the Catalog Department: A Meditation Inspired by the Business and Library Literature," *Journal of Academic Librarianship* 22, no. 1 (January 1996): 33–43; "Intellectual Freedom Toolkits: Outsourcing and Privatization in Libraries" [includes links to several documents] (available: http://www.ala.org/ala/oif/iftoolkits/ outsourcing/Default2446.htm [accessed 8/27/2005]); Marie A. Kascus and Dawn Hale, eds., *Outsourcing Cataloging, Authority Work, and Physical Processing: a Checklist of Considerations* (Chicago: American Library Association, 1995); Robert S. Martin, et al., "The Impact of Outsourcing and Privatization on Library Services and Management: A Study for the American Library Association," School of Library and Information Studies, Texas Woman's University, June 2000 (available: http://www.ala.org/ala/oif/iftoolkits/outsourcing/ outsourcing_doc.pdf [accessed: 8/27/2005]); Karen A. Wilson and Marylou Colver, eds, *Outsourcing Library Technical Services Operations: Practices in Public, Academic, and Special Libraries* (Chicago: American Library Association, 1997).

25. Dilys E. Morris and Gregory Wool, "Cataloging: Librarianship's Best Bargain," *Library Journal* 124, no. 11 (June 15, 1999): 44–46.

26. Jamshid Beheshti, "The Evolving OPAC," *Cataloging & Classification Quarterly* 24, no. 1–2 (1997): 165.

27. George Machovec, "ILS System Selection: Second Time Around," *Colorado Libraries* 23, no. 4 (Winter 1997): 6.

28. Brian Kenney, "The Future of Integrated Library Systems," *Library Journal* 128, no. 11 (June 15, 2003): 37.

29. Andrew K. Pace, "Dismantling Integrated Library Systems," *Library Journal* 129, no. 2 (Feb. 1, 2004): 35.

30. Kenney, "The Future of Integrated Library Systems," p. 36.

31. L. W. Gassie, "What Do We Expect from the Next Generation of Library Systems?" *LLA Bulletin* 60, no.2 (Fall 1997): 97; Tennant, "A Bibliographic Metadata Infrastructure," p. 179.

32. National Information Standards Organization. "Circulation Interchange Part 1: Protocol (NCIP): ANSI/NISO Z39.83-2002," available: http://www.niso.org/standards/standard_detail. cfm?std_id = 728 (accessed 2/28/2006).

33. Chris Evin Long, "The Internet's Value to Catalogers: Results of a Survey," *Cataloging & Classification Quarterly* 23, no. 3–4 (1997): 69.

34. Christine L. Borgman, "From Acting Locally to Thinking Globally: A Brief History of Library Automation," *Library Quarterly* 67, no. 3 (July 1997): 230.

35. Martha Yee, "Guidelines for OPAC Displays," prepared for the 65th IFLA Council and General Conference, Bangkok, Thailand, 20th–28th August 1999, available: http://www. ifla.org/IV/ifla65/papers/098-131e.htm (accessed 2/14/2006).

36. Ibid.

37. Ibid.

38. Roger Brisson and Janet McCue, "Retooling Technical Services," in *Encyclopedia of Library and Information Science*, vol. 58, suppl. 21 (New York: Marcel Dekker, 1996): 281–301.

39. Ibid., pp. 284–285.

40. Michael Kaplan, "Introduction," in *Planning and Implementing Technical Services Workstations* (Chicago: American Library Association, 1997): xvii.

41. "Web Cataloging Assistant," The Library of Congress Bibliographic Enrichment Advisory Team, available: http://www.loc.gov/catdir/beat/webcat.html (accessed 2/28/2006).

SUGGESTED READING

Claire-Lise Bénaud, and Sever Bordeianu. *Outsourcing Library Operations in Academic Libraries: An Overview of Issues and Outcomes*. Englewood, Colo.: Libraries Unlimited, 1998.

Evans, G. Edward, and Sandra M. Heft. *Introduction to Technical Services for Library Technicians*. 6th ed. Englewood, Colo.: Libraries Unlimited, 1994.

Foster, Donald L. *Managing the Catalog Department*. 3rd ed. Metuchen, N.J.: Scarecrow, 1987.

Harvey, Ross, and Philip Hider. *Organising Knowledge in a Global Society: Principles and Practice in Libraries and Information Centres*. Wagga Wagga, NSW, Australia: Centre for Information Studies, 2004. Chapter 14: Local systems and OPACs.

Intner, Sheila S., and Jean Weihs. *Standard Cataloging for School and Public Libraries*. 3rd ed. Englewood, Colo.: Libraries Unlimited, 2001. Chapter 15: Cataloging and Classification Policies. Chapter 16: Managing the Cataloging Department.

Potter, William Gray. "The Online Catalogue in Academic Libraries." In *Technical Services Today and Tomorrow*. 2nd ed., edited by Michael Gorman, pp. 141–155. Englewood, Colo.: Libraries Unlimited, 1998.

Sellberg, Roxanne. "Cataloguing Management: Managing the Bibliographic Control Process." In *Technical Services Today and Tomorrow*. 2nd ed., edited by Michael Gorman, pp. 111–127. Englewood, Colo.: Libraries Unlimited, 1998.

Taylor, Arlene G., with the assistance of Rosanna M. O'Neil. *Cataloging with Copy: A Decision-Maker's Handbook*. 2nd ed. Englewood, Colo.: Libraries Unlimited, 1988. Chapters 1, 9.

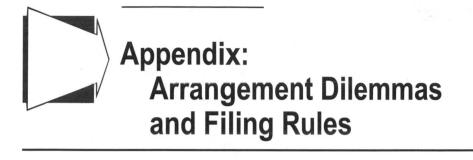

Appendix:
Arrangement Dilemmas
and Filing Rules

As mentioned in chapter 20, "Catalog Management," there is currently very little control over the arrangement of online public access catalog (OPAC) displays. When one purchases an Integrated Library System (ILS) with its OPAC, one accepts the arrangement that has been programmed into that system. However, an understanding of certain filing dilemmas can be useful in making decisions about catalog maintenance of heading forms and references. In addition, many libraries continue to maintain card shelflists as supplements to their OPACs, making understanding of notational arrangement an important part of catalog maintenance. For those who are still maintaining card catalogs, the rules for filing are essential for good catalog construction.

FILING DILEMMAS

There is a significant difference between alphabetizing straight through to the end of a phrase entry and observing the breaks in the string that occur at the end of each word. Most filers know the admonition "nothing before something," or "blank to Z." It means that library catalogs are generally arranged letter-by-letter to the end of each word and then word-by-word to the end of the heading. However, not all files in libraries are based on this premise. Reference librarians have to remember that the *American Peoples Encyclopedia*, the *Americana*, and the *World Book* are arranged word-by-word, while *Britannica*, *Collier's*, and *Compton's* prefer uninterrupted letter-by-letter filing to the close of the entry phrase. The differences are in some areas important, e.g.:

Word-by-word	Letter-by-letter
New Hampshire	Newark (N.J.)
New Haven (Conn.)	Newcastle (N.S.W.)
New York (N.Y.)	Newfoundland
New York (State)	New Hampshire
New Zealand	New Haven (Conn.)
Newark (N.J.)	Newman, Arthur
Newcastle (N.S.W.)	Newport (Isle of Wight)
Newfoundland	NEWSPAPERS
Newman, Arthur	New York (N.Y.)
Newport (Isle of Wight)	New York (State)
NEWSPAPERS	New Zealand

In entries containing dates, early historical periods usually precede later ones. However, codes differ on whether longer periods should precede or follow shorter ones starting with the same year. The American Library Association's (ALA's) *ALA Filing Rules*[1] and the Library of Congress's (LC's) *Library of Congress Filing Rules*[2] both say to arrange periods of time beginning with the same year in chronological order. They give examples from which the following selection was made:

    UNITED STATES—HISTORY—CONFEDERATION, 1783-1789
    UNITED STATES—HISTORY—1783-1865
    UNITED STATES—HISTORY—CONSTITUTIONAL PERIOD,
        1789-1809
    UNITED STATES—HISTORY—1865-
    UNITED STATES—HISTORY—1865-1898
    UNITED STATES—HISTORY—WAR OF 1898
    UNITED STATES—HISTORY—1898-
    UNITED STATES—HISTORY—20TH CENTURY

The *ALA Rules for Filing Catalog Cards*, second edition,[3] called for arranging periods of time beginning with the same year so that the longest period would file first, e.g.,

    UNITED STATES—HISTORY—1783-1865
    UNITED STATES—HISTORY—CONFEDERATION, 1783-1789
    UNITED STATES—HISTORY—1898-
    UNITED STATES—HISTORY—WAR OF 1898

If there are two or more editions or impressions of a work, edition dates or numbers may be added to the entry line, solely as filing elements. Again, codes differ on whether the earliest or latest should file first. The *ALA Filing Rules* say to arrange editions in straight chronological order, with earliest date first, e.g.,

    Schwartz, Seymour I.
        Principles of surgery. 1969.
        Principles of surgery. 2nd ed. 1974.
        Principles of surgery. 3rd ed. 1979.
        Principles of surgery. 4th ed. 1984.
        Principles of surgery. 5th ed. 1989.

In the list below, the latest ones come first, on the assumption that they are the ones the user is most likely to want:

    Sackheim, George I.
        Introduction to chemistry for biology students. 3rd ed. 1983.
        Introduction to chemistry for biology students. 2nd ed. 1977.
        Introduction to chemistry for biology students. 1966.

Numbers or digits in catalog entries give further challenges. Under current sets of rules, character strings beginning with numerals (whether Arabic or non-Arabic) are arranged before character strings beginning with letters, e.g.,

The 24th Congress of the CPSU and its contribution to Marxism-Leninism.

XXIVth International Congress of Pure and Applied Chemistry, main section lectures presented at . . . .

Twenty-four dramatic cases of the International Academy of Trial Lawyers.

The twenty-fourth session of the International Labour Conference . . . .

According to the *ALA Filing Rules*, numerals precede character strings, and all such character string/numeral combinations are interfiled regardless of the type of entry, e.g.,

HENRY I, KING OF ENGLAND, 1068-1135
HENRY V, KING OF ENGLAND, 1367-1413
Henry VIII and his wives.
HENRY VIII, KING OF ENGLAND, 1491-1547
Henry VIII's fifth wife.
Henry the Eighth and his court.
Henry the Fifth of England.

However, under *LC Filing Rules* fields with identical leading elements are subgrouped in the order of person, place, thing, title. Thus, while numerals precede character strings, the person entries are all grouped before the title entries, e.g.,

HENRY I, KING OF ENGLAND, 1068-1135
HENRY V, KING OF ENGLAND, 1367-1413
HENRY VIII, KING OF ENGLAND, 1491-1547
Henry VIII and his wives.
Henry VIII's fifth wife.
Henry the Eighth and his court.
Henry the Fifth of England.

In prior rules, however, numerals were most often filed as spelled, and spelled "as spoken," in whatever language the entry appeared. Many card catalogs and other sources still file numerals in this way. Interpretation becomes most critical when the primary filing element of a title is expressed on the chief source of information in numerals. In a catalog where numerals are filed as spoken, it is possible that the two books (one by Walter Sellar, the other by Reginald Arkell) entitled *1066 and All That* are lost forever to the patron who cannot pronounce "1066" appropriately. However, filing numerals first can also cause problems for users, regardless of kind of catalog. How would a user who has heard a title spoken (e.g., 100 classical studies for flute) know whether to look in the numerical section or the alphabetical section? References and/or added entries are required, regardless of the method of filing.

Extensive use of acronyms and initialisms has in recent years aggravated the familiar problem of how to file abbreviations. Computerized filing throws new light on the difficulties encountered in traditional approaches. In the past, initials were most often treated as one-letter words, regardless of whether spaces or punctuation intervened. For machine-readable databases it is easier to file strings of letters, or letters-and-numbers, lacking spacing or punctuation as multicharacter words. It is immaterial whether they consist entirely of capitals (e.g., FORTRAN) or of a combination of upper- and lowercase (e.g., MeSH or Unesco). Nor does pronounceability affect the filing, as it did under previous sets of filing rules that required that one determine whether or not an acronym or initialism was pronounced as a word in order to decide where to file it.

Abbreviated titles of respect or position (e.g., Mr., Dr., St.) formerly were filed as if spelled out in full. But social pressures, as well as the computer, have effected changes. For example, *Webster's New International Dictionary* (second edition) defined "Mrs." as "the form of Mistress when used as a title."[4] The problems ensuing from that edict were impressive. Fortunately, *Webster's* third edition substituted a more contemporary (and considerably more round-about) explanation that in effect recognizes the abbreviation at its face value. Meanwhile, many libraries had already decided to file "Mrs." and "Ms." as written. Under both of the 1980 sets of filing rules (ALA and LC) abbreviations are arranged exactly as they are written.

Initial articles are usually suppressed as filing words, especially in titles. The practice extends to all languages using articles, since even in inflected languages the number of articles is relatively limited. They can be tabulated for manual filing or programmed out of machine filing. But homonyms (e.g., the French article *la*, as in *la belle epoque*, and the British interjection, as in "La! she was a lady") must be differentiated. Also, articles that initiate proper names (e.g., "La Crosse, Herman Thomas" and "Los Angeles (Calif.)") are always filed as written for American or English names, and for other languages as well where usage so dictates.

In dictionary catalogs the order of entries with identical wording, which may or may not be punctuated differently, must be decided. The conventional arrangement is: author, subject, title. In practice, it is highly unusual to find an author entry, a subject entry, and a title entry, all with exactly the same wording; the question bears more often on different kinds of entries that start with the same word. Application of the "authors first" guideline leaves unanswered the ordering of surnames and given name entries that start alike (e.g., "Thomas . . ."). The *LC Filing Rules* file given name entries (e.g., "Francis, of Assisi, Saint" and "Francis Xavier, Saint") ahead of the same word used as a surname (e.g., "Francis, Connie"). The *ALA Filing Rules* undo that preference, interfiling all entries, regardless of type, word-by-word to the end of the character string. However, some older card catalogs are still filed according to the 1968 *ALA Rules*, according to which all surname entries come first, followed by all other entries that begin with the same word.

Many libraries, particularly large ones with comprehensive collections by and about certain versatile writers, have separated out main and added entries for those persons into at least two categories. However, the original edition of the *ALA Rules* discouraged the practice:

> Arrange in one file all the entries, both main and secondary, for a person as author, joint author, compiler, editor, illustrator, translator and general added entry. Subarrange alphabetically by the title of the book. *Note:* An earlier practice, still followed in some libraries, is to arrange the secondary author entries in a separate alphabet after the main author entries. This practice is not recommended because users of the catalog overlook entries so filed.[5]

It was observed in chapter 1 that divided catalogs permit a simpler filing scheme than do dictionary catalogs. The simplifications, though, depend on the way in which the division is made. Often, subject entries are alphabetized separately from author and title entries. Persons (e.g., "Shakespeare, William") who are both authors and subjects of books have entries in each catalog, rather than having all the entries about them collocated immediately behind all the entries by them. Titles that happen to be identical with a subject heading (e.g., *Freedom of the Press*) are similarly often located in a separate file. There is perhaps less danger of the title entries' being misfiled or overlooked, but closely related titles and subjects are separated from each other.

In either divided or dictionary catalogs there is seldom any doubt about where to file a *see* reference, but there are definitely two schools of thought on the location of *see also* references. Most catalogers place them immediately after those entries from which they lead, on the theory that the user will have exhausted a search at that point and be most ready for new suggestions. However, both sets of 1980 filing rules (ALA and LC) say categorically to file *see also* references before the first entry under the same word or words.

THE 1980 FILING RULES

The first edition of the *A.L.A. Rules for Filing Catalog Cards* was published in 1942. A Subcommittee of the American Library Association's Editorial Committee was established twenty years later to prepare a revision that would correlate with the 1967 publication of the *Anglo-American Cataloging Rules (AACR)*. The second edition of filing rules, like the first, was primarily designed for a dictionary catalog.[6] Except for the surname-first groupings in cases of identical entry words, single-alphabet arrangements were preferred over categorical considerations in nearly all cases. Machine filing experiments undoubtedly influenced the trend toward straight alphabetization. Yet the *ALA Rules* were designed for the manually filed catalogs that would continue to predominate for at least another two decades.

The Filing Committee of the Resources and Technical Services Division was appointed in the early 1970s to look into rules for computer filing. However, contact was maintained with the committee that was developing *Anglo-American Cataloguing Rules, Second Edition (AACR2)* so that the new rules would be applicable for *AACR2* entries. The new *ALA Filing Rules* were thought to be so different from the earlier two sets of ALA rules that they were considered to be a new work, not another edition.[7] The introduction states that they are applicable to any bibliographic displays, not just card formats, and that they can be used to arrange records formulated according to any cataloging rules.[8]

The brief summary of the *ALA Filing Rules* that follows is designed to show the rules that a filer in a modest collection would be most likely to use. In cases where the LC *Filing Rules* vary significantly, this is brought to the reader's attention.

General Rules

As already mentioned, filing is character by character to the end of each word and word by word to the end of the filing element. This is a result of applying the "nothing files before something" principle, with spaces, dashes, hyphens, diagonal slashes, and periods all considered to be "nothing." Also, as already mentioned, numerals precede letters. In addition, letters of the English alphabet precede letters of nonroman alphabets.

Modified letters (e.g., ç or ñ) are filed as if they were the plain English equivalent, and diacritical marks are ignored. Punctuation and nonalphabetic signs and symbols (except those noted above as equivalent to "nothing," ampersands, and certain such marks in numeric character strings) are also ignored.

Examples of the Basic ALA Rules

10 ans de politique social en Pologne	"Life after death"
20 a week	LIFE (BIOLOGY)
150 science experiments step-by-step	Muellen, Abraham
1918, the last act	Mullen, Allen
130,000 kilowatt power station	Müllen, Gustav
A.A.	New York
A.B.C. programs	Newark
Aabel, Marie	% of gain
$$$ and sense	One hundred best books
Camp-fire and cotton-field	Parenting guidebook
Camp Fire Girls	Rolston, Brown
Campbell, Thomas J.	Rølyat, Jane
Campfire adventure stories	Zookeeper's handbook
LIFE	πΣA: A history
Life—a bowl of rice	

The *LC Filing Rules* differ on the treatment of nonroman alphabet letters: these are to be romanized for filing.

Note that under previous rules, hyphenated prefixes and compound words written both as separate words (or hyphenated) and as single words (e.g., *campfire, camp-fire*) were interfiled as the single word. Under the new rules a hyphen is regarded as a space.

Ampersands

Ampersands may be ignored or, optionally, may be spelled out in their language equivalents, e.g.,

Without option	**With option**
Art and beauty	Art and beauty
ART AND INDUSTRY	Art & commonsense
Art & commonsense	ART AND INDUSTRY

Under *LC Filing Rules* the ampersand has the lowest filing value in alphanumeric order, e.g.,

Art & commonsense
Art and beauty
ART AND INDUSTRY

Treatment of Access Points

If access points are not identical they are filed character by character and word by word according to the general rules. The major exceptions are for initial articles, certain kinds of numerals, and certain additions to names (e.g., relators and terms of honor and address). For explanation of these exceptions, *see* below.

When access points consist of a name and a title, they are filed as two separate elements. The title portion files with all other titles under the same name heading.

Identical Access Points

When arranging identical access points, the filer should first consider the functions of the access point. As mentioned earlier, *see* and *see also* references precede the entries of their type. In addition, main and added entries are interfiled but precede subject references and subject entries, e.g.,

Philadelphia.   Free Library.   [corporate name entry]
    Annual report . . .

Philadelphia Free Library   [title added entry]
Wagner, Robert L.
    The Philadelphia Free Library . . .

PHILADELPHIA. FREE LIBRARY   [subject entry]
Bruns, Suzanne.
    A history of the Philadelphia Free Public Library . . .

As mentioned earlier, *LC Filing Rules* call for arranging entries with identical leading elements in the order: person, place, thing, title. "Thing" includes corporate body entries. Thus in the example above the title added entry would follow the subject entry.

Subarrangement of identical access points *with equivalent functions* in the *ALA Filing Rules* is determined by consideration of secondary data elements. For records with author or uniform title main entry, the next element considered is the title, followed by the date of publication, distribution, etc. For records with title main entry (not uniform title) the next element considered is the date. If the access point is a personal or corporate name added entry, the next element considered is the title, followed by the date. If the access point is a title added entry, the next element considered is the author or uniform title main entry, if there is one, followed by the date. If the access point is a series or subject added entry, the next element considered is the author or uniform title main entry, if there is one, followed by the title, followed by the date.

Examples Arranged by *ALA Filing Rules*
(examples are invented)

Love.
James, Samuel.
  Love . . .

Love and beauty.
Adams, Harriet.
  Love and beauty . . .

Love and beauty.
Hansen, Sigurd.
  Love and beauty . . .

LØVE (DENMARK)
Friis Møller, Jens.
  Life in a Danish town . . .

Love, Harold G., 1878-1926.
  The chemical industry . . .

Love, Harold G., 1911-
Symposium on the Social Organization of Anthropoid
    Apes (1st : 1954 : Berkeley, Calif.)
  Anthropoid apes and their society . . .

Love, Harold G., 1911-
  Behavior of nocturnal primates . . .

Love, Harold G., 1911-
  The primates of Africa . . .

Love, Harold G., 1911-
Atkins, Francis Harrison.
  Psychological studies of the great apes . . .

LOVE, HAROLD G., 1911-
Coffin, Lyle Warner.
  Harold Love . . .

LOVE, HAROLD G., 1911-
Driscoll, Maynard.
  Cousins, once removed . . .

LOVE, HAROLD G., 1911-   BIBLIOGRAPHY
Hennesey, Judy.
  Books by and about Harold Love . . .

LOVE (THEOLOGY)
Adam, Karl.
  Love and belief . . .

The above entries would have a somewhat different order under the *LC Filing Rules* because of the arrangement of fields with identical leading elements in the order of person (forename, then surname), place, thing (corporate body, then topical subject heading), title.

Examples Arranged by *LC Filing Rules*
(examples are invented)

Love, Harold G., 1878-1926.
   The chemical industry . . .

Love, Harold G., 1911-
Symposium on the Social Organization of Anthropoid
     Apes (1st : 1954 : Berkeley, Calif.)
   Anthropoid apes and their society . . .

Love, Harold G., 1911-
   Behavior of nocturnal primates . . .

Love, Harold G., 1911-
   The primates of Africa . . .

Love, Harold G., 1911-
Atkins, Francis Harrison.
   Psychological studies of the great apes . . .

LOVE, HAROLD G., 1911-
Coffin, Lyle Warner.
   Harold Love . . .

LOVE, HAROLD G., 1911-
Driscoll, Maynard.
   Cousins, once removed . . .

LOVE, HAROLD G., 1911-   BIBLIOGRAPHY
Hennesey, Judy.
   Books by and about Harold Love . . .

LØVE (DENMARK)
Friis Møller, Jens.
   Life in a Danish town . . .

LOVE (THEOLOGY)
Adam, Karl.
   Love and belief . . .

Love.
James, Samuel.
   Love . . .

Love and beauty.
Adams, Harriet.
   Love and beauty . . .

Love and beauty.
Hansen, Sigurd.
Love and beauty . . .

Special Rules

Abbreviations

As mentioned earlier, abbreviations are arranged as written.

Examples

Concord (Mass.)
The Concord saunterer
Concord (Va.)
CONCORD (VT.)

Doctor come quickly
Doktor Brents Wandlung
Dr. Christian's office
Dr. Mabuse der Spieler

Initial Articles

Initial articles that form integral parts of place names and personal names are filed as written. Initial articles at the beginning of corporate names, title, and subject headings are ignored unless they begin with a personal name or place name.

Examples

Las cartas largas.
El chico.
The Club.
Der Club.
Club 21 (New York)
Club accounts.
The Club (London)
El-Abiad, Ahmed H., 1926-
El Campo (Tex.)
The El Dorado Trail.
The John Crerar Library today.
La Fontaine, Jean de, 1621-1695.
Las Hurdes (Spain)
Laš, Michal.
Lasa, Jose Maria de.

Initials, Initialisms, and Acronyms

The filing of initials, initialisms, and acronyms depends upon the spacing and punctuation between the characters. If they are separated by spaces, dashes, hyphens, diagonal slashes, or periods, they are filed as if each character were a separate word. If they are separated by other marks or symbols or are not separated, the group of characters is filed as a single word.

Examples

A.A.
A., A.J.G.
A apple pie
A.B.C. programs
Aabel, Marie
AAUN news
The ABC about collecting
U.N.E.S.C.O.   See UNESCO and Unesco.
Under the old apple tree
Unesco
UNESCO bibliographical handbooks
Unesco fellowship handbook

Names and Prefixes

A prefix that forms part of the name of a person or place is filed as a separate word unless it is joined to the rest of the name without a space or is separated from it only by an apostrophe.

Examples

De Alberti, Amelia	MacAlister, James
De la Roche, Mazo	Mach, Ernst
De Marco, Clara	MACHINERY
De senectute	MacHugh, Angus
Defoe, Daniel	Maclaren, Ian
Del Mar, Eugene	MacLaren, J.
	Maclaren, James
El Dorado (Ark.)	M'Bengue, Mamadou Seyni
El-Wakil, Mohamed Mohamed	McHenry, Lawson
Elagin, Ivan	McLaren, Jack
Eldorado (Neb.)	Mead, Edwin Doak
	M'Laren, J. Wilson

Under previous ALA filing rules names beginning with the prefixes *M'* and *Mc* were filed as if written *Mac*, and card catalogs may still be filed that way.

Numerals

Numerals are arranged according to their value from lowest to highest, but there are some difficulties in reading numbers with punctuation, decimals, fractions, and non-Arabic notation and superscript/subscript numerals. If punctuation is for readability, it is treated as if it did not exist. Other punctuation is treated as a space. Decimals are arranged digit-by-digit, and if they are not combined with a whole integer, they precede the numeral 1. Fractions are arranged as if they are characters in the order numerator, line (treated as space), denominator (e.g., $2\frac{1}{2}$ is filed: 2 space 1 space 2). Non-Arabic numerals are interfiled with their Arabic equivalents. Superscript/subscript numerals are filed as if on the line and as if preceded by a space.

Examples

.300 Vickers machine gun mechanism
1:0 für Dich
$1\frac{3}{4}$ yards of silk
1.3 acres
1^3 is one
$\frac{1}{3}$ of an inch
2 x 2 = 5
3.2 beer for all
3:10 to Yuma
3 point 2 and what goes with it
$20 a week
XX Century cyclopaedia and atlas
20 humorous stories
XXth century citizen's atlas of the world
200 years of architectural drawing
2000 A.D., a documentary

Dates

Dates in titles are filed as numerals. Dates in a chronological file, such as subdivisions of subjects or personal names with dates, are arranged chronologically, with B.C. dates preceding A.D. dates. Historic time periods that are generalized or expressed only in words are filed with the full range of dates for the period (e.g., *18th century* is equivalent to 1800–1899). Subject period subdivisions are filed chronologically even when words (e.g., the name of a war) precede the dates. Geologic time periods are arranged alphabetically.

Examples

UNITED STATES—HISTORY
UNITED STATES—HISTORY—COLONIAL PERIOD, CA.1600-1775
UNITED STATES—HISTORY—REVOLUTION, 1775-1783
UNITED STATES—HISTORY—CONFEDERATION, 1783-1789
UNITED STATES—HISTORY—1783-1865
UNITED STATES—HISTORY—1865-

UNITED STATES—HISTORY—1865-1898
UNITED STATES—HISTORY—WAR OF 1898
UNITED STATES—HISTORY—1898-
UNITED STATES—HISTORY—20TH CENTURY
UNITED STATES—HISTORY—1933-1945
UNITED STATES—HISTORY—BIO-BIBLIOGRAPHY
UNITED STATES—HISTORY—DICTIONARIES

Under the *ALA Filing Rules*, subjects with subdivisions and those with qualifiers are interfiled ignoring punctuation.

Examples Arranged by *ALA Filing Rules*

COOKERY
COOKERY, AMERICAN
COOKERY, AMERICAN—BIBLIOGRAPHY
COOKERY (APPLES)
COOKERY, CHINESE
COOKERY—DICTIONARIES
COOKERY FOR DIABETICS
COOKERY, INTERNATIONAL
COOKERY—YEARBOOKS

The *LC Filing Rules*, however, are more inclined to categorize entries. Topical subject headings are grouped so that the leading element alone is first, followed by entries in the form: leading element—subject subdivision. These are followed by entries in the form: leading element, comma, additional word(s). Following these are entries in which the leading element is followed by a parenthetical qualifier. Finally, there come entries in which the word that has been the leading element in the preceding entries is the first word of a phrase.

Examples Arranged by *LC Filing Rules*

COOKERY
COOKERY—DICTIONARIES
COOKERY—YEARBOOKS
COOKERY, AMERICAN
COOKERY, AMERICAN—BIBLIOGRAPHY
COOKERY, CHINESE
COOKERY, INTERNATIONAL
COOKERY (APPLES)
COOKERY FOR DIABETICS

Subordinate elements that follow a dash are also grouped according to the *LC Filing Rules*. The order is period subdivision, form and topical subdivisions, and geographical subdivisions. This is the order in which printed versions of *Library of Congress Subject Headings* (*LCSH*) are arranged, and it is further discussed with examples in chapter 11.

SHELFLIST FILING

The notation of most modern classifications, whether pure or mixed, includes Arabic numerals (both integers and decimals) that are filed in normal mathematical sequence. A typical series of class numbers from the *Dewey Decimal Classification* (*DDC*) schedules, which use a pure decimal notation, could appear as follows:

DDC Class Number Order

001	- Knowledge
010	- Bibliography
016	- Subject bibliographies
070.01	- Theory of journalism
070.1	- News media
070.17	- Print media
070.172	- Newspapers
070.19	- Broadcast media
070.4	- Journalism
070.41	- Editing
070.509	- History of publishing
070.59	- Kinds of publishers
078	- Journalism in Scandinavia
	[etc.]

Class number notation for the LC system is mixed. In its simplest form it consists of one to three roman alphabet letters followed by one to four integers. However, decimals both in pure numeric form and in alphanumeric form may be introduced at various points. A typical sequence might be:

LC Class Number Order

T20	- History of technology in the 20th century
T26.G3	- History of technology in Germany
T26.G5B5	- History of technology in Berlin
TP572	- Directories of brewing and malting
TP573.A1	- General histories of brewing and malting
TP573.5	- Biography of brewers and malters
TP573.5A1	- Collective biography of brewers and malters
TP574	- Schools of brewing and malting
TP1107	- Exhibitions of plastics and plastics manufacture
TP1130	- Handbooks, manuals, tables, etc., of plastics
TP1135	- Plastics plants and equipment
	[etc.]

Cutter number notation also varies with the system. Libraries that use *DDC* may use cutter numbers assigned through use of the Cutter two- or three-figure alphanumeric tables or the Cutter-Sanborn tables. Two-figure Cutter and Cutter-Sanborn numbers can be filed in straight integer sequence, but those from the three-figure Cutter table must be arranged decimally, as shown:

DDC Call Numbers with Three-Figure Cutter Book Numbers

333 F189 - A work on land economics by an author surnamed Falkinson
333 F19   - A similar work by an author surnamed Fallaby
333 F191 - A similar work by an author surnamed Fallentz
333 F21   - A similar work by an author surnamed Famareus
333 F218 - A similar work by an author surnamed Fantine

Workmarks consisting of lowercase letters, and most often corresponding to the first significant word of the item's title, may be added to the cutter number as follows:

DDC Call Numbers with Workmarks

515.33 R4li   - Introduction to Differential Calculus, by an author surnamed Richmond
515.33 R41m - Mean Value Theorems, by the same author
515.33 R4lt   - Total and Directional Derivatives, by the same author

Many smaller libraries using *DDC* bypass the Cutter tables in favor of adding one to three or more capital letters from the main entry word of the item to the *DDC* class number. These book symbols are, of course, arranged alphabetically as follows. In such libraries congested files are rare, so that lowercase workmarks are not often needed:

DDC Call Numbers with Alphabetic Book Numbers

799.1 ROB   - A book on fishing by an author surnamed Robb
799.1 ROBE - A similar book by an author surnamed Robertson
799.1 ROBI - A similar book by an author surnamed Robinson

LC assigns its own unique cutter numbers to materials, as discussed in chapters 11 and 12. Many LC call numbers include two cutter numbers, of which only the final one is, or incorporates, the number for the particular item. A typical sequence might be:

HC59.7.B7	- Broekmeijer, M.W.J.M. *Fiction and truth about the decade of development.*
HC59.7.C28	- Caiden, Naomi. *Planning and budgeting in poor countries.*
HC59.7.C6	- Committee for Economic Development. *How low income countries can advance their growth.*
HN438.C5G2	- Galpern, A.N. *The religions of the people in sixteenth-century Champagne.*
HN438.P3R8	- Rudé, George F.E. *Paris and London in the eighteenth century.*
HN438.P6H52	- Higonnet, Patrice L.R. *Pont-de-Montvert; social structure and politics in a French village, 1700-1914.*

What needs to be remembered when filing LC call numbers is that the classification part of the notation up to the period files as integers, but any cutter numbers after the period file as decimals.

HN4	*but*	HN438.C15
HN5		HN438.C23
HN15		HN438.C4
HN23		HN438.C43
HN43		HN438.C5
HN59		HN438.C59

Dates or edition numbers may be added as a third element to either *DDC* or *LCC* call numbers to distinguish among different issues of the same title. These might be filed in either chronological or retrospective order, just as in catalog filing, but the majority of libraries prefer chronological shelflist filing. Location symbols of various kinds may also accompany call numbers of some materials. The shelflist filing of such additions is purely a matter of local preference.

NOTES

1. *ALA Filing Rules* (Chicago: American Library Association, 1980).

2. *Library of Congress Filing Rules* (Washington, D.C.: Library of Congress, 1980).

3. *ALA Rules for Filing Catalog Cards*, 2nd ed. (Chicago: American Library Association, 1968).

4. *Webster's New International Dictionary of the English Language*, 2nd ed., unabr. (Springfield, Mass.: G. & C. Merriam, 1959), p. 1605.

5. *A.L.A. Rules for Filing Catalog Cards* (Chicago: American Library Association, 1942), p. 25.

6. *See* Pauline Seely, "ALA Filing Rules—New Edition," *Library Resources & Technical Services* 11 (Summer 1967): 377–379; and Pauline Seely, "ALA Rules for Filing Catalog Cards: Differences between 2d and 1st Editions (Arranged by 2d Rule Numbers)," *Library Resources & Technical Services* 13 (Spring 1969): 291–294.

7. For a critique of the *ALA Filing Rules*, *see* Hans W. Wellisch, "The *ALA Filing Rules*: Flowcharts Illustrating Their Application, with a Critique and Suggestions for Improvement," *Journal of the American Society for Information Science* 34 (September 1983): 313–330.

8. *ALA Filing Rules*, pp. 1–2.

Glossary of Selected Terms and Abbreviations

Defined in this glossary are selected basic terms for students of cataloging, including a number of terms and identifiers used in bibliographic control, descriptive cataloging, classification, subject heading work, filing, document indexing, networking, and other topics treated in this text. Readers may wish to consult other sources for other terms used in the library profession.

AACR2 (Anglo-American Cataloguing Rules, Second Edition). A set of rules, published in 1978, for producing the descriptive and name-and-title access points part of a surrogate record for an information package or resource; the creation of these rules was the result of collaboration among representatives from Canada, Great Britain, and the United States.

AACR2R (Anglo-American Cataloguing Rules, Second Edition, 1988 Revision). The first revision of *AACR2*. The abbreviation *AACR2R* is also used to indicate a collection of all of the additions and changes to *AACR2* in whatever physical manifestation they appear.

AACR2R2002 (Anglo-American Cataloguing Rules, Second Edition, 2002 Revision). The most current revision of *AACR2* characterized in printed form by being issued in loose-leaf format; rules are monitored by the Joint Steering Committee (JSC) for AACR, which is made up of representatives from Australia, Canada, Great Britain, and the United States.

Aboutness. The subject of an information package. *See also* **Subject analysis**.

Abstract. A condensed narrative description of an information package that may serve as a surrogate for the information package in a retrieval system.

Abstracting. The process of creating abstracts. *See also* **Cataloging**; **Indexing**.

Access. That portion of cataloging in which access points are selected and formulated by a cataloger. *See also* **Description**; **Descriptive cataloging**.

Access point. Any word or phrase used to obtain information from a retrieval tool or other organized system; in cataloging and indexing, "access points" are specific names, titles, and subjects chosen by the cataloger or indexer, when creating a surrogate/metadata record, to allow for the retrieval of the record. *See also* **Added entry; Choice of access points; Entry; Heading; Primary access point.**

Accession number. A number assigned to each item as it is received in the library. Accession numbers may be assigned through continuous numbering (e.g., 30291, 30292) or a coded system (2005–201, 2005–202, etc.).

Accompanying materials. Dependent materials, such as answer books, teacher's manuals, atlases, portfolios of plates, slides, sound recordings, or computer disks, that accompany and are cataloged with the main component of the information package.

Add instructions. Notes in classification schedules that specify what digits to add to a base number.

Added entry. A secondary access point; i.e., any access point other than the main entry or primary access point. In COM, book, or card catalogs an added entry record may duplicate the main entry record with the addition of a heading to represent a subject, joint author, illustrator, director, conductor, series, and the like.

A-G Canada. A computer-based bibliographic network offering its database and services to a variety of Canadian libraries and also to a few libraries in the northeastern United States; formerly Utlas International, and then ISM/LIS.

Alphabetical catalog. A catalog with entries arranged or displayed in alphabetical order rather than according to the symbolic notation of a classification. *See also* **Classified catalog**; **Dictionary catalog**; **Divided catalog**.

Alphabetico-classed catalog. A catalog in which subject categories are used for arrangement of surrogate records; broad categories are subdivided by narrower categories that are placed alphabetically within each broad category.

Alternative title. The second title of a work, which is joined to the first title with *or* or its equivalent (e.g., *Maria, or, The Wrongs of Woman*). Both titles together are considered to constitute the title proper of the work. *See also* **Title proper**.

Analytical entry. An entry for a part of a work or for a whole work contained in a series or a collection for which a comprehensive entry is made. A name-title analytic (one kind of analytical entry) may be made in the form of an added entry. *See also* **Name-title added entry**.

Anonymous work. One in which the creator's name does not appear anywhere in the information package; a work of unknown authorship.

Area. A major section of an ISBD bibliographic description; e.g., edition area or physical description area.

Artifact or **Artefact**. *See* **Realia**.

Asynchronous responsibility. The situation in which the persons or corporate bodies involved in the creation of an information package have made different kinds of contributions to the creation of a work (e.g., author and illustrator; performer, conductor, choreographer, and producer; etc.); also called mixed responsibility. *See also* **Synchronous responsibility**.

Author. A person who is responsible for all or some of the intellectual or artistic content of a work; e.g., writer of a book, compiler of a bibliography, composer of a musical work, artist, photographer, etc. *See also* **Compiler**; **Creator**; **Editor**.

Author entry. The place in a retrieval tool where a surrogate record that begins with the name of the creator of an information package may be found.

Author number. *See* **Cutter number**.

Authority control. The result of the process of maintaining consistency in the verbal form used to represent an access point and the further process of showing the relationships among names, works, and subjects; also, the result of the process of doing authority work with or without the necessity of choosing one form of name or title or one subject term to be the "authorized" selection. If every variant name, title, or term is given equal status, then one form is chosen for default display. Whether or not an "authorized" form is chosen to represent the name, title, or term, a searcher may use any of the forms in the authority record to gain access to information packages related to the name, title, or subject. *See also* **Authority work**.

Authority file. A grouping of authority records.

Authority record. Printed or machine-readable documentation of the decisions made during the course of authority work. An authority record contains all the forms used for a particular name, title, or subject, and usually designates one of the forms as the "authorized" or "default" one to use in catalog records.

Authority work. The process of determining and maintaining the form of a name or title and/or determining and maintaining an "authorized" term or phrase to stand for a subject concept. In the name and title areas, the process includes identifying all variant names or titles and relating the variants to the name or title forms chosen to be access points. In some cases it may also include relating different names and/or titles to each other. In the verbal subject area, the process includes identifying and maintaining relationships among terms – relationships such as synonyms, broader terms, narrower terms, and related terms.

Auxiliary table. A generalized subdivision table appended to a classification schedule for use in building specific classification numbers where indicated in the schedule proper.

Bibliographic control. The process of describing items in the bibliographic universe and then providing name, title, and subject access to the descriptions, resulting in records that serve as surrogates for the actual items of recorded information. Bibliographic control further requires that surrogate records be placed into retrieval systems where they act as pointers to the actual information packages.

Bibliographic data. Information gathered in the process of creating bibliographic records; also refers to any discrete element(s) in a bibliographic record.

Bibliographic database. A collection of bibliographic records held in the format of a database (q.v.).

Bibliographic file. A grouping of bibliographic records. In a catalog or bibliographic database, a bibliographic file is distinct from, but might be linked to, one or more authority files and/or holdings files.

Bibliographic network. A corporate entity that has as its main resource a bibliographic database; access to the database is available for a price, and members of the network can contribute new records and download existing ones; sometimes called a "Bibliographic utility."

Bibliographic record. A catalog entry in card, microform, machine-readable, or other form carrying full cataloging information for an information package. *See also* **Metadata**; **Surrogate record**.

Bibliographic service center. A regional broker, providing intermediate communication, training, and service for libraries participating in an online bibliographic network.

Bibliographic tools. *See* **Bibliographic databases**; **Bibliography**; **Catalog**; **Index**; **Retrieval tools**.

Bibliographic universe. The concept that encompasses all instances of recorded knowledge.

Bibliographic utility. *See* **Bibliographic network**.

Bibliography. A list of information packages on a given subject, by a given author, from a particular time period or place, or the like.

Book catalog. A catalog in which surrogate records are printed on pages that are bound into book form.

Book number. *See* **Cutter number**.

Boolean operators. The terms *and*, *or*, and *not* as used to construct search topics in a retrieval tool that uses post-coordinate indexing and/or keyword searching.

Broad classification. A method of applying a classification scheme that omits detailed subdivision of its main classes or that facilitates the use in smaller libraries of only its main classes and subdivisions. *See also* **Close classification**.

Broader term (BT). A term one level up from the term being examined in a listing where terms for subject concepts have been conceived in relationships that are hierarchical. *See also* **Narrower term; Related term.**

BSO. Broad System of Ordering, a classification developed for a proposed worldwide information network covering the whole field of knowledge.

Call number. A notation on an information package that matches the same notation in the surrogate/metadata record and is used to identify and locate a particular item; it often consists of a classification notation and a cutter number, and it may also include a work mark and/or a date. It is the number used to "call" for an item in a closed stack library —thus the source of the name "call number." *See also* **Cutter number; Work mark.**

Card catalog. A catalog in which every entry is printed or typed on a card (usually 3" x 5") and placed in a file drawer in a particular order (usually alphabetical or classified order).

Catalog. An organized set of surrogate records that represent the holdings of a particular collection and/or information packages or resources to which access may be gained. It may be arranged by alphabet, by classification notation, by subject, or, in the case of an online catalog, the display may be arranged by date or any one of several other elements.

Catalog record. *See* **Bibliographic record**; **Surrogate record**.

Cataloger. Person in an archive, a library, or other such organization who creates surrogate records for the information packages collected by the organization and who works to maintain the system through which those surrogate records are made available to users; the person may also be an independent contractor. *See also* **Indexer.**

Cataloging. The process of creating surrogate records for information packages by describing the information package, choosing name and title access points, conducting subject analysis, assigning subject headings and classification numbers, and maintaining the system through which the records are made available. *See also* **Copy cataloging; Descriptive cataloging; Original cataloging; Subject cataloging.**

Cataloging in Publication. *See* **CIP.**

Categorical filing. The preference in some areas of a filing system for partially classified arrangements over a straight alphabetical sequence.

CD-ROM catalog. *See* **Online catalog.**

Centralized processing. Any cooperative effort that results in the centralization of one or more of the technical processes involved in getting material ready for use in a library.

Chief source of information. The source in an information package that is prescribed by *AACR2* as the major source of data for use in preparing a bibliographic description. *See also* **Title page.**

Choice of access points. The process of selecting the primary access point and any added entries under which an information package is to be listed in the catalog.

CIP. A program in which cataloging is provided by an authorized agency to the publisher or producer of an information package so that the cataloging can be issued with the information package; often the phrase or acronym is applied in the case of cataloging provided by the Library of Congress to the publishers of books.

Class. The first order of structure in a hierarchical classification, at which level major disciplines are represented. A class may incorporate one or more divisions, which in turn may incorporate one or more subdivisions. *See also* **Division; Hierarchical classification; Subdivision.**

Classification. The placing of subjects into categories; in organization of information, classification is the process of determining where an information package fits into a given hierarchy and then assigning the notation associated with the appropriate level of the hierarchy to the information package and to its surrogate record.

Classification notation. The set of numbers, letters, symbols, or a combination of these that is assigned to a certain level of hierarchy in a classification scheme.

Classification schedule. A listing of the hierarchy of a classification system along with the notation for each level.

Classification scheme. An organized framework for the systematic organization of knowledge, usually organized by subject.

Classification table. Supplementary part of a classification scheme in which a hierarchy is developed and notations are assigned for concepts that can be applied in conjunction with many different topical subjects. Tables commonly exist for geographic locations; time periods; standard subdivisions (e.g., dictionaries, theory, serial publications, historical treatment, etc.); ethnic and national groups; etc.

Classified catalog. A catalog arranged or displayed in the order of symbols, numbers, or other notations that represent the various subjects or aspects of subjects covered by the information packages housed in the institution. *See also* **Shelflist.**

Close classification. The use of minute subdivisions for arranging materials by highly specific topics. *See also* **Broad classification.**

Closed stacks. The name given to the situation where collections are not open to public access or are limited to only a small group of users. *See also* **Open stacks**.

Code (as a noun). (1) A set of rules. (2) A specific designation in an encoding standard that defines and limits the kinds of data that can be stored at that point.

Code (as a verb). The process of assigning the appropriate specified designations of an encoding standard.

CODEN. A system of unique letters assigned for ready identification of periodicals and serials, now administered by Chemical Abstracts Service (CAS).

Coextensive subject entry. A principle of subject analysis, by which a term, phrase, or set of terms defines precisely the complete intellectual contents, but no more than the contents, of an information package.

Collation. *See* **Physical description area**.

Collected sets. *See* **Monographs in collected sets**.

Collection. Three or more works or parts of works by one author published together, or two or more works or parts of works by more than one author published together. Each work in a collection was originally written independently or as part of an independent publication.

Collocating function. The function of bibliographic control that relates bibliographic entities to each other through the process of collocation.

Collocation. The process of bringing together records and/or information packages that are related in some way (e.g., same author, same work, same subject, etc.).

Colon Classification. Classification scheme devised by S. R. Ranganathan in the early 1930s; it was the first fully faceted classification scheme.

COM. Computer Output Microform.

COM catalog. A catalog produced on COM and requiring a microform reader for its use.

Compiler. One who brings together selections from the works of various authors or the works of a single author. *See also* **Author**; **Editor**.

Computer-produced catalog. *See* **COM**; **Online catalog**.

CONSER. Cooperative Online Serials project, a shared national database of serial records from selected libraries, now maintained on OCLC's database.

Content designation. The act of making a bibliographic or authority record machine-readable by encoding its various elements according to a specified scheme. *See also* **MARC**; **Code (as a verb)**.

Continuation. (1) A work issued as a supplement to an earlier one. (2) A part issued in continuance of a book, a serial, or a series.

Continuing resource. A work that is issued in parts, sometimes as separate entities, and sometimes with new information integrated into the existing information package. *See also* **Integrating resource**; **Serial**.

Contract cataloging. An institution's use of a contractual relationship with a person or agency to provide surrogate records that represent the institution's collection. *See also* **Outsourcing.**

Control field. A field in the MARC format (00x) that includes numeric or other encoded data for retrieval. *See also* **Field**; **Fixed field**; **Variable field.**

Controlled vocabulary. A list or database of terms (usually subject or form/genre terms) in which all terms or phrases representing a concept are brought together. Often a preferred term or phrase is designated for use in surrogate records in a retrieval tool; the terms not to be used have references from them to the chosen term or phrase, and relationships (e.g., broader terms, narrower terms, related terms, etc.) among used terms are identified. There may also be scope notes and hierarchical listings. *See also* **Subject heading list**; **Thesaurus.**

Cooperative cataloging. The working together of independent institutions to share network memberships or to create cataloging that can be used by others.

Coordinate indexing. The enabling of information retrieval through the use of single concept terms in a catalog or database. *See also* **Postcoordinate indexing**; **Precoordinate indexing.**

Copy cataloging. Adapting the original cataloging created by one library for use in another institution's catalog. *See also* **Original cataloging.**

Core record. A standard set by the Program for Cooperative Cataloging (PCC) that presents the minimum requirements for elements to be included in a nationally acceptable *AACR2* record.

Corporate body. An organization or group of persons who are identified by a name and who act as an entity.

Creator. Person who is responsible for the intellectual content of an information package.

Cross reference. *See* **Reference.**

Cutter number. The symbols, usually a combination of letters and numbers, used to distinguish among items with the same classification number in order to maintain the alphabetical order (by author, title, or other entry) of items on the shelves; sometimes called author number or book number. The word *cutter* is derived from the widespread use of the tables first devised by Charles A. Cutter for use in such alphabetical arrangement. *See also* **Call number**; **Work mark.**

Database. A set of records that are all constructed in the same way and are often connected by relationship links; the structure underlying retrieval tools.

DDC. See Dewey Decimal Classification.

Depth indexing. Assignment of subject terms to represent all of the main concepts in a document, including many subtopics and subthemes. *See also* **Exhaustivity**; **Summarization.**

Description. That portion of the descriptive cataloging process in which elements that identify an information package are transcribed into a bibliographic record; also, the portion of the bibliographic record (i.e., descriptive data) that results from this process. *See also* **Access**; **Descriptive cataloging**; **Descriptive data.**

Descriptive cataloging. That phase of the cataloging process that is concerned with the identification and description of an information package, the recording of this information in a bibliographic record, and the selection and formation of access points—with the exception of subject access points. *See also* **Access**; **Description**.

Descriptive data. Data that describes an information package, such as its title, its associated names, its edition, its date of publication, its extent, and notes identifying pertinent features.

Descriptor. Subject concept term, representing a single concept, usually found in thesauri and used in indexes. *See also* **Subject heading**.

***Dewey Decimal Classification* (*DDC*).** Classification devised by Melvil Dewey in 1876; it divides the world of knowledge hierarchically into ten divisions, which are in turn divided into ten sections, and so on, using the ten digits of the Arabic numeral system. *DDC* is enumerative but with many faceting capabilities, especially in its later editions.

Diacritic. Modifying mark over, under, or through a character to indicate that pronunciation is different from that of the character without the diacritic.

Dictionary catalog. A catalog arranged or displayed in alphabetical order with entries for names, titles, and subjects all intermixed.

Direct entry. A principle of formulation of controlled vocabularies that stipulates the entry of a concept directly under the term that names it, rather than as a subdivision of a broader concept (e.g., Child rearing, *not* Children—Development and guidance). *See also* **Specific entry**.

Divide-like note. A place in a classification schedule referring the user to another location where similar sequencing and notation set a pattern.

Divided catalog. A catalog in which different types of entries are arranged or displayed in separate files or displays. Usually the subject entries are separated from other entries, and sometimes titles are also separated. Order is usually alphabetical in each section, but the subject section may be in classified order. Online catalogs are de facto divided catalogs when authors, titles, and subjects are searched and displayed separately.

Division. In hierarchical classification, the second structural level at which major components of a discipline are represented. A division is a subset of a class and may incorporate one or more subdivisions. *See also* **Class**; **Hierarchical classification**; **Subdivision**.

Document. An information package or information resource; often associated in people's minds with text and illustrations having been produced on paper, but increasingly associated with a video, a music CD, a computer file, or other such manifestation.

Edition. Specific manifestation of the intellectual content (work) found in an information package. In the case of books, an edition refers to all the impressions of a work printed at any time or times from one setting of type. In the case of nonbook materials, an edition is all the copies of an information package made from one master copy.

Edition area. The second area of an ISBD bibliographic description, which includes the following elements: named and/or numbered edition statement and statement of responsibility relating to a particular edition, if any.

Editor. One who prepares for publication or supervises the publication of a work or collection of works or articles that are authored by others. Responsibility may extend to revising, providing commentaries and introductory matter, etc. *See also* **Author**; **Compiler**.

Electronic resource. Information resource that requires the use of a computer to access its intellectual contents.

Element. An individual category or field that holds an individual piece of description of an information package; for example, the subtitle is an element of the title and statement of responsibility area.

Encoding. The setting off of each part of a record so that the part can be displayed in certain positions according to the wishes of those creating a display mechanism, and so that certain parts of a record can be searchable.

Entity. (1) A "thing" (resource, person, name, address, etc.). (2) A term used in the field of organization of information to indicate an item; both "entity" and "item" are used in order to avoid using "book" or other such specific designation.

Entry. A representation of a bibliographic record at a particular point in a retrieval tool. One heading can be represented by more than one entry. *See also* **Access point**; **Bibliographic record**; **Heading**.

Entry word. The word by which an entry is arranged in the catalog, usually the first word (other than an article) of the heading. Also called "filing word."

Enumerative classification. A classification arrangement that attempts to assign a designation for every subject concept required in the system.

Evaluating function. The function of bibliographic control that allows a patron to make an informed choice of materials from a bibliographic tool.

Exhaustivity. The number of concepts that will be considered in the process of providing subject analysis in a document. *See also* **Depth indexing**; **Summarization**.

Expansive classification. A scheme in which a set of coordinated schedules gives successive development possibilities from very simple (broad) to very detailed (close) subdivision.

Explanatory reference. A reference that gives detailed guidance necessary for effective use of the headings involved, explaining such things as history or complex relationships.

Expression. The second level in describing a work in the *FRBR* conceptual model, where the work can actually be seen or heard or felt.

Faceted classification. A subject concept arrangement that has small notations standing for subparts of the whole topic, which, when strung together, usually in prescribed sequence, create a complete classification notation for a multipart concept.

Facsimile. A reproduction in which the producer tries to recreate the appearance of an original entity in addition to reproducing its content exactly.

FID. Fédération Internationale de Documentation (International Federation for Documentation).

Field. A separately designated segment of an encoded record. A field may contain one or more subfields. *See also* **Control field**; **Fixed field**; **Subfield**; **Variable field**.

Filing. The process of placing paper records (e.g., catalog cards, acquisition forms, etc.) in order, usually in drawers.

Filing word. *See* **Entry word**.

Finding function. *See* **Identifying function**.

Fixed field. A field in an encoded record that is of a set length. There are three major "fixed fields" in a standard *MARC 21* record, 008 (fixed length data elements), 007 (physical characteristics), and 006 (special aspects), of which the 008 field is often referred to as "The Fixed Field." *See also* **Control field**; **Field**; **Subfield**; **Variable field**.

Fixed location. A set place where a physical information package will always be found or to which it will be returned after having been removed for use. *See also* **Relative location**.

Form division. *See* **Standard subdivision**.

Form/genre heading. A controlled vocabulary term that refers to the literary genre or artistic form or the publication format of a work rather than to its topical content.

Form of entry. The specific spelling and wording used to record an access point in a catalog record. *See also* **Heading**.

FRBR. *See Functional Requirements for Bibliographic Records*.

Free-floating subdivision. A term that can be added to a subject heading in a published list, as needed, whether or not it is written in the published list following that heading. In the *LCSH* system, however, terms called "free-floating" have scope notes that express limitations on the use of some such terms.

Front matter. *See* **Preliminaries (in a book)**.

Full entry. *See* **Main entry (record)**.

Functional Requirements for Bibliographic Records (FRBR). A conceptual model of the bibliographic universe developed by IFLA that provides a way of describing entities and relationships between them. *FRBR* describes three groups of entities. Group 1 identifies entities that are the products of intellectual endeavors: work, expression, manifestation, item. Group 2 identifies entities responsible for such products: person, corporate body. Group 3 identifies entities that may serve as the subjects of intellectual or artistic endeavor: concept, object, event, and place, in addition to any group 1 or group 2 entity.

Gateway. A computer system or Web location that provides access to many different databases or other resources, using the same interface.

Gathering function. *See* **Collocating function**.

Genre heading. *See* **Form/genre heading.**

Geographic name. The place name usually used in reference to a geographic area. It is not necessarily the political name. *See also* **Political name**.

GMD. General Material Designation, a term that is given in an *AACR2* record to indicate the class of material to which an information package belongs (e.g., art original, electronic resource, motion picture, etc.).

Guide card. A labeled card with a noticeable projection that distinguishes it from other cards. It is inserted in a card catalog to help the user find a desired place or heading in the catalog.

Heading. (1) An access point printed at the top of a copy of a surrogate record or at the top of a listing of related works in an online retrieval tool. (2) The exact string of characters of the authorized form of an access point as it appears in the authority record. *See also* **Access point**; **Entry**; **Form of entry**; **Term**.

Hierarchical classification. A classification that attempts to arrange subjects according to a "natural" order—proceeding from classes to divisions to subdivisions.

Hierarchical notation. In classification, the use of symbol groups of varying combinations and lengths to reflect a hierarchy of topics and subdivisions.

Hierarchy. An arrangement by which categories are grouped in such a way that a concept (e.g., class or discipline) is subdivided into subconcepts of an equal level of specificity, each of those subconcepts are further subdivided into subcategories, and so on. In science, for example, living organisms are in the hierarchy: phylum, class, order, family, genus, species.

Holdings. Items (volumes, parts, issues, etc.) contained in a library collection.

Holdings file. A group of holdings records. In an OPAC or a bibliographic database, a holdings file is usually distinct from, but might be linked to, a bibliographic file.

Holdings note. One note in the bibliographic record for a serial that tells which parts of the serial are held by the library. *See also* **Numbering area**.

Holdings record. A record in a holdings file that gives complete holdings for an information package.

Identifying function. The function of bibliographic control that allows a user to recognize a specific information package.

IFLA. International Federation of Library Associations and Institutions, formerly International Federation of Library Associations; an international organization for the promotion of library standards and the sharing of ideas and research.

ILL. Interlibrary loan; the process of acquiring a physical information package or a copy of it from a library that owns it by a library that does not own it.

ILS. *See* **Integrated Library System.**

Imprint. The information in a textual publication that tells where it was published, who published it, and when it was published. *See also* **Publication, distribution, etc., area**.

Index. A bibliographic tool that provides access to the analyzed contents of information packages (e.g., articles in a journal, short stories in a collection, papers in a conference proceeding, etc.). Back-of-the-book indexes provide access to the analyzed contents of one work.

Indexer. A person who determines access points (usually subject terms, but may also be authors or titles) that are needed in order to make surrogate records available to searchers; an indexer also may create surrogate records.

Indexing. The process of creating surrogate records, especially the access points, for information packages; such work done in commercial enterprises is often called *indexing*, while similar work done in nonprofit agencies is usually called *cataloging*.

Indexing vocabulary. *See* **Controlled vocabulary**.

Indicators. In the MARC encoding standards, indicators for a field contain coded information that is needed for interpreting or supplementing data in the field.

Information package. An instance of recorded information (e.g., book, article, video, Internet document or set of "pages," sound recording, electronic journal, etc.); also called *information resource*. *See also* **Item**; **Work**.

Information retrieval. The process of gaining access to stored data for the purpose of becoming informed.

Integrated Library System (ILS). Computer system that includes various modules to perform different functions while sharing access to the same database.

Integrating resource. In *AACR2R* (2002 revision), a bibliographic resource that is added to or changed by means of updates that are integrated into the whole resource (includes updating looseleafs and updating websites).

ISBD. International Standard Bibliographic Description, an internationally accepted format for the representation of descriptive information in bibliographic records that standardizes the elements to be used, assigns an order to these elements, and specifies a system of symbols to be used in punctuating the elements. Multiple ISBDs have been issued to allow for specialized application to different formats of material.

ISBN. International Standard Book Number, an internationally distinctive and unique number assigned to a monographic item.

ISDS. International Serials Data System, a network of national and international centers sponsored by UNESCO. The centers develop and maintain registers of serial publications; this includes the assignment of ISSNs and key titles.

ISSN. International Standard Serial Number, a distinctive and unique number assigned to a serial by ISDS.

Item. One copy of a manifestation of a work, focusing on the physical object, such as a book, a map, or a sound recording, as distinct from its intellectual content (i.e., the work or expression of the work that it contains); the fourth level in describing a work in the *FRBR* conceptual model. *See also* **Expression; Information package; Manifestation; Work**.

Joint author. A person who collaborates with one or more associates to produce a work in which the individual contributions of the authors cannot be distinguished. *See also* **Shared responsibility; Synchronous responsibility**.

Key heading. *See* **Pattern heading**.

Keyword. A term that is chosen, either from actual text or from a searcher's head, that is considered to be a "key" to finding certain information.

Keyword indexing. Use of significant words from a title or a text as index entries. *See also* **Coordinate indexing**.

Keyword searching. The use of one or more keywords as the intellectual content of a search command.

KWIC indexing. Key Word In Context, a format for showing index entries within the context in which they occur.

KWOC indexing. Key Word Out of Context, the use of significant words from titles for subject index entries, each followed by the whole title from which the word was taken.

LC. Library of Congress.

LCC. See Library of Congress Classification.

LCRIs. See Library of Congress Rule Interpretations.

LCSH. See Library of Congress Subject Headings.

Leaf. A single thickness of paper (i.e., two sides or pages, but when referred to as a leaf or leaves, it is usually printed only on one side).

Letter-by-letter filing. An arrangement of entries in a retrieval tool in which spaces and some punctuation marks are ignored so that an entry files as if it is all run together into one word (e.g., New York is treated as Newyork and follows Newark). *See also* **Word-by-word filing**.

Library of Congress Classification (LCC). Classification scheme created by the Library of Congress beginning in the late 1890s; it divides the world of knowledge hierarchically into categories using letters of the English alphabet and then using Arabic numerals for further subdivisions. LCC is basically an enumerative scheme, allowing only a limited amount of faceting.

Library of Congress Rule Interpretations (LCRIs). A collection of the decisions that have been made by the Library of Congress's Cataloging Policy and Support Office as to how catalogers at the Library of Congress will interpret and apply *AACR2*

Library of Congress Subject Headings (LCSH). List of terms to be used as controlled vocabulary for subject concepts by the Library of Congress and any other agency that wishes to provide such controlled subject access to surrogate records.

Linkage. A relationship between or among headings or records that is manifested implicitly or explicitly in a bibliographic retrieval system.

Literary warrant. The concept that new notations are created for a classification scheme and new terms are added to a controlled vocabulary only when information packages actually exist about a new concept.

Locating function. The function of bibliographic control that allows a user to learn how to acquire or obtain access to an information package or resource.

Location device. A number or other designation on an item to tell where it is physically located.

MAchine-Readable Cataloging. *See* **MARC**.

Machine-readable data file. *See* **Computer file**; **Electronic resource**.

Main class. *See* **Class**.

Main entry (access point). *See* **Primary access point.**

Main entry (record). A full catalog record, headed by the primary access point, which gives all the elements necessary for the complete identification of a manifestation of a work. This record also bears the tracing of all the other headings under which the work is entered. This is an obsolete concept in online catalogs.

Manifestation. Any one of the formats in which one of the expressions of a work can be found; the third level in describing a work in the *FRBR* conceptual model. *See also* **Expression; Item; Work.**

Manufacturer. The agency that has made the item being cataloged (e.g., printer of a book).

Manuscripts. Papers created by an individual (not organizational papers); original handwritten or typed documents that usually exist in single copies (unless they have been carbon-copied or photocopied).

Map series. A group of map sheets having the same scale and cartographic specifications, identified collectively by the producing agency. When the series is completed, it covers a given geographic area.

MARC. MAchine-Readable Cataloging, a standard that prescribes codes that precede and identify specific elements of a catalog record, allowing the record to be "read" by machine, which then displays it in a fashion designed to make the record intelligible to users. *See also MARC 21*; **UNIMARC.**

MARC 21. A MARC standard agreed upon by Canadian and United States representatives ("21" stands for the 21st century). *MARC 21*, which represents a consolidation of USMARC and CAN/MARC, two previous national MARC schemes, has been adopted also by Great Britain, and is being adopted by other countries, as well.

MARC record. A computerized bibliographic record that has been content designated according to MARC conventions.

MARC tag. A number that designates the kind of field in a MARC record.

Material specific details area. The third area of an ISBD bibliographic description for certain special materials. *See also* **Mathematical data area; Musical presentation statement area; Numbering area.**

Mathematical data area. The third area of an ISBD bibliographic description for a cartographic information package, which includes the following elements: scale, projection, and, optionally, coordinates and equinox.

Medical Subject Headings (MeSH). List of terms to be used as controlled vocabulary for subject concepts by the National Library of Medicine and any other agency that wishes to provide controlled subject access to surrogate records in the field of medicine.

Metadata. An encoded description of an information package (e.g., an *AACR2* record encoded with MARC, a Dublin Core record, etc.); the purpose of metadata is to provide a level of data at which choices can be made as to which information resources one wishes to view or search, without having to search massive amounts of irrelevant full text.

Microfiche. A flat sheet of photographic film designed for storage of complete texts in multiple micro-images and having an index entry visible to the naked eye displayed at the top.

Microfilm. A length of photographic film containing sequences of micro-images of texts, title pages, bibliographic records, etc.

Microform. Usually a reproduction photographically reduced to a size difficult or impossible to read with the naked eye; some microforms are not reproductions but original editions. Microforms include microfilm, microfiche, microopaques, and aperture cards.

Mixed notation. A notation that combines two or more kinds of symbols, such as a combination of letters and numbers.

Mixed responsibility. A situation that occurs when two or more entities make different types of contributions during the creation of a work (e.g., one creator illustrates the story that is written by a different creator). *See also* **Asynchronous responsibility**; **Shared responsibility**.

Monograph. A complete bibliographic unit or information package; it may be issued in successive parts at regular or irregular intervals, but it is not intended to continue indefinitely. It may be a single work or a collection that is not a serial.

Monographic series. A series of monographs with a collective title.

Monographs in collected sets. Collections or compilations by one or more authors issued in two or more volumes.

Musical presentation statement. A statement in a chief source of information for music that indicates its physical form.

Musical presentation statement area. The third area of an ISBD bibliographic description for a music information package, in which a musical presentation statement (e.g., "playing score") is transcribed. *See also* **Material specific details area**.

NAL. National Agricultural Library, Washington, D.C.

Name authority file. A file containing the authority records for names used in a given catalog.

Name-title added entry. An added entry that includes the name of a person or corporate body and the title of a work (often a uniform title). It serves to identify a work that is included in a larger work that is being cataloged, to identify a work that is the subject of a work being cataloged, to identify a larger work of which a work being cataloged is part, or to identify another work to which a work being cataloged is closely related (e.g., an index).

Narrower term (NT). A term one level down from the term being considered in a listing where terms for subject concepts have been conceived in relationships that are hierarchical. *See also* **Broader term; Related term.**

NCIP. NISO Circulation Interchange Protocol; technology that offers the capacity to search different databases located in different servers.

NLA. The National Library of Australia, Canberra.

NLM. The National Library of Medicine, Washington, D.C.

Nonbook materials. Term used to designate collectively maps, globes, motion pictures, filmstrips, videorecordings, sound recordings, and other information packages that do not consist of text in book form.

Notation. A representation in a system, such as a classification system, with a set of marks, usually consisting of letters, numbers, and/or symbols.

Note area. The seventh area of an ISBD bibliographic description, reserved for recording catalog data that cannot be incorporated in the preceding parts of the record. Each note is usually recorded in a separate paragraph or separately encoded field.

NUC. The *National Union Catalog*, a publication in the Library of Congress Catalogs series that cumulated cataloging records from many libraries and indicated by "NUC symbol" those libraries that owned a particular information package; ceased publication in 2002.

Numbering area. The third area of an ISBD bibliographic description for a serial. It indicates volumes or parts of the serial, but not necessarily those held by a particular library. *See also* **Holdings note**; **Material specific details area**.

OCLC Connexion. A Web-based interface to OCLC's database; it began as CORC, a system that helped libraries provide access to Web resources.

OCLC Online Computer Library Center. A bibliographic network, based in Dublin, Ohio, that is the largest and most comprehensive bibliographic network in the world.

Online catalog. A catalog in which surrogate records are encoded for computer display and are stored in computer memory or on CD-ROM discs; arrangement within the memory or on disc is irrelevant to the user, as arrangement is created in a display in response to a query.

Online Computer Library Center. *See* **OCLC Online Computer Library Center**.

Online public access catalog. An online catalog that is available for use by the general public; also referred to as an OPAC.

Ontology. In the field of artificial intelligence, a formal representation of what, to a human, is common sense; in natural language processing, a formal representation of language that identifies specific terms, usually from a defined subject area, and lays out the relationships that exist between the terms.

OPAC. *See* **Online public access catalog**.

Open entry. A part of the descriptive cataloging not completed at the time of cataloging; used for noncompleted continuing resources (e.g., integrating resources, serials, series, etc.).

Open stacks. The name given to the situation where all users of a facility are admitted directly to the areas where information packages are stored. *See also* **Closed stacks.**

Original cataloging. The process of creating a bibliographic record for the first time, especially without reference to other records for the same information package; also, the cataloging created by this process. *See also* **Copy cataloging**.

Other title information. Words or phrases (e.g., a subtitle) that appear in conjunction with the title of an information package other than the title proper, parallel title, or alternative title. *See also* **Alternative title**; **Parallel title**; **Title proper**.

Outsourcing. A management technique whereby some activities, formerly conducted in house, are contracted out for completion by a contracting agency; technical services operations, including cataloging, are sometimes outsourced. *See also* **Contract cataloging.**

Parallel title. The title proper written in another language or in another script. *See also* **Title proper**.

Paris Principles. The conventional name of the Statement of Principles agreed upon by attendees at the International Conference on Cataloging Principles in Paris, October 9–18, 1961.

Pattern heading. A representative heading from a category of terms that would normally be excluded from a subject heading list (e.g., names of individuals), included as an example of normal subdivision practice within that category.

PCC (Program for Cooperative Cataloging). An international cooperative program coordinated jointly by the Library of Congress and participants around the world; effort is aimed at expanding access to collections through useful, timely, cost-effective cataloging that meets internationally accepted standards.

Periodical. A publication with a distinctive title, which appears in successive numbers or parts at stated or regular intervals and which is intended to continue indefinitely. Usually each issue contains articles by several contributors. Newspapers and memoirs, proceedings, journals, etc., of corporate bodies primarily related to their internal affairs are not included in this definition. *See also* **Continuing resource**; **Serial**.

Physical description area. The fifth area of an ISBD bibliographic description, which includes a statement of the extent of an item, dimensions, and other physical details.

Plate. An illustrative leaf that is not included in the pagination of the text; it is not an integral part of a text gathering; it is often printed on paper different from that used for the text (e.g., glossy paper).

Plate number. A number used by a music publisher to identify a set of printing plates used to print a musical work.

Political name. The proper name of a geographical area according to the law. This name may change with a change in government. *See also* **Geographic name**.

Postcoordinate indexing. Indexing that enters subject concepts as single concepts so that searchers are required to coordinate them using such techniques as Boolean searching in order to locate information packages on the compound and/or complex subjects in which the searchers are interested.

PRECIS. Preserved Context Indexing System, a British-designed technique for subject retrieval in which an open-ended vocabulary can be organized according to a scheme of role-indicating operators, usually for computer manipulation.

Precoordinate indexing. The assigning of subject terms to surrogate records in such a way that some concepts, subconcepts, place names, time periods, and form concepts are put together in subject strings, and searchers of the system do not have to coordinate these particular terms themselves.

Preliminaries (in a book). The title page or title pages, the verso of each title page, the cover, and any pages preceding the title page; may also include prefatory matter such as a preface or foreword; also called "Front matter."

Prescribed source of information. One of the sources in an information package that is prescribed by *AACR2* as a source from which certain parts of the description should be taken.

Primary access point. Access point that is chosen as the main or primary one; usually referred to as "main entry" in the library and archival worlds, where the other access points are called "added entries."

Processing center. A central office where the materials of more than one library are processed and distributed. Such a center may also handle the purchasing of materials for its constituents.

Producer. Person or agency responsible for financial and administrative production of a nonbook item, such as a motion picture or a computer file; also responsible for its commercial success.

Pseudonym. An assumed name used by a creator of a work to conceal identity or to establish a separate bibliographic identity.

Pseudo-serial. A frequently reissued and revised publication which, upon first being published, is usually treated as a monographic work (e.g., *Guide to Reference Books*, edited by several different editors through many editions).

Publication, distribution, etc., area. The fourth area of an ISBD bibliographic description, which includes the following elements: place of publication, distribution, etc.; name of publisher, distributor, etc.; date of publication, distribution, etc.; and sometimes place of manufacture, name of manufacturer, and date of manufacture.

Publisher. The person or corporate body responsible for issuing information packages to make them available for public use.

Pure notation. A notation that consistently uses only one kind of symbol (e.g., either letters or numbers, but not both).

Realia. Actual objects (artifacts, specimens, etc.).

Recon or RECON. *See* **Retrospective conversion**.

Record. *See* **Bibliographic record**; **Metadata**; **Surrogate record**.

Recto. In a book, the page on the right; the side of a leaf intended to be read first in cultures that read from left to right. *See also* **Verso**.

Reference (cross reference). An instruction in a catalog or other retrieval tool that directs a user to another place in the catalog or other tool.

Related term (RT). A term at the same level of specificity or bearing a non-hierarchical relationship to another term in a listing where terms for subject concepts have been conceived in relationships that are hierarchical. *See also* **Broader term; Narrower term.**

Relational database. A form of database architecture in which records are structured in such a way that information is not all stored in the same file; files for different kinds of information are created (e.g., a bibliographic file, a personal name file, a corporate name file, a subject file, a classification file, etc.); records in the bibliographic file contain pointers to records in the other files and vice versa. A relational database structure conserves storage space, allows for faster searching, and allows for easier modification of records. Pointers establish "relationships" among records.

Relative index. An index to a classification scheme that not only provides alphabetical references to the subjects and terms in the classification but also shows some of the relations between subjects and aspects of subjects.

Relative location. A classificatory arrangement of library materials, allowing the insertion of new material in its proper relation to that already on the shelves; as a result, an item might be shelved in a different physical location each time it is reshelved. *See also* **Fixed location**.

Reprint. A new printing of an item either by photographic methods or by resetting substantially unchanged text.

Retrieval tool. Device such as a catalog, an index, a search engine, etc., created for use as an information retrieval system.

Retrospective conversion. The process of changing information in eye-readable surrogate records into machine-readable form; sometimes referred to as *recon* or *RECON*.

RLG. Research Libraries Group, a consortium formed originally by the libraries of Columbia, Harvard, and Yale universities and the New York Public Library, now consisting of over 100 large research libraries.

RLG Union Catalog. RLG's main database, the basis of a bibliographic network that is particularly aimed at academic/research libraries and is especially important for special collections.

RLIN21™. Research Libraries Information Network 21, a Web-based interface to RLG's databases.

Romanization. The representation of the characters or script of a nonroman alphabet by roman characters. *See also* **Transliteration**.

Schedule. *See* **Classification schedule.**

Scope note. A statement delimiting the meaning and associative relations of a subject heading, index term, or a classification notation.

Score. An arrangement of all of the parts of a piece of music one under another on different staves. A series of staves on which is written music composed originally for one instrument is not considered a score; for example, "piano score" is used to designate, not music written originally for the piano, but music written originally for instrumental or vocal parts that has been arranged for the piano.

Search engine. A computerized retrieval tool that, in general, matches keywords input by a user to words found in documents of the site being searched; the more sophisticated search engines may allow other than keyword searching.

Sears List of Subject Headings (*Sears*). A controlled vocabulary of terms and phrases that is used mostly in small libraries to provide subject access to information packages available in those libraries.

See also **reference.** A reference indicating related entries or headings; the relationships may be lateral or hierarchical.

See from **reference.** A designation in an authority record showing a variant name or term from which a reference is to be made in the catalog to the chosen heading.

See **reference.** A reference from a name or term not used to a heading that is used.

Selecting function. *See* **Evaluating function.**

Serial. A publication issued in successive parts at regular or irregular intervals and intended to continue indefinitely. Included are periodicals, newspapers, proceedings, reports, memoirs, annuals, and numbered monographic series. *See also* **Continuing resource**; **Periodical.**

Serial record file. A group of records that contain information about receipt of specific issues of serials or other continuing resources.

Series. A number of separate works, usually related in subject or form, that are issued successively. They are usually issued by the same publisher, distributor, etc., and are in uniform style, with a collective title.

Series area. The sixth area of an ISBD bibliographic description, which contains series information, including series title and perhaps other title information, statement of responsibility if important, series numbering if applicable, and occasionally an ISSN.

Series authority file. A file of series headings used in a catalog with a record of references made to them from other forms, and a record of their treatment as to analysis, tracing, and classification.

Series title. The collective title given to volumes or parts issued in a series.

Shared authorship. *See* **Shared responsibility**.

Shared responsibility. The situation in which more than one person is responsible for the creation of the intellectual content of a work. *See also* **Asynchronous responsibility**; **Synchronous responsibility**.

Shelflist. Originally, a record of the items owned by a library with entries arranged in the order of the items on the shelves. In time the meaning has developed to indicate classification order of surrogate records for information packages, which now allows for intangible as well as physical information packages.

S.l. (sine loco). Place of publication, distribution, etc., unknown.

S.n. (sine nomine). Name of publisher, distributor, etc., unknown.

Sound recording. Aural recording, including discs, cartridges, cassettes, cylinders, etc.

Specific entry. A principle observed in application of controlled vocabularies, by which an information package is listed under the most precise term available in the controlled vocabulary (or allowed to be created by the rules of the vocabulary), rather than under some broader heading. *See also* **Direct entry; Specificity.**

Specificity. The level of subject analysis that is addressed by a particular controlled vocabulary (e.g., *LCSH* has greater specificity in its established headings than does *Sears*, as, for example, in the greater depth of subdivisions that are established under main headings by *LCSH*). *See also* **Specific entry.**

Standard number and terms of availability area. The eighth area of an ISBD bibliographic description, which includes ISBN or ISSN and, optionally, price or other terms on which the information package is available.

Standard subdivisions. Divisions used in *DDC* that apply to the form a work takes. Form may be physical (as in a periodical or a dictionary) or it may be philosophical (such as a philosophy or history of a subject). Formerly called form divisions.

Statement of responsibility. A statement in the information package being described that names persons who are responsible for intellectual or artistic content, corporate bodies from which the content emanates, or persons or bodies who are responsible for performance.

Subdivision. (1) The level of structure in a hierarchical classification at which specific concepts are represented. (2) A restrictive word or group of words added to a main subject heading to limit it to a more specific meaning or treatment. *See also* **Class**; **Division**; **Hierarchical classification**; **Subject subdivision**.

Subfield. A separately designated segment of a field in an encoded record. *See also* **Field**.

Subject access. The provision to users of the means of locating information using subject terminology and/or classification notations.

Subject analysis. The part of indexing or cataloging that deals with the conceptual analysis of an information package; translating that conceptual analysis into a framework for a particular classification, subject heading, or indexing system; and then using the framework to assign specific notations or terminology to the information package and its surrogate record.

Subject authority file. A file containing records of choices made in the development of a controlled vocabulary. The authority file contains such things as justification for the choice of one synonym over another; references from unused synonyms or near-synonyms; references for broader terms, narrower terms, and related terms; scope notes; citations for references used; etc. *See also* **Subject heading list**; **Thesaurus**.

Subject cataloging. The process of providing subject analysis, including subject headings and classification notations, when creating catalog records.

Subject entry. The place in a catalog where a surrogate record containing a particular controlled vocabulary term is found.

Subject heading. Subject concept term or phrase found in a subject heading list and used in catalog records; sometimes used in indexes. *See also* **Descriptor**.

Subject heading list. A list of authorized controlled vocabulary terms or phrases together with any references, scope notes, and subdivisions associated with each term or phrase. *See also* **Controlled vocabulary**; **Subject authority file**; **Thesaurus**.

Subject subdivision. A method of precoordinating subject headings by using terms or phrases following main concepts to show special treatment of a subject.

Subtitle. A secondary title, often used to expand or limit the title proper; considered to be one kind of "other title information." *See also* **Alternative title**; **Other title information**; **Parallel title**.

Summarization. A level of subject analysis in which only the dominant or main theme of a document is recognized. *See also* **Depth indexing**; **Exhaustivity**.

Superimposition. A Library of Congress policy decision that only entries being established for the first time would follow *AACR* rules for form of entry and that only works new to LC would follow *AACR* rules for choice of entry. When LC adopted *AACR2*, the policy of superimposition was dropped.

Surrogate record. A presentation of the characteristics (e.g., title, creator, physical description if appropriate, date of creation, subject(s), etc.) of an information package.

Switching language. A mediating or communication indexing language used to establish equivalencies between or among various subject indexing languages or classification schemes.

Synchronous responsibility. The situation in which all persons or corporate bodies involved in the creation of an information package have made the same kind of contribution to the creation of the work (e.g., joint authors). *See also* **Asynchronous responsibility**; **Shared responsibility**.

Syndetic structure. An organizational framework in which related names, topics, etc., are linked to each other via connective terms such as *See* and *See also*.

Synthetic classification. A classification that assigns designations to single, unsubdivided concepts and gives the classifier generalized rules for combining these designations for composite subjects. *See also* **Faceted classification**.

Tag. A number, set of letters, certain set of punctuation marks, or other identification, that designates the kind of field in an encoding standard.

Tagging. *See* **Content designation**.

Technical reading. The process of getting acquainted with an information package prior to cataloging, in which various internal sources of information are identified and examined.

Technical services. The group of activities in an institution that involves acquiring, organizing, housing, maintaining, and conserving collections and automating these activities. In some places circulation services are also considered to be part of technical services.

Technical Services Workstation (TSW). A client-based modular computer platform capable of running multiple applications (often vendor-supplied software) and linked to the Internet; assists local institutional personnel in the performance of acquisitions, cataloging, and maintenance functions.

Term. A separately represented concept in a thesaurus. *See also* **Descriptor**; **Subject heading**.

Thesaurus. A specialized authority list (usually restricted to a particular subject area) of controlled vocabulary terms used with information retrieval systems; terms represent single concepts together with any references, scope notes, and subdivisions associated with each term, and are organized so that the relationships between concepts are made explicit; very similar to a list of subject headings. *See also* **Controlled vocabulary**; **Subject heading list**.

Title. The name of a work, usually identified from the chief source of information of an information package. *See also* **Alternative title**; **Other title information**; **Parallel title**; **Title proper**; **Uniform title**.

Title and statement of responsibility area. The first area of an ISBD bibliographic description, which includes the title and information on who was involved in creation of the information package being described.

Title entry. The place in a retrieval tool where a surrogate record containing the name of an information package may be found.

Title page. A page that occurs very near the beginning of a book or other printed document and that contains the most complete bibliographic information about the item, such as the author's name, the fullest form of the title, the name and/or number of the edition, the name of the publisher, and the place and date of publication. In *AACR2* it is considered to be the chief source of information for published textual material.

Title proper. The title that is the chief name of an information package; excludes any parallel title or other title information. *See also* **Alternative title**; **Other title information**; **Parallel title**.

Tracing. The listing on a printed surrogate record of the set of name, title, and subject access points, other than the primary access point (i.e., main entry) under which the work is listed in the catalog; used to find (i.e., "trace") all copies of a record in a printed catalog.

Transliteration. A representation of the characters of one alphabet by those of another. *See also* **Romanization**.

TSW. *See* **Technical Services Workstation.**

UBC. *See* **Universal Bibliographic Control**.

UDC. See Universal Decimal Classification.

Uniform title. The title chosen for cataloging purposes when a work has appeared under varying titles or in more than one form; allows display of all manifestations of a work together. Uniform titles also are used to distinguish between and among different works that have the same title. *See also* **Title**; **Work**.

UNIMARC. Universal MARC format, first developed in 1977 by the Library of Congress to be an international communications format for the exchange of machine-readable cataloging records between national bibliographic agencies; now overseen by *IFLA*. A number of countries have adopted it as their national format.

Union catalog. A catalog that lists, completely or in part, the holdings of more than one library or collection.

Unit record. A basic catalog record, in the form of a main entry record, which when duplicated may be used as a unit for all other entries for that work in a printed catalog by the addition of appropriate headings.

Universal Bibliographic Control (UBC). The concept that it will someday be possible to have access to surrogate records for all the world's important information packages.

Universal Decimal Classification (UDC). A classification devised by Otlet and La Fontaine in the late 1890s; originally based on *DDC*, but has evolved into a much more faceted scheme than *DDC*.

USMARC. A machine-readable bibliographic record format developed by the Library of Congress and originally called LC-MARC. USMARC was replaced by *MARC 21*.

USNAF. United States Name Authority File, a file housed at the Library of Congress (LC), containing not only the authority records created by LC and its cooperating United States contributors, but also records contributed from Australia, Canada, Great Britain, and others.

Variable field. A field in an encoded record that can be as long or as short as the data to be placed into that field. *See also* **Control field**; **Field**; **Fixed field**.

Verification. Determining the existence of an author and the form of name as well as the correct title of a particular work; in short, using bibliographic sources to verify (i.e., prove) the existence of an author and/or work. Alternatively, verification can refer to the process of determining whether a heading input in a record matches one in an authority file. Automatic verification is a desirable feature for a cataloging subsystem of an ILS (q.v.).

Vernacular name. A name in the form used in reference sources in the country of origin of the name.

Verso. In a book, the page on the left; the side of a leaf intended to be read second in cultures that read from left to right. *See also* **Recto**.

Videorecording. A recording originally generated in the form of electronic impulses and designed primarily for television or computer playback.

Vocabulary control. The process of creating and using a controlled vocabulary.

Volume. In the bibliographical sense, a major division of a manifestation of a work distinguished from the other major divisions by having its own chief source of information.

Word-by-word filing. An arrangement of terms in a retrieval tool in such a way that spaces between words take precedence over any letter that may follow (e.g., "New York" appears before "Newark"). *See also* **Letter-by-letter filing**.

Work. A distinct intellectual or artistic creation; an abstract instance of content or ideas, regardless of the packaging in which the content or ideas may be expressed; the first level of conceptualization in the *FRBR* conceptual model. *See also* **Expression**; **Item; Manifestation**.

Workform. A structured format into which information can be placed to create a catalog record; it can also include other information pertinent to the maintenance of a collection.

Work mark. A designation (usually a letter or letters) placed after a cutter number in a call number; also called *work letter*. A work mark often is the first letter of the title of a work (exclusive of articles), but may stand for other entities, such as the name of a biographee, depending upon the circumstances. *See also* **Call number; Cutter number**.

Z39.50. A national standard that provides for exchange of information, such as surrogate records or full text, between otherwise noncompatible computer systems.

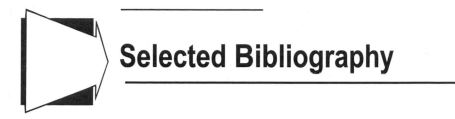

Selected Bibliography

GENERAL WORKS

Anderson, James D., and José Pérez-Carballo. *Information Retrieval Design: Principles and Options for Information Description, Organization, Display, and Access in Information Retrieval Databases, Digital Libraries, Catalogs, and Indexes*. St. Petersburg, Fla.: Ometeca Institute, 2005.

Berman, Sanford. *Joy of Cataloging*. Phoenix, Ariz.: Oryx Press, 1981.

Borgman, Christine L. *From Gutenberg to the Global Information Infrastructure: Access to Information in the Networked World*. Cambridge, Mass.: MIT Press, 2000.

Caplan, Priscilla. *Metadata Fundamentals for All Librarians*. Chicago, American Library Association, 2003.

Chan, Lois Mai. *Cataloging and Classification: An Introduction*. 2nd ed. New York: McGraw-Hill, 1994.

Evans, G. Edward, Sheila S. Intner, and Jean Weihs. *Introduction to Technical Services*. 7th ed. Greenwood Village, Colo.: Libraries Unlimited, 2002.

Functional Requirements for Bibliographic Records, *Final Report*. IFLA Study Group on the Functional Requirements for Bibliographic Records. München: K.G. Saur, 1998. Also available: http://www.ifla.org/VII/s13/frbr/frbr.htm or http://www.ifla.org/VII/s13/frbr/frbr.pdf (accessed 2/14/2006).

Hagler, Ronald. *The Bibliographic Record and Information Technology*. 3rd ed. Chicago: American Library Association, 1997.

Harvey, Ross, and Philip Hider. *Organising Knowledge in a Global Society*: *Principles and Practice in Libraries and Information Centres*. Wagga Wagga, NSW, Australia: Centre for Information Studies, 2004.

Haynes, Elizabeth, and Joanna F. Fountain. *Unlocking the Mysteries of Cataloging: A Workbook of Examples*. Westport, Conn.: Libraries Unlimited, 2005.

Intner, Sheila S., Susan S. Lazinger, and Jean Weihs. *Metadata and Its Impact on Libraries*. Westport, Conn.: Libraries Unlimited, 2006.

Intner, Sheila S., and Jean Weihs. *Standard Cataloging for School and Public Libraries*. 3rd ed. Englewood, Colo.: Libraries Unlimited, 2001.

————. *Special Libraries: A Cataloging Guide*. Englewood, Colo.: Libraries Unlimited, 1998.

Levy, David M. "Cataloging the Digital Order." Available: http://www.csdl.tamu.edu/DL95/papers/levy/levy.html (accessed 2/14/2006).

Mann, Thomas. *The Oxford Guide to Library Research*. 3rd ed. New York: Oxford University Press, 2005.

Milstead, Jessica, and Susan Feldman. "Metadata: Cataloging by Any Other Name" and "Metadata Projects and Standards." *Online* (January 1999). Available: http://www.cbuc.es/5digital/1.pdf (accessed 2/14/2006).

Oder, Norman. "Cataloging the Net: Can We Do It?" *Library Journal* 123, no. 16 (October 1, 1998): 47–51.

————. "Cataloging the Net: Two Years Later." *Library Journal* 125, no. 16 (October 1, 2000): 50–51.

Rowley, Jennifer, and John Farrow. *Organizing Knowledge: An Introduction to Managing Access to Information*. 3rd ed. Aldershot, Eng.; Burlington, Vt.: Ashgate, 2000.

Saye, Jerry D. *Manheimer's Cataloging and Classification: A Workbook*. 4th ed., revised and expanded. New York: Marcel Dekker, 1999.

Sleeman, Bill, and Pamela Bluh, eds. *From Catalog to Gateway: Charting a Course for Future Access: Briefings from the ALCTS Catalog Form and Function Committee*. Chicago: Association for Library Collections & Technical Services, American Library Association, 2005.

Smiraglia, Richard. *The Nature of "A Work": Implications for Knowledge Organization*. Lanham, Md.: Scarecrow Press, 2001.

Soergel, Dagobert. *Organizing Information: Principles of Data Base and Retrieval Systems*. Orlando, Fla.: Academic Press, 1985.

Svenonius, Elaine. *The Intellectual Foundation of Information Organization*. Cambridge, Mass.: The MIT Press, 2000.

Taylor, Arlene G. "The Information Universe: Will We Have Chaos or Control?" *American Libraries* 25, no. 7 (July/August 1994): 629–632.

————. *The Organization of Information*. 2nd ed. Westport, Conn.: Libraries Unlimited, 2004.

Taylor, Arlene G., with the assistance of Rosanna M. O'Neil. *Cataloging with Copy: A Decision-Maker's Handbook*. 2nd ed. Englewood, Colo.: Libraries Unlimited, 1988.

Zuiderveid, Sharon, ed. *Cataloging Correctly for Kids: An Introduction to the Tools*. Rev. ed. Chicago: American Library Association, 1991.

Zyloff, Ellen. "Cataloging Is a Prime Number." *American Libraries* 27, no. 5 (May 1996): 47–48, 50.

SPECIALIZED WORKS

History

A.L.A. Rules for Filing Catalog Cards. Chicago: American Library Association, 1942.

American Library Association. *List of Subject Headings for Use in Dictionary Catalogs*. Boston: Library Bureau, 1895.

Angell, Richard S. "Library of Congress Subject Headings—Review and Forecast." In *Subject Retrieval in the Seventies: New Directions*, edited by Hans Wellisch and Thomas D. Wilson. Westport, Conn.: Greenwood Publishing, 1972.

Austin, Derek. *PRECIS: A Manual of Concept Analysis and Subject Indexing*. 2nd ed. London: British Library, 1984.

———. "Progress in Documentation: The Development of PRECIS: A Theoretical and Technical History." *Journal of Documentation* 30 (March 1974): 47.

Baker, Nicholson. "Discards." *The New Yorker* 70, no. 7 (April 4, 1994): 64–86.

Coates, E. J. *Subject Catalogues: Heading and Structure*. London: Library Association, 1960.

Cutter, Charles A. *Rules for a Dictionary Catalog*. 4th ed., rewritten. Washington, D.C.: GPO, 1904; republished, London: Library Association, 1972. The original version of this work was: Charles A. Cutter. "Rules for a Printed Dictionary Catalogue." In *Public Libraries in the United States of America: Their History, Condition, and Management*, U.S. Bureau of Education. Part II. Washington, D.C.: GPO, 1876.

Dunkin, Paul S. *Cataloging U.S.A.* Chicago: American Library Association, 1969.

Dykstra, Mary. *PRECIS: A Primer*. London: British Library, 1985.

Gorman, Michael. "*AACR 2*: Main Themes." In International Conference on AACR 2, Florida State University, 1979, *The Making of a Code*, pp. 45–46. Chicago: American Library Association, 1980.

Hanson, J. C. M. "The Subject Catalogs of the Library of Congress." *Bulletin of the American Library Association* 3 (September 1909): 385–397.

Haykin, David Judson. *Subject Headings: A Practical Guide*. Washington, D.C.: GPO, 1951.

Hopkins, Judith. "The 1791 French Cataloging Code and the Origins of the Card Catalog." *Libraries & Culture* 27, no.4 (Fall 1992): 378–404.

International Conference on AACR 2, Florida State University, 1979. *The Making of a Code: The Issues Underlying AACR 2*. Chicago: American Library Association, 1980.

International Conference on Cataloguing Principles. Paris, 9th–18th October, 1961. *Report.* London: International Federation of Library Associations, 1963.

Jewett, Charles Coffin. *On the Construction of Catalogues of Libraries, and Their Publication by Means of Separate, Stereotyped Titles.* 2nd ed. Washington, D.C.: Smithsonian Institution, 1853.

LaMontagne, Leo E. "Historical Background of Classification." In *The Subject Analysis of Library Materials.* New York: Columbia University School of Library Service, 1953.

Lubetzky, Seymour. *Cataloging Rules and Principles: A Critique of the A.L.A. Rules for Entry and a Proposed Design for Their Revision.* Washington, D.C.: Processing Dept., Library of Congress, 1953.

———. *Code of Cataloging Rules, Author and Title: An Unfinished Draft . . . with an Explanatory Commentary by Paul Dunkin.* Chicago: American Library Association, 1960.

———. *Code of Cataloging Rules, Author and Title Entry: Additions, Revisions, and Changes Prepared in Light of Discussions of the March 1960 Draft for Consideration of the Catalog Code Revision Committee.* Chicago: American Library Association, 1961.

———. "The Fundamentals of Bibliographic Cataloging and *AACR 2.*" In International Conference on AACR 2, Florida State University, 1979, *The Making of a Code*, pp. 18–23. Chicago: American Library Association, 1980.

Luhn, Hans Peter. "Keyword in Context Index for Technical Literature (KWIC Index)." *American Documentation* 11 (1960): 288–295.

Mahapatra, M., and S. C. Biswas. "PRECIS: Its Theory and Application—An Extended State-of-the-Art Review from the Beginning up to 1982." *Libri* 33 (December 1983): 316–330.

Martel, Charles, "Cataloging: 1876–1926"; reprinted in *The Catalog and Cataloging*, edited by A. R. Rowland, pp. 40–50. Hamden, Conn.: Shoe String Press, 1969.

Miksa, Francis L. *The Development of Classification at the Library of Congress.* Champaign, Ill.: University of Illinois, Graduate School of Library and Information Science, 1984.

———. *The Subject in the Dictionary Catalog from Cutter to the Present.* Chicago: American Library Association, 1983.

Osborn, Andrew. "The Crisis in Cataloging." *Library Quarterly* 11 (October 1941): 393–411; also reprinted in: Carpenter, Michael, and Elaine Svenonius, eds. *Foundations of Cataloging: A Sourcebook*, pp. 90–103. Littleton, Colo.: Libraries Unlimited, 1985.

Panizzi, Antonio. "Rules for the Compilation of the Catalogue." In *The Catalogue of Printed Books in the British Museum.* London: British Museum, 1841.

Pettee, Julia. *Subject Headings: The History and Theory of the Alphabetical Approach to Books.* New York: H. W. Wilson, 1946.

Rayward, W. Boyd. "The UDC and FID: A Historical Perspective." *Library Quarterly* 37 (July 1967): 259–278.

Reynolds, Dennis. *Library Automation: Issues and Applications.* New York: R. R. Bowker, 1985.

Rohrbach, Peter T. *Find: Automation at the Library of Congress: The First Twenty-five Years and Beyond.* Washington, D.C.: Library of Congress, 1985.

Rothman, John. "Index, Indexer, Indexing," in *Encyclopedia of Library and Information Science*, Vol. 11, p. 289. New York: Marcel Dekker, 1974.

Russell, Beth M. "Hidden Wisdom and Unseen Treasure: Revisiting Cataloging in Medieval Libraries." *Cataloging & Classification Quarterly* 26, no. 3 (1998): 21–30.

Sayers, W. C. Berwick. *Sayers' Manual of Classification for Librarians.* 3rd ed., revised by Arthur Maltby. London: Andre Deutsch, 1955.

Sinkankis, George M. "A Study in the Syndetic Structure of the Library of Congress List of Subject Headings." Ph.D. dissertation, University of Pittsburgh, 1972.

Smalley, Joseph. "The French Cataloging Code of 1791: A Translation." *Library Quarterly* 61, no. 1 (January 1991): 1–14.

Strout, Ruth French. "The Development of the Catalog and Cataloging Codes." *Library Quarterly* 26 (October 1956): 254–275.

Subject Headings Used in the Dictionary Catalogues of the Library of Congress, [1st]–3rd eds. Washington, D.C.: Catalog Division, Library of Congress, 1910–1928; *Subject Headings Used in the Dictionary Catalogs of the Library of Congress*, 4th–7th eds. Washington, D.C.: Subject Cataloging Division, Library of Congress, 1943–1966; *Library of Congress Subject Headings*, 8th–12th eds. Washington, D.C.: Subject Cataloging Division, Library of Congress, 1975–1989.

Tate, Elizabeth L. "Examining the 'Main' in Main Entry Headings." In International Conference on AACR 2, Florida State University, 1979, *The Making of a Code*, pp. 109–140. Chicago: American Library Association, 1980.

Taube, Mortimer, and Associates. *Studies in Coordinate Indexing.* Washington, D.C.: Documentation, Inc., 1953.

Taylor, Arlene G. "Cataloguing." In *World Encyclopedia of Library and Information Services.* 3rd ed., pp. 117–181. Chicago: American Library Association, 1993.

———. "Development of the Organization of Recorded Information in Western Civilization." Chapter 3 in *The Organization of Information.* Westport, Conn.: Libraries Unlimited, 2004.

Thomas, Pat. "Implementing *DDC20*." *DC&* 5, no. 1 (March 1990): 7–8.

Wilson, Patrick. "The Catalog as Access Mechanism: Background and Concepts." In *Foundations of Cataloging: A Sourcebook*, edited by Michael Carpenter and Elaine Svenonius, pp. 253–268. Littleton, Colo.: Libraries Unlimited, 1985.

MARC Formats

Andresen, Leif. "After MARC – What Then?" *Library Hi Tech* 22, no. 1 (January 2004): 41–51.

Avram, Henriette D. *MARC, Its History and Implications*. Washington, D.C.: Library of Congress, 1975.

Byrne, Deborah J. *MARC Manual: Understanding and Using MARC Records*. 2nd ed. Englewood, Colo.: Libraries Unlimited, 1998.

Ferguson, Bobby. *MARC/AACR2/Authority Control Tagging: Blitz Cataloging Workbook*. 2nd ed. Westport, Conn.: Libraries Unlimited, 2005.

Fritz, Deborah A. *Cataloging with AACR2 and MARC21, for Books, Electronic Resources, Sound Recordings, Videorecordings, and Serials*. 2nd ed. Chicago: American Library Association, 2004.

Fritz, Deborah A., and Richard J. Fritz. *MARC21 for Everyone: A Practical Guide*. Chicago: American Library Association, 2003.

Furrie, Betty. *Understanding MARC Bibliographic: Machine-Readable Cataloging*. 7th ed. Washington, D.C.: Library of Congress Cataloging Distribution Service, 2003. Also available: http://www.loc.gov/marc/umb (accessed 2/14/2006).

Johnson, Bruce Chr. "XML and MARC: Which is 'Right'?" *Cataloging & Classification Quarterly* 32, no. 1 (2001): 81–90.

Library of Congress. "MARC in XML." Network Development and MARC Standards Office, Library of Congress. Washington, DC: Library of Congress. Available: http://www.loc.gov/marc/marcxml.html (accessed 2/14/2006).

MARC 21 Format for Authority Data; Including Guidelines for Content Designation. Washington, D.C.: Cataloging Distribution Service, Library of Congress, 2004; *MARC 21 Concise Format for Authority Data*. Available: http://www.loc.gov/marc/authority/ecadhome.html (accessed 2/14/2006).

MARC 21 Format for Bibliographic Data: Including Guidelines for Content Designation. Washington, D.C.: Cataloging Distribution Service, Library of Congress, 2004; *MARC 21 Concise Format for Bibliographic Data*. Available: http://www.loc.gov/marc/bibliographic/ecbdhome.html (accessed 2/14/2006).

MARC 21 Format for Classification Data: Including Guidelines for Content Designation. Washington, D.C.: Cataloging Distribution Service, Library of Congress, 2004; *MARC 21 Concise Format for Classification Data*. Available: http://www.loc.gov/marc/classification/eccdhome.html (accessed 2/14/2006).

MARC 21 Format for Community Information: Including Guidelines for Content Designation. Washington, D.C.: Cataloging Distribution Service, Library of Congress, 2004; *MARC 21 Concise Format for Community Information*. Available: http://www.loc.gov/marc/community/eccihome.html (accessed 2/14/2006).

MARC 21 Format for Holdings Data: Including Guidelines for Content Designation. Washington, D.C.: Cataloging Distribution Service, Library of Congress, 2004; *MARC 21*

Concise Format for Holdings Data. Available: http://www.loc.gov/marc/holdings/echdhome.html (accessed 2/14/2006).

"The MARC 21 Formats: Background and Principles." Prepared by MARBI in conjunction with Network Development and MARC Standards Office, Library of Congress. Washington, D.C.: Library of Congress, 1996. Available: http://www.loc.gov/marc/96principl.html (accessed 2/14/2006).

McCallum, Sally H. "An Introduction to the Metadata Object Description Schema." *Library Hi Tech* 22, no. 1 (January 2004): 82–88.

OCLC. *Bibliographic Formats and Standards.* 3rd ed. Dublin, Ohio: OCLC, 2003. Available: http://www.oclc.org/bibformats (accessed 2/14/2006).

UNIMARC/Authorities: Universal Format for Authorities. Recommended by the IFLA Steering Group on a UNIMARC Format for Authorities; approved by the Standing Committees of the IFLA Sections on Cataloguing and Information Technology. München : K.G. Saur, c1991.

UNIMARC Manual: Bibliographic Format 1994. Updated 1 March 2000. IFLA Universal Bibliographic Control and International MARC Core Programme (UBCIM). Available: http://www.ifla.org/VI/3/p1996-1/sec-uni.htm (accessed 2/14/2006).

UNIMARC: Universal MARC Format. 2nd ed., revised. London: IFLA International Office for UBC, 1980.

DESCRIPTIVE CATALOGING: DESCRIPTION, ENTRY, AND HEADING

General

ALA/ALCTS/CCS Committee on Cataloging: Description and Access. *The Future of AACR* (April 2003). Available: http://www.libraries.psu.edu/tas/jca/ccda/future1.html or http://www.libraries.psu.edu/tas/jca/ccda/docs/future1.pdf (accessed 2/14/2006).

Anglo-American Cataloguing Rules, Second Edition, 2002 Revision, prepared under the direction of the Joint Steering Committee for Revision of AACR. Chicago: American Library Association, 2002. (Also available in *Cataloger's Desktop.* Washington, D.C.: Library of Congress, Cataloging Distribution Service. Available: http://desktop.loc.gov/ [accessed 2/14/2006]. For subscription information: http://www.loc.gov/cds/desktop/ [accessed 2/14/2006].)

Baer, Eleanora A. *Titles in Series: A Handbook for Librarians and Students.* 3rd ed. Metuchen, N.J.: Scarecrow Press, 1978.

Books in Series. New York: Bowker, 1980–1989.

Books in Series in the United States. New York: Bowker, 1977–1979.

Carpenter, Michael, and Elaine Svenonius, eds. *Foundations of Cataloging: A Sourcebook.* Littleton, Colo.: Libraries Unlimited, 1985.

Ferguson, Bobby. *Cataloging Nonprint Materials: Blitz Cataloging Workbook*. Englewood, Colo.: Libraries Unlimited, 1999.

―――. *MARC/AACR2/Authority Control Tagging: Blitz Cataloging Workbook*. 2nd ed. Westport, Conn.: Libraries Unlimited, 2005.

Frost, Carolyn O. *Media Access and Organization: A Cataloging and Reference Sources Guide for Nonbook Materials*. Englewood, Colo.: Libraries Unlimited, 1989.

Gorman, Michael. *The Concise AACR2*. 4th ed. Chicago: American Library Association, 2004.

Intner, Sheila S., and Richard P. Smiraglia, eds. *Policy and Practice in Bibliographic Control of Nonbook Media*. Chicago: American Library Association, 1987.

Library of Congress Rule Interpretations. 2nd ed. Washington, D.C.: Cataloging Distribution Service, Library of Congress, 1989–date, looseleaf, with updates. (Also available in *Cataloger's Desktop*.)

Maxwell, Robert L. *Maxwell's Handbook for* AACR2R: *Explaining and Illustrating the* Anglo-American Cataloguing Rules *through the 2003 Update*. 4th ed. Chicago: American Library Association, 2004.

Mortimer, Mary. *Learn Descriptive Cataloging*. Lanham, Md.: Scarecrow Press, 2000.

RDA – Resource Description and Access. Joint Steering Committee for Revision of AACR; updated 13 February 2006. Available: http://www.collectionscanada.ca/jsc/rda.html (accessed 2/25/2006).

Rogers, JoAnn V., with Jerry D. Saye. *Nonprint Cataloging for Multimedia Collections: A Guide Based on AACR2*. 2nd ed. Littleton, Colo.: Libraries Unlimited, 1987.

Saye, Jerry D., and Sherry L. Vellucci. *Notes in the Catalog Record Based on AACR2 and LC Rule Interpretations*. Chicago: American Library Association, 1989.

Smiraglia, Richard P. "Bibliographic Control Theory and Nonbook Materials." In *Policy and Practice in Bibliographic Control of Nonbook Media*, edited by Sheila S. Intner and Richard P. Smiraglia. Chicago: American Library Association, 1987.

Statement of International Cataloguing Principles, Draft approved by the IFLA Meeting of Experts on an International Cataloguing Code, "Final" Draft Based on Responses through December 2004 showing further recommended changes from Buenos Aires, August 2004 (September 20, 2005 Draft). Available: http://www.loc.gov/loc/ifla/imeicc/source/Statement-draftsep05-clean.pdf (accessed 2/14/2006).

Weihs, Jean, ed. *The Principles and Future of AACR: Proceedings of the International Conference on the Principles and Future Development of AACR*. Chicago: American Library Association, 1998.

Weihs, Jean, with Shirley Lewis. *Nonbook Materials: The Organization of Integrated Collections*. 3rd ed. Ottawa: Canadian Library Association, 1989.

Wool, Gregory J. "Bibliographical Metadata; or, We Need a Client-Server Cataloging Code!" In *Finding Common Ground: Creating the Library of the Future without Diminishing the Library of the Past*, edited by Cheryl LaGuardia and Barbara S. Mitchell, pp. 398–401. New York: Neal-Schuman, 1998.

Material-Specific AACR2 Cataloging

American Library Association, Interactive Multimedia Guidelines Review Task Force. *Guidelines for Bibliographic Description of Interactive Multimedia*. Chicago: American Library Association, 1994.

Andrew, Paige G., and Mary Lynette Larsgaard, eds. *Maps and Related Cartographic Materials Cataloging, Classification, and Bibliographic Control*. New York: Haworth Information Press, 1999.

Association for Library Collections and Technical Services, Cataloging and Classification Section, Committee on Cataloging: Description and Access, Task Force on an Appendix of Major and Minor Changes. *Differences Between, Changes Within: Guidelines on When to Create a New Record*. April 2003. Available: http://www.libraries.psu.edu/tas/jca/ccda/docs/tf-appx10.doc (accessed 2/26/2006).

Betz, Elizabeth W., comp. *Graphic Materials: Rules for Describing Original Items and Historical Collections*. Washington, D.C.: Library of Congress, 1996. Available: http://www.itsmarc.com/crs/grph0199.htm (accessed 2/26/2006).

Cartographic Materials: A Manual of Interpretation for AACR2, 2002 Revision. 2nd ed. Chicago: American Library Association, 2003.

CONSER Editing Guide. Prepared by staff of the Serial Record Division under the direction of the CONSER operations coordinator. 2002 Cumulation. Washington, D.C.: Cataloging Distribution Service, Library of Congress, 2002–date. Looseleaf, with updates. (Also available in *Cataloger's Desktop*.)

Describing Archives: A Content Standard. Chicago: The Society of American Archivists, 2004.

Fritz, Deborah A. *Cataloging with AACR2 and MARC21, for Books, Electronic Resources, Sound Recordings, Videorecordings, and Serials*. 2nd ed. Chicago: American Library Association, 2004.

Gamble, Betsy, ed. *Music Cataloging Decisions: As Issued by the Music Section, Special Materials Cataloging Division, Library of Congress in the Music Cataloging Bulletin, Through December 1991*. Canton, Mass.: Music Library Association, 1992.

Geer, Beverley, and Beatrice L. Caraway. *Notes for Serials Cataloging*. 2nd ed. Englewood, Colo.: Libraries Unlimited, 1998.

Gorman, Michael. "Cataloging and Classification of Film Study Material." In *Film Study Collections*, edited by Nancy Allen. New York: F. Ungar Publishing, 1979.

Graham, Crystal. "What's Wrong with AACR2: A Serials Perspective." In *The Future of the Cataloging Rules*, edited by Brian E. C. Schottlaender. Chicago: American Library Association, 1998.

Hensen, Steven L. *Archives, Personal Papers, and Manuscripts: A Cataloging Manual for Archival Repositories, Historical Societies, and Manuscript Libraries.* 2nd ed. Chicago: Society of American Archivists, 1989.

Hill, Janet Swan. "Descriptions of Reproductions of Previously Existing Works: Another View," *Microform Review* 11 (Winter 1982): 14–21.

Hirons, Jean L. "Revising AACR2 to Accommodate Seriality: Report to the Joint Steering Committee for Revision of AACR." 1999. Available: http://www.collectionscanada.ca/jsc/docs.html#seriality (accessed 2/14/2006).

———, ed. *CONSER Cataloging Manual.* 2002 ed. Washington, D.C.: Cataloging Distribution Service, Library of Congress, 2002–date. Looseleaf, with updates.

Hsieh-Yee, Ingrid. *Organizing Audiovisual and Electronic Resources for Access: A Cataloging Guide.* 2nd ed. Westport, Conn.: Libraries Unlimited, 2006.

International Standard Bibliographic Description. The following ISBDs have been published by the International Federation of Library Associations and Institutions:

ISBD(A): International Standard Bibliographic Description for Older Monographic Publications (Antiquarian). 2nd Rev. ed. 1991.

ISBD(CM): International Standard Bibliographic Description for Cartographic Materials. Rev. ed. 1987.

ISBD(CR): International Standard Bibliographic Description for Serials and other Continuing Resources. Revised from the ISBD(S): International Standard Bibliographic Description for Serials. 2002.

ISBD(ER): International Standard Bibliographic Description for Electronic Resources. Revised from the ISBD(CF): International Standard Bibliographic Description for Computer Files. 1997.

ISBD(G): General International Standard Bibliographic Description. 2004 Revision. Available: http://www.ifla.org/VII/s13/pubs/isbdg2004.pdf (accessed 2/14/2006).

ISBD(M): International Standard Bibliographic Description for Monographic Publications. 2002 Revision. Available: http://www.ifla.org/VII/s13/pubs/isbd_m0602.pdf (accessed 2/14/2006).

ISBD(NBM): International Standard Bibliographic Description for Non-Book Materials. Rev. ed. 1987.

ISBD(PM): International Standard Bibliographic Description for Printed Music. 2nd Rev. ed. 1991.

John, Nancy R. "Microforms," *Journal of Library Administration* 3 (Spring 1982): 3–8.

Jones, Wayne, Judith R. Ahronheim, and Josephine Crawford, eds. *Cataloging the Web: Metadata, AACR, and MARC 21* (ALCTS Papers on Library Technical Services and Collections, no. 10). Lanham, Md.: Scarecrow Press, 2002.

Library of Congress, Program for Cooperative Cataloging, Standing Committee on Training. *Integrating Resources: A Cataloging Manual.* 2005 revision. Available: http://www.loc.gov/catdir/pcc/bibco/irman.pdf (accessed 2/14/2006).

Liheng, Carol, and Winnie S. Chan. *Serials Cataloging Handbook: An Illustrative Guide to the Use of AACR2R and LC Rule Interpretations.* 2nd ed. Chicago: American Library Association, 1998.

Olson, Nancy B. *Cataloging Computer Files,* edited by Edward Swanson. Lake Crystal, Minn.: Soldier Creek Press, 1992.

———. *Cataloging Computer Files: 1996 Update,* edited by Edward Swanson. Lake Crystal, Minn.: Soldier Creek Press, 1996.

———. *Cataloging Motion Pictures and Videorecordings,* edited by Edward Swanson. Lake Crystal, Minn.: Soldier Creek Press, 1992.

———. *Cataloging Motion Pictures and Videorecordings: 1996 Update,* edited by Edward Swanson. Lake Crystal, Minn.: Soldier Creek Press, 1996.

———. *Cataloging of Audiovisual Materials and Other Special Materials: A Manual Based on AACR 2.* 4th ed. Edited by Sheila S. Intner and Edward Swanson. DeKalb, Ill.: Minnesota Scholarly Press, 1998.

———, ed. *Cataloging Internet Resources: A Manual and Practical Guide.* 2nd ed. Dublin, Ohio: OCLC Online Computer Library Center, Inc., 1997.

O'Neil, Rosanna M. "Analysis and 'In' Analytics," *Serials Review* 13, no. 2 (Summer 1987): 57–63.

Online Audiovisual Catalogers, Inc., Cataloging Policy Committee, DVD Cataloging Task Force. *Guide to Cataloging DVDs Using AACR2r Chapters 7 and 9.* 15 October 2002. Available: http://ublib.buffalo.edu/libraries/units/cts/olac/capc/dvd/dvdprimer0.html or http://ublib.buffalo.edu/libraries/units/cts/olac/capc/dvd/dvdprimer.pdf (accessed 2/14/2006).

Sandberg-Fox, Ann, and John D. Byrum. "From ISBD(CF) to ISBD(ER): Process, Policy, and Provisions." *Library Resources and Technical Services* 42 (April 1998): 89–101.

Smiraglia, Richard P. *Cataloging Music: A Manual for Use with AACR2.* 2nd ed. Lake Crystal, Minn.: Soldier Creek Press, 1986.

———. *Music Cataloging: The Bibliographic Control of Printed and Recorded Music in Libraries.* Englewood, Colo.: Libraries Unlimited, 1989.

Soper, Mary Ellen. "Description and Entry of Serials in *AACR2.*" *Serials Librarian* 4 (Winter 1979): 167–176.

Taylor, Arlene G. "Where Does AACR2 Fall Short for Internet Resources?" *Journal of Internet Cataloging* 2, no. 2 (1999): 43–50.

Tseng, Sally C. "Serials Cataloging and AACR2: An Introduction." *Journal of Educational Media Science,* 19 (Winter 1982): 177–216.

Entry and Heading

Carpenter, Michael. "Does Cataloging Theory Rest on a Mistake?" In *Origins, Content, and Future of AACR2 Revisited*, edited by Richard P. Smiraglia, pp. 95–102. Chicago: American Library Association, 1992.

Dowell, Arlene Taylor. *AACR 2 Headings: A Five-Year Projection of Their Impact on Catalogs*. Littleton, Colo.: Libraries Unlimited, 1982.

Hagler, Ronald. "Access Points for Works." In *The Principles and Future of AACR2*, edited by Jean Weihs, pp. 214–228. Chicago: American Library Association, 1998.

Smiraglia, Richard P. "Derivative Bibliographic Relationships: Linkages in the Bibliographic Universe." In *Navigating the Networks: Proceedings of the ASIS Mid-Year Meeting, Portland, Oregon, May 21–25, 1994*, pp. 167–183. Medford, N.J.: Learned Information, 1994.

Taylor, Arlene G. "Metadata: Access and Access Control." Chapter 8 in *The Organization of Information*. 2nd ed. Westport, Conn.: Libraries Unlimited, 2004.

Tillett, Barbara B. "Bibliographic Relationships: Toward a Conceptual Structure of Bibliographic Information Used in Cataloging." Ph.D. dissertation, University of California, Los Angeles, 1987.

———. "A Taxonomy of Bibliographic Relationships," *Library Resources and Technical Services* 35 (April 1991): 150–158.

———. "A Summary of the Treatment of Bibliographic Relationships in Cataloging Rules," *Library Resources and Technical Services* 35 (October 1991): 393–405.

———. "The History of Linking Devices," *Library Resources and Technical Services* 36 (January 1992): 23–36.

———. "Bibliographic Relationships: An Empirical Study of the LC Machine-Readable Records," *Library Resources and Technical Services* 36 (April 1992): 162–188.

Vellucci, Sherry L. "Bibliographic Relationships Among Musical Bibliographic Entities: A Conceptual Analysis of Music Represented in the Library Catalog with a Taxonomy of the Relationships Discovered." D.L.S. dissertation, Columbia University, 1995.

———. "Bibliographic Relationships." In *The Principles and Future of AACR2*, edited by Jean Weihs, pp. 105–146. Chicago: American Library Association, 1998.

AUTHORITY CONTROL

Authority Control in the 21st Century: An Invitational Conference, March 3–April 1, 1996. Dublin, Ohio: OCLC Online Computer Library Center. Available: http://digitalarchive. oclc.org/request?id = oclcnum:52448562 (accessed 2/14/2006).

"Authority Control: Why It Matters," Conference sponsored by NELINET, 1 November 1999, Worcester, Mass. Available: http://www.nelinet.net/edserv/conf/cataloging/cts/ 1999/cts99.htm (accessed 2/14/2006).

Barnhart, Linda. "Access Control Records: Prospects and Challenges." In *Authority Control in the 21st Century, Invitational Conference, March 31–April 1, 1996.* Available: http://digitalarchive.oclc.org/da/ViewObject.jsp?fileid=0000003520:00000009177& reqid = 1268 (accessed 2/14/2006).

Bratton, Robert, ed. "Authority Tools for Audiovisual and Music Catalogers: An Annotated List of Useful Resources." Online Audiovisual Catalogers, Inc., 2003– . Available: http://ublib.buffalo.edu/libraries/units/cts/olac/capc/authtools.html (accessed 2/14/2006).

Burger, Robert H. *Authority Work: The Creation, Use, Maintenance, and Evaluation of Authority Records and Files.* Littleton, Colo.: Libraries Unlimited, 1985.

Clack, Doris Hargrett. *Authority Control: Principles, Applications, and Instructions.* Chicago: American Library Association, 1990.

Everett, David, and David M. Pilachowski. "What's in a Name? Looking for People Online —Humanities." *DATABASE* 9 (October 1986): 26–34.

The Future Is Now: Reconciling Change and Continuity in Authority Control: Proceedings of the OCLC Symposium, ALA Annual Conference, June 23, 1995. Dublin, Ohio: OCLC Online Computer Library Center, 1995.

Maxwell, Robert L. *Maxwell's Guide to Authority Work.* Chicago: American Library Association, 2002.

"NACO: Program for Cooperative Cataloging." Available: http://www.loc.gov/catdir/pcc? naco/naco.html (accessed 2/14/2006).

Pasterczyk, Catherine E. "Russian Transliteration Variations for Searchers." *DATABASE* 8 (February 1985): 68–75.

Patton, Glenn E. "FRANAR: A Conceptual Model for Authority Data." *Cataloging & Classification Quarterly* 38, no 3/4 (2004): 91–104; also published in *Authority Control in Organizing and Accessing Information: Definition and International Experience*, edited by Arlene G. Taylor and Barbara B. Tillett, p. 91–104. New York: Haworth Information Press, 2004.

Pilachowski, David M., and David Everett. "What's in a Name? Looking for People Online —Social Sciences." *DATABASE* 8 (August 1985): 47–65.

———. "What's in a Name? Looking for People Online—Current Events." *DATABASE* 9 (April 1986): 43–50.

Piternick, Anne B. "What's in a Name? Use of Names and Titles in Subject Searching." *DATABASE* 8 (December 1985): 22–28.

"SACO Program Description: Program for Cooperative Cataloging." Available: http://www. loc.gov/catdir/pcc/saco/saco.html (accessed 2/14/2006).

Smiraglia, Richard. "Authority Control and the Extent of Derivative Bibliographic Relationships." Ph.D. dissertation, University of Chicago, 1992.

————. "Authority Control of Works: Cataloging's Chimera?" *Cataloging & Classification Quarterly* 38, no 3/4 (2004): 291–308; also published in *Authority Control in Organizing and Accessing Information: Definition and International Experience*, edited by Arlene G. Taylor and Barbara B. Tillett, pp. 291–308. New York: Haworth Information Press, 2004.

Snow, Bonnie. "Caduceus: People in Medicine: Searching Names Online." *ONLINE* 10 (September 1986): 122–127.

Talmacs, Kerrie. "Authority Control." In *Technical Services Today and Tomorrow*, 2nd ed., edited by Michael Gorman, pp. 129–139. Englewood, Colo.: Libraries Unlimited, 1998.

Taylor, Arlene G. "Authority Control and System Design." In *Policy and Practice in the Bibliographic Control of Nonbook Media*, edited by Sheila S. Intner and Richard P. Smiraglia, pp. 64–81. Chicago: American Library Association, 1987.

————. "Authority Control: Where It's Been and Where It's Going." In "Authority Control: Why It Matters," conference sponsored by NELINET, 1 November 1999, Worcester, Mass. Available: http://www.nelinet.net/edserv/conf/cataloging/cts/1999/taylor.htm (accessed 2/14/2006).

————. "Authority Files in Online Catalogs: An Investigation of Their Value." *Cataloging & Classification Quarterly* 4 (Spring 1984): 1–17.

————. "Research and Theoretical Considerations in Authority Control." *Cataloging & Classification Quarterly* 9, no. 3 (1989): 29–56.

Taylor, Arlene G., and Barbara B. Tillett, eds. *Authority Control in Organizing and Accessing Information: Definition and International Experience.* New York: Haworth Information Press, 2004.

Tillett, Barbara B. "Authority Control: State of the Art and New Perspectives." *Cataloging & Classification Quarterly* 38, no. 3/4 (2004): 23–41; also published in *Authority Control in Organizing and Accessing Information: Definition and International Experience*, edited by Arlene G. Taylor and Barbara B. Tillett, pp. 23–41. New York: Haworth Information Press, 2004.

Tillett, Barbara B. "International Shared Resource Records for Controlled Access." In *From Catalog to Gateway: Briefings from the CFFC*, paper no. 12. *ALCTS Newsletter Online* 10, no. 1 (December 1998); also published in *From Catalog to Gateway: Charting a Course for Future Access: Briefings from the ALCTS Catalog Form and Function Committee*, edited by Bill Sleeman and Pamela Bluh, pp. 69–74. Chicago: Association for Library Collections & Technical Services, American Library Association, 2005.

Vellucci, Sherry L. "Metadata and Authority Control." *Library Resources & Technical Services* 44, no. 1 (January 2000): 33–43.

SUBJECT ANALYSIS

General

American Library Association, Association for Library Collections and Technical Services, Subject Analysis Committee, Subcommittee on Subject Reference Structures in Automated Systems. *Recommendations for providing access to, display of, navigation within and among, and modifications of existing practice regarding subject reference structures in automated systems, December 1, 2003.* Available: http://www.ala. org/ala/alctscontent/catalogingsection/catcommittees/subjectanalysis/subjectreference/ RefStructuresFinal.doc (accessed 2/14/2006).

Bates, Marcia J. "Rethinking Subject Cataloging in the Online Environment." *Library Resources & Technical Services* 33, no. 4 (October 1989): 400–419.

———. Subject Access in Online Catalogs: A Design Model." *Journal of the American Society for Information Science* 37, no. 6 (November 1986): 357–376.

Chan, Lois Mai, Phyllis A. Richmond, and Elaine Svenonius. *Theory of Subject Analysis: A Sourcebook.* Littleton, Colo.: Libraries Unlimited, 1985.

Ferguson, Bobby. *Subject Analysis: Blitz Cataloging Workbook.* Englewood, Colo.: Libraries Unlimited, 1998.

Foskett, A. C. *The Subject Approach to Information.* 5th ed. London: Library Association Publishing, 1996.

Fugmann, Robert. *Subject Analysis and Indexing: Theoretical Foundation and Practical Advice.* Frankfurt am Main: Indeks Verlag, 1993.

International Organization for Standardization. *Documentation: Methods for Examining Documents, Determining Their Subjects and Selecting Indexing Terms.* Geneva, Switzerland: ISO, 1985.

Joudrey, Daniel N. "Building Puzzles and Growing Pearls: A Qualitative Exploration of Determining Aboutness." Ph. D. dissertation, University of Pittsburgh, 2005. Available: http://edt.library.pitt.edu/ETD/available/etd-12132005-155713/ (accessed 2/14/1006).

Lakoff, George. *Women, Fire, and Dangerous Things: What Categories Reveal About the Mind.* Chicago: University of Chicago Press, 1987.

Langridge, D. W. *Subject Analysis: Principles and Procedures.* London: Bowker-Saur, 1989.

Mann, Thomas. *Doing Research at the Library of Congress: A Guide to Subject Searching in a Closed Stacks Library.* Washington, D.C.: Humanities and Social Sciences Division, Library of Congress, 1994.

———. *Library Research Models: A Guide to Classification, Cataloging, and Computers.* New York: Oxford University Press, 1993.

Markey, Karen. *Subject Searching in Library Catalogs: Before and After the Introduction of Online Catalogs.* Dublin, Ohio: OCLC, 1984.

McKiernan, Gerry. *Beyond Bookmarks: Schemes for Organizing the Web.* Available: http://www.public.iastate.edu/~CYBERSTACKS/CTW.htm (accessed 2/14/2006).

Miller, David, Tony Olson, and Sara Shatford Lane. "Promoting Research and Best Practices in Subject Reference Structures: A Decade of Work by the Subject Analysis Committee." *Library Resources & Technical Services* 49, no. 3 (July 2005): 154–166.

Olson, Hope A., and John J. Boll. *Subject Analysis in Online Catalogs.* 2nd ed. Englewood, Colo.: Libraries Unlimited, 2001.

Petersen, Toni, and Pat Molholt, eds. *Beyond the Book: Extending MARC for Subject Access.* Boston: G. K. Hall, 1990.

Šauperl, Alenka. *Subject Determination during the Cataloging Process.* Lanham, Md.: Scarecrow Press, 2002.

Subject Data in the Metadata Record: Recommendations and Rationale: A Report from the [ALA/ALCTS/SAC] Subcommittee on Metadata and Subject Analysis, July 1999. Available: http://www.ala.org/ala/alctscontent/catalogingsection/catcommittees/subjectanalysis/metadataandsubje/subjectdata.htm (accessed 2/14/2006).

Subject Indexing: Principles and Practices in the 90's: Proceedings of the IFLA Satellite Meeting Held in Lisbon, Portugal, 17–18 August 1993. München: K.G. Saur, 1995.

Taylor, Arlene G. "On the Subject of Subjects." *Journal of Academic Librarianship* 21, no. 6 (November 1995): 484–491.

Wellish, Hans H. "Aboutness and Selection of Topics." *Key Words* 4, no. 2 (March/April 1996): 7–9.

Wilson, Patrick. "Subjects and the Sense of Position." In *Theory of Subject Analysis: A Sourcebook,* edited by Lois Mai Chan, Phyllis A. Richmond, and Elaine Svenonius, pp. 253–268. Littleton, Colo.: Libraries Unlimited, 1985.

Verbal Subject Access

American Library Association. Subject Analysis Committee. "Definition of Form Data." 1993. Available: http://www.pitt.edu/~agtaylor/ala/form-def.htm (accessed 2/14/2006).

———. Subcommittee on Subject Access to Individual Works of Fiction, Drama, etc. *Guidelines on Subject Access to Individual Works of Fiction, Drama, Etc.* 2nd ed. Chicago: American Library Association, 2000.

American National Standards Institute. *American National Standard Guidelines for Thesaurus Structure, Construction, and Use,* ANSI Z39.19–1980. New York: ANSI, 1980.

Berman, Sanford. *Prejudices and Antipathies: A Tract on the LC Subject Heads Concerning People.* Metuchen, N.J.: Scarecrow Press, 1971.

———. *Prejudices and Antipathies: A Tract on the LC Subject Heads Concerning People.* Jefferson, N.C.: McFarland, 1993.

British Standards Institution. *British Standard Guide to Establishment and Development of Monolingual Thesauri*, BS 5723 [Rev. ed.] London: BSI, 1987.

Brown, A. G., in collaboration with D. W. Langridge, and J. Mills. *An Introduction to Subject Indexing*. 2nd ed. London: Bingley, 1982. [programmed text]

Canadian Subject Headings: Supplement. 3rd ed. Ottawa: National Library of Canada, 1996.

Chan, Lois Mai. *Library of Congress Subject Headings: Principles and Application*. 4th ed. Westport, Conn.: Libraries Unlimited, 2005.

Clack, Doris H. *Black Literature Resources: Analysis and Organization*. New York: Marcel Dekker, 1975.

Dean, Rebecca J. "FAST: Development of Simplified Headings for Metadata." *Cataloging & Classification Quarterly* 39, no. 1/2 (2004): 331–352; also published in *Authority Control in Organizing and Accessing Information: Definition and International Experience*, edited by Arlene G. Taylor and Barbara B. Tillett, pp. 331–352. New York: Haworth Information Press, 2004.

Dykstra, Mary. "LC Subject Headings Disguised as a Thesaurus." *Library Journal* 113 (March 1, 1988): 42–46.

Free-Floating Subdivisions: An Alphabetical Index. 1st–[current] eds. Washington, D.C.: Library of Congress, 1989–date.

Ganendran, Jacki. *Learn Library of Congress Subject Access*. Lanham, Md.: Scarecrow Press, 2000.

Getty. *Art & Architecture Thesaurus® Online*. Available: http://www.getty.edu/research/conducting_research/vocabularies/aat/ (accessed 2/19/2006).

Gross, Tina, and Arlene G. Taylor, "What Have We Got to Lose? The Effect of Controlled Vocabulary on Keyword Searching Results," *College & Research Libraries* 66, no. 3 (May 2005): 212–230.

Hemmasi, Harriette, David Miller, and Mary Charles Lasater; edited by Arlene G. Taylor. "Access to Form Data in Online Catalogs." In "From Catalog to Gateway: Briefings from the CFFC," paper no. 13. *ALCTS Newsletter Online* 10, no. 4 (July 1999); also published in *From Catalog to Gateway: Charting a Course for Future Access: Briefings from the ALCTS Catalog Form and Function Committee*, edited by Bill Sleeman and Pamela Bluh, pp. 75–81. Chicago: Association for Library Collections & Technical Services, American Library Association, 2005.

Inspec Thesaurus. 2004 [ed.] London: Institution of Electrical Engineers, 2004.

International Organization for Standardization. *Documentation: Guidelines for the Establishment and Development of Monolingual Thesauri*. 2nd ed. ISO 2788. Geneva: ISO, 1986.

Koch, Traugott. *Controlled Vocabularies, Thesauri and Classification Systems Available in the WWW. DC Subject*. Last updated 3 December 2003. Available: http://www.lub.lu.se/metadata/subject-help.html (accessed 2/14/2006).

Lancaster, F. W. *Indexing and Abstracting in Theory and Practice*. 3rd ed. Champaign, Ill.: University of Illinois, Graduate School of Library and Information Science, 2003. [Also published: London: Facet Publishing, 2003.]

————. "Trends in Subject Indexing from 1957 to 2000." In *New Trends in Documentation and Information: Proceedings of the 39th FID Congress, 1978*, pp. 223–233. London: Aslib, 1980.

————. *Vocabulary Control For Information Retrieval*. 2nd ed. Arlington, Va.: Information Resources Press, 1986.

Lee-Smeltzer, Kuang-Hwei (Janet). "Finding the Needle: Controlled Vocabularies, Resource Discovery, and Dublin Core." *Library Collections, Acquisitions, & Technical Services* 24 (2000): 205–215.

Library of Congress Subject Headings. "Introduction." Washington, D.C.: Cataloging Distribution Service, Library of Congress, 1990– . (Also available in *Cataloger's Desktop*.)

Library of Congress Subject Headings. 13th– [current] eds. Washington, D.C.: Office for Subject Cataloging Policy, Library of Congress, 1990– [date]. (Also available in *Classification Web*.)

Library of Congress Subject Headings in Microform. Washington, D.C.: Cataloging Distribution Service, Library of Congress [ceased publication 2002].

Library of Congress Subject Headings Weekly Lists. Washington, D.C.: Cataloging Policy and Support Office, Library of Congress, January 1997– [date]. Available: http://www.loc.gov/catdir/cpso/cpso.html#subjects (accessed 2/14/2006).

Lighthall, Lynne Isberg, ed. *Sears List of Subject Headings: Canadian Companion*. 6th ed. New York: H. W. Wilson, 2001.

Mann, Thomas. "Research at Risk." *Library Journal* (July 15, 2005). Available: http://www.libraryjournal.com/article/CA623006.html (accessed 2/14/2006).

————. "Will Google's Keyword Searching Eliminate the Need for LC Cataloging and Classification?" AFSCME 2910. Last updated August 15, 2005. Available: http://www.guild2910.org/searching.htm (accessed 2/14/2006).

Markey, Karen. *Subject Searching in Library Catalogs: Before and After the Introduction of Online Catalogs*, pp. 75–87. Dublin, Ohio: OCLC Online Computer Library Center, 1984.

Marshall, Joan K. *On Equal Terms: A Thesaurus for Nonsexist Indexing and Cataloging*. Santa Barbara, Calif.: American Bibliographical Center–Clio Press, 1977.

National Information Standards Organization. *Guidelines for the Construction, Format, and Management of Monolingual Controlled Vocabularies*. ANSI/NISO Z39.19-200x (draft standard). Bethesda, Md.: NISO Press, 2005.

National Library of Medicine. "PubMed." Available: http://www.ncbi.nlm.nih.gov/entrez/query.fcgi (accessed 2/14/2006).

———. "UMLS Metathesaurus: Fact Sheet." Available: http://www.nlm.nih.gov/pubs/factsheets/umlsmeta.html (accessed 2/14/2006).

———. "Unified Medical Language System (UMLS)." Available: http://www.nlm.nih.gov/research/umls/ (accessed 2/14/2006).

Noy, Natalya F., and Deborah L. McGuinness. *Ontology Development 101: A Guide to Creating Your First Ontology.* Knowledge Systems Laboratory, Stanford University, 2000. Available: http://www.ksl.stanford.edu/people/dlm/papers/ontology-tutorial-noy-mcguinness-abstract.html (accessed 2/14/2006).

Olson, Hope A. *The Power to Name: Locating the Limits of Subject Representation in Libraries.* Dordrecht, The Netherlands; Boston: Kluwer Academic Publishers, 2002.

O'Neill, Edward T., and Lois Mai Chan. "FAST (Faceted Application of Subject Terminology): A Simplified LCSH-Based Vocabulary." World Library and Information Congress: 69th IFLA General Conference and Council, 1–9 August 2003, Berlin. Available: http://www.ifla.org/IV/ifla69/papers/010e-ONeill_Mai-Chan.pdf (accessed 2/14/2006).

O'Neill, Edward T., Lois Mai Chan, Eric Childress, Rebecca Dean, Lynn M. El-Hoshy, and Diane Visine-Goetz. "Form Subdivisions: Their Identification and Use in LCSH." *Library Resources & Technical Services* 45, no. 4 (October 2001): 187–197.

Petersen, Toni. "The AAT: A Model for the Restructuring of LCSH." *Journal of Academic Librarianship* 9 (September 1983): 207–210.

"Principles of the Sears List of Subject Headings." In *Sears List of Subject Headings.* 18th ed., Joseph Miller, editor; Joan Goodsell, associate editor, pp. xv–xxxix. New York: H. W. Wilson, 2004.

Sears List of Subject Headings. 18th ed. Joseph Miller, editor; Joan Goodsell, associate editor. New York: H. W. Wilson, 2004.

Sears—Lista de Encabezamientos de Materia: Traducción y Adaptación de la 12a. Edición en Inglés, ed. por Barbara M. Westby; trans. por Carmen Rovira. New York: H. W. Wilson, 1984. [Spanish translation now out-of-print.]

Subject Cataloging Manual: Subject Headings. 5th ed. Washington, D.C.: Cataloging Distribution Service, Library of Congress, 1996. Updates, 1997– . (Also available in *Cataloger's Desktop.*)

Svenonius, Elaine. "LCSH: Semantics, Syntax and Specificity." *Cataloging & Classification Quarterly* 29, no. 1/2 (2000): 17–30.

Thesaurus of ERIC Descriptors. 14th ed. Phoenix, Ariz.: Oryx Press, 2001.

Thesaurus of Psychological Index Terms. 10th ed. Washington, D.C.: American Psychological Association, 2005.

CLASSIFICATION

Bliss Classification Association. "Bliss Classification Association: homepage." Available: http://www.sid.cam.ac.uk/bca/bcahome.htm (accessed 2/14/2006).

————. "The Bliss Bibliographic Classification: Outline of Bliss Classification (2nd ed.)." Available: http://www.sid.cam.ac.uk/bca/bcoutline.htm (accessed 2/14/2006).

Bowker, Geoffrey C., and Susan Leigh Star. *Sorting Things Out: Classification and Its Consequences*. Cambridge, Mass.: MIT Press, 1999.

British Standards Institution. *Universal Decimal Classification, Complete Edition*. London: BSI, 2005.

British Standards Institution. *Universal Decimal Classification*. 2nd ed. Abridged. London: BSI, 2003.

Chan, Lois M. *A Guide to the Library of Congress Classification*. 5th ed. Englewood, Colo.: Libraries Unlimited, 1999.

Chan, Lois Mai, and Joan S. Mitchell. *Dewey Decimal Classification: Principles and Application*. 3rd ed. Dublin, Ohio: OCLC, 2003.

Classification Research Group. "The Need for a Faceted Classification as the Basis of all Methods of Information Retrieval." In *Theory of Subject Analysis: A Sourcebook*, edited by Lois Mai Chan, Phyllis A. Richmond, and Elaine Svenonius, pp. 154–167. Littleton, Colo.: Libraries Unlimited, 1985.

Dewey, Melvil. *Abridged Dewey Decimal Classification and Relative Index*. Edition 14. Edited by Joan S. Mitchell, et al. Dublin, OH: OCLC, 2004. DDC, Dewey, Dewey Decimal Classification, and WebDewey are registered trademarks of OCLC.

Dewey, Melvil. *Dewey Decimal Classification and Relative Index*. Edition 22. Edited by Joan S. Mitchell, et al. Dublin, OH: OCLC, 2003. DDC, Dewey, Dewey Decimal Classification, and WebDewey are registered trademarks of OCLC.

Dittmann, Helena, and Jane Hardy. *Learn Library of Congress Classification*. Lanham, Md.: Scarecrow Press, 2000.

The Gale Group. [Publisher of *SUPERLCCS*™ . . . *Library of Congress Classification Schedules Combined with Additions and Changes*.] Available: http://www.gale.com/ (accessed 2/21/2006).

Gorman, Michael. "The Longer the Number, the Smaller the Spine; or, Up and Down with Melvil and Elsie." *American Libraries* 12 (September 1981): 498–499.

Herdman, M. M. *Classification: An Introductory Manual*. 3rd ed., revised by Jeanne Osborn. Chicago: American Library Association, 1978.

Hunter, Eric J. *Classification Made Simple*. 2nd ed. Aldershot, Eng.; Burlington, Vt.: Ashgate, 2002.

Koch, Traugott, and Michael Day. *The Role of Classification Schemes in Internet Resource Description and Discovery.* Available: http://www.ukoln.ac.uk/metadata/desire/classification/ (accessed 2/14/2006).

Langridge, D. W. *Classification: Its Kinds, Elements, Systems and Applications.* London: Bowker-Saur, 1992.

Library of Congress Classification: Classes A-Z. Var. eds. Washington, D.C.: Cataloging Distribution Service, Library of Congress, 1976–2006.

Marcella, Rita, and Arthur Maltby. *The Future of Classification.* Aldershot, Eng.; Brookfield, Vt.: Gower, 2000.

Marcella, Rita, and Robert Newton. *A New Manual of Classification.* Aldershot, Eng.; Brookfield, Vt.: Gower, 1994.

Markey, Karen, and Anh Demeyer. *Dewey Decimal Classification Online Project: Evaluation of a Library Schedule and Index Integrated into the Subject Searching Capabilities of an Online Catalog: Final Report to the Council on Library Resources.* Dublin, Ohio: OCLC, 1986.

McIlwaine, I. C. *The Universal Decimal Classification: A Guide to Its Use.* The Hague: UDC Consortium, 2000.

Miksa, Francis L. *The DDC, the Universe of Knowledge, and the Post-Modern Library.* Paper presented at the Fourth International ISKO Conference, July 15–18, 1996, Washington, D.C. Albany, N.Y.: OCLC Forest Press, 1998.

Mortimer, Mary. *Learn Dewey Decimal Classification (Edition 21).* Lanham, Md.: Scarecrow Press, 2000.

National Library of Medicine Classification: A Scheme for the Shelf Arrangement of Books in the Field of Medicine and Its Related Sciences. 5th ed., revised. Bethesda, Md.: NLM, 1999; *NLM Classification 2005.* Available: http://wwwcf.nlm.nih.gov/class/ (accessed 2/22/2006).

OCLC. "Dewey Services: Updates." Available: http://www.oclc.org/dewey/updates/default.htm (accessed 2/14/2006).

OCLC. "Dewey Services: Latest Versions: WebDewey." Available: http://www.oclc.org/dewey/versions/webdewey/default.htm (accessed 2/14/2006); "Dewey Services: Latest Versions: Abridged WebDewey." Available: http://www.oclc.org/dewey/versions/abridgedwebdewey/default.htm (accessed 2/14/2006).

OCLC Office of Research. "Automatic Classification Research at OCLC." Available: http://www.oclc.org/research/projects/auto_class/default.htm (accessed 2/14/2006).

Ranganathan, S. R. *Colon Classification: Basic Classification.* 6th ed., completely revised. Bombay; New York: Asia Publishing House, 1960.

Scott, Mona L. *Conversion Tables: LC–Dewey, Dewey–LC, and LC Subject Headings–LC and Dewey.* 2nd ed. Englewood, Colo.: Libraries Unlimited, 1999.

————— . *Dewey Decimal Classification, 22nd Edition: A Study Manual and Number Building Guide*. Westport, Conn.: Libraries Unlimited, 2005.

Subject Cataloging Manual: Classification. 1st ed. Washington, D.C.: Cataloging Distribution Service, Library of Congress, 1992. Update, 1995. (Also available in *Cataloger's Desktop*.)

Sweeney, Russell. "The Atlantic Divide: Classification Outside the United States," in *Classification of Library Materials*, edited by Betty G. Bengtson and Janet Swan Hill, pp. 40–51. New York: Neal-Schuman, 1990.

"Ten Taxonomy Myths," *Montague Institute Review* (November 2002; updated October 12, 2005). Available: http://www.montague.com/review/myths.html (accessed 2/22/2006).

UDC Consortium. "About Universal Decimal Classification and the UDC Consortium." Available: http://www.udcc.org/about.htm (accessed 2/14/2006).

"UDC Online." Available: http://www.udcc.org/udconline.htm (accessed 2/14/2006).

Vickery, B. C. *Faceted Classification: A Guide to the Construction and Use of Special Schemes*. London: Aslib, 1960.

Vizine-Goetz, Diane. "Using Library Classification Schemes for Internet Resources." Last edited 23 November 1999. Available: http://staff.oclc.org/~vizine/Intercat/vizine-goetz.htm (accessed 2/14/2006).

Wason, Thomas D. "Dr. Tom's Taxonomy Guide: Description, Use and Selections," IMS Global Learning Consortium, Inc., Version 1.01, 15 February 2006. Available: http://www.mindspring.com/~wason/TDW/drtomtaxonomiesguide.html (accessed 2/22/2006).

Williamson, Nancy. "Classification in the Millennium." *Online & CDROM Review* 21, no. 5 (October 1997): 298–301.

ARRANGEMENT (Including Filing)

ALA Rules for Filing Catalog Cards. 2nd ed. Chicago: American Library Association, 1968.

Buckland, Michael K., Barbara A. Norgard, and Christian Plaunt. "Filing, Filtering and the First Few Found." *Information Technology and Libraries* 12, no. 3 (September 1993): 311–319.

Comaromi, John P. *Book Numbers: A Historical Study and Practical Guide to Their Use*. Littleton, Colo.: Libraries Unlimited, 1981.

Cutter, Charles A. *Cutter-Sanborn Three-Figure Author Table*, Swanson-Swift revision, 1969. Distributed by Libraries Unlimited, Inc., Englewood, Colo.

————. *Two-Figure Author Table*, Swanson-Swift revision, 1969. Distributed by Libraries Unlimited, Inc., Englewood, Colo.

————. *Three-Figure Author Table*, Swanson-Swift revision, 1969. Distributed by Libraries Unlimited, Inc., Englewood, Colo.

Lehnus, Donald J. *Book Numbers: History, Principles, and Application*. Chicago: American Library Association, 1980.

Library of Congress Filing Rules. Washington, D.C.: Library of Congress, 1980.

Subject Cataloging Manual: Shelflisting. 2nd ed. Washington, D.C.: Cataloging Distribution Service, Library of Congress, 1995. (Also available in *Cataloger's Desktop*.)

Taylor, Arlene G. "Arrangement and Display." Chapter 12 in *The Organization of Information*. 2nd ed. Westport, Conn.: Libraries Unlimited, 2004.

ADMINISTRATIVE ISSUES

A-G Canada, Ltd. "A-G Canada, Ltd." Available: http://www.ag-canada.com/ (accessed 2/14/2006).

Bénaud, Claire Lise, and Sever Bordeianu. *Outsourcing Library Operations in Academic Libraries: An Overview of Issues and Outcomes*. Englewood, Colo.: Libraries Unlimited, 1998.

Bilal, Dania. *Automating Media Centers and Small Libraries: A Microcomputer-Based Approach*. 2nd ed. Greenwood Village, Colo.: Libraries Unlimited, 2002.

Borgman, Christine L. "From Acting Locally to Thinking Globally: A Brief History of Library Automation." *Library Quarterly* 67, no. 3 (July 1997): 215–249.

―――. "Why Are Online Catalogs *Still* Hard to Use?" *Journal of the American Society for Information Science* 47, no. 7 (July 1996): 493–503.

Brisson, Roger, and Janet McCue. "Retooling Technical Services." In *Encyclopedia of Library and Information Science*, vol. 58, suppl. 21, pp. 281–301. New York: Marcel Dekker, 1996.

Buttlar, Lois, and Rajinder Garcha. "Catalogers in Academic Libraries: Their Evolving and Expanding Roles." *College & Research Libraries* 59, no. 4 (July 1998): 311–321.

Calhoun, Karen, and Bill Kara. "Aggregation or Aggravation? Optimizing Access to Full-Text Journals." In *From Catalog to Gateway: Briefings from the CFFC*, paper no. 15. *ALCTS Newsletter Online* 11, no. 1 (Spring 2000); also published in *From Catalog to Gateway: Charting a Course for Future Access: Briefings from the ALCTS Catalog Form and Function Committee*, edited by Bill Sleeman and Pamela Bluh, pp. 91–97. Chicago: Association for Library Collections & Technical Services, American Library Association, 2005.

Carlyle, Allyson. "Fulfilling the Second Objective in the Online Catalog: Schemes for Organizing Author and Work Records into Usable Displays." *Library Resources & Technical Services* 41, no. 2 (April 1997): 79–100.

Carlyle, Allyson, and Sara Ranger. "Facilitating Retrieval of Fiction Works in Online Catalogs." *Proceedings of the 12th ASIS&T/CR Classification Research Workshop, November 4, 2001,* Silver Spring, Md.: ASIST&T, c1997 [i.e., 2001]: 1–11.

Carlyle, Allyson, and Traci Timmons. "Default Record Displays in Web-Based Catalogs." *Library Quarterly* 72, no. 2 (April 2002): 179–204.

Carter, Ruth C., and Scott Bruntjen. *Data Conversion.* White Plains, N.Y.: Knowledge Industry Publications, 1983.

Colver, Marylou, and Karen Wilson, eds. *Outsourcing Technical Services Operations.* Chicago: American Library Association, 1997.

Crawford, Walt. "The Card Catalog and Other Digital Controversies: What's Obsolete and What's Not in the Age of Information." *American Libraries* 30, no. 1 (January 1999): 52–58.

Dunkle, Clare B. "Outsourcing the Catalog Department: A Meditation Inspired by the Business and Library Literature." *Journal of Academic Librarianship* 22, no. 1 (January 1996).

Evans, G. Edward, and Sandra M. Heft. *Introduction to Technical Services for Library Technicians.* 6th ed. Englewood, Colo.: Libraries Unlimited, 1994.

Farb, Sharon. "Universal Design and the Americans with Disabilities Act: Not All Systems Are Created Equal—How Systems Design Can Expand Information Access." In *From Catalog to Gateway: Briefings from the CFFC*, paper no. 16. *ALCTS Newsletter Online* 11, no. 1 (Spring 2000); also published in *From Catalog to Gateway: Charting a Course for Future Access: Briefings from the ALCTS Catalog Form and Function Committee*, edited by Bill Sleeman and Pamela Bluh, pp. 99–106. Chicago: Association for Library Collections & Technical Services, American Library Association, 2005.

Foster, Donald L. *Managing the Catalog Department.* 3rd ed. Metuchen, N.J.: Scarecrow Press, 1987.

Gassie, L. W. "What Do We Expect from the Next Generation of Library Systems?" *LLA Bulletin* 60, no. 2 (Fall 1997): 97.

"Intellectual Freedom Toolkits: Outsourcing and Privatization in Libraries" (includes links to several documents). Available: http://www.ala.org/ala/oif/iftoolkits/outsourcing/Default2446.htm (accessed 2/14/2006).

Kaplan, Michael, ed. *Planning and Implementing Technical Services Workstations.* Chicago: American Library Association, 1997.

Kascus, Marie A., and Dawn Hale, eds. *Outsourcing Cataloging, Authority Work, and Physical Processing: a Checklist of Considerations.* Chicago: American Library Association, 1995.

Long, Chris Evin. "The Internet's Value to Catalogers: Results of a Survey." *Cataloging & Classification Quarterly* 23, no. 3–4 (1997): 65–74.

Machovec, George. "ILS System Selection: Second Time Around." *Colorado Libraries* 23, no. 4 (Winter 1997): 6.

Martin, Robert S., et al. "The Impact of Outsourcing and Privatization on Library Services and Management: A Study for the American Library Association." School of Library and Information Studies, Texas Woman's University, June 2000. Available: http://www. ala.org/ala/oif/iftoolkits/outsourcing/outsourcing_doc.pdf (accessed 2/14/2006).

Matthews, Joseph R., Gary S. Lawrence, and Douglas K. Ferguson, eds. *Using Online Catalogs: A Nationwide Survey.* Sponsored by the Council on Library Resources. New York: Neal-Schuman, 1983.

Morris, Dilys E., and Gregory Wool. "Cataloging: Librarianship's Best Bargain." *Library Journal* 124, no. 11 (June 15, 1999): 44–46.

OCLC. "OCLC Connexion." Available: http://connexion.oclc.org/ (accessed 2/14/2006).

———. "OCLC Online Computer Library Center, Inc." Available: http://www.oclc.org/ (accessed 2/14/2006).

Oddy, Pat. "Bibliographic Standards and the Globalization of Bibliographic Control." In *Technical Services Today and Tomorrow.* 2nd ed., edited by Michael Gorman, pp. 67–78. Englewood, Colo.: Libraries Unlimited, 1998.

Potter, William Gray. "The Online Catalogue in Academic Libraries." In *Technical Services Today and Tomorrow.* 2nd ed., edited by Michael Gorman, pp. 141–155. Englewood, Colo., Libraries Unlimited, 1998.

Program for Cooperative Cataloging. "About the PCC." Available: http://www.loc.gov/ catdir/pcc/2001pcc.html (accessed 2/14/2006).

Program for Cooperative Cataloging. "Introduction to the Program for Cooperative Cataloging BIBCO Core Record Standards." Available: http://lcweb.loc.gov/catdir/pcc/ bibco/coreintro.html (accessed 2/14/2006).

Program for Cooperative Cataloging. "Program for Cooperative Cataloging [PCC]." Available: http://www.loc.gov/catdir/pcc/ (accessed 2/14/2006).

RLG. "Research Libraries Group." Available: http://www.rlg.org/ (accessed 2/14/2006).

Rushoff, Carlen. "Cataloging's Prospects: Responding to Austerity with Innovation." *Journal of Academic Librarianship* 21, no. 1 (January 1995): 51–57.

Saffady, William. "Commercial Sources of Cataloging Data: Bibliographic Utilities and Other Vendors." *Library Technology Reports* 34, no. 3 (May/June 1998): 281–432.

Sellberg, Roxanne. "Cataloguing Management: Managing the Bibliographic Control Process." In *Technical Services Today and Tomorrow*, 2nd ed., edited by Michael Gorman, pp. 111–127. Englewood, Colo.: Libraries Unlimited, 1998.

Taylor, Arlene G., with the assistance of Rosanna M. O'Neil. *Cataloging with Copy: A Decision-Maker's Handbook.* 2nd ed. Englewood, Colo.: Libraries Unlimited, 1988. Chapters 1, 9.

Vellucci, Sherry L. "Future Catalogers: Essential Colleagues or Anachronisms?" *College & Research Library News* 7 (1996): 442–443.

Watson, Mark. "Top Five Reasons Why Library Administrators Should Support Participation in the Program for Cooperative Cataloging." Available: http://www.loc.gov/ catdir/pcc/topfive.html (accessed 2/14/2006).

Wilson, Karen A., and Marylou Colver, eds. *Outsourcing Library Technical Services Operations: Practices in Public, Academic, and Special Libraries*. Chicago: American Library Association, 1997.

Yee, Martha. "Guidelines for OPAC Displays." In "From Catalog to Gateway: Briefings from the CFFC," paper no. 14. *ALCTS Newsletter Online* 10, no. 6 (December 1999); also published in *From Catalog to Gateway: Charting a Course for Future Access: Briefings from the ALCTS Catalog Form and Function Committee*, edited by Bill Sleeman and Pamela Bluh, pp. 83–90. Chicago: Association for Library Collections & Technical Services, American Library Association, 2005.

————. "Guidelines for OPAC Displays." Prepared for the 65th IFLA Council and General Conference, Bangkok, Thailand, August 20–28, 1999. Available: http://www.ifla.org/IV/ifla65/papers/098-131e.htm (accessed 2/14/2006).

Yee, Martha M., and Sara Shatford Layne. *Improving Online Public Access Catalogs*. Chicago: American Library Association, 1998.

Zyroff, Ellen. "Cataloging is a Prime Number." *American Libraries* 27, no. 5 (May 1996): 47–48, 50.

CURRENT INFORMATION AND UPDATING

Banerjee, Kyle. "The Cataloging Calculator." Available: http://calculate.alptown.com/ (accessed 2/14/2006).

Cataloger's Desktop. Washington, D.C.: Library of Congress, Cataloging Distribution Service. Available: http://desktop.loc.gov/ [requires ID and password] (accessed 2/14/2006). For subscription information: http://www.loc.gov/cds/desktop/ (accessed 2/14/2006).

Cataloging & Classification Quarterly. Binghamton, N.Y.: Haworth Press, 1979– . Quarterly. Homepage available: http://www.catalogingandclassificationquarterly.com/ (accessed 2/14/2006).

Cataloging Service Bulletin, no. 1– . Washington, D.C.: Processing Services, Library of Congress, 1978– .

Classification Web. Washington, D.C.: Library of Congress, Cataloging Distribution Service. Available: http://classificationweb.net/ [requires ID and password] (accessed 2/14/2006). For subscription information: http://www.loc.gov/cds/classweb/ (accessed 2/14/2006).

Library of Congress Authorities. Available: http://authorities.loc.gov/ (accessed 2/14/2006).

Library of Congress, Cataloging Distribution Service. "Bibliographic Products & Services." Available: http://www.loc.gov/cds/ (accessed 2/14/2006).

The Library of Congress Cataloging Policy & Support Office. Available: http://www.loc.gov/catdir/cpso/ (accessed 2/14/2006).

Library of Congress Online Catalog. Available: http://catalog.loc.gov/ (accessed 2/14/2006).

Library of Congress Rule Interpretations. 2nd ed. Washington D.C.: Library of Congress, 1989– . Looseleaf, with updates. (Also available in *Cataloger's Desktop.*)

Library of Congress Rule Interpretations for AACR2, Revision 2002: Complete LCRI Texts Through Cataloging Service Bulletin *no. 109.* Compiled by Alan Boyd. Oberlin, Ohio: Oberlin College Library, 2005. Available: http://www.oberlin.edu/library/lcri-texts/ Default.html [requires ID and password] (accessed 2/14/2006).

Library Resources & Technical Services. Chicago: American Library Association, 1957– . Quarterly. Homepage available: http://www.ala.org/ala/alcts/alctspubs/librestechsvc/ Default2594.htm (accessed 2/14/2006).

OCLC. "Documentation." Available: http://www.oclc.org/support/documentation (accessed 2/14/2006).

———. "Technical Bulletins." Available: http://www.oclc.org/support/documentation/ technicalbulletins/ (accessed 2/14/2006).

Index

considerations to determine need, 179–180
defined, 179, 526
Analytical note, defined, 179
Analytical materials, *AACR2R* description of,
183
analytical added entries, 183
"In" analytic record, 184–185
monographic series and multi-part
monographs, 184
multilevel description, 185
note area, 184
Anglo-American *Rules*
(1908), 26
revised edition (1949), 26–27
Anonymous work, defined, 526
Area, defined, 526
Art & Architecture Thesaurus Online (*ATT*),
377f–378f
Artifact. *See* Realia
Asynchronous responsibility, defined, 526
Atlases, chief source of information, 70
Austin, Derek, 378
Author, 56
defined, 526
Author entry, defined, 526
Author number. *See* Cutter number
Authority control, 19–20, 283, 295. *See also*
Collocating function; Identifying
function
of catalogs, 5
and functions of the catalog, 284
lack of, 287–289, 287f, 288f
outsourcing, 488
system design, 286
system maintenance, 295
virtual international authority file concept,
33
work, 289, 488; defined, 527
name and title, 289–291
subject, 291–292, 292f
Authority files, 17–18, 20, 487–488
creation of, 293–294
defined, 527
subject, 291–293, 294
Authority record
defined, 488, 527
name, 290–291, 290f, 291f
subject, 292, 292f, 293f
Auxiliary tables
adding from in DDC, 411–417
defined, 527

Bacon-d'Alembert system, 426
Bacon, Francis, outline of knowledge, 392
Belles-lettres, headings for, 364
Berman, Sanford, 321
Bibliographic Classification, 460–462
Bibliographic control
component parts, 4–5
defined, 3, 527
Bibliographic data/database, 4–5, 527
Bibliographic file, defined, 527
Bibliographic networks
defined, 527
online, 477
A-G Canada Ltd., 21, 481
OCLC, 478–480
RLG, 480–481
Bibliographic record (entry/surrogate
record/metadata), 4, 527
Bibliographic records in catalogs (formats of)
LC pattern, 21
MARC formats, 21–22, 22f
Bibliographic service center, 477
defined, 528
Bibliographic tools, 4
functions, 5–6
collocating or gathering, 5, 285–286
evaluating, 6
identifying, 5, 284–285
overlaps, 5
Bibliographic universe, 3–4
defined, 528
Bibliographic utility. *See* Bibliographic
networks
Bibliographies, 4
defined, 528
Blind references, 271
Bliss, Henry Evelyn, 460
Bliss Classification Association, 462
Book catalog, 9, 11, 528
automated formats, 9
Book number. *See* Cutter number
Books, *AACR2R* considerations, title
illustrations, 77f–78f
Boolean operators, 381, 421
defined, 528
Broad classification, 397
and DDC, 419–420
defined, 528
Broader term (BT), defined, 528
Brown, James Duff, 459
Brunet utilitarian classification scheme, 393
BSO (Broad System of Ordering), defined,
528

About the Author

ARLENE G. TAYLOR is professor emerita, School of Information Sciences, University of Pittsburgh, and author of several works on cataloging and classification. She has received ALA's Margaret Mann Citation in Cataloging and Classification, and the ALA Highsmith Library Literature Award.